The Psychology of Women
A Lifespan Perspective

Claire A. Etaugh

Bradley University

Judith S. Bridges

University of Connecticut at Hartford

Allyn and Bacon

Boston • London • Toronto • Sydney • Tokyo • Singapore

*To my parents, Martha and Lou Teitelbaum, who taught
me that anything is possible.*

C. E.

*To my husband, Barry, my life partner and best friend, who is
always there for me, and to my children, Rachel and Jason, and
their spouse/partners, Gray and Nora, who reflect the promise of a
more gender-equal tomorrow.*

J. S. B.

Executive Editor: Carolyn Merrill
Editorial Assistant: Lara Zeises
Senior Editorial-Production Administrator: Susan Brown
Editorial-Production Service: Colophon
Composition Buyer: Linda Cox
Manufacturing Buyer: Megan Cochran

Library of Congress Cataloging-in-Publication Data

Etaugh, Claire.
    The psychology of women : a lifespan perspective /Claire Etaugh, Judith S. Bridges.
       p. cm.
    Includes bibliographical references and index.
    ISBN 0-205-28596-1 (alk. paper)
     1. Women—Psychology. 2. Gender identity. 3. Sex role. 4. Women—Socialization.
   5. Women—Physiology. 6. Feminist psychology. I. Bridges, Judith S. II. Title.
    HQ1206.E88 2000
    155.3'33—dc21   00-032284

Photo credits appear on page 540 which constitutes a continuation of this copyright page.

Printed in the United States of America

10 9 8 7 6 5 4 3 2 1   03 02 01 00

C O N T E N T S

11 Young and Middle Adulthood: Interpersonal Issues I: Close Relationships and Intimate Violence   283

12 Young and Middle Adulthood: Interpersonal Issues II: Balancing Family and Work   320

PREFACE

Over the last three decades the burgeoning interest in the psychology of women has been reflected in a rapidly expanding body of research and a growing number of college-level courses in the psychology of women or gender. *The Psychology of Women: A Lifespan Perspective* draws on this rich literature to present a broad range of experiences and issues of relevance to girls and women. Because it does not presuppose any background in psychology, this book can be used as the sole or primary text in introductory-level psychology of women courses and, with other books, in psychology of gender or interdisciplinary women's studies courses. Additionally, its presentation of both current and classical research and theory make it a suitable choice, along with supplementary materials, for more advanced courses focused on the psychology of women or gender.

Special Features Related to Content and Organization

Extensive Coverage of Women in the Middle and Later Years. Despite feminist concerns about the relative invisibility of older women, textbooks on the psychology of women provide only minimal coverage of women in the middle and later years. Thus, we include thorough coverage of women in these stages of life.

Chronological Approach. The topical, or topical combined with developmental, approach used by other texts does not communicate the complexity of issues and experiences characteristic of each stage of women's lives. Consequently, our primary goal was to write a chronologically based text that explores females' development from infancy through old age.

When we undertook this task, we realized that a major challenge of writing a book of this nature is that many issues and topics do not neatly divide themselves into time frames. However, girls' and women's physical development and health issues, their educational and employment goals and experiences, and their relationships with family and friends manifest themselves in different ways as women progress through life's stages. Thus, while acknowledging that several experiences, such as divorce or occupational choice, can occur at different points in women's lives, we discuss issues such as these during the time periods in which they most commonly occur. By doing so, we provide an overview of interconnections among physical, educational/employment, and interpersonal experiences of girls and women during each developmental stage of their lives.

Although the text is organized in a chronological framework, the topics covered in each life stage are included in most psychology of women texts and courses. For each life stage after childhood (i.e., adolescence, women in young adulthood, women in middle adulthood, and women in late adulthood), we focus on three broad areas: physical development and health, education or employment, and interpersonal relationships. In addition, we include one chapter on gender issues in infancy and childhood and begin with chapters covering topics not specific to a particular life stage—historical issues, research bias, cultural representation of gender, and gender typing. Thus, the book can be used in either a chronological or topical course format. The following list presents the text according to that latter format:

- **History, Research, and Key Definitions**—Chapter 1 (Introduction)
- **Gender Stereotypes**—Chapter 2 (Cultural Representation of Gender)
- **Gender and Language**—Chapter 2 (Cultural Representation of Gender)
- **Theoretical Perspectives**—Chapter 3 (Gender Self-Concept)
- **Prenatal Development**—Chapter 3 (Gender Self-Concept)
- **Violence Against Girls and Women**—Chapter 4 (Infancy and Childhood); Chapter 6 (Adolescence: Psychosocial and Cognitive Development); Chapter 8 (Young Adulthood: Education and Employment); Chapter 10 (Middle Adulthood: Employment); Chapter 11 (Young and Middle Adulthood: Interpersonal Issues I: Close Relationships and Intimate Violence); Chapter 15 (Later Adulthood: Interpersonal Issues)
- **Gender Similarities and Differences in Social Behaviors and Personality Traits**—Chapter 1 (Introduction); Chapter 4 (Infancy and Childhood); Chapter 11 (Young and Middle Adulthood: Interpersonal Issues I: Close Relationships and Intimate Violence)
- **Physical Health**—Chapter 5 (Adolescence: Physical Development and Health); Chapter 7 (Young Adulthood: Physical Development and Health); Chapter 9 (Middle Adulthood: Physical Development and Health); Chapter 13 (Later Adulthood: Physical Development and Health)
- **Mental Health and Psychological Disorders**—Chapter 5 (Adolescence: Physical Development and Health); Chapter 7 (Young Adulthood: Physical Development and Health); Chapter 9 (Middle Adulthood: Physical Development and Health); Chapter 13 (Later Adulthood: Physical Development and Health)
- **Sexuality**—Chapter 5 (Adolescence: Physical Development and Health); Chapter 7 (Young Adulthood: Physical Development and Health); Chapter 9 (Middle Adulthood: Physical Development and Health); Chapter 13 (Later Adulthood: Physical Development and Health)
- **Pregnancy, Childbirth, and Motherhood**—Chapter 5 (Adolescence: Physical Development and Health); Chapter 7 (Young Adulthood: Physical Development and Health); Chapter 11 (Young and Middle Adulthood: Interpersonal Issues I: Close Relationships and Intimate Violence)
- **Abilities and Achievement**—Chapter 6 (Adolescence: Psychosocial and Cognitive Development); Chapter 8 (Young Adulthood: Education and Employment)

- **Friendship and Love Relationships**—Chapter 6 (Adolescence: Psychosocial and Cognitive Development); Chapter 11 (Young and Middle Adulthood: Interpersonal Issues I: Close Relationships and Intimate Violence); Chapter 15 (Later Adulthood: Interpersonal Issues)
- **Lesbian and Bisexual Women**—Chapter 7 (Young Adulthood: Physical Development and Health); Chapter 8 (Young Adulthood: Education and Employment); Chapter 10 (Middle Adulthood: Employment); Chapter 11 (Young and Middle Adulthood: Interpersonal Issues I: Close Relationships and Intimate Violence); Chapter 12 (Young and Middle Adulthood: Interpersonal Issues II: Balancing Family and Work); Chapter 15 (Later Adulthood: Interpersonal Issues)
- **Employment**—Chapter 8 (Young Adulthood: Education and Employment); Chapter 10 (Middle Adulthood: Employment); Chapter 12 (Young and Middle Adulthood: Interpersonal Issues II: Balancing Family and Work); Chapter 14 (Later Adulthood: Employment and Economic Issues)
- **Future**—Chapter 16 (A Feminist Future: Goals, Actions, and Attitudes)

Integration of Women's Diversity throughout the Text. The text provides considerable coverage of women of color and lesbian and bisexual women. Although there is less information available, we also include material on poor women and women with disabilities whenever possible. We chose to integrate women's diversity throughout each chapter rather than in separate chapters on subgroups of women. An integrated approach demonstrates similarities and differences in life stage experiences of diverse groups of women without creating the impression that certain groups of women are treated separately because they deviate from the norm.

Thorough Examination of Balancing Family and Work. It is clear that at this point in our history, the balancing of family and work is a major issue facing North American families. We devote an entire chapter to this timely topic in order to thoroughly explore the theories, challenges, benefits, and solutions associated with this great challenge of the twenty-first century.

Up-to-Date Research. Although we include some classic studies (e.g., Horner's fear of success research), we focus most of our empirical presentation on current research. Over 90 percent of the references in the text date from 1990 on, with two-thirds published since 1995.

Pedagogical Features

Introductory Outline. Each chapter begins with an outline of the material, thus providing an organizational framework for reading the material.

Opening Vignettes. In order to grab students' attention and connect the material to real life, each chapter begins with one or two actual or hypothetical experiences illustrating one or more issues discussed in the chapter.

What Do You Think? Questions.   The text includes critical-thinking questions in every chapter. The end-of-the-chapter What Do You Think? questions foster skills in synthesis and evaluation by asking the student to apply course material or personal experiences to provocative issues from the chapter.

Get Involved Exercises.   As a means of providing firsthand involvement in the material, each chapter contains a number of student activities. Some require collecting data on a small number of respondents and others focus solely on the student. Furthermore, each exercise is accompanied by critical-thinking What Does It Mean? questions that focus on explanations and implications of the activity's findings.

The active learning involved in these activities serves several purposes. First, it reinforces the material learned in the text. Second, those exercises that involve surveys of other people or analyses of societal artifacts introduce students to the research process, which, in turn, can stimulate interest in research, increase familiarity with a variety of assessment techniques, and provoke critical evaluation of research techniques. Third, the Get Involved activities demonstrate the relevance of the course material to students' experiences or to the experiences of important people in their lives.

Learn about the Research.   To stimulate student interest in and appreciation of research as a source of knowledge about girls and women, each chapter has one or two boxed sections that focus on research. These Learn about the Research sections either highlight an interesting current study or present an overview of recent findings in an intriguing research area. We expose students to a variety of research techniques (content analysis, interviews, questionnaires) without requiring that they have any background in psychological research methods. Furthermore, to highlight the importance of diversity in research samples, our selections include studies of underrepresented populations.

Following the research presentation are What Does It Mean? questions. These provoke more critical thinking by asking the student to consider a variety of issues related to the research, such as explanations and implications of the findings.

Key Terms.   Bolded terms and italicized definitions within the text help students preview, understand, and review important concepts.

Summary.   The point-by-point end-of-the-chapter summary helps the student synthesize the material.

If You Want To Know More.   Recommended readings related to each chapter facilitate more extensive examination of the material.

Writing Style

In order to engage the student and construct a nonhierarchical relationship between ourselves and the student, we use a nonpedantic first-person writing style.

Also, to reinforce this relationship in some of the opening vignettes and within the text, we present our own experiences or those of our friends and family.

Ancillary Materials

Instructor's Manual.   The Instructor's Manual contains a variety of activities to stimulate active learning. It includes critical thinking discussion topics and offer exercises that the instructor can use instead of or supplementary to the Get Involved activities incorporated within the text. In addition, the manual includes film and video listings as well as Internet Websites. Finally, it contains multiple-choice and essay questions for each chapter.

Computerized Test Bank.   The Text Bank

Acknowledgments

We owe a great deal to the many reviewers whose expert suggestions and insights were invaluable in the development of this book. Our sincere thanks to all of you: Marlene Adelman, Norwalk Community College; Veanne N. Anderson, Indiana State University; Mary Ballard, Appalachian State University; Donna Castaneda, San Diego State University–Imperial Valley Campus; Gloria Cowan, California State University, San Bernadino; Mary Ann Drake, Mercer University; Patricia S. Faunce, University of Minnesota; Carol A. Ford, Central Connecticut State University; Grace Galliano, Kennesaw State University; Karen G. Howe, The College of New Jersey; Barbara A. Hunter, Belleville Area College; Jennifer Katz, Washington State University; Merle Kelley, Western Oregon University; Pamela Manners, Troy State University; Judy McGee, Maryville University of St. Louis; Virginia Norris, South Dakota State University; Linda M. Oliva, University of Maryland, Baltimore County; Wendy J. Palmquist, Plymouth State College; Joan Rabin, Towson State University; L. Kaye Rasnake, Denison University; Mark Reynolds, SUNY-Brockport; Toby Silverman, William Patterson University; Joanne K. Urschel, Purdue University North Central.

It has been a pleasure to work with the publishing professionals at Allyn & Bacon. In particular, we acknowledge the invaluable support and assistance of Carolyn Merrill, acquisitions editor, who provided the initial inspiration for this book. Thanks also go to Jan Ringenberg, who typed the manuscript and carried out numerous other tasks essential to the production of this book.

Thanks also to the students in our Psychology of Women courses who provided excellent editorial suggestions on earlier versions of the manuscript and for whom, ultimately, this book is written.

Finally, the book could not have been completed without the loving support of our families. Judith wishes to thank her mother, Ruth, mother-in-law, Hilde, children, Rachel and Jason, and, most important, husband Barry, for their unwavering patience and encouragement. Claire's heartfelt appreciation goes to the women who have enriched her life and encouraged her throughout this project: her mother, Martha, mother-in-law, Barbara, sisters, Paula and Bonnie, daughter, Andi, daughter-in-law, Jen, and "extended family" of friends, Suzanne, Peggy, Pat, Pat, and Ellen.

ABOUT THE AUTHORS

Claire A. Etaugh

Claire Etaugh received her bachelor's degree from Barnard College and her Ph.D. in developmental psychology from the University of Minnesota. She is Professor of Psychology at Bradley University where she has taught Psychology of Women courses since 1979. A Fellow of the Psychology of Women and Developmental Psychology divisions of the American Psychological Association, she has published over 100 articles in such journals as *Psychology of Women*, *Sex Roles*, *Child Development*, and *Developmental Psychology*. She is the co-author of *The World of Children*.

Judith S. Bridges

Judith Bridges earned her bachelor's degree from Antioch College and her Ph.D. in psychology from the University of North Carolina. She is Professor of Psychology at the University of Connecticut and has been teaching the Psychology of Women since the early 1980s. Her research, which has focused on a variety of issues related to women and gender, has been published in the *Psychology of Women* and *Sex Roles*.

1 Introduction to the Psychology of Women

History and Research

KEY TERMS

sex
gender
beta bias
alpha bias
essentialism
liberal feminism
cultural feminism
socialist feminism
radical feminism

patriarchy
women of color feminism
racism
classism
sexism
sample
population
statistical significance
meta-analysis

effect size
race
ethnicity
organizational power
interpersonal power
power-over
power-to
social construction of gender

In 1965 when I (Judith) was applying to graduate schools, the chair of one psychology department informed me that my college grades met the criterion for male, but not female, admission into the program. That department (and others) had two sets of standards and, obviously, fewer than men were admitted. When I look back at that time it is amazing to me to realize that I quietly accepted this pronouncement. I was disappointed but not outraged. I rejoiced at my acceptance by a comparable department but never thought to protest discriminatory admission policies (which were not unique to that department). A generation ago I did not identify this issue or any other gender inequality in institutional, legal, or interpersonal practices as a problem. However, over the last several decades my awareness and concern about these issues dramatically changed. Claire and I are deeply committed to gender equality in all areas of life and hope that this text will help illuminate both the progress women have made and the challenges that remain in the attainment of this important goal.

In this chapter we set the groundwork for the study of the psychology of women. We present major definitions, explore relevant history, examine research issues, and discuss the themes of the book. We begin with a look at the difference between sex and gender.

Definitions: Sex and Gender

Psychologists do not agree completely on the definitions of the words *sex* and *gender*. *Sex* is used to refer either to whether a person is female or male, or to sexual behavior. This ambiguity of definition sometimes can cause confusion. For example, Claire offered a course several years ago entitled "The Psychology of Sex Differences." The course dealt with behavioral similarities and differences of females and males. After the first day of class, some students approached her with a puzzled look on their faces. The course title had led them to believe that the subject matter of the course was human sexuality.

The words *sex* and *gender* often have been used interchangeably to describe the differences in the behaviors of women and men. One example is the term *sex roles*, which is sometimes used to refer to culturally prescribed sets of behaviors for men and women. *Sex Roles* is even the name of a highly respected journal. Yet many psychologists believe that the term *gender roles* is more appropriate to describe the concept of culturally assigned roles.

To avoid confusion, we use the term **sex** to refer to *the classification of individuals as female or male based on their genetic makeup, anatomy, and reproductive functions*. We will use **gender** to refer to *the social and cultural aspects of being female or male* (Basow, 1992).

Women and Men: Similar or Different?

Scholars who study sex and gender issues usually take one of two approaches. Either they emphasize the similarities between women and men or they focus on the differences between them.

Similarities Approach

Those who adhere to the similarities viewpoint seek to show that *men and women are basically alike in their intellectual and social behaviors. Any differences that do occur are produced by socialization, not biology* (Bohan, 1997; Kimball, 1995; Eagly & Wood, 1999). This approach, also called the **beta bias** (Hare-Mustin & Marecek, 1990a), has its origins in the work of early twentieth-century women psychologists. As we shall see later in the chapter, a number of these psychologists carried out research that challenged the prevailing belief that women were different from (and inferior to) men. Most feminist theory and research dealing with gender differences has retained this similarities approach (Bohan, 1997).

Differences Approach

The differences viewpoint, also known as the **alpha bias**, *emphasizes the differences between women and men*. Historically, these differences have been thought to arise from *essential qualities within the individual that are rooted in biology* (Bohan, 1997; Eagly & Wood, 1999; Geary, 1999). This concept is known as **essentialism**.

The differences perspective has ancient origins in both Western and Eastern philosophies, which associate men with reason and civilization and women with emotion and nature (Hare-Mustin & Marecek, 1990b). As we have seen, early psychologists often equated women's differences from men with inferiority and "otherness." Men set the standard while women were seen as deviations from that standard (Hare-Mustin & Marecek, 1990a; Eagly, 1995). For example, Sigmund

Freud stated that because women do not have a penis, they suffer from penis envy. Using the same logic, one could argue just as persuasively that men experience uterus envy because they cannot bear children. (Karen Horney [1926/1974], a psychoanalyst who challenged many of Freud's views, made this very proposal.)

Contemporary feminists regard female-male differences as arising from a culture's expectations of how individuals should behave. In other words, any behavioral differences between the genders are not inborn, but are socially constructed (Bohan, 1997; Eagly, 1995; Kimball, 1995). As we shall see at the end of the chapter, the social construction of gender is one of the three major themes of this book.

Some feminists have added still another twist to the differences approach. They embrace cultural feminism, a view that celebrates those positive qualities historically associated with women, such as a sense of human connection and concern for other people (Bohan, 1997; Kimball, 1995; Miller & Stiver, 1997). The theories of Nancy Chodorow (1990) and Carol Gilligan (1982, 1993) illustrate the cultural feminist approach. According to Chodorow, early childhood experiences forever set females and males down different paths in their development of identity, personality, and emotional needs. Girls develop an early attachment to their mother, whom they perceive as similar to themselves. This leads girls to develop relational skills and a desire for close emotional connections. Boys, on the other hand, reject their emotional attachment to their mother, who is perceived as dissimilar. Boys instead identify with male figures who are often more distant. In the process, they become more invested in separation and independence, and develop a more abstract and impersonal style (Basow & Rubin, 1999). Gilligan (1982, 1993) also sees women's identity as based on connections and relationships to others. She believes that women reason and make moral judgments in a "different voice," a voice concerned with caring and responsibility. Men, on the other hand, are more concerned with abstract rights and justice. These different patterns of reasoning are equally valid and sophisticated, according to Gilligan. We shall discuss moral reasoning in females and males in greater detail in Chapter 4.

Regardless of one's approach to gender comparisons, the study of gender and the psychology of women is rooted in a feminist perspective. Therefore, let's now examine the meaning of feminism.

Feminism

"Feminism means women working toward better rights for themselves, such as political power, equal pay, and respect in the workplace." (an undergraduate student, quoted in Jackson, Fleury, & Lewandowski, 1996, p. 690). "Women are perfect, do things better than men" (an undergraduate student, quoted in Nelson, Shanahan, & Olivetti, 1997, p. 239). "Feminism makes me think of women who are actively for equal rights. I think of them as man-haters who spend time men-bashing and demanding equality for everything" (an undergraduate student, quoted in Jackson et al., 1996, p. 690). Feminism "is a socialist, anti-family political movement that encourages women to leave their husbands, kill their children, practice witchcraft, destroy capitalism and become lesbians" (the Reverend Pat Robertson, quoted in Cranberg, August 17, 1992). Which, if any of these definitions reflects your own view of feminism? Although the term *feminism* is frequently used by the media, in opinion polls, and in casual conversation, people obviously differ in their conceptions of its meaning. There is even diversity among feminists. Although united in their belief that women are disadvantaged relative to men (Worell, 1996a), feminists differ in their beliefs about the sources of this inequality and the ways to enhance women's status. Let's examine five different types of feminism embraced by feminist scholars.

Liberal feminism is *the belief that women and men should have the same political, legal, economic, and educational rights and opportunities* (Henley, Meng, O'Brien, McCarthy, & Sockloskie, 1998; Johnson, 1997; Worell, 1996a). Liberal feminists advocate reform; their goals are to change attitudes and laws that are unfair to women and to equalize educational, employment, and political opportunities. For example, they seek the creation of an educational environment that encourages women's growth in all academic fields, removal of barriers to full participation and advancement in the workplace, and more political leadership positions for women. Liberal feminists stress the similarities between females and males and contend that gender differences are a function of unequal opportunities.

In contrast, **cultural feminism** reflects *the belief that women and men are different and that more respect should be given to women's special qualities, such as nurturance, concern about others, and cooperativeness* (Basow, 1992; Henley et al., 1998; Worell, 1996a). Cultural feminists are concerned about destructive outcomes related to masculine traits, such as aggressiveness and lack of emotional expressiveness, and want to empower women by elevating the value attached to their interpersonal orientation.

Another type of feminism, **socialist feminism**, reflects *the attitude that gender inequality is rooted in economic inequality* (Henley et al., 1998; Johnson, 1997). Socialist feminists believe that oppression based on gender, ethnicity, and social class interact with one another and cannot be eliminated until the capitalistic structure of North American society is changed.

Radical feminism, on the other hand, is *the belief that gender inequality is based on male oppression of women* (Henley et al., 1998; Johnson, 1997; Worell, 1996a). Radical feminists contend that **patriarchy**, *male control over and dominance of women*, has existed throughout history and must be eliminated to achieve gender equality. In other words, different from socialist feminists, radical feminists see men, rather than capitalism, as the source of women's oppression. Consequently, they are concerned not only about inequality in societal institutions, such as the workplace, but about power differential in the family and other types of intimate relationships.

Many women of color have argued that the feminist movement is concerned primarily about issues that confront White women. Consequently, they embrace **women of color feminism**, which is *the belief that both* **racism**, *bias against people because of their ethnicity, and* **classism**, *bias based on social class, must be recognized as being as important as* **sexism**, *gender-based bias* (Henley et al., 1998).

GET INVOLVED 1.1

How Do People View Feminism?

Answer the following questions and then ask several female and male acquaintances to do the same. Save your own answers but do not refer back to them after completing this chapter.

First, indicate which of the following categories best characterizes your identity as a feminist:

1. consider myself a feminist and am currently involved in the Women's Movement
2. consider myself a feminist but am not involved in the Women's Movement
3. do not consider myself a feminist but agree with at least some of the objectives of feminism
4. do not consider myself a feminist and disagree with the objectives of feminism

Second, on a scale from 1 (strongly disagree) to 6 (strongly agree), indicate the extent to which you disagree or agree with each of the following statements.

1. Women should be considered as seriously as men as candidates for the Presidency of the United States.

2. Although women can be good leaders, men make better leaders.
3. A woman should have the same job opportunities as a man.
4. Men should respect women more than they currently do.
5. Many women in the workforce are taking jobs away from men who need the jobs more.
6. Doctors need to take women's health concerns more seriously.
7. Women have been treated unfairly on the basis of their gender throughout most of human history.
8. Women are already given equal opportunities with men in all important sectors of their lives.
9. Women in the United States are treated as second-class citizens.
10. Women can best overcome discrimination by doing the best they can at their jobs, not by wasting time with political activity.

Reprinted with permission from Plenum Publishing Corp. from Morgan, 1996.

What Does It Mean?

Before computing your scores for the 10 items, reverse the points for statements 2, 5, 8, and 10. That is, for a rating of 1 (strongly disagree), give 6 points, for a rating of 2, give 5 points, and so on. Then sum the points for the 10 items. Higher scores reflect greater agreement with feminist beliefs.

1. Are there differences in the feminist labels and/or feminist attitude scores between your female and male respondents?
2. For each respondent, including yourself, compare the feminist attitude score to the selected feminist category. Did you

find that individuals who gave themselves a feminist label (i.e., placed themselves in category 1 or 2) generally agreed with the feminist statements and obtained a score of 40 or higher? Similarly, did the individuals who did not label themselves as feminists (e.g. category 3 or 4), tend to disagree with the feminist statements and receive a score below 40? If there was no correspondence between the feminist identity label and the feminist beliefs, give possible reasons.

3. Do you think that individuals who vary in ethnicity and social class might hold different attitudes about feminism? If yes, explain.

Clearly, there is no reason why a feminist perspective has to be limited to one viewpoint. Many individuals combine two or more into their personal definition of feminism. Now, perform the exercise in Get Involved 1.1 to more closely examine each of these types of feminism.

History of Women in Psychology

The first women in psychology faced a number of obstacles, especially in establishing their credentials, since many universities in the late 1800s and early 1900s did not welcome women who sought advanced degrees (Hogan & Sexton, 1991; Milar, in press). Judith's experience described at the beginning of this chapter indicates that this sexist policy continued well into the twentieth century. Nevertheless, several women overcame the odds to become pioneers in American psychology (O'Connell & Russo, 1990; "Once Behind", 1999).

Women and the American Psychological Association

One year after the founding of the American Psychological Association (APA) in 1892, 2 of the 14 new members admitted were women: Mary Whiton Calkins and Christine Ladd-Franklin. Calkins went on to become the first woman president of the APA in 1905. Margaret Floy Washburn, the first woman to receive a Ph.D. in psychology in America, was elected the second woman president in 1921. It would be 51 years before the APA had another female leader. From the 1930s through the 1960s, women constituted about one-third of APA membership, but they did not attain high-level offices, editorships, or important committee positions at the same rate as their male colleagues (Hogan & Sexton, 1991).

Since the early 1970s, the number of women in APA leadership roles has increased notably. Seven women have become president: Anne Anastasi (1972), Leona Tyler (1973), Florence Denmark (1980), Janet Spence (1984), Bonnie Strickland (1987), Dorothy Cantor (1996), and Norine Johnson (2001). In 1998, women represented 48 percent of the APA members, 36 percent of the council of representatives, and 42 percent of the board of directors, although fewer than one-fourth of APA fellows, the most prestigious membership category. One-third of the reviewers and 40 percent of the associate editors of APA journals (but only 15 per-

Nine women have been elected president of the American Psychological Association: Mary Whiton Calkins (shown here), *Margaret Floy Washburn, Anne Anastasi, Leona Tyler, Florence Denmark, Janet Spence, Bonnie Strickland, Dorothy Cantor, and Norine Johnson.*

cent of the editors) are women (American Psychological Association, 1999b). Of the 96 psychologists who received the APA's annual Award for Distinguished Scientific Contributions from 1956 to 1987, only 5 were women (Nancy Bayley, Eleanor Gibson, Dorothea Jameson, Brenda Milner and Beatrice Lacey). Between 1988 and 1998, however, 9 of the 30 winners were women ("Awards," 1998).

Women's Contributions

Women have been relatively invisible in psychology; their contributions to the field often have been overlooked or ignored. Coverage of gender-related topics also has been limited. However, the situation is improving. Florence Denmark (1994) examined undergraduate psychology textbooks in 1982 and 1993 for the inclusion of women's contributions and of gender-related topics. The more recent books showed progress in both areas. Claire and her students (Etaugh, Jones, & Patterson, 1995) similarly found that coverage of gender-related topics in introductory psychology textbooks increased by nearly 40 percent between the early 1970s and the early 1990s.

Even when the works of women psychologists are cited, they may still be overlooked. There are two related reasons for this apparent invisibility of many women psychologists. First, the long-standing practice in psychology books and journal articles is to refer to authors by their last name and first initials only. (Ironically, even if this practice were to change, some women authors still might choose to use their initials in order to avoid possible gender-biased devaluation of their scholarly work [Walsh-Bowers, 1999]). Second, in the absence of gender-identifying information, people tend to assume that the important contributions included in psychology books and articles have been carried out by men. When Claire learned about the Ladd-Franklin theory of color vision in introductory psychology, she assumed that two men named Ladd and Franklin had developed the theory. Only later did she discover that it was the work of Christine Ladd-Franklin. Similarly, most people assume that it was *Harry* Harlow who established the importance of touch in the development of attachment. How many individuals know that his wife, psychologist Margaret Kuenne Harlow, was his research partner and a co-developer of their groundbreaking theory? In order to make the contributions of women psychologists more visible in this book, we frequently use first names when identifying important researchers and theorists.

History of the Psychology of Women

The Early Years

Rachel Hare-Mustin and Jeanne Marecek (1990b) call the early years of psychology "womanless" psychology. Not only were there few women psychologists, but women's experiences were not deemed important enough to study. Concepts in psychology were based on the male experience. For example, as we shall see in Chapter 3, Sigmund Freud formulated his views of the Oedipus complex and penis envy from a male perspective, but applied them to both genders. The same is true of Erik Erikson's notion of the development of identity during adolescence, as we shall see in Chapter 6.

In addition, early psychologists viewed women as different from and inferior to men (Hare-Mustin & Marecek, 1990b). For example, male psychologists reported that women's brains were smaller than men's, to explain their premise that women are less rational and less intelligent than men (Spanier, 1997). This theory seemed to be discredited by the discovery that *relative* brain size—the weight of the brain relative to the weight of the body—is actually greater in women than in men. But stereotypes are not that easily erased. Scientists began comparing various segments of the brain in the two genders in an attempt to find the cause of women's purported inferior intelligence. No differences were found (Caplan & Caplan, 1999). Yet the search continued. In 1982, the prestigious journal *Science* published a study claiming that the corpus callosum (the connection between the two hemispheres of the brain) is larger in women than in men. The researchers stated that this difference might account for women's supposedly inferior spatial skills. (See Chapter 6 for a detailed discussion of this topic.) The study had many flaws, including the fact that only nine males' brains and five females' brains had been examined. Ruth Bleier, a neuroanatomist, and her colleagues did a study that corrected the flaws and used a much larger number of brains. They found no gender differences. Yet *Science* refused to publish their findings on the grounds that they were too "political" (Caplan & Caplan, 1999; Spanier, 1997).

The first generation of women psychologists carried out research that challenged assumptions of female inferiority (Milar, in press). Helen Thompson

Woolley found little difference in the intellectual abilities of women and men. Leta Stetter Hollingworth tackled the prevailing notion that women's menstrual cycles were debilitating, rendering women unfit to hold positions of responsibility. She demonstrated that intellectual and sensory-motor skills did not systematically vary across the menstrual cycle (Bohan, 1997).

The Recent Years

A number of events in the 1960s signaled the beginning of the modern feminist movement in the United States, including the publication of Betty Friedan's (1963) book *The Feminine Mystique*, the passage of the Equal Pay Act (see Chapters 10 and 14), and the formation of the National Organization for Women (NOW). In each case, the spotlight turned on glaring economic, social, and political inequities between women and men.

During these years, the psychology of women emerged as a separate field of study. In 1969, the Association for Women in Psychology was founded, followed in 1973 by the APA Division of the Psychology of Women (O'Connell & Russo, 1991). Several textbooks on the psychology of women were written, and college courses on the topic began to appear. Feminist theorists and researchers demonstrated the sexist bias of much psychology theory, research, and practice. They set about expanding knowledge about women and correcting erroneous misinformation from the past (Bohan, 1997; Denmark, 1998). Today, women make up one-third of the psychologists in nonprofit institutions, including colleges and universities. This percentage is very likely to increase because over two-thirds of doctoral degrees in psychology now are awarded to women (American Psychological Association, 1999b).

Study of the Psychology of Women

With a basic understanding of the history of the psychology of women, we now turn to an examination of issues involved in performing psychological research. As you probably learned in introductory psychology, our understanding of human behavior stems from research conducted by psychologists and other scientists who use the scientific method to answer research questions. Although you might have learned that this method is value-free, that it is not shaped by researchers' personal values, feminist scholars (e.g., Pearson & Cooks, 1995; Riger, 1992) argue that values can influence every step of the research process. Let's turn now to a brief discussion of these steps to see how researchers' own ideas about human behavior can influence our understanding of the psychology of women.

Bias in Psychological Research

Selecting the Research Topic.   The first step in any scientific investigation is selecting the topic that will be examined. Just as your personal preferences lead you to choose one term paper topic over another, scientists' personal interests influence the topics they decide to investigate. Throughout the history of psychology, most psychologists have been male; thus, for many years topics related to girls and women were rarely investigated (Riger, 1992). Since 1970, however, the increasing number of female psychologists and the growth of the psychology of women as a discipline have been accompanied by steadily increasing research attention to topics of importance to women. This progression of interest has been documented by Judith Worell (1996b), who notes a dramatic increase in publications on issues of importance to women between 1974 and 1993. For instance, she reports that, while no studies on female achievement were published in 1974, 161 were published in 1993, and published investigations of rape increased from 35 to 306 during the same period.

Another influence on topic selection is the researcher's assumptions about gender characteristics. For example, a psychologist who believes leadership is primarily a male trait is not likely to investigate the leadership styles of women.

Bias in topic selection is even more evident when we focus on women of color. Not only is there a limited number of psychologists of color (Feldman, 1998) but researchers, influenced by the biased assumption that women of color are deviant and helpless, have examined ethnic minority women in relation to only a narrow range of topics (Reid & Kelly, 1994; Wyche, 1993). For example, between 1987 and 1994, women of color were more likely to be included in examinations of poverty and teen pregnancy than in investigations of other topics (Reid & Kelly, 1994). The tendency to treat women of color as helpless deviates substantiates a negative image of ethnic minority females and denies their full personhood as women with a wide breadth of concerns and experiences.

Formulating the Hypothesis. Once the topic is selected, the researcher generally formulates a hypothesis (a prediction) based on a particular theoretical perspective. Consequently, the researcher's orientation toward one theory or another has a major influence on the direction of the research. To better understand this effect, we look at the link between two theories of rape and related research hypotheses. One theory posits that rape has evolved through natural selection, which leads to the hypothesis that rape is present in nonhuman animals (e.g., Thornhill & Palmer, 2000). A very different theory contends that rape stems from a power imbalance between women and men. One hypothesis stemming from this theory is that regions of the country with more gender inequality of power should have higher rates of rape than regions with less power imbalance (e.g., Whaley, 1999). As we see in the next section, these different hypotheses lead to very different kinds of research on rape.

Theoretical perspectives about ethnicity can similarly influence the hypotheses and direction of research. As Pamela Reid and Elizabeth Kelly (1994) noted, many studies on women of color are designed to "illuminate deficits and deviance from White norms" (p. 483). Rather than examining strengths of women of color, this deviance perspective leads to research that focuses on ethnic minority women as powerless victims.

Designing the Study.   Because the methods used to gather data stem from the underlying predictions, hypotheses based on disparate theories lead to different procedures. This, in turn, affects the type of knowledge we gain about the topic under investigation. Returning to our rape example, the hypothesis that rape is not unique to humans has led to investigations of forced copulation in nonhuman species (e.g., Wrangham & Peterson, 1996), research which would not be appropriate to the investigation of a power hypothesis. The prediction that rape is linked to the degree of gender inequality in society has led to studies of the relationship between a city's rape rate and its occupational and educational gender inequality (e.g., Whaley, 1999). Each of these procedures provides very different kinds of information about rape that can lay the foundation for different attitudes about this form of violence (see Chapter 11). Examining specific aspects of research design will show us the ways bias can also affect the choice of procedures.

Selecting Research Participants.   One of the consistent problems in psychological research has been the use of samples that do not adequately represent the general population. A **sample** refers to *the individuals who are investigated in order to reach conclusions about the entire group of interest to the researcher* (i.e., the **population**). For example, a researcher might be interested in understanding the emotional experiences of first-time mothers in the first three months following childbirth. It would be impossible, however, to assess the experiences of all new mothers (*population*). Instead, the investigator might seek 100 volunteers from among mothers who gave birth in any one of three hospitals in a specific geographical area (*sample*).

Unfortunately, research participants are not always representative of the larger population. Throughout most of the history of psychology, psychologists have focused primarily on White, middle-class, heterosexual, able-bodied males (Yoder & Kahn, 1993). This procedure can lead to unfortunate and incorrect generalizations about excluded groups. It would be inappropriate, for example, to draw conclusions about women's leadership styles by examining male managers. Furthermore, focusing on selected groups can lead to the disregard of excluded groups.

Have there been changes in the gender bias of research samples? The answer is somewhat complex. Since the 1970s there has been a progressive decline in the reliance on male-only samples (Gannon, Luchetta, Rhodes, Pardie, & Segrist, 1992). One study (Ader & Johnson, 1994) found that, although a minority of 1990 journals published studies using single-gender samples, twice as many of these studies used female-only samples than used male-only samples. Perhaps this is because of a growing interest in women's issues, at least some of which are relevant exclusively or primarily to females (e.g., personal reactions to menopause, techniques for coping with rape).

Another related issue is whether and how researchers specify the gender composition of their samples. A continuing problem is that a sizable minority of authors do not report this information. For example, between 30 percent and 40 percent of studies published in 1990 in a large variety of major psychology journals failed to mention the gender makeup of their participants (Ader & Johnson,

1994; Zalk, 1991). Therefore, the reader does not know whether the findings are applicable to both genders. Interestingly, the failure to report gender in the title of the article or to provide a rationale for sampling only one gender was more common in studies with male-only participants than in studies with female-only participants. Furthermore, discussions based on male participants were more likely to be written in general terms, whereas those based on only female participants were likely to be restricted to conclusions about females. According to Deborah Ader and Suzanne Johnson (1994, pp. 217–218), these practices suggest "there remains a significant tendency to consider male participants 'normative,' and results obtained from them generally applicable, whereas female participants are somehow 'different.'" That is, it appears that males are considered to be the standard against which all behavior is measured.

Although there has been improvement in the gender balance of participants in psychological research, samples have been limited in other ways. One problem is the invisibility of people of color. In fact, several top psychology journals have shown a steady *decline* in the examination of Black participants, and in the late 1980s, only 0.3 percent to 5 percent of the studies in these journals investigated Blacks' experiences (Graham, 1997).

Even psychologists critical of the male bias in traditional psychology have erred by using primarily White samples (e.g., Reid & Kelly, 1994; Wyche, 1993). For example, between 1989–1991, only about 10 percent of the articles published in journals that focus on women and gender roles examined the ethnicity of the participants (Reid & Kelly, 1994). A positive development is that these journals now require a description of the ethnicity of the sample even if it is restricted to typically studied White participants. However, it should be noted that specifying the ethnic composition of the sample does not imply that the researcher actually examined the relationship between the participant's ethnicity and the behavior under investigation.

Samples have been restricted, additionally, in their socioeconomic status: most participants have been middle class (Reid, 1993; Wyche, 1993). Moreover, when researchers study poor and working-class individuals, they tend to focus on people of color (Reid, 1993), perpetuating a biased assumption about ethnicity and social class as well as limiting our understanding of both poor White women and middle-class women of color.

It should also be noted that many of the middle-class individuals who serve as research participants are college students. As reported by David Sears (1997), in 1985 nearly three-quarters of the studies published in major social psychology journals were based on American undergraduates. Because this group is restricted in age, education, and life experiences compared to the general population, there are numerous findings based on these samples that cannot be generalized to other types of people.

Other groups, such as lesbian, gay, and bisexual individuals and people with disabilities, have rarely been studied in psychological research, and proportionally less research has focused on older women than on younger women or girls. What can explain researchers' narrow focus on White, middle-class, heterosexual,

GET INVOLVED 1.2

Are Samples in Psychological Research Biased?

In this exercise you are to evaluate samples used in recent psychological studies and to compare descriptions of samples published in journals oriented toward women or gender to mainstream psychological journals. At your campus library select one recent issue of *Psychology of Women Quarterly* or *Sex Roles*. Also, select a recent issue of one of the following: *Journal of Personality and Social Psychology, Journal of Experimental Social Psychology, Developmental Psychology, Child Development,* or *Journal of Consulting and Clinical Psychology*. For each article in these issues, read the brief section that describes the participants. This is found in the Method section of the article and is usually labeled Participants, Sample, or Subjects. As you read these sections, make note of the following information:

1. a. Is the gender of the participants specified?
   b. If yes, does the sample include females only, males only, or both females and males?
2. a. Is the ethnicity of the participants specified?

   b. If yes, does the sample include predominantly or exclusively Whites, predominantly or exclusively individuals of another single ethnic group, or a balanced mixture of individuals from two or more ethnic groups?
3. a. Is the social class of the participants specified?
   b. If yes, is the sample predominantly or exclusively middle class, predominantly or exclusively working class or poor, or a mixture of social classes?
4. a. Are any other characteristics of the participants (e.g., sexual orientation, presence of a disability, etc.) given?
   b. If yes, specify.

After recording the information for each article from one journal, add up the number of articles that specified the gender of the sample, the number that specified ethnicity, and so on. Similarly, sum the articles that included both genders, those that included more than one ethnic group, etc. Follow the same procedure for the other journal.

Reprinted with permission from Plenum Publishing Corp. from Morgan, 1996.

What Does It Mean?

1. Which participant characteristic was described most frequently? Explain why.
2. Which participant characteristic was represented in the most balanced way? Explain why.
3. Which participant characteristic was specified least often? Explain why.
4. Did the two journals differ in their descriptions of their samples? If yes, explain any observed differences.
5. What are the implications of your findings?

able-bodied, younger individuals? One possibility is that psychologists are more interested in understanding the experiences of people like themselves, and the majority of investigators fit the characteristics of the typical participants. Another possibility is that psychologists might use these individuals in their research because it is easier to recruit them. These are the people most likely to be located within the situational contexts—such as academic or professional environments— inhabited by researchers. Also, due to cross-group mistrust and/or misunderstanding, it might be more difficult for non-minority investigators to recruit minority individuals. Whatever the causes, the exclusion of certain groups of people from psychological examination not only devalues their experiences but can lead to inaccurate conclusions about them based on faulty generalizations. To get firsthand knowledge about the extent of biased samples in recent psychological research, complete the exercise in Get Involved 1.2.

Selecting the Measures.   Another step in the design of a study is the selection of procedures to measure the behaviors or characteristics under investigation. These procedures can determine the results that we find. For example, in their comparison of females and males aggression, Mary Harris and Kelly Knight-Bohnhoff (1996) obtained different findings depending on how they measured aggressive behavior. When participants were asked to indicate their physical aggression, males reported more aggression than females; however, when asked about their verbal aggression, there was no gender difference. As you can see, relying on only one of these measures would have distorted the conclusion.

Analyzing and Interpreting the Findings.   Once the data have been collected, the researcher performs statistical analyses to discover whether the findings support the hypotheses. Although there are numerous types of statistical tests, they all provide information about the **statistical significance** of the results, which means *that the findings are not due to chance alone.* For example, in a study of college students' perceptions of rape, Judith asked respondents to rate the degree to which a specific rape was due to the victim's failure to control the situation, from 0 (not at all) to 10 (to a great extent) (Bridges, 1991). The findings showed that females had an average rating of 2.75 and males had a rating of 4.59. These numbers have no meaning in themselves. However, a statistical analysis applied to these data indicated that the difference of 1.84 between the male and female averages was not due to chance alone; males, more than females, believed the victim failed to adequately control the situation.

Once statistical tests have been applied to the data, the researcher must interpret the findings. Statistical analyses inform us only about the likelihood that the data could have been produced by chance alone. Now, the researchers must discuss explanations and implications of the findings. One type of bias occurring at this stage is interpreting the findings in a way that suggests a female weakness or inferiority. For example, studies have shown that females use more tentative speech than males do (see Chapter 11). They are more likely than men to say, "I *sort of* think she would be a good governor" or "She *seems* to be a strong candidate."

Some researchers (e.g., Lakoff, 1975) have suggested this is an indication of females' lack of confidence—an interpretation pointing to a female deficit. Another equally plausible and more positive interpretation is that females use more tentative speech as a means of encouraging other people to express their opinions (e.g., Wood, 1994).

A second problem related to interpretation of findings is generalizing results based on one group to other groups. As discussed earlier in this chapter, psychologists frequently examine narrowly defined samples, such as White male college students, and sometimes they generalize their findings to other people, including females, people of color, and non-middle-class individuals. Linda Gannon and her associates (Gannon et al., 1992) examined evidence of generalization from one gender to the other found in several major psychology journals published from 1970–1990. Although there has been improvement since the 1970s, when inappropriate gender generalizations occurred in 19 percent to 76 percent of the articles, these researchers found that even in 1990 percentages ranged from 13 percent to 41 percent.

A third bias in the interpretation of data has been the assumption that the presence of gender differences implies biological causes. For example, Camilla Benbow and Julian Stanley (1980) found that more males than females are mathematically gifted. Although these investigators did not examine biological factors, they interpreted their findings to suggest that the difference was based on biological factors rather than on differing life experiences (Hyde, 1994).

Communicating the Findings.

Publishing.   The primary way that psychologists communicate their research findings to others is by publishing their studies, usually in psychological journals. Unfortunately, there is a publication bias. Editors and reviewers who make decisions about which studies are worthy of publication tend to favor those that report statistical significance over those that do not. This publication bias can affect the body of our knowledge about gender. Studies that show a statistically significant gender difference are more likely to be published than those that do not and can lead to exaggerated conclusions about the differences between females and males (Hyde, 1994).

Gender-Biased Language.   The language that researchers use in their research papers is another possible source of gender bias in the communication of findings. Gender-biased language, such as the use of the male pronoun to refer to both genders, can lead to serious misinterpretation. As is discussed in Chapter 2, the male pronoun tends to be interpreted as males only, not as males and females (e.g., Switzer, 1990). Fortunately, although this practice was prevalent in 1970, the *Publication Manual of the American Psychological Association* (American Psychological Association, 1994) now specifies that gender-biased language must be avoided. As of 1990 only a small minority of studies employed the inappropriate use of the male pronoun (Gannon et al., 1992).

Another, more subtle type of biased language is the use of nonparallel terms when writing about comparable female and male behaviors, thus implying an essential difference between the genders. For example, much of the research on gender and employment refers to women who work outside the home as "employed mothers" but refers to men who work outside the home as simply "employed" (Gilbert, 1994). This distinction carries the implicit assumption that the primary role for women is motherhood whereas the primary role for men is the provider role.

Conclusion.   Although it is unlikely that most researchers attempt to influence the research process in order to support their preconceived ideas about a topic, the biases they bring to the research endeavor can affect their choice of topic, hypotheses, research design, interpretation of findings, and communication about the study. Given that researchers have very human personal interests, values, and theoretical perspectives, they do not fit the image of the objective scientist (Caplan & Caplan, 1999).

Despite these inherent biases, we do not want to give the impression that psychological research is unduly value-laden or that it provides no useful information about the psychology of women. Most researchers make a concerted attempt to be as unbiased as possible, and research from psychology and other social scientific disciplines has provided a rich body of knowledge about females' experiences. However, we must read this research critically, with an understanding of its possible limitations—especially its failure to focus on the diversity of girls and women.

Feminist Research Methods

Traditional psychological research emphasizes objectivity, control, and quantitative measures as a means of understanding human behavior, and some feminist psychologists advocate adherence to this general methodology. Others, however, contend that more accurate representations of women's lives are achieved with subjective procedures, such as women's qualitative accounts of their experiences. For example, a subjective investigation of women's friendships might ask participants to describe, in their own words, the most important friendships they have had. In contrast, an objective measure might ask them to complete a questionnaire written by the researcher in which they indicate how often they have experienced a variety of feelings and interactions in their most important friendships. Whereas the subjective approach attempts to capture each participant's unique perspective, the objective approach compares participants' responses to a standard situation.

Although feminists have a variety of opinions about the most effective methods for studying girls and women, they agree that such research should increase our understanding of females and help change the world for them (Crawford & Kimmel, 1999; Riger, 1992). Thus, feminists, like all researchers, bring a set of values to the research process; values that can direct the nature and interpretation of the research. An important assumption of the feminist approach to knowledge is that research cannot be value-free (Weatherall, 1999). Accordingly, Claire and her colleague, Judith Worell, (Worell & Etaugh, 1994) have articulated a set of principles that are based on the values of feminist research. These are summarized in Table 1.1.

Drawing Conclusions from Multiple Studies

Researchers use one of two procedures to draw conclusions about gender differences on the basis of large numbers of published studies. This section examines these two techniques.

Narrative Approach

The traditional way of examining psychological gender differences has been to sift through dozens or even hundreds of studies on a particular topic and to form an impression of the general trends in their results. The first major attempt to synthesize the research on gender differences in this narrative fashion was carried out by Eleanor Maccoby and Carol Nagy Jacklin in 1974. In this massive undertaking,

TABLE 1.1   Principles Of Feminist Research

1. Challenging the traditional scientific method.
   a. Correcting bias in the research process.
   b. Expanding samples beyond White middle-class participants.
   c. Acknowledging the legitimacy of both quantitative and qualitative methods.
2. Focusing on the experiences of women.
   a. Examining diverse categories of women.
   b. Investigating topics of interest to women.
3. Considering gender imbalances in power.
   a. Recognizing that women's subordinate status is a sign of power imbalance, not deficiency.
   b. Attempting to empower women.
4. Recognizing gender as an important category for investigation.
   a. Understanding that a person's gender can influence expectations about and responses to that person.
5. Recognizing the importance of language.
   a. Changing language to be inclusive of women.
   b. Understanding that language can both influence thought and be influenced by thought.
6. Promoting social change.
   a. Creating a science that benefits women.
   b. Guiding action that will lead to justice for women.

Based on Worell & Etaugh (1994).

they tallied the results of over 1,600 published and unpublished studies appearing in the 10 years prior to 1974. Gender differences were declared to exist when a large number of studies on a given topic found differences in the same direction. Although the contribution of this pioneering work is enormous, critics have cited its use of a simple "voting" or "box-score" method, which gave each study the same weight regardless of sample size or magnitude of the reported difference (Eagly, 1995). In addition, the possibility of subtle biases is always present in any narrative review.

Meta-Analysis

A more sophisticated and objective technique of summarizing data has been developed in recent years. **Meta-analysis** is *a statistical method of integrating the results of several studies on the same topic.* It provides a measure of the magnitude, or size, of a given gender difference rather than simply counting the number of studies finding a difference (Hyde & Plant, 1995; Rosenthal, 1995).

Gender researchers using meta-analysis first locate all studies on the topic of interest. Then they do a statistical analysis of each study that measures the size of the difference between the average of the men's scores and the average of the women's scores. This difference is divided by the standard deviation of the two sets of scores. The standard deviation measures the variability or range of the scores. (For example, scores ranging from 1 to 100 have high variability, while scores ranging from 50 to 53 show low variability.) Dividing the difference between men's and women's scores by the standard deviation produces a d statistic. Finally, the researchers calculate the average of the d statistics from all the studies they located. The resulting d is called the **effect size**. *It indicates not only whether females or males score higher but how large the difference is.* This is one of the major advantages of meta-analysis over the traditional narrative method of summarizing research (Eagly, 1995; Hyde & Plant, 1995).

The value of d is large when the difference between means is large and the variability within each group is small. It is small when the difference between means is small and the variability within each group is large (Halpern, 1992). Generally a d of 0.20 is considered small, 0.50 is moderate and 0.80 is large (Hyde & Plant, 1995). However, these guidelines still do not settle the debate of whether a particular difference is *meaningful* or important (Deaux, 1999). In cancer research, for example, even a very small effect size can have powerful consequences. Suppose a treatment were discovered that completely cured a small number of women with a highly lethal form of cancer. Although the effect size might be quite small, this discovery would be hailed as a major medical breakthrough. As we discuss later in the book, the effect sizes for some psychological gender differences are greater than those found in most psychological research (Halpern, 1992) while others are close to zero (Hyde & Plant, 1995).

Now that we have explored the historical and methodological framework for understanding the psychology of women, we focus on the major themes that characterize this book.

Themes in the Text

Science is not value-free. As we have seen, the evolving belief about the importance of women has had a powerful impact on topics and methods of psychological research. Similarly, this text is not value-neutral. It is firmly rooted in a feminist belief system, which contends (1) that the diversity of women's experiences should be recognized and celebrated; (2) that men hold more power than women; and (3) that gender is shaped by social, cultural, and societal influences. These beliefs are shared by many feminist psychologists (e.g., Worell, 1996b), and are reflected throughout this book.

Theme 1: Diversity of Women's Experiences

As we saw in the discussion of research biases, minimal attention given to females throughout most of the history of psychology not only devalues women's experiences but often leads to incorrectly generalizing men's experiences to include women. Similarly, a psychology of women restricted to White, middle-class, heterosexual, able-bodied, young females minimizes the importance of women of color, poor and working-class women, lesbian and bisexual women, women with disabilities, and older women, and it can lead to the false conclusion that the experiences of the majority are applicable to all.

Consequently, this text examines the heterogeneity of females' experiences. We discuss both similarities and differences in the attitudes, emotions, relationships, goals, and behaviors of girls and women who have a diversity of backgrounds. For example, we explore interpersonal relationships of heterosexual and lesbian women (Chapters 11 and 15), health concerns of White women and women of color (Chapters 7, 9, and 13), problems on campus and in the workplace faced by women with disabilities (Chapters 8 and 10), and health, employment, and interpersonal issues of older women (Chapters 13–15). However, because most of the research to date on the psychology of women has been based on restricted samples, it is important to note that our presentation includes a disproportionate amount of information about middle-class, heterosexual, able-bodied White women and girls.

When referring to cultural variations among people we use the term *ethnicity* or *ethnic group* rather than *race*. **Race** is *a biological concept that refers to physical characteristics of people* (Feldman, 1998). However, experts disagree about what constitutes a single race (Feldman, 1998) and there is considerable genetic variation among people designated as a single race (Krieger & Fee, 1998; Winkler, 1997). **Ethnicity**, on the other hand, refers to *variations in cultural background, nationality, religion, and/or language* (Feldman, 1998), a term more closely associated with the variations in attitudes, behaviors, and roles that we discuss in this book.

Unfortunately, there are no universally acceptable labels that identify a person's ethnicity. Some terms are based on geographical origin as in *African American* and *Euro-American* whereas others are based on color, such as *Black* and *White*. Furthermore, each major ethnic category encompasses a diversity of ethnic subtypes. For example, Americans with Asian ancestry, regardless of their specific origin (e.g., Japan, China, Korea, Viet Nam) are generally grouped into a single category of Asian Americans. Similarly, Whites from countries as diverse as Ireland, Germany, and Russia are combined into one ethnic group. With the hope that our usage does not inadvertently offend anyone, ethnic group labels used in this book are Asian American, Black, Latina/o, Native American, and White, recognizing that each of these broad ethnic categories actually encompasses a diversity of cultures.

Theme 2: Gender Differences in Power

Two interlocking ideas characterize our power theme. One is that the experiences of women in North American society are shaped by both **organizational power**, *the ability to use valuable resources to influence others*, and **interpersonal power**, *the ability to influence one's partner within a specific relationship*. The greater organizational power of males compared to that of females is evident in our discussion of numerous topics, including gender differences in salary, the underrepresentation of women in high status occupations, and sexual harassment (Chapter 10). Additionally, gender differences in interpersonal power are clearly reflected in our discussions of battering, (Chapter 11), rape (Chapter 11), and the allocation of household responsibilities (Chapter 12).

Both of these power differentials reflect an undesirable imbalance in a form of power, which Janice Yoder and Arnold Kahn (1992) call **power-over**, *a person's or group's control of another person or group*. This type of power is distinguished from **power-to**, *the individual's control over her/his own behavior and goals* (Yoder & Kahn, 1992). Whereas the former is a negative type of power that restricts opportunities and choices of members of the less powerful group, the latter allows for personal growth for all. Thus, feminist psychologists want to eliminate the former and increase the latter.

A second component of our theme of power differences is that many women experience more than one type of power imbalance. In addition to a gender difference in power, women can experience power inequities as a function of their ethnicity, social class, sexual preference, age, and physical ability. Furthermore, the effects of these imbalances are cumulative. For example, women of color experience greater discrimination in the workplace than do White women (Chapter 10). As bell hooks (1990) stated, "By calling attention to interlocking systems of domination—sex, race, and class—Black women and many other groups of women acknowledge the diversity and complexity of female experience, of our relationship to power and domination." (p. 187).

One consequence of gender differences in power is that women and women's issues receive less emphasis and visibility than men and men's issues. In this chapter, for example, we saw that women's contributions to psychology often have been overlooked. We examine other instances of this problem in our discussion of specific topics, such as the underrepresentation of females in the media (Chapter 2), and the exclusion of women from major studies of medical and health issues (Chapters 7 and 13).

Theme 3: Social Construction of Gender

As indicated at the beginning of this chapter, social scientists differentiate between sex, the biological aspects of femaleness and maleness, and gender, the nonbiological components. Our third theme, the **social construction of gender,** points out that *the traits, behaviors, and roles that we associate with females and males are not inherent in one's sex; they are shaped by numerous interpersonal, cultural, and societal forces.* Even if some aspects of being a female or a male are biologically based, we live in a society that emphasizes gender, and our development as women and men as well as our conceptions of what it means to be a female or a male are significantly influenced by cultural and societal values. We do not exist in a sterile laboratory; instead, we are continually affected by an interlocking set of expectations, pressures, and rewards that guide our development as women and men.

Furthermore, our experience and conceptions of femaleness and maleness cannot be viewed as separate from our ethnicity and social class (hooks, 1990) nor from our sexual orientation and physical ability/disability. Each of these identities is also socially constructed. Lesbian women, for example, are affected not only by societal expectations about what women are like but by people's beliefs about and attitudes toward lesbianism.

The social construction of gender is discussed in relation to several topics in the text. For example, we examine theories that explain how children develop their ideas about gender (Chapter 3); we explore the processes of instilling a child with expectations about what it means to be a girl or boy (Chapter 4); and we examine social influences on gender in our discussion of gender differences in self-esteem (Chapter 6), friendship (Chapter 11) and the division of household labor (Chapter 12).

SUMMARY

1. Sex refers to classification of females and males based on biological factors. Gender refers to social expectations of roles and behaviors for females and males.

2. The similarities approach (beta bias) argues that women and men are basically alike in their behaviors and that any differences are a product of socialization. The differences approach (alpha bias) emphasizes that women and men are different and that these differences are biologically based.

3. Liberal, cultural, socialist, radical, and women of color feminism all posit that women are disadvantaged relative to men. However, they differ in their assumptions about the sources of this inequality.

4. For many years, women attained few leadership positions and awards in the American Psychological Association, but gains have been made in recent years.

5. Women's contributions to psychology often have been overlooked or ignored, but that situation is improving.

6. In the early years of psychology, women were viewed as inferior to men and their

experiences were rarely studied. Early women psychologists carried out research that challenged the assumptions of female inferiority. In the 1970s, the psychology of women emerged as a separate field of study.

7. Psychological research is not value-free. Throughout most of its history, psychology did not pay much attention to the experiences of girls and women in either the topics investigated or the participants studied. Since 1970 there has been an increase in research focus on females; however, most of this research has been focused on White, middle-class, heterosexual, able-bodied women. Generalizing results based on one type of participant to other types of people can lead to inaccurate conclusions.

8. The researcher's theoretical perspective influences the hypothesis examined in the research, which, in turn, affects the type of information learned from the research. Also, the measures used to study the research topic can influence the findings of the research.

9. Due to a publication bias, published studies are more likely to present gender differences than gender similarities.

10. Very few studies use blatantly biased gender language. However, a more subtle bias can be detected in the use of nonparallel terms for comparable female and male behaviors.

11. Some feminists advocate the use of traditional objective, quantitative research methods. Others favor the use of subjective, qualitative procedures. However, there are several principles that characterize most feminist research.

12. The narrative approach and meta-analysis are two methods of integrating results of several studies on the same topic. Meta-analysis is a statistical method that provides a measure of the magnitude of a given difference, known as the effect size.

13. Three themes are prominent in this text. First, psychology must examine the experiences of diverse groups of women. Second, the greater organizational and interpersonal power of men compared to women negatively shapes and limits their experiences. Women of color, poor and working-class women, lesbian women, and women with disabilities experience additional power inequities, with cumulative effects. Third, gender is socially constructed; it is shaped by social, cultural, and societal values.

WHAT DO YOU THINK?

1. Do you prefer the similarities approach or the differences approach to the study of gender issues? Why?

2. Which definition of feminism or combination of definitions best reflects your own view of feminism? Why?

3. Do you think it would be desirable for women and/or men if more people identified themselves as feminists? Explain your answer.

4. We noted a few experiences of women that are influenced by a gender imbalance in power, and we will cover other examples throughout the text. However, can you now identify any behaviors or concerns of women that you think are influenced by a power balance?

IF YOU WANT TO LEARN MORE

Caplan, P. J., & Caplan, J. B. (1999). *Thinking critically about research on sex and gender* (2nd ed.). New York: HarperCollins.

Johnson, A. G. (1997). *The gender knot: Unraveling our patriarchal legacy.* Philadelphia: Temple University Press.

O'Connell, A. N., & Russo, N. J. (Eds.) (1990). *Women in psychology: A bio-bibliographic sourcebook.* New York: Greenwood.

Tavris, C. (1992). *The mismeasure of women.* New York: Simon & Schuster.

Wyche, K. F., & Crosby, F. J. (Eds.) (1996). *Women's ethnicities: Journeys through psychology.* Boulder, CO: Westview.

2 Cultural Representation of Gender

KEY TERMS

gender stereotypes
communion
agency
social categorization
social role theory

ambivalent sexism
hostile sexism
benevolent sexism
neosexism (modern sexism)
male is normative

masculine generic language
spotlighting
Whorfian hypothesis

In September 1970, on the day I (Judith) enthusiastically (but somewhat nervously) began my academic career, there was a meeting of the faculty at my small campus. As is generally the custom, the campus director took this opportunity to introduce me and another new professor to the rest of the faculty and staff. His introduction of my male colleague in the physics department was both unsurprising and appropriate; he identified him as "Dr. Lantry Brooks" and then provided his academic credentials. Although my educational background was given, also, the director introduced me, quite awkwardly, as "Dr., Mrs. Judith Bridges."

What images of women's and men's roles does this dual title suggest? Is there a power difference implied by the different forms of address used for my male colleague and me?

Leap ahead to 1996. At that time, a colleague of mine went through a lengthy decision-making process about the surname she would use after her forthcoming marriage. She knew her fiancé was not going to change his name, and she considered taking his name, retaining her birth name, or hyphenating their names. She decided to hyphenate.

Does this colleague's decision have any effect on people's impressions of her? When students read her name in the course schedule, when she applies for grants, when she is introduced to new acquaintances, does her hyphenated name suggest a different image than her alternative choices would have? Why do we associate different characteristics with different surname choices; that is, what social experiences help shape these images?

These issues and similar ones are explored in this chapter as we examine stereotypes of females and males, the nature of sexism, and the representations of gender in the media and in language.

Stereotypes of Females and Males

Before we begin, think about your conception of the *typical* adult woman and the *typical* adult man. Then indicate your ideas in Get Involved 2.1.

GET INVOLVED **2.1**

How Do You View Typical Females and Males?

Indicate which of the following characteristics reflect your conception of a *typical* adult woman and a *typical* adult man. Write W next to each characteristic you associate with women and M next to each characteristic you associate with men. If you think a particular trait is representative of both women and men, write W and M next to that trait.

_____ achievement oriented	_____ emotional
_____ active	_____ gentle
_____ adventurous	_____ independent
_____ affectionate	_____ kind
_____ aggressive	_____ people-oriented
_____ ambitious	_____ pleasant
_____ boastful	_____ rational
_____ charming	_____ softhearted
_____ daring	_____ sympathetic
_____ dominant	_____ warm

Based on De Lisi & Soundranayagam, 1990; Williams & Best, 1990.

(continued on p. 28)

What Does It Mean?

Did your conceptions of a typical woman and a typical man match those reported by samples of university students from the United States and 28 other countries? These students described the typical woman with traits including: affectionate, charming, emotional, gentle, kind, people-oriented, softhearted, sympathetic, and warm; and they described the typical man with characteristics, such as: achievement-oriented, active, adventurous, ambitious, arrogant, daring, independent, rational, and showing initiative to a typical man.

1. If your impressions of the typical woman and the typical man did not agree with the descriptions reported by these samples of college students, give possible reasons.

2. What was the ethnic identity of the typical woman and man that you considered when performing this activity? If you thought about a White woman and man, do you think your conceptions would have varied had you been asked to specifically consider Blacks, Latinas/os, Asian Americans, or Native Americans? If yes, what are those differences and what can explain them?

3. Similarly, did you think of a middle-class woman and man? Would your impressions have varied had you thought about working-class or poor females and males? Explain any possible differences in gender stereotypes based on social class.

The Content of Gender Stereotypes

The characteristics shown in Get Involved 2.1 reflect **gender stereotypes**; that is, widely shared beliefs about the attributes of females and males. As this sample of traits indicates, personality characteristics associated with women, such as sympathy and warmth, reflect a concern about other people. Social scientists call this cluster of attributes **communion**. The group of traits associated with men, including achievement orientation and ambitiousness, on the other hand, reflects a concern about accomplishing tasks and is called **agency**. Interestingly, these stereotypes have remained relatively constant over time. The traits associated with females and males today are very similar to those shown in the 1970s (e.g., De Lisi & Soundranayagam, 1990; Bergen & Williams, 1991).

Consistent with the tendency to associate communal traits with females and agentic traits with males is people's tendency to expect different roles for women and men. For example, although most women are employed (U.S. Bureau of Labor Statistics, 1999b), many individuals continue to expect that women will be the primary caregivers of both children and elderly parents and that men will be the primary providers (e.g., Novack & Novack, 1996).

You might have noted that the attributes comprising the male stereotype are more highly regarded in North American society and are more consistent with a powerful image than those comprising the female cluster. In Western culture, with its strong emphasis on the value of hard work and achievement, we tend to associate agentic qualities, such as ambitiousness and independence, with power and prestige and to evaluate these traits more positively than communal attributes, such as gentleness and emotionality. Thus, gender stereotypes are the first indication of the power imbalance discussed in Chapter 1.

Gender stereotypes are relevant to another theme introduced in Chapter 1, the social construction of gender. Regardless of their accuracy, gender-related beliefs serve as lenses that guide our expectations and interpretations of other people. They can lead to the elicitation of stereotypic behaviors from others. For example, a high school teacher who believes that females are more nurturant than males might ask female students to volunteer in a day care center run by the school. This would provide females but not males the opportunity to develop their caregiving traits. Thus, the teacher's stereotype about the communal characteristics of girls and women might actually contribute to the construction of female-related traits in her female students.

The importance of gender stereotypes in the social construction of gender is also evident in the choices individuals make about their own behavior. For example, based on gender-related beliefs, more adolescent females than males might be likely to seek out baby-sitting experiences and, thus, more strongly develop traits such as nurturance and compassion.

The traits we have examined thus far are those that North Americans see as *representative* of most women and men. However, an examination of the characteristics people view as *ideal* for each gender indicates some discrepancy between people's stereotypes about most women and men and their conceptions of what women and men should be like. Sue Street and her colleagues (Street, Kromrey, & Kimmel, 1995; Street, Kimmel, & Kromrey, 1995) studied college students' and faculty's conceptions about the *ideal* woman and the *ideal* man as well as beliefs about *most* women and *most* men. Their findings showed that both students and faculty perceived most women as communal and most men as agentic. However, they viewed the ideal woman as very high in both female-related and male-related traits; that is, they believed she should be caring, sensitive, gentle, and compassionate, as well as logical, intelligent, achievement oriented, and assertive. Additionally, although these respondents saw the ideal man as highest in agentic traits, they believed he should be relatively high in compassion as well. Thus, both students and faculty believe ideal persons of both genders should have both types of characteristics.

The Perceiver's Ethnicity and Gender Stereotypes

When you performed Get Involved 2.1, did your selection of traits for females and males match those found in previous research? Alternatively, did you find that you were either less restrictive than the samples investigated in these studies or that you used different stereotypes? Possibly you indicated that some of these characteristics were reflective of both females and males or that some were more representative of the gender not usually associated with the stereotype. Although there is considerable consistency among people in their gender stereotypes, all individuals do not think alike.

In fact, there is evidence that people from different ethnic backgrounds vary in the degree to which they believe the ideal characteristics for females are different from the ideal traits for males. One early study (Pugh & Vazquez-Nuttall, 1983, cited in Vazquez-Nuttall, Romero-Garcia, & De Leon, 1987) suggested that Black women are less stereotypic in their views than are Latina or White women. When asked to describe their conceptions of the ideal woman, Blacks were the most likely and Latinas the least likely to believe that traits associated with males were important for the ideal woman.

More recently, Allen Harris (1994) approached 500 female and 500 male shopping-mall patrons from each of these three ethnic groups. He asked each person to rate the desirability of 59 personality traits for either a woman or a man in their culture. The Blacks were less likely than the Whites or Latinas/os to associate specific characteristics with each gender; instead they considered a larger variety of traits as desirable for both females and males. For example, Blacks rated assertiveness, independence, and self-reliance as equally desirable for Black women and men, whereas the other two ethnic groups evaluated these traits as more desirable for men than women in their cultural groups. Also, Blacks viewed eagerness to soothe hurt feelings as equally desirable for individuals of both genders, but Whites and Latinas/os perceived it as more desirable for women than men. However, in contrast to the earlier findings (Pugh & Vazquez-Nuttall, 1983), Latina women and Latino men viewed fewer of the characteristics as desirable for only one gender than White women and men did, and only Whites considered compassion to be more desirable for females than males.

The results of both studies indicate that among these three ethnic groups, Blacks are the least likely to adhere to rigid gender stereotypes for women and men. However, the earlier investigation (Pugh & Vazquez-Nuttall, 1983) reported that Latina women engaged in the most stereotyping whereas the later one (A. C. Harris, 1994) indicated Latinas and Latinos were less stereotypic in their perceptions than Whites were. One explanation for these different findings is that Latina/o participants in the later study were more integrated into mainstream American culture than their counterparts in the first investigation. There is evidence that the gradual acculturation of generations of Latinas/os into American society has been accompanied by a reduction in their stereotypical thinking about gender (A. C. Harris, 1994).

The Target's Characteristics and Gender Stereotypes

Ethnicity.   We have seen that people with diverse ethnic backgrounds differ somewhat in their perception of rigid stereotypes of women and men. Now let's examine whether these stereotypes vary as a function of the ethnicity of the person who is the object of the stereotype; that is, the target.

Studies that have explored the relationship between an individual's ethnic group and gender stereotypes of the person point to both commonalities and differences in stereotypes of individuals who vary in ethnicity. In one investigation, Yolanda Niemann and her colleagues (Niemann Jennings, Rozelle, Baxter, & Sullivan, 1994) asked a multiethnic sample of college students to list adjectives that came to mind when they thought of individuals in each of eight different ethnic/gender groups: White, Black, Mexican American, and Asian American females and males. Examination of the most frequently mentioned traits showed that all women, regardless of their ethnicity, were seen as pleasant. However, other traits varied as a function of ethnic identification. For example, whereas Black women were viewed as speaking loudly, Asian American women were seen as speaking softly. Further, only Mexican Americans were characterized as family oriented and only Blacks were described as antagonistic. Also, none of the most frequently listed traits for men were consistent across ethnicity. Only White and Asian American males were identified as intelligent, only Black men were viewed as athletic, and only Asian American and Mexican American men were characterized as hard workers.

Unfortunately, the study done by Niemann and her colleagues as well as one performed by Weitz and Gordon (1993) showed that college students attributed a greater number of negative traits to Black women than to other women. These studies indicate that Black women are viewed as antagonistic, unmannerly, loud, and argumentative; that is, traits connoting a threatening stereotype. Weitz and Gordon suggest two possible explanations for this image. First, it might reflect the cultural stereotype of Black women as domineering matriarchs. Second, because non-Blacks have not been exposed to a clear image of Black women, they might associate Black women with the more common threatening stereotype associated with Black men. Regardless of the explanation, this negative stereotype indicates that some Americans perceive Black women through a racist lens; a problem experienced by other ethnic minority women as well.

Social Class.   Given that stereotypes of women vary somewhat as a function of the woman's ethnicity, we might also expect them to vary according to another demographic characteristic: social class. In one of the few studies that explored class-based stereotypes, Hope Landrine (1985) found that lower-class women, compared to middle-class women, are viewed as more confused, dirty, and hostile and as less competent, happy, and vain.

Women with Disabilities.   Although there has been only minimal research on this topic, there is some evidence that people attribute very different characteristics to women with disabilities than to non-disabled women. Women with disabilities, unlike able-bodied women, are not assumed to be wives and mothers. Rather than expecting these women to function as nurturers, stereotypical images of women with disabilities emphasize their dependence on others (Hanna & Rogovsky, 1991).

In summary, we can see that gender stereotypes are not applied uniformly to all women. A woman's ethnicity, social class, and ability/disability influence stereotypes of her.

Stereotypes of Girls and Boys

We have seen that people have different expectations of the traits and behaviors of adult females and males. Now let's examine adults' gender-stereotypic expectations of children.

As early as the first few days of life, newborn girls and boys are perceived differently, at least by their parents. Studies performed two decades apart showed that parents rated newborn daughters as finer featured, less strong, and more delicate than newborn sons, despite medical evidence of no physical differences between them (Karraker, Vogel, & Lake, 1995; Rubin, Provenzano, & Luria, 1974). Additionally, the earlier study showed that parents of girls described their daughters as beautiful and their sons as big, and the more recent study found that parents rated their daughters as more feminine than their sons. Thus, it is apparent that adults hold gender stereotypes of the physical characteristics of children immediately after the child's birth.

Adults' stereotypes of children are not restricted to early infancy. In one study (Martin, 1995) Canadian college students were asked to rate the typical characteristics of four- to seven-year-old girls and boys. The evidence for gender stereotypes was quite clear. Out of 25 traits, these young adults rated 24 as being more typical for one gender than the other. Additionally, the traits seen as typical for girls versus boys reflected the communion-agency stereotypes evident in gender stereotypes of adults. For example, these students rated girls, compared to boys, as more gentle, sympathetic, and helpful around the house and they rated boys as more self-reliant, dominant, and competitive than girls.

Bases for Gender Stereotypes

Our exploration of the origins of gender stereotypes focuses on two related issues: (1) the reasons why people stereotype on the basis of gender, and (2) the reasons why these stereotypes center on communal traits for females and agentic attributes for males. In other words, we will consider explanations for both the *process* and the *content* of gender stereotyping.

Social Categorization.   The process of gender stereotyping makes sense if we consider how individuals attempt to understand their complex social environments. Because we are bombarded daily with diverse types of people, behaviors, situations, and so on, we simplify our social perceptions by *sorting individuals into categories,* a process called **social categorization**. It would be hard for us to understand and remember the multitude of people we encounter if we were to treat each as completely different from all others. Instead, we sort people into groups and focus on the characteristics they share with other members of that category. As an example, in a hospital we might categorize the individuals we encounter as doctors, nurses, patients, and visitors. Then the differential set of characteristics we associate with physicians versus nurses serves as a behavior guide when we interact with them, enabling us to ask questions appropriate to each of their skills and knowledge.

Although we make use of a variety of cues for the sorting process, social categorization is frequently based on easily identified natural characteristics, such as ethnicity, age, and gender (e.g., Brewer & Lui, 1989; Hewstone, Hantzi, & Johnston, 1991). This makes sense because these attributes are usually the first that we observe; they provide an easy basis on which to sort people. Thus, the process of gender stereotyping begins with the categorization of individuals as females or males with the implicit assumption that the members of each gender share certain attributes. Then, when we meet a new individual, we attribute these characteristics to this person.

Although the social categorization and stereotyping processes help simplify our understanding of and interactions with people, they can lead us astray: neither all females nor all males are alike. Fortunately, we are most likely to rely on stereotypes when we have little differentiating information about the person (e.g., Swim, Borgida, Maruyama, & Myers, 1989). Once more details about a person are available, we use that information in addition to the person's gender to form our impression and guide our interactions. For example, when evaluating an individual's level of ambition, we might make use of the person's gender if no other information were available. However, this information would be much less important if we knew the individual was a CEO in a major corporation.

Social Role Theory. Given that people naturally divide others into gender categories and attribute to all members of a category similar attributes, we turn now to the question of why people associate communion with females and agency with males. One possibility is that these stereotypes stem from our observations of the types of behaviors individuals typically perform in their social roles. According to **social role theory** (Eagly, 1987), *stereotypes of women and men stem from the association of women with the domestic role and men with the employee role.* This theory contends that because we have observed primarily women in the domestic role, we assume women have the nurturing traits characteristic of that role. Similarly, because more men than women have traditionally been seen in the employment role, we perceive men as having the agentic traits displayed in the workplace.

Support for this theory of gender stereotypes comes from numerous studies that show an influence of a person's social role on the application of gender-related traits to her/him. For example, there is evidence that social roles can override gender when assigning communal or agentic characteristics to others (Eagly & Steffen, 1984, 1986). Specifically, when participants are asked to describe a woman and a man who are homemakers they view them as equally communal. Similarly, when asked to describe a full-time female and male employee, they perceive both as agentic. In addition, women and men who are employed are viewed as more agentic than those who are not (e.g., Bridges, 1987; Mueller & Yoder, 1997; Riggs, 1997), mothers are seen as more communal than nonmothers (Bridges, 1987), and married women are perceived as more communal than unmarried women (e.g., Etaugh & Nekolny, 1990; Etaugh & Stern, 1984). Clearly, when people are aware of an individual's social role, their stereotypes of the person are influenced by that role information.

The influence of social roles on gender stereotypes is evident even when people are asked to describe women and men in both the past and the future. When both college and noncollege adults were asked to rate the average woman and the average man in 1950, 1975, 2025, and 2050, they viewed females as becoming dramatically more masculine over time and males as becoming somewhat more feminine (Diekman & Eagly, 1997). What accounts for these perceptions? In support of social role theory, the researchers found that the decreasing degree of gender stereotyping was related to the belief that the occupational and domestic roles of women and men during this time period have become and will continue to become increasingly similar.

Keep in mind, however, the evidence presented earlier in this chapter—that stereotypes have remained relatively constant, at least since the 1970s. What can explain the discrepancy between the increased participation of women in the labor force and the consistency of gender stereotypes over time? Although a greater number of women are now employed than was the case in the past, the proportion of women in the paid workforce continues to be lower than the corresponding proportion of men. Also, regardless of their employment role, women still have the primary caregiving responsibility in their families and are more likely than men to be employed in caregiving occupations, such as nursing and early childhood education. Although social roles are gradually changing, women remain the primary nurturers and men the primary providers. Consequently, it is not surprising that our stereotypes of females and males have been resistant to change.

Stereotypes Based on Identity Labels

Recall the experience Judith described at the beginning of the chapter when she was introduced as "Dr., Mrs. Bridges." The fact that the campus director introduced her this way but did not present her male colleague as "Dr. Lantry Brooks who happens to be married," implies he believed that a woman's identity, more than a man's, is shaped by her marital role. Although his use of a dual title was highly unusual, his belief about a woman's identity is consistent with the long-standing cultural norm that a woman is defined in terms of her relationship to a man (e.g., Lakoff, 1973). Given that a woman's title of address can signify her marital role and that her marital status has been viewed as an important aspect of her identity, we might expect different stereotypes of women who use different titles for themselves. Consider the woman who chooses not to use the conventional "Miss" versus "Mrs." labels which inform about her marital status but instead identifies herself with the neutral "Ms." Do people perceive her as different from the traditional female stereotype?

Research indicates they do. Kenneth Dion and his colleagues (Dion, 1987; Dion & Cota, 1991; Dion & Schuller, 1990) found that both college students and members of the general population hold a strong stereotype about women who prefer the modern title Ms. They perceive them as more achievement oriented, socially assertive, and competent, but less warm and likable than traditionally titled women. Thus, the Ms. title is a powerful cue eliciting a stereotype consistent with the male gender-related traits of agency and inconsistent with the female communal traits.

Given that our impressions of a woman are influenced by her preferred title, a related question is whether these stereotypes vary according to another identity label, a woman's choice of surname after marriage. Similar to the preference for Ms. as a title of address, a woman's choice of a surname other than her husband's, such as her birth name or a hyphenated name, is a nontraditional practice that separates the woman's personal identity from her identity as a wife. Thus, it is not surprising that a study performed by Claire, Judith, and their students (Etaugh, Bridges, Cummings-Hill, & Cohen, 1999) showed that college women and men view married women who use a nontraditional surname as more agentic and less communal than women who follow the patriarchal practice of taking their husband's name after marriage.

Why does a woman's preferred title and surname influence the characteristics attributed to her? One possibility is that individuals have observed more women with nontraditional forms of address (i.e., title and/or surname) in the workplace than in the domestic role and, thus, attribute her with more agentic traits. For example, there is evidence that the majority of young female executives prefer the title Ms., (Call me Madam?, 1987) and that married women who use nonconventional surnames are highly educated and career oriented (Johnson & Scheuble, 1995). Thus, consistent with social role theory (Eagly, 1987), stereotypes of women who prefer nontraditional forms of address might be due to the belief that they are in nontraditional roles.

Sexism

The definition of sexism as bias against people because of their gender can be directed at either females or males. However, women have a power disadvantage relative to men and are, therefore, more likely to be targets of sexism. Therefore, our discussion focuses on the more specific definition of sexism as *stereotypes and/or discriminatory behaviors that serve to restrict women's roles and maintain male dominance.* For example, stereotypes, such as "women are dependent and passive," "women should be the primary caregivers," and "women are not competent to be police officers or university presidents," serve to shape women's role choices. Similarly, negative treatment of women, such as the preferential hiring of a man over a woman, contributes to the maintenance of male dominance.

Consider the real-life case of Ann Hopkins, a high-achieving professional at Price Waterhouse, one of the country's most prestigious accounting firms. In 1982 Ms. Hopkins was one of 88 candidates for partner and the only female candidate. At that time she had more billable hours than any other contenders. Additionally, she had brought in $25 million worth of business and was highly esteemed by her clients. However, Ann Hopkins was turned down for the partnership. She was criticized for her "macho" style and was advised to "walk more femininely, talk more femininely, dress more femininely, wear makeup, have her hair styled, and wear jewelry" (*Hopkins v. Price Waterhouse*, 1985, p. 1117, cited in Fiske, Bersoff, Borgida, Deaux, & Heilman, 1991, p. 1050).

Ms. Hopkins filed a lawsuit, asserting that her promotion had been denied on the basis of her gender. Although she won this suit, her employer appealed the decision all the way up to the Supreme Court. The Court decided in Ann Hopkins's favor and in 1990, a federal district court judge concluded that gender-based stereotyping had played a role in the firm's refusal to promote Ms. Hopkins to partner (*Hopkins v. Price Waterhouse*, 1989, cited in Fiske et al., 1991, p. 1049). That is, in this case, the decision-makers' beliefs about Ms. Hopkins's style were inconsistent with their stereotype of femininity and this discrepancy influenced their discriminatory decision. It should be noted that, after this decision, Ann Hopkins did become a partner and was awarded financial compensation for her lost earnings (Hopkins, 1996).

Ambivalent Sexism

Generally, we consider sexism to comprise *negative* stereotypes about women, such as the beliefs that "women are fragile, submissive, and less competent than men." And, of course, we can see how stereotypes such as these are detrimental to women. Interestingly, however, Peter Glick and Susan Fiske (1997) have proposed that sexism can be **ambivalent,** encompassing both **hostile sexism**, or negative stereotypes of women, as well as **benevolent sexism**, or positive characterizations such as "women are pure" and "women should be protected."

Although hostile sexist beliefs are overtly demeaning, benevolent sexist views are usually accompanied by genuine affection and the holder of these attitudes might be unaware of their implicit sexist bias. For example, a husband who shields his wife from the family's financial difficulties because he believes she would be unable to cope might be unaware of the biased assumptions implicit in his desire to protect her. According to Glick and Fiske (1997), "Hostile and benevolent sexism . . . share common assumptions (e.g., that women are the weaker sex): both presume traditional gender roles and both serve to justify and maintain patriarchal social structures" (p. 121). In other words, ambivalent sexism includes both positive and negative beliefs about women, but both serve to channel women into traditional roles and to maintain the power imbalance between women and men.

Changes in Sexist Attitudes over Time

Since 1970 the United States has experienced a significant decrease in overt sexism. For example, in 1970 48 percent of a sample of college students expressed the belief that married women with children should stay home; however, only 26 percent expressed agreement with this belief in 1992 (Higher Education Research Institute, 1993, as cited in Twenge, 1997a). Further, a comparison of undergraduates' beliefs about the appropriate behaviors and roles for women at four points in time between 1972 and 1992 (Spence & Hahn, 1997) and a meta-analysis of 71 undergraduate samples from 1970 to 1995 (Twenge, 1997a) showed a steadily decreasing adherence to overt sexism by both females and males.

Of course, we must note that the studies that demonstrated decreasing sexism over time were all based on the attitudes of college students. There is little information available about the sexist beliefs of noncollege adults, such as working or middle-class women and men or adults on welfare.

Neosexism or Modern Sexism

It is likely that the reduction in sexism is due, in part, to legislative actions (e.g., 1960s legislation prohibiting education and workplace discrimination on the basis of sex) and other social changes (e.g., the significant influx of married women into the workplace in the last few decades). However, some of the decline in overt sexism might actually reflect the decreased social acceptability of blatantly sexist views, rather than a real weakening of beliefs that serve to maintain traditional roles and power differences. Several theorists have suggested that a more subtle type of sexism has emerged in North America. This ideology, called **neosexism** (Tougas, Brown, Beaton, & Joly, 1995) or **modern sexism** (Swim & Cohen, 1997), is based on the coexistence of conflicting attitudes. According to this perspective, some people hold egalitarian values but, at the same time, harbor negative feelings toward women. The resulting ideology is *characterized by the belief that gender discrimination is no longer a problem in society and is manifested by harmful treatment of women in ways that appear to be socially acceptable.* For example, a neosexist might argue that policies that foster gender equality, such as affirmative action, should not be implemented. Thus, it is possible for a person to espouse sexist beliefs such as these but not appear to be prejudiced against women.

Do you know anyone who endorses neosexism? See Get Involved 2.2 for examples of neosexist beliefs.

Experiences with Sexism

Have you ever experienced unfair treatment by teachers, employers, strangers, romantic partners, and others because of your gender? Have you ever been the target of inappropriate or unwanted sexual advances or sexist name calling? Have you ever been forced to listen to sexist jokes? Elizabeth Klonoff and Hope Landrine (1995) asked 631 culturally diverse college and non-college women how

GET INVOLVED 2.2
Who Holds Neosexist Beliefs?

On a scale from 1 (strongly disagree) to 7 (strongly agree), indicate the extent to which you disagree or agree with each of the following statements. Also, ask several female and male acquaintances who vary in age to respond to these statements.

1. It is rare to see women treated in a sexist manner on television.
2. Society has reached the point where women and men have equal opportunities for achievement.
3. Over the past few years, the government and news media have been showing more concern about the treatment of women than is warranted by women's actual experiences.
4. Discrimination against women is no longer a problem in the United States.
5. Women's requests in terms of equality between the sexes are simply exaggerated.
6. Universities are wrong to admit women in costly programs such as medicine, when in fact, a large number will leave their jobs after a few years to raise their children.
7. Due to social pressures, firms frequently have to hire underqualified women.

Based on Swim, Aikin, Hall, & Hunter, (1995); Tougas et al., (1995).

What Does It Mean?

Sum the ratings you gave to these seven statements. Do the same for each of your respondents. Note that each statement reflects a sexist belief; therefore, the higher the score, the greater the sexism.

1. Are there differences between the views of your female and male respondents? Explain your finding.
2. Are there differences between the views of respondents who vary in age? Explain your finding.
3. Do you think it is possible that a person could endorse one or more of these beliefs but not be supportive of traditional roles and male dominance? Why or why not?

often incidents like these had happened to them. All except 6 women (99 percent) reported experiencing sexist discrimination at least once in their lives. Among the most commonly experienced events, reported by more than 80 percent of the women, were being forced to listen to sexist jokes, being sexually harassed, and experiencing a lack of respect. Although less common, 40 percent of the women reported some type of employment discrimination and 19 percent indicated they had taken legal or institutional action to pursue discrimination on the basis of gender.

Other studies (e.g., Krieger, 1990) also report widespread sexist behavior against women. However, the perception of sexism is dependent, in part, on a woman's interpretation. To one woman a joke that sexually degrades women is sexist but to another woman that joke is simply funny.

Not only do women vary in their interpretation of sexist incidents but they differ from one another in their willingness to acknowledge their own experience with discrimination. In a study of college students, Kobrynowicz and Branscombe (1997) found that women who have a strong desire for social approval are less likely to acknowledge they had experienced discrimination than those willing to risk disapproval are. According to these researchers, claiming sexism might be perceived as socially undesirable for women who are greatly concerned about the amount of approval they receive from others.

Another factor that can explain variations in the interpretation of a specific behavior as discriminatory is the perpetrator's gender. When people decide whether a behavior is sexist they take into account the gender of the person who performed the action. For example, in one study (Baron, Burgess, & Kao, 1991), researchers asked college students to read vignettes in which a woman or a man responded to a woman in accordance with traditional roles and stereotypes (e.g., discouraged a female applicant who applied for a job as a tractor-trailer driver; counseled a female student to change from premed to nursing). The results showed that the same behaviors were more likely to be perceived as sexist if they were performed by a male than by a female perpetrator. Possibly, people consider it unlikely that women will discriminate against other women; thus, they fail to label women's gender-stereotypic comments and behaviors as sexist.

Representation of Gender in the Media

As we have seen, there is considerable evidence that North American adults have different conceptions of females and males. We turn now to the depiction of these stereotypes in the media. On a daily basis we are bombarded with differential images of females and males on television, in the movies, in books, and in magazines. Are these images consistent with gender stereotyping? Try the exercise in Get Involved 2.3 to examine television portrayals of gender.

Numerous investigations of the depiction of females and males in both electronic and print media have revealed several themes: the underrepresentation of females, the underrepresentation of specific groups of women, the portrayal of gender-based social roles, the depiction of female communion and male agency, and the emphasis on female attractiveness and sexuality. Our first task is to examine these themes. Then we consider the effects of media images on gender stereotypes and attitudes.

GET INVOLVED **2.3**

How Are Females and Males Portrayed on Prime-Time Television?

Watch 5 different prime-time shows and record the following information: (1) the number of major female and male characters, (2) the ethnicity of these characters, (3) the employment status and occupation, if employed, of each major female and male character, (4) the marital and parental status of these characters, (5) the approximate age of each of these characters (e.g., twenties, thirties, etc), and (6) whether or not each character's physical appearance was mentioned or otherwise appeared to be an important characteristic of that person. After recording this information, examine commonalities and differences in the depiction of females and males and in the portrayal of different age groups. Also, if these shows featured women and/or men of color, compare portrayals of characters of varying ethnicities.

What Does It Mean?

1. Are your findings consistent with those presented in this chapter? If not, what do you think might explain any differences you observed?
2. Do your findings indicate that members of each gender are depicted similarly, regardless of their ethnicity or age? If you found differences related to ethnicity or age, explain them.
3. Do you think that media images of gender, as described in this chapter and as shown by your analysis, help shape our construction of gender? Explain your answer.

Theme 1: Underrepresentation of Females

As we have previously seen, women are perceived as less powerful than men; men's roles are viewed as more important. This imbalance of power and value is reflected in the media's underrepresentation of females. Although the percentage of female characters in television shows increased from 28 percent in the 1970s to 39 percent in the 1990s (Signorielli & Bacue, 1999), it is clear that the proportion of females continues to be low. Similarly, the percentage of female characters in TV commercials (Allan & Coltrane, 1996; Signorielli, 1997), including animated spokes-characters (Peirce & McBride, 1999), MTV music videos (Signorielli, 1997; Sommers-Flanagan, Sommers-Flanagan, & Davis, 1993), and movies (Bazzini, McIntosh, Smith, Cook & Harris, 1997; Signorielli, 1997) ranges from approximately 20 percent to 40 percent. Furthermore, this underrepresentation is mirrored in children's television programs (Calvert, Stolkin, & Lee, 1997; Thompson & Zerbinos, 1995) and commercials (Ogletree, Williams, Raffeld, Mason, & Fricke, 1990) and in video games (Dietz, 1998).

A similar underrepresentation of females is found in many types of children's books. Although children's readers (Purcell & Stewart, 1990) show nearly equal numbers of females and males as central characters, picture books tend to feature more males than females in titles, as central characters, and in pictures (Kortenhaus & Demarest, 1993; Tepper & Cassidy, 1999; Turner-Bowker, 1996).

Theme 2: Underrepresentation of Specific Groups of Females

The invisibility of females is most evident when considering females in less powerful social categories. Women and girls of color, especially Latinas, Asian Americans, and Native Americans are featured very infrequently in both children's and adult's television shows and commercials (Calvert et al., 1997; Furnham, Abramsky, & Gunter, 1997; Greenberg & Brand, 1993; Hall & Crum, 1994). Also, they are underrepresented in advertisements in a wide variety of periodicals, including mainstream fashion, business, and general interest magazines (Jackson & Ervin, 1991; Taylor, Lee, & Stern, 1995) and are nearly invisible in fiction stories in large-circulation women's magazines (Peirce, 1997). Moreover, even college-level textbooks pay little attention to women of color. For example, a study of 11 developmental psychology texts reported that ethnic minority women were mentioned only four times (Conti & Kimmel, 1993), and an analysis of 20 leading marriage and family texts found that only 2 percent of the material dealt with people of color, and this coverage completely excluded Native Americans (Shaw-Taylor & Benokraitis, 1995). Similarly, a study of sociology textbooks noted that Latina women were nearly invisible (Marquez, 1994).

Another seriously underrepresented group is older women. In both television shows (Davis, 1990; Fouts & Burggraf, 1999; Signorielli & Bacue, 1999) and movies (Bazzini et al., 1997) female characters are younger than male characters, with most women under age 35. In fact, women over 50 are portrayed in only 12 percent of the roles in popular movies and, among the top actors aged 50 or older, only 20 percent are women (Haskell & Harmetz, 1998).

Theme 3: Portrayal of Gender-Based Social Roles

Females and males are portrayed differently in the media not only in terms of their numbers but in relation to their social roles. Over the last few decades there has been an increase in the percentage of prime-time TV shows that feature female characters who are employed, with 60 percent of female characters depicted as working in the 1990s (Signorielli & Bacue, 1999). Furthermore, their range of jobs has broadened; in the 1990s only one-quarter were shown in traditional female jobs, such as secretary or nurse (Signorielli & Bacue, 1999).

On the other hand, consistent with the stereotypical association of men in the worker role and women in the family role, popular television shows (Signorielli & Bacue, 1999), commercials (Allan & Coltrane, 1996; Coltrane & Adams, 1997; Signorielli, 1997), and movies (Signorielli, 1997) still show more men than women with jobs, and in both commercials (Coltrane & Adams, 1997) and prime-time programs (National Partnership for Women & Families, 1998) women are more likely than men to be shown in families. Also, although most married men in TV shows are employed, there are few married working women in these shows (Signorielli, 1993). Thus, despite the presence of several positive employed-female role models on television and the fact that the majority of American married women are employed (U.S. Bureau of Labor Statistics, 1999c), there is little depiction of women who successfully combine a job and marriage.

Similarly, the Sunday comics feature more women than men at home and fewer women than men in career activities (Brabant & Mooney, 1997). Also, children's picture books reflect this role difference by depicting females with household objects and males with objects related to non-household productive activities (Crabb & Bielawski, 1994). In addition, when females are portrayed as working, children's readers (Purcell & Stewart, 1990) and cartoons (Spicher & Hudak, 1997) show them in a smaller variety of occupations, and teen magazines for girls portray both genders in gender-stereotypical occupations (e.g., men as physicians and women as nurses) (Peirce, 1993). Furthermore, the majority of feature articles in the leading teen magazine for girls, *Seventeen*, focus on traditional topics, such as appearance and relationships (Schlenker, Caron, & Halteman, 1998). Only 40 percent address more feminist themes, such as self- and career development. Thus, the portrayal of social roles for women and men reflects the common expectation that women have the primary domestic responsibility and men have the primary provider role.

Theme 4: Depiction of Female Communion and Male Agency

Consistent with the depiction of females and males in different social roles, the communion stereotype for females and the agency stereotype for males are both evident in the media. Boys and men are depicted as more assertive, aggressive, and powerful than females in a range of media, including adult films (Hedley, 1994), MTV music videos (Sommers-Flanagan, Sommers-Flanagan, & Davis, 1993), children's cartoons (Browne, 1998; Spicher & Hudak, 1997; Thompson & Zerbinos, 1995), Disney films (Levant, 1997), and picture books (Kortenhaus & Demarest, 1993; Turner-Bowker, 1996). Also, the lack of agency on the part of females is reflected in both teen (Peirce, 1993) and women's (Peirce, 1997) magazine fiction where the female main character generally has to depend on other people to help her solve her problems. Furthermore, consistent with their greater power, males are presented as narrators in approximately 90 percent of commercials that use voice-overs (e.g., Craig, 1992; Ogletree et al., 1990), thus projecting an image of authority and expertise.

Although less pervasive than the agentic images of males, the media feature females as communal, as oriented toward other people. Many plots of teen-magazine fiction stories center on conflicts with boys (Peirce, 1993), and in both television and movies, women more than men focus on their romantic relationships (Signorielli, 1997). Furthermore, picture books describe more females than males as sweet (Turner-Bowker, 1996), a trait associated more with an interpersonal (communal) orientation than with a goal-directed (agentic) orientation.

Theme 5: Emphasis on Female Attractiveness and Sexuality

A last theme is that the media define females more than males by their looks and sexuality. For example, commercials are likely to show more women than men as physically attractive (Lin, 1998), and commercials, television shows, and movies portray women as more likely than men to receive comments about their appearance (Signorielli, 1997). Even commercials directed at children feature more female than male characters when marketing appearance-enhancing products (Ogletree et al., 1990). Both commercials and MTV portray more females than males as sex objects (Coltrane & Adams, 1997; Craig, 1992; Hall & Crum, 1994; Lin, 1998; Sommers-Flanagan et al., 1993) and prime-time television programs show more females than males in provocative clothing (Davis, 1990).

This emphasis on females' appearance is apparent in print as well as electronic media. In 1996, 78 percent of the covers of the most popular magazines for women presented text about bodily appearance, such as messages about diet or exercise. However, none of the covers of frequently read men's magazines contained comparable messages (Malkin, Wornian, & Chrisler, 1999). Kate Peirce (1997) contends that new magazines targeted at working women focus as much on appearance as beauty and fashion magazines do. She notes that in one 1995 issue of *New Woman*, 12 pages of makeup ads preceded the table of contents. Moreover, the depiction of women, more so than men, tends to be sexualized. For example, female fashion ads are more likely than male ads are to feature models in sexual attire (Plous & Neptune, 1997).

Not only is a woman's attractiveness portrayed as highly important but that attractiveness is depicted as overly thin. For example, most *Playboy* centerfolds are underweight, and approximately one-third are so thin that they meet the World Health Organization's standard for anorexia nervosa, a severe eating disorder (see Chapter 5) (Spitzer, Henderson, & Zivian, 1999). Gregory Fouts and Kimberley

Burggraf (1999) examined the body weight of characters in Canadian situation comedies and found that the number of below-average-weight female characters was greater than that found in the general population. Additionally, they observed that positive comments from male characters were contingent on a female character's weight. The thinner the female, the more positive reinforcement she received.

Thus, the media still portray appearance and sexuality as two highly valued aspects of a woman's identity. More specifically, they present the message that it is White beauty that is valued. Black actresses and models who are depicted as physically desirable are likely to be light-skinned and to possess White facial features (Perkins, 1996), thus informing the Black viewer that not just beauty but White beauty, is important.

Significance of Gender-Role Media Images

As this discussion indicates, despite the nearly equal numbers of North American females and males, the media portray a world more heavily populated by males than by females, a world in which males are more likely than females are to have jobs and be active and assertive and where beauty and romantic relationships are central to females' identity. Many researchers (e.g., Peirce, 1990; Wilson & Gutierrez, 1995) have argued not only that the media reinforces existing stereotypes but that media portrayal of gender can influence the development of gender stereotypes (e.g., Davis, 1990; Peirce, 1993; Signorielli, 1993). Kyra Lanis and Katherine Covell (1995) found that male college students viewing a series of magazine ads depicting women as sex objects reported more stereotypical gender beliefs than males who viewed neutral ads, indicating that the media can play an important role in shaping our construction of gender and in providing us with expectations of what females and males are like—their personality traits, social roles, and value to society. In addition, the very limited depiction of non-White or older females can reinforce perceptions of the powerlessness of these groups and communicate that their experiences are not important.

Consider other types of media that might portray females and males stereotypically. See, for example, Learn about the Research 2.1 to find out about stereotypes in greeting cards.

Representation of Gender in the English Language

The last section demonstrated how communication via the mass media, such as television and magazines, portrays different images of females and males. This section examines language itself: at the different ways females and males are depicted in the English language and how this differential portrayal can shape our conceptions of gender.

LEARN ABOUT THE RESEARCH 2.1

Are Babies Portrayed Stereotypically in Birth Congratulations Cards?

Previous studies demonstrated that girls and boys are portrayed stereotypically in children's literature (e.g., Purcell & Stewart, 1990) and in toy catalogs and packages (Schwartz & Markham, 1985). However, none of these examined societal expectations about baby boys and girls. In order to explore these stereotypes, Judith and her assistants systematically examined the visual images and verbal messages present in 61 birth congratulations cards for girls and 61 cards for boys.

Their detailed examination of the visual and verbal content of these cards showed several differences. Not surprisingly, pink was the most common color used on the cards for girls and blue on the cards for boys. In terms of activities, boys were more likely to be shown performing physical activities, such as walking or building, whereas girls were pictured passively sitting or lying down. Similarly, more of the cards for boys featured toys, such as sports equipment and vehicles, that require considerable action; whereas girls were pictured with baby toys, such as rattles and mobiles, that required less physical involvement. Larger animals, including bears and dogs, were more common on the cards for boys and smaller, less aggressive birds and rabbits were shown on the cards for girls.

Although there were few gender-specific verbal messages in the cards, there were several interesting differences. Girls, more than boys, were described as "little" and "sweet," while the happiness of parents or the child was included more often in the verbal message to boy's than in the message to girls.

What Does It Mean?

Answer these questions before reading the remaining part of the research description.

1. The pictures on the cards for girls and boys differed in terms of the types of activities the children were doing, as well as the types of toys and animals presented. How do these differential images fit in with gender stereotypes of females and males as discussed in this chapter?
2. Do any of the study's findings suggest that one gender is more culturally valued than the other? Explain your answer.
3. If you were buying a birth congratulations card for a friend or relative, would you look for a gender-stereotypic or a nonstereotypic card? Why?

One conclusion of this study was that birth congratulations cards do portray newborns in gender-stereotypic ways. In keeping with the stereotypical conception that males are more active than females, the types of activities, toys, and animals shown on the cards portrayed boys as more active than girls. Similarly, the tendency to characterize girls more than boys as "little" and "sweet" is consistent with the stereotypic conception of more passive and less powerful females. It is possible that the more frequent reference to happiness on the cards for boys might reflect a greater societal value placed on males than on females and/or it might be indicative of a stronger preference for a son than for a daughter.

(Bridges, 1993).

Language Practices Based on the Assumption That Male Is Normative

Numerous language practice reflect the assumption that **male is normative**; that is, that *male behaviors, roles and experiences are the standards (i.e., norms) for society.* Integral to this perspective are the assumptions that males are more important than females and that female behaviors, roles, and experiences are deviant, that is, different from the norm (Wood, 1994). One indication of this assumption is that adults tend to think of males as persons, as standard or normative individuals in society. For example, Mykol Hamilton (1991) found that college students were more apt to describe typical persons as males than as females and to refer to a male as a *person* but a female as a *woman.* Try Get Involved 2.4 and see if your findings match those reported by Hamilton.

G E T   I N V O L V E D   **2.4**

Are Both Women and Men Persons?

Ask two acquaintances of each gender to help you with this activity. Tell them you are studying people's choices about grammatical structure; that is, you are examining students' selections of specific words in a sentence. Therefore, you would like them to fill in the blank in each of the following:

1. "Debra Cook won the raffle at the charity fund-raising event. The event organizers will send the prize to this _____ in two weeks."

   person   woman

2. "Dave Sherman moved to a new town and went to the Town Hall to register to vote. The registrar of voters gave this _____ the application form."

   person   man

Based on Hamilton, 1991.

What Does It Mean?

Examine the selections made by your respondents.

1. Did they select different terms depending on the gender of the person?
2. Were there any differences between the answers of the females and males?

3. Did these answers correspond to the findings of Hamilton, as discussed in this chapter?
4. What interpretation can you offer for your findings?

Now let's examine some of the language practices that reflect this belief of male as normative.

Masculine Generic Language. Consider the following situation:

> At the first session of a training program called "Reducing Man's Addictions" the program's director informed participants that they would be divided into small groups for discussion of the material and that each group should appoint a chairman to facilitate its discussion. Also, the director indicated that at the end of the training program each participant would have sufficient knowledge so that he could work at a drug rehabilitation center.

Describe your image of this event. Does the program deal with addiction problems of both women and men or men only? Will the chairs of the groups be men or women? What is the gender of the participants? Are these gender images clear?

Now substitute, *woman's* for *man's*, *chairwoman* for *chairman*, and *she* for *he*. Ask yourself the same questions.

Regardless of your own interpretations of these two verbal descriptions, note that the latter was written using gender-specific (i.e., female) terms whereas the former was written in **masculine generic language**, which is *language that uses male terms but purports to be inclusive of females and males*. Both male pronouns, such as *he* and *his*, as well as male nouns, such as *chairman, freshman, businessman, man-hours*, and *forefathers*, are used not only in reference to males but as inclusive of both genders (reflecting the assumption that male is standard).

Are these masculine generic terms actually interpreted as gender neutral; that is, are they as likely to elicit images of females as males? An abundance of research suggests they are not. Far from communicating gender-neutral images, these terms tend to be exclusionary, connoting just what they directly indicate; that is, men and boys. For example, in one study (Switzer, 1990) first- and seventh-grade children listened to the following story:

> Pretend that [teacher's name] told you that a new student is coming to be a part of your class. Tomorrow will be ＿＿ first day. Describe how you think ＿＿ will feel on the first day. (p. 74)

Students heard the story with one of the following pronouns inserted in the blanks: *he, he or she,* or *they*. The results clearly showed that *he* is not assumed to mean both females and males. Its exculsionary interpretation was demonstrated by the finding that 93 percent of the children who heard the *he* story, wrote that the student was a boy. On the other hand, when the pronouns were the inclusive *he or she* or *they*, the girls were more apt to write about a girl than a boy and the boys were more likely to write about a boy than a girl.

A comparable study with adults (Gastil, 1990) similarly indicates the male bias of the pronoun *he*. In response to sentences with these different pronouns, college students visualized more males when the pronoun *he* was used than when either *he/she* or *they* was specified.

Given that male pronouns are evidently not gender neutral, it is not surprising that the use of male nouns as gender neutral similarly connotes male images. In one study (McConnell & Fazio, 1996) college students rated a *chairman* as more masculine than either a *chair* or a *chairperson*, suggesting that the former leads to more male-related mental imagery than the other two. Therefore, it is not surprising that the newer, gender-neutral terms, chair and chairperson, are more likely used in reference to women whereas the traditional term, chairman, is more often used to indicate a man (Romaine, 1999).

Spotlighting.   **Spotlighting** refers to *the practice of emphasizing an individual's gender*, as in "*Female* professor receives prestigious grant" or " *Woman* attorney wins the case." Consistent with the male as normative perspective, this practice of highlighting a woman's gender serves to reinforce the notion that males are the standard (Wood, 1994, p. 127). That is, although spotlighting does give recognition to specific females, at the same time, it conveys the message that these females are exceptions.

One investigation of gendered spotlighting involved the examination of televised broadcasts of the 1989 women's and men's National Collegiate Athletic Association final four basketball tournaments (Messner, Duncan, & Jensen, 1993). The researchers observed spotlighting an average of 26 times per game during the women's tournament with commentary, such as ". . . is a legend in *women's* basketball" or "this NCAA *women's* semifinal is brought to you by . . ." (p. 125). However, there was no evidence of spotlighting during the men's games.

Diminutive Suffixes for Female Terms.   The English language sometimes differentiates genders by using a root word to designate a male and an added suffix to specify a female. This language feature, like others discussed in this section, is based on the assumption of the male as the standard. A suffix is needed to indicate the non-normative exception, the female. Examples of this include *actor/actress*, *poet/poetess*, and *author/authoress*. In fact, according to Suzanne Romaine (1999), the only English words where the female term is the root word with a male suffix added are *widower* and *bridegroom*. Why do these words have female roots? Perhaps the term, *widower*, reflects the fact that women generally outlive men and *bridegroom* might be based on the traditional expectation that women's roles are linked to marriage and the family.

Romaine (1999) contends that this practice of marking the female with a suffix added to the male root is one way the English language signifies that a woman is a "lesser man" (p. 140). Similarly, Casey Miller and Kate Swift state (1991, p. 171), "the significance of a word like authoress is not that it identifies a female but that it indicates deviation from what is consciously or unconsciously considered the standard."

Negative Terms for Females

Another language practice that reflects the differential treatment of females and males is the greater number of negative terms depicting women than men.

Tide twists Vols' title plans

Disappearing act won't help Vols' status

TUSCALOOSA, Ala.

If you're a Tennessee men's basketball fan, you can rest easy today.

You no longer have to fret about those whispers concerning the possibility of one or more Vols jumping to the NBA early.

Let's just put it this way: junior Tony Harris and sophomore Vincent Yarbrough should be thankful there was only one NBA scout in the building to witness the second half of UT's 80-75 loss to Alabama on Saturday.

"Both of those Tennessee guys have a tremendous future," Seattle SuperSonics regional scout Yvan K. Kelly said diplomatically.

Note: The key word is "future."

As for the present, that's another story.

Harris was 1 for 9 against Alabama and scored four points.

"It's going to be a big transition for Tony to play the point in the pros, and size (under 6 feet) is going to be more of a problem in the pros than in college," Kelly said.

GARY LUNDY

Hot second half helps Alabama ambush No. 7 UT

By Mike Strange
News-Sentinel sportswriter

TUSCALOOSA, Ala. — Among the several costly turnovers Tennessee fumbled away in the closing minutes Saturday, the biggest was this: the chance to control its own destiny.

The SEC men's basketball championship the Vols covet hasn't fallen completely out of reach, but now it also will be decided in places such as Gainesville and Lexington.

"We just put the ball in somebody else's hands," said UT's Vincent Yarbrough, assessing the damage after No. 7-ranked Tennessee was upset by Alabama 80-75.

UT arrived at Coleman Coliseum in the driver's seat of a tight SEC race. However, the Vols got unseated by a young Alabama team that rose to the occasion, cheered on by a crowd of 9,063.

The Crimson Tide (13-13, 6-8 SEC) overturned a 10-point Tennessee lead early in the second half and held the cold-shooting, fumble-fingered Vols at bay down the stretch.

The intensity Tennessee showed in its victory over Kentucky three days earlier was nowhere to be found.

"We came in thinking because we're Tennessee, they'd lay down for us," senior C.J. Black said, searching for an explanation.

"You look at our defense against Kentucky," UT coach Jerry Green said, "and our offense and how much enthusiasm and energy we've got to expend.

Lady Vols seek a repeat defense against LSU

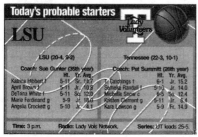

Today's probable starters

LSU (20-4, 9-2)				Tennessee (22-3, 10-1)			
Coach: Sue Gunter (35th year)				Coach: Pat Summitt (26th year)			
	Ht.	Yr.	Avg.		Ht.	Yr.	Avg.
Katrica Hibbert f	5-11	Sr.	13.7	Gwen Jackson f	6-1	Jr.	15.2
April Brown f	5-11	Jr.	10.9	Semeka Randall f	5-10	Jr.	14.0
DeTrina White f	5-11	Sr.	12.0	Michelle Snow c	6-5	So.	12.4
Marie Ferdinand g	5-9	Jr.	18.0	Kristen Clement g	5-11	Jr.	6.4
Angelia Crockett g	5-10	Jr.	4.1	Kara Lawson g	5-9	Fr.	14.9

Time: 3 p.m.	Radio: Lady Vols Network	Series: UT leads 25-5.

By Dan Fleser
News-Sentinel sportswriter

A visit from LSU today recalls the finest hour for Tennessee's defense.

The 3 o'clock tip-off at Thompson-Boling Arena is the second regular-season meeting for these SEC rivals. The first game, Jan. 6 in Baton Rouge, La., probably was second to none for the Lady Vols.

"That could've been our best game of the year," UT coach Pat Summitt said of the 86-50 victory.

One of the biggest reasons for the one-sided result was Tennessee's defenders helping limit the Tigers to 36.8 percent shooting

from the floor. They also played a part in 25 LSU turnovers.

Striving for a repeat performance would be a noble quest, but probably not realistic. Summitt conceded to the one-of-those-nights nature of the first encounter.

"We were on a roll," she said. "They couldn't get on track. It snowballs."

Nonetheless, taking a stab at better defensive consistency would be a useful objective. Before the first LSU-Tennessee game, the defense was viewed as good but not great. Thirteen games later, the same perspective applies.

The Lady Vols are more apt to have their moments on defense.

Obviously they've had their share, as evidenced by their record (22-3, 10-1 SEC) and their national ranking (2nd). A nine-game winning streak adds to their stature.

"I believe we can get a (defensive) stop against any team in the country at any time," freshman guard Kara Lawson said.

She offered this assessment after UT's defenders held Mississippi State scoreless during the final 2:35 of last Thursday's 79-75 comeback victory. This work was a crucial accompaniment to the Lady Vols' 11-point finishing kick across the same time span.

The defensive stand was a

Please see **LADY VOLS**, page C7

Highlighting the female gender but not the male gender reinforces the assumption that males are the standard and females are the exception.

Parallel Terms. There are numerous pairs of words in the English language in which the objective meaning of the female and male term are comparable, but the female word has a negative connotation. Consider, for example, *bachelor* and *spinster* or *old maid*. All three refer to unmarried persons, but the female terms connote an undesirable state reflecting rejection and old age. Another example is *master* versus *mistress*. Originally these referred to a man and woman in charge of a household, a usage that still pertains to *master*. *Mistress*, however, has developed a sexual connotation with negative overtones (Romaine, 1999).

Childlike Terms.   Have you ever heard the term *girl* in reference to an adult woman? Perhaps you have noted a male manager say something like the following to one of his associates: "I'll have my *girl* phone your *girl* to schedule a lunch meeting for us." Given that neither of the secretaries to whom he is referring is likely to be "a female child" a dictionary definition of girl (Neufeldt & Guralnik, 1994), the term *girl* is not appropriate. However, it is more common for people to refer to adult women as *girls* than to adult men as *boys*. For example, in the investigation (Messner et al., 1993) of televised commentary of women's and men's sports discussed above, the researchers found that, although the female athletes were not younger than their male counterparts, the broadcasters referred to female basketball and tennis players as *girls* but never called the male athletes *boys*.

Other childlike terms that are applied more to women than to men include *baby*, *babe*, and *sweetie*. Although these terms might be perceived as signs of affection in an intimate relationship, their use by nonintimates reflects the childlike quality of many terms used to identify women.

Is the use of these terms detrimental to women? Research suggests that it might be. For example, when female and male respondents in a study were asked about their impressions of adult women, they described women who were referred to as *girls* as being less responsible than women who were labeled *women* (Kitto, 1989). Such a negative depiction could clearly apply to other childlike terms.

Animal and Food Terms.   Researchers of the gender biases of language (e.g., Wood, 1994) point to the heavy use of animal names and food products in reference to women as another example of the negative depiction of females. Examples of these include the animal labels *fox, chick, bitch,* and *cow,* and the food-related terms *honey, cookie, dish,* and *feast for the eyes.*

Sexualization of Women.   As discussed earlier in this chapter, the media treat a woman's sexuality as an important aspect of her identity. American English also places a strong emphasis on a woman's sexuality. One study (Stanley, 1977) identified 220 terms that refer to a sexually permissive woman, compared to only 22 terms that refer to the male counterpart. In another investigation (Grossman & Tucker, 1997), college students were asked to list all of the slang words they could think of for either a woman or a man. Although there was no difference in the number of terms associated with each gender, approximately 50 percent of the terms used for females were sexual (e.g., *slut*) whereas less than 25 percent of those used for males were.

Negative Slang for Females.   In addition to the strong sexualization of women, Grossman and Tucker's study of slang noted that the terms used for women were more negative than those used for men. For example, among the most frequently listed terms were *bitch* and *slut* for women and *guy* and *dude* for men

Significance of the Differential Treatment of Females and Males in Language

We have examined several indications that English depicts males as the societal standard and that many language conventions portray females in negative terms. Do these practices matter?

Although language certainly reflects our conceptions of females and males, some scholars contend that it can, additionally, shape our images of gender. That is, it is influential in forming our social construction of gender. Specifically, a psycholinguistic theory, the **Whorfian hypothesis** (Whorf, 1956), states that *language influences our thoughts*; that is, the way we think is affected, in part, by the words we use. Certainly, research such as Kitto's (1989) investigation of perceptions of the term *girl*, points to the strong influence of words on thoughts. Therefore, it is not surprising that some scholars believe language practices, such as the use of the male as the norm, help promote an image of the more powerful male. As stated by Julia Wood (1994): "In Western society, our language negates women's experience by denying and dismissing women's importance and sometimes their very existence. In so doing, it represents men and their experiences as the norm and women and their ways as deviant. This marginalizes women" (p. 125). Furthermore Grossman and Tucker (1997) expressed concern about the impact of negative and sexual slang terms for females. They commented, "To the extent that gender-related slang not only reflects how the sexes are viewed within a particular culture, but may also shape perceptions, these results do not appear to bode well for women" (p. 109).

SUMMARY

1. Based on the natural tendency to sort others into gender categories, we assume that certain characteristics, behaviors, and roles are more representative of females and others of males. These are called gender stereotypes.

2. Stereotypes vary according to the ethnicity of the person holding the stereotype and the ethnicity and social class of the target person. Also, stereotypes of women with disabilities differ from stereotypes of able-bodied women.

3. According to social role theory, because we associate females with the domestic role and males with the employment role, our female stereotype tends to center on communion and our male stereotype on agency.

4. Women who choose to be called "Ms." or who use a nontraditional name after marriage are perceived as more agentic than women who prefer conventional titles of address.

5. Several different forms of sexism have been proposed by scholars. Ambivalent sexism comprises both hostile and benevolent attitudes. Neosexism (modern sexism) is a subtle form of sexism, based on egalitarian values combined with underlying negative feelings toward women. Studies indicate that large numbers of women have experienced either minor or major sexist incidents.

6. Females are underrepresented in the media. First, there are fewer female than male characters. Second, women of color,

especially Latinas, Asian Americans, and Native Americans, are infrequently featured. Third, few of the female TV or movie characters are over the age of 35.

7. Although the media do depict women in occupational roles, TV features few women who combine family and work roles. Similarly, the Sunday comics, children's books, and teen magazines present messages consistent with the importance of the domestic role for women and the provider role for men. Also, many forms of media portray males as more agentic than females. Although less prevalent than the image of the agentic male, the media show females as being relationship oriented.

8. Media images emphasize the importance to females of physical attractiveness and sexuality.

9. The media both reinforce and contribute to our stereotypes of gender.

10. Numerous English-language practices, including the use of the masculine generic, spotlighting, and diminutive suffixes for female terms, are based on the assumption that the male is normative. Other practices that deprecate women include the use of parallel terms, childlike terms, animal and food terms, sexual terms, and negative slang.

11. The differential treatment of females and males in language both reflect and helps shape our gender images.

WHAT DO YOU THINK?

1. We have seen that women who use the title Ms. or who do not take their husband's surname after marriage are perceived as more agentic and less communal than women who use Miss or Mrs. or who take their husband's name. One explanation for this is provided by social role theory. Can you think of any other possible explanations?

2. Consider the work by Glick and Fiske on ambivalent sexism.

   a. Do you agree that positive stereotypes of women can serve to maintain patriarchal roles and relationships? Why or why not?

   b. Do you believe that benevolent and hostile sexism are equally detrimental to women? Why or why not?

3. We have examined numerous sources of societal representations of gender, such as greeting cards, children's books, and television commercials. What other types of media might reflect gender stereotypes?

4. Which of the various language features that treat females and males differently do you think has the most detrimental effect on girls and women? Why?

5. Provide evidence, from the chapter or from your own experience, that language influences our perceptions of gender.

IF YOU WANT TO LEARN MORE

Basow, S. A. (1992). *Gender: Stereotypes and roles* (3rd ed.). Pacific Grove, CA: Brooks/Cole.

Dines, G., & Humez, J. M. (Eds.) (1995). *Gender, race and class in media: A text-reader*. Thousand Oaks, CA: Sage.

Douglas, S. J. (1995). *Where the girls are: Growing up female with the mass media*. NY: Times Books.

Miller, C., & Swift, K. (1991). *Words and women: Updated*. New York: HarperCollins.

Tannen, D. (1990). *You just don't understand*. New York: William. Morrow.

3

Gender Self-Concept

Developmental Processes and Individual Differences

KEY TERMS

gender identity
transgendered individual
gender attitudes
sexual orientation
prenatal sex differentiation
androgens
estrogens
mullerian ducts
wolffian ducts
testosterone
mullerian inhibiting
    substance
Turner's syndrome
intersexuality

congenital adrenal
    hyperplasia
androgen-insensitivity
    syndrome
5 alpha-reductase deficiency
gender typing
psychoanalytic theory
Oedipus complex
castration anxiety
identification
penis envy
social learning theory
observational learning
social cognitive theory

cognitive developmental
    theory
gender constancy
gender schema theory
femininity
masculinity
androgyny
undifferentiation
traditional gender attitude
nontraditional or egalitarian
    gender attitude
social status hypothesis
sexual orientation hypothesis

In 1965 shortly after starting graduate school, I (Judith) participated in a discussion about graduate student issues with my eight male classmates. During this conversation, much to my surprise and dismay, one of the men offered his impression of my lack of femininity. When asked for clarification, Dick said without hesitation, "Judith is too highly achievement oriented to be feminine."

Now consider the lighthearted mockery of gender-expected behaviors shown by my daughter and son-in-law during their wedding ceremony. On the one hand, the setting was traditional with the bride in a long white gown, the groom in a formal tuxedo, and an entourage of bridesmaids and ushers. On the other hand, inconsistent with traditional expectations, at the end of a beautiful and serious service celebrating the bride and groom's love for each other, the officiate concluded with "Now you may kiss the groom!"

My classmate's comment suggests that, in his mind, people cannot combine female-stereotypic and male-stereotypic characteristics. Do you see problems with this type of thinking?

Do you know people, who like Judith's daughter and her husband, believe our behaviors should not be dictated by our gender? Do you know others who see value in separate roles for women and men? In this chapter we focus on issues like these as we examine the integration of gender into one's personal identity. After a brief look at the components of gender self-concept, we look at prenatal sex development and its influence on these gender concepts. Then we explore theoretical perspectives of gender learning and conclude with an examination of variations among people in their gender self-concepts .

Gender Self-Concept

One component of gender self-concept is **gender identity**; *one's self-definition as a female or male.* This identity generally develops between the ages of 2 and 3 and is usually consistent with anatomy. In other words, most individuals establish a gender identity in accordance with their external reproductive organs. **Transgendered individuals**, however, do not. They have *a gender identity inconsistent with their reproductive organs.* They firmly believe they were born with the body of the wrong sex and really feel that they are the other sex.

Despite the usual consistency between anatomy and gender identity, there are variations in the degree to which people incorporate gender stereotypes into their own personalities and attitudes. As we saw in Chapter 2, there are numerous commonly held expectations about the appropriate traits and roles for females and males. However, these gender stereotypes reflect *beliefs* about individuals; they do not tell us what anyone is *actually* like. Although these stereotypes are descriptive of some people, they are not representative of all. Instead, individuals differ from one another in their adherence to cultural stereotypes about gender. That is, they differ in the extent to which their traits, behaviors, interests, and roles conform to those expected for their gender. Moreover, they differ in their **gender attitudes**, their *beliefs about the appropriate traits, interests, behaviors, and roles of females and males.*

Are various domains of an individual's gender self-concept associated with one another? Although most people's gender identity is consistent with their anatomy, that does not imply a connection between gender identity and gender-related attributes. A person can feel that she is a female but have male-related traits, such as ambitiousness and independence, or engage in roles generally associated with men, such as construction worker or engineer. Furthermore, a person's gender-related attributes are not linked to her or his **sexual orientation**. *Preference for a same- or other-gender sexual partner* does not reflect the individual's gender-related traits, behaviors, interests, or roles.

Prenatal Development

Our journey toward understanding the development of a personal sense of gender begins with an examination of **prenatal sex differentiation**; that is, *the biological processes that influence the making of our physical sex.* As we shall see, prenatal sex differentiation consists of a highly complex set of processes. The first step, the joining of the sex chromosomes in the fertilized egg, is followed by several other prenatal events that collectively contribute to the determination of sex (see Table 3.1). Furthermore, not only is the biological process highly complex, but the meaning of biological sex is multidimensional; it is defined by our chromosomes, hormones, reproductive organs, and brain organization.

TABLE 3.1   Stages of Prenatal Sex Differentiation of Females and Males

Stages	Females	Males
1. Chromosomes	XX	XY
2. Gonads & Hormones	ovaries (estrogens)	testes (androgens)
3. Internal Reproductive Organs	uterus, fallopian tubes, and upper vagina	vas deferens, seminal vesicles, & prostate
4. External Genitalia	clitoris, labia, and vaginal opening	penis and scrotum
5. Brain	female differentiation of the hypothalamus	male differentiation of the hypothalamus

Stages of Prenatal Sex Differentiation

Chromosomes.   Sex differentiation begins with the combining of the sex chromosomes at conception. Normally individuals inherit 23 pairs of chromosomes from their parents. Twenty-two of these pairs contain genes that determine the general nature of the human species and the individual's specific characteristics (e.g., eye color), and one pair consists of the sex chromosomes, containing the genetic material that begins the process of sex differentiation. Genetic females have two X chromosomes, one received from each parent, and genetic males have one X chromosome received from their mother and one Y from their father. Although the XX or XY chromosomal combination is found in every cell in the body, the contribution of the sex chromosomes to sex development is restricted to their influence on the next stage, the development of the gonads; that is, the sex glands.

Gonadal Development.   Until the sixth week of development there are no anatomical differences between XX and XY embryos. In fact, all embryos contain the same undifferentiated tissue that will later develop along sexual lines. However, at that point in time, the Y chromosome in XY embryos directs the previously undifferentiated gonadal tissue to develop into testes, the male sex glands.

Scientists know less about the genetic basis of female differentiation. They do know that in XX embryos gonadal development begins at approximately the twelfth week after conception; the previously undifferentiated gonadal tissue develops into ovaries, the female sex glands. Although many researchers have stated that this occurs in the absence of the Y chromosome, recent evidence suggests that the X chromosome might direct this development (Angier, 1994).

Once the gonads develop, the remaining process of sex differentiation is regulated by the sex hormones. Most research has examined XY development and we know that prenatal male differentiation requires the presence of the *male sex hormones*, collectively known as **androgens**. Unfortunately, we know less about the possible hormonal basis for the making of a biological female (Fitch, Cowell, & Denenberg, 1998). Until recently, it was believed that no gonadal hormones were necessary for female development; differentiation of female sex organs would proceed in the absence of androgens (e.g., Hood, Draper, Crockett, & Petersen, 1987). Now, although not yet fully understood, there is evidence suggesting that the *female sex hormones,* collectively known as **estrogens**, play a more active role in female development than previously believed (Fitch et al., 1998)).

Development of Internal Reproductive Organs.   The female and male internal reproductive organs develop from the same previously undifferentiated tissue. Both XX and XY fetuses contain two sets of tissues. One of these, the **mullerian ducts**, are *the foundation for female structures*, and the other, the **wolffian ducts**, serve as *the basis for male internal reproductive structures*. In XX individuals, the mullerian ducts differentiate into the uterus, fallopian tubes, and upper vagina and the wolffian tissue degenerates. In XY development, two substances produced by the testes govern the process of developing male internal reproductive structures. **Testosterone**, an androgen, is necessary for the transformation of the wolffian ducts into the male organs, including the vas deferens, seminal vesicles, and prostate; and the **mullerian inhibiting substance** is necessary for the degeneration of the mullerian ducts.

External Genitalia.   Similar to the development of the internal reproductive structures, the external structures develop from previously undifferentiated tissue present in both XX and XY individuals. In XX fetuses this tissue differentiates as the clitoris, labia, and vaginal opening. In XY development, testosterone is converted into another substance, dihydrotestosterone, which then transforms this tissue into the penis and the scrotum (Kimura, 1992).

Brain Differentiation.   Sex differences in the brain are less observable and, predictably, more controversial than sex differences in reproductive organs. However, experimentation on lower animals and case histories of humans whose prenatal exposure to androgens was abnormal for their genetic sex shows there is a critical period of time during which exposure to sex hormones can affect the hypothalamus and, thereby, influence the threshold for subsequent behaviors. The evidence indicates that, in animals, early exposure to androgens lowers the threshold for aggression and increases the likelihood of male sexual behaviors (Money & Ehrhardt, 1972). Also, in both animals and humans, this exposure to androgens organizes the hypothalamus so that it becomes insensitive to estrogen (Hood et al., 1987). The result is the elimination of the normal hormonal cyclical pattern associated with the menstrual cycle. We explore behavioral and sexual effects in humans in the next section as we examine the outcomes of various anomalies in prenatal sex differentiation.

Anomalies of Prenatal Development

The pattern of sex differentiation just described is the normal one that character-izes the prenatal development of most individuals. However, several types of anomalies can occur, and examination of these can help elucidate the role of the chromosomes and hormones on gender identity and gender-related attributes.

Turner's Syndrome.   **Turner's syndrome** is *a chromosomal disorder in which the individual has a single X chromosome rather than a pair of sex chromosomes.* The missing chromosome could have been an X or a Y but is defective or lost. Because two chromosomes are necessary for the development of the gonads, the individual has neither ovaries nor testes. Externally, the genitalia are female and the individual is reared as a girl. Estrogen therapy at puberty enables girls with Turner's syndrome to develop female secondary sex characteristics, such as breasts and pubic hair.

Now let's examine several disorders that result in **intersexuality**, *the pres-ence of both female and male sex characteristics*

Congenital Adrenal Hyperplasia (CAH).   **Congenital adrenal hyperplasia** is *an inherited disorder in which the adrenal glands of a genetic female malfunction and pro-duce an androgen-like hormone* (Kelso, Nicholls, & Warne, 1999). Because this hor-mone is not produced until after the internal reproductive organs develop, these individuals have a uterus. However, the disorder causes either a partial or com-plete masculinization of the external genitals with the formation of an enlarged clitoris or a penis. Usually CAH is diagnosed at birth and the baby is reared as a girl, requiring some degree of surgical feminization of the genitals. Additionally, because this condition does not cease at birth, the individual generally receives hormonal therapy to prevent continued masculinization of her body.

Androgen-Insensitivity Syndrome.   The **androgen-insensitivity syndrome** is *an inherited disorder in which the body of a genetic male cannot utilize androgen* (Hood et al., 1987). Analogous to CAH in which prenatal exposure to androgen mas-culinizes the external genitals of a genetic female, this inability of body tissue to respond to androgen feminizes the external genitals of a genetic male. Usually, the feminization of the external genitalia is complete and there is no suspicion that the baby is a genetic male (see Figure 3.1). Similarly, the inability of the body to respond to androgen prevents the wolffian ducts from differentiating into the internal male reproductive structures. However, because of the presence of the mullerian inhibiting substance, the mullerian ducts do not develop into the inter-nal female organs. Consequently, the individual has no internal reproductive organs.

5 Alpha-Reductase Deficiency.   The **5 alpha-reductase deficiency** is *an inher-ited deficiency in a genetic male which prevents the prenatal differentiation of the external genital tissue into a penis* (Hood et al., 1987). In other ways, prenatal development

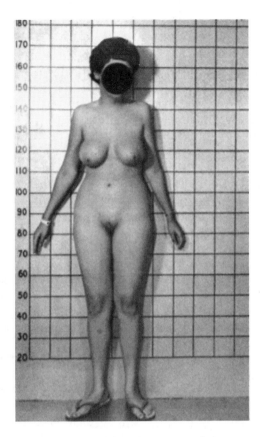

FIGURE 3.1 *An Adult with the Androgen-Insensitivity Syndrome.* (From Money, J., & Ehrhardt, A. A. [1972]. *Man & woman, boy & girl: The differentiation and dimorphism of gender identity from conception to maturity,* [p. 116, Figure 6.4]. **Baltimore: Johns Hopkins.)**

follows a male blueprint; testes and male internal reproductive organs develop. Usually at birth these genetic males appear to be girls and are labeled as such. However, the surge of testosterone at puberty causes a belated masculinization of the external genitals and the development of male secondary sex characteristics, such as a deepening voice and facial hair. Thus, these genetic males, generally raised as girls, now develop the body of a male.

Case Studies.   The relative influence of prenatal and postnatal experiences on gender-related development has been the focus of considerable controversy. Case histories of intersexuals and girls with Turner's syndrome have examined the role of prenatal hormones on the development of nonsexual gender-related attributes, gender identity, and sexual orientation and have produced inconsistent findings. Several researchers contend that prenatal biological factors are highly influential, whereas others conclude that experiences after birth play the most significant role in shaping individuals' gender-related attributes.

First, let's examine the effects of prenatal hormones on nonsexual gender-related interests and activities. On the one hand, some studies show that girls with CAH, who were exposed to an androgen-like substance prenatally, show stronger than average preferences for boys' toys and activities and for boys as playmates. (e.g., Berenbaum, 1999; Berenbaum, Duck, & Bryk, 2000; Berenbaum & Hines, 1992; Hines & Kaufman, 1994) However, other findings indicate that the greater physical activity of these girls does not translate into more rough-and-tumble play (Hines & Kaufman, 1994), and evidence about aggressive behavior is mixed (Berenbaum & Resnick, 1997; Money & Ehrhardt, 1972)

Investigations on the effects of prenatal estrogen suggest that it might not be necessary for the development of female gender -related interests or role expectations (Hood et al., 1987). In one study, girls with Turner's syndrome who lack prenatal estrogen were found to be similar to matched controls in their preferences for female playmates and female-style clothing (Money & Ehrhardt, 1972). Additionally, the Turner's syndrome girls did not differ from the controls in terms of satisfaction with the female gender role or interest in marriage and motherhood. Similarly, androgen-insensitive (XY) individuals raised as females tend to have female-related interests, although they, also, lack prenatal estrogen. As children, they enjoy playing with girls' toys and have fantasies about motherhood and homemaking (Money & Ehrhardt, 1972).

Turning to the development of gender identity, research similarly provides inconsistent findings. Some investigators have pointed to the importance of the gender of rearing, that is, experiences after birth, on gender identity (Money & Ehrhardt, 1972; Zucker, Bradley, Oliver, & Blake, 1996). However, Milton Diamond (1997) contends that individuals are not sexually neutral at birth and that their prenatal experiences predispose them toward a female or male identity. He notes, for example, that prenatal processes influence some intersexuals to switch from the gender of rearing to an identity of the other gender. Possibly, both biological and social factors are involved in shaping gender identity (Slijper, Drop, Molenaar, de Muinck, & Sabine, 1998)

There is some evidence that cultural values might, additionally, play a role in the development of gender identity. Studies of individuals who have experienced a female-to-male body change (5 alpha-reductase deficiency) show that the decision to remain a female or to change to a male depends, at least in part, on one's culture. A study in the United States showed that individuals identified with this disorder maintained their female gender identity despite their changing bodies (Rubin, Reinisch, & Haskett, 1981). In the Dominican Republic, on the other hand, 16 of 18 who were raised as girls elected to reverse their gender identity at puberty and become males (Imperato-McGinley, Peterson, Gautier, & Sturla, 1979). Still another study, this one conducted in New Guinea, found that some changed and some did not but that those who did switch from a female to a male identity did so as a result of social pressure stemming from their inability to fulfill their female role (Herdt & Davidson, 1988). Although there might be a variety of explanations for these cultural differences, the researchers suggest that cultural expectations have some influence in shaping gender identity, at least for individuals with conflicting body signals.

Last, in examining influences on sexual orientation, case studies of intersexual individuals have led some researchers to contend that sexual orientation has its origins in prenatal development (e.g., Diamond, Binstock, & Kohl, 1996). John Money (1993), for example, points to a higher-than-average same-gender orientation among adolescent and adult females with CAH and states that prenatal exposure to androgen has an effect on the brain, which serves as one influence on sexual orientation. However, based on their review of research on the topic, Amy Banks and Nanette Gartrell (1995) conclude that atypical prenatal hormone exposure is not related to increased same-gender sexual orientation.

What can we conclude about this controversial issue? Unfortunately, it is difficult to evaluate the relative contribution of biological and postnatal factors because case studies do not enable adequate control. For example, CAH girls have somewhat masculinized genitalia. Consequently, it is difficult to separate effects of their atypical exposure to prenatal hormones from the psychological and interpersonal reactions they might experience after birth. Both CAH girls and their parents are aware of their masculinization and this knowledge might serve as a powerful influence on the girls' gender-related self-concept and on their parents' treatment of them (Bem, 1993; Ruble & Martin, 1998).

Theories of Gender Typing

Now we turn to an exploration of the major theories that attempt to explain *the acquisition of the traits, behaviors, and roles that are generally associated with one's gender*, a process known as **gender typing**. Although these theories posit different processes involved in the learning of gender, only one (psychoanalytic theory) contends that the development of gender-related attributes is rooted in biological sex differences. The other perspectives share the assumption that gender traits, behaviors, and roles are socially constructed; that they develop from children's interactions with others and are not inherent in our biology. Furthermore, even psychoanalytic theory emphasizes the perceived significance of anatomical differences, rather than the effect of hormonal or other biological sex differences on gender development.

Psychoanalytic Theory

We begin our theoretical exploration with an examination of psychoanalytic theory, a complex theory of personality and psychotherapeutic treatment developed by the Viennese physician, Sigmund Freud. **Psychoanalytic theory** proposes that *gender typing stems from children's awareness of anatomical differences between females and males combined with their strong inborn sexual urges*. According to this theory, children have sexual urges that shift from one bodily region to another as they develop. During each psychosexual stage of development a different body part produces pleasure and children's attempts to obtain this pleasure can have major effects on their personality development.

The first two psychosexual stages of development, the oral and anal stages, do not have direct relevance to the acquisition of gender-related traits. It is the third stage, the phallic stage, occurring between the ages of three and six years, that plays a significant role. According to psychoanalytic theory, during the phallic stage, two very important experiences occur that have dramatic consequences for gender-related development. The first is the child's discovery of the anatomical differences between females and males and the second is her/his love for the parent of the other gender.

The child's sexual attraction for the other-gender parent, known as the **Oedipus complex,** runs a different course in the development of boys than it does in girls and leads to very different outcomes. For the little boy, the sexual attraction for his mother is accompanied by a belief that his father is a rival for his mother's affections and that his father, similarly, perceives him as a competitor. At the same time, the boy becomes aware of the anatomical differences between males and females, and it is this awareness that serves to resolve his Oedipus complex. The boy's interpretation of the genital differences is that females have been castrated. He then assumes that he, too, can be castrated and the likely person to do this is his powerful rival, his father. Because the boy is very attached to his prized organ, *his fear of castration by his father*, called **castration anxiety**, is strong enough to induce him to give up his Oedipal feelings for his mother. When he does so, he forms *a close emotional bond* with his father, an attachment called **identification**. It is through this identification process that the boy adopts his father's masculine behaviors and traits and incorporates his father's values into his superego (the moral component of personality) thus developing a strong sense of morality.

The phallic stage of development follows a different sequence of events for the little girl. Her discovery of the anatomical distinction between females and males has different implications for her than we saw for the little boy. Whereas for the boy, the awareness led to castration fears and the consequent resolution of the Oedipus complex, for the little girl, the discovery sets the foundation for the development of Oedipal feelings (sometimes referred to as the Electra complex in girls). The girl's awareness of the boy's "far superior equipment" (Freud, 1933/1965, p. 126) leads to the development of **penis envy**, *a desire to possess the male genitals*, and to blaming the mother for her castrated state. Then, her desire for a penis is replaced by a desire for a child and she turns to her father to fulfill that wish. Because the girl lacks the fear of castration (having already been castrated), the chief motive for resolving the Oedipus complex is absent. Thus, she does not completely resolve her Oedipal feelings. However, with the realization that she will never possess her father, the girl gradually gives up her Oedipal feelings, identifies with her mother, and begins the acquisition of her mother's feminine traits and behaviors. Although she, too, begins superego development, this development is weak. Freud maintained that, for the girl, "the formation of the super-ego must suffer; it cannot attain the strength and independence which give it its cultural significance" (Freud, 1933/1965, p. 129).

Freud believed that the experiences of the phallic stage have lifelong consequences for the little girl, besides the acquisition of her mother's feminine qualities and the development of a weak superego. The little girl's wish for a penis does not disappear at the end of this stage. Instead, her strong desire for the male organ accounts for the fact that "envy and jealousy play an even greater part in the mental life of women than of men" (Freud, 1933/1965, p. 125). Further, it contributes to her sense of inferiority, her "little sense of justice" (Freud, 1933/1965, p. 134), and her sharing of the "contempt felt by men for a sex which is the lesser in so important a respect" (Freud, 1925/1959, p. 192). In addition, penis envy contributes to women's physical vanity "since they are bound to value their charms more highly as a late compensation for their original sexual inferiority" (Freud, 1933/1965, p. 132).

Evaluation.   First, as is fairly obvious, Freud's theory is highly male-biased. His use of the male term *phallic* to label the third stage of psychosexual development, his strong emphasis on the superiority of the male organ, and his assumption that females are doomed to feelings of inferiority because they lack a penis are a few of the numerous indications of Freud's pro-male bias. For these reasons, psychoanalytic theory is not widely embraced by feminist scholars. Second, psychoanalytic theory cannot be subjected to empirical examination. Important psychoanalytic concepts, such as penis envy and castration anxiety, are conceptualized as unconscious; thus, they are not translatable into clearly defined scientific measures. Third, Freud has been criticized for his emphasis on the anatomical foundations of gender development to the virtual exclusion of societal influences. From Freud's perspective, gender is constructed from the presence or absence of a penis. That is, the importance bestowed on this piece of male anatomy, and not the societal value attached to males, shapes boys' and girls' personality development.

Social Learning Theory

Whereas psychoanalytic theory envisions the growing child as pushed around by her/his inborn desires, **social learning theory**, originally proposed by Mischel (1966) and Bandura (1969), views *gender development as influenced by the social environment.* Based on learning theory principles, this perspective posits that the same processes that influence the development of other types of social behavior account for the development of gender-related behaviors. Specifically, *children acquire behaviors associated with their gender because those behaviors are more likely to be imitated and to be associated with positive reinforcement.*

Observational Learning.   One mechanism through which gender-related behaviors are acquired is **observational learning** (Mischel, 1966) (also called imitation or modeling); that is, *the acquisition of behaviors via the observation of role models.* Children are continually exposed to both real-life and media models who engage in gender-stereotypic behaviors. Because they are more likely to emulate similar models than to emulate dissimilar models, they are more likely to observe and imitate same-gender individuals rather than other-gender individuals (Bussey & Bandura, 1984). Through observation of these models children learn which behaviors are considered appropriate for someone of their gender. For example, five-year-old Jenny sees her mother bake cookies and then uses her play kitchen to pretend she is baking. And, because the nurses in her pediatrician's office are females, Jenny believes that only women can be nurses. Also, Jenny learns that it is important for women to be pretty because she sees televised female role models who are frequently concerned about their appearance.

Reinforcement and Punishment.   Social learning theory maintains that even though children sometimes engage in cross-gender observational learning in addition to same-gender imitation, they are likely to perform primarily gender-appropriate behaviors. The mechanisms that explain this phenomenon are reinforcement and punishment. The likelihood that individuals will engage in any particular behavior is contingent on the anticipated consequences of that behavior. If people expect a positive reinforcement (reward) for performing the behavior, it is likely they will engage in that behavior. On the other hand, if they anticipate a negative consequence (punishment), they are not likely to perform that act. Thus, girls and boys learn, both through observing the con sequences to models and as a result of the outcomes received for their own behaviors, that girls are more likely to be rewarded for certain actions and boys for others. For example, a girl playing "dress-up" might be praised for her beauty as she parades around wearing her mother's old dress and high heels. If her brother wears the same outfit, however, his parents might tell him to take off the clothes.

Cognition.   A modification of social learning theory, known as **social cognitive theory**, posits that *observational learning and rewards and punishments following behavior cannot alone account for gender typing; thought processes (cognitions), also, play a role.* As children develop, they not only receive rewards and punishments from others but begin to internalize standards about appropriate gender-related behavior (Bussey & Bandura, 1999). Consequently, children initially engage in gender-appropriate behaviors because of the anticipation of rewards from others. However, as they gain experience and maturity, they develop internal standards about gender-related behavior, which motivates them to engage in gender-appropriate activities in order to gain self-satisfaction and avoid self-censure. For example, Pablo might refuse to play with his sister's dolls because playing with them would violate his personal standard of appropriate behavior for boys.

Evaluation.   Unlike psychoanalytic theory, the concepts of the social learning perspective are clear and observable. Therefore, numerous studies have examined the theory's assumptions. These studies have provided support for some aspects of the theory and are inconclusive about others.

One assumption of social learning theory is that girls and boys receive encouragement and reinforcement for different behaviors. In support of this perspective, several studies show that parents do treat their daughters and sons differently, at least in regard to some behaviors. For example, there is some evidence that mothers encourage their preschool daughters more than their sons to talk about interactions with other people; thus fostering a greater interpersonal interest and concern (Flannagan, Baker-Ward, & Graham, 1995). In addition, on the basis of their extensive review of the research, Hugh Lytton and David Romney (1991) conclude that parents are most likely to engage in gender-based treatment of their children when it comes to play activities and household chores. For example, they buy different types of toys for their daughters and sons from preschool through middle school (Etaugh & Liss, 1992; Robinson & Morris, 1986).

According to social learning theory, the other process in gender typing is observational learning. You probably can think of several examples in your own life where you learned from observing the behaviors of others; and numerous studies indicate that children's actions are, at times, imitative of adults' behavior (e.g., Bandura, 1965). However, more debatable is whether this imitation is restricted to the behavior of same-gender models. Here the evidence is mixed. Some studies show that girls and boys are, indeed, more likely to imitate same-gender adults than to imitate other-gender adults. Kay Bussey and Albert Bandura (1984), for example, had nursery school children view videotapes of adult females and males engaging in a variety of play behaviors. When these children were then placed in a similar play situation, the girls tended to imitate the behaviors of the women and the boys imitated the behaviors of the men.

Although children do imitate same-gender role models, observational learning is not restricted to the behaviors of individuals of the same gender as the child. Other characteristics can influence the selection of role models. One factor is a model's power. Children, especially boys, are more likely to imitate the behavior of role models who have control over valuable resources such as attractive toys (Bussey & Bandura, 1984). Second, children are more likely to imitate others if the model's behavior receives positive reinforcement (Mischel, 1966). Thus, it is likely that children do, indeed, learn from the behaviors of important adults in their lives, including parents and teachers. However, this learning is not restricted to adults of the same gender as the child.

Recall that social cognitive theory includes internal cognitive processes in addition to external rewards, punishments, and observation as influences on the acquisition of gender-appropriate behavior. This concept of the cognitive control of behavior has received support. For example, Kay Bussey and Albert Bandura (1992) asked nursery school children to anticipate how they would feel if they played with same-gender and cross-gender toys. If a child has incorporated personal standards about appropriate gender-linked conduct, they should expect to feel good if they play with same-gender toys and bad if they play with other-gender toys. This is exactly what the researchers found when they examined the anticipated reactions of four-year-olds. On the other hand, the three-year-old children in their study did not show any difference in anticipated reaction to these activities, although they did disapprove of peers' playing with cross-gender toys. These findings suggest the three-year-old children were aware of gender-linked activities but had not yet developed an internal mechanism that could guide their own behavior.

Cognitive Developmental Theory

Cognitive developmental theory, originally formulated by Kohlberg (1966), accepts neither the psychoanalytic postulate that young children's gender typing is a function of their inborn sexual urges nor the social learning assumption that this development is a product of environmental learning. In other words, **cognitive developmental theory** contends that *children are neither pushed by their biological desires nor pulled by external rewards and punishments. Instead, children are active learners, attempting to make sense of the social environment.* As part of that process, they organize the environment on the basis of gender and develop conceptions about what females do and what males do. That is, children actively search for patterns and rules that govern the functioning of females and males and then follow these in an attempt to best adapt to social demands.

By approximately three years of age, children can correctly label their own gender. However, they do not yet know that gender is unchangeable; that neither time nor behavioral and appearance modifications can alter one's gender. For example, Kohlberg (1966) reported that most four-year-olds believe that a girl could become a boy if she wanted to, if she engaged in boy-related activities, or if she wore a boy's clothes. As an example of this thinking, he reported the following conversation between two preschool children (p. 95):

JOHNNY: I'm going to be a airplane builder when I grow up.

JIMMY: When I grow up, I'll be a Mommy.

JOHNNY: No, you can't be a Mommy. You have to be a Daddy.

JIMMY: No, I'm going to be a Mommy.

JOHNNY: No, you're not a girl, you can't be a Mommy.

JIMMY: Yes, I can.

It appears that Johnny, but not Jimmy, has developed the concept of **gender constancy**, *the belief that gender is permanent regardless of changes in age, behavior, or appearance*, a belief that generally develops between the ages of four and seven years.

According to Kohlberg (1966), the absence of gender constancy in young children is not a function of their lack of knowledge of genital differences. Even children who have this awareness at an early age do not conclude that gender cannot be altered. Instead the absence of gender constancy is due to the young child's reliance on obvious physical characteristics, such as clothing or hair length, as informative, even if they are not. Kohlberg notes that this type of thinking parallels children's beliefs about the changeability of other entities. Preschool children do not recognize that changes in any object's visible characteristics do not necessarily alter its quality. For example, Kohlberg (1966) writes that most four-year-olds believe a cat would become a dog if its whiskers were cut off.

Gender constancy is an important concept in cognitive developmental theory. The theory contends that gender typing cannot take place until children understand that their gender is unchangeable. Once they acquire that understanding, they begin to behave in gender-appropriate ways and their motivation to do so stems from several sources. First, children "naturally" value behaviors that are consistent with their self-image (Kohlberg, 1966, p. 108). Therefore, they now value gender-consistent activities. Second, children view conformity to their gender role as a moral imperative. They believe there is a moral order in the world and do not distinguish between social expectations, such as those based on gender, and moral laws and responsibilities, such as religious teachings. Therefore, they see any deviations from gender-related behaviors as immoral and punishable. Third, boys recognize the power and strength associated with the male role and girls value the niceness of the female role. For these reasons, engaging in gender-consistent activities enables children to effectively master the environment and to competently adapt to the social world. To learn which behaviors are performed by females and which are performed by males, children actively observe parents and other role models. In this process they seek out information and use rewards and punishments as a source of information about which behaviors are gender-appropriate and which are not. Then they engage in the gender-appropriate behaviors because behaving in a gender-consistent manner is, in itself, rewarding.

You might think this sounds similar to the social learning theory assumption that children learn about gender from external rewards and punishments and from observation of others. However, Kohlberg (1966) notes that the cognitive developmental view of children's use of the social environment is very different from the social learning perspective. According to social learning theory, rewards for gender-appropriate behavior lead to the development of gender-appropriate behaviors and attitudes. Cognitive developmental theory, on the other hand, argues that rewards for gender-consistent behavior are merely informative of what is gender-appropriate and that children engage in these behaviors because acting in a gender-consistent manner is, in itself, rewarding. Let's look at an example to help clarify the distinction. Six-year-old Caitlin has been praised for helping her mother cook dinner. According to social learning theory, she then wants to cook again because she anticipates positive reinforcement from others (and possibly from herself) for cooking. The attainment of gender constancy would not be necessary because her desire to cook stems from her expectation of positive reinforcement, not because cooking is defined as a female activity. According to cognitive developmental theory, on the other hand, the praise received by Caitlin serves as information that cooking dinner is a female activity. If she has attained gender constancy, she now wants to cook because behaving in a gender-consistent manner is, in itself, rewarding.

Evaluation.   The concepts of cognitive developmental theory, like those of social learning theory, are clearly defined and easily measured and have generated considerable research. One important assumption of this perspective is that gender typing is dependent on an awareness of the unchangeability of gender. Examination of this assumption has provided mixed results. Some studies have shown that children who understand gender constancy are more likely than their peers who do not to select gender-appropriate activities (e.g., Frey & Ruble, 1992; Newman, Cooper, & Ruble, 1995). However, other research has found no consistent relationship between gender constancy and children's understanding of gender stereotypes or involvement in gender-appropriate behaviors (e.g., Levy, 1998; Levy, Barth, & Zimmerman, 1998). Similarly, whereas there is some evidence that gender-constant boys are more interested in viewing male television characters than are their peers without gender constancy (Luecke, Anderson, Collins, & Schmitt, 1995), other research shows no relationship between the attainment of gender constancy and children's imitation of same-gender models (Bussey & Bandura, 1984).

A second assumption of cognitive developmental theory is that, children tend to value same-gender activities once they attain gender constancy. On this point the theory receives considerable support; numerous studies show that children value their own gender more highly than they value the other gender (e.g., Bussey & Perry, 1982; Etaugh, Levine, & Mennella, 1984).

Although children do seem to place more value on their own gender, one criticism of this theory is that it fails to adequately explain why girls learn to appreciate the female role. For boys the value of the male role comes not only from the desire for consistency with oneself but from the obvious prestige and power associated with the male role. It is not as clear how the niceness and goodness of the female role get translated into placing a positive value on femininity.

Another criticism of cognitive developmental theory is that it does not specify why children use gender as a classifying concept. Kohlberg (1966) asserts that children want to adhere to social rules so as to best master the social environment, but his theory does not explain why these rules are structured around gender. In fact, his emphasis on gender classification as natural seems to ignore societal influences on making gender a salient characteristic. As Bem (1983, p. 601) stated, "The theory fails to explicate why sex will have primacy over other potential categories of the self such as race, religion, or even eye color."

Gender Schema Theory

Gender schema theory, proposed by Sandra Bem (1983), incorporates elements of cognitive developmental and social learning theories. Like the former, it proposes that *children develop an interrelated set of ideas or schema about gender that guides their social perceptions and actions.* However, unlike cognitive developmental theory, gender schema theory postulates that the use of gender as an organizing principle is not inevitable; it does not naturally stem from the minds of children. Similar to social learning theory, it assumes that *gender schema development stems from learning the gender norms and practices of society.*

The theory posits that children formulate conceptions of the traits and roles associated with females and males on the basis of societal expectations. Then they use this information to regulate their own behavior, and their self-esteem becomes contingent on their adherence to these gender schemas (Bem, 1981).

A significant difference between gender schema and cognitive developmental theories lies in the basis for gender schema development. Whereas Kohlberg

(1966) assumes the development of cognitive conceptualizations about gender is a natural process, Bem (1981) contends that the use of gender as a way of processing social information occurs because societal norms and practices emphasize its importance. Thus, children do not organize the social environment on the basis of physical attributes, such as eye color or hair color, because society does not give these characteristics the same significance it applies to gender. Bem does not rule out the possibility that the development of gender schemas to organize the social world has a biological basis. However, she contends that any evolutionary basis for this is strengthened by the societal emphasis on the importance of gender. According to Bem (1981), society insists

> that an individual's sex makes a difference in virtually every domain of human experience. The typical American child cannot help but observe, for example, that what parents, teachers, and peers consider to be appropriate behavior varies as a function of sex: that toys, clothing, occupations, hobbies, domestic chores—even pronouns—all vary as a function of sex. (p. 362)

What specific examples depict this societal emphasis on gender? As one illustration, Bem (1983) points out that elementary school teachers do not line up children separately by race because they do not want to emphasize race as a distinguishing characteristic. They might, however, group children by gender, thus increasing its perceived importance as a distinguishing characteristic.

Bem (1983) claims that individuals vary in the degree to which they use gender schemas to understand and evaluate others and to guide their own behavior. That is, some individuals strongly associate behaviors and roles with one gender and not the other, whereas other people are less likely to perceive behaviors and roles as gender-specific. According to Bem, people who have strong gender schemas consider a narrower range of activities as acceptable for individuals of each gender, including themselves. For example, a high school girl who thinks of mathematics as a male domain would be less likely than her friend who does not view math as gender-related to sign up for advanced math classes.

Why do some individuals have stronger, less flexible gender schemas than do others? Bem suggests that variations among people might be influenced by individual differences in exposure to gender as an organizing characteristic. Consequently, she proposes several strategies parents can use for minimizing the development of gender schemas and, consequently, for reducing the development of gender-stereotypic attitudes and behavior. Can you think of parental practices that might be effective? Read Get Involved 3.1 and answer the questions to learn about Bem's proposal.

Evaluation. We saw that cognitive developmental theory Kohlberg (1966) does not explain why children structure their social perceptions around gender. One strength of gender schema theory, on the other hand, is that it illustrates how societal messages can influence the formation of gender schemas.

In addition, there is considerable research support for the theory. For example, one of its assumptions is that gender schemas help individuals organize their

GET INVOLVED **3.1**

Parental Strategies for Minimizing Gender Schemas in Children

Bem (1983) suggests that the following parental practices might help reduce gender schema development in children:

1. Elimination of gender stereotyping from parental behavior. For example, parents could share household duties instead of dividing them along gender lines.
2. Elimination of gender stereotyping from the choices parents present their children. That is, they could offer toys, activities, and clothing associated with both females and males.
3. Definition of femaleness and maleness along anatomical and reproductive lines only. That is, parents could reduce children's tendency to organize the social world according to gender by teaching their children that one's sex is relevant only for reproduction. Bem offers the

following anecdote about her four-year-old son Jeremy and his nursery school classmate as an illustration of the limiting outcomes of a cultural definition of gender and the greater flexibility of a biological definition:

One day Jeremy decided to wear barrettes to school. Several times that day, another little boy told Jeremy that he, Jeremy, must be a girl because "only girls wear barrettes." After trying to explain to this child that "wearing barrettes doesn't matter" and that "being a boy means having a penis and testicles," Jeremy finally pulled down his pants as a way of making his point more convincingly. The other child was not impressed. He simply said, "Everybody has a penis; only girls wear barrettes" (p. 612).

What Does It Mean?

1. Do you agree that each of the practices proposed by Bem could help reduce gender schema development? Why or why not?
2. Which of these, if any, do you think you would use, or are using, in raising your own children? Explain your answer.
3. According to gender schema theory, minimizing the use of gender schemas

for perceiving the social world should reduce the development of gender stereotypes. Are there other practices that might help reduce gender stereotyping?
4. What advantages and/or disadvantages might result if all children were raised to restrict their definition of gender to reproductive characteristics only?

memories, thus facilitating the recollection of gender-consistent information. In support of this assumption, there is evidence that children are better able to remember information consistent with gender stereotypes than to remember gender-inconsistent information (e.g., Fyock & Stangor, 1994). Similarly, gender-schema theory contends that individuals are more likely to form more detailed schemas about their own gender than they are about the other gender, thereby facilitating memory of information consistent with own-gender stereotypes. In support of this view, research shows that, children remember material consistent with their own gender better than they remember material consistent with the other gender (Signorella, Bigler, & Liben, 1997). For example, Isabelle Cherney and Brigette Ryalls (1999) asked adults to recall items that were located in a room where they were waiting for an experiment to begin. Females were better able to remember female-related items, such as a makeup kit, a cookbook, and a purse, whereas males were better at recalling male-related objects, including aftershave, a sports video, and a necktie.

In another study, Gary Levy and his colleagues (Levy et al., 1998) investigated the theory's assumption that there is a relationship between the degree to which individuals use gender as an organizing structure and their tendency to exhibit behaviors considered stereotypical for their gender. These researchers found that preschool children who are more likely to use gender to organize their social perceptions are more gender-stereotyped in their own behaviors.

Gender-Related Traits

We have explored a variety of theories that explain gender typing. Now let's examine variations in individuals' conformity to stereotyped expectations about their gender. As mentioned previously, people differ in the degree to which their own traits, behaviors, interests, and roles are consistent with gender stereotypes.

The most commonly measured variation has been in the gender-related traits individuals ascribe to themselves; that is, in their personal identification with female-related and male-related characteristics. Historically, these two sets of traits were viewed as bipolar; that is, as opposite extremes of a single continuum. In the opening vignette, we saw that Judith's classmate believed she could not be both feminine and achievement oriented. This belief reflects the bipolar view that a person cannot have characteristics stereotypically associated with both females and males.

In the 1970s, there was a change in this characterization of female-related and male-related traits. At that time psychologists began to conceptualize the two dimensions as independent, rather than opposite, of one another. Unlike a bipolar dimension, such as tall-short, in which it is impossible to be described by both traits, the new perspective posited that individuals can exhibit any combination of female-stereotypic and male-stereotypic characteristics. That is, a high degree of one does not imply a low degree of the other.

In 1974 Sandra Bem proposed that femininity and masculinity should be assessed independently and developed the Bem Sex Role Inventory (BSRI) to accomplish that goal. The BSRI includes one set of traits viewed as more desirable for females than for males and another set of items seen as more desirable for males than for females. At approximately the same time, Janet Spence, Robert Helmreich, and Joy Stapp (1974) published the Personal Attributes Questionnaire

(PAQ), which also has two separate dimensions to measure gender-related personality characteristics. On the PAQ these two scales comprise personality characteristics seen as desirable for both females and males but viewed as more representative of one gender than the other. On both instruments the female-related scale comprises communal traits and the male-related scale reflects agentic traits (see Chapter 2); however, when used as measures of gender-related trait identification, they have typically been labeled either "femininity" and "masculinity" or "expressiveness" and "instrumentality".

The scoring of the BSRI and the PAQ reflects the goal of each to evaluate femininity/expressiveness and masculinity/instrumentality as independent dimensions. Thus, the respondent receives a score on each dimension and the combination of the two indicates which of four categories best describes her/his gender-related traits. These categories are: (1) **femininity**, *a high score on the femininity/expressiveness scale and a low score on the scale for masculinity/instrumentality*, (2) **masculinity**, *a high score on the masculinity/instrumentality scale and a low score on the femininity/expressiveness scale*, (3) **androgyny**, *high scores on both scales*, and (4) **undifferentiation**, *low scores on both scales*. Any individual, regardless of gender, can be characterized by any of these categories. To assess your own gender-related traits, try Get Involved 3.2.

GET INVOLVED **3.2**

What Are Your Gender-Related Traits?

The following is a partial set of characteristics from the Personal Attributes Questionnaire. For each item, choose the letter that best describes where you fall on the scale. Choose **A** if you feel the characteristic on the left strongly describes you and choose **E** if the trait on the right is strongly descriptive of you. Choose **C** if you are in the middle, and so on. Also, ask a friend to rate you on these characteristics.

1. Not at all independent	A . B . C . D . E	Very independent
2. Not at all emotional	A . B . C . D . E	Very emotional
3. Very rough	A . B . C . D . E	Very gentle
4. Not at all competitive	A . B . C . D . E	Very competitive
5. Not at all helpful to others	A . B . C . D . E	Very helpful to others
6. Not at all kind	A . B . C . D . E	Very kind
7. Not at all self-confident	A . B . C . D . E	Very self-confident
8. Gives up very easily	A . B . C . D . E	Never gives up easily
9. Not at all understanding of others	A . B . C . D . E	Very understanding of others
10. Goes to pieces under pressure	A . B . C . D . E	Stands up well under pressure

From Masculinity and Femininity: Their Psychological Dimensions, Correlates and Antecedents by Janet T. Spence and Robert L. Helmreich, Copyright (c) 1978. By permission of the University of Texas Press.

(continued on p. 73)

What Does It Mean?

To score yourself, give 0 points to a response of **A**, 1 point to **B**, and so on. Then add up your points for items 2, 3, 5, 6, and 9; this comprises your femininity/expressiveness score. Similarly, sum your points for items 1, 4, 7, 8, and 10; this comprises your masculinity/instrumentality score. Use the same procedure to score your friend's ratings of you.

1. Are your two scores similar to each other or is one much higher than the other? Does your pattern of scores reflect the gender-related trait category you think best describes you? Why or why not?
2. Is your pattern of scores similar to the pattern based on your friend's ratings? If not, describe the differences. Also, explain why your friend views your gender-related traits differently than the way you perceive them.
3. Although the Personal Attributes Questionnaire is widely used today, it was based on 1970s' perceptions of traits more typical of either females or males. Are there any characteristics presented here that no longer seem to be more representative of one gender than the other? Which ones? What evidence do you have for the gender similarity on those traits?

Changes in Gender-Related Traits over Time

In the 1970s studies showed that more female than male college students scored high on femininity whereas more males than females scored high on masculinity and approximately one-third of both genders were androgynous (e.g., Spence & Helmreich, 1978). To determine whether there has been any change over time, Jean Twenge (1997b) performed a meta-analysis of femininity and masculinity scores based on samples from over 50 different college campuses since the 1970s. Interestingly, the most notable change found by Twenge was the dramatic increase in masculinity scores of women. Additionally, there was a significant increase in androgyny among women and a weaker increase among men.

Twenge (1997b) suggests that these changes in gender-related traits may be accounted for by several societal changes that have occurred over this time period. First, there has been a dramatic increase in the percentage of women who are employed. Therefore, college women in the 1990s, more than their counterparts in the 1970s, had mothers who worked outside the home. Second, there has been a significant increase in the professional aspirations of college women. Third, more girls and women now participate in sports.

As we saw in Chapter 2, according to social role theory (Eagly, 1987), we perceive a connection between role participation and perceived role-related traits. Thus, given that the employment role, professional careers, and sports participation all involve agentic traits, such as self-reliance, competitiveness, and ambitiousness, young women in the nineties might be more likely than their counterparts in the seventies to have witnessed or experienced roles that involve male-stereotypic characteristics. This could have contributed to the development of their greater masculinity and, in turn, their greater androgyny. Thus, consistent with the view that gender is socially constructed, changes in women's personal sense of gender seem to be related to their social experiences.

Gender-Related Traits and Ethnicity

Although most investigations of gender-related traits have focused on White college students; a few have examined college and/or noncollege women with diverse ethnic backgrounds. These have shown that Black college women report greater masculinity than White (De Leon, 1995; Harris, 1993) or Puerto Rican (De Leon, 1995) women. Also, a study of women from a broad range of educational backgrounds found that a higher percentage of Blacks than Whites were androgynous (Binion, 1990).

Gender-Related Traits and Psychological Adjustment

Once psychologists started to conceptualize gender-related traits as being more complex than a single dimension of femininity-masculinity, they began to examine the psychological well-being of individuals who varied in their pattern of gender-stereotypic traits. For example, when Bem formulated her concept of androgyny, she hypothesized that because androgynous individuals are comfortable engaging in both feminine and masculine behaviors, they can adapt more adequately to various situational demands and should report greater well-being than nonandrogynous individuals (Bem, 1975). Research shows, however, that it is high masculinity, and not the specific combination of high masculinity and high femininity, that is strongly related to well-being and self-esteem (e.g., Helgeson, 1994; Whitley, 1983).

What can explain the positive relationship between masculinity and psychological adjustment? As we saw in Chapter 2, male-related traits are more highly valued in North America than female-related traits are. Therefore, people with male-stereotypic traits feel better about their ability to function effectively. Derek Grimmell and Gary Stern (1992) found support for this explanation in college students' BSRI self-ratings, their BSRI ratings of the ideal person, and their psychological well-being. These investigators found that students' masculinity score was related to their psychological adjustment. Moreover, respondents' adjustment was predicted by the difference between their self-reported masculinity and their ratings of masculinity for the ideal person. The higher their own masculinity in relation to their perception of ideal masculinity, the higher their own self-esteem and the lower their anxiety and depression. Thus, it appears that the degree to which we feel we possess highly valued masculine traits is a good predictor of our psychological adjustment.

However, before we conclude that androgyny is not related to psychological well-being, let's consider a different conceptualization of androgyny. See Learn about the Research 3.1 for a new approach to androgyny measurement and its psychological benefits.

A Real-Life Approach to Androgyny

Examination of gender-related traits indicates that masculinity, and not the co-existence of masculinity and femininity, best predicts psychological adjustment. Recently, however, Jayne Stake argued that the psychological benefits of androgyny should not be dismissed on the basis of measuring individuals' ratings of their gender-related traits. Instead, she suggested we consider androgyny as the integration of communal and agentic behaviors given in response to expectations demanded by specific life situations. That is, measurement of these behaviors must be grounded in situational contexts.

Stake focused on work-related expectations because job settings tend to require a wide range of behaviors from the worker. Her specific interest was in individuals' responses to demands on the job that required both communal and agentic behaviors. She wanted to discover whether people who use both types of behaviors when they respond to these situations experience any benefits compared to those who rely on one type or neither type. Accordingly, in individual interviews, 194 undergraduate students were asked to describe a work situation in which they were expected to behave with both "sensitivity and caring" (e.g., "Be sensitive to the needs of others," "Show others you care about them") and

"mastery and independence" (e.g., "Always show that you can handle things on your own—without the help of others," "Show you have technical know-how"). Then they were asked to describe the behaviors they used to cope with these dual expectations. Similarly, they were asked to consider the overall expectations in their job and to describe what they usually did to respond to these expectations. These coping strategies in both the specific situation as well as in the job setting overall were coded into one of the four categories generally used to classify gender-related traits. In addition, students indicated to what extent their well-being was affected by work situations that expected both types of behaviors.

The results showed that androgynous coping behaviors used in response to dual expectations in specific job situations and dual expectations in the job overall were related to the highest level of well-being. Individuals who used both communal and agentic behaviors experienced more rewards and fewer negative outcomes than those using other types of strategies. Thus, it is possible that examining gender-related attributes as behavioral responses to specific situations rather than as general personality traits might be a fruitful approach to understanding the beneficial effects of various gender-related orientations.

Source: Stake, J. E. (1997).

What Does It Mean?

1. Stake examined expectations for communal and agentic behaviors in the workplace. Can you think of other situations that might make simultaneous demands?
2. Identify a job experience you had where both types of demands were made.

Describe how you handled it and how you felt in this situation. Was your experience consistent with the results reported here?

Evaluation of the Concept of Androgyny

When the psychological measurement of androgyny was introduced in the 1970s, it was received enthusiastically by feminist scholars. It replaced the notion that psychological health required that females be feminine and males be masculine. By embodying socially desirable traits for both females and males, androgyny seemed to imply the absence of gender stereotyping. Furthermore, by incorporating both feminine and masculine behaviors it appeared to broaden the scope of behaviors that can be used to handle different situations and, thus, lead to more flexible and adaptive behaviors.

Although androgyny continues to be viewed by feminist scholars as more positive than restrictions to either femininity or masculinity, several feminist criticisms have been leveled against this concept. One is that the notion of androgyny, similar to the bipolar differentiation of femininity-masculinity, is based on the division of gender into female-stereotypic and male-stereotypic characteristics (Bem, 1993). Rather than making traits *gender-neutral*, androgyny involves the combination of *gender-specific* orientations. A second concern is that androgyny might be erecting unrealistic goals for individuals—the requirement that people be competent in both the communal and agentic domains. Third, according to Bem (1993), the concept of androgyny does not deal with masculinity and femininity in their unequal cultural context. It neither acknowledges nor attempts to eliminate the greater cultural value placed on male activities. Last, Bem is concerned that androgyny will not lead to the elimination of gender inequality, a goal that requires *societal* rather than *personal* change. That is, the mere existence of individuals with both feminine and masculine traits does not alter the patriarchal power structure in society.

Gender Attitudes

Let's turn now to an examination of variations in gender attitudes. People differ in the degree to which they believe that gender should dictate females' and males' roles. Some individuals hold a **traditional gender attitude**, *the belief that females should engage in communal behaviors and roles and males should engage in agentic behaviors and roles.* They might believe, for example, that women should be the primary rearers of children whereas men should be the primary financial providers or that women are better suited than men to nursing whereas men are better suited than women to corporate management. Others adhere to a **nontraditional or egalitarian gender attitude**, *the belief that behaviors and roles should not be gender-specific.* To get more familiar with the meaning of gender attitudes, take the test in Get Involved 3.3.

The Sex-Role Egalitarianism Scale (King & King, 1990), which is shown in part in Get Involved 3.3, illustrates the multidimensional nature of gender attitudes. This scale comprises beliefs about appropriate roles within five life domains: marital, parental, employment, social-interpersonal-heterosexual, and educational;

GET INVOLVED 3.3

What Is Your Gender Attitude?

On a scale from 1 (strongly agree) to 7 (strongly disagree), indicate the degree to which you agree or disagree with each of the following statements:

1. The husband should be the head of the family.
2. Keeping track of a child's out-of-school activities should be mostly the mother's responsibility.
3. Home economics courses should be as acceptable for male students as for female students.
4. A person should generally be more polite to a woman than to a man.
5. It is more appropriate for a mother rather than a father to change their baby's diaper.
6. It is wrong for a man to enter a traditionally female career.
7. Things work out best in a marriage if a husband leaves his hands off domestic tasks.
8. Women can handle pressures from their jobs as well as men can.
9. Choice of college is not as important for women as for men.

Reproduced by permission of Sigma Assessment Systems, Inc., P.O. Box 610984, Port Huron, MI 48061-0984. Tel: (800) 265-1285.

What Does It Mean?

Before computing your score, reverse the points for statements 3 and 8. That is, if you answered "1" (strongly agree) to these two questions, give yourself 7 points, if you answered "2," give yourself 6 points, and so on. Then sum the points for the 9 items. Note that higher scores reflect more nontraditional or egalitarian gender attitudes.

1. These statements come from the Sex-Role Egalitarianism Scale, developed in the 1980s. Are there any questions that you think are no longer adequate measures of egalitarian gender beliefs? If yes, give your reasons.
2. Look at your answers to Get Involved 3.2. Is there any consistency in the extent to which you describe yourself as communal and/or agentic and your beliefs about appropriate gender-related behaviors and roles? For example, if you received high scores on both communion and agency, reflecting an androgynous identity, did your answers to the questions in this activity indicate egalitarian beliefs? Can you explain why a person's gender-related traits might not be associated with her or his gender attitudes?
3. If most North Americans were to endorse egalitarian gender beliefs, what positive outcomes might be experienced by women and girls? By men and boys? Would there be any negative consequences for either gender? Explain.

and there is considerable evidence that gender attitudes are not uniform across these dimensions. Instead, North American college students tend to have more nontraditional beliefs about women's employment roles than they do about women's combined family and work roles (e.g., Holland & Andre, 1992; Powell & Yanico, 1991). For example, Holland and Andre found that approximately 84 percent of a college student sample disagreed with the statement that it is more important for a wife to help her husband with his career than for her to have a career of her own. However, only 42 percent believed a woman should accept an employment opportunity if it meant her husband would have to find another job and her family would have to move.

Individual Differences in Gender-Related Attitudes

As we have seen, gender attitudes can vary from traditional to egalitarian. Now let's examine demographic and personality characteristics that might be related to differences in gender attitudes.

Gender.   Not surprisingly, one of them is gender. Dozens of studies have shown that, among Whites, males have more traditional beliefs about the appropriate roles for women than females do (e.g., Hoffman & Kloska, 1995; Lottes & Kuriloff, 1992; Powell & Yanico, 1991; Willetts-Bloom & Nock, 1994). However, this gender difference might not be true of Blacks. Although there has been only limited research, one study found that Black women and men do not differ in their views of gender-related behaviors and roles (Brenner & Tomkiewicz, 1986).

Ethnicity.   Another demographic characteristic that is related to gender attitudes is ethnicity. As we saw in Chapter 2, Black women are less likely than White or Latina women to adhere to gender stereotypes. Thus, we might think their attitudes about gender-related behaviors and roles would be uniformly more egalitarian.

Interestingly, research comparing Black and White views about gender roles shows a complex pattern. On the one hand, Black women seem to hold more traditional views about the domestic domain. They have more stereotypical views about children's domestic roles (Dugger, 1988) and women's responsibilities for housework and childcare (Binion, 1990). According to Dugger (1988, p. 439) this traditional view might reflect a defensive reaction against the "labeling of Black women as 'matriarchs' . . . who rob their sons and men in general of their manhood." On the other hand, there is some evidence that Black women hold more egalitarian views about women's employment and political roles than White women do (Harris & Firestone, 1998). Also, Black college women, compared to White college women, perceive less conflict in the combination of the provider and domestic roles (e.g., Bridges & Etaugh, 1996; Murrell, Frieze, & Frost, 1991), a difference possibly due to Black women's longer history of combining work and family roles.

What about gender attitudes of Latinas? Traditionally, Latina/o families have been characterized as patriarchal with a dominant, powerful husband/father and a submissive, self-sacrificing wife/mother. Thus, it is not surprising that Latina women have been found to hold more traditional views about women's employment and political roles than either Black or White women (Harris & Firestone, 1998). However, there is evidence that the views held by Latina women are becoming less traditional, over time. The Latina/o family has been undergoing many changes related to gender (Castaneda, 1996). They have been experiencing an increasingly greater flexibility in the division of household responsibilities and a more egalitarian approach to family decision making (Gonzalez & Espin, 1996). For example, Donna Castaneda (1996) notes that second- and third-generation Latinas/os are less likely than first-generation women and men to believe that the husband should be the sole provider and decision maker within the family and that females should do all of the housework and obey the husband's/father's demands. Thus, the degree of acculturation of Latina women and Latino men seems to be strongly related to their gender attitudes.

Research on Native Americans has focused on their actual gender-related behaviors and roles rather than on their attitudes and has shown great variations over time and across tribal groups. According to Theresa LaFromboise and her associates (LaFromboise, Heyle, & Ozer, 1990), women's behaviors and roles in traditional Native American life included caregiving, spiritual continuation of their people, and transmission of cultural knowledge. Many Native American societies were characterized by complementary but equally powerful roles for some women and men while other groups institutionalized alternative female roles. For example, within several Plains tribes, women's roles included masculine ones, such as the "warrior woman" and the "manly hearted woman" (aggressive and independent) in addition to the traditional role of the submissive, hard-working wife. Other tribes, such as the Navajo and Iroquois, were matrilineal; women owned the material goods and passed these on to their daughters and sisters and played important economic, political, and spiritual roles.

Interestingly, LaFromboise and her colleagues (1990) contend that colonization by Europeans and the continuing acculturation process by which Native Americans have become more involved in the dominant White culture have contributed in several Native-American societies to a breakdown in complementary female-male roles and to an increase in male dominance and the subjugation of women. However, in many tribes women continue to experience considerable political power because of their traditional roles of caretakers for the community and transmitters of the culture.

Consistent with our discussion of the differences in gender attitudes across ethnic groups in the United States is evidence for cross-nation differences. For example, in one study (Morinaga, Frieze, & Ferligoj, 1993), gender attitudes of college students from the United States, Japan, and Slovenia were compared. The results showed that students in the United States and Slovenia had more egalitarian attitudes than did Japanese students. These differences might be due, at least in part, to the greater labor-force involvement of women in both the United States and Slovenia compared to Japan.

In order to more directly learn about the gender attitudes of women of different ethnicities, perform the interviews described in Get Involved 3.4.

GET INVOLVED **3.4**

Ethnic Variations in Gender Attitudes

Interview two college women of approximately the same age (i.e., both traditional-age students or both older adults), from each of two different ethnic groups. Ask the following questions:

1. Do you think there should be different roles for women and men in the family? In dating relationships? In the workplace? If your respondent answered "yes" to any of these, ask her to be specific.

2. What is your career goal?
3. How important is your future/current career to your personal identity?
4. Do you want to get married and have children? If yes, do you think you will have any difficulty balancing your family and work roles?
5. Who do you think should be the primary provider in your family?
6. How do you think you and your spouse/partner will divide up the household responsibilities, including child care?

What Does It Mean?

1. Although your sample is very small, did you observe any ethnic differences? Did these differences match those discussed in the text? If yes, show the connections. If no, explain why your results might differ from those reported in past research.

2. You interviewed college women. Do you think your findings might have been different had your respondents been college graduates? Working-class or poor women without a college education? Explain your answers.

Other Factors.   There is some evidence that gender attitudes are related to religious factors. Among college students, Jews, for example, tend to have less traditional gender beliefs than do Protestants (Lottes & Kuriloff, 1992; Willetts-Bloom & Nock, 1994), and Catholics fall somewhere in between (Lottes & Kuriloff, 1992). Moreover, the more strongly students embrace religion in their lives, the more traditional their gender attitudes are. Specifically, those who attend religious services frequently (Willetts-Bloom & Nock, 1994) and whose religious beliefs reflect internal values and a commitment to live by these values (Jones & McNamara, 1991) tend to have more traditional gender attitudes than students who are less committed to their religious beliefs.

Two other demographic characteristics related to gender attitudes are social class and academic achievement. Among both Blacks and Whites, higher social class and educational level tend to be associated with more nontraditional views about gender (Hoffman & Kloska, 1995). Similarly, a high GPA among college women, is related to nontraditional gender attitudes (Ahrens & O'Brien, 1996).

Perceived Value of Female versus Male Gender-Related Attributes

Derek Grimmell and Gary Stern (1992) found that college students value masculinity more strongly than femininity. This is consistent with our previous discussion of the greater power held by males in North American society. Is it, therefore, more advantageous to be a male than to be a female? Alternatively, are gender-related advantages and disadvantages equally distributed between the genders or, perhaps, balanced in favor of females? To examine this question, try the exercises in Get Involved 3.5.

GET INVOLVED **3.5**

Would You Rather Be A Female or a Male ?

Have you ever considered what life would be like if you were the other gender? Think about what is has been like to be a female or male. Then think about any advantages and/or disadvantages that would occur if you were the other gender. For each of the following three categories, list any advantages and/or disadvantages of being the other gender: (1) *social roles*, i.e., opportunities that are not equally available to the two genders and/or behaviors that are considered more appropriate for one gender than the other, (2) *physical appearance expectations*, and (3) *physical differences*, e.g., reproductive, size, or strength differences. Also, ask an other-gender friend to perform the same exercise. Discuss your answers with your friend.

(Cann & Vann, 1995)

What Does It Mean?

1. Did you imagine more advantages and/or disadvantages in one category than the others? If yes, how can you explain the pattern of perceived advantages and disadvantages?
2. Are the responses of your other-gender friend complementary to your own responses? In other words, are your friend's perceptions of the advantages of being your gender consistent with your perceptions of the disadvantages of being your friend's gender? Why or why not?
3. Examine the number of advantages relative to disadvantages that you associated with being the other gender and consider the relative importance of each. Do the same for your friend's responses. Do you and/or your friend attach greater value to one gender or the other? If yes, how can you explain this?
4. If you or your friend perceive a relative advantage of one gender over the other, discuss some societal changes that would have to occur to reduce this discrepancy?

When Arnie Cann and Elizabeth Vann (1995) asked college students to list as many advantages and disadvantages as they could associate with being the other gender, they found that, overall, both women and men associated more advantages with being male. Specifically, these students considered differences in physical appearance requirements and actual physical differences as more disadvantageous to females than to males. For example, they believed that more females than males must be concerned about their appearance and that biological differences, such as pregnancy and menstruation, are disadvantageous to females. Interestingly, these students did not perceive males to have more social-role advantages than females. Although females were seen to be limited by workplace discrimination and the expectation to be subordinate in their relationships, males were viewed as hurt by the social pressure on them to be successful and to play a leadership role. Thus, these students seemed to be aware that the gender imbalance in power puts women at a disadvantage and that the social construction of the agentic, achievement-oriented male role establishes potentially difficult expectations for men.

Given the evidence that males are seen as having more advantages than females, it is not surprising that people evaluate males more negatively than they do females who violate gender expectations (e.g., Lytton & Romney, 1991; Martin, 1990). Scholars have posited two possible explanations for this difference. The **social status hypothesis** contends that *because the male gender role is more highly valued than the female role is, a male is seen as lowering his social status by engaging in female-stereotypic behaviors, whereas a female performing male-stereotypic behaviors is perceived as raising her status* (e.g., McCreary, 1994). Consequently, males who engage in cross-gender behaviors are viewed more negatively than are females who deviate from gender expectations. As stated by Bem (1993), our society

> so thoroughly devalues whatever thoughts, feelings, and behaviors are culturally defined as feminine that crossing the gender boundary has a more negative cultural meaning for men than it has for women—which means, in turn, that male gender-boundary-crossers are much more culturally stigmatized than female gender-boundary-crossers. (pp. 149–150)

Although there has been only minimal investigation of the social status hypothesis, it receives some support from the finding that male behavior, regardless of the gender of the person engaging in that behavior, is seen as more desirable than female behavior (Feinman, 1984). That is, people associate a higher value with the male role than they do with the female role.

The other explanation of the more negative evaluation of male gender-role violation is the **sexual orientation hypothesis** (e.g., McCreary, 1994). This perspective argues that *cross-gender behavior in boys but not girls is considered a sign of actual or potential same-sex sexual orientation.* Several investigations have provided support for this perspective. For example, Carol Martin (1990) asked college students to report their attitudes toward sissies and tomboys. Not only did they believe it was more acceptable for girls to be tomboys than for boys to be sissies but they believed that sissies, more than tomboys, would be likely to develop a same-sex sexual orientation. Similarly, when Donald McCreary (1994) asked college students to evaluate either a child or an adult who had cross-gender traits and interests, he found they considered it more likely that the feminine male was or would become a gay man than that the masculine female was or would become a lesbian.

SUMMARY

1. Prenatal sex differentiation is a multistage process. The joining of the sex chromosomes at conception is followed by the differentiation of the gonads, the development of the internal and external reproductive organs, and the organization of the hypothalamus. After the gonads develop, the presence or absence of androgens influences the development of the reproductive organs and the brain. Additionally, estrogens might play a role in female development.

2. Some individuals experience anomalies in their prenatal development. Turner's syndrome is a chromosomal disorder in which the individual has a single X chromosome. These individuals are raised as girls and tend to have female gender expectations although they have no sex glands and no prenatal estrogen.

3. There are several forms of intersexuality. Genetic females with the CAH are usually reared as girls, although they have a partial or complete masculinization of their external genitals. Genetic males with the androgen-insensitivity syndrome have feminized external genitals and are reared as girls. Genetic males with a 5 alpha-reductase deficiency experience a female-to-male body transformation at puberty.

4. Case studies of both females with Turner's syndrome and intersexuals provide mixed evidence regarding the influence of prenatal biological factors on nonsexual gender-related attributes, gender identity, and sexual orientation. Some researchers claim that gender-related development is dependent on prenatal

factors and others point to the importance of the gender of rearing.

5. Psychoanalytic theory proposes that gender typing stems from the child's identification with the same-gender parent, a process that occurs when the child resolves the Oedipus complex. For the boy the resolution stems from fear of castration by the father. For the girl it stems from the realization that she will never possess her father. However, because the girl's desire for a penis, which started her Oedipal feelings, does not stop, she experiences jealousy and inferiority feelings throughout her life.

6. Social learning theory posits that children acquire gender behaviors via imitation of same-gender models and positive reinforcement of their own gender-consistent behaviors.

7. Cognitive developmental theory contends that once children attain gender constancy, they are motivated to behave in gender-appropriate ways. Thus, they actively seek out the patterns and rules that characterize female behavior and male behavior. They then engage in gender-consistent behaviors because it enables them to competently adjust to the social environment.

8. Gender schema theory proposes that children develop an interrelated set of ideas about gender. They are aware of the numerous societal norms and practices that signify the importance of gender. Thus, children learn to organize the social world on the basis of gender and guide their own actions accordingly.

9. On the basis of their gender-related traits, individuals can be categorized as feminine, masculine, androgynous, or undifferentiated. Research has shown an increase in masculinity and androgyny in women over time. Masculinity is related to psychological adjustment. Androgyny was once considered to be highly desirable, but recently feminist scholars have criticized it.

10. Gender attitudes are multidimensional. There is some evidence that college students have less-traditional beliefs about the value of the employment role for women but more-traditional views about the combination of women's employment and family roles.

11. Individuals differ in their gender attitudes. Among Whites, women are generally more nontraditional in their beliefs than men are. Among women, Blacks hold more traditional views about domestic responsibilities than Whites do but they have more nontraditional views about the combination of women's employment and family roles. The roles of Latina/o women and men have become more egalitarian over time, but Latinas have more traditional views than do Black and White women. The gender-related behaviors and roles of Native American women vary greatly across tribes and in several societies increased acculturation has been accompanied by greater male dominance.

12. College women and men associate more advantages with being male than with being female. Also, males, compared to females, are more negatively evaluated for engaging in cross-gender behavior.

WHAT DO YOU THINK?

1. Evidence indicates that boys, more than girls, select role models who are powerful. Explain this finding.

2. As discussed in Chapter 2, it is possible that the media not only reflect gender stereotypes but help shape them. Now that you are familiar with theories of gender typing, use one of these theories to explain how the media might contribute to an individual's acquisition of gender stereotypes.

3. Which gender-typing theory or theories best explain(s) the development of gender-related traits, behaviors, and roles? Explain. To help you develop your reasons, critically think about the evaluations presented in the text. Indicate why you believe that some of the evaluative comments seem to be more credible than others. Additionally, if you have had any contact with young children, try to provide anecdotal support for some of the theoretical concepts.

4. Discuss the advantages and disadvantages to girls/women and boys/men of gender-related trait identifications consistent with stereotypes; i.e., femininity in females and masculinity in males. Can you think of the advantages and disadvantages of an androgynous identity?

5. There is some evidence that individuals who internalize their religious beliefs and attempt to live by them hold more traditional gender attitudes than individuals who do not. Consider possible explanations for this finding.

IF YOU WANT TO LEARN MORE

Anselmi, D. L., & Law, A. L. (1998). *Questions of gender: Perspectives and paradoxes*. Boston: McGraw Hill.

Basow, S. A. (1992). *Gender: Stereotypes and roles* (3rd ed.). Pacific Grove, CA: Brooks/Cole.

Bem, S. L. (1993). *The lenses of gender: Transforming the debate on sexual inequality*. New Haven, CT: Yale University Press.

Money, J., & Tucker, P. (1975). *Sexual signatures: On being a man or a woman*. Boston: Little, Brown & Co.

Children's Knowledge and Beliefs about Gender
   Distinguishing between Females and Males
   Gender Identity and Self-Perceptions
   Gender Stereotypes

Gender-Related Activities and Interests
   Physical Performance and Sports
   Toys and Play
   Gender Segregation

Gender-Related Social Behaviors and Personality Traits
   Aggression
   Prosocial Behavior
   Influenceability

   Emotionality
   Moral Reasoning

Influences on Gender Development
   Parents
   School
   Peers
   Media

Child Sexual Abuse
   Incidence
   Consequences
   Memories of Child Sexual Abuse:
      Repressed or False?
   Prevention
   Treatment

KEY TERMS

gender identity
rough-and tumble-play
relational aggression
prosocial behavior

persuasion studies
group pressure conformity
  studies
empathy

socialization
child sexual abuse
incest

What are little girls made of?

What are little girls made of?

Sugar and spice and everything nice.

That's what little girls are made of.

What are little boys made of?

What are little boys made of?

Frogs and snails and puppy dogs' tails,

That's what little boys are made of.

(old nursery rhyme)

My family was very traditional. I have two older brothers and they would follow my father and learn from him. I, on the other hand, followed and learned from my mother. I learned to cook at a very young age. I played house with my friends and dressed up in fancy clothes. I would pretend I was a waitress, a model or a teacher. (Angie, 21-year-old college senior)

Are girls and boys really as different as the nursery rhyme suggests? Is there even a kernel of truth in these age-old stereotypes? And if so, what factors might be responsible? Angie's recollection of her childhood indicates the important contributions made by parents. In this chapter, we focus on the development of girls in infancy and early childhood and examine both similarities and differences between girls and boys during these early years. We also explore factors that influence gender development, including the roles played by parents, schools, peers, and the media. Finally, we examine a bleaker aspect of childhood for all too many youngsters: Sexual abuse.

Children's Knowledge and Beliefs about Gender

Distinguishing between Females and Males

From birth, infants are surrounded by abundant cues signifying gender. They are given gender labels, and are outfitted in color-coded clothing, diapers, and blankets (Eisenberg, Martin, & Fabes, 1996). It is not surprising that children learn to differentiate between females and males at an early age. Six-month-old infants can tell the difference between pictures of adult females and males (Walsh, Katz, & Downey, 1991), and 10-month-olds are able to distinguish between their faces (Leinbach & Fagot, 1993; Younger & Fearing, 1999). By the age of 18 months, children can match the face and voice of men and women (Poulin-Dubois, Serbin & Derbyshire, 1998). Between the ages of 2 and 2½ years, they can accurately label pictures of girls and boys (Etaugh & Duits, 1990; Etaugh, Grinnell, & Etaugh, 1989; Leinbach & Fagot, 1993). Young children who learn to identify females and males early show more gender-typical preferences for toys and peers than children of the same age who do not make this distinction (Martin, 1999).

Gender Identity and Self-Perceptions

Gender identity refers to *an individual's sense of being female or male* (Bradley & Zucker, 1997). As we saw in Chapter 3, children develop gender identity between 2 and 3 years of age. By that time they can accurately label their own gender and place a picture of themselves with other same-gender children (Ruble & Martin, 1998).

As children grow aware of their membership in a particular gender category, they begin to view their own gender more favorably than the other gender (Powlishta, 1995, 1997; Ruble & Martin, 1998). In one study of children in second through tenth grade, for example, girls believed that girls were nicer, harder workers, and less selfish than boys. Boys, on the other hand, felt that *they* were nicer, harder workers, and less selfish than girls (Etaugh, Levine, & Mennella, 1984).

Gender Stereotypes

In Chapter 2, we discussed how gender stereotypes are formed. This process begins early in life. Rudimentary knowledge about gender-typical objects and activities develops during the second year. Children as young as 24 months know that certain objects (e.g., ribbon, dress, purse) are associated with females and that others (e.g., gun, truck, screwdriver) are associated with males (Levy et al., 1998; Poulin-Dubois, Serbin & Eischedt, 1997). By age 3, they display knowledge of gender stereotypes for toys, clothing, work, and activities (Fagot, Leinbach, & O'Boyle, 1992; Weinraub et al., 1984). For example, children of this age generally agree that boys play with cars and trucks and help their fathers, whereas girls play with dolls and help their mothers (Etaugh & Rathus, 1995). Gender-stereotyped knowledge of activities and occupations increases rapidly between ages 3 and 5 and is mastered by age 7 (Martin & Little, 1990; Serbin, Moller, & Gulko, 1993; Signorella, Bigler, & Liben, 1993). For a closer look at how occupational stereotypes develop throughout childhood, read Learn about the Research 4.1.

In addition, preschoolers demonstrate a rudimentary awareness of gender stereotypes for personality traits. Traits such as "cries a lot," "gets feelings hurt easily," "needs help," "likes to give hugs and kisses," and "can't fix things" are applied to girls, while "hits people," "likes to win at playing games," "is not afraid of scary things," and "fixes things," are seen as characteristics of boys (Bauer, Liebl, & Stennes, 1998; Ruble & Martin, 1998). In general, knowledge of gender-typical

---

LEARN ABOUT THE RESEARCH 4.1

Gender Stereotypes about Occupations

The stereotype that certain occupations are more appropriate for one gender than the other emerges early in childhood (Helwig, 1998; Phillips & Imhoff, 1997). Even children as young as 2 and 3 years of age make a distinction between "women's jobs" and "men's jobs" (Etaugh & Rathus, 1995). Girls generally are less rigid in their occupational stereotypes than boys (Helwig, 1998; Jessell & Beymer, 1992). In addition, girls are more likely to have nonstereotyped career aspirations for themselves (Belansky, Early, & Eccles, 1993; Kresevich, 1993). In one study (Etaugh & Liss, 1992), kindergarten-through-eighth-grade children were asked about their occupational aspirations. Through the third grade, most girls chose traditional feminine occupations, such as nurse and teacher. About 25 percent

listed traditionally male occupations, such as doctor and pilot. Older girls, however, were more likely than younger ones to choose a traditionally masculine career and were less likely to pick a feminine one. Boys, on the other hand, aspired to masculine careers at all ages and *never* chose a feminine occupation. The results for females may be related to the finding that, by fourth grade, children view stereotypical feminine occupations less favorably than masculine occupations (Bukatko & Shedd, 1999). In studies done in the early 1970s, boys aspired to a wider variety of occupations than did girls. However, more recent studies report that girls now are selecting more varied occupations than boys (Helwig, 1998; Phipps, 1995; Trice, Hughes, Odom, Woods, & McClellan, 1995).

What Does it Mean?

1. Why are girls more flexible in their career aspirations than boys?
2. Why are male-dominated careers more attractive to both girls and boys than female-dominated careers are?
3. What are some ways that gender stereotypes about occupations can be reduced?

personality traits emerges later than other stereotype information (Eisenberg, Martin, & Fabes, 1996) and increases throughout elementary school (Best & Williams, 1993).

Stereotypes are held quite rigidly until about 7 or 8 years of age and then become more flexible until adolescence (Ruble & Martin, 1998). For example, Thomas Alfieri and his colleagues (Alfieri, Ruble, & Higgins, 1996) presented 12 trait-related terms, half of them feminine and half masculine, to children ranging in age from 9 to 16 years. The children were asked whether the items described males, females or both. Gender-trait flexibility, indicated by choosing the "both" option, peaked at ages 11 and 12 and declined thereafter (see Chapter 6). Boys showed less flexibility than girls, particularly regarding masculine traits. Similarly, Lisa Serbin and her colleagues (Serbin et al., 1993) found that 11-year-olds knew more about stereotypes than 5-year-olds, but were also more aware of gender-role exceptions, such as girls using tools and sports equipment, and boys engaging in domestic chores. While these older children retain the broad stereotypes, their increasing cognitive maturity allows them to recognize the arbitrary aspects of gender categories, and they are more willing to accept and even try behaviors that are typical of the other gender (Etaugh & Rathus, 1995; Katz & Walsh, 1991).

Gender-Related Activities and Interests

Physical Performance and Sports

In the preschool and elementary school years, girls and boys are fairly similar in their motor skills. Boys are slightly stronger, and they typically can throw a ball farther and jump higher. Their activity levels also tend to be greater, at least in some settings (Danner et al., 1991). Girls are better at tasks requiring overall flexibility, precise movement, and coordination of their arms and legs. This gives them an edge in activities such as jumping jacks, balancing on one foot, and gymnastics (Etaugh & Rathus, 1995).

Gender differences in motor skills favoring boys become increasingly pronounced from childhood through adolescence (Small & Schultz, 1990; Thomas & French, 1985). What might account for this change? Thomas and French suggest that childhood gender differences in motor skills (with the exception of throwing) are more likely a result of environmental factors than biological ones. They note that boys receive more opportunities, encouragement, and support for participating in sports. It is not surprising that by middle childhood, boys in most cultures spend more time than girls in vigorous, competitive, athletic activities (Larson & Verma, 1999).

During puberty, hormonal changes increase muscle mass for boys and fat for girls, giving boys an advantage in strength, size and power (see Chapter 5). But hormones are only part of the story. Social pressures on girls to act more feminine and less "tomboyish" intensify during adolescence, contributing to girls' declining interest and participation in athletic activities (Ruble & Martin, 1998). This trend is troubling, given that involvement in sports is associated with high self-esteem among adolescent girls (Denmark, 1999). The good news is that the participation of girls and young women in sports has increased dramatically since the passage in 1972 of Title IX of the Education Amendments Act. This Federal legislation bars discrimination in all educational programs, including athletics. Prior to Title IX, only 7.5 percent of high school athletes and 15 percent of college athletes were women. By 1995, these percentages had risen to 39 percent of high school athletes and 37 percent of college athletes (Marklein, 1997; Women's Sports Foundation, 1998). The bad news is that schools still spend disproportionately more money on scholarships, recruiting, and operating expenses for men's sports and on the salaries of coaches (mostly male) of men's teams (Suggs, 2000; Women's Sports Foundation, 1998).

Toys and Play

Gender differences in children's play activities and interests are more evident than they are in other areas such as personality qualities or attitudes (McHale, Crouter, & Tucker, 1999). Girls and boys begin to differ in their preference for certain toys and play activities early in life. By the time they are 12 to 18 months old, girls prefer to play with dolls, domestic equipment, and soft toys, while boys choose vehicles, sports equipment, and tools (Etaugh & Rathus, 1995). By 3 years of age, gender-typical toy choices are well established (Eisenberg et al., 1996) and these differences persist throughout childhood (e.g., Rodgers, Fagot, & Winebarger, 1998). However, girls are more likely than boys to display cross-gender toy choices and activities (Bussey & Bandura, 1992; Frey & Ruble, 1992; Lobel & Menashri, 1993). For example, girls are more likely to request transportation toys and sports equipment as gifts than boys are to ask for dolls (Etaugh & Liss, 1992).

Why are girls more likely to depart from the stereotype? In most cultures, masculine activities have greater prestige than feminine ones. A girl who plays with "boys' toys" might be viewed as showing an acceptable desire to aspire to a higher social status, whereas a boy who plays with "girls'" toys might be seen as engaging in an inferior role (Etaugh & Rathus, 1995). Moreover, children generally find boys' toys more interesting and appealing than girls' toys (Rosenblum, 1991). You can do lots more things with Legos than with a tea set!

Because of their preferences, girls and boys experience very different play environments (Eisenberg et al., 1996). During the preschool and elementary school years, boys spend more time than girls in vigorous physical outdoor activities such as playing with large vehicles, climbing, exploratory play, and **rough-and-tumble play**, which consists of *playful chasing, tumbling, and wrestling* (Bornstein et al., 1999; Fabes et al., 1999; Harper & Huie, 1998; Lindsey, Mize, & Pettit, 1997). Boys are more likely to engage in competitive activities and to play in large groups of five or more children. In conflict situations with other children, they are more likely to use powerful, controlling strategies (Sims, Hutchins, & Taylor, 1998). Girls play preferences, on the other hand, include dolls, domestic play, and arts and crafts. They engage in more symbolic (i.e. "pretend") play than boys

(Bornstein et al., 1999). Girls' play is more sedentary, more cooperative, more socially competent, and more supervised and structured by adults. Also, girls are more likely than boys are to play with a small group of children or just one child (Fabes et al., 1999; Harper & Huie, 1998; Hartup & Stevens, 1999; Neppl & Murray, 1997; Pellegrini & Smith, 1998). To take a closer look at play patterns of girls and boys, try Get Involved 4.1.

Gender Segregation

Between the ages of 2 and 3 years, children begin to prefer playing with children of the same gender, with girls showing this preference somewhat earlier than boys (Fagot, 1995; Moller & Serbin, 1996; Serbin et al., 1994). Gender segregation increases during childhood and is especially strong in the elementary school years (Boyatzis, Mallis, & Leon, 1999; Etaugh & Liss, 1992; Gray & Feldman, 1997; Lewis & Phillipsen, 1998). One study by Eleanor Maccoby and Carol Nagy Jacklin (1987) found that 4-year-olds interacted with same-gender peers 3 times more often than with peers of the other gender, while 6-year-olds played with same-

GET INVOLVED **4.1**
Play Patterns of Girls and Boys

Observe preschool-aged children in a day care center or preschool during a free-play session. Keep a record of the following behaviors:

1. The toys that girls choose and those that boys choose.

2. The activities girls engage in and those that boys engage in.
3. How often: (a) girls play with other girls; (b) boys play with other boys; (c) girls and boys play with each other.

What Does It Mean?

1. Did boys and girls show different patterns of toy choice and activity preference? If so, describe these patterns. How do you account for the differences you observed (if any)?
2. Which toys in general were most in demand? Were these "girl" toys, "boy" toys or gender-neutral toys?

3. Did boys prefer to play with same-gender peers more than girls did, was it the other way around, or were there no differences? How do you account for the differences you observed (if any)?

gender peers 11 times more often. Even when elementary school children choose seats in the lunchroom or get into line, they frequently arrange themselves in same-gender groups. Peer pressure can be a powerful motivator, as illustrated in Barrie Thorne's (1993) observation of second graders seating themselves in the lunchroom. One table was filling with both boys and girls, when a high-status second-grade boy walked by. He commented loudly, "Too many girls" and headed for a seat at another table. The boys at the first table picked up their trays and moved and no other boys sat at the first table, which had now been declared taboo. Children who cross the "gender boundary" are unpopular with their peers, although there are certain conditions under which contact with the other gender is permissible (see Table 4.1).

Why do children play primarily with children of their own gender? According to Eleanor Maccoby (1998a, 1998b), there are two reasons why girls may avoid boys. One is that they don't like the rough, aggressive, dominant play style of boys. A second is that boys are unresponsive to their polite suggestions. Analogously, boys may avoid girls because girls are not responsive to their rough play (Eisenberg et al., 1996). An alternative view is that rather than actively trying to avoid children of the other gender, children simply prefer the company of their own gender (Sippola, Bukowski, & Noll, 1997). This, in turn, may be because they share a preference for gender-typed toys (Etaugh & Liss, 1992).

TABLE 4.1. Knowing the Rules: Under What Circumstances Is it Permissible to Have Contact with the Other Gender in Middle Childhood?.

Rule:	The contact is accidental.
Example:	You're not looking where you are going, and you bump into someone.
Rule:	The contact is incidental.
Example:	You go to get some lemonade and wait while two children of the other gender get some. (There should be no conversation.)
Rule:	The contact is in the guise of some clear and necessary purpose.
Example:	You may say "pass the lemonade" to persons of the other gender at the next table. No interest in them is expressed.
Rule:	An adult compels you to have contact.
Example:	"Go get that map from X and Y and bring it to me."
Rule:	You are accompanied by someone of your own gender.
Example:	Two girls may talk to two boys though physical closeness with your own partner must be maintained and intimacy with the others is disallowed.
Rule:	The interaction or contact is accompanied by disavowal.
Example:	You say someone is ugly or hurl some other insult or (more commonly for boys) push or throw something at them as you pass by.

From Sroufe, Bennett, Englund, Urban & Schulman, 1993. Reproduced with permission of the Society for Research in Child Development, Inc.

Gender-Related Social Behaviors and Personality Traits

In Chapter 2, we examined numerous gender stereotypes. How accurately do these stereotypes reflect actual differences in the behaviors and personality characteristics of females and males? As we shall see, some stereotypes have at least a grain (or more) of truth to them, whereas others are not supported by the evidence. Two cautionary notes: First, even when gender differences are found, they typically are small. Second, there is considerable overlap in the characteristics of females and males. For example, girls generally are more nurturant toward younger children than boys are, but some boys show greater nurturance than some girls. Also keep in mind that the differences we discuss here are not limited to childhood, but generally continue into adulthood as well.

Aggression

Few gender differences in aggression are noted in the infancy and toddler years. By the time children begin to interact with each other during the preschool period, however, the differences become striking. Boys are more physically aggressive than girls and this difference increases over time (Coie & Dodge, 1998; Loeber & Hay, 1997; Loeber & Stouthamer-Loeber, 1998). The differences hold across socioeconomic groups and across cultures (Coie & Dodge, 1998; Eley, Lichtenstein, & Stevenson, 1999). Girls, however, are more likely than boys to use **relational aggression**, which involves *harming others through nonphysical hurtful manipulation of their peer relationships* (Crick & Bigbee, 1998; McNeilly-Choque, Hart, Robinson, Nelson & Olsen, 1996; Zuger, 1998b). For example, girls might exclude a peer from their play group, or spread malicious rumors and gossip about her. Girls also are more likely than boys to be victims of relational aggression (Crick, Casas, & Ku, 1999).

Both biological and environmental influences probably contribute to gender differences in aggression. On the biological side, it has been noted that the gender difference emerges early and appears across most cultures. In addition, the sex hormone testosterone appears to play a role, at least in animal aggression (Eisenberg et al., 1996). Research on the relationship between aggressive behavior and testosterone in humans has produced mixed results (Björkvist, 1994; Tremblay, et al., 1998). Some studies yield little evidence of a correlation between testosterone and behavior. When relationships are found, they generally are quite modest in size. Jacquelyn White and Robin Kowalski (1994) suggest that studies showing a connection between aggression and testosterone may be unduly emphasized because they are consistent with the stereotype of the aggressive male and the submissive female.

Environmental factors may be even more important than biological ones in producing gender differences in aggression. For one thing, teachers and peers are more likely to ignore girls' aggression, which helps to terminate the behavior (Coie & Dodge, 1998). Although parents do not discourage girls' aggression more than boys' aggression (Lytton & Romney, 1991), their encouragement of boys' physical play and the use of gender-typical toys such as guns may serve to promote aggression. Moreover, the rougher, dominance-oriented play of boys' groups may contribute to the maintenance of higher aggression levels in boys (Coie & Dodge, 1998). In addition, girls expect more guilt, more peer and parental disapproval, and fewer material gains for aggression than boys do (Eisenberg et al., 1996).

Prosocial Behavior

Prosocial behavior is *voluntary behavior intended to benefit someone else*. It includes helping, comforting others, sharing, and cooperating (Eisenberg & Fabes, 1998). The stereotype is that females are more nurturant, supportive and helpful than males. Are they?

Most studies of children have found no gender differences in prosocial behavior, but when differences are found they favor girls (Eisenberg & Fabes, 1998; Eisenberg et al., 1996). For example, girls show greater interest in and more interaction with babies as early as the preschool years (Blakemore, 1998). Girls also help others more than boys do (Eisenberg & Fabes, 1998) but studies have found that the opposite is true for adults. This is partly because studies with adults frequently involve male-oriented situations, such as rescuing strangers, sometimes in potentially dangerous situations (for example, helping to change a tire or picking up a hitchhiker). Women, on the other hand, are more likely to offer psychological assistance and help to friends and family members (Eisenberg & Fabes, 1998; Eisenberg et al., 1996). Unfortunately, this aspect of helpfulness has largely been overlooked by researchers.

Gender differences in helping styles are consistent with stereotyped expectations for males and females. How do the differences arise? In many societies, girls are expected to be more nurturant, kind, and emotionally supportive than boys, and they are rewarded for these behaviors. Boys, meanwhile, are more often rewarded for helping behaviors that involve rescuing, risk taking, and chivalry (Eagly, 1998).

Influenceability

Females tend to be stereotyped as more easily influenced and more conforming than males. Is there any evidence to support this view? Again, the answer depends on several factors, such as the type of measure used and even the gender of the researcher. The two major types of tasks used to measure influenceability are **persuasion studies** and **group pressure conformity studies**. In persuasion studies, *participants indicate their position on a controversial topic. A different position supported by arguments is presented by another individual and the participant's position is again measured.* Conformity studies *are similar, except that a group of people, not just one individual, supports a position discrepant with the participant's.*

Alice Eagly and Linda Carli (1981) performed a meta-analysis on both kinds of studies and found that women were more easily influenced than men. The gender difference was somewhat greater for the conformity studies, but all differences were small. Females were influenced more when masculine topics, such as technology or sports, were used. The gender difference also was greater when the researchers were male.

Several factors may account for these findings. For one thing, females are socialized to yield to social influence, while males are trained to do the influencing. Remember also that from an early age, females show more cooperation and less conflict in group settings. Accepting the views of others can be viewed as a mechanism for maintaining social harmony and avoiding conflict. In addition, consistent with our theme that females have less power than males, women are accorded a lower status than men in most societies. Individuals of lower status generally learn to conform to the wishes of higher-status individuals (Eagly & Wood, 1985).

Emotionality

Females are thought to be more emotional than males: more fearful, anxious, easily upset, and emotionally expressive. Males are viewed as more likely to express anger and to hide or deny their emotions (Ruble & Martin, 1998). Is there any truth to these stereotypes?

Preschool girls express less anger and more fearfulness than boys. In elementary school, boys start to hide negative emotions such as sadness, while girls begin to hide negative emotions, such as disappointment, that might hurt others' feelings. By adolescence, girls report more sadness, shame, and guilt, whereas boys deny experiencing these feelings. Girls also report experiencing emotions more intensely than boys (Eisenberg et al., 1996; Polce-Lynch, Myers, Kilmartin, Forssmann-Falck, & Kliewer, 1998). Note that these findings do not answer the question of whether females are actually more emotional than males or whether they simply are more likely to report their feelings.

Another aspect of emotionality is **empathy,** which involves *feeling the same emotion that someone else is feeling*. The stereotype is that women are more empathic than men. Are they in reality? The answer depends on how you measure empathy. When individuals are asked to report how they feel in certain situations (for example, "Does seeing people cry upset you?"), females show more empathy than males (e.g., Karniol, Gabay, Ochion, & Harari, 1998). However, when individuals' behaviors are observed unobtrusively or when their physiological reactions are measured, no gender differences in empathy are found (Eisenberg et al., 1996). These findings suggest that when people know what is being measured and can control their reactions, they may act in the socially acceptable gender-typical manner.

Socialization seems to be an important factor in the development of differences in emotionality (or in the willingness to report emotions). Parents report being more accepting of fear in girls and anger in boys. Mothers focus more on emotions, particularly positive emotions, when talking to their daughters (Adams, Kuebli, Boyle, & Fivush, 1995; Flanagan & Perese, 1998). In addition, parents put more pressure on sons to control their emotions, while encouraging their daughters to be emotionally expressive (Eisenberg et al., 1996). Parents emphasize closer emotional relationships with daughters than with sons. As early as preschool, mothers and daughters already are closer emotionally than mothers and sons (Benenson, Morash, & Petrakos, 1998).

A series of five studies done by Penelope Davis (1999) on adults' memories of childhood events provides an interesting illustration of the apparent social construction of gender differences in emotionality. She found that, in general, females and males did not differ either in the number of memories recalled or in how quickly they recalled them. However, females consistently recalled more childhood memories of events associated with emotion and were faster in accessing these memories. Furthermore, this difference was observed across a wide range of emotions experienced by both the individuals and others.

Moral Reasoning

Are there gender differences in moral reasoning? The question has been hotly debated ever since Lawrence Kohlberg (1985) proposed that males show higher levels of moral reasoning than females. In his research, Kohlberg asked individuals to respond to moral dilemmas. In one dilemma, a druggist refuses to lower the price of an expensive drug which could save the life of a dying woman. Her husband, who cannot afford the drug, then steals it. Was he right or wrong in doing so, and why? Kohlberg reported that males' answers emphasized abstract justice and "law and order," which he believed to be more advanced than the emphasis on caring and concern for others expressed by females. As we saw in Chapter 1, Carol Gilligan (1982, 1993) argued that females' moral reasoning is just as advanced as that of males, but that females speak "in a different voice" that emphasizes personal connections rather than abstract legalities.

Research, however, generally fails to support Kohlberg's and Gilligan's view that there are gender differences in the underlying basis of moral reasoning. Most studies have found that both females and males are concerned with caring *and* with justice in resolving moral conflicts (Crandall, Tsang, Goldman, & Pennington, 1999; Turiel, 1998). Extensive reviews by Lawrence Walker (1984, 1991) also reveal that females score as high as males on Kohlberg's measure of moral reasoning. On another measure of moral reasoning, the Defining Issues Test, females score higher than males at every age and educational level (Thoma, 1986).

Influences on Gender Development

Socialization *refers to the process by which each generation passes along to children the knowledge, beliefs, and skills which constitute the culture of the social group.* Since societies prescribe somewhat different social roles for adult females and males, girls and boys typically are socialized differently in order to prepare them for the adult roles they will play (Maccoby, 1998b). This is a restatement of the third theme of our book; namely, that much of gender is socially constructed. A variety of sources help shape the behaviors and interests of boys and girls. These include parents, teachers, peers, and the media. In Chapter 3, we briefly mentioned the role of these influences when we discussed theories of gender typing. In this section, we examine these factors in greater detail.

Parents

One of the most obvious ways in which parents influence gender development is by providing their sons and daughters with distinctive clothing, room furnishings, and toys. Infant girls are likely to be dressed in a ruffled pink outfit (sometimes with a bow attached to wisps of hair), whereas baby boys typically wear blue (Pomerleau, Bolduc, Malcuit, & Cossette, 1990; Shakin, Shakin, & Sternglanz, 1985). The bedrooms of infant and toddler girls contain dolls and are decorated in pastel colors, frills, and flowery patterns. Baby boys' rooms feature animal themes, sturdy furniture, blue bedding, and a variety of sports equipment, vehicles, and military toys (Pomerleau et al., 1990). Clearly, infants are too young to express their preference in these matters.

Could it be that infant girls and boys give off subtle cues that influence their parents' gender-typed behavior? Research suggests that this is not the case. For example, in some studies, adults are asked to play with an unfamiliar infant who has a girl's name and is dressed in girls' clothing. Other adults play with an infant who wear boys' clothes and has a boy's name. (In fact, it is actually the same baby, who is dressed and named according to whether it is introduced as one gender or another). Adults who believe the child is a boy are more likely to offer "him" a football or hammer, and to encourage physical activity. Those who think the baby is a girl are more apt to offer a doll (Etaugh & Rathus, 1995; Stern & Karraker, 1989).

Parents and other adults are less likely to purchase cross-gender toys than to purchase gender-typical toys for children, even when children request the cross-gender toy (Etaugh & Liss, 1992). Boys are even less likely than girls to receive such toys (Fisher-Thompson, Sausa, & Wright, 1995). Parents, especially fathers, also tend to offer gender-typical toys to children during free play, and are more supportive when children engage in gender-typical activities than in cross-gender activities (Ruble & Martin, 1998). Both mothers and fathers play more roughly with little boys than with little girls, and fathers in particular roughhouse with their young sons (Maccoby, 1998b). Given that fathers treat children in more gender-typical ways than mothers do, it is not surprising that children's gender-typical activity preferences are more closely linked to their father's gender-related attitudes than to their mother's (McHale, Crouter, & Tucker, 1999).

Parents both in North America and Europe react negatively to children who do not adhere to traditional gender roles. As we saw in Chapter 2, this is especially true for boys (Ruble & Martin, 1998; Sandnabba & Ahlberg, 1999). In a recent study (Sandnabba & Ahlberg, 1999), for example, Finnish parents expected cross-gender boys to be less well-adjusted psychologically and more likely to become homosexual than cross-gender girls.

Young children whose parents strongly encourage gender-typical play learn gender labels at an earlier age than other children (Fagot & Leinbach, 1995; Fagot, Leinbach, & O'Boyle, 1992). Moreover, preschool boys choose more stereotyped toys when they believe that their fathers think cross-gender play is "bad" (Raag & Rackliff, 1998). More than one male college student has confided to Claire that as a child he longed to play with his sister's Barbie dolls, but would do so only when no one else was home.

Parents also shape their children's environment by assigning chores based on gender. In many cultures around the world, daughters are more likely to be given domestic and child-care tasks centered around the home, whereas boys typically are assigned outside chores such as yard work and taking out trash (Eisenberg et al., 1996; Larson & Verma, 1999). For a closer look at the relationship between toy giving, chore assignments, and children's gender-related development, read Learn about the Research 4.2.

LEARN ABOUT THE RESEARCH 4.2
Learning Gender-Related Roles at Home and at Play

Are the toys children request and receive and the chores adults assign them related to gender differences in play activities and occupational goals? To study this question, Claire Etaugh and Marsha Liss (1992) gave questionnaires to 245 five- to thirteen-year-olds before and after Christmas, asking which gifts they requested and which ones they received. The children also were asked to name their friends, play activities, assigned chores, and occupational aspirations. Children generally requested and received gender-typical toys. They were less likely to receive requested cross-gender toys (such as a girl asking for a baseball glove). Children who wanted and received gender-typical toys also were more likely to be assigned gender-typical chores (such as yard work and taking out the garbage for boys; and kitchen work and dusting for girls), to engage in gender-typical play activities and to have same-gender friends. Girls preferred masculine toys and jobs more than boys preferred feminine ones. As they got older, both girls and boys increasingly preferred masculine toys, and girls increasingly chose masculine occupations.

What Does it Mean?

1. Why do you think parents and other adults are more likely to give children a requested gender-typical toy than a requested cross-gender toy? What message does this send? Did you ever ask for a gender-atypical toy? Did you get it?

2. Why do girls prefer masculine toys and jobs more than boys like feminine ones? Explain.
3. How might the assignment of gender-typical chores help influence the formation of gender roles?

Parents help to shape their children's environment by encouraging activities based on gender.

Parents treat daughters and sons differently in other ways than encouraging activities or assigning chores. For example, mothers talk more and use more supportive speech with daughters than with sons (Leaper, Anderson & Sanders, 1998). Earlier, we saw that mothers also talk more about emotions with their daughters. In addition, parents control their daughters more than their sons, while granting their sons greater autonomy. For example, parents are more likely to make decisions for girls and to give them help even if it is not requested. Boys, on the other hand, are encouraged to make their own decisions and to solve problems on their own (Pomerantz & Ruble, 1998). Parents also emphasize prosocial behaviors and politeness more with their daughters than their sons (Eisenberg & Fabes, 1998).

Parents serve as role models for their children's development of gender concepts. Take the case of maternal employment. More mothers work outside the home today than ever before. Also, although to a much lesser degree, more fathers are participating in child care and household chores (See Chapter 10). Not surprisingly, researchers have found that maternal employment is associated with less stereotyped gender-related concepts and preferences in boys and girls from the preschool years through adolescence (Etaugh, 1993a). Children also show less stereotyping in their activity preferences if their fathers are highly involved in sharing housework and if their mothers frequently engage in traditional "masculine" household and child-care tasks such as washing the car, doing yard work and, taking the children to ball games (Serbin et al., 1993; Turner & Gervai, 1995; Weisner, Garnier, & Loucky, 1994).

Boys growing up in single-parent homes tend to be less traditional in their gender stereotypes and activities than boys from two-parent homes (Serbin et al., 1993). One reason for this is that a single parent engages in activities normally carried out by both parents, such as housework, child care, home repairs, and going to work. In addition, the absent parent is most often the father, who usually encourages children's adherence to gender norms more strongly than the mother does (Etaugh & Rathus, 1995; Katz, 1987).

School

Schools convey powerful messages to children about gender typing. For one thing, the school social structure is biased. Women hold most of the low-paying elementary school teaching positions, while males occupy more than half of the higher-paying high school teaching jobs. Additionally, men more often are in the leadership positions of principal and superintendent (Ruble & Martin, 1998). A clear signal is sent that men hold more power than women, one of the themes of this book.

In the classroom, girls often are treated unequally by their teachers. That was the conclusion of the American Association of University Women (AAUW, 1992) in a report reviewing over 1,000 publications about girls and education. According to the report, teachers pay far less attention to girls than to boys, a finding strikingly documented by Myra and David Sadker (1994) in their book. *Failing at Fairness*. The Sadkers found that teachers call on boys more often and give them more time to answer questions. Boys are more likely to be praised, corrected, helped, and criticized constructively, all of which promote student learning. Girls are more likely to receive a bland and ambiguous "okay" response. Black girls are the least likely to be given clear feedback. Teachers are more likely to accept calling out from boys, while girls are reprimanded for the same behavior. Boys are rewarded for being smart, while girls are rewarded for being neat, pretty, and compliant. Unfortunately, teachers generally are unaware that they are treating boys and girls differently. In Chapter 6, we will see how such unequal treatment may contribute to the declining self-esteem of adolescent girls.

As we saw in Chapter 2, girls also are shortchanged in school textbooks, which often ignore or stereotype females (AAUW, 1992; DeZolt & Henning-Stout, 1999). Worksheets and other teaching materials may also reflect such biases. A few years ago, for example, a friend of Claire's was very upset when her 5-year-old brought home a particular worksheet from school. At top of the page were the pictures of a woman and a man. At the bottom were various objects, such as a lawnmower, pots and pans, a hammer, and a vacuum cleaner. The instructions were to draw a line from the woman to the objects that belong with her, and a line from the man to the objects that go with him. In their home, Claire's friend did the yard work and her husband vacuumed and cooked. Their child drew the lines accordingly and received an F on the worksheet!

Peers

Children exert strong pressures on each other to engage in gender-appropriate behavior. As early as the preschool years, they modify their activity and toy preferences to conform to the patterns their peers reward. The mere presence of other children inhibits gender-inappropriate play (Eisenberg et al., 1996). Children who dare to violate gender norms are teased, ridiculed, rejected, or ignored by their playmates (Etaugh & Liss, 1992).

Boys who routinely engage in traditionally feminine activities are viewed more negatively than girls who display masculine activities (Martin, 1990, 1995; Rubin, Bukowski, & Parker, 1998). Even the label given to boys who show cross-gender behavior—"sissy"—has negative overtones, whereas the term used for girls who display cross-gender behavior—"tomboy"—does not.

Media

We saw in Chapter 2 that females are underrepresented in the media and that females and males are portrayed in stereotyped ways. What is the impact of these media messages on children's gender-related learning? Most of the research has focused on television. Children between the ages of 2 and 11 watch about 22 hours of television per week (Fabrikant, 1996), but there are large individual differences in viewing. Children who are heavy viewers have greater knowledge of gender stereotypes (Huston & Wright, 1998; Signorella et al., 1993; Signorielli & Lears, 1992). In these correlational studies, it is difficult to know the direction of influence. Television may cause children to develop stronger stereotypes. On the other hand, children with stronger stereotypes may choose to watch more television because it shows images that are consistent with their beliefs (Ruble & Martin, 1998). A third alternative is that both factors are involved.

Stronger evidence of the impact of television comes from experiments that examined whether television can undo or counter the stereotypic messages. These studies found that exposure to characters who engage in nontraditional behaviors and roles (nurturing boys and girl auto mechanics, for example) reduced children's gender stereotypes about activities, domestic roles, and occupations (Comstock, 1991; Huston & Wright, 1998). The most ambitious effort was the program *Freestyle*, which involved 13 episodes broadcast over the course of a semester to school children in grades 4 to 6. When the viewing was accompanied by classroom discussions, changes in gender stereotypes and attitudes occurred and were still evident at a follow-up nine months later (Huston & Wright, 1998; Johnston & Ettema, 1982).

For a closer and more personal look at influences on gender role development, try the exercise in Get Involved 4.2.

Child Sexual Abuse

Sexual abuse of children is viewed by many as among the most heinous of crimes (Rathus, Nevid, & Fichner-Rathus, 2000). While definitions vary, a typical definition of **child sexual abuse** *includes both contact and noncontact sexual experiences in*

GET INVOLVED **4.2**

Influences on Gender Development

Describe your own gender socialization. Focus on specific things that were said, done, or modeled by: (a) your parents and other family members; (b) your teachers; (c) your peers; (d) television, books, and other media. Then ask two female friends and two male friends to do the same.

What Does it Mean?

Include your own responses when answering the following questions:

1. Did the females and the males you interviewed describe different kinds of socialization experiences? If so, what were they?
2. Identify aspects of your own socialization and that of your friends that are consistent with the material presented in the chapter.
3. When did you realize there were social expectations for your gender?
4. What happened in situations when you crossed gender lines?
5. How have your socialization experiences affected your current choices in activities friends, major, career, etc.?

Based on Gilbert and Scher, 1999

---

which the victim is below the age of 18 and the abuser is significantly older or in a position of power over the child (Rathus et al., 2000). Sexually suggestive language or exhibitionism are examples of noncontact experience, while contact abuse may range from kissing, fondling, and sexual touching to oral sex and vaginal or anal intercourse (Boston Women's Health Book Collective, 1998).

Incest is a form of child abuse. **Incest** *may be defined narrowly as sexual contact between a child and a close blood relative, or more broadly as any sexual behavior committed toward a child by a trusted or needed adult* (Godbey & Hutchinson, 1996). The broader definition goes beyond family members to include anyone who has authority or power over the child, including baby-sitters, teachers, scout leaders, and clergy. Incest may be particularly devastating emotionally to a child. It involves a loss of trust in and deep sense of betrayal by the abuser and perhaps other family members—especially the mother—whom the child may perceive as failing to provide protection (Rathus et al., 2000).

Incidence

The incidence of child sexual abuse is difficult to pinpoint precisely. Recent federal government reports indicate approximately 120,000 children were victims of *substantiated* sexual abuse in 1996 (U.S. Department of Health and Human Services,

1998). Because many cases of abuse are never reported, this figure unfortunately is quite conservative. In a comprehensive national health survey of American women (Commonwealth Fund, 1993a), 10 percent of women and 2 percent of men said they had been sexually abused as children. These percentages translate into about 9.5 million women and 1.7 million men. Black, Latina, Native American and White women reported similar rates of child sexual abuse (Commonwealth Fund, 1996b). A recent survey of adolescent girls and boys similarly found that 12 percent of girls and 5 percent of boys reported being sexually abused as a child (Commonwealth Fund, 1997a; Roosa, Reinholtz, & Angelini, 1999).

For both females and males, most sexual abuse is committed by a family member or a family friend, takes place at home and occurs more than once. The large majority of cases involve a female victim and a male perpetrator (U.S. Department of Health and Human Services, 1998), a blatant illustration of the power differential between females and males. The most frequently reported and publicized type of incest is between a daughter and her father or stepfather, but surveys indicate that brother-sister incest may actually be more common (Adler, 1991; Canavan, Meyer, & Higgs, 1992). In one study of college students, for instance, 39 percent of the women and 21 percent of the men reported an incestuous relationship with a sibling of the other gender, while just 4 percent reported such a relationship with their father (Finkelhor, 1990). These figures for sibling incest are much higher than the reported incidence of sexual abuse mentioned above. Perhaps brother-sister incest is less likely to be perceived or reported as incest.

Few girls and even fewer boys tell anyone about being sexually abused. When girls talk to anyone about it, they are most likely to confide in their best friend or their mother (Commonwealth Fund, 1997a). Why do so few children talk about being sexually abused? For one thing, they are relatively powerless, and they may fear retaliation from the abuser. Second, the offender is often a trusted and beloved adult whom the youngster may be reluctant to accuse. In addition, the child may feel embarrassed, humiliated, and responsible for encouraging or allowing the abusive behavior to occur (Daniluk, 1998). Claire knows this from personal experience. As she walked home from school one day at age 12, a nicely dressed man who introduced himself as a doctor began chatting with her about the possibility of baby-sitting for his two young sons. He became increasingly graphic about the details of bathing them. When they reached her apartment building, he began fondling her breasts ("My boys don't have anything like this") until she broke away and ran upstairs, flushed with shame and guilt. It was days before she was able to tell her best friend and weeks before she told her mother. Until this moment, she has told no one else, and even now it is difficult for her to write these words.

Consequences

Sexual abuse can result in devastating consequences for children, not only in the short term, but well into their adult lives. Females are more adversely affected than males (Rind, Tromovitch, & Bauserman, 1998). Sexually abused children are more likely than other children to be depressed, anxious, or angry, to have behavioral and school problems, and to have low self-esteem (Barnett, Miller-Perrin, & Perrin, 1997; Cicchetti & Toth, 1998b; Spaccarelli & Fuchs, 1997). Symptoms of post-traumatic stress disorder (PTSD) have also been identified frequently in sexually abused children. These include fears, nightmares and sleep disturbances, and "flashbacks" (that is, reexperiencing the traumatic event) (Cicchetti & Toth, 1998b; Emery & Laumann-Billings, 1998; Teegen, 1999). Inappropriate sexual behavior directed toward themselves or other children and adults, and play or fantasy with sexual content also are common reactions to sexual abuse (Azar, Ferraro, & Breton, 1998; Trickett & Putnam, 1998).

Adolescents who were sexually abused in childhood begin sexual intercourse at an earlier age, have more sex partners, and are more likely to become pregnant (Fiscella et al., 1998; Luster & Small, 1997; Roosa, Tein, Reinholtz, & Angelini, 1997; Stock, Bell, Boyer, & Connell, 1997). They also are more likely than other teenagers to have eating disorders, to use drugs and alcohol, and to try to injure themselves or commit suicide (Garnefski & Diekstra, 1997; Swanston, Tebutt, O'Toole, & Oates, 1997; Teegen, 1999; Wiedeman, Sansone, & Sansone, 1998).

In adulthood, victims of child sexual abuse continue to be more anxious, depressed, and angry; to have interpersonal problems and impaired self-concept; to feel isolated, stigmatized, and distrustful; to have sexual and substance-abuse problems; to have medical problems such as chronic pelvic pain, chronic headaches, and gastrointestinal problems; and to be more suicidal. They also are more likely to have experienced further sexual assault or physical abuse as adults (Azar et al., 1998; Commonwealth Fund, 1998a; Golding, 1999; Krahé, Scheinberger-Olwig, Waizenhöfer, & Kolpin, 1999; Neumann, Houskamp, Pollock, & Briere, 1996; Roosa et al., 1999). In a recent government study, more than a third of the women in state prisons and jails reported that they were sexually or physically abused as children, twice the rate of child abuse reported by women overall (High percentage, 1999). Estimates of child sexual abuse among women on welfare range from 25 to over 40 percent (DeParle, 1999b). The effects of sexual abuse are greatest when the abuser is someone close to the child, when the abuse is frequent and has continued over a long period of time, when force has been used, and when vaginal, oral, or anal penetration has occurred (Barnett et al., 1997; Kendall-Tackett, Williams, & Finkelhor, 1993).

Memories of Child Sexual Abuse: Repressed or False?

How accurate are children's memories of sexual abuse? Can memories of childhood abuse which have been repressed (forgotten) for years emerge during adulthood? Or are such memories actually false, created by the suggestive probing of a therapist or other health professional? These questions have been hotly debated by psychologists in recent years (e.g., Bruck, Ceci, & Hembrooke, 1998; Goodman, Emery, & Haugaard, 1998; Freyd & Quina, 2000; Pope, 1997). The outcome of the debate has enormous implications. If all allegations of child sexual abuse are accepted uncritically, innocent people could stand unjustly accused, their lives thrown into turmoil. On the other hand, if allegations of sexual abuse are dismissed simply as products of "false memories," many abused individuals will not be believed, causing them further trauma and permitting their abusers to continue victimizing children (Goldberg, 1998).

Researchers appear to have reached broad agreement on the following points (see Bruck et al., 1998; Bruck & Ceci, 1999; Goldberg, 1998; Goodman et al., 1998):

1. The vast majority of child sexual abuse accusations are true.
2. Most children give highly accurate accounts of intimate and/or stressful situations in the absence of suggestive interviewing techniques.
3. If children are interviewed in suggestive ways, however, they may give inaccurate reports.
4. Preschool children tend to be more suggestible than older children, who in turn are more easily influenced than adults.
5. Even adults' recollections are impaired by suggestive interviewing techniques. For example, researchers have implanted false childhood memories of being lost in a shopping mall in 25 percent of adult participants (Loftus & Pickrell, 1995), or of spilling a punch bowl at a wedding for 38 percent of adult participants (Hyman & Pentland, 1996).
6. The success of implanting false memories in both children and adults increases when certain conditions prevail, such as repeating the misinformation multiple times, inducing visual imaging of the supposed event, and having an interviewer of high status (Bruck et al., 1998).

Recently, psychologists and other professionals who deal with accusations of child sexual abuse have developed guidelines for interviewing children more accurately and sensitively (e.g., Poole & Lamb, 1998). Many of these would apply equally well to interviews or therapy sessions with adults. One important guideline is that individuals should not be asked leading or suggestive questions, but instead should be encouraged to describe events in an open-ended manner. For example, instead of asking, "Uncle Jim touched your bottom, didn't he?" (leading question) or "Did Uncle Jim touch your bottom?" (suggestive question), the interviewer should say "Tell me everything that happened at Uncle Jim's house from the beginning to the end" (Goldberg, 1998).

Prevention

Increasing numbers of schools are offering sexual-abuse prevention programs. According to one estimate, about two-thirds of children in the United States have participated in such programs (Goleman, 1993). The programs help children learn what sexual abuse is and how they can avoid it. Children are taught to distinguish between "good" touching, such as an affectionate pat on the back and "bad" touching. They also are encouraged to tell someone about any abuse that does occur. Children who participate in comprehensive school-based programs are more likely to use effective strategies such as refusing, running away, or yelling when confronted by an abuser, and they are more apt to report incidents to adults (Rathus et al., 2000).

In addition, many state legislatures recently have enacted laws designed to inform communities of the presence of known sex offenders who have been released from prison. These laws collectively are referred to as Megan's Law, after a 7-year-old girl who was raped and murdered in 1995, allegedly by a male neighbor who had recently completed a prison sentence for child sexual abuse (Donatelle & Davis, 1998).

Treatment

Healing from childhood incest and other forms of sexual abuse is a long and arduous process (Faria & Belohlavek, 1995; Godbey & Hutchinson, 1996). Group or individual psychotherapy helps women break their silence, gain perspective and realize they are not alone, relinquish feelings of responsibility for the abuse and grieve for what they have lost (Bass & Davis, 1994; Boston Women's Health Book Collective, 1998). Ultimately, therapy can improve survivors' self-esteem and their ability to have intimate relationships.

The effectiveness of treatment for victims of child sexual abuse depends on several factors (Stevenson, 1999). For example, one study evaluated the outcome of group therapy for 65 women who had been sexually abused by their fathers, stepfathers, or another close male relative (Follette, Alexander, & Higgs, 1991). Women with the best treatment outcomes were those who had more education, had experienced only fondling and not oral sex or intercourse, and had lower levels of distress and depression prior to treatment.

Therapy programs for sexually abused children and adolescents also are available. A comprehensive approach usually is recommended. This may involve play therapy or art therapy for very young children; group therapy for adolescents; individual therapy for the child and each parent; marital therapy for the parents; and family therapy (Cohen & Mannarino, 1998; Gagliano, 1995; Lutzker et al., 1999).

S U M M A R Y

1. Children are able to distinguish females and males as early as 6 months of age. By age 2 or 3 years, they can label their own gender and they show some awareness of gender-typical objects, activities, and occupations. Awareness of gender stereotypes for personality traits emerges later in the preschool years. Stereotypes become more flexible after ages 7 or 8.

2. Preschool girls and boys are similar in their motor skills. Differences favoring boys become more pronounced in adolescence as a result of both environmental and biological factors.

3. By age 3, gender differences in toy choices and activities are well established. Gender segregation, the preference for same-

gender children, emerges by age 2 or 3 and increases during childhood.

4. Girls and boys are more alike than different in their social behaviors and personality traits. Gender differences, when found, generally are small.

5. Boys are more physically aggressive than girls, whereas girls are more likely to use relational aggression. Girls and boys are similar in prosocial behavior, but the few observed differences favor girls. Females are somewhat more easily influenced than males are in certain situations.

6. Girls are more likely than boys are to express their emotions and to report feeling empathy. Whether this reflects actual differences in emotionality or in the willingness to report feelings remains an open question.

7. Research does not support Kohlberg's and Gilligan's claim of gender differences in the underlying basis of moral reasoning. Both females and males show caring and justice concerns in resolving moral conflicts.

8. Both parents, but fathers more than mothers, encourage gender-typical toys, play activities, and chore assignments for their children. Parents talk more to their daughters, give them less autonomy, and encourage their prosocial behaviors. Maternal employment is associated with less stereotyped gender-related concepts and preferences in sons and daughters.

9. Boys receive more attention from teachers than girls do. They are more likely to be called on, praised, and criticized constructively. Girls also are shortchanged in school textbooks.

10. Children exert strong pressures on each other to engage in gender-typical behavior. Boys are viewed more negatively than girls when they engage in cross-gender activity.

11. Children who are heavy TV viewers are more aware of gender stereotypes. Exposure to characters who show nontraditional behaviors reduces children's gender stereotypes.

12. The incidence of child sexual abuse may run as high as 10 to 12 percent of females and 2 to 5 percent of males. Most abuse is committed by a relative or family friend (usually male). The issue of whether emerging adulthood memories of child abuse have been repressed or created through suggestion remains controversial. Sexual abuse can have a devastating impact on the mental health of children, both immediately and in the long term. School-based sexual-abuse prevention programs may help children avoid and report abuse. Psychotherapy can help abused children and women heal.

WHAT DO YOU THINK?

1. Should parents attempt to raise their children in gender-neutral ways? If so, why? What would be the advantages? What would be the disadvantages? Incorporate material from Chapters 2 and 3 into your answers.

2. Why do you think teachers pay more attention to boys than to girls? What can be done to ensure more equal treatment of girls in the classroom?

3. In your opinion, why are boys who engage in feminine activities viewed more negatively than girls who engage in masculine activities?

4. Lois Gould (1990), in her fictional *X: A Fabulous Child's Story*, wrote about Baby X, whose gender was concealed from everyone except its parents. This created considerable consternation among relatives and family friends. Why do you think that was?

5. Why are family members often the perpetrators of child sexual abuse? What actions can be taken to prevent such behaviors?

IF YOU WANT TO LEARN MORE

American Association of University Women. (1992). *How schools shortchange girls: The AAUW report.* Washington, DC: AAUW Educational Foundation.

Goodman, G. S., & Bottoms, B. (Eds.) (1993). *Child victims, child witnesses.* New York: Guilford.

Sadker, M., & Sadker, D. (1994). *Failing at fairness: How America's schools cheat girls.* New York: Scribner.

Yelland, N. (Ed.) (1998). *Gender in early childhood.* New York: Routledge.

5 Adolescence

Physical Development and Health Issues

KEY TERMS

puberty
primary sex characteristics
secondary sex characteristics
adolescent growth spurt
menarche
secular trend

dysmenorrhea
prostaglandins
premenstrual syndrome (PMS)
premenstrual dysphoric
   disorder (PMDD)
vacuum aspiration

body image
anorexia nervosa
bulimia nervosa
female athlete triad
acquired immunodeficiency
   syndrome (AIDS)

One of the most moving accounts of a young woman's entry into adolescence was written by Anne Frank, a Jewish girl who lived in Nazi-occupied Holland in World War II. Anne kept a diary during the two years she and her family hid from the Germans in an attic. Anne wrote about her sudden physical growth, commenting on the shoes that no longer fit her and the undershirts that became "so small that they don't even cover my stomach" (Frank, 1995, p. 101). She also grew concerned about her appearance and asked her sister "if she thought I was very ugly" (p. 55). A few months before she and her family were discovered and sent to die in a concentration camp, Anne wrote the following entry about the "wonders that are happening to [my] body": "I think what is happening to me is so wonderful, and not only what can be seen on my body, but all that is taking place inside . . . Each time I have a period (and that has only been three times) I have the feeling that in spite of all the pain, discomfort, and mess, I have a sweet secret, and that is why, although it is nothing but a nuisance to me in a way, I always long for the time that I shall feel that secret within me again" (pp. 158–159).

In this chapter we explore the physical transformations of adolescence. First we describe puberty. We next discuss menstruation, and then examine sexuality. Finally, we look at some health issues that affect adolescent females.

Puberty

Puberty is the *period of life during which sexual organs mature and the ability to reproduce emerges.* Increasing levels of sex hormones stimulate development of primary and secondary sex characteristics. **Primary sex characteristics**—in girls, the ovaries, fallopian tubes, uterus, and vagina—*are structures that make reproduction possible.* **Secondary sex characteristics** are *visible signs of sexual maturity that are not directly involved in reproduction,* such as breast development and the appearance of pubic and underarm hair (Rathus et al., 2000). Table 5.1 summarizes these changes.

TABLE 5.1   Stages of Pubertal Development in Females

Beginning sometime between ages 8 and 11

Pituitary hormones stimulate ovaries to increase production of estrogen.

Internal reproductive organs begin to grow.

Pubic hair begins to appear.

Breast development begins.

Beginning sometime between ages 9 and 15

First the areola (the darker area around the nipple) and then the breasts increase in size and become more rounded.

Pubic hair becomes darker and coarser.

Growth in height continues.

Body fat continues to round body contours.

A normal vaginal discharge becomes noticeable.

Sweat and oil glands increase in activity, and acne may appear.

Internal and external reproductive organs and genitals grow, which makes the vagina longer and the labia more pronounced.

Beginning sometime between ages 10 and 16

Areola and nipples grow, often forming a second mound sticking out from the rounded breast mound.

Pubic hair begins to grow in a triangular shape and to cover the center of the mons.

Underarm hair appears.

Menarche occurs.

Internal reproductive organs continue to develop.

Ovaries may begin to release mature eggs capable of being fertilized.

Growth in height slows.

Beginning sometime between ages 12 and 19

Breasts near adult size and shape.

Pubic hair fully covers the mons and spreads to the top of the thighs.

The voice may deepen slightly (but not as much as in males).

Menstrual cycles gradually become more regular.

Some further changes in body shape may occur into the early 20s.

Note: This table is a general guideline. Changes may appear sooner or later than shown, and not always in the indicated sequence.

Source: Rathus et al., 2000, p. 396. Reprinted with permission from Allyn & Bacon.

Most White girls begin to show signs of puberty by the age of 10, and Black girls do so a year earlier (Kaplowitz et al., 1999). Other studies confirm that feelings of sexual attraction, one of the behavioral hallmarks of puberty, also first appear between the ages of 9 and 10 (Marano, 1997). However, recent research shows that many girls start puberty far earlier than previously thought. For example, Marcia Herman-Giddens and her colleagues (Herman-Giddens et al., 1997) found that by the age of 8, 15 percent of White girls and almost half of Black girls have some breast development, pubic hair, or both. Even among 7-year-olds, 7 percent of White girls and 27 percent of Black girls show these signs of puberty.

Gender Differences in Puberty

Besides the obvious differences in secondary sex characteristics, girls and boys differ in other ways as they move through puberty. For one thing, girls begin and finish puberty about two years before boys, on average. The **adolescent growth spurt**, *a rapid increase in height and weight,* also starts earlier in girls, at about age 9, while boys start their spurt at about age 11. The period of peak growth occurs 2.5 years after it begins (age 11.5 for girls and 13.5 for boys, on average) and then tapers off for two years or so. Boys grow more than girls during their spurt, adding an average of 12 inches to their height, while girls grow slightly over 11 inches (Abbassi, 1998). Boys also gain more weight than girls do during their growth spurt (Etaugh & Rathus, 1995).

Body shape changes in puberty as well. Girls gain almost twice as much fatty tissue as boys, largely in the breasts, hips, and buttocks, while boys gain twice as much muscle tissue as girls (Scholl, 2000). These changes produce the more rounded shape of women as compared to men.

Early and Late Maturation in Girls

The timing of the events of puberty vary considerably from one girl to another (see Table 5.1). Early-maturing girls may feel awkward and self-conscious because they begin the physical changes of puberty earlier than their peers. Boys may tease them about their height and developing breasts. Some early-maturing girls may slouch so they don't appear so tall (Etaugh & Rathus, 1995). Not surprisingly, early maturers tend to have lower self-esteem and a poorer body image than girls who mature later (Graber & Brooks-Gunn, 1998; O'Dea & Abraham, 1999).

Early-maturing girls tend to associate with older peers (Petersen, 1993). This may explain why they begin sexual activity at an earlier age, and are more likely to engage in risky behavior such as smoking and drinking (Alsaker, 1995; Dick, Rose, & Vicken, 2000; Ge, Conger, & Elder, 1996). But not all early maturing girls suffer negative consequences. Instead, early maturation seems to accentuate behavioral problems in girls who already had shown adjustment difficulties earlier in childhood (Caspi & Moffitt, 1991).

Once early-maturing girls reach high school, they come into their own socially. They are envied by other girls because of their grown-up looks. Also, they may serve as advisers to their later-maturing girlfriends on such increasingly important topics as makeup, dating, and sex. They are likely to cope better than their peers with the challenges of adolescence, perhaps because of skills developed in dealing with problems of early maturation (Etaugh & Rathus, 1995). By the end of high school, early-maturing girls appear to be as well-adjusted as other girls (Brody, 1999g).

Late-maturing girls may have relatively low social status during the middle school and junior high school years. They look and are treated like "little girls," and often are excluded from boy-girl social activities. Late-maturing girls often are dissatisfied with their appearance and lack of popularity. By tenth grade, however, they are noticeably showing the physical signs of puberty. They often wind up more popular and more satisfied with their appearance than early-maturing girls (Simmons & Blyth, 1987). One reason for this may be that late maturers are more likely to develop the culturally valued slender body shape than early maturers, who tend to be somewhat heavier.

Menstruation

The Menstrual Cycle

The menstrual cycle involves the release of a mature egg or ovum from its surrounding capsule or follicle. The cycle, which occurs in four phases, averages 28 days in length. (*Menstruation* is derived from the Latin word for *month*.) The menstrual cycle is governed by a feedback loop involving two brain structures—the hypothalamus and the pituitary gland—and the ovaries and uterus.

In the *follicular* phase, Days 4 to 14, low levels of estrogen and progesterone cause the hypothalamus to stimulate the pituitary gland to secrete follicle-stimulating hormone (FSH). This causes the ovaries to increase estrogen production and bring several follicles and their eggs to maturity. Estrogen stimulates development of the endometrium (uterine lining) in order to receive a fertilized egg. Estrogen also signals the pituitary to stop producing FSH and to start producing luteinizing hormone (LH). The LH suppresses development of all but one follicle and egg.

In the second or *ovulatory* phase, about Day 14, LH levels peaks, causing rupture of the follicle and release of the egg near a fallopian tube. During ovulation, some women experience *mittelschmerz* ("middle pain") on the side of the abdomen where the egg has been released.

During the *luteal* phase, LH stimulates the follicle to form a yellowish group of cells called the *corpus luteum* ("yellow body"), which produces large amounts of progesterone and estrogen. These hormones, which reach their peak around Day 20 or 21 of the cycle, cause the endometrium to secrete nourishing substances in the event an egg is fertilized and implanted in the uterine lining. If fertilization does not occur, high progesterone levels cause the hypothalamus to stop the pituitary's production of LH. This causes decomposition of the corpus luteum and a sharp drop in levels of estrogen and progesterone through Day 28.

The fourth phase, *menstruation* (Days 1 to 4), occurs when the low levels of estrogen and progesterone can no longer maintain the uterine lining, which is shed and exits through the cervix (the lower end of the uterus) and vagina as menstrual flow. The low hormone levels trigger the beginning of another cycle. Should the egg be fertilized, however, the hormone levels remain high and a new cycle does not occur.

Changes in the levels of the ovarian and pituitary hormones over the menstrual cycle are shown in Figure 5.1

Menarche

Menarche, *the first menstrual period*, is a dramatic and meaningful event in women's lives. In one study of 137 women from 18 to 45 years old, almost all remembered their first menstrual period and most could describe the details surrounding it (Golub & Catalano, 1983). (If you, the reader, are female, can you?)

The average age of menarche in the United States is about 12.5 years, although it is quite normal for a girl to begin to menstruate any time between 9 and 16 (Golub, 1992). *Over the past 150 years, the onset of puberty and the attainment*

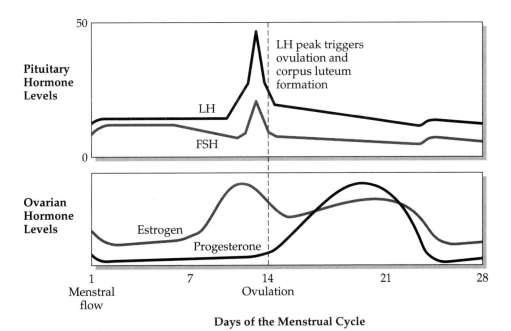

FIGURE 5.1   Changes in hormone levels during the menstrual cycle.
Source: Donatelle & Davis (1998), p. 190. Reprinted with permission from Allyn & Bacon.

of adult height and weight have occurred at progressively earlier ages in the United States and western Europe (Tanner, 1991). This **secular trend** most likely is a result of better nutrition and medical care. The onset of puberty is triggered when individuals reach a certain body weight. Improved diet and living conditions have led to the achievement of that weight at a younger age (Etaugh & Rathus, 1995).

Environmental stress also is linked to an earlier onset of puberty. Research has found that girls from divorced families or families high in parental conflict begin to menstruate earlier than girls whose parents are married or have lower levels of conflict (Ellis & Garber, 2000; Ellis, McFadyen-Ketchum, Dodge, Pettit, & Bates, 1999; Graber, Brooks-Gunn, & Warren, 1995). Several explanations for these findings have been proposed. Stress may lead to overeating, which increases body weight, which then triggers the onset of puberty. Alternatively, evolution may induce people who grow up in stressful conditions to reproduce early to ensure that their genes are passed to the next generation (Belsky, Steinberg, & Draper, 1991). For some girls, there may be yet another explanation for the relationship between parental conflict, divorce, and early puberty (Rowe, 1999). Early-maturing mothers tend to have early-maturing daughters because of genetic factors. Early maturers become sexually active, marry, and give birth at younger ages than others. But early marriages are more likely to end in divorce. So, girls who parents divorce may reach puberty early *not* because of parental conflict and divorce, but simply because their own mothers matured early.

In the United States, girls have mixed feelings about starting to menstruate (Koff & Rierdan, 1995; Moore, 1995). In one study of 9- to12-year-old girls, most of whom were premenarcheal, nearly two-thirds looked forward to menstruation as a sign of "growing up" (Williams, 1983). According to one adolescent girl, "It's a great feeling knowing that one day when you want to have a baby, that you can do it. To me that's just amazing" (Commonwealth Fund, 1997b, p. 39).

Still, one-third of the girls also believed that menstruation was embarrassing and over one-quarter felt it was disgusting. Young adolescent girls also worry about having an "accident" and about someone knowing they have their menstrual period. "When you're in middle school and you're getting your period, you don't want to tell anyone. I was ashamed when I got my period," (Commonwealth Fund, 1997b, p. 39) and they envy boys for not having to menstruate (Stubbs, Rierdan, & Koff, 1989).

Feminine hygiene advertisements targeted toward adolescent girls reflect and reinforce these concerns by focusing on the discomfort and messiness of menstrual periods and the potential embarrassment of "showing" (Merskin, 1999).

A negative attitude toward menstruation before menarche is associated with greater menstrual discomfort. For example, girls whose mothers lead them to believe that menstruation will be uncomfortable or unpleasant later report more severe menstrual symptoms. Moreover, girls who begin to menstruate earlier than their peers, or who are otherwise unprepared and uninformed about pubertal changes, find menarche especially distressing (Koff & Rierdan, 1996; Stubbs et al., 1989). When 14- and 15-year-old girls were asked what advice they would give to younger girls about menarche, they recommended emphasizing the normalcy of menstruation, providing practical information on handling menstrual periods, and discussing what menarche actually feels like (Koff & Rierdan, 1995).

Menstrual Pain

Menstrual pain, or **dysmenorrhea**, includes painful abdominal cramps and lower back pain during menstruation. About 50 to 75 percent of adolescents and young women experience menstrual pain each month. The cause of this discomfort is thought to be **prostaglandins**, *hormone-like chemicals secreted by the uterine lining and other tissues as menstruation approaches*. These substances cause uterine contractions, decreased blood flow, and increased sensitivity to pain, which lead to cramping. Adolescents and women who suffer from severe menstrual pain have unusually high levels of prostaglandins (Golub, 1992). Antiprostaglandin drugs, available both in prescription form and over the counter—such as Motrin, Naprosyn, Anaprox, and Ponstel—help relieve menstrual pain in 80 to 85 percent of women. Aspirin, a mild antiprostaglandin, also is helpful (Golub, 1992), as is a low-fat vegetarian vegan diet, which includes grains, legumes, vegetables and fruits, but no eggs or dairy products (Barnard, Scialli, Hurlock, & Bertron, 2000).

Attitudes toward Menstruation

Throughout history, menstruation has had a "bad press." Menstrual blood has been viewed as having magical and often poisonous powers. Menstruating women have been isolated and forbidden to prepare food or to engage in sexual activity (Golub, 1992). Menstrual myths and taboos still exist, although in somewhat less extreme form. For example, some adolescent girls and women believe that menstruating women should not swim or get a hair permanent (Walker, 1998). In addition, many euphemistic terms are used to avoid the word *menstruation*: "period," "that time of the month," "I've got my friend," "she's on the rag" (Golub, 1992; Gordon, 1993). Have you heard or used other expressions? How many are positive? Many Americans believe that a woman cannot function normally when menstruating. Yet there is little evidence that athletic performance, academic performance, problem solving, memory, or creative thinking show meaningful fluctuations over the menstrual cycle (Golub, 1992).

Menstrual Joy

Despite the prevalence of negative attitudes toward menstruation, some women experience their menstrual periods as self-affirming, creative, and pleasurable (Boston Women's Health Book Collective, 1998). Negative expectations about menstruation may influence many women to focus more on its associated unpleasant symptoms. But what would happen if menstruation were portrayed in a more positive light? Joan Chrisler and her colleagues (Chrisler, Johnston, Champagne, & Preston, 1994) studied the effects of presenting positive and negative views on women's reported responses to menstruation. The researchers administered both the Menstrual Joy Questionnaire (MJQ) and the Menstrual Distress Questionnaire (MDQ) to college women (see Get Involved 5.1). The MJQ lists positive feelings that might be experienced before or during menstruation, such as self-confidence, creativity, and power. The MDQ lists negative feelings that might occur at these times, such as irritability, anxiety, and fatigue. The researchers

GET INVOLVED **5.1**

Menstrual Symptoms

Ask six female friends or relatives to complete both parts of the following questionnaire. Give half of them Part I, followed by Part II. Give the other half Part II first, then Part I. The instructions are: *Rate each item on a 6-point scale,* *using 1 if, shortly before and during your menstrual period, you do not experience the feeling at all; 2, if you experience the feeling slightly; 3, if you experience it moderately; 4, if you experience it quite a bit; and 5, if you experience it intensely.*

Part I Menstrual Joy		Part II Menstrual Distress	
Energetic	_____	Irritated	_____
Affectionate	_____	Sad	_____
Cheerful	_____	Tense	_____
Creative	_____	Moody	_____
Powerful	_____	Fatigued	_____
Self-confident	_____	Out of control	_____
Active	_____	Anxious	_____
Sense of well-being	_____	Angry	_____

Add the score for the Menstrual Joy items. Do the same for the Menstrual Distress items.

Adapted from The Menstrual Joy Questionnaire in Delaney, J., Lupton, M. J., & Toth, E., *The Curse: A Cultural History of Menstruation*, rev. ed. Copyright 1988 by the Board of Trustees of the University of Illinois; based on the Menstrual Distress Questionnaire from Moos, 1985.

What Does it Mean?

1. Did individuals who completed the Menstrual Joy items first report less menstrual distress than those who completed the Menstrual Distress items first? If so, why?
2. Why do you think some women have more positive feelings than others before and during their menstrual periods?
3. Why have the negative aspects of menstruation been emphasized much more than the positive aspects?
4. What might be done to focus more on the positive side of menstruation?

found that women who completed the MJQ before they were given the MDQ reported less menstrual distress and more favorable attitudes toward menstruation than those who received the questionnaires in reverse order. It appears that the way menstruation is portrayed can affect the way women react to their menstrual cycles. Try the questionnaires in Get Involved 5.1 and see whether you find the same results as Joan Chrisler and her colleagues did.

Premenstrual Syndrome (PMS)

For most women, mild to moderate physical and emotional fluctuations are part of the normal menstrual cycle experience. Women may experience breast tenderness, bloating, anxiety, or mood swings that may be annoying but do not disrupt their daily lives (Brody, 1996; Hardie, 1997). A small minority of women, about 2.5 to 5 percent, experience *symptoms so severe that their normal functioning is impaired for the week of each month preceding menstruation* (Mortola, 2000). These women are considered to suffer from **premenstrual syndrome (PMS)**. No marked ethnic differences in the prevalence of PMS have been identified (Mortola, 2000).

What is PMS?   For years, controversy has swirled around the validity of PMS as a disorder because scientists have not agreed upon its definition (Derry, Gallant, & Woods, 1997). In addition, some theorists object to treating normal reproductive system functioning in women as a disease. Since 1987, the American Psychiatric Association has included PMS in its diagnostic handbook, labeling it **premenstrual dysphoric disorder (PMDD)**. *To be diagnosed with PMDD, a woman must experience multiple symptoms during the week before her menstrual period, including depression, anxiety, mood swings, or anger/irritability. The symptoms must interfere markedly with work or social relationships and must be present only in the premenstrual phase of the cycle* (American Psychiatric Association, 1994; Derry et al., 1997).

Given that only a small minority of women meet this definition of PMS, it is surprising to find that a majority of North American women report that they have the disorder (McFarlane & Williams, 1994). Societal attitudes and expectancies may be responsible for this discrepancy. For example, a widely held stereotype in North America is that women experience negative moods before their menstrual periods (Nash & Chrisler, 1997). Thus, if a woman feels anxious, sad, irritable, or moody and believes she is in the premenstrual phase of her cycle, she may attribute her feelings to PMS (Hardie, 1997). The role of cultural factors in determining one's reaction to menstruation is further illustrated in a study of Samoan women who were exposed to modern Western culture and who reported increased numbers of menstrual symptoms (Fitzgerald, 1990). Even within the same culture, differences in the life circumstances of individual women may influence their experiences with menstrual symptoms. For example, women who acknowledge high levels of stress related to work, family, or finances report increased severity of PMS (Gallant & Derry, 1995). Biological factors also may be involved. For instance, the brains of women with and without PMS react differently to normal fluctuating levels of estrogen and progesterone (Brody, 1998c;

Schmidt, Nieman, Danaceau, Adams, & Rubinow, 1998). It is unclear, however, whether these differences contribute to the development of PMS or result from it.

Treating PMS.   Various treatments for PMS have been tried. While some women report that dietary changes, vitamin supplements, or progesterone supplements provide some relief, these approaches generally have been shown to be ineffective (Mortola, 2000). Taking daily 1,200 milligram doses of calcium, however, reduces the symptoms of PMS by over 50 percent (Thys-Jacobs, Starkey, Bernstein, & Tian, 1998). Antidepressants that raise levels of the substance serotonin in the brain—including Prozac, Paxil and Zoloft—relieve emotional and often physical symptoms in over 70 percent of women with PMS (Mortola, 2000; "Study Shows," 1997). The anti-anxiety drug Xanax also is effective in more than 70 percent of women with the disorder (Mortola, 2000).

Sexuality

Sexual Activity

Most adolescents begin having sexual intercourse in their mid- to late teens. Males become sexually active at younger ages than females (Upchurch, Levy-Storms, Sucoff & Aneshensel, 1998) and Black female teens typically become sexually active before other female teens (Erkut & Tracy, 1999). The likelihood of teenagers having intercourse increases steadily with age. Among 15-year-olds, for example, 24 percent of females and 27 percent of males have had intercourse, compared with 77 percent of 19-year-old females and 85 percent of 19-year-old males (Alan Guttmacher Institute, 1999a). Rates of teenage sexuality reached near-record highs in the late 1980s, but declined somewhat during the 1990s ("Trends in HIV-Related," 1999). The percentage of females 15 to 19 years old who had intercourse rose steadily from 29 percent in 1970 to 57 percent in 1988, but decreased to 52 percent by 1997 ("Fewer High School Students," 1998). This drop may be the result of efforts to educate young people about safe sex and about the risks of pregnancy and sexually transmitted diseases such as AIDS (Annie E. Casey Foundation, 1999).

Many factors affect the onset of sexual activity. These include the effects of puberty, family, and peers, as well as individual characteristics. Hormone levels do not predict the onset of sexual experience and intercourse in girls, but the level of pubertal development does (American Academy of Pediatrics, 1999). One possible reason for this is that the development of breasts, curves, and other secondary sex characteristics may attract sexual attention from males (Udry & Campbell, 1994).

Teenagers who are close to their parents and communicate well with them delay the onset of sexual activity (Murry, 1994; Resnick et al., 1997). Other factors associated with a later start of sexual activity include a two-parent family, higher income level, better-educated parents, and firm, consistent parental discipline (American Academy of Pediatrics, 1999; Billy, Brewster, & Grady, 1994; Hetherington, 1999; Udry & Campbell, 1994; Upchurch et al., 1998). Teenagers who begin sexual activity at a later age are more apt to be religious, have higher grades in school, be socially mature, have low levels of alcohol and drug use and, for girls, participate in sports (Billy et al., 1994; Erkut & Tracy, 1999; Perkins, Luster, Villarruel, & Small, 1998; Udry & Campbell, 1994).

An early onset of sexual activity for both girls and boys is linked to having sexually active siblings and peers, having parents with permissive values about sex, and being in a committed dating relationship (East, Felice, & Morgan, 1993; Perkins et al., 1998; Small & Luster, 1994; Udry & Campbell, 1994). Girls who have sexual intercourse at an early age, as well as those who fail to use contraceptives, tend to have low self-esteem and little sense of control over their lives (Brody, 1998d). Sexual abuse in childhood, which may contribute to these negative feelings about oneself, also increases the likelihood of both early sexual activity and early pregnancy (Fiscella, Kitzman, Cole, Sidora, & Olds, 1998; Perkins et al., 1998; Storkamp & McCluskey-Fawcett, 1998). Unfortunately, 7 in 10 girls who have sex before age 13 report being coerced into it (Alan Guttmacher Institute, 1998).

Despite the relaxing of sexual prohibitions over the past few decades, the double standard of sexuality in our society—acceptable for boys, but not girls—remains alive and well. Parents may be willing to condone sexual experimentation in their sons ("Boys will be boys"), but rarely sanction it in their daughters. Girls, more than boys, are encouraged to express their sexuality only within the context of a committed, socially approved relationship (Daniluk, 1998). Consequently, it is not surprising to find that adolescent girls are more likely than adolescent boys to consider affection a prerequisite for sexual intimacy. They also are less inclined to believe that sexual coercion is justifiable. In addition, there is a positive correlation between expectations for sexual intercourse and the length of relationship for adolescent boys, but not for girls (Werner-Wilson, 1998).

Two problematic aspects of adolescent sexuality are teenage pregnancy and sexually transmitted diseases. We begin with a discussion of teenage pregnancy. Later in the chapter we address the topic of sexually transmitted diseases.

Teenage Pregnancy

Each year almost one million American girls age 15 to 19 become pregnant, and nearly 80 percent of these pregnancies are unplanned (Alan Guttmacher Institute, 1999a). Asian American teenagers have the lowest birth rate (2.3 percent), followed by Whites (3.5 percent), Native Americans (7.2 percent), Blacks (8.5 percent), and Latinas (9.4 percent) (Ventura, Mathews, & Curtin 1999). Since 1991, the birth rate among teenagers has declined, with a bigger decrease among young teenagers and an especially big drop among Black adolescents (Alan Guttmacher Institute, 1999b; Ventura et al., 1999). Among those teens who do have babies, however, the proportion who are unmarried has jumped from 15 percent in 1960 to 79 percent in 1998 (Ventura et al., 1999). The decrease in teenage births is not a result of abortion, which has declined among teenagers in the 1990s (Alan Guttmacher Institute, 1999b). Rather, young people are delaying sex until they are older, having sex less frequently, and using birth control, especially condoms, more often and more responsibly (Brindis, 1999; Donovan, 1998).

Despite the decline in births among American teenagers, the United States still has one of the highest teen pregnancy rates among industrialized nations, second only to the Russian Federation. The U.S. rate is nearly twice that of the United Kingdom, and at least four times the rates in France, Germany, and Japan (Singh & Darroch, 2000). The major reason is that teens' use of contraceptives is higher in other countries, where teenage sexual activity is more accepted and contraceptive services are much more widely available (Coley & Chase-Lansdale, 1998).

Consequences of Teenage Pregnancy.   The consequences of unplanned teenage pregnancy often are grim. Teenage mothers are likely to live in poverty and to suffer from a lack of psychological and social support. In addition, they typically drop out of school, have less stable employment patterns, and are more likely to be on welfare. Their marriages are less apt to be stable and they are more likely to have additional children out of wedlock (Coley & Chase-Lansdale, 1998; Kaufmann, 1996; Parke & Buriel, 1998).

Children born to teenagers have an increased risk of prematurity and birth complications, which may result partly from inadequate prenatal care and partly from the young age of the mother (Fraser, Brockert, & Ward, 1995; Ventura et al., 1999). The children also are more apt to have emotional, behavioral, and cognitive difficulties, most likely as a result of their impoverished caregiving environment (Coley & Chase-Lansdale, 1998; Sommer, Keogh, & Whitman, 1995), and they are more likely to be abused or neglected (Annie E. Casey Foundation, 1999). In adolescence, children of teenagers show higher rates of school failure, delinquency, and early sexual activity and pregnancy than teens born to older mothers (Coley & Chase-Lansdale, 1998).

Support for Pregnant Teenagers.   Support programs for pregnant teenagers have met with some success in improving the lives of teenage parents and their children (Kaufmann, 1996; Seitz, 1996). Programs include one or more of the following components: family planning services, child care provisions, and education about parenting and job skills. Teenage mothers who participate in such programs have fewer children in the long run. They are more likely to complete high school and to become economically self-sufficient. Their babies are healthier, suffer less abuse, and have fewer developmental problems (Chira, 1994; Furstenberg, 1991; Seitz, 1996).

Preventing Teenage Pregnancy.   Programs aimed at preventing teen pregnancy have taken various approaches: providing knowledge of sexuality and contraception, teaching abstinence, building decision-making and social skills, and discussing life options (Coley & Chase-Lansdale, 1998). Programs that teach that abstinence is best for preteens and young teens and provide information and access to contraceptives for older or sexually experienced teens are most successful in delaying sexual activity, increasing contraceptive use, and reducing pregnancy (Allen, Philliber, Herrling, & Kupperminc, 1997; Coley & Chase-Lansdale, 1998; Frost & Forrest, 1995; Jemmott, Jemmott, & Fong, 1998). While an overwhelming majority of American parents favor sex education in school, there is considerable debate on what should be taught, when, and by whom (Brick & Roffman, 1998; Lickona, 1998). Consequently, many school-based programs discuss abstinence but are prohibited from mentioning contraception (Lewin, 1999b). Unfortunately, this approach has little effect on reducing sexual activity or pregnancy (Bronner, 1998a; Coley & Chase-Lansdale, 1998).

Contraception

The use of contraceptives, especially condoms, has increased among sexually active adolescents in recent years, due in part to the growing awareness of the danger of AIDS and other sexually transmitted diseases (Abma et al., 1997; Alan Guttmacher Institute, 1999a; "Trends in HIV-Related," 1999). Still, a substantial number of adolescents use contraceptives inconsistently or not at all. Almost one-quarter of girls ages 15 to 19 do not use contraceptives the first time they have sexual intercourse (Brody, 1998d). The average time between an adolescent female's becoming sexually active and seeking medical services for contraception is 12 months. Unfortunately, about half of all adolescent pregnancies occur within 6 months after the onset of sexual activity and one-fifth occur in the first month (American Academy of Pediatrics, 1999).

Many adolescent girls and women resist initiating condom use. Nicola Gavey and Kathryn McPhillips (1999) suggest several reasons for this. First, some females do not have enough power and control in their relationship with a male partner to be able to persuade him to wear a condom, particularly if he is reluctant to do so. Second, females may reject condom use because it diminishes their own sensations and pleasure. Third, sexual intercourse without condoms may symbolize feelings of trust, commitment, and "true love" in the relationship. Finally, Gavey and McPhillips contend that for some women, taking control of a sexual situation—even if just to introduce a condom—may disrupt their feminine sexual identity and threaten potential rewards they expect in the form of love and protection. Other factors that contribute to lack of contraceptive use in adolescent females include reluctance to acknowledge one's own sexual activity, a sense of invincibility ("*I* won't get pregnant."), and misconceptions regarding use of contraception (American Academy of Pediatrics, 1999).

Which individuals are most likely to practice contraception? The older teenagers are when they begin sexual activity, the more likely they are to use contraception. Other factors associated with contraceptive use in teenagers and college students include: being in a committed relationship, having high educational aspirations and achievement, having knowledge about sex and contraception, fearing HIV infection, having good communication and a supportive relationship with parents, discussing contraceptive use with parents and with one's partner, and having high self-esteem and feelings of control over one's life (Christ, Raszka, & Dillon, 1998; Etaugh & Rathus, 1995; Miller et al., 1998; Sheeran, Abraham, & Orbell, 1999).

A wide variety of contraceptive choices are available in addition to abstinence, the one totally foolproof method (see Table 5.2). Among all women in the

TABLE 5.2   Effectiveness Rates of Contraceptive Methods

Method	Percent Effectiveness		Disadvantages
	Correct Use	Typical Use	
Birth control pills (combined hormones)	99.9	95.0	Risk of blood clots in smokers over 35
Norplant (implant)	99.9	99.9	Menstrual bleeding
Depo-Provera (injection)	99.7	99.7	Menstrual bleeding
Intrauterine device (placed in uterus)	99.4	99.2	Heavy menstrual flow; cramps; pelvic infections
Diaphragm (cup placed in vagina) plus spermicide	94.0	80.0	Need to insert before intercourse; genital irritation
Cervical cap (cup placed over cervix) plus spermicide	91.0	82.0	Urinary tract infection; high failure rate
Sponge (placed in vagina) plus spermicide	90.0	85.0	Need to insert before intercourse; high failure rate
Spermicide only	94.0	74.0	Need to insert before intercourse; genital irritation
Condom (sheath placed over penis)	97.0	88.0	Need to put on before intercourse; may lessen male's sensations; may tear, slip off
Withdrawal (of penis before ejaculation)	96.0	75.0–81.0	High failure rate
Rhythm method (fertility awareness)	1.0–9.0	80.0	High failure rate
Tubal ligation (cutting and tying fallopian tubes)	99.6	99.5	Slight surgical risk
Vasectomy (cutting and tying sperm-carrying ducts)	99.9	99.8	Slight surgical risk

Sources: Adapted from "Achievements in Public Health," 1999; Rathus et al., 2000, pp 346–347, Table 12.1; Trussell & Vaughn, 1999.

childbearing years, the most popular method is tubal ligation or "having one's tubes tied" (used by 28 percent of women). The next most commonly used methods are the pill (used by 27 percent), and condoms (used by 20 percent) (National Center for Health Statistics, 1999). Of these, the condom is the only method providing any protection against sexually transmitted diseases. In addition to these methods, emergency contraception, or the so-called "morning after pill," also is available under the trade name Preven. This method, which involves taking high doses of birth control pills within 72 hours after having sex, and then again 12 hours later, blocks fertilization of the egg or prevents a fertilized egg from attaching itself to the lining of the uterus (Canedy, 1999; Glasier & Baird, 1998).

As women's reproductive goals change during their childbearing years, the type of contraception they choose also changes. Birth control pills are used most often by women under age 25, by unmarried women, and by those who intend to have children. Tubal ligation is more commonly used by women over 35, by previously married women, by Black women, and by less well-educated and low-income women. Tubal ligation for women has become far more common than vasectomy has for their male sexual partners (Chandra, 1998).

Abortion

Abortion is one of the most commonly performed medical procedures and also one of the most controversial. In the United States, the debate over abortion centers around two opposing views: Abortion as a right and a means for attaining individual freedom and equity for women versus abortion as a threat to morality, the family, and society. These differing attitudes toward abortion in turn stem from different socially constructed beliefs, attitudes, and values about gender roles and female sexuality (Adler & Smith, 1998; Beckman, 1999).

The 1973 landmark Supreme Court decision in *Roe v. Wade* gave women the legal right to terminate pregnancy by abortion during the first trimester (3 months) of pregnancy. It allowed individual states to set conditions for second-trimester abortions and ruled third-trimester abortions illegal except when the mother's life was endangered (Donatelle & Davis, 1998). Since then, a number of restrictions on abortion have been enacted (Beckman & Harvey, 1998; Solinger, 1998). Nearly two-thirds of the states require parental consent or notification for minors seeking abortion. Congress has barred the use of federal Medicaid funds to pay for abortion except when the mother's life is endangered or in cases of rape or incest. Since poor families rely on Medicaid for health care, low-income women now are less able to afford abortion (Alan Guttmacher Institute, 2000).

Several nationwide polls conducted in 1998, 25 years after the *Roe v. Wade* ruling, found that public opinion has shifted away from general acceptance of legal abortion toward a more ambivalent acceptance, favoring choice but only under certain conditions (Goldberg & Elder, 1998; Reibstein, 1998). The proportion of first-year college students believing that abortion should be legal was 53 percent in 1999, a drop of 12 percentage points since 1990 (Reisberg, 2000).

Incidence.   Over half of pregnancies among American women are unplanned and half of these are terminated by abortion (Alan Guttmacher Institute, 2000). In 1996, 1.2 million women in the United States had abortions (Centers for Disease Control and Prevention, 1998a). In recent years, the abortion rate has been declining steadily. Teens have shown the most dramatic drop: a 24 percent decrease between 1987 and 1994 (Reibstein, 1998).

Not surprisingly, nearly 90 percent of abortions take place within the first trimester. In fact, new tests that can detect pregnancy before women have missed a menstrual period make it possible to have abortions as early as 8 to 10 days after conception (Centers for Disease Control and Prevention, 1998a; Lewin, 1998a).

Three-fourths of women obtaining abortions are under 30. Two out of three are unmarried, over half are already mothers and almost half had a previous abortion. White women account for 60 percent of all abortions, but their abortion *rate* is below that of women of color. Black women are nearly 3 times as likely as White women to have an abortion and Latinas are twice as likely. Also, women who have no religious affiliation are more likely to obtain an abortion than those who do (Alan Guttmacher Institute, 2000; Lewin, 1998a).

Methods of Abortion.   The safest and most common method of abortion is **vacuum aspiration**, in which *the contents of the uterus are removed by suction* (Stotland, 1998; Strong, DeVault, & Sayad, 1999). While most American women prefer this surgical procedure, those up to nine weeks pregnant can choose to take certain drugs to induce abortion. One of these, methotrexate, has long been used to treat cancer. The other is mifepristone, the French abortion pill known as RU-486. Mifepristone, when combined with the drug misoprostol, is 98 percent effective when used within the first 49 days of pregnancy (Spitz, Bardin, Benton, & Robbins, 1998; Talbot, 1999). Many women's rights advocates have fought to make these drugs more widely available. They argue that since the pills can be taken at home, abortion becomes a private matter, and women are spared the taunts and threats of protestors at abortion clinics (Lewin, 1997b; Talbot, 1999).

Consequences of Abortion.   Abortion is a physically safe procedure. The risk of death from childbirth (1 in 10,000) is about 10 times higher than the risk of abortion performed within the first 12 weeks by a health professional (1 in more than 100,000) (Alan Guttmacher Institute, 1997; Boston Women's Health Book Collective, 1998). What about the psychological consequences of abortion? Since abortion is a planned response to an unwanted pregnancy, the woman may experience positive emotions to it, such as feelings of relief or of having made a good decision. On the other hand, negative emotions such as regret or guilt also may arise because of moral and social sanctions against abortion (Zucker, 1999). Brenda Major and her colleagues (Major, Richards, Cooper, Cozzarelli, & Zubek, 1998) found that a woman's reaction to abortion is affected by her particular circumstances, including her coping skills and the degree of social support she has. For example, a woman is more likely to experience postabortion stress if she has little social support from her partner, family, and friends, poorer coping skills, and if she blames herself for the pregnancy (Major & Cozzarelli, 1992). The most negative feelings occur *before* the abortion (Adler & Smith, 1998). While some women report mild distress afterwards—guilt, anxiety, and regrets—the strongest feeling is one of relief (Adler & Smith, 1998). Research on the long-term psychological aftereffects of abortion has found no link between abortion and subsequent mental health (Adler & Smith, 1998; Mirkin & Okun, 1994). When women seek but are *denied* abortions (as was the case in some eastern European countries) their children are more likely than children of mothers who did not seek abortion to feel neglected or rejected, to drop out of school, and to have social problems at work and with friends (David, 1992).

So far in this chapter, we have focused on the sexual and reproductive lives of female adolescents in the United States. For a more global picture, turn to Learn about the Research 5.1.

LEARN ABOUT THE RESEARCH 5.1

Young Women's Sexual and Reproductive Lives around the World

In order for adolescent women throughout the world to best fulfill their future roles as mothers, workers, and leaders, they need improved access to education and to reproductive health services. How are their reproductive health needs currently being met? (We look at education in chapter 6.) A new report by the Alan Guttmacher Institute (1998) gathered information on this question from 47 developing and 6 developed countries around the globe. Here are some of the key findings:

- Up to 60 percent of adolescent births throughout the world are unplanned.
- Contraceptive use by married and unmarried adolescents is greater than in the past, but in most of the world is still low. Among married adolescents, for example, contraceptive use is less than 5 percent in India and Pakistan and under 30 percent in Africa and the Middle East.
- Adolescent childbearing is declining in countries where it had been common,

as access to education increases and the advantages of delayed childbearing are recognized. Still, in many parts of the developing world, 25 to 50 percent of women—especially rural adolescents and those with little education—have their first child before age 18. In the developed world, by contrast, fewer than 1 in 10 have an early first birth.

- Sexually transmitted diseases that threaten the lives and health of young women and their newborns are on the rise, particularly in the developing world. For example, in some African countries, over 20 percent of pregnant women test positive for HIV.
- Sexual relationships that result from force, coercion, and abuse, and cultural practices such as a genital mutilation and sexual exploitation of young girls and adolescents for commercial gain, endanger the reproductive and mental health of young women.

(continued on p. 128)

What Does It Mean?

1. What role does education play in helping to delay marriage and childbearing among adolescents?

2. What steps can communities and governments take to address the reproductive health needs of young women? What services need to be provided?

Health Issues

Body Image

The weight gain associated with puberty occurs within a cultural context that emphasizes a female beauty ideal of extreme thinness. As a consequence, it is typical for adolescent girls to experience intense dissatisfaction with their **body image** (*attitude toward one's physical appearance*) (Striegel-Moore & Cachelin, 1999). Adolescent and young adult females are much more concerned with body weight and appearance than are males of the same age. They have a less positive body image, are less satisfied with their weight, and are more likely to be dieting (Kassirer & Angell, 1998; Sobal & Maurer, 1999; Thompson, 1996). Gender differences in body dissatisfaction emerge between the ages of 13 and 15. During adolescence, girls become increasingly dissatisfied with their appearance, whereas boys become more satisfied with theirs (Rosenblum & Lewis, 1999). American adolescent girls and women often view themselves as overweight even at average weight levels, and about half of them have a negative view of their overall appearance (Cash, Ancis, & Strachan, 1997; Cowley, 1999). The importance of body image to adolescent females is indicated by the close association between teenage girls' body image and their self-esteem. The more negative their body image is, the lower their self-esteem. However, no such relationship exists for adolescent boys (Fallon, 1994; Joiner & Kashubeck, 1996; Knox, Funk, Elliott, & Bush, 1998).

Gender differences in body image have grown over the past 50 years, according to a meta-analysis of 222 studies by Alan Feingold & Ronald Mazzella (1998). Their analysis showed a dramatic increase in the number of women with a poor body image, particularly during the adolescent years. Along these same lines, Joan Jacobs Brumberg (1997), after reviewing 150 years of girls' diaries, concluded that the focus of adolescent girls has shifted from developing their talents, interests, character, and contributions to society to worrying about their weight, shape, and appearance.

A major factor contributing to this change, as noted earlier, is the increasing emphasis in Western culture on thinness as the ideal female body shape (Kassirer & Angell, 1998; Thompson, Heinberg, Altabe, & Tantleff-Dunn, 1999). Studies of Playboy centerfolds, Miss America contestants, and fashion models over the last few decades have found that the average size and shape of the idealized woman has become thinner and more boyish (Cusumano & Thompson, 1997; Spitzer, Henderson, and Zivian, 1999). Magazines designed for an audience of women or girls are far more likely than magazines aimed at men or boys to focus on becoming slim and trim through diet, exercise, and cosmetic surgery (Malkin, Wornian, and Chrisler, 1999). As an example of this media emphasis on female appearance, 43 percent of articles in the 1995 issues of *Seventeen* magazine focused on this topic, compared with only 14 percent that dealt with career development (Schlenker, Caron, & Halteman, 1998). Furthermore, as mentioned in Chapter 2, thin central women characters are overrepresented in television situation comedies, and receive more positive comments from male characters the thinner they are (Fouts & Burggraf, 1999). So powerful is the cultural emphasis on slenderness that simply viewing photographs of physically attractive women with idealized physiques diminishes self-evaluations of attractiveness, body-image satisfaction, and self-esteem in some adolescent girls and young women (Thornton & Maurice, 1999). In one study (Commonwealth Fund, 1997b), adolescent girls generally agreed that there is considerable pressure to be thin, especially from the media:

> *There's such pressure. I look at movie stars and I'm like, "Oh, my God. She's so pretty. She's so thin. I want to look like that." I'm not a small person. I am never going to be like a size 2. I should be happy with what I am and just accept that. But inside I'm freaking out because I can't eat.* (p. 67)

In their search for the "perfect look," more teenage girls are choosing to undergo cosmetic surgery. At least 14,000 American adolescents had such surgery in 1996, an increase from previous years. Moreover, the procedures requested are changing from a generation ago. While nose reshaping still is the most popular surgery, girls increasingly are choosing breast augmentation, liposuction, and tummy tucks (Gross, 1998; Kalb, 1999).

Adolescent girls and adult women of color are more satisfied with their bodies and are less concerned about weight loss and dieting than are White females (Jackson & McGill, 1996; Molloy & Herzberger, 1998; Parnell et al., 1996; Schwartz & Abell, 1999). Standards of beauty and attractiveness in minority cultures appear to place less emphasis on thinness than in White culture (Cash & Henry, 1995; Cash & Roy, 1999; Harris, 1995). However, even though females of color may be more satisfied with their bodies than their White counterparts, they still have concerns about weight and are more likely than males of color to be dieting (DeAngelis, 1997a; Mintz & Kashubeck, 1999; Serdula et al., 1999). Both body dissatisfaction and eating disorders have been reported among Asian, Black, Latina, and Native American girls and women, and among the urban poor as well as the suburban middle class (Davis & Gergen, 1994; Fisher et al., 1995; LaFromboise, Berman, & Sohi, 1994; Pastore, Fisher, & Friedman, 1996; Robinson et al., 1996; Schreiber et al., 1996).

Lesbians are less preoccupied with weight and dieting than are heterosexual women but still are more concerned than heterosexual men (Beren, Hayden,

Wilfley, & Striegel-Moore, 1997; Bergeron & Senn, 1998; Gettelman & Thompson, 1993, Guille & Chrisler, 1999; Lakkis, Ricciardelli, & Williams, 1999). Why are lesbians less concerned about their body image? According to Judith Daniluk (1998), lesbians are branded by society as sexually unappealing because of their sexual orientation, no matter how slender and beautiful they might be. This decoupling of physical attractiveness and sexual appeal may help protect lesbians from developing a negative body image. Another explanation (Heffernan, 1999) is that lesbians may be less likely than heterosexual women to base romantic relationships on physical appearance (See Chapter 11).

Eating Disorders

The prevalence of eating disorders among women has increased dramatically in the 1980s and 1990s, paralleling the increase in women's body dissatisfaction (Feingold & Mazzella, 1998; Litt, 1997; Muth & Cash, 1997). The two most prevalent eating disorders are anorexia nervosa and bulimia nervosa.

Anorexia Nervosa.

Anorexia nervosa is characterized by *a refusal to maintain a minimal normal body weight (defined as 85 percent of ideal weight), intense fear of gaining weight, a distorted body image (feeling fat even when too thin), and amenorrhea* (lack of menstruation) in females. Anorexic individuals diet, fast, and exercise excessively in order to lose weight (Nye & Johnson, 1999; Striegel-Moore & Cachelin, 1999; Williamson, Bentz, & Rabalais, 1998). Unlike "normal" dieters, anorexics may lose 25 percent of their original body weight. Dramatic weight loss can damage body organs and become life-threatening. Between 10 and 20 percent of anorexics die from the physical complications of self-starvation or from suicide (Kassirer & Angell, 1998; Nye & Johnson, 1999).

Girls and women account for more than 90 percent of cases of anorexia nervosa. About 1 percent of female adolescents and young adults suffer from the disorder. While anorexia is often thought of as a White, middle-class or upper-class

Young women with anorexia nervosa literally starve themselves to attain the cultural ideal of slenderness.

disease, its incidence is increasing among women of color and poor women (Henriques, Calhoun, & Cann, 1996; Litt, 1997). Although the usual age of onset is at ages 12 to 18, females can become anorexic at virtually any age (Pike & Striegel-Moore, 1997). In fact, it is no longer rare for 10- and 11-year-old girls to have the disorder (Litt, 1997) and a case involving a 7-year-old girl was reported recently (Bostic et al., 1997).

Bulimia Nervosa. The primary features of **bulimia nervosa** are *recurrent episodes of uncontrolled binge eating, followed by purging activities aimed at controlling body weight.* Purging activities include self-induced vomiting, exercise, extreme dieting or fasting, and the abuse of laxatives, diuretics, or enemas (Nye & Johnson, 1999; Striegel-Moore & Cachelin, 1999; Williamson et al., 1998). One young woman, bulimic since the age of nine, graphically describes her binge-purge cycles:

> *At my lunch break, I would eat a quarter-pounder with cheese, large fries, and a cherry pie. Then I would throw up in the antiseptic-scented bathroom, wash my face and go back on the floor, glassy-eyed and hyper. After work, I would buy a quarter-pounder with cheese, large fries, and a cherry pie, eat it on the way home from work, throw up at home with the bathtub running, eat dinner, throw up, go out with friends, eat, throw up, go home, pass out.*
> (Hornbacher, 1998, p. 91)

Individuals with bulimia seem to be driven by an intense fear of weight gain, and a distorted perception of body size similar to that seen in anorexics (Cash & Deagle, 1997). Unlike anorexics, however, bulimics usually maintain normal weight (Williamson et al., 1998). Although usually not life-threatening, bulimia can cause intestinal and kidney problems, as well as extensive tooth decay because of gastric acid in the vomited food ("Eating disorders—Part I," 1997)). Bulimia also may result in an imbalance of electrolytes, the chemicals necessary for the normal functioning of the heart (Boston Women's Health Book Collective, 1998; Litt, 1997).

As with anorexia nervosa, young women account for more than 90 percent of the cases of bulimia. About 1 to 3 percent of females in late adolescence and early adulthood have bulimia. The typical onset is in late adolescence (Nye & Johnson, 1999; Williamson et al., 1998). Black and White women have about the same rates of bulimia nervosa (DeAngelis, 1997a).

Causes of Eating Disorders. Biological, psychological, and cultural factors all seem to play a part in the development of eating disorders (Foote & Seibert; 1999; Williamson et al., 1998). Let us consider each of these in turn.

Studies of identical twins (who share the same genetic material) have found that if one twin is anorexic, then chances are 55 to 65 percent that the other also will have the disorder (Halmi, 1996). Similar results have been found with bulimic twins. Together, this research suggests the existence of a genetic predisposition toward eating disorders (Woodside & Kennedy, 1995; Hopkins, Raja, Ruderman,

& Tassava, 1997). Keep in mind, however, that these findings could also reflect identical twins' highly similar social and cultural environments. Anorexics and bulimics also have disturbances in certain aspects of their metabolic functioning. For example, bulimic women have low levels of serotonin, a mood- and appetite-regulating chemical in the brain (Smith, Fairburn, & Cowen, 1999). However, these disturbances may result *from* the eating disorder rather than cause it.

Certain psychological characteristics also put young women at higher risk for eating disorders. These include low self-esteem, high levels of anxiety, depression, perfectionism, extreme competitiveness, difficulty in separating from parents, strong need for approval from others, and perceived lack of control in their lives (Burckle, Ryckman, Gold, Thornton, & Audesse, 1999; Campion & Garske, 1998; Halmi, 2000; Pryor & Wiederman, 1998; Williamson et al., 1998). Eating disorders also reflect family problems (Hopkins et al., 1997). For example, parents of anorexics are overly nurturant and overprotective and place undue emphasis on achievement and appearance. Families of bulimics are more hostile, conflicted, and disorganized as well as less nurturant and supportive than families of anorexics or normal adolescents are (Halmi, 2000; Nye & Johnson, 1999; Rollins, 1996). Another risk factor for eating disorders is sexual or physical abuse (Tripp & Petrie, 1999; Wiederman et al., 1998). One study, for example, found that adolescent girls who had been abused were nearly three times as likely as other girls to show bulimic behavior (Commonwealth Fund, 1997a).

As mentioned earlier, cultural pressure to be slim also is an important factor in eating disorders. The powerful role of the media in transmitting this message is illustrated dramatically in Anne Becker's recent study of adolescent girls living in Fiji (reported in Goode, 1999b). When interviewed in 1995, just as television was introduced to the island, only 3 percent of girls reported they vomited to control their weight. In 1998, 15 percent reported the behavior. Similarly, 29 percent scored highly on a test of eating-disorder risk in 1998 compared with just 13 percent in 1995. The more television the girls watched, the more likely they were to diet and to report feeling "too big or fat." Several girls mentioned that they wanted to look like the Western women they saw on television shows. The study does not conclusively prove that television helps cause eating disorders. Still, Becker notes that the increases are dramatic in a culture that traditionally has equated a robust, nicely rounded body with health, and that considers considerable weight loss ("going thin") a sign of illness.

In North America, the effect of cultural pressures to be thin perhaps is seen most vividly among girls and young women who are involved in sports. The incidence of disordered eating (ranging from excessive dieting to anorexia or bulimia) among female athletes is estimated to be as high as 62 percent, far greater than the estimate of 3 percent among the general population of girls and young women (Gilbert, 1999a). *The combination of disordered eating accompanied by amenorrhea and premature bone loss, or osteoporosis* (discussed in Chapter 9), is sometimes referred to as the **female athlete triad**. The prevalence of this condition appears to have grown along with girls' participation in sports, particularly gymnastics, figure skating, diving, and long-distance running, in which a slim figure is considered ideal

(Stedman, 1999; Villarosa, 1999). According to one feminist perspective, starvation and purging are drastic attempts to attain this beauty ideal of extreme thinness (Fredrickson & Roberts, 1997). Another feminist viewpoint is that eating disorders in teenagers are a form of resistance to entering an adult world in which females are devalued (Steiner-Adair, 1990).

Treatment.   Eating disorders are difficult to cure. Cognitive-behavioral therapy, which helps people to change both their behaviors and the way they think about themselves and others, appears to be more effective than other forms of therapy. Antidepressants such as fluoxetine (Prozac) also are of use in treating bulimia (Halmi, 2000; Nye & Johnson, 1999; Thompson et al., 1999; Williamson et al., 1998). Bulimic adolescents also benefit when massage therapy is added to standard therapeutic treatment (Field et al., 1998).

Regardless of type of treatment, only about 40 percent of anorexics fully recover, and about 30 percent show improvement; for the rest the disorder is chronic (Pike & Striegel-Moore, 1997). In follow-up studies, 40 to 50 percent of treated anorexic patients continued to be underweight and to show disordered eating behavior (Deter & Herzog, 1994). Treatment for bulimia tends to be more successful. About half of women diagnosed as bulimic show full recovery 5 to 10 years later, while 30 percent show some symptoms and 20 percent still have the full-blown disorder. Ten to 15 years later, 30 percent continue to display symptoms, but only 11 percent have the disorder (Keel, Mitchell, Miller, Davis, & Crow, 1999). Nearly one-third of recovered women relapse within four years, but a second recovery is common ("Eating disorders—Part II," 1997; Keel & Mitchell, 1997).

Sexually Transmitted Diseases

Sexually transmitted diseases (STDs) have reached epidemic proportions and are among the most common infectious diseases in the United States today (Stolberg, 1998c). Each year, over 3 million teens contract an STD, accounting for about one-fourth of the 12 million Americans infected annually (Annie E. Casey Foundation, 1999). Rates of gonorrhea and chlamydia among teenagers are extremely high in the United States, compared to other countries, perhaps because European nations provide more widespread and intensive prevention policies and better access to STD health care (Panchaud, Singh, Feivelson, & Darroch, 2000) If untreated, STDs can have serious consequences. For example, chlamydia and gonorrhea can lead to pelvic inflammatory disease (PID), which may result in infertility. As many as 30 percent of cases of infertility in women are caused by STDs. In addition, the human papilloma virus that causes genital warts increases the risk of cervical cancer (Centers for Disease Control, 1998b, 1999). Moreover, people with syphilis, gonorrhea, chlamydia, or herpes are two to five times as likely as others to become infected with the AIDS virus, in part because they have open sores that allow the virus to enter the body (Stolberg, 1998c). (See Table 5.3).

STDs have a disproportionate impact on women. They are transmitted more easily to women than to men and are more difficult to diagnose in women

TABLE 5.3 **Major Sexually Transmitted Diseases (STDs)**

STD	Mode of Transmission	Symptoms	Treatment
Gonorrhea	Vaginal, oral or anal sex, or from mother to new-born during delivery	In women, vaginal discharge, burning urination, irregular menstrual periods	Antibiotics, e.g., ceftriaxone
Chlamydia (Most common STD)	Vaginal, oral or anal sex, or from mother to new-born during delivery	In women, painful urination, lower abdominal pain, vaginal discharge	Antibiotics, e.g., doxycycline, azithromycin
Syphilis	Vaginal, oral or anal sex, or touching an infectious chancre (sore)	Initially, hard, round painless chancre (sore)	Antibiotics, e.g., penicillin, tetracycline
Genital herpes	Vaginal, oral or anal sex; most contagious during active outbreaks	Painful sores around genitals, thighs, buttocks	Acyclovir (Zovirax) promotes healing but isn't a cure
Trichomoniasis	Sexual contact	In women, yellowish odorous vaginal discharge; itching, burning in vulva. Often, no symptoms	Metronidazole (Flagyl)
Genital warts	Sexual and other contact, such as infected towels, clothing	Painless warts on genital area or anus, or in vagina, cervix, or rectum	Cryosurgery (freezing), burning, surgical removal
Acquired immune deficiency syndrome (AIDS)	Sexual contact; infected blood transfusions; mother to fetus during pregnancy or through childbirth or breastfeeding	Fever, weight loss, fatigue, opportunistic infections such as rare forms of cancer and pneumonia	No cure. Antiviral drugs like AZT may delay progress of the disease

Source: Rathus et al., 2000, pp. 489–491, Table 16.1. Reprinted with permission from Allyn & Bacon.

(Centers for Disease Control, 1999). In a single act of unprotected intercourse with an infected partner, a woman is twice as likely as a man to contract gonorrhea or chlamydia and is nearly eighteen times more likely to contract HIV, the virus that causes AIDS (EDK Associates, 1994). Women most at risk for contracting STDs are those who are under 25, use latex condoms inconsistently, if at all, are sexually active at an early age, have sex frequently and with multiple partners, and use drugs or alcohol (Boyer, Tschann, & Shafer, 1999; S. Brody, 1997; Finer, Darroch, & Singh, 1999: Sieving et al., 1997). Black and Latina females are at higher risk than White females (Buzi, Weinman, & Smith, 1998; Shain et al.,

1997). Because the risk of woman-to-woman sexual transmission of STDs is small, the prevalence of STDs in lesbians is low (Solarz, 1999).

One factor behind the rapid increase in STDs is that the majority of American women have relatively little knowledge of STDs and even less concern about contracting one. In one recent poll, for example, women and men were asked to name the two most common STDs. Only 13 percent of women named the human papilloma virus and only 3 percent mentioned trichomoniasis. Yet these two diseases account for about two-thirds of the new cases of STDs that occur annually in the United States (Dogar, 1999). Moreover, women are not very comfortable communicating with their partners or doctors about STDs (EDK Associates, 1994). For more on this subject, see Learn about the Research 5.2.

AIDS.   **Acquired immunodeficiency syndrome (AIDS)** is *caused by the human immunodeficiency virus (HIV)*. It is the most devastating of all the STDs, ultimately resulting in death (Rathus et al., 2000). Women—particularly women of

---

LEARN ABOUT THE RESEARCH **5.2**

Knowledge and Communication about Sexually Transmitted Diseases

In 1997, a telephone survey was conducted with a national sample of women from 18 to 44 years old who had been to a new gynecologist or obstetrician for the first time within the previous year (Lewin, 1997a). Only 3 percent of the women believed they were at risk for sexually transmitted diseases. When asked what STDs they were aware of, less than one-quarter could name chlamydia, the most common STD. Most of the women did not know that chlamydia and other STDs increased susceptibility to HIV infection. Only 15 percent of the women discussed STDs other than AIDS with their physician, and just 3 percent raised the topic themselves. HIV and AIDS were discussed in 21 percent of the visits, but only 2 percent of patients initiated the topic. Most women believed it was up to the physician to bring up the subject.

What Does It Mean?

1. Why do you think that most obstetricians and gynecologists do not discuss STDs with their patients?
2. What actions can be taken to better educate women about STDs? What do we need to teach young people in school on this topic?

3. What can be done to increase communication between a woman and her reproductive health care provider?

color—are the fastest-growing but invisible group of Americans infected with HIV. While the overall number of AIDS cases in the United States began to drop in 1996, cases of HIV infection and AIDS among females and males of color have continued to increase (Altman, 1999a; "HIV Infection Rate," 1998; Morrow, 1999). Although injection drug use is the major source of AIDS infection in the United States, heterosexual sex has become the leading method of transmission for women (National Center for Health Statistics, 1999).

AIDS is the leading cause of death in America for women age 20 to 29 and the second leading cause of death for Black female adolescents (Rabasca, 1998). Women accounted for 23.5 percent of AIDS cases in 1998, up from 19.7 percent in 1995 (Morrow, 1999). Even more disturbing, women now account for an estimated 30 percent of new HIV infections (Altman, 1999a). Many are young, low-income women of color who live in urban areas, although the incidence of HIV-infected rural White women also is on the rise (Belluck, 1998). About 60 percent of American women with AIDS are Black, one-fifth are White, and nearly one-fifth are Latina. Black women are about 15 times more likely than White women to have AIDS; Latinas are nearly 7 times more likely (Morokoff, Mays, & Coons, 1997; National Center for Health Statistics, 1999). Women, especially those of color, are sicker at the time of diagnosis with HIV or AIDS and die at least twice as quickly as men with the disease (Boston Women's Health Book Collective, 1998). Why are women often diagnosed at a later stage of HIV than men? For one thing, women generally are viewed as being at low risk for the disease and so they and their physicians may overlook signs of HIV infection that they exhibit. Second, women usually serve as caregivers for family members and, increasingly, as breadwinners. As a result, they may delay seeking health care for themselves until they are very ill (Strong et al., 1999).

Decisions about childbearing are difficult for HIV-infected women. The chances of passing the virus to their children are about one in four. Recent research shows that this risk can be cut in half if the mother delivers the baby by cesarean section prior to the onset of labor. An infected woman who has a cesarean and who also takes the drug AZT during pregnancy has only about a 1 to 2 percent chance of infecting her child (International Perinatal HIV Group, 1999; Mandelbrot et al., 1998). Even when the mother does not have a cesarean or take AZT, starting the newborn on the drug at birth reduces the rate of HIV transmission by two-thirds (Wade et al., 1998). A recently developed drug, nevirapine, cuts the transmission risk to 13 percent. Because it is much less costly than AZT and needs to be administered only once to the mother during labor and once to her newborn, nevirapine is likely to be used widely in many developing countries (Altman, 1999b; DeCock et al., 2000).

Still, women with HIV must wrestle with the fact that their children may be infected and also may be motherless at a young age (Armistead, Forehand, Steele, & Kotchik, 1998; Meredith & Bathon, 1997; Strong et al., 1999). It is helpful for HIV-infected women to share dilemmas such as this with a support group. Many of these women feel isolated and have not disclosed their illness out of fear of rejection and ostracism. Often, a support group is a woman's first opportunity to meet other women with HIV or AIDS (Morokoff et al., 1997).

The best way to prevent AIDS is to practice "safer sex": that is, avoid unprotected sex with multiple partners, and always use latex condoms during sexual intercourse (Kalichman, 1998). The good news is that during the 1990s, American teenagers have shown improvement in these HIV-related sexual risk behaviors ("Trends in HIV-Related," 1999). Unfortunately, many young people, including college students, still fail to engage in safer-sex practices. Factors underlying these risky sexual behaviors include a perceived low risk of infection and negative attitudes toward condom use (Rathus et al., 2000; Sheeran et al., 1999).

Mental Health

Compared to boys, girls show fewer adjustment problems in childhood. Girls, however, are more likely than boys are to first manifest psychological difficulties during the adolescent years (Wangby, Bergman, & Magnusson, 1999). Stress levels increase for both genders during these years. However, the patterns of stress girls encounter may leave them more vulnerable to emotional disorders, such as depression, than do those experienced by boys (Rudolph & Hammen, 1999).

Depression is characterized by prolonged depressed moods and loss of pleasure in most activities (American Psychiatric Association, 1994). Higher rates of depression among females first appear in early to middle adolescence and continue into adulthood (Cicchetti & Toth, 1998a; Cole, Martin, Peeke, Seroczynski, & Fier, 1999; Schwartz, Gladstone, & Kaslow, 1998; Wichstrom, 1999). We examine adult depression in greater detail in Chapter 9. For now, we take a closer look at the stresses of adolescence that are linked to higher rates of depression in girls than in boys. Karen Rudolph and Constance Hammen (1999) found that teenage boys were more likely to complain of stressful situations such as doing poorly in school, getting sick, moving to a new school, getting in trouble with the police, or other events unrelated to interpersonal problems. Girls, on the other hand, experienced most of their stress from relationship problems, including fights with peers, siblings, or friends. Girls reported more symptoms of depression in response to stress than boys did. Their symptoms included being sad, feeling like crying, and feeling alone and unloved. According to Karen Rudolph, girls have closer, more intimate relationships with family and friends than boys do. Consequently, disruptions in these relationships can lead to depression (Berger, 1999).

Adjustment problems that are more common in girls and women, such as depression, anxiety, and social withdrawal, are often labeled "internalizing problems." They are harder to detect and easier to overlook than the externalizing problems more often shown by boys and men: aggression, conduct disorders, antisocial behaviors, and hyperactivity. Ironically, girls with externalizing disturbances rarely are studied because of the male predominance in these types of disorders. However, a recent longitudinal study of 500 Swedish girls from late childhood to adulthood (Wangby et al., 1999) found that girls with externalizing problems in adolescence were at greater risks of all types of maladjustment in adulthood than were those without such problems. On the other hand, there was little or no relationship between having internalizing problems during adolescence and later maladjustment.

SUMMARY

1. During puberty, sexual organs mature and secondary sex characteristics appear. Girls who mature early tend to adjust less easily than late-maturing girls.

2. The menstrual cycle is regulated by hormones, brain structures, and reproductive organs. Menarche is a major event of puberty. Attitudes toward menstruation remain somewhat negative, despite evidence that physical and psychological performance do not change meaningfully over the menstrual cycle. Only a small minority of women experience the symptoms of premenstrual syndrome (PMS). However, a majority believe they suffer from the disorder.

3. Rates of teenage sexuality have been decreasing. The onset of sexual activity is influenced by pubertal development, and individual characteristics as well as by family and peers.

4. The teenage pregnancy rate is higher in the United States than in most industrialized nations, but the teenage birth rate is declining, probably due to increased condom use. Teen pregnancy has serious economic, social, and medical costs. Programs stressing abstinence and contraception can delay sexual activity and reduce pregnancy rates.

5. Contraceptive use has increased among adolescents, but many use contraceptives sporadically or not at all. The type of contraception chosen by women changes as their reproductive goals change.

6. Most abortions occur within the first trimester by means of the vacuum aspiration method. Early abortion is physically safe and generally has no negative psychological aftereffects.

7. Adolescent girls, compared to boys, have a more negative body image and are more likely to diet and to have eating disorders. Cultural pressures for slimness are partly responsible.

8. Anorexia nervosa is marked by severe weight loss and fear of being overweight. Bulimia nervosa is characterized by cycles of bingeing and purging. Biological, psychological, and cultural factors are involved in these disorders, which occur most often in adolescent girls.

9. Sexually transmitted diseases (STDs) are transmitted more easily to women than to men and are harder to diagnose in women. Women, especially those of color, are the fastest-growing group of Americans with HIV.

10. Stress levels increase for girls and boys during adolescence. Most of girls' stress stems from relationship problems and is linked to higher rates of depression. Externalizing problems in girls are less common than internalizing problems, but are more likely to be associated with adult maladjustment.

W H A T   D O   Y O U   T H I N K ?

1. The earlier onset of puberty in the United States and western Europe has not been accompanied by earlier gains in social and emotional development that would help children successfully manage their sexuality. What are the implications for individual adolescents and for society?

2. If a friend of yours unexpectedly became pregnant, what factors might influence her decision about whether or not to terminate the pregnancy?

3. How does the social construction of gender influence women's body images versus men's body images?

4. Why do you think that even though many college students have heard about the risks of sexually transmitted diseases, including HIV infection, they fail to use condoms regularly or to engage in other self-protecting behaviors? What actions could be taken to make more of your friends engage in "safer sex" practices?

I F   Y O U   W A N T   T O   L E A R N   M O R E

Brumberg, J. J. (1997). *The body project: An intimate history of American girls.* New York: Random House.

Golub, S. (1992). *Periods: From menarche to menopause.* Newbury Park, CA: Sage.

Gullotta, T. P., Adams, G. R., & Montemayor, R. (Eds.), (1993). *Adolescent sexuality.* Newbury Park, CA: Sage.

Hornbacher, M. (1999). *Wasted: A memoir of anorexia and bulimia.* New York: Harper Perennial.

Kalichman, S. C. (1998). *Understanding AIDS: Advances in research and treatment* (2nd ed.). Washington, DC: American Psychological Association.

6 Adolescence

Psychosocial and Cognitive Development

Psychosocial Development
  Identity
  Self-Esteem
  Gender Intensification
  Friendships
  Dating

Education and Cognitive Skills
  The Educational Environment for Girls
  Gender Comparison of Cognitive Abilities

KEY TERMS

identity
individuate
self-esteem
gender intensification
dating script

sexual harassment in an
   educational setting
mental rotation
spatial perception
spatial visualization

lateralization
critical filter
mathematics self-efficacy

How much do I like the kind of person I am? Well, I like some things about me, but I don't like others. I'm glad that I'm popular since it's really important to me to have friends. But in school I don't do as well as the really smart kids. That's OK, because if you're too smart you'll lose your friends. So being smart is just not that important. But what's really important to me is how I look. If I like the way I look, then I really like the kind of person I am. I've also changed. It started when I went to junior high school. I got really depressed. There was this one day when I hated the way I looked, and I didn't get invited to this really important party, and then I got an awful report card, so for a couple of days I thought it would be best to just to end it all. I was letting my parents down, I wasn't good-looking anymore, and I wasn't that popular and things were never going to get better. I talked to Sheryl, my best friend, and that helped some. (adapted from Harter, 1990, pp. 364–365)

This self-description from a 15-year-old girl illustrates some of the characteristics of adolescent females. Notice how important physical appearance is to her self-esteem. Note also that she discloses her private thoughts to her best friend. Can you recall what was important to *you* at age 15?

In this chapter we explore three aspects of female adolescence. First, we focus on psychosocial development, including identity formation, self-esteem, gender intensification, friendships, and dating. Next, we examine the educational environment of adolescent girls. We finish with a discussion of gender comparisons of cognitive abilities.

Psychosocial Development

Identity

One of the most important tasks of adolescence is to develop a sense of **identity**: that is, *deciding who we are and what we want to make of our lives.* According to Erik Erikson (1968, 1980), adolescent identity formation involves commitment to a vocation and a philosophy of life. In order to do so, adolescents must **individuate** (*see themselves as separate and unique*). Carol Gilligan (1982), Sally Archer (1992), Ruthellen Josselson (1994), and others maintain that this model describes the traditional identity development of males better than that of females. They believe that achieving identity for both female and male adolescents requires an interplay between separateness (meeting one's own needs) and connectedness (satisfying the needs of those one cares for) (Jaffe, 1998).

Research supports the view that adolescent females and males take similar paths in their quest for identity. Elements of career choice, personal competence, and interpersonal relationships are central to the identity of both genders (Archer, 1992; Giesbrecht, 1998; Murray, 1998). For one thing, adolescent girls' educational and career aspirations have increased in recent years and now parallel those of boys (Denmark, 1999). In addition, an increasing number of teenagers (83 percent of females and 72 percent of males) say that having a good marriage and family life is extremely important to them as a life goal (Popenoe & Whitehead, 1999). However, whereas most adolescent girls see interconnections between their career goals and family goals, most adolescent boys perceive no connection between the two. For example, young women place greater emphasis than young men do on flexible working hours that facilitate the coordination of employment and child-rearing (see Chapter 8). Still, it appears that nowadays, individual differences in identity development may be more important than gender differences (Archer, 1993; Marcia, 1993).

Unfortunately, little research has been conducted on the identity formation of ethnic minority adolescent girls. The studies that have been done, however, find that one key factor in this process is the family unit, often an extended kinship network, which is a highly valued part of life among Asian Americans, Blacks, Latinas/os, and Native Americans. Identity with the family and community seems to provide strength and resources for adolescent girls of color as they strive to integrate their ethnicity and their femaleness within a larger society that devalues both (de las Fuentes & Vasquez, 1999; Vasquez & de las Fuentes, 1999).

Self-Esteem

Self-esteem is *the sense of worth or value that people attach to themselves*. High self-esteem has long been associated with healthy psychological adjustment (DuBois, Bull, Sherman, & Roberts, 1998; Kling, Hyde, Showers, & Buswell, 1999). Beginning in early adolescence, self-esteem diminishes for both genders, with girls showing lower self-esteem than boys (Chubb, Fertman, & Ross, 1997; Eccles, Wigfield, & Schiefele, 1998; Harter, 1998; Major, Barr, Zubek, & Babey, 1999). According to a recent meta-analysis of over 97,000 respondents by Kristen Kling and her colleagues (Kling et al., 1999), this gender gap becomes greatest in late adolescence, with a small to moderate effect size of 0.33 (see Chapter 1). For example, in one survey of 2,400 girls and 600 boys in grades 4 through 10, 60 percent of girls and 69 percent of boys 8 and 9 years old reported feeling confident and happy with themselves. By the ages of 16 and 17, however, the percentage who reported these positive feelings dropped to only 29 percent for girls compared with 46 percent for boys. Many more Black adolescent girls, 58 percent, remained confident and positive than did White girls or Latinas (American Association of University Women [AAUW], 1992). A recent meta-analysis revealed a similar increasing gap between the self-esteem of Black and White females during late adolescence and young adulthood (Gray-Little & Hafdahl, 2000). Other studies have found that, compared to White adolescent girls, Black girls have more confidence in their physical attractiveness, sports ability, femininity, popularity, and social relations (Eccles, Barber, Jozefowicz, Malenchuk, & Vida, 1999).

What causes girls' self-esteem to drop in adolescence and why do Black girls remain more self-confident than others? For one thing, perceived physical appearance is closely linked to self-esteem (Polce-Lynch et al., 1998). Girls are more dissatisfied with their appearance than are boys, a difference that increases during adolescence (Harter, 1998). But Black girls, as we saw in Chapter 5, are less concerned about body shape and size than are White girls, and physical appearance is less important to their sense of self-worth (Erkut, Marx, Fields, & Sing, 1999; Schwartz & Abell, 1999). Upon entering adolescence, for example, the self-esteem of obese Latina and White girls drops more than that of nonobese girls, but obese Black girls do not show this decline (Strauss, 2000).

In addition, as we saw in Chapter 4, schools appear to short-change girls in ways that undermine girls' perceptions of their competence and importance (AAUW, 1992; Orenstein, 1994; Sadker & Sadker, 1994). Black girls, however, seem less dependent on school achievement for their self-esteem. Their view of themselves is more influenced by their community and family (Daley, 1991; Vasquez & de las Fuentes, 1999). Some researchers believe that Black females are socialized early in life by their mothers and other female relatives to be strong, independent women who can cope with a society in which racism, sexism, and classism can be barriers to the development of a positive identity (Vasquez & de las Fuentes, 1999; Way, 1995). In one study of African American female college students, for example, over 75 percent mentioned a sense of strength as a key component of their sense of identity (Shorter-Gooden & Washington, 1996).

Several theorists, notably Carol Gilligan (1993; Taylor, Gilligan, & Sullivan, 1995) and scholars at the Stone Center (Jordan, Kaplan, Miller, Stiver, & Surrey, 1991; Jordan, 1997) maintain that as girls make the transition to adolescence, they become aware of growing up in a patriarchal society which devalues women and which views the desirable stereotype of the "good woman" as being nice, pleasing to others, and unassertive. This places girls in conflict with their view of themselves as self-sufficient, independent, and outspoken. Many girls respond to this conflict by losing confidence in themselves and by suppressing their thoughts, opinions, and feelings; that is, by "losing their voice."

However, research by Susan Harter and her colleagues (Harter, 1998, 1999) found that adolescent boys and girls did not differ with respect to the loss of voice. About a third of young people of both genders said they disguised their true feelings and thoughts in dealing with certain categories of individuals, but a large majority of these females and males did not report doing so. Harter and her colleagues found that *gender role identity*, not gender itself, predicted the level of voice.

Masculine and androgynous adolescents of both genders reported higher levels of voice and higher self-esteem than those with a feminine orientation. Along the same lines, adolescent girls who are involved in sports (and who tend to be more androgynous) are found to have higher self-esteem, as well as better social skills and better grades, than adolescent girls who are not athletes (Denmark, 1999). Although the feminine girls in Harter's study reported loss of voice in public contexts, such as school and group social situations, this did not occur with parents or close friends. Parental support, approval, and acceptance appear critical to the development of high esteem and to the expression of one's thoughts and feelings (Harter, 1998). Students also need their teachers' encouragement and support for expressing themselves.

Gender Intensification

> All through grade school, I had been very active in sports. Basketball was my favorite and I was really good at it. Basketball gave me self-esteem. When I was 13, I set my life's goal—to one day coach the Boston Celtics. I will never forget the reactions I got when I told people this. Everyone—my friends, my parents' friends, other adults—all said the same thing: A girl could never coach a professional men's team. Until then, it hadn't occurred to me that gender mattered. I just thought you needed talent and desire, which I had. I was totally heart-broken. Then I began to question whether women were as good as men in basketball. If not, why was I playing? I didn't ever again want people to tell me I couldn't do something because I was a girl. So I quit basketball and became a cheerleader. I didn't really want to, but I felt people wouldn't like me unless I became a "complete and total girl." (Liz, 21-year-old college senior)

Early adolescence is marked by an increase in rigidity of gender-role stereotypes, although girls continue to remain more flexible than their male peers (Basow & Rubin, 1999). Gender differences in value orientation also become pronounced at the onset of adolescence. For example, a study by Kimberly Badger and her colleagues (Badger, Craft, & Jensen, 1998) of geographically diverse American adolescents found that as early as sixth grade, girls were more likely than boys to place a high value on: (1) compromising; (2) being kind and forgiving; (3) expressing feelings; (4) wanting to know what people are like inside; (5) enjoying people; (6) getting along with others; and (7) having friends, cooperating, and helping. This *increasing divergence in gender-related behaviors and attitudes of girls and boys that emerges in early adolescence* is known as **gender intensification** (Crouter, Manke, & McHale, 1995; Galambos, Almeida, & Petersen, 1990).

Several factors contribute to the development of gender intensification. For one thing, the physical changes of puberty accentuate gender differences in appearance. Peers, parents, and other adults, especially those with traditional views of gender, apply increasing pressure on girls to display "feminine" behaviors (Crouter et al., 1995), as illustrated poignantly by Liz's experience. This magnification of traditional gender expectations is stronger for girls than for boys, probably because girls have been given more latitude than boys have to display cross-gender behaviors in middle childhood (Crockett, 1991; Huston & Alvarez,

1990). In addition, when adolescents begin to date and enter romantic relationships, they may increase their gender-stereotypical behavior in order to enhance their appeal to the other gender. Furthermore, cognitive changes make adolescents more aware of gender expectations and more concerned about what others think of them (Crockett, 1991). The resulting adherence to a traditional construction of gender seems at least partly responsible for the gender differences in self-esteem, friendship patterns, dating behaviors and cognitive skills that we discuss in this chapter.

Gender intensification starts to decrease by middle to late adolescence. Gender-related occupational stereotypes (see Chapter 4) become more flexible, and sexist attitudes (see Chapter 2) become less pronounced. Also, the understanding that gender-related traits, behaviors, and roles are culturally created and modifiable increases (Crockett, 1991).

Friendships

Throughout life, our closest friends tend to be people of our own gender. Even though romantic attachments increase during adolescence, most teenagers still choose members of their own gender as best friends (Hartup, 1993). Starting in early adolescence, girls report greater satisfaction with their same-gender friendships than do boys (Veniegas & Peplau, 1997). Adolescent girls also spend more time than adolescent boys do thinking about their friends, both female and male (Richards, Crowe, Larson, & Swarr, 1998).

Intimacy, the sharing of thoughts and feelings with someone else, is a key characteristic of adolescent friendships (Rubin, Bukowski, & Parker, 1998). Girls' relationships are more intimate than those of boys (Brown, Way, & Duff, 1999; Buhrmester, 1996; Lundy et al., 1998). Girls show greater increases in intimacy from early to late adolescence, they report more self-disclosure and emotional support, and they spend more time with their friends than do boys (Brown et al., 1999; Buhrmester, 1996; Seiffge-Krenke, 1993). Adolescent girls also expect and receive more kindness, loyalty, commitment, and understanding from their best friends than do boys (Clark & Bittle, 1992). In addition, adolescent girls rate the importance of close friendships more highly, show more satisfaction with the closeness of their friendships, and are more likely to maintain close relationships with an absent friend (Moore & Boldero, 1991).

Girls tend to have a few very close friends, whereas boys are more likely to have larger, less intimate friendship groups (Seiffge-Krenke, 1993). Boys' friendships focus on shared group activities, mostly sports and competitive games. Girls' friendships, on the other hand, are more apt to emphasize self-disclosure and emotional support (Buhrmester, 1996; Gibbons, Lynn, & Stiles, 1997; Ringle & LaVoie, 1997). In the words of one adolescent girl:

I've had a best friend for about five years now, and she pretty much knows everything about me. I'd probably turn to her for all of my problems because she's always helped me out and always gave me the right answers for everything. (Commonwealth Fund, 1997b, p. 19)

Studies of ethnically and socioeconomically diverse adolescents have found friendship patterns that differ somewhat from those commonly seen among White, middle-class adolescents (Brown et al., 1999). For example, Julia Duff (1996) found differences in how upper- and middle-class suburban White girls and poor and working-class urban girls of color describe their closest friendships with other girls. Whereas 95 percent of the White girls reported competition as an aspect of their friendships, only 38 percent of girls of color did so. Similarly, the White girls were five times as likely to report feeling "used" by a close friend and were nearly three times as likely to indicate that jealousy was an issue. Other research suggests that differences in adolescent girls' friendship patterns may be more strongly related to social class than to ethnicity. In one study (Gallagher & Busch-Rossnagal, 1991), for example, middle-class Black and White girls were more likely to disclose beliefs and attitudes to their friends than were Black and White girls of lower socioeconomic status.

Dating

While same-gender friendships continue to be important during early adolescence, mixed-gender peer groups also start to form. These groups are central to the emergence of dating and romantic relationships that begin to blossom at this time (Connolly & Stevens, 1999). Dating serves a variety of purposes apart from its obvious role as a courting ritual that can lead to serious commitment and marriage. Dating can help one learn how to establish intimacy with other individuals. It can provide entertainment, serve as an opportunity for sexual experimentation, enhance a teenager's social status and popularity, and help develop a sense of identity (Furman, Brown, & Feiring, 1999; Sanderson & Cantor, 1995; Savin-Williams & Berndt, 1990).

Since the beginning of the century, the age when U.S. adolescents start dating has decreased. Many girls now begin to date at age 12 or 13, and many boys at 13 or 14. Some start as early as age 10 (Jarrell, 2000). By the senior year in high school, 90 percent or more of teenagers have dated (Savin-Williams & Berndt, 1990).

You will recall from Chapter 5 that the age when sexual activity begins depends on a number of factors. Many of these same factors are related to the age at onset of dating. For example, Black teenagers begin both dating and sexual activity earlier than White and Latina/o adolescents. Other factors related to early dating include early age at puberty, being poor, and not having a strong religious identity (Bingham, Miller, & Adams, 1990; Miller & Moore, 1990). Girls from divorced or stepparent families initiate dating and sexual activity earlier than girls whose parents are married.

Young people usually bring to their early dating encounters a set of beliefs regarding how they should behave in order to appeal to the other gender. The advice passed along to girls by girlfriends, mothers, older siblings, and the media frequently includes such helpful hints as massaging the boy's ego, bringing up subjects that he enjoys talking about, admiring his accomplishments (but not mentioning yours), and not being too assertive or confrontational (Maccoby,

1998b). A boy, on the other hand, learns to "take care" of a girl he dates by making the arrangements, being chivalrous (opening the door, helping her put her coat on), paying for the date, and taking her home (Maccoby, 1998b). Notice how traditionally gender-typed these dating expectations are.

Suzanne Rose and Irene Hanson Frieze (1993) explored this subject in greater detail by studying the expected **dating scripts** and actual dating behavior of college students on a first date. A dating script is a *culturally developed sequence of expected events that guide an individual's behavior while on a date.* (The task they used is described in Get Involved 6.1. Try it with some of your friends.) Students' expected dating behaviors and their actual behaviors were very similar. Some aspects of the dating script were the same for females and males. These included worrying about one's appearance, talking, going to a show, eating, and kissing goodnight. Many of the elements of the date, however, were strongly gender-stereotypical. Males were the initiators. They asked for and planned the date, drove the car and opened doors, and started sexual interaction. Females, on the

---

GET INVOLVED **6.1**

Dating Scripts of Women and Men

Complete the following task from the study by Rose and Frieze (1993, p. 502). Then ask two unmarried female and two unmarried male undergraduates to do the same.

From the perspective of your *own* gender, list the actions which a woman (use the word "man" for male participants) would typically do as she (he) prepared for a first date with someone new, then met her (his) date, spent time during the date, and ended the date. Include at least 20 actions or events which would occur in a routine first date, putting them in the order in which they would occur.

What Does It Mean?

1. What elements of a dating script were shared by your female and male respondents?
2. In what ways were the dating scripts gender-stereotypical?
3. How do your results compare to those of Rose and Frieze (1993) described above?
4. Based on your knowledge of gender stereotypes, gender-related attitudes and socialization experiences, what might account for the differences in the dating scripts of females and males?
5. Do you think that the degree of traditional gender-stereotypical behavior in dating scripts would be the same on a fifth date as on a first date? Explain your answer.

other hand, reacted to what men did: being picked up, having doors opened, and responding to sexual overtures. They also focused more on the private domain, such as concern about appearance and enjoying the date (Rose & Frieze, 1993). Dating scripts of lesbians and gay males are similar in many respects to those of heterosexuals, but they are not as strongly gender-typed (Klinkenberg & Rose, 1994). We shall discuss the dating relationships of young adults in greater detail in Chapter 11.

A darker and rarely mentioned side of high school dating relationships is physical aggression toward a dating partner. Dating violence among high school students occurs with alarming frequency. Studies show that anywhere from 9 percent to 59 percent of adolescents report having had at least one experience of physical aggression in a dating relationship, ranging from being pushed, shoved, and slapped to being punched, threatened with a weapon, and forced to engage in sexual activity (Cano, Avery-Leaf, Cascardi, & O'Leary, 1998; Feldman & Gowen, 1998; Jezl, Molidor, & Wright, 1996; Schwartz, O'Leary, & Kendziora, 1997). While a few studies have found that adolescent girls and boys experience equal amounts of dating aggression (e.g., Bennett & Fineran, 1998), most, perhaps surprisingly, find that males are more likely than females to report being victims of such abuse (Jezl et al., 1996; O'Keefe, 1997; Schwartz et al., 1997).

One possible explanation of these findings is that females underreport aggression and/or that males overreport it (Jezl et al., 1996). Males might overreport their victimization in order to rationalize their own aggression (e.g., "She hits me, so I hit her back"). Another possibility is that females actually *are* more aggressive in their dating relationships. For one thing, females may feel freer than males to be physical without fear of injuring their dating partners (Jezl et al., 1996; Schwartz et al., 1997). Alternatively, females may inflict more violence than males in self-defense, or in retaliation for sexual assault, which is more commonly committed by males (O'Keefe, 1997).

Certain factors increase the likelihood that high school students will inflict dating violence. In Maureen O'Keefe's (1997) study of a large ethnically and socioeconomically diverse high school, the strongest predictor of dating aggression for both girls and boys was being the recipient of dating violence. This finding supports the self-defense explanation. Believing that dating violence is justifiable was another strong predictor for both females and males. (Interestingly, both genders were more accepting of dating violence in females.) In addition, dating violence is more prevalent among adolescents who were abused as children (Wolfe, Wekerle, Reitzel-Jaffe, & Lefebvre, 1998), are exposed to family violence (Foshee, Bauman, & Fletcher, 1999), and have a history of problem behaviors such as stealing, fighting, and destroying things (Feldman & Gowen, 1998). Other warning signals that a young couple's relationship may turn violent include possessiveness, controlling behavior, unpredictable mood swings, and use of alcohol or drugs (Kelley, 2000). These factors continue to be involved in violent adult relationships (see Chapter 11). Such findings highlight the need to implement programs early in high school to curtail the use of dating violence (Cano et al., 1998).

Education and Cognitive Skills

The Educational Environment for Girls

In Chapter 4, we saw that American girls are often shortchanged in school. For example, girls are less likely than boys to be called on, praised, and given constructive feedback. Girls and women continue to experience a less-than-friendly classroom and campus climate throughout the high school and college years (See Chapter 8 for a further discussion of this topic).

Girls also are subjected to sexual harassment by boys during school hours. **Sexual harassment in an educational setting** includes *unwelcome verbal or physical behavior of a sexual nature when (a) submission to or rejection of the behavior forms the basis for decisions about the student (e.g., admission, grades); or (b) the behavior creates an intimidating, hostile, or offensive study environment.* In most cases, boys harass girls, rather than the other way around.

Reports of student sexual harassment are on the rise among junior and senior high school students. In the American Association of University Women (AAUW) (1992) survey discussed in Chapter 4, more than three-quarters of junior and senior high school girls said they had received sexual comments or looks (see Figure 6.1). Two-thirds reported being touched, grabbed or pinched in a sexual way. Nearly three-quarters of girls, but less than one-quarter of boys said they were "very upset" or "somewhat upset" when they were the targets of sexual harassment. About one-third of the girls reported that the unwanted activity made them not want to go to school or talk in class. Two additional recent studies of middle school and high school students in New York and Texas confirmed these results ("Two Studies Show," 1998). A troublesome finding in all three studies was that teachers rarely intervened, even when they were informed of serious incidents of sexual harassment. Instead of considering sexual harassment to be serious misconduct, school authorities too often treat it as harmless instances of "boys will be boys" (AAUW, 1992).

That attitude may be changing, however. In a landmark decision on May 24, 1999, the U.S. Supreme Court ruled that any school or college receiving federal funds must protect students from severe and pervasive sexual harassment by other students. The case involved a 10-year-old girl, LaShonda Davis, who was subjected to five months of unwanted sexual touching and taunting by a male classmate whose seat was next to hers. Despite repeated complaints and pleas for help, school officials took no action. It was three months before her teacher agreed to move the boy's desk across the room. As the harassment continued, LaShonda Davis's grades declined, she became increasingly despondent and upset, and wrote of suicide. At that point her mother, Aurelia Davis, filed a criminal complaint against the boy, who was convicted in juvenile court of sexual battery. She also sued the school district for their failure to respond, a suit which the Supreme Court upheld after five years of litigation ("Students and Sexual Harassment," 1999; V. L. Williams, 1999).

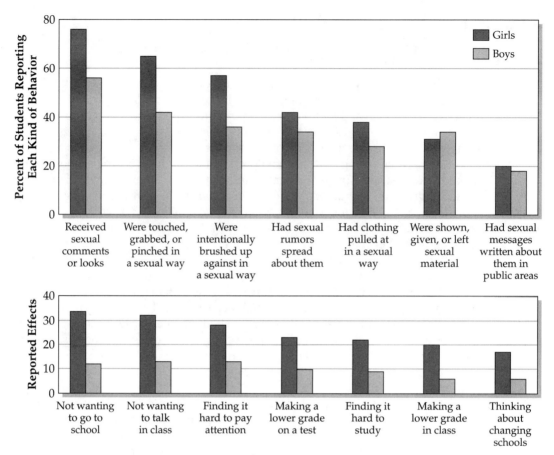

FIGURE 6.1 **Percentage of junior and senior high school students who reported experiencing unwelcomed sexual behavior at school, and its effects.**
Data from: American Association of University Women, 1992.

In developing societies, educational biases against girls often are even more severe. Many girls are not able to attend school at all, or attend for just a few years before they drop out (Larson & Verma, 1999). For a closer look at this serious problem, see Learn about the Research 6.1.

Gender Comparison of Cognitive Abilities

Although females and males do not differ in general intelligence, they do vary in certain cognitive skills. Some differences emerge in childhood while others do not appear until adolescence (Halpern, 1992). Some of these differences may have a bearing on the career choices made by females and males, a process which accelerates during adolescence. For these reasons, we will discuss gender comparisons of

LEARN ABOUT THE RESEARCH 6.1

Educating Girls Worldwide: Gender Gaps and Gains

What is the state of education for girls around the world? A recent study of 132 developing and developed nations (Population Action International, 1998) reports both good news and bad. The good news is that between 1985 and 1995, access to education improved worldwide, particularly for girls at the secondary (high school) level. More than half the countries studied now have no gender gap, including the United States, where 99 percent of girls and boys go to school.

The bad news is that 51 countries still have serious gender gaps, with 75 million fewer girls than boys in school. Gender disparities are greatest in South Asia, the Middle East, and sub-Saharan Africa. In Africa and Latin America, increasing numbers of unmarried girls are dropping out of school because of unplanned pregnancy. School policies often *require* the expulsion of pregnant girls. (Before you become too outraged, keep in mind that such policies also existed in the "enlightened" United States until a generation or so ago.)

An important benefit of educating girls is that women who have finished secondary school have fewer, healthier, and better educated children. Not only do these women delay childbearing, as we saw in Chapter 5, but the mortality rate of their infants also declines (Bellamy, 1999). How can girls' enrollment in school be increased? The Population Action International report (1998) recommends the following:

- Build more schools, especially in rural areas of developing countries.
- Recruit more female teachers.
- Lower the costs to families of educating their daughters.
- Provide programs to prevent teenage pregnancy.
- Encourage teen mothers to stay in school.
- Educate parents about the importance of educating daughters as well as sons.

What Does It Mean?

1. Why do many parents in developing countries consider it more important to educate their sons than their daughters? Why do some North American parents also stress the importance of educating their sons?

2. How might the recruitment of more female teachers help increase girls' enrollment in school?
3. What do you think are the reasons for requiring expulsion of pregnant girls from school?

cognitive abilities in this chapter. Remember our cautionary notes from Chapter 4. Gender differences, where they exist, generally are small. Females and males are much more alike in cognitive abilities than they are different. Even when there is a small *average* difference favoring one gender on a test of a particular cognitive skill, many individuals of the other gender will score well above the average. Also, recall from Chapter 1 that the presence of a gender difference does not tell us any-thing about the *causes* of the difference. Finally, keep in mind that cognitive skills, like the social behaviors and personality traits we discussed in Chapter 4, develop within a social context. As we see throughout this section of the chapter, attitudes and expectations about the cognitive performance of females and males play an important role in socially constructing that performance.

Verbal Ability.   Verbal abilities include a variety of language skills such as vocab-ulary, reading comprehension, writing, spelling, grammar, and word fluency. Females show superior performance on most verbal tasks, although the differences are small (Ruble & Martin, 1998). Gender differences in verbal ability appear earlier than other cognitive gender differences. Girls are more vocal than boys during infancy (Bjorklund, 2000), they talk at an earlier age, produce longer utterances, have larger vocabularies, and are more fluent (Bornstein & Haynes, 1998; Haden, Haine, & Fivush, 1997; Halpern, 1992, 1997; Morisset, Barnard, & Booth, 1995).

Girls continue to show an edge in verbal skills throughout the grade school years (Feingold, 1993; Halpern, 1992). They achieve higher scores on tests of reading comprehension and are less likely to display reading problems such as reading disability (dyslexia) and reading below grade level (Mullis et al., 1994; U.S. Department of Education, 1999). In adolescence, girls continue to outperform boys in reading, writing, and speech production (Halpern, 1997; Nowell & Hedges, 1998; Stumpf & Stanley, 1998; U.S. Department of Education, 1997, 1999).

Some researchers have suggested that gender differences in verbal skills and other cognitive abilities are becoming smaller (Feingold, 1988; Hyde & Linn, 1988). More recent reviews, however, have concluded that these differences are not diminishing and have remained relatively stable for decades (Nowell & Hedges, 1998; Voyer, Voyer, & Bryden, 1995).

What might account for the greater verbal ability of girls? In Chapter 4, we noted that parents vocalize more to their infant daughters than to their infant sons. This may lead to increased vocalization by female infants which in turn may encourage parents to talk even more to their young daughters. Girls' early advan-tage with language may lead them to rely more on verbal approaches in their interactions with others, further enhancing their verbal ability (Halpern, 1992).

Parental expectations also may play a role in girls' superior verbal skills. One study of grade school children in Japan, Taiwan, and the United States found that as early as first grade, children and their mothers generally believed that girls are better than boys are at reading (Lummis & Stevenson, 1990). In addition, girls whose mothers thought that girls were better readers received higher scores on reading comprehension and vocabulary than girls whose mothers thought girls and boys read equally well.

Visual-Spatial Ability.   Visual-spatial ability refers to skill in visualizing objects or shapes and in mentally rotating and manipulating them. Visual-spatial skills are used extensively in engineering, architecture, and navigation and in everyday activities such as doing jigsaw puzzles or reading maps.

Gender differences in visual-spatial ability are larger and more consistent than in other cognitive skills, with males outperforming females (Nordvik & Amponsah, 1998; Ruble & Martin, 1998). The pattern of differences, however, depends on the spatial ability being measured. For example, females do better than males on remembering the location of various objects (Cherney & Ryalls, 1998; James & Kimura, 1997). Three separate facets of visual-spatial ability have been identified by Marcia Linn and Anne Petersen (1986). Tasks used to measure these three components are shown in Figure 6.2.

Mental rotation involves *the ability to rapidly manipulate two- or three-dimensional figures* (See Figure 6.2a). Meta-analyses (see Chapter 1) show that the largest gender difference in spatial skills occurs on tests of this ability, with an overall *d* value of 0.60 (Collins & Kimura, 1997; Voyer et al., 1995). Boys outperform girls as early as age four (Levine, Huttenlocher, Taylor, & Langrock, 1999), consistently do so by age nine, and the gender difference increases into adolescence and adulthood (Ruble & Martin, 1998; Voyer et al., 1995).

Tests of **spatial perception** involve *the ability to locate the vertical or the horizontal while ignoring distracting information.* For example, individuals may be seated in a dark room and asked to position a rod inside a tilted frame so that it is vertical (see Figure 6.2b). Gender differences on spatial perception tests like this are smaller than those found on mental rotation tasks (overall *d* = 0.40) (Voyer et al., 1995; Ruble & Martin, 1998). Boys begin to perform better than girls by age nine and this difference gets larger during the adolescent and adult years.

Tasks measuring **spatial visualization** include *finding simple shapes hidden within larger, complex shapes* (see Figure 6.2c). Gender differences favoring males are much smaller or absent on these tasks (overall *d* = 0.20) (Voyer et al., 1995).

The size of gender differences on spatial visualization and spatial perception tasks has been decreasing over time (Feingold, 1993; Voyer et al., 1995). Differences on mental rotation tests, however, have remained stable or even increased (Ruble & Martin, 1998; Voyer et al., 1995).

Several biological and environmental theories have been proposed to account for gender differences in visual-spatial abilities. Biological theories focus on genes, hormones, or the organization of the brain. According to one theory, visual-spatial ability is influenced by sex-linked recessive genes on the X chromosome. Research does not support this view, however (Halpern, 1992).

Another biological theory is that sex hormone levels affect visual-spatial skills (Halpern, 1997). Hormones could exert their effects in one of two ways. One possibility is that hormones circulating in the bloodstream might directly affect visual-spatial performance (Kimura, 1996). Studies have shown that women with higher testosterone levels achieve better spatial scores than women with lower testosterone levels, whereas the reverse is true in men (Moffat & Hampson, 1996). Keeping in mind that women's testosterone levels, on average, are lower than those of men, these findings suggest that the optimal level of testosterone for certain spatial skills is in the low male range (Kimura, 1996). In addition, the scores of both women and men on tests of spatial and verbal ability rise and fall in a pattern that corresponds to fluctuations in their daily or monthly levels of estrogen (for

A. MENTAL ROTATION

Mental Rotation Test. Are these pairs of figures the same except for their orientation?

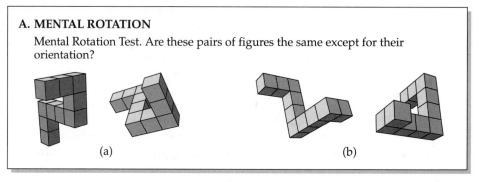

(a) (b)

B. SPATIAL PERCEPTION

Rod and Frame Test. Align a rod within these frames so that the rod is vertical.

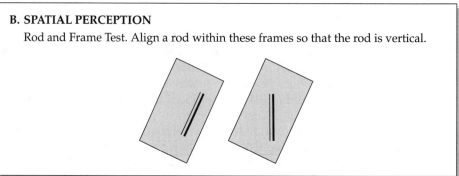

C. SPATIAL VISUALIZATION

Embedded Figure Test. Is figure (a) part of figure (b)?

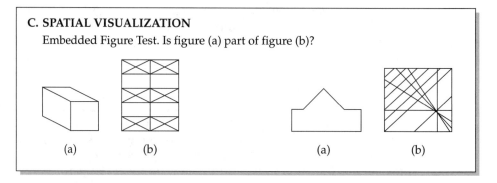

(a) (b) (a) (b)

FIGURE 6.2 Examples of Tests of Visual-Spatial Ability

Source: Reprinted with permission from Halpern, D. F. (1992). *Sex differences in cognitive abilities* (2nd ed.) Hillsdale, NJ: Erlbaum.

women) and testosterone (for men). Women, for example, perform better on visual-spatial tasks in the low-estrogen phase of the menstrual cycle and do better on verbal tasks in the high-estrogen phase (Halpern, 1997; Kimura, 1996).

Another possibility is that prenatal sex hormones might irreversibly organize the brain to enhance certain spatial functions. Evidence for this view comes from studies of girls with adrenogenital syndrome (see Chapter 3), which exposes them to high levels of prenatal androgens. At birth, the hormone imbalance is corrected and they are raised as girls, yet they display better visual-spatial skills than their unaffected sisters (Berenbaum, Korman, & Leveroni, 1995). Some psychologists (e.g., Bem, 1993), however, point out that parents' awareness of the possible masculinizing effects of androgens may influence their treatment of and expectations for their daughters.

Some theorists have attributed gender differences in visual-spatial skills to differences in the lateralization of female and male brains. **Lateralization** refers to the *specialization of the cerebral hemispheres of the brain to perform different cognitive functions*. For most of us, the left hemisphere is involved in language and mathematical computation, whereas the right hemisphere is more involved in processing visual and spatial information (Halpern, 1992). Some evidence suggests that male brains may be more completely lateralized or specialized than female brains (Halpern, 1997). But it is not clear that lateralization leads to better performance in visual-spatial or other cognitive skills (Caplan & Caplan, 1999).

Numerous environmental theories have been proposed to explain gender differences in visual-spatial skills. Most of these focus on the impact of cultural gender stereotypes, observational learning, and encouragement of gender-typed activities and interests in shaping the experiences and attitudes of females and males (see Chapter 4). Participation in spatial activities fosters the development of spatial abilities, yet females engage in fewer spatial activities than males (Baenninger & Newcombe, 1989; Bjorklund & Brown, 1998; Halpern, 1997). Why is this? For one thing, gender-stereotyped "boys'" toys, such as blocks, Erector sets, Legos, and model planes and cars, provide more practice with visual-spatial skills than gender-stereotyped "girls'" toys. Boys also are encouraged more than girls to participate in sports, which often involves moving balls and other objects through space (Etaugh & Rathus, 1995). Action video games, which are especially popular with boys, also appear to exercise and develop spatial skills (Huston & Wright, 1998). If experience enhances the development of visual-spatial skills, appropriate training ought to improve these skills. Research indicates that it does, for both females and males (Law, Pellegrino, & Hunt, 1993; Lawton & Morrin, 1999; Halpern, 1997). Some training procedures have reduced or eliminated gender differences (Baenninger, 1997; Vasta, Knott, & Gaze, 1996).

The stereotyping of visual-spatial activities as masculine also influences performance. Studies have found that females and males with more masculine self-concepts perform better on visual-spatial tasks than those with less masculine self-concepts (Halpern, 1992). For example, college men and women who describe themselves as having few stereotypical feminine traits or many stereotypical masculine traits get better scores on visual-spatial tests than students who show the reverse pattern (Signorella & Frieze, 1989). Simply changing the instructions on spatial tests also has a marked effect on the performance of females and males. In one study (Sharps, Welton, & Price, 1993), college students were given one of two sets of instructions before performing a mental rotation task. One set of instructions emphasized that the test measured spatial abilities and that these abilities are involved in mechanical skills, navigation, map reading, and work with tools. The other instructions made no mention of spatial ability or masculine-typed activities. The "spatial" instructions lowered the performance of women but not men. Under the "nonspatial" instructions, women improved and performed as well as men.

Mathematical Ability.   In the most comprehensive review to date of gender differences in mathematics performance, Janet Hyde and her colleagues (Hyde, Fennema & Lamon, 1990), did a meta-analysis of 100 studies involving more than 3 million individuals. They found a small difference in computation skills favoring girls up to age 15. Girls and boys did equally well at understanding mathematical concepts at all ages. In tests of problem solving, boys began to do better than girls starting at age 15. In studies that sampled from the general population, overall gender differences were smallest, with females showing a slight edge over males. However, in highly select samples (for instance, college students or mathematically precocious youth), differences in mathematics performance were larger and favored males. Although gender differences in mathematics performance have decreased over time (e.g., Feingold, 1993), they still exist. For example, in a recent large-scale study of college-bound juniors and seniors, boys outperformed girls on standardized tests of mathematics, as well as on tests of physics, chemistry, computer science, and biology (Stumpf & Stanley, 1998). In an international study of high school seniors (Bronner, 1998b), the same pattern of results for math and sciences was found in 18 out of 21 countries.

When we shift from scores on standardized tests to grades in mathematics classrooms, a different picture emerges. Girls receive higher grades than boys, a pattern found in a number of countries including the United States and Canada (Kimball, 1998). This female advantage in grades is found even in samples of mathematically precocious youth, where the male advantage on standardized tests is greatest (Benbow & Arjmond, 1990). When female and male college students in the same mathematics courses are compared, females earn the same or higher grades than do males who have received higher scores on the mathematics portion of the SAT (Wainer & Steinberg, 1992). (This finding applies to other academic subjects as well. In other words, women receive higher grades in college than their SAT scores would predict [Leonard & Jiang, 1999]. Thus, of the women and men who would receive the *same grades* in college, fewer of the women are admitted because of their lower SAT scores.)

The single best predictor of scores on mathematics achievement tests is the number of mathematics courses an individual has taken. But starting in adolescence, girls are less likely than boys to take advanced mathematics courses, even when they show superior math ability (Catsambis, 1999; Kimball, 1989). A recent synthesis of 1,000 studies by the AAUW (1998) reports both good news and bad news. The good news is that since 1992, high school girls' enrollment in math and science courses has increased. Moreover, they are reducing the gender gap in scores on standardized tests of computer science (Stumpf & Stanley, 1998). The bad news is that girls still are less likely than boys to take advanced mathematics

Girls receive higher grades than boys in math courses but lower scores on standardized math tests such as the SAT. Why the discrepancy?

and any of the three core science courses—biology, chemistry, and physics—before they graduate. Girls also take fewer computer science and computer design courses (AAUW, 1998; Adelman, 1999).

In college, many women avoid choosing math and science courses and careers even when they are gifted in mathematics (Chipman, 1996; Halpern, 1992). This is troubling, since mathematics is the so-called **critical filter** of career development (Sells, 1982), *the factor that paves the way to high-status and high-salary careers in the sciences, engineering, and business*. Why, then, do girls begin to avoid math in high school and college?

One important clue is found in the attitudes and feelings that girls and boys develop toward mathematics. Nancy Betz and Gail Hackett (1997) have developed the concept of **mathematics self-efficacy** to refer to *a person's beliefs concerning her or his ability to successfully perform mathematical tasks*. Numerous studies show that males have greater mathematics self-efficacy than females (Betz & Hackett, 1997; Nosek, Banaji & Greenwald, 1998; Schweingruber, 1997). Females have less confidence than males in their ability to learn math despite their equal or superior performance on tests and in the classroom. This self-perception emerges as early as elementary school and continues into adolescence (Catsambis, 1999; Kimball, 1998; Manger & Eikeland, 1998). By early adolescence, students generally view mathematics as part of the male domain (Chipman, 1996; Henrion, 1997). The more that girls endorse this stereotype, the less effort they exert in their mathematics classes (Greene, DeBacker, Ravindran, & Krows, 1999). During the high school years, girls begin to perceive themselves as less competent in mathematics than boys do, even when they earn the same grades (Eccles, Barber, & Jozefowicz, 1999; Steele, 1997a).

Adolescent girls also are less likely than adolescent boys are to view mathematics as useful and important for their future careers (Eccles, Barber, & Jozefowicz, 1999). In addition, girls are more apt than boys are to express math anxiety, and to have negative feelings about math (Eccles, 1994). These negative attitudes have been found in Black, Latina, and White girls (Catsambis, 1999).

Several theories have been proposed to account for gender differences in math performance and attitudes. One viewpoint is that genetic, hormonal, and/or structural brain differences underlie gender differences in mathematic ability (Lubinski & Benbow, 1992; Geary, 1996). Critics have argued that research fails to support this interpretation (Halpern, 1992; Kimball, 1995), and the biological approach remains controversial.

The most frequently offered explanations for gender differences in mathematics focus on differences in the socialization of girls and boys (Duffy, Gunther, & Walters, 1997). Parents and peers give less encouragement and support to girls than to boys for studying math (Clewell, 1991; Eccles et al., 1993). As early as first grade, parents in the United States, Japan, and China believe that boys are better than girls in mathematics (Lummis & Stevenson, 1990). These beliefs and expectations influence parents' perceptions and behaviors toward their children and also the children's own perceptions and behaviors (Ruble & Martin, 1998). For example, a series of studies by Jacquelynne Eccles and her colleagues (e.g., Eccles et al., 1993; Eccles et al., 1998) found that parents with stronger stereotypes about the abilities of girls and boys in math, English, and sports had different expectations of their own daughters' and sons' abilities in these areas. These expectations, in turn, were linked to their children's performance and self-perceptions of competence regardless of their actual ability levels.

How are parents' expectations transmitted to their children? Among other things, parents provide different experiences for their daughters and sons. For example, they are more likely to buy their sons science-related toys (Fisher-Thompson, 1991) and to enroll them in summer computer camps (D'Amico, Baron, & Sissons, 1995). (See Learn about the Research 6.2 for a discussion of gender, computers and video games).

Children receive the same message in the math classroom. Teachers have higher expectations for boys than for girls in math courses (Fennema, 1990; Halpern, 1992), and they spend more time instructing, interacting with, and giving feedback to boys than to girls (AAUW, 1992; Jovanovic & Dreves, 1997). In many other subtle ways, children learn that mathematics is essentially a male activity. For example, teachers of mathematics and science are predominantly men (Crawford & Chaffin, 1997), and fathers are more likely than mothers are to help children with math homework (Raymond & Benbow, 1986).

How can teachers make the math classroom more "girl friendly"? Females respond more positively to math and science instruction if it is taught in a cooperative manner, using an applied perspective and a hands-on approach rather than in the traditional competitive manner, using a theoretical perspective and a book-learning approach. When the former practices are used, both girls and boys are more likely to continue taking courses in math and science and to consider future careers in these fields (Eccles et al., 1998; Eccles & Roeser, 1999).

LEARN ABOUT THE RESEARCH **6.2**
Gender, Computers and Video Games

Girls and boys both like to play video games, but boys spend more time than girls do playing them (Huston, Wright, Marquis, & Green, 1999; Roberts, Foehr, Rideout, & Brodie, 1999; Siann, 1997). Why is this? One major reason is the content of video games, most of which have violent themes (Dietz, 1998; Elrich, 1997). The few females who appear in the games are portrayed either as helpless victims (Provenzo, 1991) or as "Barbies in sexy combat gear" (Vogt, 1997, p. 6). Presenting women in this negative manner may decrease the attraction of many video games for girls and thus their time commitment. One large survey of 8- to 14-year-old girls found that they like games that solve problems or tell stories (Vogt, 1997). Unfortunately, very little software is designed to appeal to girls or to children of both sexes, although that situation is beginning to change (Cassell & Jenkins, 1998; Elrich, 1997). Between 1995 and 1998, the number of games designed for girls jumped from 10 to 65. Girls' games are as stereotyped as those designed for boys, featuring Barbies, makeovers, jewelry, and cooking (Hafner, 1998).

The gender gap in video game usage has important implications for girls' experience with computers. Video games often provide a child's introduction to the computer. As early as the preschool years, boys are more likely than girls to use computers and to have positive attitudes toward them (D'Amico et al., 1995). This trend continues into adolescence (AAUW, 2000; Fielding, 1999). Boys are more likely than girls to have a computer at home, to attend summer computer camps and enrichment programs, and to enroll in computer programming courses in high school and college (AAUW, 1998; D'Amico et al., 1995; Morahan-Martin & Schumacher, 1998; Newman, Cooper, & Ruble, 1995). The AAUW (1998) report discussed earlier in the chapter reached the troubling conclusion that a new gender gap in technology has developed. Boys are using computers to program and solve problems while girls use computers for word processing, the 1990s version of typing.

Computer ownership as well as greater experience with programming and games may account for male adolescents' greater degree of competency and comfort with computers (Morahan-Martin & Schumacher, 1998). How can girls' experience with computers be increased? One solution may lie in the kinds of computer programs children are exposed to. Like video games, even educational software often takes the form of games constructed around male themes of violence and adventure (Newman et al., 1995). One study (Littleton, Light, Barnes, Messer, & Joiner, 1993) found that when educational software included only male characters and a "treasure quest" theme, 11- and 12-year-old girls performed more poorly than boys. When a less masculine-stereotyped theme was used, however, girls did just as well as boys.

What Does It Mean?

1. Why are most video games and educational software dominated by themes of violence and adventure?
2. What do you think accounts for gender differences in computer-related attitudes?
3. What can be done to minimize or eliminate these differences?
4. Why are positive attitudes toward computers important in today's society?

SUMMARY

1. Adolescent girls and boys show similar patterns of identity development, focusing both on occupational choices and interpersonal relationships.

2. Girls begin to show lower self-esteem than boys in early adolescence, and the gender gap widens during adolescence. Explanations include girls' dissatisfaction with their physical appearance, short-changing of girls in school, and girls' "losing their voice."

3. Early adolescents show an increasing divergence in gender-related behaviors and attitudes, known as gender intensification.

4. Girls' friendships are more intimate than those of boys. Girls tend to have a few close friendships whereas boys have larger, less intimate friendship groups.

5. The age when adolescents start to date has decreased. Many dating behaviors are strongly gender-stereotypical. Substantial numbers of teenagers experience violence in their dating relationships. More males than females report being victims of such violence.

6. Reports of sexual harassment are increasing among junior and senior high school students. Girls are more likely than boys to be sexually harassed by their schoolmates and they are more upset by it.

Schools now are legally obligated to protect students from severe and pervasive harassment by other students.

7. Females and males do not differ in general intelligence, but show some differences in certain cognitive skills.

8. Girls have a slight advantage in verbal skills beginning in infancy. Girls outperform boys in reading, writing, and speech production and are less likely to have reading problems.

9. On visual-spatial tests, gender differences favoring boys are greatest in mental rotation, less in spatial perception, and smaller or absent in spatial visualization.

10. Girls are better than boys in mathematics computation skills and get better grades in mathematics courses. Boys are better at problem solving starting in mid-adolescence and perform better on standardized mathematics tests.

11. Biological explanations for gender differences in cognitive skills focus on genetics, hormones, and brain structure or organization. Environmental explanations include differential socialization of girls and boys by parents and teachers, gender typing of activities as feminine or masculine, and gender differences in attitudes toward various cognitive skills.

WHAT DO YOU THINK?

1. Using what you know about gender-role identity, explain why masculine and androgynous adolescents have higher self-esteem than feminine adolescents.

2. What actions can parents and teachers take to help enhance the self-esteem of adolescent girls?

3. Some people have criticized the recent U.S. Supreme Court ruling that obligates schools to protect students from severe and pervasive sexual harassment by other

students. Some argue that sexual taunting and even touching is a normal rite of adolescence. Others contend that even such apparently innocent gestures as the exchange of Valentine's Day cards by first graders will now be classified as sexual harassment and thus forbidden. What is your position on this issue, and why?

4. What can parents do to maximize girls' potential for learning and liking math?

IF YOU WANT TO LEARN MORE

Brown, L. M. (1998). *Raising their voices: The politics of girls' anger*. Cambridge, MA: Harvard University Press.

Johnson, N. G., Roberts, M. C., & Worell, J. (Eds.), (1999). *Beyond appearance: A new look at adolescent girls*. Washington, DC: American Psychological Association.

Maccoby, E. E. (1998). *The two sexes: Growing up apart, coming together*. Cambridge, MA: Harvard University Press.

Orenstein, P. (1994). *School girls: Young women, self-esteem, and the confidence gap*. New York: Doubleday.

Pipher, M. (1994). *Reviving Ophelia: Saving the selves of adolescent girls*. New York: Grosset/Putnam.

7 Young Adulthood

Physical Development and Health

Sexuality
Sexual Anatomy and Sexual Response
Sexual Attitudes
Sexual Behaviors
Sexual Dysfunctions

Lesbians and Bisexual Women
Bisexual Women
Attitudes toward Lesbians
Lesbian Health and Health Care
Mental Health of Lesbians
Explanations of Sexual Orientation

Pregnancy and Childbirth
Pregnancy
Childbirth
Postpartum Distress
Infertility

Mental Health and Illness
Alcohol Use and Abuse
Other Types of Substance Abuse

Health Services
The Physician-Patient Relationship
Women of Color and Health Care

KEY TERMS

vulva
mons pubis
labia majora
labia minora
clitoris
vagina
sexual response cycle
vasocongestion
orgasmic platform
sexual double standard
inhibited sexual desire
sexual aversion disorder

female sexual arousal
    disorder
female orgasmic disorder
dyspareunia
vaginismus
lesbian
bisexual
heterosexism
homophobia
cesarean section
Lamaze method
doula

maternity blues
postpartum depression
infertility
endometriosis
in vitro fertilization
surrogate motherhood
telescoping
binge drinking
fetal alcohol syndrome
fetal alcohol effect

I felt godlike—a miracle worker. It was the best moment of my life. I felt my baby's head, then saw his face—I got to cut his cord and put him to my breast. I felt like I did the impossible. I couldn't believe he was finally out into the light. I felt holy. (Boston Women's Health Book Collective, 1992, p. 447)

Giving birth to a child can be one of the major events of a woman's life. Childbirth typically (although not exclusively) occurs during young adulthood, the years from about 20 to 40. In this chapter, we focus on physical and health issues related to young women, including sexuality, pregnancy, and childbirth. We discuss lesbians and bisexual women, and conclude with an examination of mental health and illness, and health services. Many of these issues also are relevant to women in middle age and later life and will be addressed again when we explore those years.

Sexuality

Sexual Anatomy and Sexual Response

External Female Sexual Anatomy.   The *external female sexual organs*, collectively called the **vulva** are shown in Figure 7.1. Women can get a clear view of their own vulva by squatting and looking into a hand mirror. The **mons pubis** (also *mons veneris*, mountain of Venus) is *a pad of fatty tissue covering the pubic bone*. During puberty, it becomes covered with coarse hair. The hair continues between the legs and around the anus, the opening of the large intestine. The *fatty hair-covered area between the legs forms flaps called* the **labia majora** (outer lips). They surround *soft hairless flaps of skin*, the **labia minora** (inner lips). Between the inner lips and the anus lies the perineum. Spreading the inner lips apart reveals that they join at the upper end to form a fold of skin, or *hood* over the **clitoris**. *This highly sensitive organ, whose only known function is sexual pleasure, consists of erectile tissue that swells during sexual stimulation* (somewhat like the penis). Right below the clitoris is the urethral opening, through which urine passes. Below that is the larger vaginal opening. The **vagina** is *the canal leading to the uterus*. The menstrual blood passes through it and it is the birth canal during childbirth (Boston Women's Health Book Collective, 1998; Donatelle & Davis, 1998).

The Sexual Response Cycle.   William Masters and Virginia Johnson (1966) first described the **sexual response cycle**, *the physiological responses of women and men to sexual stimulation from any source* (sexual intercourse, masturbation, etc.). They pointed out that women and men respond similarly during the four phases of the cycle. Here we discuss women's responses.

In the *excitement phase*, a major response is **vasocongestion**, *the swelling of genital tissues with blood*. Vasocongestion produces vaginal lubrication within 30 seconds after stimulation. The clitoris and labia swell with blood. The inner two-thirds of the vagina expand, the uterus elevates, the breasts enlarge, the nipples

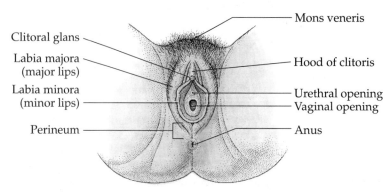

FIGURE 7.1   Female external sex organs
Source: Rathus et al., 1997, p. 63, Fig. 3.1. Reprinted with permission from Allyn & Bacon.

become erect, and the skin becomes flushed. Heart rate, breathing rate, and muscle tension increase.

During the *plateau phase,* the clitoris, now extremely sensitive, shortens and withdraws under the clitoral hood. *The low third of the vagina becomes engorged with blood, forming* the **orgasmic platform**. Heart rate, blood pressure, and breathing rate continue to rise.

In the *orgasmic phase*, the orgasmic platform, uterus, and anal sphincters contract strongly between 3 and 15 times, at intervals of less than a second. These contractions constitute the orgasm.

During the *resolution* phase, the *body returns to its prearousal state* within 15 to 30 minutes. Blood is released from engorged areas, the clitoris, vagina, uterus, and labia return to normal size, and muscle tension dissipates. Heart rate and breathing rate return to prearousal levels.

Multiple Orgasms.   Alfred Kinsey and his colleagues (Kinsey, Pomeroy, Martin, & Gebhard, 1953) reported that 14 percent of the women they interviewed experienced multiple orgasms. However, Masters and Johnson (1966) reported that most women are capable of multiple orgasms. In a more recent survey of over 700 nurses, 48 percent reported reaching multiple orgasms (Darling, Davidson, & Jennings, 1991). Unlike women, few, if any, men are physiologically capable of multiple orgasms. This is one of the major gender differences in sexual response, the other being that men but not women ejaculate during orgasm. While having multiple orgasms can be a good thing, some women feel that they are sexually inadequate if they don't. One orgasm can be quite satisfying, as can sex that does not culminate in orgasm.

One or Two Kinds of Orgasm?   Freud (1938) proposed that there were two types of female orgasm: clitoral and vaginal. Clitoral orgasms were achieved through clitoral stimulation during masturbation. This form of orgasm, practiced by young girls, was considered immature and sexually inadequate in adult women. Women were expected to shift to vaginal orgasms, brought on by sexual intercourse. Masters and Johnson (1966), however, demonstrated that there is only one kind of orgasm, physiologically, whether it is brought on by clitoral or vaginal stimulation. Furthermore, the clitoris is indirectly stimulated even in vaginal intercourse. While orgasms resulting from clitoral and vaginal stimulation are physiologically the same, there may be psychological or subjective differences. For example, the context of sexual intercourse includes a partner to whom one may be emotionally attached, whereas masturbation is often (but not always) done without the presence of a partner.

Sexual Attitudes

The Sexual Double Standard.   Historically, women's sexuality was discouraged and denied, especially outside of marriage. The social construction of norms about female and male sexuality is nowhere seen more clearly than in this **sexual**

double standard, *which allowed and even encouraged premarital sex for men, but not for women.* As premarital sex became more acceptable, the double standard has evolved into a belief that casual sexual activity is acceptable for men, but that women's sexual experiences should occur only in the context of a serious relationship (Hynie, Lydon, & Taradash, 1997; Gentry, 1998). As one example of the double standard, sexually permissive women are perceived by males as more attractive casual dating partners, but as less acceptable partners for long-term relationships (Oliver & Sedikides, 1992).

Gender Differences in Attitudes.   Women generally have less permissive attitudes toward sexual behavior than men do. In a review of a large number of studies on sexual attitudes and behavior, Mary Oliver and Janet Hyde (1993) found that women reported much more negative attitudes than men about casual premarital sex. Women were moderately less approving than men were of extramarital sex and of premarital sex when couples are committed or engaged. They were somewhat more likely to feel anxious or guilty about sex and to endorse the double standard. No gender differences were found in attitudes toward masturbation, however. In general, gender differences in attitudes towards sexual behavior overall narrowed as people got older. These differences also diminished from the 1960's through the 1990's.

Attitudes toward Women with Disabilities.   A common assumption is that women with disabilities are asexual beings who have no sex life and do not want one (King, 1997; Nosek et al., 1994). While able-bodied women often resent being treated as sex objects, some disabled women resent being treated as asexual objects and would relish a wolf whistle from a passing motorist (Lisi, 1993). The view of disabled women as asexual is based on misconceptions about the sexual desires and abilities of women with disabilities. Most individuals with disabilities have the same sexual desires as able-bodied persons. Their ability to perform sexually depends on their adjustment to the physical limitations of their disability, and the availability of partners (Rathus et al., 2000).

Sexual Behaviors

There is considerable consistency between sexual attitudes and sexual behaviors. Those with more permissive attitudes toward premarital, extramarital, or homosexual relations are more likely to have engaged in those behaviors. For example, 75 percent of women and men who say extramarital relations are not at all wrong have had such relations, whereas only 10 percent of those who believe extramarital relations are always wrong have been unfaithful (Smith, 1994). The consistency between sexual attitudes and behaviors may mean that people act in accordance with their attitudes, but can also mean that people rationalize their sexual activity by adopting matching attitudes. Both may be involved.

In the National Health and Social Life Survey (NHSLS), the most comprehensive study of sexuality in America in the 1990s, researchers surveyed a representative sample of over 3,400 Americans from ages 18 to 59 (Laumann, Gagnon, Michael, & Michaels, 1994; Michael, Gagnon, Laumann , & Kolata, 1994). They found that the vast majority of married Americans reported having sexual relations either a few times per month or two to three times a week, with an average of seven times a month (Laumann et al., 1994; Michael et al., 1994). The frequency of sexual relations declined gradually with age, with 50- to 59-year-olds reporting an average of four to five times a month. The most sexually active women were those ages 25 to 29, 96 percent of whom reported sexual activity during the past year as compared to 59 percent of the 55- to 59-year-old women. Both women and men expressed fairly high levels of satisfaction with marital sex, although women were slightly less satisfied.

Gender Differences. A number of gender differences in sexual activity have been reported, largely corresponding to gender differences in attitudes toward sexuality. Oliver and Hyde (1993) found that men, compared to women, had a higher incidence of intercourse, more frequent intercourse, a greater number of partners, and a younger age at first intercourse. Interestingly, the largest gender difference was in the incidence of masturbation, even though attitudes toward masturbation were the same. The size of this difference is shown in the NHSLS study which found that 7 percent of women but 28 percent of men reported masturbating at least once a week (Michael et al., 1994). This study also revealed gender differences in the frequency of extramarital sex. Over 90 percent of married women, but only 75 percent of men stated that they were faithful to their spouses.

Two limitations of research on sexual attitudes and behaviors must be kept in mind. One is the problem of volunteer bias. Many people refuse to participate in surveys of their sexual views and practices. Thus, samples are biased because they include the responses only of those individuals who are willing to discuss their intimate behavior. Such individuals tend to be more sexually permissive and to have more liberal attitudes toward sexuality than nonvolunteers. Therefore, survey results based on volunteer samples may not be representative of the population at large (Rathus et al., 2000).

A second problem is that all the results are based on self-reports, not on direct observations of behavior. It is possible that there are gender differences in reporting behaviors, but few if any differences in sexual behaviors or attitudes. Women may underreport their sexual experiences and men may exaggerate theirs (Oliver & Hyde, 1993). As a result of these two problems, we must take findings regarding gender differences in sexuality with a grain of salt.

Sexual Dysfunctions

Sexual dysfunctions are problems that can interfere with sexual pleasure. The four major types of sexual dysfunction are sexual desire disorders, sexual arousal disorders, orgasm disorders, and sexual pain disorders. In most instances, sexual dysfunctions can be treated successfully if both partners are willing to work together to solve the problem (Donatelle & Davis, 1998; "Silence about Sexual Problems," 1999).

Sexual Desire Disorders.   The most frequent sexual problem among women is *a lack of desire for sexual activity*, or **inhibited sexual desire**. Nearly one in four women report having this problem (Laumann, Paik, & Rosen, 1999). Persons who are distressed by this situation are diagnosed as having sexual desire disorder. Individuals who have little interest in sex but are not concerned by it, are not considered to have the disorder. **Sexual aversion disorder**, another type of desire dysfunction, *is marked by anxiety about sexual contact*. These desire disorders may be caused by stress, depression, negative attitudes toward sex, or a history of sexual trauma (Donatelle & Davis, 1998).

Female Sexual Arousal Disorder.   About one in seven women have **female sexual arousal disorder**, which involves *insufficient lubrication or a failure to be aroused* (Laumann et al., 1999). Most women with the disorder also have problems with desire and/or orgasm as well (Segraves & Segraves, 1993). The causes may be physical or psychological. Childhood sexual abuse often is linked to sexual arousal disorder (Rathus et al., 2000).

Female Orgasmic Disorder.   Women with **female orgasmic disorder** *experience the excitement phase of the sexual response cycle, but do not achieve orgasm*. In the past, such women were referred to as "frigid," but this term has been abandoned because it suggests that the woman is at fault. The term "preorgasmic" is now used, since most women can be taught to become orgasmic. Women who reach orgasm through manual or oral stimulation of the clitoris may not reach orgasm during intercourse. If a woman is satisfied with this situation, she is not considered to have an orgasmic disorder. A woman who does not reach an orgasm during intercourse may fake orgasm in order to not disappoint her partner. Studies find that up to two-thirds of women have faked an orgasm at some time in their lives (Donatelle & Davis, 1998).

Sexual Pain Disorders.   One form of sexual pain disorder is **dyspareunia** or *painful intercourse*. About 7 percent of women report this sexual problem (Laumann et al., 1999). Often a physical condition, such as a vaginal infection, sexually transmitted disease, lack of lubrication, or a structural problem, is involved. Psychological factors such as anxiety about sex or prior sexual trauma also may be responsible (Rathus et al., 2000).

The other sexual pain disorder is **vaginismus**, the *involuntary contraction of vaginal muscles*, making intercourse painful or impossible. Vaginismus often is caused by factors such as childhood sexual abuse, rape, a family upbringing that included negative attitudes toward sex, and a history of painful intercourse (Donatelle & Davis, 1998; Rathus et al, 2000).

How common is sexual dysfunction? A recent study by Edward Laumann and his colleagues (Laumann et al., 1999) of American adults ranging in age from

18 to 59 years found that sexual problems are widespread. In their survey, 43 percent of women and 31 percent of men reported having such problems.

The researchers found that factors such as age, marital status, ethnicity, education, and economic status are related to the incidence of sexual dysfunction. For women, the prevalence of sexual problems declines as they get older, except for those who report trouble lubricating. Men, on the other hand, have more problems with age, such as trouble achieving and maintaining an erection and lack of interest in sex. Single, divorced, separated, and widowed individuals show an elevated risk of sexual problems. Formerly married women, for example, are roughly one and one-half times more likely than married women to experience sexual anxiety and trouble reaching orgasm. Ethnicity also is associated with sexual problems. White women are more likely to have sexual pain, while Black women more often experience low levels of desire and pleasure. Latinas, on the other hand, report lower rates of sexual problems than other women.

Women and men with lower educational attainment report more sexual problems than more highly educated individuals do. Women without high school diplomas are twice as likely as college educated women to experience low desire, problems achieving orgasm, sexual pain, and sexual anxiety. Lower levels of household income are associated with an increase in all categories of sexual dysfunction for women, but only in erectile dysfunction (impotence) for men.

Another factor related to problems with sex is poor physical or emotional health. Underlying physical conditions that can cause sexual dysfunction include diabetes, heart disease, neurological disorders, side effects of medications, alcoholism and drug abuse, or heavy smoking. Psychological causes of sexual problems include stress or anxiety from work, concern about poor sexual performance, marital discord, depression, or previous traumatic sexual performance ("Silence about Sexual Problems," 1999).

Lesbians and Bisexual Women

Before reading this section, try the exercise in Get Involved 7.1. Compare your findings with the information that follows.

A **lesbian** is a women who is *emotionally and sexually attracted to other women*. A **bisexual** woman is *attracted to both men and women* (Firestein, 1996). It is difficult to estimate the number of women who are lesbian and bisexual because negative attitudes toward homosexuality discourage some individuals from reporting this behavior. In addition, the sexual identities of sexual-minority woman may change over time. For example, a two-year longitudinal study of lesbian and bisexual women found that half of the participants had changed sexual-minority identities more than once in their lives and one-third had done so over a two-year period (Diamond, 2000). In recent research, 2 percent of American women *identified* themselves as having a lesbian sexual orientation, 2 to 4 percent reported *engaging in sexual behavior* with women in the past five years, and 8 to 12 percent reported some *sexual attraction* to other women, but no sexual interaction since age

GET INVOLVED **7.1**

Attitudes toward Lesbians

Ask two female and two male friends to complete the following exercise:

Our society views some groups of unmarried women as having higher social status or acceptability than other groups of unmarried women. Give each group below a Social Status Score based on how you think these groups are viewed in our society. Assign each group a score ranging from 1 to 100, with *high* scores indicating *high* status and *low* scores indicating *low* status.

Social Status Score

divorced heterosexual women   _____

never-married homosexual women   _____

widowed heterosexual women   _____

never-married heterosexual women _____

Source: Etaugh & Fulton, 1995.

What Does It Mean?

1. In what ways are your female and male respondents' answers alike? In what ways are they different? Explain the differences and similarities.
2. How does the social status of lesbians compare to that of the three groups of heterosexual women?
3. How would you account for the differences in social status of these four groups of women?

15. About 1 percent of women reported having a bisexual identity, and 1.4 percent reporting having both female and male partners (Laumann et al., 1994).

Bisexual Women

Women often become bisexual after first being exclusively heterosexual or exclusively homosexual (Blumstein & Schwartz, 1993). Lesbians may move toward bisexuality for several reasons. First, nearly all have had some heterosexual experience (Nichols, 1994). Second, a heterosexual lifestyle is the norm in our society; thus, bisexuality can be a "cover" for a woman who still desires lesbian experiences. However, lesbians risk ostracism from the lesbian community if they become bisexual. Third, some women who label themselves bisexual are making the transition from a heterosexual to a lesbian lifestyle. Some women experience a need for relationships with both men and women at the same time, while others simply feel attracted to both sexes (Nichols, 1994). Heterosexual women often are reluctant to express their bisexual feelings because of the social stigma attached to homosexuality. The dilemma faced by a bisexual woman was expressed this way:

> *Invisibility is a problem. Few people know we exist because we don't "fit" into either the heterosexual or the lesbian world. When we are open, both worlds judge us* (Boston Women's Health Book Collective, 1992, p. 214).

One of Claire's students described the following experience in her journal:

> *If I hear "The lesbian's dating a boy?!" one more time . . . So I met a boy and we've started dating, not a big deal to me but obviously to others. My main issue here is pigeon-holing. "I thought you were supposed to be gay," as if I have become a caricature of a human.* (Angelique, age 22)

Attitudes toward Lesbians

Heterosexism *is the view that heterosexuality is the norm and that homosexuality is abnormal.* This view often leads to **homophobia**, *negative reactions to homosexuality and irrational fear of homosexuals.* Such reactions are pervasive in American and Canadian society (Brooke, 1998; Schellenberg, Hirt, & Sears, 1999; Solarz, 1999; Wolfe, 1998). In a 1998 survey of American adults, for example, nearly sixty percent felt that sex between adults of the same sex is always wrong (Smith, 1999). A recent survey of more than 261,000 first-year college students found that nearly one-third believed there should be laws banning homosexual relationships. Interestingly, over 40 percent of male students but only 22 percent of females endorsed this statement (Reisberg, 2000). A 1998 poll found that about half of American adults felt that homosexuals should not be allowed to legally marry or to adopt children. On the other hand, 80 percent felt homosexuals should have equal rights in employment and housing and nearly 60 percent supported health insurance and inheritance rights for gay spouses (Leland, 2000). Americans who believe that individuals cannot change their homosexuality are more sympathetic toward homosexual issues than those who see it as a choice (Leland & Miller, 1998). For a look at other factors that influence attitudes towards lesbians and gay men, turn to Learn About the Research 7.1.

Women of Color.   According to Beverly Greene (1996), lesbian women of color are in triple jeopardy. They face societal barriers of sexism, racism, and homophobia. While most lesbians of color look to their ethnic communities as a source of support, these communities may be more homophobic than the White community

LEARN ABOUT THE RESEARCH 7.1
Who Is Homophobic?

Although negative attitudes toward lesbians and gays are prevalent in American society, the degree of homophobia varies markedly from one individual to another and some people are not homophobic at all. Homophobic attitudes are more likely to be found among individuals who are older, less well-educated, politically conservative, and from the Midwest, South, and rural areas. Those who hold traditional gender-role attitudes, fundamentalist religious beliefs, and authoritarian right-wing views also have more negative attitudes toward lesbians and gays (Bohan, 1996; Herek, 1996; Murphy, Kinnaird, Sellers, Crutchfield & Jordan, 1999; Peyser, 1998; Whitley & Richardson, 2000). Men are more homophobic than women (remember the study of the first-year college students?), particularly toward gay men. Gender differences in attitudes toward lesbians generally are small or absent (Kite & Whitley, 1996; Lee & Kite, 1998).

What Does It Mean?

1. Individuals with traditional gender role attitudes are also more likely to have negative attitudes toward gays and lesbians. Propose a possible connection between these two sets of attitudes.
2. Why do you think men are more homophobic than women?
3. What steps can be taken by individuals and communities to ensure more equal treatment of lesbians and gays?

(Bohan, 1996; Jones & Hill, 1996). In ethnic minority cultures, women who do not adhere to traditional gender roles or who are not subordinate to men often are ostracized. Lesbian members of these communities may be more reluctant to "come out," choosing to remain invisible rather than be rejected (Greene, 1994).

Discrimination. Discrimination against lesbians can take many forms. The most virulent form of homophobia is expressed in violent "hate crimes" committed against homosexuals, mostly by groups of adolescents or young adult males (Bohan, 1996; Moore, 1999; Waldo, Hesson-McInnis, & D'Augelli, 1998). In 1997, the reported number of such crimes rose 7 percent over the previous year while the overall crime rate dropped 4 percent (Peyser, 1998). The most frequent forms of harassment experienced by gay and lesbian youth in school are being called names and being ridiculed in front of others (Rivers, 1999). A recent survey of community college students by Karen Franklin (1998) found that nearly one-quarter admitted to verbally harassing people they thought were gay or lesbian. Among men, 18 percent said they had physically assaulted or threatened to assault gays or lesbians. In a nationwide survey, nearly 2000 lesbians were asked if they had experienced discrimination because they were lesbians. Over half of the sample had been verbally attacked for being lesbian. Thirteen percent had lost their jobs, 6 percent had been physically attacked, 4 percent had their health affected, and 1 percent had been discharged by the military for being lesbian (Bradford, Ryan, & Rothblum, 1994).

Although some states have laws that ban discrimination on the basis of sexual orientation in employment, credit, housing, and public accommodation, many do not. Some states prohibit same-sex partners of government employees from receiving domestic partner benefits. Same-sex marriage is specifically banned in over 30 states and is not legal in any state, although Vermont now gives same-sex couples spousal rights (Goldberg, 2000).

Lesbian Health and Health Care

There is some evidence that lesbians may be at increased risk for certain health problems. These risks do *not*, however, arise simply from having a lesbian sexual orientation. Rather, certain risk factors may be more common among lesbians because of lifestyle considerations. For example, lesbians may face heightened risks of breast, ovarian, and cervical cancer because they are less likely than heterosexual women to experience the hormonal changes associated with pregnancy (Bradford & White, 2000; Solarz, 1999).

The social stigma attached to homosexuality also contributes to elevated health risks for lesbians by reducing access to health care. Surveys have found that many lesbians avoid going to the doctor for routine checkups—especially gynecological exams—because they feel uncomfortable talking about issues that may reveal their sexual orientation and consequently may elicit negative reactions from the physician. In the words of one young woman, "If you lie, then you may not get the information you need to take care of yourself. And if you come out, your doctor may become really uncomfortable with you" (Thompson, 1999, A25). Lesbians also tend to limit their visits to doctors because they are less likely to have health insurance, since lesbians generally cannot share spousal benefits. Even for lesbians who do have coverage, managed health care plans often limit women's ability to choose lesbian-friendly health care providers. (See Chapter 13 for a discussion of health insurance for women.) The reduced access to health care that results from fear of discrimination and from financial barriers puts lesbians at greater risk for preventable illnesses and makes them more likely to die from diseases that are treatable if detected early (Thompson, 1999). Surveys of the health care choices of lesbians have found preferences for female practitioners, holistic approaches, preventive care and education, and woman-managed clinics (Lucas, 1992; Trippet & Bain, 1992).

Mental Health of Lesbians

Reviews of research consistently find that lesbians and heterosexual women do not differ in overall psychological adjustment (Gonsiorek, 1996; Rathus et al., 2000; Rosenbluth, 1997). The American Psychiatric Association (1994) no longer classifies homosexuality as a mental disorder, dropping this designation in 1973. Among lesbians and gays, better mental health is linked with accepting one's homosexuality, having relationships with other homosexual individuals, and being active in the lesbian and gay community (Evans & D'Augelli, 1996; Gonsiorek, 1996; Perry & O'Hanlan, 1998; Zea, Reisen, & Poppen, 1999).

Lesbians and gays often face special challenges, however. The process of "coming out"—accepting one's homosexual orientation and declaring it to others —is often a slow and painful process (Savin-Williams, 1998; Savin-Williams & Dubé 1998). Lesbian and gay teens and adults may be rejected by family members and peers. Compared to heterosexual teens, lesbian and gay adolescents have higher rates of substance abuse, poor school performance, truancy, running away from home, conflicts with the law, depression, and suicide (Bernstein, 1999; D'Augelli, 1996, 1998; "For Gay Teens," 1999; Remafedi, 1999).

Adult lesbians are much more likely than nonlesbians to seek psychological counseling. About three-quarters of lesbians have used mental health services compared with anywhere from 14 to 29 percent of heterosexual women (Bradford, Ryan, & Rothblum, 1994; Morris, 1998; Solarz, 1999). What accounts for this disparity, given that lesbians are as well adjusted as other women? For one thing, homophobia can cause considerable stress in the lives of lesbians. In addition, lesbians have higher rates of alcohol use than heterosexual women, and their rates, unlike those of other women, do not decline with age, (Bux, 1996; Solarz, 1999). But perhaps the biggest factor is that lesbians put a high value on personal growth and have a much more positive attitude toward seeking counseling than do nonlesbians (Morgan, 1992).

Explanations of Sexual Orientation

The origins of homosexuality are complex and controversial (Ruble & Martin, 1998). A number of psychological and biological theories have been proposed. According to Sigmund Freud (1925/1989), all individuals initially are bisexual. The mother is the original love object for both girls and boys. In heterosexual development, the father becomes the girl's love object and she substitutes other males for him as she gets older. When the mother remains the love object, lesbian development occurs. Little evidence exists in support of this theory, however. From a learning theory point of view, early positive sexual activity with members of one's own gender or negative sexual experiences with members of the other gender could lead to homosexuality. However, many lesbians and gay males are aware of their sexual orientation before they have engaged in any sexual activity (Bohan, 1996; Etaugh & Rathus, 1995).

Biological theories focus on genetic or hormonal factors. In one study, 48 percent of identical twin sisters of lesbians also were lesbians, compared with just 16 percent of fraternal twin sisters, and 6 percent of adopted sisters (Bailey, Pillard,

Neale, & Agyei, 1993). But if genetics were the whole story, 100 percent of the identical twin sisters would have been lesbian (Ellis, 1996).

Is sexual orientation determined by sex hormones? In adulthood, there is no link between levels of female and male sex hormones and sexual orientation (Friedman & Downey, 1994). *Prenatal* sex hormones may be a factor, however. Studies of intersexuality discussed in Chapter 3 pointed to the prenatal influence of androgen on the development of females' sexual orientation. One recent study found that the inner ears of lesbians function more like the inner ears of men than those of heterosexual women (McFadden & Pasanen, 1998). Similarly, finger-length patterns of lesbians resemble those of men more than those of heterosexual women (Williams et at., 2000). These findings suggest that high levels of androgens (male sex hormones) during the prenatal period partially masculinize certain physiological and anatomical characteristics of lesbians, including the brain structures responsible for sexual orientation.

Most likely, complex interactions among genetic, hormonal, and environmental factors determine sexual orientation, and different causal mechanisms may operate for different individuals (Savin-Williams & Diamond, 1997).

Pregnancy and Childbirth

Pregnancy

Pregnancy begins when an egg and sperm cell unite in the fallopian tube. The fertilized egg begins to divide as it travels toward the uterus, a 3- or 4- day journey. When it arrives, it implants itself into the thick lining of the uterus. Pregnancy typically lasts 40 weeks and is divided into three trimesters of 3 months each. A missed menstrual period is often the first indication of pregnancy although new tests may detect pregnancy within 10 days after conception (Strong et al., 1999).

Physical Changes during Pregnancy.   Early signs of pregnancy include breast tenderness, more frequent urination, fatigue, and nausea. Nausea usually is confined to the first trimester and, despite being called "morning sickness," can occur anytime during the day (Boston Women's Health Book Collective, 1998). (Claire's and Judith's personal experiences attest to the value of eating crackers or toast slowly in the morning before getting up.) During the second trimester, most of the nausea and fatigue disappear. Around the four or fifth month, women begin to feel fetal movements ("quickening").

During the third trimester, weight gain and protrusion of the abdomen become quite noticeable. Some of the activities of daily living, such as tying one's shoes, may become a challenge. The expanding uterus exerts increasing pressure on other internal organs, causing feelings of pressure and discomfort (Strong et al., 1999).

In the past, pregnancy was viewed as an illness, but that is less true today. Most women feel that their pregnancy is a normal and healthy—if somewhat inconvenient—experience. Regular exercise along with good nutrition reduces or eliminates many discomforts (Boston Women's Health Book Collective, 1998). Claire played pool well into her first pregnancy, until her bulging abdomen made it too difficult to bend over the pool table. During her pregnancy with her second child, a summer baby, she swam until the day she gave birth.

Psychological Changes During Pregnancy. A woman's feelings during pregnancy vary tremendously depending on such factors as her economic circumstances, her desire to be pregnant, her physical condition, and her childhood experiences (Boston Women's Health Book Collective, 1998; Seegmiller, 1993). At each stage, women sometimes feel positive and sometimes negative. Feelings of being more sensual, potent, creative, and loving may occur. Negative feelings include loss of individuality, worries about whether the baby will be normal, distress at gaining weight and looking awkward, and concerns about whether one can cope with the responsibilities of parenting (Boston Women's Health Book Collective, 1998; Rathus et al., 2000).

Reactions to Pregnant Women. A pregnant woman elicits a variety of reactions from those around her. Many women have had the experience of having their pregnant abdomen patted by people who would not consider such a gesture with a nonpregnant woman (Bergum, 1997). In an interesting study by Shelly Taylor and Ellen Langer (1977), two women—one who was made to look pregnant through the use of padding and another who carried a box in front of her so that she took up as much space as the "pregnant" woman—stood in the back corners of the same elevator. The reactions of people boarding the elevators were dramatic. Men went to great lengths to avoid standing close to the "pregnant" woman. Women also avoided her, but not to the same extent. Much to the discomfort of the "pregnant" woman, both women and men frequently stared at her. People often react this way when encountering a physically disabled person. Research by Hilary Lips (1997) shows that young adults perceive pregnant women as irritable, emotional, and suffering from physical maladies. The discomfort some people feel around pregnant women was made abundantly clear to Claire in the end-of-semester course evaluations filled out by students when she was seven months pregnant. Some made negative comments about her teaching while pregnant; one said "Go home and have your baby."

Childbirth

Women describe the birth of their first child as a physically and psychologically transforming experience (DiMatteo & Kahn, 1997; also see the quotation at the beginning of the chapter). In Chapter 11, we examine some of the psychological aspects involved in making the transition to motherhood. In this section, we focus on the biological aspects.

Stages of Childbirth. In the first stage, the cervix becomes dilated to about 4 inches in diameter, a process that may last from a few hours to a day or more. In the second stage, which lasts from a few minutes to several hours, uterine contractions move the baby through the vagina. At the end of this stage, the baby is born. During the third stage, which lasts from a few minutes to an hour, the placenta detaches from the uterine wall and is expelled. Progesterone and estrogen levels drop dramatically during the second and third stages (Rathus et al., 2000).

Methods of Childbirth.   Throughout most of the twentieth century, women gave birth in hospitals, attended by obstetricians using surgical instruments and anesthetics. While use of these medical procedures has saved lives and reduced pain, it also has depersonalized childbearing. Feminists argue that it has taken from women control over their own bodies and, through drugs, denied many women the experience of giving birth (Etaugh & Rathus, 1995; Rathus et al., 2000).

One example of the "medicalization" of the birth process is the **cesarean section** (or C-section). *Incisions are made in the abdomen and uterus and the baby is surgically removed.* C-sections are performed if vaginal delivery is expected to be difficult or threatens the health of the mother or baby—as when the mother's pelvis is small or misshapen, the baby is very large, or the baby is not in the normal birth position. The cesarean delivery rate is higher in the United States than in other industrialized countries, rising from 5 percent in 1970 to 25 percent by 1988. Several health professionals feel that many C-sections are unnecessary. These concerns have led to a drop in the C-section rate during the 1990s, down to 21 percent in 1997 (Curtin & Park, 1999; Sachs, Kobelin, Castro, & Frigoletto, 1999).

Parents now can choose among more family-centered approaches to childbearing. The most popular method in the United States is prepared child birth, or the **Lamaze method**. *Pre-labor classes teach the mother to control her pain through relaxation, breathing techniques, and focusing exercises.* A labor coach, usually the husband or partner, provides moral support and coaches techniques of breathing and relaxation during childbirth (Donatelle & Davis, 1998). Others also may serve as a labor coach: a woman's mother, sister, friend, or *an experienced and knowledgeable female labor and birth coach* known as a **doula**. Doula comes from the Greek word meaning "woman caregiver of a woman." Studies have found that women who are randomly assigned a doula during labor have less pain and anxiety during labor, need less medication, have fewer C-sections, and have shorter labors and less postpartum depression than women without a doula (Kennell & McGrath, 1993; Kennell, Claus, McGrath, Robertson, & Hinkley, 1991; Scott, Berkowitz, & Klaus, 1999). In addition, women assigned doulas are found to be more sensitive, loving, and responsive to their infants two months later (Gilbert, 1998a).

Home birth also has increased in recent years, providing families with familiar settings and enhancing the feeling that the woman and her family are in control. More women also are choosing to deliver in homelike birthing centers outside a hospital. Family members and friends may be present during labor and delivery. Many hospitals now provide similar family-friendly birthing rooms (Strong et al., 1999). Other aspects of family-centered birth include minimizing the use of anesthesia, eliminating practices such as enemas and shaving of the genital area, and use of the more natural sitting position to give birth.

Using certified nurse-midwives for prenatal care and delivery also has become increasingly popular in the United States. Certified nurse-midwives attended only 1 percent of births in 1975, but nearly 7 percent of births in 1997 (Curtin & Park, 1999). Mortality rates are lower and birth weights are higher for infants delivered by nurse-midwives than for those delivered by physicians even though nurse-midwives tend to serve traditionally higher-risk women such as teenage mothers and those with less education (MacDorman & Singh, 1998). The most likely explanation for this is that nurse-midwives, compared to physicians, spend more time with patients during prenatal visits, provide more patient education, counseling, and emotional support and are with their patients throughout labor and delivery.

Childbirth after 40.   A growing number of women are having children after the age of 40. These women have a harder time conceiving and have more miscarriages than younger women. They have higher levels of complications during pregnancy and are more likely to have cesarean sections. The good news is that almost all older mothers, like their younger counterparts, have healthy babies, and that infant mortality rates are comparable for the two groups (O'Neil, 1999).

To find out more about individual women's experiences with pregnancy and childbirth, try Get Involved 7.2.

GET INVOLVED 7.2
Pregnancy and Childbirth Experiences

1. Briefly interview two women in their twenties, two middle-aged women, and two older women about their experiences with pregnancy and childbirth. It is helpful, but not essential, if you know your respondents fairly well. You may interview your sisters, cousins, friends, mother, aunts, grandmothers, etc. Keep a record of your respondents' comments.
2. Compare and contrast the responses of the women in the three age groups.

What Does It Mean?

1. In what ways are the pregnancy experiences of the three groups of women different? In what ways are they alike?
2. In what ways are the childbirth experiences of the three groups different? In what ways are they alike?
3. What social and historical conditions may have influenced the pregnancy and childbirth experiences of these three generations of women?

Postpartum Distress

During the postpartum period, the first weeks after birth, many women experience some psychological distress. The mildest and most common form, called **maternity blues** or baby blues, is experienced by 40 to 85 percent of new mothers. *This mood state, characterized by crying, anxiety, and irritability, typically begins 3 to 4 days after childbirth and lasts about 2 to 4 days.* Maternity blues are more common following a first birth, and may reflect the mother's adjustment to parenthood (Gotlib, 1998; Lamberg, 1999).

About 10 to 15 percent of women have *severe feelings of depression that last for weeks or months after delivery.* These changes, called **postpartum depression**, are characterized by anxiety or panic attacks, loss of interest in daily activities, despair, feelings of worthlessness and guilt, sleep and appetite disturbances, fatigue, difficulty in concentrating, and thoughts of harming the baby (Gotlib, 1998; Greenberg & Westreich, 1999). One in 1,000 women experience postpartum psychosis, a serious condition that often includes delusions and hallucinations (DeAngelis, 1997c; Miller, 1999).

Women are more likely to develop postpartum depression if they are young, less educated, or first-time mothers. Risk factors also include a history of mental illness, previous depression, marital difficulties or other stressful life events, major role changes such as the transition from employed woman to stay-at-home mother, and lack of support from family and friends. It is unclear whether the drastic drop in levels of estrogen and progesterone after birth also plays a role. Studies examining the relationship between hormonal levels and postpartum distress have produced mixed and inconclusive findings (Kendall-Tackett & Kantor, 1993).

The important role of social support in reducing the risk of postpartum depression is illustrated in a recent study of mothers who, immediately after their child's birth, participated in a supportive informal counseling session of up to 2 hours with a midwife (Lavender & Walkinshaw, 1998). Three weeks after delivery, only 9 percent of the mothers received a high score on a measure of depression, compared with 55 percent of new mothers in a control group who had not been assigned to a counseling session. While support and counseling clearly help prevent postpartum depression, about 75 percent of women recover from the condition without any treatment (Berthiaume, David, Saucier, & Borgeat, 1996; DeAngelis, 1997c).

Infertility

Infertility is *the failure to conceive a child after a year of trying* (teVelde & Cohlen, 1999). About one couple in six in the United States cannot conceive and the likelihood of being infertile increases with age. In about one-third of the cases, the difficulty is traced to the woman, in another third the problem originates with the man, and in the other third, both partners have problems (Grady, 1999e). Causes of infertility in women include blockage of the fallopian tubes, failure of the ovaries to produce eggs, and **endometriosis**, *the presence of uterine lining tissue in abnormal locations* (Goldman, Missmer, & Barbieri, 2000; Miller & Raymond, 1999).

About 10 percent of infertile women have tried recently developed reproductive technologies (Fein, 1998). In 71 percent of the cases, couples use IVF or **in vitro fertilization** in which *the couple's own sperm and egg are fertilized in a glass laboratory dish ("in vitro" means "in glass") and the resulting embryo is transferred into the woman's uterus* (Centers for Disease Control and Prevention, 1998). Louise Brown, born in England in 1978 as a result of IVF, was the first of these so-called test-tube babies, now numbering 300,000 strong worldwide (Goldberg, 1999a). In 14 percent of infertility treatments, the couples' frozen embryos are used, and in 8 percent, donor eggs are used (Stolberg, 1997b). Donated eggs typically are used for older women who do not produce eggs or whose eggs are damaged (Kolata, 1998b; Stolberg, 1998b). On rare occasions a "donor uterus" is used when a woman can produce eggs but cannot carry a pregnancy to full term. An embryo is produced by IVF using the couple's egg and sperm, and is then placed in the donor's uterus. In one well-known case, 53-year-old Geraldine Wesolowski carried a child for her daughter-in-law, who had no uterus and gave birth to her own grandson (Etaugh & Rathus, 1995).

The "success rate," that is, the percentage of times a live birth results, is about 17 percent for frozen embryos, 26 percent for IVF, and 47 percent for egg donation (Centers for Disease Control and Prevention, 1998). The treatments are expensive. For example IVF costs $11,000 and up per try (Lang, 1999). Only 14 states require insurance companies to cover the treatments and some insurers now are eliminating coverage for fertility treatments (Fein, 1998; Freudenheim, 1998; Phillips, 1998).

Another, more controversial approach to infertility is *to pay a woman to be artificially inseminated with the sperm of an infertile woman's husband and to give birth to the child*. This practice, known as **surrogate motherhood**, raises a number of social, legal, and financial questions ("Assisted Reproduction," 1999; Boston Women's Health Book Collective, 1998; Monaghan, 1999). Can a contract signed before a baby's conception be legally binding after birth? Who are the legal parents? Should the surrogate mother be paid for her services? Some critics argue that surrogate motherhood exploits women physically, economically, and emotionally (Leiblum, 1997; Raymond, 1993). Others believe that surrogate motherhood can benefit all parties as long as the interests of the surrogate mother are protected (Purdy, 1992). A recent study found that women who had served as surrogate mothers more than ten years earlier reported few regrets, although some were sad and disappointed over losing contact with the children they bore (Grady, 1998).

Mental Health and Illness

Overall, rates of mental illness are almost identical for women and men. There are, however, striking differences in the prevalence of specific mental disorders. Women have higher rates of depression, anxiety disorders (including phobias), and eating disorders. Men are more likely to have personality and substance abuse disorders (Commonwealth Fund, 1995b; Culbertson, 1997; Gater et al., 1998). Eating disorders were discussed in Chapter 5. In this chapter, we examine alcohol use and abuse as well as other forms of substance abuse. It is appropriate to discuss this topic here because the incidence of alcohol consumption, heavy drinking and alcohol problems is higher among young women than older women. In Chapter 9, we examine depression and anxiety disorders.

Alcohol Use and Abuse

Incidence. Women are less likely than men to use alcohol and to be heavy drinkers. In addition, when women drink they drink less than men: 15 percent of women are moderate to heavy drinkers compared with 36 percent of men (Brown et al., 1995; Vogeltanz & Wilsnack, 1997). Overall, about 4 percent of women and 11 percent of men have been diagnosed with alcohol problems, a male-to-female ratio of nearly 3 to 1. *However, while women's alcoholism starts later than to men's alcoholism, it progresses more quickly*, a pattern called **telescoping** (Donatelle & Davis, 1998).

Problem drinking in young women has been increasing at an alarming rate. For example, the number of college women who drink abusively has tripled since the mid-1970s. Over one-third of college women report that they drink to get drunk, a percentage equal to that of college men (Celis, 1994). Furthermore, college women now are almost as likely as college men to engage in **binge drinking**, defined as *having five drinks in a row for men or four in a row for women at least once in the last two weeks*. Half of college men and 39 percent of college women are binge drinkers (Hitt, 1997).

The percentage of women drinkers declines considerably with age (Russell, Testa, & Wilsnack, 2000). About three-quarters of American women ages 21–34 drink at least occasionally, compared with two-thirds of women 35–49, half of women ages 50–64, and less than a third of those 65 and older.

Ethnicity. The rate of alcoholism among Native Americans is two to three times the national average. Their death rate from alcohol-related causes is about eight times the national average (Donatelle & Davis, 1998; Kauffman & Joseph-Fox, 1996). Native American women have higher rates of alcohol use than women in other ethnic groups. White women have the next highest rate of drinking, followed by Latinas and Black women. Asian American women have much lower rates of alcohol use than other groups of women (Brown et al., 1995). The course of alcohol abuse during adulthood differs for Black and White women. Alcoholism rates in White women peak during young adulthood (ages 18–29) and decline thereafter. Among Black women, on the other hand, the incidence of alcoholism rises between 18 and 44 years of age and does not decrease until after age 65 (Caetano, 1994).

Physical Consequences. Women have more body fat and less of the enzyme that breaks down alcohol than men do. As a result, they have higher levels of alcohol in their blood even when they consume the same amount of alcohol per unit of body weight. (For example, 3 ounces of alcohol consumed by a 120-pound woman has a greater effect on her than the equivalent 6 ounces of alcohol consumed by a 240-pound man has on him.) One consequence is that women develop cirrhosis of the liver, hepatitis, high blood pressure, and ulcers at lower levels of alcohol intake than men. Prolonged heavy drinking also increases the risk of breast cancer (Cirillo, 1996; Rohsenow, 1998; Russell et al., 2000). In addition, alcohol use contributes to the development of osteoporosis (see Chapter 9).

Drinking alcohol during pregnancy can lead to **fetal alcohol syndrome**, *a disorder characterized by mental retardation, growth deficiencies, facial deformities, and learning and behavioral problems.* One of every 750 newborns is born with FAS, the third most common birth defect and the leading cause of mental retardation in the United States (Donatelle & Davis, 1998; Streissguth, Barr, Bookstein, Sampson, & Olson, 1999). Among mothers who drink heavily during pregnancy, about 40 percent have children with FAS, and many others have children with impaired cognitive and motor skills (Kaemingk & Paquette, 1999; Mattson, Riley, Gramling, Delis, & Jones, 1998). Even light drinkers risk having children with **fetal alcohol effect (FAE)**, *a milder but still serious form of FAS* (Rohsenow, 1998; Streissguth et al., 1999).

Risk Factors.   Children of alcoholic parents have increased rates of alcoholism. Genetic factors appear to play about as strong a role for daughters as for sons (McGue, 1999; Rohsenow, 1998). Women who have low self-esteem, depression, and difficulties in coping with stressful life events are more likely than other women to develop alcohol problems (Gomberg, 1994; Walitzer & Sher, 1996). Women who were sexually abused in childhood, or who lost a parent through divorce or death early in life also are at greater risk for alcohol problems. Adolescents whose parents and peers consume alcohol and tolerate its use are more likely to start drinking at an early age (National Center on Addiction and Substance Abuse, 1999; National Institute on Alcohol Abuse and Alcoholism [NIAAA], 1997). Early initiation of drinking is an important risk factor for later alcohol-related problems (Grant & Dawson, 1997).

Treatment.   Society has set up several double standards for women and men. The double standard of sexuality was discussed earlier in this chapter. There is also a double standard with regard to drinking. Heavy drinking in men is often expected and seen as normal whereas heavy drinking in women is strongly criticized. As a result, women tend to hide their alcohol use, making them less likely to seek help and to be more seriously ill before the disease is diagnosed (Cirillo, 1996; McDonald, 1999). Moreover, physicians ask more questions about alcohol use and give more advice and information to male than to female problem drinkers (Liu, Kahan, & Wilson, 1999). One study, (Brown et al., 1995) for example, found that only one-third of women who had a checkup during the past year were asked about their drinking patterns. For women over 65, the rate dropped to one-sixth. (Older women are particularly invisible.) Twelve-step alcoholism treatment programs such as Alcoholics Anonymous have been criticized for being based exclusively on research with alcoholic men. Alternative programs, such as Women for Sobriety, focus on the special issues and needs of women with drinking problems (Rohsenow, 1998).

Other Types of Substance Abuse

In both adolescence and adulthood, males are more likely than females to use most illegal drugs, such as marijuana, cocaine, heroin, hallucinogens, and steroids (U.S. Department of Health and Human Services [USDHHS],1999). Use of these substances is somewhat lower among Black women than among Latinas or White women (Johnston, O'Malley, & Bachman, 1999a, 1999b). Males also are likely to use illegal drugs more heavily than females do. One possible reason for this gender gap is that drug use among women is less acceptable in our society. The only consistent exception to the rule that males are more frequent users of illicit drugs than females occurs for amphetamines, which females use as much as or slightly more than males. Recently, the gender gap in substance use has declined as a result both of increasing use among females and decreasing use among males ("Gender Gap," 1996; Johnston et al., 1999a, 1999b). One disturbing trend, for example, is a sharp increase in the use of anabolic (muscle-building) steroids by adolescent girls. According to health experts, some teenage girls are moving away from a preoccupation with thinness toward a lean, more muscular look, a trend labeled "reverse anorexia" (Noble, 1999). Unfortunately, not only does steroid use expose females to the same severe health risks as boys, but it also may damage their ability to bear children.

Typically, women and men who use illegal substances use more than one and also use or abuse alcohol. In women, the problem is compounded because they are more likely than men to be given prescription drugs, such as tranquilizers, antidepressants, and sleeping pills (Lex, 1994; Marecek & Hare-Mustin, 1998).

Health Services

About 10 years ago, Dr. Annette Stanton, a professor of psychology at the University of Kansas, attended a university reception with a colleague. She reacted strongly when her colleague referred to a recent study concerning the connection between heart disease and caffeine consumption, which had received a great deal of media coverage. "I guess our hearts are safe if we have a cup of coffee," he said. "Your heart may be safe; I have no idea about the safety of my heart! That study was conducted on over 45,000 men," retorted Dr. Stanton. (adapted from Stanton, 1995, p. 3)

Only a decade or so ago, little was known about many aspects of women's health. Women were routinely excluded as research participants in large studies designed to examine risk factors and potential treatments for various diseases. Even the first clinical trials to examine the effects of estrogen on heart disease were conducted solely on men! Scientists gave two principal reasons for confining medical experiments to men. First, women's monthly hormonal fluctuations "complicated" research results. Second, potential ethical and legal problems might arise from experimenting on women who would later bear children (McDonald, 1999). One wonders if the "male is normative" assumption (see Chapter 2) played a role as well.

In any case, the recognition that women have a number of poorly understood medical problems and that diseases sometimes affect women and men in radically different ways has increasingly led health researchers to include women in their studies (McDonald, 1999). The federal government has established an Office of Research on Women's Health, and the National Institutes of Health (NIH) now requires the inclusion of women in federally funded medical research (National Institutes of Health, 1999). Today, the Food and Drug Administration requires evidence that new drugs are effective and safe for women before it approves them (Legato, 1998). The health issues of ethnic minority women, however, still have not been sufficiently explored.

Unfortunately, gender biases still exist within the health care system, leading to differences in the way health professionals interact with women and men and to differences in the care women and men receive. In this section, we examine issues of gender discrimination in health services.

The Physician-Patient Relationship

Sexism in the physician-patient interaction is well documented. Feminist analysis of the interaction between female patients and male physicians describe it as paternalistic, with women patients treated as subordinates. Male physicians frequently trivialize women's experiences by interrupting female patients and making jokes in response to their concerns. Physicians tend to belittle women's health complaints by attributing them to psychosomatic factors. This stereotype may account for the fact that nearly two-thirds of all tranquilizers, antidepressants, and anti-anxiety drugs are prescribed for women (Pincus et al., 1998).

Sexist views of women are perpetuated in medical journal advertisements as well. For example, White males are pictured as physicians while nearly 70 percent of their patients are portrayed as women. Female patients also are much more likely than male patients to be shown nude or provocatively dressed (Hawkins & Aber, 1993).

A nationwide survey of women's health by the Commonwealth Fund (1993a) found that women are much more likely than men to change physicians because they are dissatisfied (41 percent of women compared to 27 percent of men). The major reason women change their doctors is communication problems. One-fourth of women (compared to 12 percent of men) report that they are "talked down to" or treated like a child by a physician. Moreover, 17 percent of women (compared to 7 percent of men) have been told that a medical condition they felt they had was "all in their head." Female physicians are more likely than male physicians to establish interpersonal rapport with their patients and to provide them with information (Cooper-Patrick et al., 1999; Roter & Hall, 1997; Zuger, 1998b). They also spend more time with their patients and tend to focus on them as people rather than on the procedures they need (Steinhauer, 1999). Patients of female physicians report a greater willingness to reveal personal problems such as family violence or sexual abuse (Clancy, 2000). Not surprisingly, both women and men express more satisfaction with women physicians (Bertakis, 1998; Delgado, López-Fernández, & deDios Luna, 1993).

Women of Color and Health Care

Women of color are more likely than White women to be poor and uninsured (Kilborn, 1999b; Kuttner, 1999). For example, about 42 percent of Latinas, 23 percent of Black women, and 13 percent of White women are uninsured (Commonwealth Fund, 1998b). Because the lack of health insurance often is a financial barrier to seeking preventive health care, women of color are less likely to get the medical care they need (Centers for Disease Control, 1998c). Furthermore, experiences with prejudice or culturally inappropriate health care cause many women of color to visit the doctor less frequently than White women do (National Institutes of Health, 1999). In 1993, 17 percent of Latinas, 14 percent of Black women, and 13 percent of White women did not receive needed medical care. In addition, 27 percent of Latinas have no regular source of care (such as a physician), compared with 22 percent of Black and 21 percent of White women. Moreover, women of color have lower rates than White women for many preventive health services—Pap smear, pelvic exam, clinical breast exam, and complete physical exam—(Blackman, Bennett, & Miller, 1999; Commonwealth Fund, 1993a).

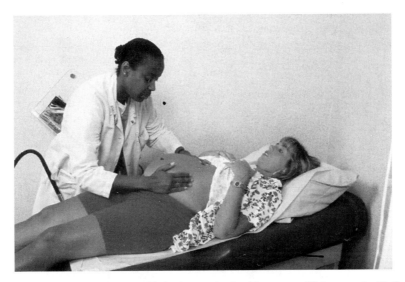

Female physicians are more likely than male physicians to establish rapport with their patients.

SUMMARY

1. The external female organs (vulva) consist of the mons pubis, labia majora, labia minora, and clitoris.

2. The four phases of the sexual response cycle are excitement, plateau, orgasm, and resolution. Women, unlike men, are capable of multiple orgasms. Orgasms resulting from clitoral and vaginal orgasm are physiologically the same.

3. The sexual double standard condones casual sexual activity for men but not for women. Women have less permissive attitudes toward sexual behavior than men do. There is considerable consistency between sexual attitudes and sexual behaviors. Women are less likely than men are to masturbate and to have extramarital sex.

4. The four major types of sexual dysfunction are sexual desire disorders, sexual arousal disorders, orgasm disorders, and sexual pain disorders.

5. Homophobia is pervasive in North American society. It is most commonly found in older, less-educated, politically conservative males, who hold traditional gender-related attitudes and fundamentalist religious beliefs.

6. Lesbians and heterosexual women are equally well adjusted. Lesbian and gay teens, however, face special challenges.

7. Complex interactions among genetic, hormonal, and environmental factors appear to determine sexual orientation.

8. Physical effects of pregnancy include nausea, fatigue, and weight gain. Women have both positive and negative feelings during pregnancy. People may react negatively to a pregnant woman.

9. The three stages of childbirth are dilation of the cervix, birth of the baby, and expulsion of the placenta. The cesarean delivery rate is high in the United States, but is dropping. Family-centered approaches to childbearing include the Lamaze method, home birth, birthing rooms and centers, and use of midwives. Many women experience maternity blues shortly after birth. A small percentage experience the more severe postpartum depression.

10. About 10 percent of infertile women have tried reproductive technologies, such as in vitro fertilization, frozen embryos, donor eggs, and surrogate motherhood.

11. Women are less likely to be heavy drinkers than men are, but binge drinking is increasing in college women. Women's alcoholism starts later than men's, progresses more quickly, and is diagnosed at a more advanced stage. Drinking in pregnancy can cause FAS or FAE. Women are less likely than men to use most illegal drugs.

12. Women increasingly are being included in health research. Unfortunately, they continue to be treated with less respect within the health care system and receive poorer medical care than men. Women of color are more likely than White women to be poor, uninsured, and to lack medical care.

WHAT DO YOU THINK?

1. Why do you think women generally have less permissive attitudes toward sexual behavior than men do?

2. Why do you think that our society holds negative attitudes toward gays and lesbians?

3. Who is the baby's real mother—the surrogate mother who conceived and carried the baby or the wife of the man who fathers the baby? Is motherhood primarily a biological or psychological concept? Explain your answers.

IF YOU WANT TO LEARN MORE

Blechman, E., & Brownell, K. (Eds.). (1998). *Behavioral medicine and women: A comprehensive handbook*. New York: Guilford.

Boston Women's Health Book Collective (1998). *Our bodies, ourselves for the new century: A book by and for women*. New York: Touchstone.

Gallant, S. J., Keita, G. P., & Royak-Schaler, R. (Eds.). (1997). *Health care for women: Psychological, social and behavioral influences*. Washington, DC: American Psychological Association.

Jansen, R. (1997). *Overcoming infertility: A compassionate resource for getting pregnant*. New York: W. H. Freeman.

Ponticelli, C. M. (Ed.) (1997). *Gateways to improving lesbian health and health care*. Binghamton, NY: Haworth.

Strong, B., DeVault, C., & Sayad, B. W. (1999). *Human sexuality: Diversity in contemporary America* (3rd ed.). Mountain View, CA: Mayfield.

Travis, C. B., & White, J. W. (Eds.). (1999). *Sexuality, society, and feminism*. Washington, DC: American Psychological Association.

8 Young Adulthood

Education and Employment

KEY TERMS

chilly classroom climate   achievement attributions
achievement motivation   self-efficacy
fear of success

You might recall from the opening vignette in Chapter 1 that when I (Judith) applied to graduate school in 1965 I was told that several psychology departments had higher admission standards for female than male graduate program applicants. The unofficial explanation for this discriminatory practice was the need to limit the number of female students because they were more likely than men to drop out of lengthy graduate programs for marriage and/or childrearing. This view that women would or should not pursue both family life and a career was evident, also, in the comment of a male graduate student who asked why I wanted a doctorate given that, at some point, I hoped to get married and have children. Similarly, when I later did get married, a female cousin suggested I now give up my Ph.D. aspirations and become a mother instead.

This perceived dichotomy between career and family might seem strange today. The cultural milieu has changed dramatically since the 1960s. Today the majority of college women want to have it all—both a career and a family (e.g., Davey, 1998; Schroeder, Blood, & Maluso, 1992). On the other hand, some women today experience conflicts between their career goals and their commitment to relationships. As educational psychologist Sally Reis states: "Smart ambitious young women come to college with all these big plans, but then they fall in love, and all their priorities change. It happens during college, in terms of the workload they take. It happens as they graduate, and many put off graduate school to feed the relationship. Maybe they work to support their partners, or they follow them. Then once they have children, those original goals are pushed far off" (D'Arcy, 1998, p. F3).

In this chapter we set the framework for understanding women's experiences in the workplace (see Chapters 10 and 14). First, we examine females' educational attainment and college experiences. Next we explore young women's expectations about both their careers and the coordination of their careers with family life. Then we turn to influences on their career choices, issues related to career counseling, and gender bias in the hiring process.

Women's Educational Expectations and Values

As we discuss in more detail in Chapter 10, men earn higher salaries than women (U.S. Bureau of Labor Statistics, 1999d) and occupy higher positions in their jobs (e.g., Dobrzynski, 1996). Further, more men than women achieve prominence in domains such as politics, literature, and entertainment. It has been suggested that these discrepancies indicate that women, compared to men, place a lower value on education and have a lower level of educational attainment. Does the evidence support these assumptions?

To answer the question about value, Barbara Banks (1995) examined females' and males' reasons for seeking a bachelor's degree. Her results showed that female and male respondents placed a similar value on college education and reported similar explanations for desiring a degree. Commonly, they mentioned enjoyment, determination, and skill, as well as career plans, occupational prestige, and financial rewards. Furthermore, in a study of Black and White college students, Lawrence Ganong and his colleagues (Ganong, Coleman, Thompson, & Goodwin-Watkins, 1996) found no differences between women and men in their expectations about the level of education they will achieve and the likelihood they will be professionally successful. Thus, the evidence indicates that women and men have similar educational expectations. Now we turn to their actual educational experiences.

Women's Educational Experiences

Educational Attainment

Approximately 83 percent of both females and males graduate from high school and until recently, men earned the majority of higher education degrees (U.S. Bureau of the Census, 1999c). However, women's participation in higher education now surpasses men's, and there is evidence that college women obtain higher grades than college men (Betz, 1994).

One way to look at gender differences in higher education attainment is to compare the percentage of traditional-college-age women who complete at least four years of college education with their male counterparts. As can be seen in Table 8.1, among Blacks, Latinas/os, and Whites in the 25 to 29-year-old age group, the percentage of women with at least four years of college is higher than the corresponding percentage of men.

Another way to look at gender and educational attainment is to determine the percentage of degrees awarded to women versus those awarded to men. Table 8.2 presents these data and indicates that, within each ethnic group, women obtain the majority of associate's and bachelor's degrees. Similarly, with the exception of Asian Americans, women are granted more than half of all master's degrees. However, men continue to complete the most advanced levels of education. Among Asian Americans, Latinas/os, and Whites, women earn less than half of all doctoral degrees and women in all ethnic groups except Blacks earn a minority of the professional (e.g., medical, dental, law) degrees. However, even these advanced levels of education have experienced a dramatic change in the participation of women. For example, in 1965 women obtained only 11 percent of doc-

TABLE 8.1   Percent of Persons Ages 25–29 Who Completed Four Years or More of College, by Ethnicity and Gender, 1998

Gender	Ethnicity		
	Blacks	**Latinas/os**	**Whites**
Females	17%	11.0%	30.0%
Males	14%	9.5%	26.5%

Source: ACE Fact Sheet on Higher Education, January 1999, presented in *Higher Education and National Affairs* (1999).

toral and 3 percent of professional degrees (U.S. Bureau of the Census, 1999c), compared to the 1996 figures of 40 percent and 42 percent, respectively. Furthermore, projections indicate that women will earn 50 percent of all Ph.D.'s in the year 2006 (U.S. Department of Education, National Center for Educational Statistics, 1996).

This high level of educational attainment by women is, unfortunately, more true of able-bodied women than of women with disabilities. Women with disabilities also have less education than men with disabilities (Fulton & Sabornie, 1994). and are less likely than these groups to graduate from high school or attend college (Hanna & Rogovsky, 1991). Furthermore, they are less likely than males with disabilities to receive occupationally oriented vocational training that can provide them with the skills needed in the job market (Wagner, 1992).

TABLE 8.2   Degrees Conferred by Ethnicity and Gender, 1995–1996

Type of Degree	Ethnicity									
	Asian Americans		**Blacks**		**Latinas/os**		**Native Americans**		**Whites**	
	women	men	women	men	women	men	women	men	women	men
Associate's	56%	44%	66%	34%	59%	41%	64%	36%	60%	40%
Bachelor's	52%	48%	64%	36%	57%	43%	59%	41%	55%	45%
Master's	49%	51%	68%	32%	60%	40%	61%	39%	58%	42%
Doctorate	36%	64%	55%	45%	49%	51%	50%	50%	46%	54%
Professional	47%	53%	58%	42%	44%	56%	45%	55%	40%	60%

Source: U. S. Department of Higher Education, presented in The Chronicle of Higher Education, (1998).

Campus Climate

Although women comprise slightly more than half of the undergraduate population, the campus climate—that is, the social and academic atmosphere on campus—is not as comfortable for women and other less powerful groups of students as it is for White men (Ponterotto, 1990). In one study, approximately one-third of the female undergraduate respondents, compared to only one-tenth of the male undergraduates, reported experiencing demeaning, intimidating, or hostile behavior related to their gender from other students, faculty members, and/or administrators (Sands, 1998).

The more negative campus climate experienced by women can be compounded for ethnic minority women, lesbian and bisexual women, and women with disabilities. What is the nature of the discomfort or exclusion experienced by these students? Socially, this can include blatant sexist, racist, homophobic, and other prejudicial acts, such as placing signs that bar members of certain groups on residence hall room doors. Alternatively, it can involve subtle insensitivity to the feelings of women and other oppressed groups, as might be reflected in a "joke" about women's bodies. Because the campus climate can have a profound and lasting impact on students' education and lives, we turn to a more detailed examination of this issue.

Instructors' Behaviors.   In 1982 Roberta Hall and Bernice Sandler contended that college faculty engage in unfair treatment of female students. This behavior is generally inadvertent, but can produce a **chilly classroom climate**, that is, *an atmosphere that negatively affects women's feelings of confidence and worth.*

To what extent does the chilly climate characterize college campuses today? It is not easy to answer this question because it can be difficult to evaluate the gender fairness of faculty-student interactions. Many behaviors, such as eye contact, questions and answers, smiles, positive reinforcement, and lecture content, contribute to the atmosphere in the classroom and to each student's own feeling of comfort and involvement. Although some overt behaviors, such as sexist jokes, might be conspicuous to some students, other more subtle acts, such as eye contact with some students more than others, might be harder to identify or criticize.

Perhaps because of the difficulty of measuring these types of behaviors, findings are not consistent across studies. Whereas Mary Crawford and Margo MacLeod (1990) reported no difference between women's and men's perceptions of the participatory climate established by professors, Lilia Cortina and her colleagues (Cortina, Swan, & Fitzgerald, 1995) found that women more than men felt mistreated by professors. Also, they expressed greater agreement with statements such as "Some instructors tend to ignore women students" (p. 6).

Another indication of a chilly climate for women is the presence of sexist behavior in the classroom. For example, one of Crawford and MacLeod's (1990) male respondents stated: "The instructor sometimes uses language (especially in the course of an anecdote or humorous example) that is sexist. Also, on occasion he treats female students in a manner that shows he feels females are less able to learn the material than males" (p. 119). Other evidence of sexism in the classroom comes from a study by Sharon Shepela and Laurie Levesque (1998). In this investigation more female (55 percent) than male (44 percent) university students reported that they had experienced sexist language, comments, or jokes from faculty members.

A chilly climate is not limited to undergraduate women. Female graduate students, also, confront problems on campus. As one example, Daniel Myers and Kimberly Dugan (1996) examined graduate students in psychology, sociology, and political science and found that a sizeable minority of both female and male students reported that their professors engaged in a variety of behaviors, reflecting a bias against women. These included rarely included material related to female authors or theorists, rarely using examples containing women, and seldom portraying women in nontraditional roles. In addition, approximately three-quarters of these students reported their professors used the male generic pronouns at least some of the time. Not surprisingly, these sexist behaviors on the part of faculty had negative effects on the students. In fact, although more female than male students felt bothered by and angry about their professors' behaviors, a majority of the students of both genders experienced these negative feelings.

The chilly climate for women is another reflection of the gender inequality of power in North American society. Sexist treatment of women on campus, whether blatant or subtle, reflects a greater value attached to males and serves to maintain an already existing power imbalance. Furthermore, this treatment reinforces constructions of women as inferior or less valued than men.

Single-Gender Institutions Compared to Mixed-Gender Institutions.   Given the existence of an uncomfortable climate on some mixed-gender campuses, it is not surprising that several scholars (e.g., Astin, 1993; Ledman, Miller, & Brown, 1995; Tidball, Smith, Tidball, & Wolf-Wendel, 1999) point to the benefits of single-gender campus environments for women's academic and personal development. They note, for example, that graduates of women's colleges compared to female graduates of mixed-gender institutions report greater satisfaction with all aspects of their college experience except the social life (Tidball et al., 1999). Furthermore, M. Elizabeth Tidball and her colleagues contend that women's colleges provide more leadership opportunities for women students, higher achievement expectations for them, and more female role models within the faculty and administration. As an example of the last point, they note that as of 1997, 87 percent of the presidents of women's colleges were women compared to 16 percent of the presidents of mixed-gender institutions.

Other benefits of women's colleges are the greater likelihood of close student-faculty relations and more female class participation (Trice, in Gose, 1995). Also, examination of postcollege achievement shows that women's-college graduates are more likely than graduates of mixed-gender institutions to have majored in male-dominated fields, such as the physical sciences and mathematics (Tidball et al., 1999), to reach high levels of achievement in their careers (e.g., Ledman et al., 1995), and, for both reasons, to earn higher salaries (Tidball et al., 1999).

Some educators believe that women's colleges provide a more effective educational environment for female students.

Despite these positive findings, it should be noted that not all researchers have drawn the same conclusions about the value of women's colleges. Faye Crosby (in Gose, 1995), for example, claims that studies of women's colleges have been flawed in that many have compared students at highly selective women's institutions to students at less selective mixed-gender colleges and universities. Furthermore, some students believe that isolation from men in the college environment can hinder academic development (Gose, 1995).

The Academic Environment for Women of Color.   Not surprisingly, the climate for female students of color on college campuses is more problematic than that for White women. Some women of color experience primarily White campuses as unwelcoming and unsupportive (Rocha-Singh, in Hackett, Betz, Casas, & Rocha-Singh, 1992), and Black students who drop out of college are more likely than Whites are to attribute their college withdrawal to frustration and a lack of social and academic support (Allen, 1996). Moreover, some of the students examined in the previously discussed Crawford and MacLeod study (1990) reported instances of racist comments on the part of their professors. For example, one female student stated that a male "instructor makes sexual and racial 'jokes' and comments that I find offensive. There has {sic} been repeated allusions to the 'stupidity' of Native Americans and the inferiority of cultures other than his own" (Crawford & MacLeod, 1990, p. 119).

Claude Steele (1997a) suggests another problem that can seriously affect the college experience of women of color. He contends that Black female and male students' awareness of the societal devaluation of Black people creates a pressure to defy negative stereotypes about ability. According to Steele, in addition to concern about their own academic performance, Black students must deal with the possibility that their poor performance will confirm the inferiority of their ethnic group in the eyes of others. In an attempt to feel less vulnerable, they may choose not to identify with achievement; that is, with the importance of achievement to self-esteem. Furthermore, although Steele focused on Blacks, the same argument might apply to other ethnic minority students.

Another problem for some students of color is that they experience the individualism prominent in academic life as inconsistent with the collectivistic values of their culture. The individualistic value system of Western, primarily North American and European, cultures emphasizes personal achievement, independence, and individual uniqueness. The collectivistic values of Asian, Native American, and Latina/o cultures, on the other hand, stress the importance of the group, including the family, the community, and the work team. This competitive style of college education can be uncomfortable for these students. Native Americans, for example, have difficulties adjusting to the competitive climate (Canabal, 1995; LaFromboise, Heyle, & Ozer, 1990). As one Native American senior stated, "When I was a child I was taught certain things, don't stand up to your elders, don't question authority, life is precious, the earth is precious, take it slowly, enjoy it. And then you go to college and you learn all these other things and it never fits" (Canabal, 1995, p. 456).

Although the clash between individualism and collectivism can produce conflicts for some students, Angela Lew and her colleagues (Lew, Allen, Papouchis, & Ritzler, 1998) note that these value systems can coexist. These researchers examined the achievement values of Asian American students and found that some students adopted both sets of values; they saw individual achievement as a way to fulfill both personal and family goals. Lew and her associates suggest that internalization of both value systems can be helpful because it enables the student to function effectively in two different cultural environments. Of course, it may be easier for some students than for others to integrate and reconcile the disparate sets of values.

The Academic Environment for Working-Class and Poor Women.   Research on working class and poor women's adjustment to college life is very limited. However, one interesting study (LePage-Lees, 1997) of high-achieving women from working-class or poor families found that many of these women felt they had to hide their backgrounds from others in order to achieve during undergraduate and graduate school. Also, they felt their socioeconomic backgrounds put them at an intellectual disadvantage, that other students were better prepared and more intelligent. One respondent said: "People now think the only issue is ethnicity, and I still think that economic level is an important issue regardless of ethnicity. Economics doesn't explain everything but it explains a lot" (p. 380).

Another type of poor woman with special needs and difficulties in the college environment is the woman on welfare. Those who decide to better themselves and their children through their own higher education anticipate and receive many benefits. However, they also face numerous obstacles. As Erika Kates (1996) points out, these women must cope with child care responsibilities, transportation costs, reductions in federal assistance, and other difficulties. On the positive side, higher education is an important route to a reasonable income and greatly reduces reliance on federal aid (e.g., Kates, 1996). Illustrative of the obstacles and benefits is the story of Pauline. This Black woman attended college at age 17 but dropped out after falling in love. She then had three children and was deserted by the children's father. Once her youngest child was in child care, she began community college as a welfare recipient. While in school she faced several obstacles; however, Pauline successfully completed college and then found a job in her town's school department (Kates, p. 550).

Women with Disabilities and the Physical Campus Environment.   The institutional environment we have discussed thus far focuses on behavioral issues. Women with disabilities face not only these issues, but also must cope with challenges in bureaucracy and the physical environment. According to Lillian Holcomb and Carol Giesen (1995), women with disabilities on college campuses face obstacles such as inadequate funding of support services, old buildings not designed to be barrier-free, and campus grounds made inaccessible by not having curb cuts. In addition, they can experience increased burdens in the time needed to engage in activities such as traversing an inaccessible campus or using Braille to study.

Use the survey in Get Involved 8.1 to assess the academic climate on your campus.

GET INVOLVED **8.1**

Does Your Campus Have a Hospitable Environment for Women?

Answer the questions presented below, and ask three female students the same questions. If possible, select interviewees who vary in ethnicity, physical ability/disability, and/or sexual orientation.

1. Did you ever hear a professor tell a sexist or racist "joke" during or outside of class?
2. Did you ever hear a professor make a derogatory comment about a student's gender, ethnicity, physical disability, or sexual orientation? If yes, indicate the nature of that comment.

3. Do you feel that women and men receive the same degree of encouragement and support from their instructors? If not, explain.
4. Do you feel that women of color, women with disabilities, and lesbian women receive the same degree of encouragement and support from their instructors as White, able-bodied, heterosexual women? If not, explain.
5. Do you experience any conflict between the values that characterize this campus and the values of your cultural group?

(continued on p. 197)

What Does It Mean?

1. Did you find any evidence of sexism, racism, bias against women with disabilities, and/or prejudice against lesbians? If yes, do you think these experiences affect the educational process of students who are targets of these behaviors? Why or why not?

2. Did you find any evidence of differential support for students because of their gender, ethnicity, physical ability, or sexual preference? If yes, do you think this can affect the educational process of students who receive less support? Why or why not?

3. Did you note any conflict between campus and cultural values? If yes, is this conflict similar to that described in the text?

Sexual Harassment of Students.   Another factor that can contribute to a negative campus climate for female students is sexual harassment. Interestingly, although sexual harassment is legally defined (see Chapter 6), there are wide variations in people's conceptions of harassing behaviors. Before reading this section, perform the exercise in Get Involved 8.2 to examine the behaviors and situations that you and your acquaintances classify as sexual harassment.

The research shows there are gender differences in the tendency to classify behaviors, such as those listed in Get Involved 8.2, as sexual harassment. Women perceive more situations as harassing than men do (e.g., Katz, Hannon, & Whitten, 1996; LaRocca & Kromrey, 1999; Marks & Nelson, 1993). Also, whether an individual perceives a behavior as harassment depends, in part, on the role relationship between the harasser and target. When students are targets, behaviors are more likely to be seen as harassment if they are performed by a professor than by another student (e.g., Bursik, 1992; Pryor & Day, 1988). Did you find these two patterns when you performed the Get Involved activity?

The questions in Get Involved 8.2. raise two controversial issues related to power. One is whether sexual harassment by definition is restricted to behaviors performed by a person with authority (e.g., a professor) over a target (e.g., a student). The other is whether a sexual relationship between individuals who differ in power, as in a professor-student relationship, constitutes sexual harassment even if the student gives consent. In the first issue, the crucial criteria are (1) the target perceives the behavior as unwelcome; and (2) the unwanted behavior creates a hostile or offensive atmosphere for the target. If these conditions are met, it is not necessary that the perpetrator have power over the target (e.g., Fitzgerald, 1996).

There is greater controversy surrounding the second issue. Does a romantic relationship between a professor and student constitute sexual harassment, regardless of whether it is consensual? One view is that as long as the student is an adult and expresses willingness to enter into a sexual relationship with a professor, that relationship is acceptable. However, this view is not shared by all.

GET INVOLVED **8.2**

What Constitutes Sexual Harassment on Campus?

Check each of the following items that you believe is a form of sexual harassment if expe- rienced by a student. Then ask one female student and one male student to do the same.

____ comments on personal appearance by a student

____ comments on personal appearance by a professor

____ unwanted letters or phone calls of a sexual nature from a student

____ unwanted letters or phone calls of a sexual nature from a faculty member

____ unwanted sexually suggestive looks or gestures from a student

____ unwanted sexually suggestive looks or gestures from a faculty member

____ offensive sexually suggestive stories or jokes told by a student

____ offensive sexually suggestive stories or jokes told by a faculty member

____ inappropriate staring by a student that causes discomfort

____ inappropriate staring by a faculty member that causes discomfort

____ unwelcome seductive remarks or questions by a student

____ unwelcome seductive remarks or questions by a faculty member

____ unwanted pressure for dates by a student

____ unwanted pressure for dates by a faculty member

____ unwanted leaning, touching, or pinching by a student

____ unwanted leaning, touching, or pinching by a faculty member

____ unwanted pressure for sexual favors by a student

____ unwanted pressure for sexual favors by a faculty member

____ nonforced sexual relationship between a faculty member and a student

____ nonforced sexual relationship between two students

____ forced sexual intercourse by a student

____ forced sexual intercourse by a faculty member

Based on Shepela & Levesque, (1998).

What Does It Mean?

Separately sum the behaviors you classified as sexual harassment if performed by a student and those seen as sexual harassment if performed by a faculty member. Do the same for each of your respondents.

1. Compare the number of behaviors seen as harassment if performed by a student to those if performed by a faculty member. Is there a difference in your answers or in those of your respondents? Try to explain any differences you might have found. Are these differences consistent with the evidence presented in the text?

2. Is there any difference in the number of behaviors seen as harassment by your female and male respondents? If yes, does it match the difference presented in the text? What do you think can explain this?

Another perspective is that whenever a formal power differential between two people is present, a sexual relationship involves some degree of coercion because the target is not really in a position to freely consent or refuse. In other words, this viewpoint contends that *any* sexual behavior directed at a student by a professor is harassment (Fitzgerald, 1996).

Incidence of Sexual Harassment.   The frequency of sexual harassment on college campuses is hard to assess for a number of reasons. Not only do few students submit formal complaints of harassment, but surveys of harassment experiences show that the incidence varies from campus to campus. Also, the frequency of sexual harassment, varies according to the specific type of unwanted conduct and the nature of the power relationship between the harasser and the target. Despite these problems, however, we can draw certain conclusions from recent surveys. First, although some studies report no gender difference in students' experience of sexual harassment (e.g., Shepela & Levesque, 1998), most indicate that females are more likely than males to be sexually harassed (e.g., Cochran, Frazier, & Olson, 1997; Malovich & Stake, 1990). Second, women are more likely to experience subtle forms of harassment, such as unwanted sexually suggestive jokes or body language than they are to encounter more blatant forms, such as unwanted sexual advances, although the latter do occur (e.g., Brooks & Perot, 1991; Cortina, Swan, Fitzgerald, & Waldo, 1998; Shepela & Levesque, 1998). Third, students are more likely to experience unwanted sexual behaviors by other students than by faculty members (e.g., Cochran et al., 1997; Shepela & Levesque, 1998).

One illustrative study (Shepela & Levesque, 1998) found that approximately three-quarters of the women sampled at a New England university experienced unwanted sexually suggestive jokes from other students, and one-third received inappropriate comments about their appearance or their body language from faculty. When questioned about sexual advances 40 percent of students reported unwanted physical contact from another student, and 20 percent experienced this conduct from a faculty member.

What about the experiences of doubly oppressed groups of women? There is some evidence that lesbian and bisexual women are more likely than heterosexual women to experience sexual harassment (Cortina et al.,1998). Incidence rates are highest for Black and Latina women, lowest for Asian American women, and in between these extremes for White women (Cortina et al., 1998).

College women have reported harassment not only in the academic environment but within collegiate sports. Since the passage of Title IX in 1972 (see Chapter 4), women's participation in athletics has grown significantly. However, this growth has been accompanied by a dramatic decrease—from 90 percent to 47 percent—in the percentage of female coaches of women's sports (Finn, 1999). Unfortunately, female student athletes are also experiencing a rising incidence of harassment by their coaches (Heywood, 1999; Finn, 1999).

Responses to Sexual Harassment.   What do people do when they experience sexual harassment? Caroline Cochran and her associates (Cochran et al., 1997) examined the responses of students, faculty, and staff to unwanted sexual attention. Their results showed that the most common response was to ignore the behavior (60 percent). Avoidance of the harasser and talking to others about the harassment were other common reactions. Only 5 percent filed a formal complaint. Researchers are concerned (e.g., Brooks & Perot, 1991; Bursik, 1992) that this lack of formal response—due, in part, to misconceptions about what constitutes, harassment—hinders attempts to reduce its frequency. Unless people acknowledge that harassment occurs, it is difficult to take action against it. See Table 8.3 for recommended ways to reduce sexual harassment on campus.

Women's Work-Related Goals

Career Aspirations

In an address to a women's-college graduating class, feminist author Gloria Steinem noted a major difference between the goals of her generation of female college graduates in 1956 and those of young women today: "I thought we had to marry what we wished to become. Now you are becoming the men you once would have wanted to marry" (in Goldberg, 1999b, G3). This quote suggests that college women are striving for—and attaining—high achievement goals; they are no longer living vicariously through the accomplishments of their husbands. In the following discussion we see that women do, indeed, have high aspirations. However, we also see that there continue to be some differences in the career goals of females and males.

Research has shown that high school girls and boys aspire to careers that are relatively similar in prestige (Betz, 1994) and that college women are as motivated as college men to pursue a career and to achieve success in their field (Ganong, Coleman, Thompson, & Goodwin-Watkins, 1996; Morinaga, Frieze, & Ferligoj,

TABLE 8.3   Recommended Procedures for Reducing Sexual Harassment on Campus

Michele Paludi (1996) has made several recommendations about actions students can take to ensure that a campus environment is free of sexual harassment. Here is a sampling of these.

1. Find out whether your campus has policies and procedures for dealing with sexual harassment.
2. Establish a Sexual Harassment Awareness Week during which campuswide activities related to sexual harassment take place. These events can include activities such as plays, movies, and group discussions about sexual harassment.
3. Establish a peer educators program. Peer educators can provide both information to the campus community at large and support to those who have been harassed.

Based on Paludi, (1996).

LEARN ABOUT THE RESEARCH **8.**1

The Illinois Valedictorian Project

The Illinois Valedictorian Project followed a group of 46 female and 35 male 1981 high school valedictorians as they proceeded through college and into adulthood. Seventy-two were White, five were Black, three were Mexican American, and one was Asian American. While in high school, 21 percent of the women and 23 percent of the men rated their intelligence as far above average. After two years of college, however, only 4 percent of the women but 22 percent of the men said their intelligence was far above average. By senior year, not a single woman reported her intelligence in this category, while 25 percent of men did. Yet the women had maintained a grade-point average of 3.7 on a 4-point scale throughout college, compared to 3.6 for the men. By the sophomore year in college, women had lowered their

career aspirations more than men. The women expressed persistent concerns about combining career and family, leading six of them to abandon plans for medical school. Two-thirds of the women valedictorians, but none of the men, planned to reduce or interrupt their employment to accommodate childrearing.

In 1991, six years after college graduation, both women and men were pursuing careers in the male-dominated fields of science, business, and the professions of law, medicine, and college teaching. However, a substantial proportion of women (but not men) were employed in the traditionally female fields of precollege teaching, nursing, physical therapy, and secretarial work. A few were employed in nonprofessional positions or were working as full-time homemakers.

Source: Arnold, (1993)

What Does It Mean?

1. What do you think accounts for the drop in women's intellectual self-confidence during the college years?
2. What can be done to prevent this from happening?

3. Why do you think some women maintained their original career aspirations while others changed or reduced theirs?

1993). However, during college, women sometimes lower their aspirations, majoring in less prestigious career fields and, therefore, eventually ending up in lower-level careers (Farmer, 1997; Leung, Conoley, & Scheel, 1994). See Learn about the Research 8.1 to read more about this phenomenon.

As we saw in Chapter 4, girls are socialized toward communal behaviors. Consistent with the social construction of women as caring and nurturant, they are encouraged to develop a strong interest in and concern for other people . Not surprisingly, women tend to earn degrees in academic disciplines that focus on people, such as education and psychology. (See Table 8.4.)

TABLE 8.4   Degrees Conferred in Selected Fields by Gender, 1995–1996

Educational Field	Type of Degree					
	Bachelor's		Master's		Doctorate	
	women	men	women	men	women	men
Biological/life sciences	53%	47%	53%	47%	42%	58%
Business & marketing	49%	51%	38%	62%	29%	71%
Communications	59%	41%	63%	37%	46%	54%
Computer & information sciences	28%	72%	27%	73%	15%	85%
Education	75%	25%	76%	24%	62%	38%
Engineering	18%	82%	17%	83%	13%	87%
English	66%	34%	64%	36%	62%	38%
Mathematics	46%	54%	39%	61%	20%	80%
Physical sciences	36%	64%	32%	68%	23%	77%
Psychology	73%	27%	72%	28%	66%	34%

Source: U. S. Department of Higher Education, presented in *The Chronicle of Higher Education* (1998).

The data in Table 8.4 also show that few female students aspire toward computer and information sciences, engineering, and physical sciences. In 1997, the only leading technology institution in which more than 28 percent of the undergraduates were women was the Massachusetts Institute of Technology , with 40 percent (Selingo, 1998). Several scholars (e.g., Hackett et al., 1992) believe this is unfortunate, given the high status and high pay associated with these careers.

What might account for women's continued low participation rate in these academic areas? As we saw in Chapter 6, the possibility that females are less mathematically or scientifically skilled can be ruled out; however, parents and teachers are less likely to encourage the development of math or science skills in girls than boys. Furthermore, females are less likely than males are to enroll in science or advanced math courses and are less confident of their math ability. These factors can play an important role in steering women away from careers in the sciences.

Interestingly, even those college women who venture into the sciences and engineering are more likely than college men are to drop out of these programs. For example, among biology majors with A averages, 80 percent of the women, compared to 60 percent of the men, change majors. In the physical sciences, these percentages are 69 percent of women versus only 1 percent of men, and in engineering 71 percent compared to 18 percent (Selingo, 1998). The dearth of female role models (e.g., Zirkel, 1996, in Zirkel, 1997) and insufficient faculty encouragement (e.g., Betz, in Hackett et al., 1992; Hackett et al., 1992) may be other factors that contribute to these unfortunate trends for women in the sciences. Female graduate students in science and engineering have even been told by male professors that women do not belong in those fields (e.g., Hollenshead, Wenzel, Lazarus, & Nair, 1996).

Do women who differ in ability/disability or ethnicity have different career aspirations? There tend to be few differences between the career interests of college women with disabilities and those without disabilities (DeLoach, 1989) or between the career aspirations of White, Black, and Latina college women. (Arbona & Novy, 1991; Murrell, Frieze, & Frost, 1991). Although college women in these ethnic groups do not differ much in terms of aspiration level or specific career choice, there is some evidence that Black college women expect success more than White women do (Ganong et al., 1996). One study comparing Asian American and White college women found that the former are more likely than the latter to aspire toward male-dominated and more prestigious occupations (Leung, Ivey, & Suzuki, 1994). One explanation, according to S. Alvin Leung and his colleagues, may be that although Asian culture values traditional gender roles, Asian American families encourage their daughters to pursue nontraditional prestigious occupations associated with social recognition (Leung et al., 1994).

Work-Family Expectations

Most college women desire marriage, motherhood, and a career (e.g., Schroeder, Blood, & Maluso, 1992; Spade & Reese, 1991), and young adulthood is a time when women think about scheduling these roles. If you are interested in both employment and parenthood, have you considered how you would like to combine these? Research shows that most college women want to work before they have children and interrupt their employment for some period during their children's early years (e.g., Bridges & Etaugh, 1996; Schroeder et al., 1992). According to Karen Schroeder and her colleagues (1992), the female respondents they examined during the late 1980s had not considered potential situations, such as divorce or financial demands, that might require adjustments in their preferred patterns. Perhaps this is slowly changing. In Learn about the Research 8.2, a recent study (Davey, 1998) found more realistic expectations on the part of young women. Still, Lesley Novack and David Novack (1996) believe that "modern women receive mixed messages. They are told that they can be whatever they want to be, while they are simultaneously sent subliminal messages espousing the virtues of traditional femininity which may lead to lower self-esteem and less satisfaction" (p. 73). This can create conflicts for women as they try to reconcile their career goals with their perceived family obligations.

Although most college women want to interrupt their employment for child-drearing, Black college women want to discontinue their employment for a shorter period of time than do White women (e.g., Bridges & Etaugh, 1996; Murrell et al., 1991). For example, Judith and Claire found that Blacks want to return to employment when their first child was approximately $2\frac{1}{2}$ years old, whereas Whites want to delay employment until their child was approximately 4 (Bridges & Etaugh, 1996).

LEARN ABOUT THE RESEARCH **8.2**

Young Women's Preferred and Expected Patterns of Employment and Childrearing

E. Heather Davey assessed the views of 54 White Canadian college and non-college young women in the 1990s. She asked questions about their preferences and expectations for combining employment and childrearing. Respondents were given a choice of three options: leaving work before the birth of the first child, working until the birth of the first child and again after the youngest child reaches an age deemed appropriate by the respondent, or working continuously, with maternity leaves as needed.

She found that only a small minority either wanted or expected to leave employ-ment prior to motherhood. Interestingly, there was a difference in preferences for and expectations about the other two options. Although 50 percent desired a long interruption of employment, only 29 percent expected to follow this pattern. Furthermore, whereas 46 percent wanted to work continuously, taking maternity leaves as needed, 59 percent expected to do so. The researcher points out that this last pattern more realistically conforms to current employment trends and she suggests that the more realistic expectations shown by these young women reflect their increasing awareness of economic realities.

Source: E. H. Davey (1998).

What Does It Mean?

1. What are other explanations of the discrepancies between these women's preferred and expected employment-childrearing patterns?
2. Do you think there are differences between young men's preferred and expected employment-fatherhood patterns? Explain your answer.
3. Do you think it would be useful for young women thinking about their careers to have realistic expectations about how they will combine the employment and parenting roles? If yes, what can be done to guide young women toward a realistic appraisal of their future roles?

Why do Black college women prefer an earlier return to employment after childbirth than do White college women? One possible explanation is that White college women are more likely than their Black peers to believe that maternal employment is harmful to young children (Bridges & Etaugh, 1996; Murrell et al., 1991). For example, Whites are more likely than Blacks to think that continuous maternal employment produces negative outcomes for children, such as low self-esteem, feelings of neglect, and lack of maternal guidance (Bridges & Etaugh, 1996). The more positive attitude of young Black women might, in turn, be related to Black women's long history of combining the roles of mother and provider (e.g., Gump, 1980). Further, there is some evidence that more college-educated Black women are encouraged by their parents to consider an occupation as essential to success than their White counterparts are (Higginbotham & Weber, 1996), indicating that employment might be a more integral aspect of Blacks' construction of women's roles than it is for Whites.

Some educated women of color face another role-related problem: finding an appropriate mate within one's ethnic group. Evidence suggests that uneducated Native American men are reluctant to marry college-educated women (LaFromboise et al., 1990) and that Native American college women fear they will not be able to marry native men (Medicine, 1988). Similarly, Black college women express the desire to marry a person of equal or greater educational and occupational status. However, because, they earn a higher proportion of every type of higher education degree than do Black men, they may be frustrated in this desire (Ganong et al., 1996).

Salary Expectations

Consistent with a tendency to have less prestigious career aspirations than men do, women expect lower salaries in their jobs. Kenneth Sumner and Theresa Brown (1996) asked college students in a variety of majors to give their salary expectations. Students' assessments of their entry-level incomes were closely linked to their college major. Given that salaries tend to be higher in male-dominated occupations than in female-dominated occupations (AFL-CIO & The Institute for Women's Policy Research, 1999), it is not surprising that students in male-dominated majors expected higher starting salaries than did those in female-dominated fields. However, when asked to indicate their peak salaries, students revealed large gender differences regardless of major. Males in male-dominated, female-dominated, and gender-neutral majors expected higher peak salaries than women in these fields did. For example, in male-dominated majors, males expected an average $67,500 whereas females expected only $48,600, and in female-dominated majors, the averages were $55,600 and $34,000, respectively.

What can explain women's lower salary expectations? One possibility is that women know that females earn lower salaries than males and base their own salary expectations accordingly. (e.g., Brown & Allgeier, 1995). Another possibility is that women might lower their salary expectations because they place importance on making accommodations in their job to fulfill their family obligations (Jackson, Gardner, & Sullivan, 1992). A third possibility is that women, compared to men, believe they deserve less (e.g., Major, 1989) (see Chapter 10).

Influences on Women's Achievement Level and Career Decisions

Although this chapter focuses on education and employment, it is essential to note that achievement goals can be satisfied in diverse ways. Raising a well-adjusted and loving child, providing emotional and physical support to a spouse recovering from a stroke, and helping the homeless in one's community are only a few of the numerous forms achievement can take that are independent of education and occupation. However, despite the diversity of achievement directions, researchers have focused primarily on the traditional areas of education and occupation, and if we define achievement in this manner, it appears that women have achieved less than men. As discussed earlier in this chapter, more men than women attain the highest educational levels, aspire to the most prestigious careers, and hold high positions within their occupational fields. Now we examine possible internal and external influences on women's achievement level and occupational decisions. First, we look at their orientation to achievement in general and the personality traits that might be related to their career decision making. Then, we explore social and cultural influences on young women's educational and occupational pursuits.

Orientation to Achievement

For several decades psychologists attempted to explain women's lower achievement compared to men's as due, in part, to their orientation to achievement.

Achievement Motivation.   One explanation was that females' **achievement motivation**; that is, their *need to excel*, was lower than males'. However, in their narrative review of the research on achievement motivation, Martha Mednick and Veronica Thomas (1993) noted that the early studies on which this conclusion was based used male-biased procedures. For example, investigators (e.g., McClelland, 1961) used achievement-arousing instructions to intensify respondents' achievement motivation. This procedure was effective in increasing men's but not women's achievement drive. What was overlooked, however, was that females showed a higher level of achievement motivation than did males when a different procedure was used, that is, when these achievement-arousing instructions were not given (Stewart & Chester, 1982).

At the present time, researchers believe that women and men are similarly motivated to achieve. However, females' and males' social construction of gender, including their beliefs about gender-appropriate interests and family responsibilities, can shape the direction of their achievement goals. That is, both women and men acquire gender-related expectations and values from families, peers, teachers, and other socializing forces. Through this socialization, they learn not only the importance of achievement but also the "appropriate" direction it should take for their gender. For example, women tend to learn that, if they have children, they should be the primary caregiver. Consequently, women might adjust their achievement goals in order to meet this expectation.

Fear of Success.   Another view of women's lower achievement in comparison to men's came from Matina Horner (1972), who proposed that women want to achieve but have a *fear of success*; that is, *a motive to avoid situations of high achievement.* Horner contended that women were concerned about the negative social consequences that can result from success, especially social rejection and loss of femininity. This suggestion might seem strange as you read this book at the beginning of the twenty-first century. However, in the 1970s and 1980s the idea was embraced by many scholars who performed investigations of females' fear of success.

To support her concept of the fear of success, Horner devised the following statement: *After first-term finals, Anne/John finds herself/himself at the top of her/his medical school class.* She asked female respondents to write a paragraph about Anne and male respondents to write about John. Approximately two-thirds of the females wrote negative stories involving themes such as Anne's physical unattractiveness, her inability to have romantic relationships, rejection by her peers, and her decision to transfer into a less prestigious occupation. Most of the stories told by the males about John, on the other hand, reflected positive outcomes.

Although Horner believed these results indicated a motive to avoid success on the part of women, subsequent research points to a different conclusion. It now appears that these stories did not reflect women's fear of high-achieving situations in general but rather their awareness of negative consequences that can occur when individuals violate gender stereotypes. Medicine, especially in the 1970s when Horner performed her study, was strongly dominated by men. Thus, it is likely that females' negative stories reflected their concern about the problems individuals face in gender-atypical occupations, rather than their desire to avoid a high level of achievement. A subsequent study showed that both women and men wrote negative stories about a successful woman in medicine *and* a successful man in nursing (Cherry & Deaux, 1978). Furthermore, considerable evidence now shows that women and men do not differ in their fear of success (e.g., Mednick & Thomas, 1993; Paludi, 1998); therefore, psychologists today do not believe that women's lower level of educational or occupational achievement can be accounted for by their fear of success.

Achievement Attributions.   A third explanation given for gender differences in levels of achievement is that females and males make different **achievement attributions**; that is, *explanations about their good and poor performance.* Researchers assume that internal attributions (ability and effort) for success and external attributions (task difficulty and luck) for failure help protect one's self-esteem (e.g., Mullen & Riordan, 1988). That is, taking responsibility for good performance (e.g., "I did well on the test because I know the material") but attributing poor performance to external factors (e.g., "I failed the test because it was unfair") enables a person to maintain a good self-image. The reverse pattern, on the other hand, can lead to self-blame and an unwillingness to persevere in a challenging situation (Dweck, Goetz, & Strauss, 1980).

Early studies suggested that females and males made different attributions about their performance. Researchers concluded that males were more likely to attribute their success to ability and females were more likely to attribute their success to luck (e.g., Simon & Feather, 1973). However, a more recent meta-analysis (Whitley, McHugh, & Frieze, 1986) and narrative review of the research (Mednick & Thomas, 1993) showed that gender differences in attributions of performance are actually very small and are associated with the type of performance situation. For example, there is evidence that in male-stereotyped domains, such as mathematics, males attribute success to ability more than do females, but in female-stereotyped domains, such as languages or English, the reverse pattern occurs (Beyer, 1997; Birenbaum & Kraemer, 1995).

Achievement Self-Confidence.   Another internal barrier that has been used to explain women's lower achievement in comparison to men's is their lower self-confidence. Many studies show that males are more self-confident in academic situations than females are. For example, when asked to estimate their grades on exams or on cognitive tasks, females generally give lower estimates than males (Beyer, 1999; Mednick & Thomas, 1993). Also, Mary Crawford and Margo MacLeod (1990) found that when asked why they don't participate in class discussion, college women's responses reflected questionable confidence in their abilities, such as "might appear unintelligent in the eyes of other students" and "ideas are not well enough formulated" (p. 116). Men's reasons, on the other hand, focused on external factors, as in "have not done the assigned reading" or participation might "negatively affect [their] grade" (p. 116). Other research suggests that even among high achievers in the sciences, fewer women than men believe their scientific ability to be above average (Cross, n.d.; Sonnert & Holton, 1996).

Despite the evidence for gender differences in achievement self-confidence, females do not show lower levels of confidence in all situations. Studies indicate that females' confidence is lower than males', especially in male-linked tasks (e.g., Beyer, 1990; Beyer & Bowden, 1997) and when performance estimates are made publicly rather than privately (e.g., Daubman, Heatherington, & Ahn, 1992). Also, research by Kimberly Daubman and her colleagues (Daubman & Sigall, 1997; Heatherington et al., 1993) suggests that, at least in some situations, what appears to be lower self-confidence (e.g., publicly predicting lower grades for oneself) might really reflect women's desire to be liked or to protect others from negative feelings about themselves.

Conclusion.   Early conclusions that women have lower aspirations than men because they are not as highly motivated to excel and because they fear the negative consequences of success have not been supported. Although some evidence exists for gender differences in achievement attributions and self-confidence, these differences are not observed in all situations. Furthermore, as is the case with all types of psychological gender differences, the differences are small and do not apply to all females and males. Thus, most social scientists point to other factors to help explain different career aspirations and attainment levels of women and men.

Personality Characteristics

Are personality characteristics related to women's career aspirations? In their narrative review of research related to women's occupational choices, Susan Phillips and Anne Imhoff (1997) note that women who aspire toward male-dominated careers tend to be high in agency and to have nontraditional gender attitudes. This suggests that they have a more flexible construction of gender; in other words, their assumptions of what women can or should do is not rooted in traditional expectations. In addition, there is some evidence that pursuit of a nontraditional skilled labor job is related to a woman's positive sense of her identity (Greene & Stitt-Gohdes, 1997). That is, women who choose a career in the trades tend to have high self-esteem and to be unconcerned about other people's judgments of their career choice.

Another personality factor related to career choice is the individual's **self-efficacy**; that is, *the belief that one can successfully perform the tasks involved in a particular domain*. Individuals with high self-efficacy for a particular field are more likely to aspire toward that field as a career (Jozefowicz, Barber, & Eccles, in Eccles, 1994). For example, overall, females tend to have lower mathematics self-efficacy than males (e.g., Betz & Hackett, 1997) (see Chapter 6), but women who select careers in science or engineering have high self-efficacy for mathematics (e.g., Farmer, 1997) as well as low levels of math anxiety (Chipman, Krantz, & Silver, 1992). Furthermore, females, compared to males, have higher self-efficacy for health-related professions and female-dominated skilled labor occupations. These gender differences, in turn, correspond to differences in occupational choice.

Sexual Orientation

For some lesbians, the career decision-making process can be complicated by sexual identity formation. Many lesbians become aware of their sexual identity during late adolescence or adulthood, at the same time that they are selecting a career. According to Ruth Fassinger (1995), the overlap of these two processes can complicate career development. Lesbians might put career selection on hold as they explore their sexuality and intimate relationships. Also, as a result of coming out, many lose the family support that can be beneficial to the career-selection process.

In addition, lesbians' career choices might be directly affected by their perception of the occupational climate for lesbians and gays. Whereas some lesbians select occupations they perceive as employing large numbers of lesbians and gays in order to experience an environment in which there is safety in numbers (Morrow, Gore, & Campbell, 1996), lesbians who are closeted or anxious about their sexual identity might steer away from these occupations (Fassinger, 1995). Also, occupations that are oppressive for lesbians and gays (e.g., teaching and the military) might not be considered, thus narrowing lesbians' field of choices (Fassinger, 1995).

On the positive side, Ruth Fassinger (1995) notes that lesbians tend to be less traditional in their attitudes about gender than are heterosexual women. Consequently, they tend to consider a broader range of occupational options including those that are nontraditional for women.

Social and Cultural Factors

Although some internal characteristics are related to individuals' career choices, career decisions are made within a sociocultural context in which the attitudes of significant people and the values of one's culture contribute to career selection as well. Not surprisingly, support and encouragement from the family are very important. High-achieving Black and White women report receiving considerable family support for pursuing their highly prestigious careers and being strongly influenced by their families' values regarding the benefits of hard work (Richie et al., 1997; Simpson, 1996). For example, a Black female attorney whose father was a janitor, commented: "They wanted me to have a better life than they had. For all of us. And that's why they emphasized education and emphasized working relationships and how you get along with people and that kind of thing" (Higginbotham & Weber, 1996, p. 135). Similarly, women who select a career in the trades point to the importance of their families' and teachers' support for their nontraditional choice (Greene & Stitt-Gohdes, 1997).

In addition to social support, cultural values play a role in women's career development. According to McAdoo (in Higginbotham & Weber, 1996), many Black families believe that college education and professional attainment are family, as well as individual, goals. Moreover, there is evidence that high-achieving Black women who move up from their lower social-class backgrounds feel a sense of obligation to their families. In one study (Higginbotham & Weber, 1996), almost twice as many Black as White upwardly mobile women expressed this sense of familial debt. A Black occupational therapist said: "I know the struggle that my parents have had to get me where I am. I know the energy they no longer have to put into the rest of the family even though they want to put it there and they're willing. I feel it is my responsibility to give back some of that energy they have given to me. It's self-directed, not required" (p. 139). In contrast, here is the comment of a White library administrator: "Growing up in a family, I don't think it's that kind of a relationship—that's their job. I feel that way with my son. I certainly love him but I don't want him ever to be in a position to think he owes me" (p. 140).

Another cultural value shown by Black women is their concern for their communities. Many successful Black women are committed to ending both sexism and racism in the workplace and community (Richie et al., 1997) and see their achievements as ways of uplifting Black people (Collins, in Higginbotham & Weber, 1996). As expressed by a high-ranking Black female city official: "Because I have more opportunities, I've got an obligation to give more back and to set a positive example for Black people and especially for Black women. I think we've got to do a tremendous job in building self-esteem and giving people the desire to achieve" (Higginbotham & Weber, 1996, p. 142).

Many high-achieving Latina women receive family encouragement and have a supportive social network (Kitano, 1998). However, some experience a conflict between traditional cultural values that guide them toward family-oriented goals and other socialization factors that encourage high educational and career attainment (Kitano, 1998).

Conflicting values are evident, also, in the experiences of educated Native American women. Although research on Native Americans' achievement goals is sparse, it suggests that family and community members often try to discourage native women from attending college. Consequently, those that persist in seeking a college education feel they are going against their culture (Kidwell, in LaFromboise et al., 1990).

To more directly learn about family and cultural influences on women's career goals, perform the interviews described in Get Involved 8.3.

In addition to cultural variations across ethnic groups, values associated with social class can influence career decisions. According to Constance Flanagan (1993), working-class families tend to hold more traditional gender attitudes than do middle-class families and to see less value in academic achievement. Thus, lower-class women who have an interest in school and a willingness to be independent of their families are likely to become invested in employment immediately after high school whereas middle-class women with those attributes are apt to seek higher education.

GET INVOLVED **8.3**

Family and Cultural Values about Education and Career Goals

Interview two female students who vary in ethnicity. Select your interviewees from any two of the following ethnic groups: Asian American, Black, Latina, Native American, and White. Inform them you are exploring connections between women's family and cultural values and their education and career goals.

First, ask each respondent to indicate her college major, career goal, and expected educational attainment (i.e., highest educational degree). Second, ask her to evaluate the degree to which her family's values support her specific educational aspirations and career goals. Third, ask her to evaluate the degree to which her specific educational aspirations and career goals were influenced by her ethnic or national cultural values.

What Does It Mean?

1. Did you find any differences among respondents in the extent to which they received support from their families? If yes, refer to information presented in the text or to your own ideas and explain these differences.

2. Did your respondents report that their goals were influenced by their values? Is the information you obtained consistent with the material presented in the text? If not, explain the discrepancies.

Job-Related Characteristics

Individuals vary in the benefits they want from working in a particular job, and these benefits can play a role in guiding career selections. Research shows that college women and men strongly value interesting or challenging work, a sense of personal fulfillment, a good salary, and an opportunity for advancement (Bridges, 1989; Browne, 1997); thus, both women and men would like careers that lead to these outcomes. However, college females and males differ in the importance they attach to other job-related attributes, which can account for some of the differences in their occupational choices.

Consistent with the traditional social construction of gender, women more than men want to help others through their job (Bridges, 1989; Jozefowicz, Barber, & Eccles, in Eccles, Barber, & Jozefowicz, 1999; Morinaga et al., 1993). Thus, it is not surprising that women are more likely than men to aspire toward careers that involve caring for others. In one study of women and men with an interest in science or technology, almost half of the women but only 4 percent of the men pursued helping sciences, such as nursing and health technician careers (Crabtree, Farmer, Anderson, & Wardrop, in Farmer, 1997). Furthermore, although there are gender differences in preferred job-related attributes, variations exist within each gender. Therefore, it is not surprising that females who aspire toward non-health-related sciences have an extremely low interest in helping or working with people (Eccles et al., 1999).

Another gender difference in job values is the greater emphasis college women place on flexibility of working hours and ease of job reentry after breaks for childrearing (Bridges, 1989; Redman, Saltman, Straton, & Young, 1994). For example, one reason women give for choosing nursing as their career is the flexibility of hours, which facilitates the coordination of employment and childrearing (Farmer, 1997).

What accounts for women's and men's differential emphasis on flexibility? This gender difference probably reflects college women's continuing belief that mothers should stay home and care for infants (Novack & Novack, 1996), a value that is expressed during many stages of females' lives. For example, high school girls report a greater willingness than boys do to make occupational sacrifices for their future families (Jozefowicz et al., in Eccles et al., 1999). Furthermore, a sample of rural women indicated that throughout their lives they assessed occupational alternatives according to how easily a particular job would accommodate their role as mother (Vermeulen & Minor, 1998).

Career Counseling

Historically, several problems have been related to career counseling for women. Until the 1960s women were largely invisible to career counselors, because women were not viewed as pursuing careers. In the 1960s and 1970s, career counselors tended to steer girls and women toward traditionally female careers and away from male-dominated occupations (Betz, 1994). Although there is now greater acceptance of females' pursuit of traditionally male occupations, counselors, teachers, and parents continue to show gender-biased attitudes toward career choices (Betz, 1994; Phillips & Imhoff, 1997). Many girls are discouraged from taking advanced math and science courses or from choosing high-status professions dominated by males. Gender bias also permeates vocational interest inventories and aptitude testing (Betz, 1994).

What can career counselors do to support, encourage, and expand the career aspirations of young women? Nancy Betz (1994) suggests that counselors should help women in the following four areas: (1) dealing with realistic concerns, such as managing career and family roles; (2) obtaining necessary education, training, and job-hunting skills; (3) locating support systems, mentors, and role models; and (4) dealing with discrimination and sexual harassment, if necessary. Cherry Greene and Wanda Stitt-Gohdes (1997) recommend that career counselors increase young women's awareness of career opportunities in the traditionally male skilled trades. Career counselors also need to become aware and understand that a woman's views and needs are shaped by culture, ethnicity, and disability (Bingham & Ward, 1994; Brooks & Forrest, 1994; Hopkins-Best, Winamaki, & Yurcisin, 1985). For example, Carla McCowan and Reginald Alston (1998) suggest that counselors working with Black college women set up mentoring programs that pair them with Black professionals in order to expose them to information about career options and to help them develop realistic goals.

Entering the Workplace

We have seen that a variety of personal, social, and cultural factors contribute to women's career choices. Once they have made their selections, do women run into any obstacles in the workplace? In Chapter 10 we look into women's experiences on the job, but we begin here by examining the hiring process.

Antidiscrimination laws prohibit the use of gender (as well as ethnicity, national origin, or age) as a determinant in hiring or in other employment decisions. However, gender-based and other forms of discrimination still occur (Reskin & Padavic, 1994). Both gender and ethnic discrimination in hiring have been reported in studies of Black and White female professionals and managers (Richie et al., 1997; Weber & Higginbotham, 1997). Also, discrimination on the basis of sexual orientation is legal in most workplaces (Ragins, 1998), and studies report considerable hiring discrimination against lesbians and gays (Badgett, Donnelly, & Kibbe, in Ragins, 1998), especially among those who reveal their sexual orientation (Croteau & Von Destinon, 1994). Furthermore, a meta-analysis of research on gender bias in the evaluation of women's work provided some evidence for discrimination against female job applicants (Swim, Borgida, Maruyama, & Myers, 1989). As an example of this bias, Rhea Steinpreis and her colleagues (1999) sent a job resume to psychology academicians and asked them to evaluate the quality of the work-related experience that was presented. Although the resumes were identical, those who were told the applicant was a man evaluated the credentials more positively and indicated a greater willingness to hire than did their colleagues who were told the applicant was a woman.

Although gender discrimination can influence hiring decisions, it does not occur in all situations. Not surprisingly, one factor that influences evaluation of job applicants is the gender-dominance of the occupation. There is evidence of a pro-male bias for male-dominated jobs (Fritzsche & Mayfield, 1997; Glick, 1991; Marlowe, Schneider, & Nelson, 1996) and a pro-female bias for female-dominated jobs (Glick, 1991; McRae, 1994).

Another factor that affects bias in hiring decisions is the amount of information provided about the applicant. Gender bias is most likely when little information is provided about the candidate's qualifications (Tosi & Einbender, 1985). In this situation, the gender of the applicant is highly salient and can give rise to stereotyped impressions and decisions. On the other hand, when the candidate's academic and employment records are presented, her or his qualifications strongly influence the evaluator's impression (Foschi, Sigerson, & Lebesis, 1995; Olian, Schwab, & Haberfeld, 1988).

SUMMARY

1. College women and men have similar expectations about their educational attainment. However, women obtain the majority of associate's and bachelor's degrees and men earn the majority of doctorates and professional degrees.

2. The campus climate can be problematic for some women. There are concerns of sexism in the classroom and a sizeable minority of women perceive the academic environment as hostile and demeaning. Further, women of color, poor women, and women with disabilities experience additional problems on campus.

3. More female than male students experience sexual harassment on campus. Most incidents involve subtle forms of harassment and most are perpetrated by other students. However, a minority of students do experience harassment by a faculty member, and some students are targets of severe harassment.

4. College women generally aspire to less prestigious careers than college men. Few women decide to enter the physical sciences or engineering.

5. Most college women envision their futures as involving employment, marriage, and motherhood. However, many plan to interrupt their employment for childrearing.

6. Women have lower salary expectations compared to men. Possible explanations are women's knowledge that females earn less than males, their willingness to accommodate their jobs to their family life, and their belief that they deserve less.

7. There is no evidence that women have less motivation to achieve than men do or that women stay away from high-achieving situations because they fear success. Also, gender differences in attributions for performance are very small and are more likely to occur when making attributions

in gender-stereotypic domains. There is evidence that women display less self-confidence than men, especially in relation to male-linked tasks and when estimates of one's performance are made publicly.

8. Women with nontraditional gender-related traits or attitudes are more likely to aspire toward male-dominated careers. Women's feelings of self-efficacy for particular occupational fields are related to their aspirations for those fields.

9. Lesbians' career decisions are sometimes influenced by their perceptions of the job climate for lesbians and gays.

10. Family support and family and cultural values can influence women's career development.

11. Job-related characteristics highly important to both college females and males include interesting work, a good salary, and an opportunity for advancement. Characteristics valued more strongly by females than males are helping others and scheduling flexibility. Both of these attributes are more likely to be found in female-dominated occupations than in male-dominated occupations.

12. Several scholars have made recommendations about ways to expand the career goals of young women.

13. There is some evidence of gender discrimination in hiring, especially when the job is dominated by the other gender.

WHAT DO YOU THINK?

1. Discuss your opinion about the relative advantages and disadvantages for women of attending a women's college versus a mixed-gender college.

2. This chapter discusses several issues faced by women of color and women with disabilities on college campuses. Select two or three of these concerns and suggest institutional procedures that could address these problems and improve the academic climate for these groups.

3. Which of the recommended procedures for reducing sexual harassment on campus do you think would be particularly effective at your school? Can you think of other activities that might be beneficial on your campus?

4. Many women who desire both employment and motherhood want to interrupt their employment for childrearing. What can explain this? As part of your answer,

discuss the extent to which gender differences in power (see Chapter 1) and gender socialization (see Chapter 4) explain this.

5. The traditional conception of achievement as the attainment of high academic and occupational success has been criticized as reflecting the achievement domains of men more than of women. Do you agree with this criticism? Give a rationale for your answer. Also, if you agree, suggest other indices of success that would more accurately reflect women's achievement.

6. Discuss the relationship between gender stereotypes and common career choices of young women and men. Also, several changes have occurred in the educational attainment and career aspirations of women over time. Show how a changing social construction of gender has contributed to this.

IF YOU WANT TO LEARN MORE

Farmer, H. S. (Ed.). (1997). *Diversity and women's career development: From adolescence to adulthood.* Thousand Oaks, CA: Sage.

Gmelch, S. B. (1998). *Gender on campus: Issues for college women.* New Brunswick, NJ: Rutgers.

Josselson, R. (1996). *Revising herself: The story of women's identity from college to midlife.* New York: Oxford University Press.

Katz, M. (1996). *The gender bias prevention book: Helping girls and women to have satisfying lives and careers.* Northvale, NJ: Jason Aronson Inc.

Paludi, M. A. (1996). *Sexual harassment on college campuses: Abusing the ivory power.* Albany, NY: SUNY.

9

Middle Adulthood

Physical Development and Health

Physical Development

    Physical Appearance

    The Double Standard of Aging

Reproductive Functioning and Sexuality

    Menopause

    Osteoporosis

    Hormone Replacement

       Therapy

    Sexuality

Physical Health

    Heart Disease

    Breast Cancer

    Reproductive System Disorders

Mental Health and Illness

    Depression

    Anxiety Disorders

    Diagnosis and Treatment of

       Psychological Disorders

KEY TERMS

double standard of aging	phyto-estrogens	fibroid embolization
late mid-life astonishment	vaginitis	endometriosis
menopause	mammogram	cervix
perimenopause	radical mastectomy	Pap smear
hot flashes	modified radical mastectomy	specific phobia
osteoporosis	simple mastectomy	agoraphobia
raloxifene	lumpectomy	nonsexist therapy
hormone replacement	fibroid tumors	feminist therapy
therapy	hysterectomy	

Sometimes I think of the alternatives to looking older, and I wonder what it would be like to have my face frozen the way it was in my thirties, and I think—that would be ridiculous! That's not me, that doesn't reflect the years I've lived and all the things I've experienced. I don't want to deny my experiences and I feel that if I dislike my aging looks I'm denying all the wonderful parts of my life. I don't want to do that (a forty-eight year-old woman, in Doress-Worters & Siegal, 1994, p. 39).

Women in middle-age—the years from about 40 to 65—experience a number of physical changes. Physical appearance begins to show signs of aging, and illness or chronic health conditions may emerge. But it is a mistake simply to equate getting older with getting sicker. Throughout life, women can take active steps to maintain good health and decrease the impact of any health problems that develop. Lifestyle choices involving good nutrition, physical activity, and not smoking can prevent and even reverse many of the changes of aging once thought to be inevitable (Boston Women's Health Book Collective, 1998). In this chapter, we first examine changes in physical appearance, then turn to reproductive functioning and sexuality and finally, explore physical and mental health.

Physical Development

Physical appearance begins to change in midlife. People often react negatively to the changes that occur in women's appearance.

Physical Appearance

The early aging changes that occur in the skin and hair are probably the most visible. The hair becomes thinner and grayer. The skin becomes drier and, along with the muscles, blood vessels, and other tissues, begins to lose its elasticity. These changes result in wrinkling of the skin, especially on the face, neck, and hands. Lines appear on the forehead as a result of smiling, frowning, and other facial expressions repeated over time. The skin begins to sag and lose color, and age spots appear. Skin which has been exposed to the sun is affected most, especially in light-skinned individuals (Whitbourne, 1998). Fat becomes redistributed, decreasing in the face, legs, thighs, and lower arms, and increasing in the abdomen, buttocks, and upper arms. Starting at about age 40, the discs between the spinal vertebrae begin to compress, resulting in an eventual loss in height of 1 to 2 inches. Bones begin to lose density and, in later years, become more brittle and porous, especially in women, sometimes resulting in the collapse of vertebrae and the appearance of a so-called "dowager's hump" in the upper back (Etaugh, 1993b).

The Double Standard of Aging

How do women react to these changes in physical appearance? In our youth-oriented society, the prospect of getting older generally is not relished by either sex. *For women, however, the stigma of aging is greater than it is for men.* Susan Sontag (1979) has labeled this phenomenon the **double standard of aging**. The same gray hair and wrinkles that enhance the perceived status and attractiveness of an older man appear to diminish the attractiveness and desirability of an older woman. Some researchers account for this by noting that a woman's most socially valued qualities—her ability to provide sex and bear children—are associated with the physical beauty and fertility of youth. As she ages, she is seen as less attractive because her years of social usefulness as childbearer are behind her. Men, on the other hand, are seen as possessing qualities—competence, autonomy, and power—which are not associated with youth but rather increase with age (Wilcox, 1997). Middle-aged women themselves are more critical of the appearance of middle-aged women than are women of other age groups, or men. Midlife women, compared with midlife men, are more dissatisfied with their bodies (Janelli, 1993), and use more age concealment techniques (M. B. Harris, 1994). Concern with one's appearance is important to both Black and White women in middle age (Etaugh, 1993b).

The more a woman has based her sense of identity and self-esteem upon her youthful physical attractiveness, the greater the impact of midlife changes in her physical appearance. Sarah Pearlman (1993) describes a transition experienced by women in their fifties which she calls **late mid-life astonishment**, *a sudden* *awareness of diminished physical/sexual attractiveness which produces feelings of amazement and despair.*

It may be difficult for women to feel comfortable about aging in a culture where older women do not often appear in the media, and those who do are praised for their youthful appearance and for hiding the signs of aging. Editors of women's magazines admit that signs of age are removed from photographs through computer imaging, making 60-year-old women look 45. *Lear's*, a magazine for midlife women, rarely shows photographs of gray-haired women (Chrisler & Ghiz, 1993). In addition, as we saw in Chapter 2, a study of popular films from the 1940s to the 1980s found that "older" women (over age 35) were underrepresented compared with older men. Furthermore, they were portrayed as more unfriendly, unintelligent, unattractive, and wicked (Bazzini et al., 1997). Attractive actresses such as Meryl Streep, Jessica Lange, and Diane Keaton are labeled "geezer babes"—and thus too old for romantic parts—while male actors many years their senior are paired with young ingenues (Haskell, 1998). Along the same lines, an analysis of Academy Award nominations for Best Actress and Best Actor from 1927–28 to 1990 found that women over the age of 39 accounted for only 27 percent of all winners for Best Actress, while men in the same age category won 67 percent of Best Actor awards (Markson & Taylor, 1993). Before going further, try Get Involved 9.1.

GET INVOLVED 9.1
Media Ads and the Double Standard of Aging

Look though newspapers and magazines for advertisements that include middle-aged adults. Then answer the following questions:

1. Are there differences in the appearance of the women and the men?

2. Do females and males advertise different products?
3. In ads with two or more people, what is the role of the principal male or female in relationship to others?

Source: Berk, Wholeben, & Bouchey, 1998.

What Does It Mean?

1. Do the ads show evidence of a double standard of aging?
2. What can advertisers do to minimize differences in the portrayal of middle-aged females and males?

3. How do media images of mid-life adults help shape our perceptions of middle-aged women and men?

Reproductive Functioning and Sexuality

Declining estrogen production results in menopause, one of the most obvious biological events of women's middle years, and also hastens the development of osteoporosis. Hormone replacement therapy can alleviate many menopausal changes. Some physical changes accompanying menopause may affect sexual activity, but women can continue to enjoy sex throughout their lives.

Menopause

Menopause is the *cessation of menstrual periods for a full year*. For most American women, menopause occurs between the ages of 45 and 55, with an average age of 51 (American College of Obstetricians and Gynecologists, 1997b; Dennerstein & Shelley, 1998). Menopause occurs because of the decline in the number of ovarian follicles (egg-producing cells), which results in a decline in the production of both estrogen and progesterone. Some estrogen continues to be produced after menopause by the adrenal glands and fat cells. *The months and years preceding the beginning of menopause*, known as the **perimenopause**, are marked by increasing irregularity of the menstrual cycle and variations in the amount of menstrual flow.

Physical Symptoms. The frequency and severity of physical symptoms associated with menopause vary widely among women. In fact, the *only* symptom that all menopausal women experience is the end of menstruation. In North America, the most commonly reported symptom is the **hot flash**, *a sudden feeling of heat that spreads over the body, and that is often accompanied by perspiration*. Surveys report that anywhere between 50 and 80 percent of menopausal women experience hot flashes. For example, in a recent nationwide study of adult Americans by the MacArthur Foundation, half of the postmenopausal women surveyed reported having no hot flashes at all, only 25 percent said they had hot flashes at least once a week, and 13 percent reported having them almost daily (Goode, 1999a). Some women will have hot flashes for a few months, some for a few years, and many not at all. Hot flashes at night (sometimes called *"night sweats"*) can interfere with the sleep of some menopausal women, but most women find hot flashes to be only a minor inconvenience (American College of Obstetricians and Gynecologists, 1997b; Boston Women's Health Book Collective, 1998).

Loss of estrogen also causes thinning of the vaginal lining and decreased vaginal lubrication. These changes can lead to painful sexual intercourse and also make the vagina more prone to infection. Headaches, fatigue, joint and muscle pains, and tingling sensations are other physical symptoms that occasionally are reported (American College of Obstetricians and Gynecologists, 1997b; Baram, 1997; Begley, 1999). Women who smoke or who are less physically active have more of all types of symptoms (DeAngelis, 1997b). The most serious physical consequence of menopause, osteoporosis, is discussed later in this chapter.

Women in different ethnic and cultural groups vary in the kinds and degree of menopausal symptoms they report. Black women are more likely than other ethnic groups to experience hot flashes and vaginal dryness, but are least likely to have headaches, joint pains, and sleeping difficulties. Latinas are more apt to report racing heart and urinary leakage. Asian American women experience fewer symptoms than other groups. Women in non-Western cultures often have menopausal experiences very different from those reported by Western women, indicating that menopausal symptoms are at least in part socially constructed. For example, women of high social castes in India report very few negative symptoms, and hot flashes are virtually unknown among Mayan women (Feldman, 2000). Similarly, Japanese women are much less likely than American and Canadian women to report hot flashes (Lock, 1993).

Psychological Reactions.   It is popularly believed that menopausal women are more likely to display such psychological symptoms as depression, irritability, or mood swings. There is no evidence, however, that these or other psychological symptoms are more prevalent among menopausal women (Morse, 1997; Nicol-Smith, 1996). Some women may feel irritable or tired, but these feelings may be linked to disruptions in sleep caused by hot flashes (American College of Obstetricians and Gynecologists, 1997b).

Even if some women do show heightened psychological distress during the menopausal years, this cannot be attributed solely to biological processes. Changes in social roles that occur in midlife (see Chapters 11 and 12) may be largely responsible for increased distress. Women not only are confronting their own aging during this time, but also may be coping with stressful changes in the family: the illness or death of a spouse, divorce, separation, difficult teenagers, children who are preparing to leave home, and/or aging parents who increasingly require care (Gise, 1997).

Attitudes toward Menopause.   Popular images and stereotypes of menopausal women are overwhelmingly negative in North America. Menopause continues to be defined in the medical and psychological literature by a long list of negative symptoms and terms such as "estrogen deprivation" and "total ovarian failure" (Gannon, 1999; Rostosky & Travis, 1996). The popular press reinforces the notion of menopause as a condition of disease and deterioration that requires treatment by drugs (Gannon & Stevens, 1998). Even Gail Sheehy's (1991) best-selling book *The Silent Passage*, which attempts to shatter negative myths about menopause, describes it as a "lonely and emotionally draining experience" (p. 14).

Not surprisingly, women express more positive attitudes toward menopause when it is described as a normal life transition than when it is described as a medical problem (Gannon & Ekstrom, 1993). A woman who expects menopause to be unpleasant is apt to focus on its negative aspects. For example, women with a negative attitude toward menopause are more likely to report vaginal dryness, decreased sexual interest, and negative mood (Collins, 1997).

Most middle-aged American women, however, minimize the significance of menopause. In a classic study, Bernice Neugarten and her colleagues (reported in

Neugarten & Datan, 1974) found that women in their mid-forties to mid-fifties viewed menopause as only a temporary inconvenience. Many looked forward to menopause as marking the end of menstruation and childbearing. More recent research confirms that middle-aged women generally have positive views toward menopause and do not view it as an illness ("Menopause," 1999). In the MacArthur Foundation survey mentioned earlier, the majority of postmenopausal women reported feeling "only relief" when their menstrual periods stopped, while only 2 percent said they experienced "only regret" (Goode, 1999a). Post-menopausal women have more positive attitudes toward menopause than younger middle-aged women, with young women age 35 or less holding the most negative views of all (Gannon & Ekstrom, 1993; Sommer et al., 1999).

Attitudes toward menopause also differ according to a woman's ethnic and cultural background. For example a recent study of over 16,000 Asian American, Black, Latina, and White women found that Black women had the most positive attitudes toward menopause whereas Asian American women who were less acculturated to American society were least positive (Sommer et al., 1999). Across ethnic groups, better-educated women held more positive views.

In some cultures, menopause is an eagerly anticipated event. For example, when high-caste Indian women reach menopause, they are freed from menstrual taboos which restrict their full participation in society (Feldman, 2000). No wonder these women experience few negative menopausal symptoms!

Some intriguing recent research suggests that menopause may actually have evolved as a mechanism to help ensure the survival and success of the human species. For more information, read Learn about the Research 9.1.

Osteoporosis

What is Osteoporosis? **Osteoporosis** is an *excessive loss of bone tissue in older adults which results in the bones becoming thinner, brittle, and more porous.* Osteoporosis affects more than 25 million Americans, 80 percent of them women (Turner, Taylor, & Hunt, 1998). Bone density in women and men increases until age 30 when gradual bone loss begins. The rate of bone loss accelerates sharply for five to seven years after menopause begins, as estrogen levels drop (Levinson & Altkorn, 1998). Each year, more than 1.3 million fractures related to osteoporosis occur in the United States. One-third of women older than 65 will have a fracture of the spine and one-third of the women who live to extreme old age will experience a hip fracture. A woman's risk for hip fracture alone is equal to the *combined* risk of developing breast, uterine, and ovarian cancer. Fractures can be crippling and painful and can cause permanent loss of mobility. Up to 20 percent of patients with a hip fracture die within a year from problems caused by lack of activity, such as blood clots and pneumonia (American College of Obstetricians and Gynecologists, 1997c; Crose, Leventhal, Haug, & Burns, 1997; Greenspan, 1999; Older Women's League, 1995).

LEARN ABOUT THE RESEARCH 9.1
Menopause and the Grandmother Hypothesis

Anthropologist Kristen Hawkes and her colleagues (Hawkes, O'Connell, & Blurton-Jones, 1997), in their studies of the Hadza hunter-gatherers of Northern Tanzania, found that women in their fifties, sixties, seventies, and beyond are the ones who "bring home the bacon" (in this case, the berries and other edible plants). Working for long hours each day, they gather more food than any other members of the group. Nursing Hadza women, unable to provide for their older children while tending their infants, rely not on their mates but on these postmenopausal women relatives—their mothers, aunts, or elder cousins—to make sure that the other children are well fed.

This intriguing finding challenges a long-held belief that menopause is simply an accidental by-product of modern medicine, with most women outliving their childbearing years. According to this view, a woman's contribution to survival of the species ends when she has successfully procreated and reared her children. Postmenopausal women are of little biological use (Angier, 1999a).

But Hawkes and her colleagues propose a Grandmother Hypothesis, arguing that in prehistoric times postmenopausal women helped ensure the survival and fitness of their grandchildren and other young relatives. This,

they say, made possible the colonization of new territory and the success of the human species. The hypothesis lends support to the view that menopause is far from being an accident of modern medicine, but instead is a uniquely human product of Darwinian natural selection.

Female humans are the only primates to experience menopause. Our closest relatives, the great apes, can continue bearing young throughout their lives. But human children take a much longer time to rear than the young of other species. In addition, childbirth can be risky, especially as women get older. Let us assume that in prehistoric times, some women were genetically programmed to cease their childbearing capacity in their late forties or early fifties. These women were spared the risks of later childbirth and the time-consuming burden of continually raising young children. Instead, they were able to invest their energies in helping to ensure the survival of their grandchildren and other young relatives. These descendants in turn passed on the older women's genes to future generations. Those women who were genetically programmed to bear children throughout their lives, however, were less likely to have surviving descendants. Their genes, according to the theory, eventually died out.

What Does It Mean?

1. How could the helping role of grandmothers in prehistoric times lead to the spread of humans around the globe?
2. In what ways are grandmothers of today important in ensuring the well-being of their grandchildren?

3. If the Grandmother Hypothesis were substantiated, would negative views of postmenopausal women be changed? Explain your answer.

Some women are more likely to develop osteoporosis than others. For a list of risk factors, see Table 9.1.

Detection.   Until recently, the first sign of osteoporosis was a bone fracture. Conventional X-rays cannot detect osteoporosis until one-fourth or more of a bone's mineral content is gone. Now, imaging techniques can spot osteoporosis before any bones break (Brody, 1998e; "U.S. Approves Device," 1998). The most sensitive of these bone density tests can detect even a 1 percent loss. Who should take the test? The best candidates are postmenopausal women with one or more of the risk factors listed in Table 9.1, and all women over 65 (S. Williams, 1999). But steps to help prevent or slow bone loss should begin much earlier, in a young woman's reproductive years, while bone growth is still occurring.

Prevention and Treatment.   A look at Table 9.1 indicates some ways to build and keep as much bone as possible. Increasing calcium intake during childhood, adolescence, and young adulthood is a highly effective way of building denser

TABLE 9.1   Risk Factors for Osteoporosis

Biological Factors
- Gender: Women's risk is greater because their bones are smaller and lighter
- Age: After the mid-30s, bone loss begins
- Menopause: Drop in estrogen levels increases bone loss
- Thin, small-framed body
- Blonde, fair-skinned; Northern European ancestry
- Ethnic background: White, Latina, and Asian American women are at higher risk than Black women, who have heavier bone density
- Family history of osteoporosis (older relatives who have had fractures or spinal curvature)

Lifestyle Factors
- Diet low in calcium and vitamin D
- High salt intake, leading to excretion of calcium
- Lack of physical activity
- Alcohol and tobacco use
- Caffeine consumption

Medical Factors
- Removal of ovaries before menopause
- Eating disorders (anorexia or bulimia)
- Certain medications: diuretics ("water pills"), steroids, anticonvulsants
- High blood pressure

Sources: National Osteoporosis Foundation, 2000; Doress-Worters & Siegal, 1994, p. 281; S. Williams, 1999; Cappuccio et al., 1999.

bones. In order to suppress bone loss, the National Institutes of Health recommends consumption of 1,200 to 1,500 milligrams of calcium per day for adolescents and women through age 25, 1,000 milligrams for women 25 to 50 and 1,200 milligrams for postmenopausal women. Low-fat and no-fat milk and dairy products such as skim milk, low-fat cheese, and yogurt are the best sources of calcium. Dark-green leafy vegetables such as kale, collard greens, and turnip greens, and canned fish (sardines and salmon, with the bones) are other good sources (Brody, 1998f).

Most women consume only about half the daily amount of calcium they need. Calcium supplements are good additional sources, especially those containing calcium carbonate, the ingredient found in Tums. The body can absorb up to 600 milligrams of calcium at a time so if a person takes 1,000 to 1,200 milligrams per day, it should be divided into two doses (Greenspan, 1999).

Calcium cannot be absorbed without vitamin D. Many women do not get the 800 international units of vitamin D per day shown to sharply decrease the likelihood of osteoporosis and bone fractures (LeBoff et al., 1999; Utiger, 1998). Milk fortified with vitamin D and sunlight are two of its best sources. As little as 15 minutes per day in the sun helps the body produce Vitamin D (American College of Obstetricians & Gynecologists, 1997c; Brody, 1998f). Still, most adults may need dietary supplements in order to prevent vitamin D deficiency.

Decreasing or eliminating smoking and decreasing consumption of alcohol and caffeine are good not only for strong bones but confer many other health benefits, as we shall see later in the chapter.

Exercise increases bone mass during adolescence and young adulthood and slows bone loss after menopause. The exercise should be weightbearing, such as brisk walking, low-impact aerobics, or lifting weights. Although swimming is a good all-around exercise it is *not* weight bearing, and will do little to strengthen bones. Even everyday activities such as climbing stairs, walking the dog, doing yard work, or playing actively with children can be beneficial. It is never too late to start exercising (see Chapter 13) and a little bit of physical activity is better than none (American College of Obstetricians & Gynecologists, 1997c; Karlsson et al., 2000; O'Neill, 2000; "Prevent Hip Fractures," 1999).

Estrogen helps build and maintain strong bones (Raisz, 1998; S. Williams, 1999). Taking birth control pills (which contain estrogen) during the childbearing years can slow the rate of bone loss. One study found that women who had taken birth control pills had more bone mass than women who had never used them. Hormone replacement therapy increases estrogen levels after menopause. In addition to slowing bone loss, it can actually increase bone mass, even in women who start using it in their sixties (Writing Group for the PEPI Trial, 1996). Estrogen after menopause has been linked to a 90 percent decrease in spinal deformities and a 50 percent decline in hip fractures.

For those women who do not take estrogen, some medications developed in the late 1990s can be of help (Cummings et al., 2000). Fosamax, the brand name for alendronate, has been shown to increase bone mass in the spine and hip by 4 to 7 percent in only 2 years, comparable to the increase produced by estrogen replacement. One 4-year study found that Fosamax decreased the risk of spinal fractures in women with osteoporosis (Cummings et al., 1998). In addition, the medication reduces spinal fractures by nearly 50 percent among healthy thin-boned women. **Raloxifene**, a *synthetic estrogen* marketed as Evista, similarly increases bone density both in healthy postmenopausal women and in those with osteoporosis when taken for 2 to 3 years (Delmas et al., 1997; Ettinger et al., 1999; Walsh et al., 1998). Raloxifene also reduces the risk of spinal fractures by up to 50 percent in women with osteoporosis. It is not, however, as effective as natural estrogen or alendronate in building bone mass. Another drug, calcitonin, inhibits bone loss and increases spinal bone density in individuals who consume high levels of calcium. It is the least powerful of the bone builders, but is offered in an easy-to-take nasal spray known as Miacalcin. Sodium fluoride (the same chemical that protects teeth) also increases bone density and reduces fracture rates (Brody, 1997b), but has yet to be marketed for this use.

Hormone Replacement Therapy

What Is It?   **Hormone replacement therapy** (HRT) is *a medical treatment that replaces hormones whose levels drop after menopause.* Women who have had their uterus removed are advised to take estrogen alone. Most physicians advise women who still have their uterus to take a combination of estrogen and synthetic progesterone (progestin). Because hormone replacement therapy has risks as well as benefits (summarized in Table 9.2), only one in three postmenopausal women have chosen to use it. Usage is even lower among older women. In one recent study, for example only 6 percent of women 65 and older currently were using hormone replacement therapy, and about 19 percent had done so in the past (Rochon & Gurwitz, 1999). Should a woman use HRT after menopause? That decision must be based on each woman's evaluation of the benefits and risks to

TABLE 9.2   Benefits and Risks of Hormone Replacement Therapy

Benefits	Risks/Side Effects
• Ends hot flashes	• Causes breast tenderness in some women
• Relieves vaginal dryness	• May cause menstrual bleeding (when
• Delays bone loss	progesterone is used along with estrogen)
• Increases bone density	• Increases risk of endometrial cancer if
• Decreases risk of heart disease	estrogen is taken without progesterone
• Protects against Alzheimer's disease	• Increases risk of gallbladder surgery
• Decreases risk of colon cancer	• May increase risk of breast cancer after
• May decrease risk of breast cancer	long-term use
when used less than 10 years	

Sources: AARP, © 1992, American Association of Retired Persons. Reprinted with permission; Azar, 1997, Copyrighted 1997 by the American Psychological Association. Adapted by permission.

herself given her personal and family medical history (Brody, 2000b; Commonwealth Fund, 1998b; "Menopause," 1999).

Benefits.   Hormone replacement therapy relieves the symptoms of low estrogen: hot flashes and vaginal dryness. But the major benefits are that HRT helps prevent osteoporosis and reduces the risk of heart disease—problems that can have long-term effects on a woman's life and health (Mendelsohn & Karas, 1999; Peyser, 1999). As we saw earlier in the chapter, estrogen protects against osteoporosis by slowing bone loss after menopause and by helping increase bone mass. Estrogen decreases the risk of heart disease by lowering the level of "bad," low-density lipoprotein (LDL) cholesterol and raising the level of "good," high-density lipoprotein (HDL) cholesterol ("Menopause," 1999). It was once thought that adding progestin to estrogen might diminish estrogen's protective effects against heart disease, but research has not supported that claim (Brinton & Schairer, 1997; Grodstein et al., 1997). In fact, postmenopausal women who take both estrogen and progestin reduce their risk of heart disease by 60 percent, compared to a 40 to 50 percent reduction for women who take estrogen alone (McDonald, 1999). Two recent studies, however, suggest that estrogen use—with or without progestin—may provide no benefits to the heart and may even slightly increase the risk of heart attack and stroke for some women (Kolata, 2000a).

Studies have found that hormone replacement therapy reduces the risk of death from several kinds of cancer including colon and breast cancer (Col et al., 1997; Grodstein et al., 1997). In addition, hormone therapy lowers the risk of osteoarthritis, the most common form of arthritis, which mostly affects women over age 45 (George & Spector, 1997; Gilbert, 1996). Studies have shown that estrogen also helps combat age-related memory loss (Peyser, 1999), macular degeneration (a leading cause of blindness), and Alzheimer's disease, which causes early dementia (Grady, 2000b). The latter condition is more common in women than in men and is more prevalent among Latina and Black women than White women (American College of Obstetricians & Gynecologists, 1997a; Tang et al., 1998; Yaffe, Sawaya, Lieberburg, & Grady, 1998).

Risks and Concerns.   The risk of endometrial (uterine) cancer increases if estrogen is taken without progestin. Adding progestin decreases this risk, but may cause the inconvenient return of menstrual bleeding. Hormone replacement therapy also increases the risk of gallbladder surgery.

But women's biggest concern by far is whether hormone replacement therapy increases the risk of breast cancer. Many studies of this issue have been conducted, with most showing no increase in risk (Bush & Whiteman, 1999). As previously mentioned, several large-scale studies have found hormone therapy is linked to a decrease in fatal breast cancer, at least up to about 10 years of use. Longer periods of use (ranging from 15 to 20 years), however, may be associated with an increase in the risk of breast cancer (Col et. al., 1997; Grodstein et al., 1997; Hunt, 1997). Although researchers long believed that estrogen was the major hormonal culprit in breast cancer, two recent studies found a substantially higher risk of breast cancer when progestin was combined with estrogen than when estrogen was taken alone. The irony is that, as we have seen, the addition of progestin prevents estrogen from inducing endometrial cancer (Brody, 2000). One piece of encouraging news is that the breast cancers linked to hormone therapy appear to be forms of the disease that are slow-growing and highly treatable (McDonald, 1999). In addition, the risk of breast cancer exists primarily for women who are current or recent users of the hormones (Schairer et al., 2000). Once HRT is stopped the risks (and benefits) dissipate.

Even if there is an increased risk of breast cancer with long-term hormone therapy, the increase appears small—especially compared with the risks of diseases against which hormones protect. Long-term hormone use might increase the incidence of breast cancer from 10 women per 10,000 each year to 13 per 10,000 each year (American College of Obstetricians & Gynecologists, 1997a). Coronary heart disease, the number one killer of women, is responsible for 30 percent of deaths among American women, and hip fracture accounts for another 3 percent. The percent of women who die from breast cancer also is 3 percent. The benefits of hormone use thus appear to outweigh the risks (Brinton & Schairer, 1997; Grady, 1999a).

Many women, however, appear either to be unaware of these facts or to be so concerned about breast cancer that they neglect far more serious risks to their health and life. A number of polls conducted in the past few years illustrate some of the misconceptions women have about breast cancer relative to other diseases. In one 1997 survey, more than half the women thought they were more likely to die of breast cancer than heart disease. Another 1997 poll found that women ranked breast cancer as a greater threat to their health than heart disease and lung cancer (Brody, 1997a). (In fact, although the *incidence* of lung cancer is lower than that of breast cancer among women, lung cancer is the leading cause of cancer *deaths* among women.) In addition, a 1997 national survey of women ages 45 to 64 found that over 60 percent of women feared cancer more than any other disease, with 24 percent fearing breast cancer most. Only 9 percent said they feared heart attack. About 75 percent did not realize that lung cancer is the foremost cancer killer in women (National Council on Aging, 1997). In addition, most women are not aware that colon cancer is the leading cause of cancer death for women aged 75 and older (Wilcox & Stefanik, 1999).

Who Should Not Take Hormones?   Despite the benefits of HRT, there are some women who definitely should *not* use hormones. These include women who already have had cancer of the breast or uterus, a stroke, heart attack, severe liver disease, or chronic impairment of liver function. Women should *consider* avoiding hormones if they have gallbladder disease, uterine fibroid tumors, high blood pressure, migraine headaches, seizure disorders, and blood clots in the leg. These conditions do not absolutely rule out use of hormones. Women should discuss risks and benefits with their physicians (Boston Women's Health Book Collective, 1998; Doress-Worters & Siegal, 1994; Wingo & McTiernan, 2000).

Alternatives to Standard Hormone Replacement Therapy.   The usual dose of estrogen given in HRT is 0.625 milligram. Recent research indicates that lower doses may confer similar benefits while lowering risks and side effects. Robert

Recker and his colleagues (1999) found that half the usual dose of estrogen (0.30 milligrams), combined with calcium and vitamin D supplements, increased bone density in women over 65 at least as much as the usual dose but without unpleasant side effects such as weight gain and breast tenderness. Other researchers (Genant et al., 1997) have found that the lower dose also has favorable effects on cholesterol and other fats circulating in the blood, suggesting that its potential for protecting postmenopausal women from heart disease might also be considerable. In addition, the low dose does not produce changes in the uterine lining that are associated with the development of uterine cancer.

Another alternative approach is the use of synthetic estrogens that have some of the benefits but fewer of the risks of natural estrogen. One such hormone, raloxifene, was mentioned in our discussion of osteoporosis. The same research (Delmas et al., 1997; Walsh et al., 1998) found that healthy postmenopausal women who took raloxifene for up to two years experienced a drop in blood levels of heart-damaging LDL cholesterol. While the hormone was not as effective as natural estrogen in elevating levels of the "good" cholesterol HDL, it did not stimulate precancerous growth of the uterus or breast. In fact, raloxifene has been found to *reduce* the risk of breast cancer in postmenopausal women with osteoporosis (Cummings et al., 1999).

Lifestyle modifications, especially those involving exercise and dietary modifications, appear to be beneficial in reducing menopausal symptoms. For example, women who exercise regularly have a lower incidence of hot flashes than women who do not. Limiting or eliminating caffeine and alcohol also reduces the frequency of hot flashes. Consuming foods and herbs that contain estrogen-like substances, such as soy products, wild yams, flaxseed and black cohosh also is helpful (Brody, 1999a, 1999f; "Menopause," 1999). Known as **phyto-estrogens**, these *plant foods do not contain estrogen but affect the body in a similar manner.* Phyto-estrogens are many times weaker than pharmaceutical estrogens and may not help women experiencing severe effects of menopause. Furthermore, there is as yet no evidence that these estrogen substitutes provide the same long-term benefits against heart disease and osteoporosis that estrogen provides (Burros, 2000; "Estrogens au Naturel," 1997).

Sexuality

Sexual activity and satisfaction vary among midlife women just as they do among young women. Women who in their earlier years found sexual expression to be fulfilling typically continue to enjoy sex in their middle years and beyond. Other women, whose sexual desires were not strong earlier, may find that their interest diminishes further during middle age (Leiblum, 1990). In this section, we examine the sexuality of women in midlife.

Physical Changes.   Most women experience a number of physical changes as they enter menopause (Doress-Worters & Siegal, 1994; Lamont, 1997). Decline in the production of estrogen is responsible for many of these changes. The vaginal walls become less elastic, thinner, and more easily irritated, causing pain and bleeding during intercourse. Decreases in vaginal lubrication also can lead to painful intercourse. This situation can be relieved by the application of lubricants such as KY Jelly. Normal acidic vaginal secretions become less acidic, increasing the likelihood of **vaginitis** (*an infection caused by yeast organisms*). Vaginitis can cause burning, itching, discharge, and painful intercourse. Signs of sexual arousal—clitoral, labial, and breast engorgement and nipple erection—become less intense, and sexual arousal is slower. Most menopausal women, however, experience little or no change in *subjective* arousal (Leiblum, 1990). Painful contractions, similar to menstrual cramps, may occur during orgasm. Although the number and intensity of orgasmic contractions are reduced, few women either notice or complain about these changes (Leiblum, 1990).

Patterns of Sexual Activity.   Research on patterns of sexuality in midlife women has produced mixed results. While some women report a decline in sexual interest and the capacity for orgasm during these years, others report the opposite pattern (Mansfield, Koch, & Voda, 1998; Mansfield, Voda & Koch, 1995). In one study by Phyllis Mansfield and her colleagues (Mansfield et al.,1998), one-fifth of the women reported an increased desire for nongenital sexual expression such as cuddling, hugging, and kissing. Changes in sexual physiology and hormone levels are not the only factors determining female sexuality in the middle years. The extent of sexual activity in middle-aged women is strongly influenced by past sexual enjoyment and experience. Women who have been sexually responsive during young adulthood are most likely to be sexually active as they get older (Hodson & Skeen, 1994).

    Many postmenopausal women find that their sexual interest and pleasure are heightened. What are some possible reasons for this? One is freedom from worries about pregnancy (Crose et al., 1997; Leary, 1998). This factor may be especially relevant for older cohorts of women for whom highly effective birth control methods were unavailable during their childbearing years. A second reason is the increase in marital satisfaction which often develops during the postparental ("empty nest") years (Etaugh, 1993b). In addition, slower arousal time for both women and men may lengthen the time of pleasurable sexual activity (Weg, 1989).

    Sexual activity decreases only slightly and gradually for women in their forties and fifties. Greater declines may result from physical or psychological changes. Physical causes include various medical conditions, surgery, certain medications, and heavy drinking. Psychological causes include dissatisfaction with one's partner and worries about family matters, finances, or work (American Association of Retired Persons [AARP], 1999; Rathus et al., 2000). Hysterectomy does not impair sexual functioning. In fact, a recent study found that following a hysterectomy, women experienced greater sexual desire, an increase in orgasms, and a drop in painful intercourse (Rhodes et al., 1999). However, if a woman feels that her ability to enjoy sex after a hysterectomy is diminished, counseling can be helpful. Mastectomy also does not interfere with sexual responsiveness, but a woman may lose her sexual desire or her sense of being desired. Talking with other women who have had a mastectomy often helps. One resource is the American Cancer Society's Reach to Recovery program (American Cancer Society, 1999b; Leiblum, 1990).

Sexual activity and contentment during middle age is more likely to diminish for individuals who have lost their partners. For example, a recent nationally representative study of sexuality in Americans age 45 and over found that just over half of those polled, but two-thirds of those with sexual partners, were satisfied with their sex lives (AARP, 1999). Women in their forties and fifties, the study found, are nearly as likely as men to have a sexual partner (78 percent compared to 84 percent). The "partner gap" between women and men grows as people age, however (see Chapter 13).

Physical Health

Most middle-aged Americans are in good health, with 83 percent reporting their health to be good, very good, or excellent (USDHHS, 1996). Heart disease, stroke, and cancer become the leading causes of death for both women and men in midlife. Reproductive system disorders also may emerge during the middle years.

Heart Disease

One out of every three women develops coronary heart disease after the age of 40 (Lloyd-Jones, Larson, Beiser, & Levy, 1999). As we noted earlier, heart disease is the number one killer of American women. More women in the United States die of heart disease than from all forms of cancer combined, including breast cancer (Centers for Disease Control and Prevention, 2000).

Gender Differences.   Women typically develop heart disease about 10 years later than men (Underwood, 1999a). Illness and death from heart disease increase dramatically in women after menopause. By her seventies, a woman has the same risk of heart attack and heart disease as a man her age (Donatelle & Davis, 1998; Grady, 1999a). Women are more likely than men to die after a heart attack, especially if they are under age 50 (Wexler, 1999). If they survive, they are more likely to have a second attack (Collins, Rowland, Salganicoff, & Chait, 1994; Marrugat et al., 1998). Since women are older than men when they develop heart disease, their prognosis is poorer (American Heart Association, 1997, Malacrida et al., 1998). But women are more likely than men to die after heart bypass surgery, even when they are equally old and ill (Edwards, Carey, Grover, Bero, & Hartz, 1998).

Risk Factors.   Some risk factors for heart disease are unchangeable. These include gender, age, ethnicity, and family history. More men develop heart disease and develop it earlier than women, but women narrow the gap in the postmenopausal years. The risk of heart disease increases with age. For women, this is due partly to declining estrogen levels after menopause. The death rate from heart attack is 40 percent higher for Black women than White women, who, in turn, are much more likely to die from heart disease then are Latina, Native American, and Asian American women (Centers for Disease Control and Prevention, 1999). In addition, the risk of heart disease and stroke increases if close family members have had these diseases (Newton, Lacroix, & Buist, 2000; Winkleby, Kraemer, Ahn, & Varady, 1998).

Major risk factors over which women have control include smoking, physical inactivity, high cholesterol levels, and high blood pressure. Women who have lower cholesterol levels, lower blood pressure, and who don't smoke add up to six years to their life expectancy (Stamler et al., 1999). Even young women, who have a low rate of heart disease, should begin controlling these risk factors early in life (Bousser, 1999).

Smoking is a powerful risk factor for heart disease and stroke in women. A woman who smokes is 2 to 6 times as likely to have a heart attack as a nonsmoker and is more apt to die from the heart attack (American Heart Association, 1997). Smoking is especially harmful in women because it decreases estrogen's protective effects and can cause menopause to occur about two years early. Nearly half of all heart attacks before age 55 can be attributed to smoking. Smoking only 1 to 4 cigarettes a day doubles a woman's risk of heart disease. Women who smoke slightly over a pack a day are 15 times more likely to develop the disease ("Heart Disease," 1993; Newton et al., 2000). The good news is that chances of having a heart attack are cut by 25 percent within 2 years of quitting smoking and are as low as a nonsmoker's chances within 5 to 10 years after stopping (Newton et al., 2000).

Inactivity is another major risk factor in heart disease and stroke. Sedentary women are nine times more likely to die from cardiovascular disease than women who are very active. Women benefit from vigorous exercise such as aerobics, running, biking, or swimming for at least 30 minutes, three to four times a week. But even moderate everyday activities such as a brisk walk, gardening, household chores, and climbing stairs for a total of 30 minutes on most days provide health benefits (Andersen et al., 1999; Dunn et al., 1999; Kujala, Kaprio, Sarna, & Koskenvuo, 1998; Lemaitre et al., 1999). In one recent study, for example, Jo Ann Manson and her colleagues (Manson et al., 1999) found that brisk walking reduced the incidence of heart disease in middle-aged and older women by up to 40 percent, comparable to the reduction produced by more vigorous exercise. Another piece of good news was that sedentary women who did not become active until middle age or later lowered their risk of heart disease compared to those who remained sedentary. Unfortunately, more than 80 percent of American women are sedentary or do not engage in any regular physical activity. In addition, women become even less active as they get older, when they most need the cardiovascular benefits of exercise (U.S. Bureau of the Census, 1998c).

In our discussion of hormone replacement therapy, we talked about the two types of *cholesterol*. High levels of "bad" cholesterol (LDL) *raise* the risk of heart disease and stroke. High levels of "good" cholesterol (HDL) *lower* the risk of both diseases. Low levels of HDL are a stronger risk factor for women than for men. Women with a family history of early heart attack or stroke should have their

Everyday activities such as brisk walking provide health benefits to women.

cholesterol levels checked starting at age 20. Regular physical activity and losing weight (if overweight) helps raise HDL (American Heart Association, 1997).

High blood pressure (hypertension) is another major risk factor for heart attack and the most important risk factor for stroke (Bousser, 1999). By their sixties, at least half of all women—but nearly 80 percent of postmenopausal Black women—have high blood pressure (Newton et al., 2000). Reducing salt intake, losing weight (if overweight), exercising, and taking medication (if needed) can bring blood pressure under control.

Women with *diabetes* are more likely to have a heart attack or stroke than are nondiabetic women. Diabetes may be delayed by controlling blood sugar, eating less saturated fat, staying physically active, and maintaining a normal weight (American Heart Association, 1997; Gu, Cowie, & Harris, 1999). Being *overweight*, especially by 15 percent or more, also increases the risk of both heart attack and stroke. Overweight individuals are more likely to develop high blood pressure, high cholesterol levels, and diabetes (Calle, et al., 1999; Kolata, 1998a; Stevens et al., 1998).

Eating less saturated fat is just one dietary modification that reduces a woman's risk of heart disease. Another is increasing her daily intake of Vitamin B_6 and folic acid. Three milligrams of B_6 and 400 micrograms of folic acid provide the greatest protection (Oakley, 1998; Rimm et al., 1998) and also may decrease the risk of breast cancer (Zhang et al., 1999). Women who eat a diet high in fiber, especially the fiber in whole grain cereals, also reduce their risk of heart disease ("Are You Getting?," 1999). Other heart-healthy foods include fish, soy, nuts, and vegetables and fruits such as dried beans and peas, garlic, apples, and citrus fruits (Brody, 1999e, 2000a). Drinking tea also appears to protect against heart disease, especially in women. In one recent study, for example, people who drank one to two cups of tea daily lowered their risk of heart disease by 46 percent; those who consumed four cups a day decreased their risk by 69 percent (Geleijnse et al., 1999). In addition, women who consume one alcoholic drink per day have at least a 40 percent lower death rate from heart disease than women who do not drink (Rimm et al., 1998; Thun et al., 1997; Valmadrid et al., 1999) and they are only half as likely to suffer a stroke (Sacco et al., 1999). Red wine appears to be especially beneficial (Brody, 1999e).

Hormones also affect heart disease. Older forms of *birth control pills*, which contained high levels of estrogen and progestin, increased women's risk of heart disease and stroke. Newer versions of the pill contain lower hormone doses and may not increase the chances of these diseases (Beral et al., 1999; Thorogood, 1999). However, taking oral contraceptives and smoking greatly increases the risk of stroke, especially for women over 35 (American Heart Association, 1997; Underwood, 1999a). As noted earlier in the chapter, *hormone replacement therapy* may substantially reduce the risk of heart disease in postmenopausal women, although recent research casts some doubt on this conclusion (Kolata, 2000a).

Treatment. Women with heart disease often do not receive the aggressive treatment from physicians that men do (Holubkov & Reis, 2000). For one thing, physicians often miss the symptoms of heart disease and heart attack in women because women can show symptoms that occur less often in men, such as nausea, dizziness, shortness of breath, chest discomfort, fatigue, and heart palpitations. Women may be misdiagnosed as simply suffering from indigestion, muscle pain, stress or anxiety (McSweeney, 1998; Underwood, 1999a). In addition, women are often believed to be less threatened by heart disease or less responsive to treatment, both of which are untrue (Schulman et al., 1999; "Women's Cholesterol Undertreated," 1997).

Women are less likely than men to receive one of the most important diagnostic heart tests, the angiogram. This X-ray test releases dye into the heart and determines whether blockages in arteries need to be repaired. In the event of serious blockages, doctors often perform angioplasty, which uses a balloon to clear the arteries, or coronary bypass surgery. Women are less likely than men are to receive either treatment. They also are less likely to receive clot-dissolving drugs in the hours following a heart attack (Knox & Czajkowski, 1997; Roger et al., 2000; Underwood, 1999a; Wexler, 1999). Do these gender differences occur because physicians hesitate to give risky procedures to women, who are older and more ill than men when they are diagnosed? This may be part of the answer. But even when women and men are the same age and have identical symptoms and conditions, women are less likely to receive these treatments (Knox & Czajkowski,

1997). Women also get fewer referrals for cardiac rehabilitation programs following heart attacks, even though they benefit from therapy as much as men do (Woods & Jacobson, 1997).

Psychosocial Factors.   Women and men with a so-called Type A personality—competitive, time-driven, impatient, perfectionistic, and angry—are more prone to develop heart disease. Those Type A's who are high in hostility, distrust of others, and cynicism are particularly at risk (Donatelle & Davis, 1998). Depression also is strongly associated with heart disease for both women and men. Since women are more likely than men to be depressed (as we saw in Chapter 7), this factor increases women's risk.

The psychosocial health of women following a heart attack or coronary bypass surgery is worse than that of men. Women are more anxious and depressed, return to work less often, take longer to recuperate physically, and resume their sex lives later than men. In spite of their poorer heath, women resume household activities sooner than men and are more likely to feel guilty that they cannot quickly resume the chores they once did (Knox & Czajkowski, 1997; Martin, 1994). Women's poorer psychosocial functioning after heart attack and heart surgery can take a toll on their well-being, productivity, and quality of life. In addition, the greater depression experienced by women after heart attack or heart surgery is associated with a greater risk of death and of second heart attacks. Health care providers need to become aware of the potential difficulties faced by women with heart disease and to take steps to enhance the recovery of their female patients (Knox & Czajkowski, 1997).

Breast Cancer

As we noted earlier, women fear breast cancer more than any other disease including heart disease, the top killer of women (Grady, 1999d). One out of every eight women will develop breast cancer at sometime in her life (Hewitt & Simone, 1999). Although this statistic sounds frightening, it represents a lifetime risk. At age 40, only one in 217 women develops breast cancer. At age 50, the risk increases to one in 50 women and at age 70, it rises to one in 14. Only for women who are 90 years and older is the risk one in eight ("Half of America's Women," 1997).

The majority of women in whom breast cancer is diagnosed—70 percent—do not die of the disease. Moreover, the death rate from breast cancer has been dropping in recent years as a result of earlier detection and improved treatments (Phillips, Glendon, & Knight, 1999; Wingo et al., 1998, 1999). The five-year survival rate for women with localized breast cancer has risen from 78 percent in the 1940s to 97 percent in 1998. Even if the cancer has spread to lymph nodes, 76 percent of women will be alive five years later. If it invades bones or other organs, the rate drops to 21 percent (Grady, 1999d).

Why is the prospect of getting breast cancer so terrifying? According to Jane Brody (1999c) and Ellen Ratner (1999), both breast cancer survivors and authors, the extensive publicity given to the disease in recent years in order to stimulate research and raise women's awareness has created the misleading impression that breast cancer is more common and more deadly than it actually is. In addition, while only a small number of women die of breast cancer in their thirties and forties, their untimely deaths may trigger greater alarm than the heart attack deaths of a far greater number of women later in life.

Risk Factors. *Age*, as we have just seen, is the greatest risk factor for breast cancer. In fact, 70 percent of women who develop breast cancer have no risk factors other than age ("Half of America's Women," 1997).

Ethnicity is another risk factor. White women are slightly more likely than Black women to get breast cancer overall, but Black women are far more likely to die from it (Campbell, 1999; Jetter, 2000; Wingo et al., 1998). Part of the reason is that Black women have poorer access to state-of-the-art medical care, but this accounts for only about half of the increased death rate. The tumors of Black women appear to be faster-growing and more malignant. Even when Black and White women wait the same amount of time to see a doctor after they first detect signs of breast cancer, the Black women's cancers are already more advanced (Collins, Bussell, & Wenzel, 1997; Jetter, 2000; Lannin et al., 1998).

Family history of breast cancer—especially in one's mother, sister, or daughter—is another risk factor, accounting for 10 to 15 percent of breast cancers. A small percentage of women with a family history of breast cancer have unusually high risk—50 to 80 percent—as a result of inheriting one of two breast cancer genes, BRCA-1 and BRCA-2. Inherited breast cancer occurs at younger ages, is more likely to affect both breasts, and often appears in multiple family members over several generations. The genes are more common in Jewish women of eastern European origin than in other groups (Grady, 1999f; Stolberg, 1998a).

A recently discovered risk factor in young women is an elevated level of an *insulin-like growth factor* called IGF-1. This hormone, produced by most tissues in the body, is involved in normal growth but also helps cancer cells grow. Among premenopausal women younger than 50, the risk of breast cancer for those with high levels of the hormone is about seven times greater than for those with low levels of the hormone (Hankinson et al., 1998).

Age, family history, and growth-hormone levels are risk factors women cannot change. Other factors over which they have little or no control include *early age at menarche, late age at menopause, late age at first birth* (after 30), and *having no or few children*. All these events lengthen the amount of time women's breast tissue is exposed to high levels of estrogen (Grady, 1999f; Hortobagyi, 1998; "Know Your Options," 1999).

Women can reduce the chances of breast cancer by making certain lifestyle choices. Women who have *smoked* a little over a pack of cigarettes a day since the age of 15 increase their risk of breast cancer by 80 percent. Those who have smoked for more than 30 years face a 60 percent increase (Brody, 1997a). The more *alcohol* a woman consumes, the greater is her risk of developing breast cancer (Smith-Warner et al., 1998). Women who have more than one drink a day and who started drinking before age 25 more than double their breast cancer risk.

Even the one daily drink that dramatically lowers death rates from heart disease may increase a woman's risk of breast cancer by 10 percent, although recent research disputes this conclusion (Brody, 1999b). Since women are much more likely to die of heart disease than of breast cancer, many women would benefit from decreasing their chances of getting heart disease. However, the decision to have one drink per day should be based on each woman's assessment of her own risks and benefits given her personal and family medical history.

The role of *fat consumption* in breast cancer is controversial. Most studies have found no link between overall fat intake and incidence of breast cancer (e.g., Holmes et al., 1999). Some recent research, however, has shown that the *type* of fat is important (Wolk et al., 1998). Monounsaturated fat (olive oil, canola oil) may reduce the risk of breast cancer, whereas polyunsaturated fat (corn, safflower, and soybean oil) may increase it.

The more *weight* a woman gains during adulthood, the greater are her chances of developing breast cancer. One study (Huang et al., 1997) found that women who put on at least 45 pounds were twice as likely to develop the disease as women who gained fewer than five founds. Body fat produces estrogen which, as we have noted, may be linked to breast cancer. One way to reduce fat is to engage in *physical activity*. Strenuous exercise in adolescence and young adulthood can delay onset of menstruation or interrupt it. This lowers a woman's overall exposure to estrogen, possibly inhibiting development of breast cancer. Even among premenopausal and postmenopausal women, physical activity reduces breast cancer risk, most likely because it reduces body fat (Gammon, John, & Britton, 1998; Rockhill et al., 1999; Thune, Brenn, Lund, & Gaard, 1997). While use of *birth control pills* may slightly increase breast cancer risk, women who have stopped using them for at least 10 years have the same risk as women who have never used the pill. Finally, we have seen that long-term use of *hormone replacement therapy* (10 to 15 years) may also increase risk. However, a woman needs to evaluate her relative risks of heart disease and breast cancer before deciding whether to use HRT (Brody, 2000b; Peyser, 1999). To assess your risk of breast cancer, try Get Involved 9.2.

Detection.   The American Cancer Society (1998) recommends that women age 20 and older do a monthly breast self-examination about a week after their menstrual period ends (during menstruation breasts have normal lumps). Figure 9.1 provides instructions. Many women do not examine their breasts, partly out of fear of finding a lump. (Keep in mind that 80 to 90 percent of all lumps are noncancerous). Only two-thirds of women over 40 do regular breast exams (American Cancer Society, 1998). This is unfortunate, because a substantial portion of breast cancers are found during self-examination, particularly among women under 50 (Zuger, 1998a). Women also should have a clinical breast exam by a health professional every 3 years from ages 20 to 39 years and annually from age 40 onward (American Cancer Society, 1998).

A **mammogram**, *a low-dose X-ray picture of the breast* detects small suspicious lumps up to two years before they are large enough to be felt. Regular mammo-

GET INVOLVED **9.2**

Assessing Your Risk of Breast Cancer

Read each question below and circle the number in the parentheses following your response. Individual numbers for specific questions should not be interpreted as an exact measure of relative risk, but the totals give a general indication of your risk.

Then give the questionnaire to female friends and relatives, including both young and older women.

Breast Cancer Risk

1. Age group: a. Under 35 (10) b. 35–39 (20) c. 40–49 (50) d. 50 and over (90)
2. Ethnicity: a. Asian (10) b. Latina (10) c. Black (20) d. White (25)
3. Family history: a. None (10) b. Mother, sister, daughter with breast cancer (30)
4. Your history: a. No breast disease (10) b. Previous lumps or cysts (15) c. Previous breast cancer (100)
5. Maternity: a. 1st pregnancy before 30 (10) b. 1st pregnancy at 30 or older (15) c. No pregnancies (20)

Detecting Cancer Early

6. I do a monthly breast self-exam (if yes, subtract 10 points).   Yes   No
7. I have had a negative mammogram and examination by a physician. (if yes, subtract 25 points).   Yes   No

Total _____

Under 100 indicates low risk; 100–199 shows moderate risk; 200 or higher means high risk.

Source: Donatelle & Davis, 1998, pp. 445–449. Reprinted with permission from Allyn & Bacon.

What Does It Mean?

1. How did breast cancer risk vary with the age of your respondents?
2. Did you find age differences in the use of early detection procedures?

3. What advice can you give to your respondents who have moderate to high risk of breast cancer?

gram screening reduces breast cancer death rates by 30 percent in women over 50, and by at least 15 percent in women between ages 40 and 49. For these reasons, the American Cancer Society recommends a mammogram every year for women age 40 and older. Yet only 56 percent of women 50 and older and 45 percent of women 70 and older have had a mammogram in the past year or two. Among women age 50 and older with low income or less than a high school education,

How to Examine Your Breasts

Do you know that 95% of breast cancers are discovered first by women themselves? And that the earlier the breast cancer is detected, the better the chance for a complete cure? Of course, most lumps or changes are not cancer. But you can safeguard your health by making a habit of examining your breasts once a month – a day or two after your period or, if you're no longer menstruating, on any given day. And if you notice anything changed or unusual – a lump, thickening, or discharge – contact your doctor right away.

How to Look for Changes

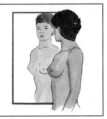

Step 1
Sit or stand in front of a mirror with your arms at your side. Turning slowly from side to side, check your breasts for
- changes in size or shape
- puckering or dimpling of the skin
- changes in size or position of one nipple compared to the other

Step 2
Raise your arms above your head and repeat the examination in Step 1.

Step 3
Gently press each nipple with your fingertips to see if there is any discharge.

How to Feel for Changes

Step 1
Lie down and put a pillow or folded bath towel under your left shoulder. Then place your left hand under your head. (From now on you will be feeling for a lump or thickening in your breasts.)

Step 2
Imagine that your breast is divided into quarters.

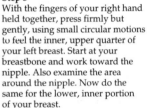

Step 3
With the fingers of your right hand held together, press firmly but gently, using small circular motions to feel the inner, upper quarter of your breast. Start at your breastbone and work toward the nipple. Also examine the area around the nipple. Now do the same for the lower, inner portion of your breast.

Step 4
Next, bring your arm to your side and feel under your left armpit for swelling.

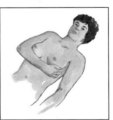

Step 5
With your arm still down, feel the upper, outer part of your breast, starting with your nipple and working outwards. Examine the lower, outer quarter in the same way.

Step 6
Now place the pillow under your right shoulder and repeat all the steps using your left hand to examine your right breast.

FIGURE 9.1   Doing a Breast Self-Examination
Source: From American Cancer Society, 1997. Reprinted with permission.

fewer than half have had a recent mammogram (American Cancer Society, 1998; National Center for Health Statistics, 1998; UK Trial, 1999). Low-income Latinas and Black women with strong social ties to family and friends are more likely to get mammograms than those with fewer social ties (Royak-Schaler, Stanton, & Danoff-Burg, 1997).

Treatment.   When breast cancer is diagnosed, several treatment options are available. For many years, the standard treatment was **radical mastectomy**, *the removal of the breast, underlying chest wall, and underarm lymph nodes.* Because of disfigurement and side effects, it now is rarely done. **Modified radical mastectomy** involves *removal of the breast and underarm lymph nodes* and **simple mastectomy**, *removal of the breast only.* In **lumpectomy**, also known as partial mastectomy or breast-conserving surgery, only *the lump and some surrounding tissue are removed.* Lumpectomy is almost always followed by several weeks of radiation. Research has shown that for small tumors in the early stages of disease, lumpectomy followed by radiation is as effective in terms of five-year survival as mastectomy (American Cancer Society, 1999a; "Know Your Options," 1999).

Chemotherapy may be used to kill cancer cells that the surgeon was not able to remove. The addition of the drug Taxol to standard chemotherapy dramatically reduces the risk of breast cancer recurrence (Pollack, 1998). An alternative procedure involves hormone therapy with an estrogen blocker called tamoxifen. Tamoxifen treatment for five years reduces the recurrence of breast cancer and improves survival rates over a 10-year period (Early Breast Cancer Trialists' Collaborative Group, 1998; Peto et al., 1998). In addition, tamoxifen helps *prevent* breast cancer among women at high risk for the disease. However, it also increases the risk of uterine cancer and life-threatening blood clots (Altman, 1998b; Cowley & Underwood, 1999). Nonetheless, the American Society of Clinical Oncology has recently suggested that physicians consider prescribing tamoxifen for women with an elevated risk of developing breast cancer, including all women over age 60 (Stephenson, 1999). Raloxifene, the estrogen blocker used to treat osteoporosis, also reduces the incidence of breast cancer, but without raising the risk of uterine cancer or blood clots (Altman, 1998c; Delmas, Mitlak, & Christiansen, 1998). Clinical trials comparing the effectiveness of tamoxifen and raloxifene are underway (Stephenson, 1999). Another recently developed drug, Herceptin, shrinks tumors in women whose advanced breast cancer is not responsive to other treatments (Altman, 1998a; Cowley & Underwood, 1999).

Psychological Impact.   The diagnosis of breast cancer and the surgery that often follows causes depression, anxiety, and anger in most women. If the cancer recurs at some point after treatment, women may experience even higher levels of distress. Concerns about bodily appearance can be substantial for women who have had breast surgery. Lumpectomy has a more positive effect on body image and sexual functioning than mastectomy (Royak-Schaler et al., 1997). Individual differences in reactions to breast cancer vary considerably. Women with higher levels of hostility and a "fighting spirit" survive breast cancer longer than those who show passive acceptance, stoicism, emotional inhibition, or feelings of hopelessness (Ott & Levy, 1994; Watson et al., 1999).

The importance of support groups in helping women cope with cancer cannot be underestimated. David Spiegel and his colleagues (Spiegel, Bloom, Kraemer, & Gottheil, 1989; Spiegel, 1998) found that after attending weekly group therapy sessions for a year, women with advanced breast cancer showed less emotional distress and more adaptive coping responses than women who had been assigned to a control group. A 10-year follow-up found that the women in group therapy had lived on average twice as long (36.6 versus 18.9 months from entry in the study to death) as women in the control group. In addition, recent research by Barbara Andersen and her colleagues (Andersen & Emery, 1999) found that women with breast cancer who participated for 8 months in a psychological intervention program showed lower levels of a stress hormone and higher levels of an antibody that fights breast tumors than did a control group of other breast cancer patients. Participants in the program, which included social support, muscle relaxation training, and information on diet and exercise, also reported less depression, more energy, and better tolerance of chemotherapy.

Reproductive System Disorders

A number of sexually transmitted infectious diseases of the reproductive system were discussed in Chapter 5. Here we will discuss other disorders including benign (noncancerous) conditions such as uterine fibroid tumors and endometriosis, as well as various cancers.

Benign Conditions.   **Fibroid tumors** are *noncancerous growths of the uterus* that occur in 20 to 40 percent of women of reproductive age. Fibroids are not dangerous but they can cause severe pelvic pain, heavy bleeding, and possibly infertility and miscarriage. They occur more often in Black women than in White women and are the most common reason for **hysterectomy** (*removal of the uterus*) (Boston Women's Health Book Collective, 1998; Harden, 1999). **Fibroid embolization**, *which reduces the size of tumors by blocking their blood supply*, is a recently developed, less invasive alternative to hysterectomy for some women (Gilbert, 1999b).

Endometriosis occurs when *the lining of the uterus (endometrium) migrates and grows on pelvic structures, such as the ovaries, fallopian tubes, and bladder.* About 7 percent of women are affected. Severe endometriosis is a major cause of infertility (Queenan & Beauregard, 1997).

Cancers.   Endometrial or uterine cancer is the most common cancer of the female reproductive tract and is often characterized by vaginal bleeding. It occurs most often in women between 50 and 70 years old and is more common in White women than in Black women. Because most cases are detected early, this is one of the most curable cancers of the reproductive system, with an overall survival rate of about 85 percent (Cook & Weiss, 2000; Strong et al., 1999; Wingo et al., 1999).

Cancer of the **cervix**, *the lower end of the uterus*, has cure rates of 80 to 90 percent in its early stages. Black, Latina, and Native American women, however, have a much higher death rate, probably because their more limited access to medical care prevents early diagnosis and treatment (Campbell, 1999; Collins et al., 1997; Queenan & Beauregard, 1997). The **Pap smear**, *an inexpensive and effective screening technique*, has been used for over 50 years to identify precancerous changes in the cervix. The test has slashed cervical cancer deaths by 70 percent and saved tens of thousands of lives ("Better Pap Smear," 1998; Solomon & Schiffman, 2000). Of those women who die of cervical cancer in the United States, over 60 percent either have never had a Pap smear or have not had one in five years ("For Pap Smears," 1999). Sexually active women or women over the age of 18 (whichever comes first) should get a Pap smear once a year ("The Importance of a Pap Test," 1999). Unfortunately, fewer than 60 percent of women have annual Pap smears. Low-income, uninsured, and elderly women are least likely to get regular Pap tests (Blackman et al., 1999; Collins et al., 1997). A recently developed laboratory test is even more accurate than the Pap test in detecting cervical cancer in women over 40. Moreover, since the test can be done by women themselves and does not require a pelvic exam, it is likely to greatly increase the number of women tested worldwide (Grady, 2000a). Factors that increase the risk of cervical cancer include smoking, obesity, early age at first intercourse, multiple sex partners, and infection with HIV or with human papilloma virus, the common virus that causes genital warts (Centers for Disease Control, 1999; Protect Against Cervical Cancer, 2000). Until very recently, radiation was the standard treatment for cervical cancer that had spread within the pelvic area. In 1999, however, five studies found that adding chemotherapy to the radiation decreases the risk of death by 30 to 50 percent (Grady, 1999c).

Ovarian cancer is a major killer of women, accounting for 25 percent of all reproductive system cancers, but half of all deaths from these cancers. It is a so-called silent disease because its symptoms do not appear until the cancer is in an advanced stage. The five-year survival rate is under 50 percent (Troisi & Hartge, 2000). Ovarian cancer received attention during the past decade after the comedian Gilda Radner (1991) and the editor-in-chief of Harper's Bazaar, Liz Tilberis (1998), wrote books about their courageous fight against the disease, which ultimately killed them. The lifetime risk of ovarian cancer is 2 percent, compared with 12 percent for breast cancer. Women who take fertility drugs may increase their risk, but longtime use of oral contraceptives cuts the incidence at least in half (Godard et al., 1998; Underwood, 1999b). Use of acetaminophen (the pain reliever marketed as Tylenol) also reduces the risk of ovarian cancer (Cramer et al., 1998).

Hysterectomy.   Each year, about 560,000 women in the United States undergo a hysterectomy. By age 60, more than one in three American women have had their uterus removed, one of the highest rates in the world (Agency for Health Care Policy and Research, 1998). By comparison, one in six Italian women and only one of eighteen French women of the same age will have undergone the procedure. For years, many critics have questioned the high rate of hysterectomy in this country. While removal of the uterus is considered appropriate in cases of cancer of the uterus, cervix, or ovaries, these situations account for only 10 percent of the total (Angier, 1997a; Dickersin & Lemaire, 2000). The most common reason for having a hysterectomy is the presence of fibroid tumors. Because Black women are more likely than White women to have fibroid tumors, their hysterectomy rates are higher (DeAngelis, 1997c). Endometriosis, heavy menstrual bleeding, and unexplained pelvic discomfort are other common reasons for hysterectomy.

While some researchers regard the uterus as a useless organ after the childbearing years are over, others argue that it continues to play a key role in regulating bodily functions. Another common practice, which has been heavily criticized, is the removal of the ovaries along with the uterus, even when the ovaries are normal and healthy. Physicians who carry out such surgery contend that when a women is in her mid-forties or older, the ovaries' major function is over and that removing them forestalls the possibility of ovarian cancer (Angier, 1997a). Can you see the sexist bias in this argument? Could one not equally argue that the prostate and testes of middle-aged men should be removed to prevent cancer of these organs?

Women who have heavy menstrual bleeding, the cause of almost 30 percent of hysterectomies, now have an alternative to removal of the uterus. In December 1997, the Food and Drug Administration approved a procedure in which a small balloon is inserted into the uterus, inflated with salt solution and heated to 188 degrees for 8 minutes. The procedures destroys most of the endometrial lining of the uterus that is the source of the bleeding ("Device Offers," 1997; Harden, 1999).

Mental Health and Illness

In Chapters 5 and 7, we investigated gender differences in eating disorders and substance abuse, including alcohol problems. In this section, we focus on depression and anxiety disorders, the diagnosis of psychological problems, and treatment approaches.

Depression

Incidence.   We saw in Chapter 5 that higher rates of depression in females first appear in early to middle adolescence and continue into adulthood. Women in the United States and in other industrialized countries are two to four times as likely as men to suffer from depression, although there is less evidence for gender differences in developing countries (Culbertson, 1997; Nolen-Hoeksema, 1995; Weissman et al., 1996). Although the incidence of depression is lower among Whites than among Blacks and Latinas/os, the 2:1 gender ratio holds across all three ethnic groups (Fredrickson & Roberts, 1997).

Theories.   Many theories have been offered to explain the gender difference in depression. Gender differences in help-seeking behavior or willingness to report symptoms have been ruled out as possible reasons (Commonwealth Fund, 1995b). One explanation is biological, linking depression to hormonal changes that occur during the menstrual cycle, the postpartum period, and menopause. As we saw earlier in this chapter, however, menopause is not associated with an increase in depression. In Chapters 5 and 7, we also noted that direct relationships between menstrual and postpartum hormonal changes and depression are weak, temporary, and far from universal (Fredrickson & Roberts, 1997). One biological factor that is strongly linked to depression is having a low level of the neurochemical serotonin. Recent research has found that men produce 50 percent more serotonin than women do, possibly making women more susceptible to depression (Angier, 1997a; Foote & Seibert, 1999).

A second possible explanation is that stressful life events may precipitate depression, and that women's lives are more stressful than men's. Women are more likely than men are to have low social status, undergo economic hardship, face discrimination in the workplace, experience marital and family strains, and be subjected to domestic violence, sexual abuse, and sexual harassment (Sprock & Yoder, 1997). Research has documented that economic hardship, family-based strains, and childhood sexual abuse are indeed contributing factors to depression in women (Angier, 1997a; Rickert, Wiemann, & Berenson, 2000; Wu & DeMaris, 1996).

A third proposed explanation is that the feminine role makes women more vulnerable to depression by making them feel helpless and powerless to control aspects of their lives (Fredrickson & Roberts, 1997). Females are expected to be less competent and more in need of help than males. Their efforts and achievements are more likely to be ignored or devalued (Etaugh & Rathus, 1995). The sense that one's actions do not count can lead to a feeling of "learned helplessness," which in turn is linked to depression. In support of this view, girls and women with more masculine behavior traits are less likely to experience depression than those with more feminine traits (Obeidallah, McHale, & Silbereisen, 1996; Sprock & Yoder, 1997).

A fourth theory known as *silencing the self* (Jack, 1991, 1999) is based on the assumption that women are socialized to place a high value on establishing and maintaining close relationships. According to this view, women defer to the needs of others, censor their self-expression, repress anger, and restrict their own initiatives, which increases their vulnerability to depression (Carr, Gilroy, & Sherman, 1996; Hart & Thompson, 1996).

Susan Nolen-Hoeksema has proposed a fifth theory based on the way that females and males respond when they are depressed. She and her colleagues have found that when adolescent girls and women are depressed, they focus on their inner feelings and try to analyze the causes and consequences of their depression. This so-called *ruminative style* leads to more severe and longer-lasting depressed moods. Adolescent boys and men, on the other hand, tend to engage in activities to distract themselves when they are depressed. (Nolen-Hoeksema & Girgus, 1994, 1998; Nolen-Hoeksema, 1999).

These explanations of depression are not mutually exclusive. For example, a recent large-scale study of adults suggests that women are more likely than men to get caught in a cycle of despair and passivity because of a lower sense of control over important areas of life, compounded by more chronic strain caused by women's lesser social power. In the study, chronic strain led to more rumination, which in turn increased feelings of powerlessness and depression (Nolen-Hoeksema, Grayson, & Larson, 1999).

Anxiety Disorders

Almost everyone feels anxious now and again. When you have to give a speech in class, for instance, it is normal to feel anxious. But when anxiety is irrational, excessive, and persists over several months, it is called an anxiety disorder (American Psychiatric Association, 1994). Most anxiety disorders, including specific phobias and agoraphobia, occur twice as frequently in women as in men. Black women are more likely than White or Latina women to experience phobias (Commonwealth Fund, 1995b; Frank, 2000; Merikangas & Pollack, 2000).

A **specific phobia** is *a fear of a specific object, such as a spider, or a specific situation, such as flying.* Specific phobias appear to originate in childhood. Social construction of gender-specific attitudes and behaviors may account for the higher prevalence of these phobias in females. Expression of fear is more socially acceptable in girls and women than in boys and men, who are discouraged from displaying their fears (Merikangas & Pollack, 2000).

Agoraphobia is *a fear of being in public places where escape might be difficult if one were suddenly incapacitated* (*agora* is the Greek word for marketplace). The disorder often begins with the onset of *panic attacks* marked by intense anxiety, racing heartbeat, dizziness, chest pain, and fear of dying or of being out of control. Sufferers become so afraid of having an attack in public that many ultimately do not venture outside their homes. Because agoraphobia often begins within a few years of marriage, it may be triggered by a woman's conflict between being dependent and passive (the traditional feminine role) and her desire to become competent and independent (Rollins, 1996).

Diagnosis and Treatment of Psychological Disorders

Gender Bias in Diagnosis.   Is there a double standard of mental health for women and men? In a classic study, Inge Broverman and her colleagues (Broverman, Broverman, Clarkson, Rosenkrantz, & Vogel, 1970) reported that mental health professionals gave similar descriptions for a "healthy" adult (gender unspecified) and a "healthy" male. A "healthy" woman, however, was seen as less healthy in several ways: more submissive, more excitable in minor crises, more emotional, more illogical, more easily hurt, more sneaky, and less independent.

Over the years, other researchers have repeated this study with mixed results. Some have found less bias in later studies than in earlier ones (Smith, 1980). Others have found that gender bias in diagnosis is alive and well. In one study (Waisberg & Page, 1988), for example, female patients who showed "masculine" symptoms (alcohol abuse or antisocial personality) were rated as more seriously disturbed than males with the same symptoms. Similarly, male patients with "feminine" symptoms (anxiety or depression) were viewed as more disturbed than females with these symptoms. Drug treatment was more likely to be recommended for females, especially by male therapists. In another study (Robertson & Fitzgerald, 1990), therapists viewed one of two videotapes in which the same male actor discussed having symptoms of depression such as sleeplessness, poor appetite, and boredom. In one video, the male was portrayed in the traditional role of sole breadwinner with a full-time homemaker wife. In the other video, the employment and domestic roles of the husband and wife were reversed. Therapists rated the nontraditional male as less masculine and, more important, as more depressed than the traditional male. These studies suggest that individuals are judged as more psychologically disturbed when they violate traditional gender expectations. As a final example of gender bias in diagnosis, a recent book on clinical diagnosis (Ratey & Johnson, 1997) described the employed woman who chafes when her husband does not help with housework and child care as suffering from a mild form of obsessive-compulsive disorder.

Gender Bias in Psychotherapy.   Gender bias also exists in psychotherapy. It may take the form of fostering traditional gender roles (e.g., "be a better wife"), telling sexist jokes, not taking violence against women seriously, and seducing female clients (American Psychological Association, 1975). In a recent study (Fowers, Applegate, Tredinnick, & Slusher, 1996), for example, over 200 clinical psychologists were asked to recommend strategies that would best help hypothetical females and males with identically described problems. The psychologists indicated that male clients could best be helped by increasing their instrumental (traditionally masculine) actions, whereas females could benefit more by enhancing their expressive (traditionally feminine) behaviors. Therapists are more likely to see women's emotional problems as internally caused (intrapsychic) than they are to regard men's emotional problems in this way and they may fail to perceive the external stresses of women's lives (Boston Women's Health Book Collective, 1998; Marecek & Hare-Mustin, 1998).

Therapy Issues for Women of Color and Poor Women.   Women of color and poor women face a number of external stresses which can cause or intensify mental health problems: racism, poverty, culturally approved subordinate status, and living in contexts of violence and chronic strain (Comas-Díaz & Greene, 1994; Commonwealth Fund, 1995b). Unfortunately, financial constraints and time and transportation problems prevent many poor women from seeking help. In addition, people of color are underrepresented in the mental health professions, so that members of these groups often have a therapist who does not know their culture or speak their language. Nonminority providers may apply racial stereotypes to their minority patients instead of seeing them as individuals. Moreover, they can be insensitive to the social and economic conditions in which women of color and poor women live (Adams, 1995; Gil, 1996; Greene 1996; LaFromboise, Berman, & Sohi, 1994; Shum, 1996).

Traditional Therapies. Traditional psychotherapies are based on a medical model in which emotional pain is viewed as a "disease" which must be "treated" by an expert. This leads to a therapeutic relationship marked by an imbalance of power between therapist (often male) and patient (often female). In addition, the individual's emotional problems are seen as having internal, not external causes. The goal of therapy is to promote the person's adjustment to existing social conditions (Boston Women's Health Book Collective, 1998; Rollins, 1996).

Nonsexist and Feminist Therapies. According to **nonsexist therapy**, *women and men should be treated equally and viewed as individuals.* In addition, there is less of a power imbalance between therapist and client. Nonsexist therapy is similar to traditional therapies, however, in its focus on internal causes of psychological problems. **Feminist therapy** on the other hand, *emphasizes the role of social, political, and economic stresses facing women as a major source of their psychological problems.* Feminist therapy encourages women to become psychologically and economically independent, and to try to change a sexist society rather than adjust to it. Another component of feminist therapy is that therapists should not be more powerful than their clients, but should build egalitarian relationships with them. In addition, feminist therapy stresses awareness of the ethnic and cultural differences between client and therapist (Greene & Sanchez-Hucles, 1997; Simi & Mahalik, 1997; Sparks & Park, 2000; Wyche & Rice, 1997). Feminist therapy is a philosophy underlying therapy rather than a specific therapeutic technique, and it can be integrated with other treatment approaches (Brown & Brodsky, 1998; Gilbert & Scher, 1999).

SUMMARY

1. Physical appearance changes as women age, and include thinning and graying of hair, wrinkling and loss of elasticity in the skin, redistribution of fat, and greater porosity of the bones.

2. The stigma of aging is greater for women than men. This double standard is based on society's emphasis on youthful physical beauty for women.

3. Menopause, caused by a decrease in estrogen production, causes hot flashes and vaginal dryness, but is not linked to heightened psychological distress. Middle-aged women usually have positive attitudes toward menopause.

4. Osteoporosis, the loss of bone tissue, increases after menopause and can lead

to disabling and even fatal fractures. Building and maintaining bone mass is enhanced by increasing calcium intake, decreasing use of alcohol, caffeine, and tobacco, increasing physical activity, and taking estrogen or certain medications.

5. Hormone replacement therapy (HRT) has benefits and risks. Benefits include decrease in menopausal symptoms and decrease in the risk of heart disease, osteoporosis, colon cancer, and Alzheimer's disease. Risks include increase in breast cancer risk after long use. Alternatives to HRT include synthetic estrogens and phyto-estrogens.

6. Postmenopausal physical changes can lead to painful intercourse. Some women show a decline in sexual interest and

capacity for orgasm, while others show the opposite pattern.

7. Heart disease, the leading killer of women, increases dramatically after menopause. Women develop heart disease later than men and are twice as likely to die of it. Risk factors for heart disease include gender, age , ethnicity, family history, smoking, physical inactivity, high cholesterol levels, high blood pressure, diabetes, and overweight. Women with heart disease receive less aggressive treatment than men.

8. One in eight women will develop breast cancer, but survival rates have been increasing. Risk factors include age, ethnicity, family history, drinking, smoking, weight gain, and physical activity. Many women do not do monthly breast self-exams or get regular mammograms. For small early tumors, lumpectomy with radiation is as effective as mastectomy. Support groups helps women cope with cancer.

9. Benign disorders of the reproductive system include fibroid tumors and endometriosis. Uterine and cervical cancers have higher survival rates than ovarian cancer. The Pap smear is an effective screening device for cervical cancer. American women have one of the highest hysterectomy rates in the world.

10. Depression is two to four times more common in women than men. Possible explanations for this difference include biological factors, stressful life events, learned helplessness, self-silencing, and women's ruminative style in responding to depression.

11. The anxiety disorders of specific phobias and agoraphobia are much more common in women than men.

12. Gender bias exists in diagnosis and treatment of psychological disorders. Women of color face external stresses which can intensify mental health problems and prevent them from seeking help.

13. Traditional psychotherapies are marked by a power imbalance between therapist and client, and a focus on internal causes of emotional problems. Nonsexist therapy treats women and men equally. Feminist therapy is nonsexist, encourages equal power between therapist and client, and focuses on societal causes of women's problems.

WHAT DO YOU THINK?

1. In your opinion, why do young women have more negative views of menopause than middle-aged women?

2. Why do you think women's heart disease risks were largely ignored until fairly recently? What actions can individuals take to help improve this situation? What actions can members of the medical community take?

3. Why do you think there is a difference between mammogram screening rates for women who differ in socioeconomic status? What actions could be taken to change these disparities?

4. Of the health conditions mentioned in this chapter, which ones can you prevent? Which ones can you delay? What actions can you take now to protect yourself from these problems? Which of these are you currently doing, and why?

5. How might stereotypes about women and men affect the way psychotherapists work with female and male clients?

IF YOU WANT TO LEARN MORE

Dennerstein, L., & Shelly, J. (Eds.). (1998). *A woman's guide to menopause and hormone replacement therapy*. Washington, DC: American Psychiatric Press.

Comas-Díaz, L., & Greene, B. (Eds.). (1994). *Women of color: Integrating ethnic and gender identities in psychotherapy*. New York: Guilford.

Gilbert, L. A., & Scher, M. (1999). *Gender and sex in counseling and psychotherapy*. Boston: Allyn and Bacon.

Goldman, M. B., & Hatch, M. C. (Eds.). (2000). *Women and health*. New York: Academic Press.

Northrup, C. (1998). *Women's bodies, women's wisdom*. New York: Bantam Books.

Notelovitz, M., & Tonnessen, D. (1996). *The essential heart book for women*. New York: St. Martin's Griffin.

Ratner, E. (1999). *The feisty woman's breast cancer book*. New York: Hunter House.

CHAPTER

10 Middle Adulthood

Employment

KEY TERMS

index of segregation
glass ceiling
job ladder
mentor
rational bias theory
human capital perspective

sexual harassment in the
    workplace
quid pro quo harassment
hostile environment
sex-role spillover theory
feminist theory

internally focused responses
externally focused responses
pay equity
affirmative action

The work environment for Lois Robinson, a welder in a shipyard with a predominantly male workforce, was one where profanity, obscenity, and overt anti-female hostility were common, where the work space was "decorated" with graffiti, calendars, and magazine photos depicting female nudity and sexually explicit poses, where female employees were called by demeaning or sexual terms, such as baby, honey, pussy, or cunt, and where women workers were subjected to physical touching and sexual propositions. Disturbed by these conditions, Ms. Robinson complained to shipyard managers. However, not only were her accusations dismissed, but she was even told by one manager that he, also, posted pinups (Fiske & Stevens, 1993).

Ronnie Falco experienced a different form of negative gender-based treatment. A graduate of prestigious Stanford University with a major in computer science, Ms. Falco began a successful career as a software designer, work that she loved. Unfortunately, however, due to the frustrating interactions she had with her male colleagues, her computer career was short-lived. Her coworkers did not look at her when they spoke to her, directed questions at male colleagues even when she had greater expertise, and seemed to resent her successful solutions to problems. Consequently, after 10 years in the computer industry, Ronnie Falco left and went into the health field (Piller, 1998).

In this chapter we examine the nature of women's employment. We begin with an overview of why women work, how many women work, what kinds of jobs they have, and the salaries they receive. Then we focus on negative experiences that women can experience in the workplace, like those illustrated in these vignettes. Next we look at women's evaluations of their jobs and the work-related review process experienced by some women during midlife. Last, we consider procedures and policies that can improve the work environment for women.

In our exploration of these topics, we use the terms *employment* and *work* interchangeably, so it is important that we clarify their meaning. According to Barbara Reskin and Irene Padavic, authors of *Women and Men at Work* (1994), the term *work* refers to "activities that produce a good or a service" (p. 1). Thus, it includes myriad behaviors, such as cooking dinner, mowing the lawn, writing a term paper, teaching a class, fixing a car, volunteering in a nursing home, or running a corporation. The kind of work that we cover in this chapter is a qualified subset of work activities—work for pay. We examine this form of work because it is a major focus of the lives of women (and men) in terms of both time and personal identity. However, our focus on paid employment does not imply that this form of work is more valuable than other types of productive activities. Our society would not function without the unpaid labor that contributes to family and community life.

Women's Preference for Employment

"If you had enough money to live as comfortably as you'd like, would you prefer to work full time, work part time, do volunteer-type work, or work at home caring for the family?" (Families and Work Institute, 1995, p. 54). Two national surveys asking this or a similar question in the 1990s indicated a diversity of opinions. Approximately 50 percent of women reported they would desire employment even if it were not financially necessary, and 50 percent reported they would not want to work (Boxer, 1997; Families and Work Institute, 1995). Furthermore, these studies showed that several factors contribute to women's decision to work or not under this circumstance. One factor is age. As we will see in Chapter 12, child care responsibilities continue to be viewed as primarily women's domain. Therefore, it is not surprising that women in the 25- to 34-year-old age group tend to be least likely to desire employment. Instead, many of these women want to stay home and care for their families (Families and Work Institute, 1995)

Other factors that differentiate between women who would and would not prefer employment are education and salary. The Families and Work Institute study (1995) showed that a desire for employment was strongest among the most educated and highly paid women in the sample: 58 percent of the college-educated respondents and 65 percent of those earning at least $50,000 desired paid work. Possibly these women were more likely than less-educated or lower-paid women to see their jobs as careers important to their personal identities and to have more psychologically rewarding experiences at work.

What work do women do? What percentage are employed? In which occupations do they work? What job levels do they hold in the workplace?

Employment Rates

In 1999, 58 percent of White women and 61 percent of Black women 20 years old and over were employed. These rates are lower than the comparable rates for men (75 percent and 68 percent, respectively) (U.S. Bureau of Labor Statistics, 1999b). For women with disabilities, the gender difference is even greater. For example, the rate of employment for White women with disabilities is half the rate of White men with disabilities (Asch & Fine, 1992). However, although the percentage of employed women is smaller, women's labor force participation has increased dramatically over several decades, especially among mothers. Whereas in 1975 only 44 percent of all married women and 37 percent of married women with children under age 6 were in the labor force, by 1998 these numbers had increased to 68 percent and 61 percent, respectively (U.S. Bureau of Labor Statistics, 1999c).

What might account for the influx of women into the workplace? Several factors probably have contributed. First, the women's movement provided encouragement for women to consider other role options in addition to the homemaker role. Second, women's current higher level of educational attainment (see Chapter 8) has better prepared them for careers that provide greater challenge, stimulation, and a sense of accomplishment. Third, many women must work for financial reasons. There is evidence that over 80 percent of Americans believe two salaries are necessary to support a family (Coltrane, 1997). Also, the Families and Work Institute survey (1995) found that the majority of women sampled (67 percent of Blacks, 55 percent of Whites, and 52 percent of Latinas) earned at least half of their family's income. Economic necessity is particularly strong for women who are single heads of households. In 1998, 22 percent of all families with children were headed by an unmarried mother, and 72 percent of these mothers were employed (U.S. Bureau of Labor Statistics, 1999c). Unfortunately, for poor women who are heads of households, the employment opportunities are greatly limited, and numerous obstacles block the way to employment. Read Learn about the Research 10.1 for an exploration of employment issues for sheltered homeless and low-income women.

Gender Differences in Occupational Distribution

One way to examine the occupational distributions of women and men is to look at the occupations that employ the greatest number of women and those that employ the greatest number of men. At the time of the 1990 U.S. census, a comparison of the 10 most frequent occupations for women and men showed that only two occupations (manager/administrator and sales supervisor/proprietor) were among the most common for both genders. Also the top three occupations

Employment Decision Making of Sheltered Homeless and Low-Income Single Mothers

As policy makers at both the federal and state levels are grappling with ways to overhaul the welfare system, employment options for poor, single mothers remain very limited. In order to understand both the obstacles to and positive influences on the employment of poor mothers, Margaret Brooks and John Buckner interviewed 220 homeless mothers living in shelters and 216 housed mothers on welfare. Most of these women were White, Latina, or Black, the majority had never been married, and they had an average of two children.

One purpose of the study was to determine the types of jobs obtained by poor women. Among those respondents who had been employed during the preceding five years, nearly 40 percent had worked in service occupations, primarily food service and cashier jobs. This figure is significantly higher than the percentage of women in general who work in these occupations. Because these jobs are frequently of limited duration, pay low wages, provide little opportunity for advancement, and offer limited benefits, the authors concluded that they do not readily lead to self-sufficiency.

A second purpose of the study was to identify characteristics and experiences that differentiated women who had been employed from those who had not. Findings showed that having a high school diploma or GED and a primary female caregiver who had been employed during the respondent's childhood were more common among women who had worked. On the other hand, one characteristic more prominent among women who did not work was difficulty speaking or understanding English.

Given their living and financial conditions, these women experienced numerous barriers to employment. The greatest were child care and family responsibilities. The majority of respondents reported the need for child care assistance in order to be able to seek employment. In addition, more than one-quarter expressed the need for transportation and job training.

The authors concluded their study by stating:

> Until work opportunities for low-skilled individuals are created, until women receive job training and education, and until affordable, quality child care is available, the task of becoming self-supporting will remain a daunting one for single mothers. Welfare reform that ignores these needs is fraught with peril for thousands of families and our society as a whole. (p. 536)

Source: Brooks & Buckner, (1996).

What Does It Mean?

1. How can some of the problems raised by this study be addressed by government, the private sector, educational institutions, or other societal institutions? Be specific.

2. What can poor women do to ensure that their children have better opportunities?

3. Most of the research on women's achievement and career aspirations has focused on middle-class women. Which factors examined in Chapter 8 do not appear to be relevant to the lives of poor women? Explain your answer.

were different for females and males. The most frequent occupations for women were secretary, elementary school teacher, and cashier, whereas the top three for men were manager/administrator, sales supervision/proprietor, and truck driver (Reskin & Padavic, 1994).

Another way of looking at occupational segregation is to determine the **index of segregation**, that is, *the proportion of workers of either gender that would have to change their occupations in order to achieve equal gender representation across all occupations*. This figure would be 0 if every occupation employed equal numbers of each gender and it would be 100 if every occupation employed only one gender. In 1990 the index was 53 percent. In other words, 53 percent of all workers of one gender would have had to shift to jobs dominated by the other gender in order to attain equal gender representation across the workplace (Reskin & Padavic, 1994).

There are indications, however, of some reduction in occupational segregation. Paralleling the influx of women into the workplace over the last several decades, major changes have occurred in the gender distributions of many occupations. Women have increased their numbers in both managerial and professional jobs and in the 1990s approximately equal percentages of women and men were employed in these occupations. However, a closer look at the gender distribution within professions overall shows significant differences in the types of occupations pursued by women and men. In 1998, 83 percent of elementary school teachers were women compared with only 28 percent of computer systems analysts and 6 percent of engineers (U.S. Bureau of the Census, 1999c). Further, although more women have entered the skilled trades (e.g., as carpenters and electricians), they still comprise a very small percentage of these workers (Castro, 1997). Thus, the workplace continues to be characterized by significant gender segregation, with men tending to dominate the most prestigious occupations (e.g., medicine, engineering, banking).

The workplace is segregated not only by gender but by ethnicity. More Whites than Blacks are employed in high-status and high-paying managerial or professional occupations and more Blacks than Whites hold service jobs (U.S. Bureau of Labor Statistics, 1999a). In 1990 two professions (elementary school teaching and nursing) were among the 10 top occupations for Black and White women, but teaching was the only profession among Latinas' most common jobs and accounting was the only one for Asian American women (Reskin & Padavic, 1994). However, the ethnic differences among women are not as great as the gender differences. For example, secretary work and cashiering are among the three most common jobs for Asian American, Black, Latina, and White women.

Gender Differences in Job Levels

Comparative Job Levels

In addition to gender differences in several occupations, there are large differences in the levels of jobs held by women and men within their occupations. To get a picture of the positions women attain in occupations that vary in gender dominance we start with management, a field that employs comparable numbers of women and men. In the United States, although women hold approximately 45 percent of all managerial jobs (U.S. Bureau of Labor Statistics, 1999a), they rarely occupy upper-management positions. Women hold fewer than 5 percent of senior management jobs, and only 2.4 percent of the top executive positions (i.e., executive vice president or above) in the 500 largest companies in the United States (Dobrzynski, 1996). In Canada, women similarly are employed in approximately 41 percent of management positions but in only 8 percent of upper-level management jobs (Employment and Immigration Canada, 1992). Also, women of color are greatly underrepresented at high managerial levels. Approximately 95 percent of the female top managers at large U.S. corporations are White (Federal Glass Ceiling Commission, 1995a).

Now we look at the occupational levels held by women and men in a male-dominated occupation, college teaching. This profession offers five levels of advancement, from lecturer (lowest level) to full professor (highest level). One-third of college faculty in the United States are women. If women and men were equally distributed among the five levels of college teaching, one-third at each level would be women. However, women comprise only 19 percent of faculty at the full professor level and 56 percent of those at the lecturer level. Looking at these figures another way, whereas 45 percent of male faculty are full professors, only 21 percent of female faculty hold this job position (*Academe*, 1998).

The gender and ethnic differences in job levels that we have examined reflect the **glass ceiling**; that is, *invisible barriers that prevent qualified women and people of color from upward mobility in their occupations*. Do men experience these barriers in traditionally female-dominated occupations?

It is disturbing to note that, contrary to women's difficulties advancing in gender-neutral or male-dominated fields, men in female-dominated occupations (e.g., nursing, elementary school teaching, and social work) seem to have an advantage. A study by Christine Williams (1992) shows that men in nontraditional fields are encouraged to take supervisory positions; in fact, it is expected of them. Rather than a glass ceiling, Williams states that men are on a "glass escalator," a quick ride to the top. Thus, men hold a disproportionate number of supervisory positions in occupations dominated by women. For example, a report in 1991 noted that in administrative support and clerical work, 12 percent of middle-aged and older male workers were supervisors, compared to only 3 percent of female workers (Older Women's League, 1991). What is the nature of glass ceiling barriers and why do they occur?

Barriers That Hinder Women's Advancement

Job Ladders.   One of the obstacles women experience is their placement in jobs that have little or no room for growth. Many traditional female jobs have either no **job ladder**; that is, no *path toward higher positions* or a short job ladder where the final step is a low-level position (Reskin & Padavic, 1994). Clerical work exemplifies an occupation with little room for job growth.

Mentors and Social Networks.   What prevents women and people of color from climbing the job ladder in fields that have long job ladders, such as the two we examined, management and college teaching? One factor is the limited availability of mentors for these workers. A **mentor** *is a senior-level person who takes an active role in the career planning and development of junior employees.* Mentors help their mentees develop appropriate skills, learn the informal organizational structure, meet appropriate people, and have access to opportunities that enable them to advance.

Although women workers can receive benefits from both female (e.g., Collison, 1994; Gilbert, 1993) and male (Ragins & Cotton, 1999) mentors, the problem for women employees is the difficulty in identifying an appropriate mentor. The limited number of women in senior-level positions makes it hard for a woman to find a female mentor. Also, the Federal Glass Ceiling Commission (1995a) observed that many male middle-level managers do not want to mentor women or people of color. One male manager had this to say about mentoring women (Nicolau, in the Federal Glass Ceiling Commission, 1995a, p. 28): "It's always going to be tough to figure out how to treat the women, but now it's worse and I'd rather not be in a mentoring relationship with them."

A second vehicle for advancement that is limited for women and people of color is access to informal social networks. These networks can provide information about job opportunities as well as opportunities to meet important members of the organization. Furthermore, they offer social support and can serve as an important precursor to developing a mentoring relationship with a senior-level person. However, White male reluctance to deal with women and people of color means these groups are less likely than White men to be invited to informal social events (e.g., golf outings, lunches) or to be included in informal communication networks (Cianni & Romberger, 1995). The frustration this can produce is voiced by a Black female administrator in higher education who said, "Unless you are able to deal with the old White boy network you will continue to face obstacles and barriers" (Ramey, 1995, p. 116).

Discrimination.   Another factor limiting the job advancement of women and ethnic minorities is discrimination, that is, unfavorable treatment based on gender or ethnicity. Decisions about promotion should reflect an employee's training and experience and, indeed, these factors do have an influence on employer's judgments. However, they do not fully account for the gender difference in promotions. For example, there is evidence that supervisors view female managerial and professional employees and especially those who are ethnic minorities as having less promotion potential than White men (Landau, 1995). Also, laboratory research makes a strong case that women have to demonstrate a greater degree of ability than their male counterparts in order to be viewed as highly competent (Eagly, 1999). As stated by a Black community college professor: "We have to prove more, be twice as good, and be damned near flawless to meet even their mediocre standards. And that to me is not right!" (Weber & Higginbotham, 1997, p. 167). It is not surprising that, in one large-scale study of career women, approximately one-fifth claimed they had experienced discrimination in promotions (Hamrick, 1994).

What form does this discrimination take? An extensive study of gender discrimination within the School of Science at the Massachusetts Institute of Technology, the most prestigious science and engineering university in the United States, revealed discriminatory practices that shocked the university community. Women were disadvantaged not only in promotions and salary but in research grants, appointments to important committees, types of teaching assignments, and even in the size of their research laboratories. Furthermore, not one woman had ever served as head of a science department ("Gender Bias," 1999). What can explain the discriminatory treatment experienced by women and people of color in the workplace?

Stereotypes.   One important factor is the operation of gender stereotypes. The visibility of gender, especially when women are in the minority, can increase the likelihood that male coworkers and supervisors will rely on stereotypes when appraising women's work performance (Stokes, Riger, & Sullivan, 1995). That is, the salience of female workers' gender in male-dominated work environments can lead decision-makers to use gender stereotypes when evaluating the work performance of these employees. Management-level positions, for example, are seen as requiring male gender-stereotypic traits, such as ambition, decisiveness, and self-reliance; hence, reliance on traditional gender stereotypes will lead to the conclusion that a woman is not qualified. In the words of a Black health care administrator in a major hospital: "You can't be just a normal woman in that environment. They take you too much for granted and they want to treat you like you're helpless. You've got to be very aggressive, which they consider abrasive . . . They still promote men because men 'need' it and women don't 'need' it. You're still fighting the same old 'isms.' When I'm upset, they say it's because I need a husband. When John [a coworker] is upset it's because John has so many important things on his mind" (Weber & Higginbotham, 1997, p. 161).

Obviously when stereotypes about a person's gender (or ethnicity) influence job decisions, these decisions are less fair and accurate than they would be if they were based on the individual's experience, training, and skills. According to Ann Morrison, an expert on leadership diversity (Federal Glass Ceiling Commission, 1995a, p. 28): ". . . of all the barriers to corporate advancement identified, it is prejudice that tops the list." That is, Morrison claims, the prejudgment of lack of ability serves as a major obstacle in the career development of women and people of color.

Under what conditions are unfavorable gender stereotypes most likely to operate? First, stereotypes are more likely to hurt women when the evaluators are men (Eagly et al., 1992). In one study, female college students perceived female managers as high in agentic traits, but male college students did not (Deal & Stevenson, 1998). In fact, male respondents characterized female managers very negatively, viewing them as bitter, easily influenced, hasty, nervous, passive, and shy. Given that more than half of all managers and administrators are men and that men dominate higher-level management positions, many female workers are evaluated by men and, therefore, face the possibility of similar stereotype-based judgments and decisions.

Second, gender stereotypes are more likely to negatively influence the perceptions of women performing male-related activities. When functioning in a male domain, women are less likely than men are to be selected as leaders (Hebl, 1995) or to receive positive evaluations for their leadership (Eagly, Makhijani, & Klonsky, 1992). Third, women are more negatively evaluated when they adopt a masculine style of leadership; that is, an autocratic, nonparticipative approach (Eagly et al., 1992).

The operation of negative stereotyping when women work in male-related jobs or use masculine styles is clearly illustrated by the experience of Ann Hopkins (see Chapter 2). Ms. Hopkins was an extremely competent, high-achieving accountant who did not receive her earned promotion to partner because her employers claimed she was not sufficiently feminine. Apparently Ann Hopkins was punished for her masculine style in a male-dominated field. According to Alice Eagly and her colleagues (Eagly et al., 1992) female managers "pay a price" for intruding in men's domains, in terms of either their leadership position or their leadership style.

Cultural Differences. In addition to gender stereotypes, the perception of cultural differences between the evaluator and subordinate can influence discrimination in the workplace. Differences between White male managers and females or people of color can create tension that managers attempt to avoid. As one corporate manager stated: "What's important is comfort, chemistry, relationships, and collaborations. That's what makes a shop work. When we find minorities and women who think like we do, we snatch them up" (Federal Glass Ceiling Commission, 1995a, p. 28). His need to emphasize minorities and women suggests that he thinks achieving rapport with these groups is less likely to occur than rapport with other White men.

Perceived Threat. A third factor influencing discrimination in the workplace is the perception of threat. Many White middle and upper-middle managers view the career progression of women or people of color as a direct threat to their own advancement. "If they are in, there's less of a chance for me. Why would I want a bigger pool? White men can only lose in this game. I'm endangered" (Federal Glass Ceiling Commission, 1995a; p. 31). In one study, of a large Canadian federal agency 126 male managers estimated the number of women at their level in their department and indicated their perception of whether men in management are disadvantaged relative to women (Beaton, Tougas, & Joly, 1996). Not surprisingly, there was a positive relationship between these factors: the more women estimated to be in a department, the greater the perception that women pose a threat to men.

Perceived Benefits of Discrimination. A last explanation of discrimination in the workplace is that people view discrimination as potentially beneficial to the organization. **Rational bias theory** contends that *under some conditions managers will* *deliberately engage in discrimination if it seems beneficial to business interests* (Trentham & Larwood, 1998). Thus, if managers perceive that superiors support discrimination or that a particular personnel decision would jeopardize the company's relationship with a major client, they might favor the use of discriminatory policies. Some comments by business graduate school alumni working primarily as managers or professionals are illustrative of this perspective (Trentham & Larwood, 1998, pp. 16–17): "I would select a male. Customers deal with men on a similar level rather than a woman." "Heads of companies seem to relate better to men and seem to like to do business with men." "Select the male—the male will generally be taken more seriously."

What do all of the barriers against the advancement of women and people of color have in common? Consistent with one of our major themes, these obstacles are clear reflections of power differences in the workplace. White men have higher status and more resources; that is, they have higher organizational power. Although there has been progress in recent years, they continue to have the ability to control opportunities and decisions that have major impact on women and ethnic minorities. However, on the positive side, as more and more women and people of color enter higher-status occupations and gradually advance within these fields, they will acquire greater organizational resources, thus contributing to a reduction in this power inequality.

Gender Differences in Salaries

Comparative Salaries

Although, the earnings gap between women and men has declined over the last few decades, in 1999 women still earned only 75.6 percent of what men earned (U.S. Bureau of Labor Statistics, 1999d). Moreover, when we look at the earnings ratio of women of varying ethnicities to that of White men, we see that women of color fare even more poorly than White women. Whereas White women earn 76 percent of what White men earn, these figures drop to 64 percent and 55 percent for Black and Latina women, respectively. Among Asian Americans, women also have lower incomes than men (Espiritu, 1997) and Native American women earn lower wages than workers in all other ethnic groups (Hunter College Women's Studies Collective, 1995). Similarly, women with disabilities have lower earnings than their male counterparts and are more apt to live near or below the poverty level (Hanna & Rogovsky, 1991). Given that the majority of employed women provide at least half of their families' income and that a sizeable minority of families are headed by employed single women, this pay differential has important implications for families. Not only is it detrimental to the financial well-being of many families, both two-parent and single-parent, but it places more women than men at risk of poverty.

To get a more detailed picture of the gender gap, let's examine wage differentials within selected occupations. In management, 1992 data show that the ratio of female-to-male earnings varied from a low of 50 percent in banking to a high of 85 percent in human services, with Black women in top management positions earning only 60 percent of the income of White men in comparable jobs. Furthermore, among MBA graduates from the top 20 business schools, women's beginning salaries averaged $6,600 less than men's (Federal Glass Ceiling Commission, 1995a).

In college teaching, the ratio of women's-to-men's salaries is higher than the 75.6 percent average. In the 1997–98 academic year, women's average salaries ranged, depending on faculty position, from 85 percent of men's (at the level of full professor) to 96 percent (at the level of instructor). Despite these relatively high ratios, it is important to note what these differences signify in dollars. At the full professor level, women earned, on average $9,000 less than men; among instructors, the average difference was nearly $1,300 (*Academe*, 1998).

Even in occupations that employ primarily women, women's salaries are lower than men's. In 1998 female nurses earned 95 percent of the earnings of male nurses, the wages of female cashiers were 86 percent of the wages of male cashiers, and, among restaurant servers, women earned 82 percent of what men earned (U.S. Department of Labor, Women's Bureau, 1999).

What is the economic meaning of the gender pay gap? Unfortunately, it is far from trivial. For the average 25-year-old woman, the wage gap translates into $523,000 over her lifetime (AFL-CIO and the Institute for Women's Policy Research, 1999). Furthermore, according to sociologist Lois Haignere (in DeAngelis, 1997d), if a woman's starting salary is $1,000 less than a man's (less than the average difference) and both receive yearly raises of 3.5 percent, at the end of 40 years, the woman will have earned $84,550 less than the man.

For poor single mothers the earnings gap poses an additional set of problems. Many unmarried women who are employed do not earn enough to support their families. In fact, there is evidence that if single mothers were paid the same as men, who are comparable in education and number of hours worked, the poverty rate for their families would be reduced by 50 percent (AFL-CIO and the Institute for Women's Policy Research, 1999). Instead, these women are at high risk for both welfare and homelessness (Bassuk, 1993).

Reasons for Differences in Salaries

Several factors have been offered as explanations of the pay differential. In considering these reasons, keep in mind the societal power differential in the workplace.

Gender Differences in Investments in the Job.   According to the **human capital perspective**, *salaries reflect investments of human capital (e.g., education and work experience) and because of their family responsibilities, women, relative to men, reduce their investment in their education and jobs* (e.g., Reskin & Padavic, 1994). That is, women are paid less than men because they have less training and put less time into their careers. Does the evidence support this viewpoint?

We first look first at the influence of educational background. Although education does influence earnings (Reskin & Padavic, 1994), gender differences in education do not account for the wage differences. Recall that similar numbers of females and males graduate from high school and males do not surpass females in education except at the highest levels of educational degrees (see Chapter 8). Furthermore, in the United States, a bachelor's degree increases a man's salary by an average of $28,000 but adds only $9,000 to a woman's salary (Angier, 1999a).

Also, if educational differences could explain salary differences, females and males with comparable levels of education should earn similar wages. The facts speak otherwise. Income data from 1995, for example, show that at every level of educational attainment, from high school to master's degree, Black, Latina, and White women earned less than men in the same ethnic group. These salary differences ranged from $5,000 for Blacks with a high school diploma, to $23,000 for Whites with a master's degree. Moreover, it is disheartening that the average salary of *women with a college degree* ($26,841) was comparable to the earnings of *men with only a high school education* ($26,333) (Institute for Women's Policy Research, 1997).

What about investment of time on the job? Women spend an average of 42 hours per week at work compared to men's 49 hours (Lewin, 1998b), and time at work does play some role in the wage gap (Reskin & Padavic, 1994). Another indicator of time investment is the interruption of employment. Because of their childbearing and childrearing responsibilities, women are more likely than men to temporarily leave employment (Wilson & Wu, in Reskin & Padavic, 1994). However, employment interruptions are becoming less common because there is a greater dependence on two incomes, thus shortening parental leaves, and because women are having fewer children. Furthermore, a survey of senior managers (Korn/Ferry, in the Federal Glass Ceiling Commission, 1995a) showed that only one-third of the women in their study had ever taken a leave, most leaves were for less than 6 months, and excluding interruptions for maternity, men took more leaves than women.

We have seen that there are few differences in educational investment but that women work somewhat fewer hours than men and take more family leaves. Now let's examine whether differences in investment help explain pay differences. According to Reskin and Padavic (1994), human capital differences were a major source of the gender wage gap in the 1970s but that influence is now minimal. One study found that educational background and number of hours worked per week did not account for the salary difference between women and men in the beginning stages of business management careers (Tsui, 1998). Also, an examination of school psychologists demonstrated gender differences in salaries despite similarities in work experience and time spent at work (Thomas & White, 1996). Even though job interruptions can have a negative impact on salary (e.g., Eliason, 1995), studies that have taken into account all human capital differences show that these differences explain only 50 to 75 percent of the gender wage gap (AFL-CIO & the Institute for Women's Policy Research, 1999). In other words, 25 to 50 percent of the salary difference cannot be explained by differences in educational background and time commitment.

Occupational and Job-Level Distribution.   The major factor that contributes to both gender and ethnic differences in pay is the difference in jobs held by women and men and by individuals in different ethnic groups (Reskin & Padavic, 1994). As we saw earlier in this chapter, the workplace is characterized by gender and ethnic segregation. Women, compared to men, and Whites, compared to ethnic minorities, are congregated in different occupations and at different levels within occupations. It is not surprising that employees in higher positions earn higher salaries. Higher-level positions generally involve more responsibility and are associated with factors, such as seniority and productivity, that reflect investment in the job. However, the problem for women and people of color is that they are less likely than White men to attain these higher-paying positions.

Now let's turn to type of occupation. As we have seen, women tend to be congregated in female-dominated occupations, and these occupations are at the low end of the salary scale. According to the National Committee on Pay Equity (1998), the greater the number of women or people of color in an occupation, the lower the wages. As an example, child care workers, including workers with a college degree, earn a lower hourly wage than parking lot attendants (Schodolski, 1998). In fact, if women in female-dominated occupations earned as much as women similarly educated and aged and who work a comparable number of hours in all other occupations, their annual earnings would increase by approximately 18 percent (AFL-CIO & the Institute for Women's Policy Research, 1999).

Why is it that occupations employing mostly women pay less than those employing mostly men? One answer is that women's occupations are devalued relative to men's. In Chapter 3 we saw that people more highly value males and male-related attributes. In the workplace this value difference gets translated into employers' higher evaluation of male-dominated jobs and job-related skills associated with men than of female-dominated occupations and job skills associated with women. For example, physical strength, which characterizes men more than women, is highly valued and well-compensated in metal-working jobs. Nurturance, a trait associated with females more than males, on the other hand, is not highly valued. Consequently, occupations that rely on caregiving, such as child care, are on the low end of the pay scale. Similarly, employers devalue the jobs held by large numbers of people of color and pay them less (Reskin & Padavic, 1994).

Wage Discrimination.   Wage discrimination refers to differential payment for work that has equal or substantially similar value to the employer. Unequal pay scales were once considered justifiable by employers on the basis that women work only for "extras" or "pocket money" or that women can function with less money than men can (Reskin & Padavic, 1994). Since passage of the 1963 Federal Equal Pay Act, however, unequal pay for equal work has been illegal. Nevertheless, according to Shirley Wilcher, head of the Office of Federal Contract Compliance Programs, "old biases are still at work against women" (U.S. Department of Labor, 1999).

Because wage discrimination laws are poorly enforced, equal pay legislation has not guaranteed equality (National Committee on Pay Equity, 1998). As one example, in the early 1990s, a female assistant editor at a major national newspaper earned $2,400 less than the man she succeeded and over $7,000 less than the man who replaced her (Reskin & Padavic, 1994). It should not be surprising, therefore, that thousands of women have filed discrimination claims (Reskin & Padavic, 1994), and settlements have been made for women employed in a range of occupations, including both female-dominated jobs (e.g., clerical workers) and male-dominated jobs (e.g., executives).

Discriminatory policies contribute to ethnic differences in pay as well as to gender differences (National Committee on Pay Equity, 1998). A study conducted by the Fair Employment Council of Washington sent out pairs of Black and White women, matched in work experience and backgrounds, to apply for the same advertised jobs. Not only did more White than Black women receive job offers, but they were more likely to be offered a higher starting salary (Bendick, in Frye, 1996).

Women's Perceptions of Their Salaries

Most studies show that women believe their salaries are not commensurate with the value of their work or their abilities and experience. For example, information provided by the Women's Bureau of the U.S. Department of Labor shows that women, regardless of their age, ethnicity, occupation, or income, believe that the most necessary change in the workplace is better pay (Castro, 1997). Similarly, a study of career women, primarily managers and professionals, reported that 55 percent believed their salaries did not reflect their skills and experiences (Hamrick, 1994) although 61 percent felt their salaries were comparable to the salaries of men in similar positions (Hamrick, 1994). Interestingly, women who interrupt their careers for childraising are more likely than those who do not to believe their salaries are lower than those of men (Hamrick, 1994).

Although most studies of employed women show that they tend to be dissatisfied with their salaries, recall that women have lower salary expectations than men do (see Chapter 8). Do you think these lower expectations can have an impact on satisfaction? Turn to Learn about the Research 10.2 for some intriguing perspectives on this question.

Sexual Harassment

Analogous to the definition of sexual harassment in academic settings (see Chapter 6), **sexual harassment in the workplace** comprises *unwelcome verbal or physical behavior when (a) submission to, or rejection of the behavior forms the basis for work-related decisions* (**quid pro quo harassment**) *or (b) the behavior creates an intimidating, hostile, or offensive work environment* (**hostile environment**). Examples of quid pro quo harassment would be the offer of a promotion in exchange for sex and the threat of a layoff if sex were refused. The hostile environment form of harassment, on the other hand, is illustrated by the experience of Lois Robinson, the welder described in the opening vignette.

LEARN ABOUT THE RESEARCH 10.2
How Do Women Perceive Their Wages?

Salary expectations are closely related to perceptions of entitlement. That is, the higher the salary a person feels entitled to, the higher the salary the person expects. In addition, several scholars contend that salary satisfaction is influenced by the consistency between actual salary and salary believed to be deserved (Bylsma & Major, 1994; Crosby, 1982; Jackson, 1989). One study (Bylsma & Major, 1994) showed that, women, compared to men, feel they deserve lower pay and are more likely to feel satisfied with objectively lower earnings. What could possibly explain women's feelings of lower pay entitlement?

According to Linda Jackson and her colleagues (Jackson, Gardner, & Sullivan, 1992; Jackson & Grabski, 1988), women perceive lower salaries as fair salaries. These researchers suggest that, as a result of differential socialization, women and men have different attitudes toward money, which affect their views of a fair wage.

Brenda Major and Wayne Bylsma (Bylsma & Major, 1994; Major, 1989) offer another explanation. They contend that women and men have different perceptions of personal entitlement because they have different standards of comparison. People tend to evaluate what they deserve by comparing themselves to similar others. Because women's salaries have historically been lower than men's, the standard women use to judge entitlement is lower than the standard used by men. This lower comparison standard then influences women to feel they deserve less than men feel they deserve. Consequently, they are satisfied with lower pay.

What Does It Mean?

1. Jackson and her colleagues suggest that women compared to men have lower standards for fair salaries. Additionally, they claim that this might be because women and men have different attitudes toward money. First, show how different views about money could lead to different perceptions of fair salaries. Then, use information from any chapters in the text to formulate an argument that either supports or refutes the assumptions of gender differences in perceived fairness and attitudes toward money.

2. Use material from any chapters in the text to frame an argument that either supports or refutes Bylsma and Major's claim that women and men have different perceptions of what they deserve and that these differences are due to different comparison standards.

3. Bylsma and Major contend that the lower comparison standards and feelings of entitlement are applicable to any less-powerful group. If this assumption is correct, can you suggest ways to counteract the influence of lower comparison standards?

Incidence

How common is sexual harassment in the workplace? Although few incidents reach the legal standard of harassment (Fitzgerald & Ormerod, 1997), unwanted sexual behaviors in the workplace are commonplace. Based on her narrative review of numerous studies, Barbara Gutek (1993) estimated that between one-third and one-half of all employed women experience sexual harassment. They most commonly experience sexual remarks and jokes, whereas sexual coercion is relatively rare (e.g., Bingham & Scherer, 1993; Gruber, Smith, & Kauppinen-Toropainen, 1996). This does not mean, however, that the latter does not occur. In a particularly disturbing case, Central American immigrant women working in a food plant on the East Coast in 1996 were forced to have sex with their supervisors or risk being fired, being given more physically demanding work, or receiving a cut in pay (Simon, 1998).

Although any woman in any work situation might experience harassment, there are certain factors associated with the greater likelihood of its occurrence. We now turn to an examination of these.

Occupational Characteristics Related to Sexual Harassment. Sexual harassment is more common in male-dominated blue-collar occupations, such as public safety, firefighting, custodial work, skilled repair, construction, and transit, than in other male-dominated, female-dominated, or gender-balanced jobs (Mansfield et al., 1991; Ragins & Scandura, 1995; Yoder & Aniakudo, 1996). Moreover, the type of harassment experienced in these occupations, compared to other jobs, is more severe and brings greater risk of physical injury (Fitzgerald, 1993).

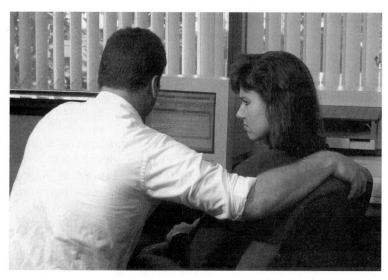

Sexual harassment in the workplace can take many forms.

To investigate the job climate for women in different occupations, Phyllis Mansfield and her colleagues (Mansfield et al., 1991) examined female workers in two male-dominated (blue-collar) jobs and one traditional female-dominated job (school secretary). Among their respondents, 60 percent of the tradeswomen and 36 percent of the transit workers, compared to only 6 percent of the school secretaries, reported experiencing sexual harassment (Mansfield et al., 1991). Moreover, the blue-collar workers were more likely than the clerical employees to feel isolated and to perceive their supervisors and coworkers as sexist and disrespectful. Also, not surprisingly, they expressed less job satisfaction.

In another study of women in blue-collar occupations, Janice Yoder and Patricia Aniakudo (1996, 1997) interviewed and surveyed 22 Black female firefighters about their experiences on the job and their feelings about their job. These researchers concluded that, "encounters with sexual harassing behaviors were almost universal" (1996, p. 257). These women were subjected to unwanted sexual behaviors including teasing and jokes, suggestive looks, deliberate touching, and unwelcome pressure for dates. In addition to sexual harassment, they reported isolation, lack of support, hostility, and hypercritical training, as well as racism. Consider one woman's experience: "No one really talked to me. It was difficult the first, I'd say, six months, because I was basically alone. I'd walk in and everything would get quiet. I'd go to eat; everybody leaves the room . . . As I said, I've been on the job now seven years, and there're still guys that don't talk to me" (Yoder & Aniakudo, 1997, p. 330). Also, another woman described her first interaction with her White male captain as follows: "The first day I came on, the first day I was in the field, the guy told me he didn't like me. And then he said: 'I'm gonna tell you why I don't like you. Number one, I don't like you cuz you're Black. And number two, cuz you're a woman'" (Yoder & Aniakudo, 1997, p. 329).

Another historically male-dominated field associated with a high incidence of sexual harassment is the military. Studies of military personnel in general (Firestone & Harris, 1997), Army women (Wolfe et al., 1998), and Navy personnel (Culbertson & Rosenfeld, 1994) show that between 44 and 78 percent of military women report being sexually harassed. Furthermore, an investigation of blue-collar civilian workers in the U.S. Navy (Palmer & Lee, 1990) found that male coworkers admitted they generally treated their female coworkers less favorably than they treated their male colleagues.

Why is sexual harassment of women more common in male-dominated blue-collar occupations and the military than in other jobs? This is possibly because these fields are strongly associated with the male gender stereotype and male-related physical attributes and skills are highly salient in the performance of these jobs. For example, the Navy blue-collar workers indicated that their unfavorable treatment of women workers was primarily due to their acceptance of gender stereotypes suggesting women's inability to perform the requisite job-related tasks.

In addition to the type of occupation, another job characteristic that affects the likelihood of harassment is an organization's standards about acceptable behavior (Koss et al., 1995). Theresa Glomb and her colleagues (Glomb, Munson,

Hulin, Bergman, & Drasgow, 1999) interviewed both nonacademic and academic female university employees about their sexual harassment experiences. These researchers found a positive relationship between their respondents' perceptions that the work environment was tolerant of sexual harassment and their experiences with harassment. Not surprisingly, employers' and supervisors' attitudes regarding the appropriateness and seriousness of harassment can set the tone for behavior in the workplace.

Target Characteristics Related to Sexual Harassment. Sexual harassment tends to target certain groups more than others. One key characteristic is gender. Sexual harassment is a problem primarily for women. Not only are women, more than men, likely to be targets (e.g., Gutek, 1993; Koss et al., 1995), but women and men tend to have different reactions to harassing behaviors. Women are more likely than men to feel frightened and degraded, whereas men are more likely than women to feel flattered by these behaviors (Koss et al., 1995).

Age and marital status are two other target characteristics associated with harassment. Younger or unmarried women are more likely than older or married females to be harassed (e.g., Koss et al., 1995). This is possibly because younger and single women are seen as more powerless and vulnerable than their older or married counterparts.

Lesbian women are another group at higher risk (Koss et al., 1995). If their sexual identity is not known, they are seen as single women; thus, their risk goes up for that reason. Alternatively, if they are open about their identity, antilesbian prejudice can increase the likelihood that they will be targets of harassment.

Several researchers have examined the incidence of sexual harassment among women of different ethnic groups and have found mixed results (e.g., Mansfield et al., 1991: Wyatt & Riederle, 1994). However, most of the research has been restricted to Black and White women. Audrey Murrell (1996) notes that there are no large-scale surveys of ethnically diverse women. She posits that ethnic stereotypes of Black women as permissive and hypersexual, Latinas as submissive and hypersexual, and Asian American women as submissive might increase the likelihood that these women are seen as suitable targets for harassment. In addition, she suggests that the marginalization of women of color within the work environment can lower their perceived power, further increasing their risk for harassment. However, these hypotheses have not yet been thoroughly investigated.

Characteristics of Offenders. There has been only minimal investigation of the attributes of offenders. However, the picture that emerges from this research is that the way these men construct gender might serve as a foundation for their harassing behaviors. Specifically, harassers tend to have negative attitudes toward women, hold traditional gender attitudes, and perceive sexual relationships as manipulative and exploitative (Pryor, 1987; Pryor, LaVite, & Stoller, 1993). That is, the most likely offenders appear to be traditional men who do not view women as equals.

Explanations

How can we account for the occurrence of sexual harassment in the workplace? According to **sex-role spillover theory** (Gutek, 1985), *in workplaces with unequal concentrations of women and men, gender is a highly salient attribute. Consequently, in these environments men respond to female employees more as women than as workers. That is, they allow gender roles to spill over into the workplace and to influence their interactions with female workers.* The high incidence of sexual harassment among blue-collar workers, supports this theory and points to the importance of an employment context in which male-related physical attributes are very prominent (Ragins & Scandura, 1995). In this type of situation harassment reflects a restrictive construction of gender that specifies separate behaviors and roles for women and men. This inflexibility results in viewing women not as competent workers but as targets of male-female interactions.

The **feminist theory** of sexual harassment, also known as the power perspective, posits that *sexual harassment is seen as an abuse of power to gain sexual favors or to reinforce the imbalance in power* (e.g., MacKinnon, 1979). Because society accords greater power to men than to women, men generally have more power in the workplace, and some men abuse this power for sexual ends (e.g., Kurth, Spiller, & Travis, 2000). Other men use sexual harassment to reinforce the imbalance in power (e.g., Hoffman, 1986). That is, as a means of intimidation in order to protect their own power base.

The male-dominated blue-collar occupations, where sexual harassment is most frequent, once again provide a good example. According to Fiske and Glick (1995), men in these occupations hold most of the power for several reasons. First, men historically view the blue-collar workplace as their own territory. Second, they are in the great majority. Third, they view the few women who enter these occupations as being on probation. Fourth, the generally male supervisors support male workers' power. Fifth, men's overall greater physical strength is an important attribute for most blue-collar jobs. Sixth, men have higher status in society in general. These factors not only maintain a power imbalance in which men are more likely to harass but contribute to an organizational climate in which the negative effects of sexual harassment tend to be minimized and in which complaints about harassment might not be seen as serious.

Women's Responses

How do women respond to sexual harassment? Louise Fitzgerald (in Fitzgerald, Swan, & Fischer, 1995) proposes a two-category framework that classifies the large variety of responses to sexual harassment as either internally focused or externally focused. **Internally focused responses** are *responses that attempt to manage the emotions and cognitions associated with the incident(s).* For example, attempting to forget about the event or convincing oneself that it won't affect one's job performance are adjustments that aim to reduce negative emotions or thoughts about the situation. **Externally focused responses**, on the other hand, are *responses that attempt to solve the problem*. Examples are avoiding the harasser or seeking organizational assistance. Targets of harassment use both types of strategies. A common internally focused response is ignoring the situation, and frequently used externally focused strategies include avoiding the harasser, asking him to stop, and quitting one's job (Firestone & Harris, 1997; Fitzgerald et al., 1995; U.S. MSPB, in Murrell, 1996).

Atypical responses are those that use the system to seek redress, such as filing a complaint or lawsuit. Both formal claims and informal complaints to authorities are rare responses, and filing a lawsuit is the least likely response (Fitzgerald et al., 1995). According to Fitzgerald and her colleagues, the primary reasons targets do not report the harasser are fear, shame and embarrassment. Sexually harassed women, similar to other victimized women (see Chapter 11), frequently experience shame and embarrassment as a result of their harassment (Koss et al., 1995). This, combined with their fear of retaliation or humiliation, increases the likelihood they will not report the harassment. Furthermore, fears of retribution or trivialization are justified. Research reviewed by Fitzgerald and her associates (Fitzgerald et al., 1995) indicates that women who used more active measures to deal with their harassment reported negative outcomes, such as lowered job evaluations, humiliation, and health problems, from their attempts. These researchers conclude that those women who do turn to organizational or legal routes do so only after other efforts have failed.

Consequences

There is considerable evidence that numerous negative consequences for women can result from sexual harassment in the workplace. A broad variety of psychological consequences, such as decreased self-esteem, lowered life satisfaction, fear, depression, interpersonal difficulties, and sexual problems can occur (Fitzgerald & Ormerod, 1997; Glomb et al., 1999; Koss et al., 1995). Additionally, women can experience undesirable job-related outcomes, including reduced job satisfaction, decreased morale, increased absenteeism, and a decline in organizational commitment. Furthermore, they may suffer from stress-related physical symptoms, such as headaches, gastrointestinal problems, sleep disturbances, and disordered eating.

Are these negative reactions affected by whether or not women label their experience as harassment? That is, do women who acknowledge they have been harassed have more negative outcomes than those who do not? Vicki Magley and her colleagues (Magley, Hulin, Fitzgerald, & DeNardo, 1999) examined a large number of female employees in diverse occupations to try to answer this question. Interestingly, they found that women who were targeted with unwelcome sexual behaviors had negative psychological and physical reactions whether or not they labeled their experience as harassment. The authors note that women might not realize certain behaviors fit the definition of harassment or, alternatively, they might want to avoid the label of victim. The lack of labeling unwanted sexual acts as harassment does not, however, affect the consequences of those behaviors. It is the experiencing of these behaviors on the job, and not the labeling of them as harassment, that leads to unpleasant psychological and physical outcomes.

Now that you are familiar with some of the problems experienced by women in the workplace, perform the interviews in Get Involved 10.1 to gain firsthand knowledge about women's experiences with wage or promotion discrimination and with sexual harassment.

Women's Evaluations of Their Jobs

Earlier in this chapter, we saw that women and men congregate in different jobs and that the most prestigious occupations employ more men than women. Also, we noted that women's job levels and salaries are generally lower than men's. Do these gender differences in occupational dimensions correspond to differences in job satisfaction?

Given the existence of the glass ceiling, it is not surprising that women express less satisfaction than men do about their promotional opportunities (Chiu, 1998; Lyness & Thompson, 1997). More than three-quarters of the women in the Families and Work Institute sample (1995) discussed earlier in this chapter indicated concern about insufficient opportunities for women to get ahead or to grow.

GET INVOLVED **10.1**

Gender-Based Treatment in the Workplace

Interview two employed women. If possible, select full-time employees, but if they are not available, include any working women, including students with part-time jobs. Ask each respondent to discuss her experiences with the following: (1) discrimination in salary, (2) discrimination in promotion, (3) gender stereotyping by coworkers or supervisors, and (4) any other types of gender-based unfair treatment.

What Does It Mean?

1. Compare the reported experiences of your respondents with the information reported in the chapter. Describe both the differences and similarities between your findings and the material presented in the text. Give possible reasons for the differences, if any.

2. What kinds of changes do you think could be instituted so that the specific problems your respondents identified would be eliminated or greatly reduced?

However, research on gender differences in overall job satisfaction provides mixed results. Although numerous studies show that women are less satisfied than men (Chiu, 1998; Singh, Robinson, & Williams-Green, 1995), there are many exceptions. Some investigations indicate no gender differences in overall job satisfaction (Lyness & Thompson, 1997; Mason, 1995; Weeks & Nantel, 1995), whereas others show higher satisfaction in some occupations among females than among males (Mason, 1995). The fact that women are not consistently less satisfied than men suggests that many factors contribute to the overall satisfaction gained from one's job. Job and salary level are two sources. However, women (as well as men) get other rewards from their jobs, such as recognition, pride, and social stimulation, which can influence job satisfaction.

The great variation across studies may reflect the differences in the occupations sampled. For example, among workers in high-status occupations (e.g., health care practitioners), men show greater job satisfaction than women do, whereas in lower-status jobs (e.g., clerical workers, factory workers), women have higher rates of job satisfaction than men (Mason, 1995; Varca, Shafer, and McCauley, in Chiu, 1998). Given that people's contentment with their jobs is influenced by their expectations (e.g., Crosby, 1982), women in higher status occupations possibly experience a greater discrepancy between their expectations and their actual benefits than do women in lower-status jobs. Put another way, the male advantage in job level and salary might be more important for women in higher-status, compared to lower-status, occupations.

Now let's look at concerns women have about their jobs. We saw previously that they are disturbed by a lack of advancement opportunities. Given the nature of women's experiences in the workplace and their work-family balancing experiences (see Chapter 12), it is not surprising that women are concerned—about their employer's evaluation of them, about challenges associated with balancing work and family, and about sexual harassment (Families and Work Institute, 1995).

For lesbian women, the organizational climate for lesbians and gays is another important concern that influences job satisfaction (Driscoll, Kelley, & Fassinger, 1996). Also, although disclosure of lesbian or bisexual identity does not seem to influence job satisfaction (Croteau & Lark, in Driscoll et al., 1996), the decision of whether or not to come out is a major concern for lesbian workers. A positive consideration is that coming out enables the lesbian or bisexual woman to display an honest public identity that reflects her actual self (Hollingsworth, Tomlinson, & Fassinger, 1997). Coming out can lead to greater self-knowledge and self-confidence (Hollingsworth et al., 1997) and to the development of a beneficial support system (Fassinger, 1995). On the negative side, lesbian and bisexual women fear that sexual identity disclosure might precipitate workplace discrimination, including job loss, salary reduction, harassment (Driscoll et al., 1996; Fassinger, 1995), or reprimand (Frankie & Leary, 1991). Lesbian women of color experience an extra burden because they risk adding homophobia to the gender or ethnic prejudice which they might already experience. Given the perceived risks of coming out in the workplace, it is not surprising that the majority of lesbians do not disclose their sexual identity at work (Fassinger, 1995; Levine & Leonard, 1984).

As we have seen, women's perceptions of their work experiences, develop as a result of many societal and cultural factors. But many women evaluate their lives during their middle adult years, and this evaluation process merits a closer look.

Midlife Transitions

Many middle-aged women (and men) go though a process of life review, that is, an intensive self-evaluation of numerous aspects of their lives, including their job or career. They reexamine their occupational values and goals, evaluate their accomplishments, and sometimes consider new career directions. Some make transitions to different jobs during their middle adult years while others begin their paid work role at this point in their lives.

Women who are in their middle adult years at the beginning of the twenty-first century are members of a generation of women who experienced profound changes in gender role expectations. Born in the mid-twentieth century, they were raised, at least for a period of their lives, with traditional attitudes about gender roles. Many women, especially White middle-class women, were socialized to marry and raise children and not to consider jobs or careers. However, the women's movement of the late 1960s and 1970s, coupled with the significant increase in women's labor force participation, changed some of the rules and expectations for these women. New possibilities arose and some women followed new paths. Thus, many midlife women of today were exposed to two different social constructions of their gender, one dictating traditional roles and the other allowing for nontraditional alternatives.

Given changing societal standards about appropriate roles for women, it is not surprising that one characteristic theme in the life reviews of midlife women today has been the search for an independent identity. As stated by Ravenna Helson (1992), "For countless women, the need to rewrite the life story has been related to the experience of dependence and restriction associated with marriage and motherhood, followed by a lessening of that dependence and restriction as children grow up" (p. 344). Thus, many women attempt to affirm their own being, independent of their husbands, through graduate education, entering the workforce, or a change in careers (Helson, 1992; Stewart & Vandewater, 1999). The development of an independent identity, however, does not imply a lack of desire for connectedness. Many midlife women, whether heterosexual, lesbian, or bisexual, attempt to balance the establishment of autonomy with the maintenance of an intimate relationship (Josselson, 1996; Kimmel & Sang, 1995).

Because of the multiple societal gender-role messages encountered by the current cohort of midlife women, it is not surprising that some followed traditional roles early in adulthood and continued these roles at midlife while others began their adult lives committed to traditional roles but made changes in their middle adult years. Still others deviated from traditional expectations by committing themselves to careers in early adulthood. Because each of these patterns of choices can be fulfilling (Vandewater & Stewart, 1997), many women are satisfied with their life paths and, therefore, make no or minimal changes at midlife.

Satisfaction with Life Roles

First, let's look at the midlife satisfaction of women with jobs or careers. Is their life satisfaction related to their work experience? For some of these women, a general sense of psychological well-being is connected to a feeling of satisfaction with work (Vandewater, Ostrove, & Stewart, 1997). The more satisfied they are with their jobs, the better they feel in general.

Several factors may account for this connection. Satisfying work can provide an independent source of fulfillment, and job-related rewards can help balance problems originating in other life domains. Another job-related factor associated with midlife satisfaction for these women is the achievement of previously established goals. Women who have attained the career goals they set for themselves in young adulthood are generally satisfied. They have a greater sense of life purpose and are less depressed in midlife than those who fall significantly short of their expectations (Carr, 1997). This might be because fulfilling one's career goals represents an important accomplishment that contributes to both self-worth and well-being (Carr, 1997; Roberts, 1997).

Many women who have followed traditional paths also report midlife satisfaction. There is some evidence that midlife women who are full-time homemakers experience the same degree of psychological well-being as those who work for pay (McQuaide, 1998). Furthermore, they have a comparable sense of purpose, or directedness, in life (Carr, 1997). Perhaps a key factor influencing midlife role evaluation is not a woman's *role per se* but fulfillment of her *preferred role* (Carr, 1997).

Regrets about Life Direction

Let's turn now to women who are not satisfied with their role choices and who experience some regrets about the direction their lives have taken. Abigail Stewart and Elizabeth Vandewater (1999) examined the experiences of two samples of women who, as young adults, devoted themselves to marriage and motherhood but in middle adulthood had regrets about their earlier traditional choices. The women in these samples were some of the members of the 1964 class of Radcliffe College and the 1967 University of Michigan class. During midlife many expressed regrets about their earlier traditional role choices. They reported disappointment about not pursuing a more prestigious career, marrying before establishing a career, and not returning to work after having children: "I would not have let my husband take sole responsibility for determining the course of our lives. His career has always been the *only* deciding factor in our lives[,] which has not been fair to me or the children"; "I would have chosen a profession less traditionally female and would have gone into something with more long-range challenge" (p.272).

Making Changes

Was the experience of regret sufficient to alter the life direction of these women? Not for all; some who regretted previous decisions followed new paths but others did not change course. However, as might be expected, those who had regrets and then made changes in their lives benefited from these changes. These women were better adjusted psychologically and even experienced greater physical well-being than their counterparts who had regrets but did not use those regrets as a basis for altering their life direction (Stewart & Vandewater, 1999). Why did some women have regrets but did not act on them? Interestingly, it was not the presence of external constraints, such as the number of children they had, that seemed to prevent these women from making goal-related changes. Instead, it was the tendency to focus on negative life events; to engage in self-pity, moodiness, and negativism. These women seem to have been constrained by personality characteristics rather than external obstacles.

Pursuing a new direction at midlife involves making significant changes in one's life role during the middle adulthood years. A midlife woman who chooses to switch direction at this point must be willing to leave one long-term role (e.g., full-time homemaking or career) that has been a significant part of her identity and proceed down a new and as yet unfamiliar path. In so doing, she is leaving a role to which she has devoted considerable time and energy during her adult years. What are the psychological experiences of women who begin a work role or alter occupational directions in midlife?

To attain a partial answer to this question, let's look at Vandewater and Stewart's (1997) sample of 1964 Radcliffe College graduates who made major work-related changes in midlife. After an earlier, full-time commitment to the traditional roles of wife and mother or to traditional female jobs, such as elementary or secondary school teaching, they realized there was a broader set of options available to them and decided to follow a new career interest or return to an earlier interest that they had never pursued. What precipitated their new directions? For many, the women's movement made a strong impact on their midlife development by raising their awareness of the increasing possibilities open for women and, consequently, changing the way they constructed the female role. As they described it: "[The] women's movement taught me that I could be a doer and not a helper" and "[The] women's movement and political activism of the '60s led me to law school" (p. 404). These women were happy about the changes they made and felt a sense of accomplishment and pride. However, despite new directions suggested by the increasing societal acceptance and encouragement of women's diverse roles, making these significant life changes was often difficult.

Limited Samples of Midlife Women

We saw in Chapter 1 that generalization on the basis of one type of respondent can lead to false conclusions about individuals who are not represented in the sample. For at least two reasons the research findings presented here are relevant to a very specific group of midlife women and should not be extended to other females. First, the respondents in these studies reflect a homogeneous educational and socioeconomic group of women. They were primarily White, highly educated, middle-class women, whose experiences at midlife are vastly different from those of women of color, less educated women, and poor women. Large variations in the range of options for these different groups of women can affect their choices and life reviews both during early adulthood and at midlife. When Terri Apter (1996) interviewed 80 middle-aged women about changes involved in their lives, she found that her two very poor respondents felt they had no choices available to them at midlife because they had no control over their own direction. These women reported feeling so constrained by poverty that significant change and growth at midlife were outside the realm of possibility.

Second, the midlife evaluations and decisions shown by these women must be placed in their historical context. Social constructions of gender have evolved over time and, along with these changes, women have experienced differing perceptions of their own options. Women examined in the studies reported here are in their middle adult years at the beginning of the twenty-first century. The gender-based social climate that shaped their development was different from the societal attitudes influencing the lives of future generations of midlife women. As we discussed earlier, these midlife women were exposed to both traditional and flexible gender role expectations at different points of their lives. Thus, it is likely that they experienced more regrets about previous traditional choices than future generations of midlife women will. Because there are greater options for young women today than there were in the 1960s and 1970s when current midlife women were making life choices, it is possible that fewer young women today will find the need to make significant revisions in their life paths during middle age (Stewart & Ostrove, 1998). Furthermore, older women who were in midlife prior to or during the 1960s and 1970s, experienced different constructions of women's roles than did current midlife women. Thus, during their middle years, they did not experience the career and role opportunities encountered by today's midlife women and, consequently, were not faced with decisions about major role changes.

Changing the Workplace

During the past several decades, there has been a dramatic influx of women in the workplace, an increase in the number of women in male-dominated occupations, and a reduction in the pay differential between men and women. At the same time, women continue to be more heavily congregated in lower-status occupations, to have limited opportunities for advancement, to earn lower salaries than men, and to be targets of biased behavior. What can be done to continue improvements in the work environment that have begun during the last few decades?

Organizational Procedures and Policies

Pay Equity. We have seen that equal pay legislation has not eliminated the gender or ethnicity wage gaps. As long as women and men or Whites and people of color are segregated in different occupations, it is legal to pay them different wages. One way of narrowing these earnings gaps is **pay equity**, *pay policies based on workers' worth and not their gender or ethnicity* (National Committee on Pay Equity, 1998). Pay equity would require that employees in different jobs that are similar in skill, effort, and responsibility receive comparable wages.

Affirmative Action. Think of what affirmative action means to you. To what extent do you characterize affirmative action as a set of procedures that ensures equitable treatment of underrepresented individuals or, alternatively, as a policy that fosters preferential treatment and reverse discrimination? Affirmative action goals and procedures are highly misunderstood. Let's examine the legal conception of affirmative action as well as typical misconceptions of its meaning.

    Affirmative action in employment refers to *positive steps taken by a company, institution, or other type of employer to ensure that the workplace provides equal opportunity for all*. That is, affirmative action involves deliberate actions that facilitate the recruitment and advancement of historically underrepresented workers. To achieve equity, these procedures involve weighing candidates' qualifications as well as group membership. Is this definition consistent with your conception of affirmative action?

    Jennifer Eberhardt and Susan Fiske (1998) contend that perceptions of affirmative action are highly unfavorable. According to these researchers, many people attribute the achievements (e.g., job attainment, promotion) of less powerful individuals (e.g., women, people of color) to group-based preferential treatment but ascribe the accomplishments of more powerful individuals (e.g., White males) to merit. Consequently, they think that affirmative action results in reverse discrimination that hurts qualified White males in favor of unqualified women or people of color. Contrary to these misperceptions, Eberhardt and Fiske claim that the recruitment and promotion of unqualified individuals and the reliance on group membership only, without consideration of qualifications, are highly unusual and illegal practices. Furthermore, the U.S. Department of Labor (n.d.) reports that accusations of reverse discrimination comprised less than 2 percent of the 3,000 discrimination cases filed in federal court between 1990 and 1994 and that few of these were upheld as legitimate claims.

    Despite criticisms of its practices, affirmative action has played an important role in reducing gender inequity in the workplace (Frye, 1996; U.S. Department of Labor, n.d.), and there is evidence that it has done so without negatively affecting performance, productivity, or company profits (Murrell & Jones, 1996). Its success in bringing more women into the workplace and in increasing the gender similarity in occupations, job levels, and salaries, is likely to result in even further reductions in gender imbalances in the future.

One drawback of affirmative action is that it produces ambiguity about the basis for selection of targeted individuals (Eberhardt & Fiske, 1996). Both targets and coworkers might be unsure about the extent to which employment decisions are influenced by gender and ethnicity versus background and performance. However, this problem can be greatly reduced by making clear that both merit and group membership influence the selection of targets.

What kind of actions would be most effective in improving the workplace for women? The exercise in Get Involved 10.2 explores this issue.

Other Organizational Procedures.   Improvements for women and other underrepresented groups must also involve changes in the workplace itself. It is essential for employers to develop a work environment that values diversity and to back up this attitudinal climate with well-publicized antidiscrimination policies. Managers and other workers can be sensitized about both subtle and blatant forms of prejudice and discrimination in the work environment and can learn that the employer will not tolerate any form of discrimination. This can be accomplished through workshops aimed at increasing awareness of how stereotypes operate in evaluating and treating less powerful individuals, including women, people of color, lesbians and gays, and people with disabilities. A nationwide study of the effectiveness of policies such as these found that antidiscrimination policies were

---

G E T   I N V O L V E D   **10.2**

Ways to Make the Workplace Better for Women

Listed below are 6 factors that can contribute to an improvement in women's opportunities and experiences at work. Indicate how important you think each would be to making the workplace better for women in the future, by rank ordering these from 1 to 6. Give a 1 to the factor you think would be most beneficial to improving future conditions for women, give a 2 to the factor you consider would be next most helpful, and so on. Also, ask a woman who differs from you in ethnicity to do the same.

_____ 1. women's hard work

_____ 2. the efforts of feminists to improve conditions for women

_____ 3. women's past contributions that demonstrate their value as workers

_____ 4. laws that make it less likely for employers to discriminate

_____ 5. greater number of women who know how to succeed in the workplace

_____ 6. a workplace that is more responsive to women's needs

Based on Konek, Kitch, & Shore, (1994).

(continued on p. 280)

What Does It Mean?

Factors 1, 3, and 5 (Set A) all point to actions on the part of working women. Factors 2, 4, and 6 (Set B) reflect adaptations resulting from political/social activism, legal mandates, and adaptations within the workplace. Determine the number of items in the each set that you included among your top 3 items. Do the same for your other respondent.

Konek and her colleagues asked a large number of career women to rank these influences and found that these women ranked the items in Set A higher than those in Set B. The researchers interpreted this as an emphasis on individualism; a belief that one's success is due to one's own efforts.

1. Did your answers match the responses of the study's respondents? If yes, was the reason the same? That is, do you more heavily value self-reliance and hard work over external changes that provide increased opportunities?

2. Make the same comparison for your other respondent. Do her answers reflect an emphasis on individualism?

3. Did you notice any differences between the answers given by you and your other respondent? If yes, is it possible that these differences reflect a different emphasis on individualism versus collectivism?

4. Which actions mentioned in the text but not included on this list would be effective? Additionally, are there other strategies that might be beneficial?

---

highly successful in protecting lesbian and gay workers from discrimination (Ragins, 1998).

Another strategy, recommended by the Federal Glass Ceiling Commission (1995b), is for organizations to identify employees with high potential, including women and people of color, and provide them with career development opportunities, such as specialized training, employer-sponsored networks, and job assignments that expand their experience and organizational visibility. Equally important, the Commission stresses, is that senior management clearly communicate throughout the organization its firm commitment to a diverse workforce.

In order to facilitate reporting of complaints, organizations also should make use of clear, well-publicized procedures for filing and evaluating claims of discrimination. Organizations that enact such procedures and ensure that claims can be filed without fear of recrimination produce more favorable work environments for women (Stokes, Riger, & Sullivan, 1995).

Strategies for Women

Although organizational efforts have more far-reaching effects, there are several actions that women can take as they either prepare themselves for employment or attempt to improve their own situation while in the workplace. Beth Green and Nancy Russo (1993) suggest that women can benefit from workshops or work-related social networks that arm them with information that can help them better understand and fight against discriminatory practices in the workplace.

A useful strategy for women who experience discrimination is to join together with others who are experiencing similar inequities. Reporting a shared problem can, in some situations, receive both attention and a commitment to institutional change. As an example of this, recall the pervasive discrimination reported at the Massachusetts Institute of Technology. Documentation of this discrimination resulted from a collective effort by women in the School of Science. Fortunately, the dean of this school responded quickly to redress inequities, and several women within the School of Science received salary increases, research money, and larger or improved laboratories (Hopkins, 1999).

SUMMARY

1. Approximately half of women surveyed in national surveys would prefer to work even if they had no financial need. This percentage is higher among highly educated and more highly paid women and lower among women of childbearing and early childrearing age.

2. More than half of women 20 years and older, including those who are married and have young children, are employed. Economic necessity is a major reason for women's employment.

3. Although the last several decades have seen a decrease, gender and ethnic segregation in the workplace continues to be highly prevalent. The most prestigious occupations are dominated by White men.

4. Women and people of color are less likely than White males to attain high positions in their occupations. Numerous factors contribute to this glass ceiling: shorter job ladders, limited availability of mentors, exclusion from informal social networks, and discrimination. Discriminatory treatment is due, in part, to the operation of gender stereotypes, cultural differences between managers and subordinates, White males' perception of threat, and beliefs that discrimination can produce business benefits.

5. Women earn approximately 76 percent of what men earn. The gender discrepancy is even greater between women of color and White men. These income differences are explained by a variety of factors, including gender differences in job investments, in occupations, and in job levels as well as discrimination. Women tend to be dissatisfied with their incomes, although under some circumstances, they express less pay dissatisfaction than men.

6. It is estimated that between one-third and one-half of employed women experience sexual harassment. Sexist remarks and jokes are common forms of harassment; sexual coercion is relatively rare.

7. Women in blue-collar occupations and the military are more likely to be targets of harassment than women in other types of jobs. This might be due to the high prevalence of both the male gender stereotype and male-related physical traits in these fields.

8. The sex-role spillover explanation of sexual harassment states that harassment occurs because men respond to females in the workplace as women rather than workers. Feminist theory posits that harassment is used by more powerful individuals either to gain sexual favors or to reinforce their position of greater power.

9. Most targets of sexual harassment use informal strategies for dealing with the harassment, such as ignoring it or asking the harasser to stop. They rarely file formal complaints or seek legal redress.

10. Numerous negative psychological, job-related, and physical outcomes can stem from sexual harassment.

11. Findings regarding women's and men's overall satisfaction with their jobs are mixed, but, women are less satisfied with their advancement opportunities than men are. One factor contributing to job satisfaction for lesbian women is the organizational climate for lesbians and gays.

12. Many women go through a life review during their middle adult years. Because those who are in midlife at the beginning of the twenty-first century were exposed to traditional gender role expectations during their early years and flexible gender roles later, many now seek an identity independent of their husband's.

13. Some midlife women are satisfied with either the career or traditional paths they have followed. Others experience regrets about previous traditional role choices, and some of these women choose to make significant changes in their life direction.

14. Organizational strategies that can improve the workplace for women and people of color include implementation of pay equity, establishment of clearly defined affirmative action policies and procedures, and maintenance of an organizational environment characterized by sensitivity to diversity.

WHAT DO YOU THINK?

1. The Families and Work Institute survey showed that approximately one-half of female respondents would like to work even if they had no financial need to work. What kinds of rewards, other than financial, are provided by employment? How does gender socialization affect the particular values women attach to work? Explain your answers.

2. Why do you think many people have negative impressions, including misconceptions, of affirmative action? Incorporate information about stereotypes, gender socialization, gender differences in power, and/or any other material related to this course.

3. This chapter discussed several procedures for improving the workplace for women and people of color. What other actions can be undertaken by employers or individuals in these groups to decrease gender and ethnicity inequities in the work environment?

4. How might greater gender equity in the workplace change the current social construction of gender? Would this, in turn, influence the gender acquisition of gender-related traits, behaviors, and roles and/or the career goals of future generations of females? Explain your answers.

IF YOU WANT TO LEARN MORE

Ellis, A. L., & Riggle, E. D. B. (Eds.). (1996). *Sexual identity on the job—Issues and services.* Binghamton, NY: Harrington Park Press.

Konek, C. W., & Kitch, S. L. (Eds.). (1994). *Women and careers: Issues and challenges,* Thousand Oaks, CA: Sage.

Koss, M. P., Goodman, L. A., Browne, A., Fitzgerald, L. F., Keita, G. P., & Russo, N. F. (1995). *No safe haven: Male violence against women at home, at work, and in the community.* Washington, DC: American Psychological Association.

Reskin, B. F., & Padavic, I. (1994). *Women and men at work,* Thousand Oaks, CA: Pine Forge Press.

11 Young and Middle Adulthood

Interpersonal Issues I: Close Relationships and Intimate Violence

KEY TERMS

affiliative interruption
intrusive interruption
cohabitation
selection effect
Boston marriage
motherhood mandate
matriarch stereotype

welfare mother stereotype
superwoman stereotype
extended families
augmented families
postparental period
rape
acquaintance rape

sexual script
rape myths
evolutionary theory
feminist theory
social learning theory
domestic violence

A middle-aged lesbian couple had been together for 15 years when their daughter was born. To celebrate the joyous occasion, they held a naming ceremony attended by their closest friends. The nonbiological mother held the baby and presented her with her full name consisting of her given name and each of her parents' surnames. Then each parent lit a candle and made a wish for their baby girl. Following this, they expressed their feelings for one another and for the new family they had created. (Muzio, 1996)

R., a first-year college student at a large university, was flattered by the attention she received from a six-foot-five-inch, 265-pound football player at a residence hall party. After encouraging her to have several drinks, the man asked her to his room, down the hall from the party. R. thought there would be other students there and was surprised to find the room empty. "We started kissing and then he started taking off my clothes. I kept telling him to stop and I was crying. I was scared of him and thought he was going to hurt me . . . He had a hand over my face. I was five-foot-two and weighed 110 pounds. I didn't have any choice." (Warshaw, 1988, p. 30)

These vignettes portray vastly different experiences with close relationships. In this chapter we explore the nature of women's close relationships—including friendships, dating relationships, marriage and other long-term relationships, unattached lifestyles, and motherhood. Also, we look at the disturbing, violent side of some relationships, with an examination of rape and domestic violence. Because interpersonal interaction is strongly based on both verbal and nonverbal communication, we begin our examination of interpersonal issues with a look at women's and men's communication styles.

Communication Style

Verbal Communication

Stereotypes suggest that females are always talking, that they speak more than males do and, according to a best-selling book, that women and men are so different in their communication styles that it is as if *Men Are from Mars, Women Are from Venus* (Gray, 1992). What does science tell us about differences between females and males in their communication styles?

There is evidence of a number of gender differences, and one of these is, indeed, a difference in talkativeness. However, interestingly, the talking behavior of females and males is opposite of the stereotype. In most situations examined by researchers males talk more than females; they speak more frequently and for longer periods of time. Furthermore, this gender difference is apparent as early as the preschool years and continues throughout adulthood (Wood, 1994).

Given the gender difference in talkativeness, we might expect that males also interrupt others more than females do. Research indicates that gender differences in the number of interruptions are not consistent across different types of situations, but that women and men have different goals when they interrupt others. One purpose of an interruption is *to show interest and affirm what the other is saying*—an **affiliative interruption**—for example, by saying "uh-huh." A second reason for interrupting is *to usurp the floor and control the conversation*—an **intrusive interruption**. This might be accomplished by taking over the conversation even though the previous speaker shows no signs of relinquishing the floor. It might not surprise you to learn that women are more likely to engage in the former type of interruption and men in the latter (Anderson & Leaper, 1998; Wood, 1994). These differences are consistent both with the social construction of females as other-directed and caring and with the gender inequality in power. Affiliative interruptions are one way to express an interest in other people, and females might have learned through their socialization that this was one means of showing concern about and reinforcing others. Also, intrusive interruptions and talkativeness are both associated with the desire to maintain dominance and the power to do so. More powerful individuals are seen as having the right to dominate the conversation and to usurp the floor. This connection between power and communication behavior is illustrated in a study by Elizabeth Cashdan (1998), who observed female and male college students in group discussions and asked them to rate their housemates on characteristics of power. Her findings showed that the more powerful students were the ones who talked the most.

Let's turn now to individuals' manner of communicating or conversational style. Consistent with communal and agentic stereotypes, studies show that females use more emotional language while males use more direct, goal-oriented language (Guerrero & Reiter, 1998; Mulac, 1998). For example, women are more likely than men to refer to emotions and use intensive adverbs (e.g., "She is *really* friendly"), whereas men tend to use directives (e.g., "Think about this") and judgmental adjectives more than women do.

Another gender difference in conversational style is that females use more uncertainty verbs (e.g., "It *seems* that the class will be interesting"), hedges (e.g., "*I kind of feel* you should not be too upset about this") and questions ("Do you agree?") (Mulac, 1998). One explanation for this difference is that females have lower self-esteem than males do and, consequently, are more tentative in their speech (e.g., Lakoff, 1975). However, other interpretations indicate women's tentativeness might result not from women's uncertainty but from their lower status (e.g., Wood, 1994). Less powerful individuals are more likely to use more tentative speech, regardless of their own confidence in what they are saying, and as we have noted throughout this text, women have less power than men. In support of this explanation, research suggests that females use more tentative language in their conversations with men but not in their interactions with other women (e.g., Carli, 1990). Still another perspective on this gender difference in conversational style is that the language features used by women do not reflect tentativeness at all but instead are due to women's communal orientation—their desire to leave open the lines of communication and encourage the participation of others (e.g., Wood, 1994).

Despite some gender differences in style, it is important to note that these characteristics are subtle; it is difficult to detect the gender of communicators simply from their words. For example, Mulac and his colleagues (see Mulac, 1998) performed several studies in which college students were asked to determine the gender of a communicator after reading a written communication, such as a transcription of a speech from a public speaking class or an essay describing landscape photos. In none of these situations were respondents able to accurately guess the gender of the communicator. Mulac concludes, "spoken and written language used in everyday communication by women and men, as well as girls and boys, displays a high degree of similarity" (p. 131).

Similar to conversational style, the content of females' and males' conversations, at least with their same-gender friends is characterized by both gender similarities and differences. In an attempt to learn what young adult women and men talk about with their friends, Ruth Anne Clark (1998) asked college students to list all the topics discussed in a recent conversation with a same-gender close friend and to indicate the dominant topic. Not surprisingly, given the importance of romantic relationships to young adults, her findings showed that both females and males talked about the other gender. However, women's conversations more than men's were dominated by interpersonal issues. Whereas 64 percent of the women reported that other people (both other- and same-gender) were the dominant topic of their conversations, this was true for only 40 percent of the men. Furthermore, 36 percent of the men said that sports and other leisure activities were their primary focus. Another difference in content was the type of discussion about other people, with women more likely than men to discuss the nature of their relationships or problems in these relationships. Despite these gender differences, it is important to keep in mind that this study was done with college students and tells us little about the topics of interest to older women and men or to girls and boys.

Nonverbal Communication

Consistent with the communal stereotype, people believe that females are more likely than males to engage in nonverbal behaviors that demonstrate interpersonal interest and warmth. Are these beliefs accurate? Considerable evidence (Briton & Hall, 1995a) shows that they are, that females are more likely than males to smile (e.g., Briton & Hall, 1995b; Hall, 1998) and look at their partner (e.g., Guerrero, 1997); to be more sensitive to the meanings of nonverbal messages portrayed by others; to accurately interpret their emotions (Hall, 1998); and to perceive themselves as skilled in nonverbal interpretation (Guerrero & Reiter, 1998).

One explanation for these gender differences is the differential socialization of females and males and the societal encouragement for females more than males to be socially concerned (Guerrero & Reiter, 1998). Smiling and gazing communicate an interest and involvement in another person. Furthermore, women's ability to accurately decipher other people's emotional states might stem from their greater interest in others and their more extensive experience with emotional communication.

A different explanation of females' superior sensitivity skills lies in their subordinate status within society. In order to best adapt socially—to know how to respond appropriately and to structure their own action—less powerful individuals must be good interpreters of the nonverbal cues of more powerful people (LaFrance & Henley, 1994; Wood, 1994). They must be able to anticipate the reactions of those with power. In other words, the ability to decipher the nonverbal behavior of others might serve as a protective mechanism that guides the interpersonal relationships of all lower-status individuals, including women.

Touch is another form of nonverbal communication. In 1973 Nancy Henley proposed a framework for understanding gender differences in tactile communication. She contended that there is an unwritten societal rule that high-status individuals can touch low-status individuals but those of low status cannot touch those of high status. For example, it is more likely that the president of a corporation will pat a janitor on the back than the reverse. Based on this assumption, Henley asserted that because males in North America have a greater degree of power than females, there is more male-to-female touching than the reverse. Despite the inherent logic of this perspective, research on gender differences in touching has provided mixed findings, with some studies even showing more female-to-male touching (e.g., Jones, 1986).

Of course, tactile communication can vary widely—from hugs that show affection to inappropriate sexual touching that is harassing to formal handshakes that communicate respect. Given the complexity of the types of touch and the nature of relationships in which touching can take place, it is not surprising that researchers have failed to observe any overall gender differences in the tendency to use touch (Hall, 1996). One investigation, however, suggests an interesting relationship among gender, status, and touching. Judith Hall (1996) trained college students to unobtrusively observe and record touching behavior that occurred among professionals attending either a psychology or a philosophy convention. Her results indicated no overall tendency for one gender to touch the other gender more nor for more touching to be initiated by higher-status professionals (based on factors such as the prestige of their university or the academic rank of the individual) than by lower-status professionals. However, when the toucher and recipient were of similar status, males were more likely to touch females than vice versa. Hall suggested that when individuals are similar in professional status, gender serves as a status cue that can dictate rules about touching. Obviously, gender and status differences in touching are more complex than were originally believed. Additional variables, such as age and type of relationship, also can affect who touches whom (Hall & Veccia, 1992).

Friendship

Gender Differences in Friendship

Both women and men highly value their friendships. These close relationships provide mutual support and encouragement (Duck & Wright, 1993) as well as interpersonal intimacy (Wright, 1998). However, there is some evidence that women care about their close friends more than men do (Guse, 1998). Furthermore, despite the importance of friendship to both females and males, they achieve closeness with their friends somewhat differently. Whereas men develop closeness by sharing activities with their friends (e.g., Wood, 1994), women are more apt to do so by sharing thoughts and feelings (e.g., Reis, 1998).

The greater emphasis on emotional expressiveness shown by women (Duck & Wright, 1993; Samter, Whaley, Mortenson, & Burleson, 1997) is reflected in several ways. Adult and adolescent females (see Chapter 6) disclose more to their friends and reveal more intimate information than males do (Dindia & Allen, 1992; Dolgin & Minowa, 1997; Reis, 1998). Also, when helping a friend with a problem women are more likely than men to express greater empathic understanding of their friend's problem (George, Carroll, Kersnick, & Calderon, 1998).

How can we account for gender differences in emotional intimacy and expressiveness in friendships? Consistent with our assumption that gender is socially constructed, experiences and attitudes shape orientations toward friendship. As we saw in Chapter 4, parents are more likely to encourage emotional expression in their daughters and discourage it in their sons, and females and males carry these messages into their peer relationships. Furthermore, because emotional expression is viewed as a female trait and many males think of gay men as having feminine traits, males might associate emotional closeness between males with homosexuality, a perceived connection that can be threatening and might steer men away from expressing emotions to their male friends (Nardi, 1992).

Most of the research on friendship discussed thus far has focused on young, unmarried, heterosexual college students (e.g., Dolgin & Minowa, 1997; Duck & Wright, 1993). Next we examine the friendship patterns of working-class and middle-class married individuals and those of lesbian women.

Marriage, Social Class, and Friendship

Women's friendships continue to be characterized by emotional intimacy after marriage (Wellman, 1992); however, an interesting study by Karen Walker (1998) suggests that the degree of intimacy might vary by social class. Walker interviewed 24- to 48-year-old working- and middle-class couples and found that the former reported greater intimacy in their friendships. Walker offered several possible explanations for this difference. First, her working-class respondents were less geographically mobile than those in the middle-class, thus enabling their friendships to deepen over time. Second, the working-class women and men engaged in considerable single-gender socializing, which facilitated the development of intimacy, whereas the middle-class individuals socialized in couples. Third, the middle-class respondents, especially those who were parents with professional careers, experienced extensive demands on their time, leaving little opportunity for developing or maintaining intimate friendships.

Lesbian Friendships

The emotional support shown in heterosexual female friendships is a particularly important quality of lesbian friendships (Weinstock, 1997), because lesbians are frequently subjected to antagonism in their social environment (Nardi & Sherrod, 1994). The reinforcement and empathy that are part of close relationships can help lesbians cope with prejudice from the broader society. Also, social support can help them develop and maintain their lesbian identity (Weinstock, 1997).

For some lesbians, friendships function as an extended family (Weinstock, 1997). Many midlife and older lesbians who came out during a period that was more hostile toward lesbianism than is true today were not accepted by their families. For them, and for other lesbians who have been rejected by their families of origin, lesbian friendships serve this familial role. And because most lesbians have not been married and have not created a traditional family, these social networks of friends can be an important source of support to midlife and older women (Rothblum, Mintz, Cowan, & Haller, 1995).

Dating Relationships

Importance of Physical Attractiveness

What do females and males look for in a romantic partner? Although both genders value physical attractiveness, men put more emphasis on looks than women do (e.g., Feingold, 1990; Milette & Howard, 1998; Pines, 1998). Personal advertisements written by women and men are good illustrations of this gender difference. Consider this hypothetical ad: "Attractive, slender blonde seeking financially stable partner." Who comes to mind, a woman or a man? Studies show that heterosexual women's and men's ads complement one another. Women are more likely to offer physical attractiveness and ask for financial stability (e.g., Gonzales & Meyers, 1993; Willis & Carlson, 1993). On the other hand, men are more apt to ask for physical attractiveness, including specific facial and bodily features (e.g., blue eyes, long legs, thin) and offer financial security (e.g., Smith, Waldorf, & Trembath, 1990; Gonzales & Meyers, 1993; Willis & Carlson, 1993). The personal ads of gays and lesbians similarly show that gay men are more interested in the attractiveness of their partners than are lesbian women (Hatala & Prehodka, 1996). Lesbians also are less likely than heterosexual females to offer attractiveness (Rothblum et al., 1995) as an attribute, perhaps because they are less likely to base their relationships on physical appearance (Gonzales & Meyers, 1993).

This great value placed on physical appearance has very unfortunate consequences for heterosexual women. Not only can it contribute to a distorted body image and eating disorders (see Chapter 5), but it denigrates women by placing more importance on superficial characteristics than on behaviors and accomplishments. Emphasizing characteristics beyond a person's control (e.g., facial attractiveness) rather than qualities that are achievable (e.g., conscientiousness) can lower self-esteem (Hamida, Mineka, & Bailey, 1998). The impact on women with disabilities is particularly negative. These women are less likely than nondisabled women to be perceived as attractive and may even evoke reactions of repulsion and rejection (Hanna & Rogovsky, 1991). Not surprisingly, the resulting poor self-image and fear of rejection can lead women with disabilities to avoid social and intimate relationships (Hanna & Rogovsky, 1991).

Gender-Related Behaviors and Roles in Dating Relationships

Given the strong societal emphasis on women's physical attractiveness, it is understandable that college women, more than men, put a lot of time into getting ready for dates (Laner & Ventrone, 1998). According to Dorothy Holland and Margaret

Eisenhart (1990), this behavior is consistent with the heterosexual romantic script whereby women try to look attractive to men who, in turn, compete for their attention.

Are there other gender-based behaviors that characterize dating relationships? Although young adults' beliefs about appropriate behaviors and roles for women have become more egalitarian over time (Spence & Hahn, 1997; Twenge, 1997a), females and males still have traditional expectations about heterosexual dating (see Chapter 6). Consistent with societal stereotypes, college women will "try to act very feminine" when they want to impress a man (Sherman & Spence, 1997, p. 270) and college men like a woman "who dresses in feminine styles" and who "is soft and feminine" (Sherman & Spence, 1997, p. 269). Also, we see the operation of stereotypes in people's construction of appropriate behavior for males on a first date. Consistent with the stereotype of male agency, many college students expect males to play the more active role by planning the date and carrying out these plans, and a sizeable minority believe men should pay for the date (Laner & Ventrone, 1998; Ross & Davis, 1996).

These views about appropriate dating behaviors reflect not only the stereotype of the agentic male but suggest that heterosexual dating relationships are characterized by a continuing power imbalance between women and men (Laner & Ventrone, 1998). Does research evidence support this assumption of greater male power? Studies of late adolescents and young adults report wide variations in respondents' perceptions of the distribution of power in their heterosexual relationships. Judgments of equality were found in 29 to 79 percent of samples (Felmlee, 1994; Galliher, Rostosky, Welsh, & Kawaguchi, 1999; Sprecher & Felmlee, 1997) with variations reflecting the gender of the perceiver, differences among the samples in different studies, and types of power examined. Thus, some dating couples view their relationships as egalitarian, at least in terms of certain types of power, whereas others perceive a power imbalance. When there is inequality, who is seen as having more control? Consistent with males' greater power in society, couples are more likely to view males than females as the powerful partner (Felmlee, 1994; Sprecher & Felmlee, 1997). The status and value attached to males in North America might provide men with interpersonal resources to control outcomes in their romantic relationships with women. Moreover, men are more likely than women to view the male as the more powerful partner, possibly reflecting men's greater endorsement of a masculine power ideology (Sprecher & Felmlee, 1997).

Perception of Sexual Interest

How do young adults determine sexual interest of their partner? In heterosexual relationships both males and females interpret certain nonsexual behaviors as cues that one's partner is interested in sex. For example, some young adults believe that asking someone out on a date indicates the requester is interested in having sex (Kowalski, 1993). Also, some assume that how much a partner spends on a date influences how far things go sexually—a belief held more strongly by Blacks than Whites (Ross & Davis, 1996).

In general, however, men are more likely than women to perceive sexual interest in nonsexual behaviors. For example, college men are more likely than college women to attribute sexual characteristics (e.g., sexy, promiscuous) to women they observe or converse with (Edmondson & Conger, 1995; Tomich & Schuster, 1996) and to interpret a female's nonsexual behaviors, such as asking out a male (Kowalski, 1993; Mongeau, Carey, & Williams, 1998) or maintaining eye contact with him (Kowalski, 1993), as an indication that she is interested in having sexual intercourse with him. Possibly, men's emphasis on sexuality is a reflection of the societal link between masculinity and sexual potency (Hupka & Bank, 1996). Whatever its cause, can you identify problems stemming from the cues men use to perceive sexual interest? Unfortunately, the sexual meaning men give to many nonsexual behaviors can lead to a misunderstanding of women's desires and to possible sexual aggression.

Almost all of the research on dating has focused on nondisabled women and men. Persons with disabilities face other issues in dating relationships. To examine some of these issues for women with disabilities, see Learn about the Research 11.1.

LEARN ABOUT THE RESEARCH 11.1
Dating Issues for Women with Physical Disabilities

Because previous research had shown that women with physical disabilities are considered asexual and not acceptable as romantic partners, Diana Rintala and her colleagues examined dating issues experienced by women with and without disabilities. Their national sample included 475 women with disabilities (average age, 41.5) and 425 nondisabled women (average age—38). These women responded to mailed questionnaires.

There were some differences in the dating histories of these groups of women. Women who were disabled before their first date began dating approximately $2\frac{1}{2}$ years later than nondisabled women. However, there was no difference in the percentage of women with or without disabilities who had ever had sex with a man, although somewhat fewer women with disabilities reported having had sex with a woman.

The findings indicated several differences between these two groups of women in

issues related to dating. Compared to nondisabled women, the women with disabilities were less satisfied about their dating frequency and perceived more problems trying to attract dating partners. Also, they were more concerned about both physical obstacles in the environment and societal barriers to dating, including people's assumptions that women with disabilities are uninterested in or unable to have sexual intimacy. Last, women with disabilities experienced more personal barriers to dating, such as pressure from family members not to date and low frequency of getting out of the house to socialize.

Based on these findings, the authors suggest several interventions that might improve the dating experiences of women with disabilities. Some of these are: (1) removal of physical barriers in public places, (2) educating the public about disability and sexuality, and (3) educating families about the appropriateness of dating for women with disabilities.

Source: Rintala et al., (1997).

(continued on p. 293)

What Does It Mean?

1. Rintala and her colleagues offered some general forms of intervention. What specific strategies could be used to educate the public about disability and sexuality and to change families' feelings about the appropriateness of dating? What solutions other than those presented here might improve the dating situation for women with disabilities?

2. This investigation focused on women only. Do you think men with disabilities experience similar problems? Explain your answer.

Committed Relationships

Marriage

Most women view marriage positively, although some variation occurs across ethnic groups. Specifically, Latinas are more oriented toward marriage than either Black or White women, and Black women show less interest than do women of other ethnic groups (Tucker & Mitchell-Kernan, 1995). How can these differences be explained? Latina women's commitment to marriage might reflect the strong value placed on family in Latina/o culture (Tucker & Mitchell-Kernan, 1995), while the more negative attitude of Black women might be because they see few financial benefits from marriage, given the high unemployment rate of Black men (Schwartz & Rutter, 1998).

Marriage Rates. High marriage rates indicate the continuing value placed on marriage in our society. In 1997 82.5 percent of White, 75 percent of Latina, and 63 percent of Black women 18 years or older were married or had been married at some point, with percentages for men at 75 percent, 64 percent, and 58.5 percent, respectively (U.S. Bureau of the Census, 1998e). However, these rates reflect a slight decline over time and a rise in the age of first marriage. For example, the percentage of ever-married females dropped from 83 percent in 1980 to 80 percent in 1997 and the corresponding decline for males was 76 to 73 percent (U.S. Bureau of the Census, 1998e). Also, in 1998 the median age was 25 for women and 26.7 for men, an increase of approximately 4 years since the beginning of the 1970s (U.S. Bureau of the Census, 1999a). This increase in age of marriage is due in part to changes in economic conditions, leading both women and men to desire some degree of financial security before embarking on a long-term commitment, and in part to changes in women's roles. Specifically, a greater number of women are now seeking higher education and aspiring toward careers; consequently, they are delaying marriage.

Nature of the Relationship. Not surprisingly, emotional expressiveness is very important for marital satisfaction. Disclosure of personal information to one's spouse and a willingness to express positive feelings about him or her lead to happier marriages (Culp & Beach, 1998; Oggins, Veroff, & Leber, 1993; Vangelisti & Daly, 1997). Also, wives tend to be happier and more satisfied when their husbands display an understanding of the relationship, perhaps because it reflects an interest in her (Acitelli, 1992) and/or a willingness to work on the marriage.

Consistent with the social construction of females as emotionally expressive and concerned about the feelings of others, women are more involved than men in maintaining this important emotional communication (e.g., Ragsdale, 1996). They are more likely to think about marital interaction patterns and the quality of the relationship (Acitelli, 1992) and are more apt to try to listen to their spouses and make them feel loved (Lynch, 1998). Among White newlyweds, wives communicate more with their husbands about themselves and their relationship than husbands communicate with their wives. However, this difference does not characterize Black newlyweds, possibly because Blacks do not endorse the cultural prohibition against men's emotional expressiveness as much as Whites do (Oggins et al., 1993).

Gender differences in social-emotional involvement might seem to indicate that women's marital outcomes would be less positive than men's. However, this is not necessarily the case. Some studies do show that men experience greater marital satisfaction than women (e.g., Fowers, 1991; Schumm, Resnick, Bollman, & Jurich, 1998; Schumm, Webb, & Bollman, 1998) and greater fulfillment of their relational needs (Vangelisti & Daly, 1997); however, other research shows no gender difference in marital satisfaction (e.g., Mookherjee, 1997; Oggins et al., 1993). Further research is needed before any firm conclusions can be drawn.

Whether or not men experience more satisfaction from their marriages than women do, it is clear that marriage provides women and men with many benefits. Both married women and men are happier than their unmarried counterparts (Marano, 1998), a finding shown in 14 of 17 industrialized nations studied (Stack & Eshleman, 1998). Moreover, married individuals experience fewer symptoms of psychological distress (Angier, 1998) and are more satisfied with life in general (Mookherjee, 1997).

Why are married people happier than single individuals? One obvious answer is the emotional support they receive from their spouse, although, as we have seen, women provide more support than they receive. Second, married couples often benefit financially because they have a combined household and, frequently, two incomes (Stack & Eshleman, 1998). Third, married people are physically healthier than their nonmarried counterparts because spouses tend to encourage health-promoting behaviors in one another (Angier, 1998). Physical health, in turn, contributes to general happiness (Stack & Eshleman, 1998).

Cohabitation

Cohabitation, *the state in which an unmarried couple lives together*, has dramatically increased in the United States over the last several decades. Approximately one-quarter of women age 25–39 are currently living with an unmarried partner (Popenoe & Whitehead, 1999) and about half of young adults cohabit at some time (U.S. Bureau of the Census, 1998c). Furthermore, more than half of all first marriages follow a period of cohabitation (Nagourney, 2000).

For many couples, cohabitation serves as a trial marriage; for others, especially divorced persons, it is seen as an alternative to marriage (Nock, 1995; Popenoe & Whitehead, 1999). The prevalence of the view that cohabitation can be a tryout for marriage is shown by the fact that the majority of high school seniors think that cohabitation is desirable so that the couple can determine before marriage whether they are compatible (Monitoring the Future Surveys, in Popenoe & Whitehead, 1999).

Despite its popularity, not all people are in favor of cohabitation. One factor related to a willingness to cohabit is lower religiosity (Huffman, Chang, Rausch, & Schaffer, 1994; Popenoe & Whitehead, 1999), perhaps because cohabitation is counter to the teachings of many religions. Furthermore, women who hold more liberal sexual views and less traditional gender attitudes have more positive views of cohabitation (Huffman et al., 1994). Clearly, this lifestyle is inconsistent with traditional views about premarital chastity for women and is less likely than marriage to enable fulfillment of traditional gender roles.

How happy are cohabiting couples and how do they feel about their relationship? Cohabitors tend to be happier than single individuals who are not living with a partner, but not as happy as married couples (Stack & Eshleman, 1998). Also, although cohabitors are no more depressed than married individuals (Horwitz & White, 1998), those who do not expect to marry do not feel as good about their relationship (Brown & Booth, 1996; Nock, 1995). Cohabitation, by definition, embodies less legal commitment. Therefore, it is not surprising that cohabitors report less emotional commitment to their partner than do married individuals and that their lower degree of commitment contributes to their lower level of satisfaction with their relationship (Nock, 1995). Interestingly, there is some evidence that the differences between married and cohabiting couples' satisfaction and level of commitment are greater among Latinas/os than Blacks or Whites (Nock, 1995) . Perhaps the strong value on family within Latina/o culture creates greater problems for Latina/o cohabiting couples.

Other comparisons show that married individuals who previously cohabited have more problems than those who did not (Rogers & Amato, 1997). In fact, couples who cohabit prior to marriage are more likely than noncohabitors to get divorced (e.g., Bumpass, Martin, & Sweet, 1991; DeMaris & Rao, 1992; Wu & Penning, 1997). It might seem surprising that previous cohabitors seem to fare less well in marriage than noncohabitors. This does not necessarily mean that cohabitation fosters marital instability. Possibly, these findings are accounted for by a **selection effect** whereby *the attitudes of individuals who cohabit are more accepting of divorce and less committed to marriage than the attitudes of noncohabitors* (Nock, 1995).

Lesbian Relationships

Close to 75 percent of lesbians are in committed relationships (Bohan, 1996). In fact, many lesbians are in long-term relationships of 20 years or more and symbolic signs of commitment, such as an exchange of rings, are common (Bryant & Demian, 1990). Lesbians are likely to meet their partners through friends or feminist or lesbian activities and are very unlikely to meet them at bars or through personal ads (Bryant & Demian, 1990). Although most lesbian women live with their partners on a full-time basis, approximately 25 percent do not (Bryant & Demian, 1990). What might account for this? According to Janis Bohan (1996), several reasons center on the problems of being identified as a lesbian in our heterosexist society. By living apart, couples might reduce the risk of employers and families discovering the nature of their relationship. Further, those who parented children with heterosexual men might avoid custody battles by living apart from their partner.

Lesbian relationships tend to be egalitarian. Although in mid-century many lesbians adopted rigid male (butch) and female (femme) gender-related behaviors and roles, these are now very rare, in part because the feminist movement awakened concerns about sexism inherent in traditional gender expectations (Bohan, 1996). Instead, lesbians engage in household activities, decision-making tasks, and other relationship behaviors based on their individual skills and interests rather than on rigid conceptions of appropriate behaviors. In fact, lesbian relationships are characterized by more equality of power than are either heterosexual or gay relationships (Bohan, 1996). Interestingly, bisexual women who have had relationships with partners of both genders report more conflicts over power in their heterosexual than in their same-gender relationships, in part because of dissatisfaction with the power balance in heterosexual relationships (Weinberg, Williams, & Pryor, 1994).

Most lesbians are involved in sexually exclusive relationships (Klinger, 1996). Although they engage in less frequent sex than either heterosexuals or gays (Bohan, 1996; Klinger, 1996), they experience considerable nongenital physical expression, such as hugging and cuddling, and are as satisfied with their sexual relationships as are heterosexual and gay couples (Bohan, 1996; Klinger, 1996). In addition, some lesbians are involved in a **Boston marriage**, which is a *nonsexual romantic relationship between two lesbians* (Rothblum & Brehony, 1991). The partners feel love and affection for one another and consider themselves a couple, and receive acceptance by the lesbian community, which is rarely aware of the nonsexual nature of the relationship.

Although lesbians are generally satisfied with their relationships, lesbian couples experience a variety of unique stressors. First, the coming-out process can be problematic (Bohan, 1996). Conflicts can arise when one partner is more open about her sexual orientation than the other partner. Second, close same-gender friendships, which are common for women, might be threatening to the partners of lesbian women in these friendships (Bohan, 1996). Third, lesbians must cope with the frequent lack of societal acceptance of their relationship (Bohan, 1996). Fourth, lesbian couples frequently face economic difficulties, in part because their income is based on the earnings of two women and women tend to earn less than men (Klinger, 1996) (see Chapter 10) and because many lesbian couples are denied domestic partner insurance benefits typically awarded to married individuals (Browning, 1998). Fifth, lesbian women often are denied custody of their children (Browning, 1998).

Despite these stressors, lesbians do not differ from heterosexual women in psychological adjustment (see Chapter 7) or in how much they love their partner (Bohan, 1996). Also, lesbians are as satisfied with their relationships as are heterosexuals (Bohan, 1996; Kurdek, 1994), and their satisfaction is based on similar factors. For example, both lesbians and heterosexuals feel better about their relationships when they and their partners share equal power and decision making, equal commitment to the relationship, and similar interests and backgrounds (Bohan, 1996). In addition, the quality of lesbians' relationships is dependent on their degree of openness about their sexual orientation. Lesbians who are open, especially to family and friends, tend to perceive their relationship more positively than those who are not in part because approval from one's family is highly related to relationship satisfaction (Caron & Ulin, 1997).

Unattached Lifestyles

Divorce

Most couples probably do not walk down the aisle with expectations of splitting up. Nevertheless, approximately 50 percent of all marriages end in divorce, and the risk is higher for remarriages (Popenoe & Whitehead, 1999). Marriages end for numerous reasons—including incompatibility, communication problems, infidelity, alcoholism, and physical abuse (Gander, 1992; Parra, Arkowitz, Hannah, & Vasquez, 1995). Furthermore, although separation and divorce are most likely to occur when partners are young (Hiedemann, Suhomlinova, & O'Rand, 1998), marriages can dissolve at any point in the life cycle. It is estimated that approximately 11 percent of women in the United States experience the end of their first marriage when they are 40 or older (Uhlenberg, Cooney, & Boyd, 1990).

While divorce occurs throughout the population, divorce rates do vary across ethnic groups and socioeconomic categories. Marital disruption is considerably more common among Black woman than among other women (Hiedemann et al., 1998) and among lower-income couples compared to higher-income couples (McLanahan & Sandefur, 1994).

Women with disabilities are more likely than nondisabled women to be divorced (Hanna & Rogovsky, 1991; Kilborn, 1999a). Not surprisingly, both financial pressure and interpersonal problems can be contributing factors. If the spouse with a disability is unable to continue working or if the nondisabled partner must quit work to care for her or his spouse, the couple might experience considerable financial strain. In addition, psychological reactions, such as anger or moodiness, on the part of either spouse or stress stemming from an overload of responsibilities for the nondisabled partner can damage the quality of the relationship. Consistent with the social construction of females as caregivers and the resultant socialization of girls to be responsive to the emotional needs within a relationship, wives are less likely than husbands to leave a spouse who has a disability (Kilborn, 1999).

Effects of Divorce on Women and Their Children.   Although divorced mothers view themselves as better parents than do mothers in high-conflict marriages, single parenting after a divorce can be highly stressful (Hetherington & Stanley-Hagan, 1995). The breakup of a marriage produces numerous stressors for custodial parents and their children. Not only must both deal with strong emotional reactions, such as grief, anger, and guilt, but their daily routines often involve major adjustment. Financial pressures can require the mother to begin or extend her employment, there can be major modifications in household responsibilities and the family might have to change residence.

Given these and other stressors associated with parental divorce, children tend to experience a variety of emotional and behavioral problems in the immediate aftermath (e.g., Forehand et al., 1991; Hetherington et al., 1992; Hetherington, 1999), but according to psychologist Abigail Stewart (1997), most rebound within a year and are as psychologically healthy as children from two-parent homes. In fact, a meta-analysis comparing children from divorced and nondivorced families concluded that differences are very small and that children in conflict-ridden intact families experience lower levels of psychological well-being than do children in divorced families (Amato & Keith, 1991b).

Divorced women also experience initial problems followed by satisfactory adjustment. Immediately following the breakup, it is common for divorced women to experience higher levels of depression and distress than married women. These negative reactions are greatest in the first few years after the divorce and decline somewhat over time (e.g., Lorenz et al., 1997), with little long-term effects on women's psychological adjustment (Amato & Keith, 1991a; Thabes, 1997). Not surprisingly, other life conditions can affect a woman's adjustment to divorce. For example, studies suggest that Latinas experience more distress than do White women, perhaps due to the triple burdens stemming from racism, sexism, and economic hardship (Parra et al., 1995). A woman's postdivorce income is important. Many women experience a dramatic decline in family income (e.g., McLanahan & Sandefur, 1994; Wagner, 1993) after divorce, which places them in a significantly worse financial situation than divorced men (McLanahan & Booth, 1989; Uhlenberg, Cooney, & Boyd, 1990). In the early 1990s, less than two-thirds of divorced mothers with children under 21 were awarded child support, and only half of these received full child support on a regular basis (U.S. Bureau of the Census, 1992). Furthermore, the lower their postdivorce income, the lower women's satisfaction with life and the greater their depression (Thabes, 1997).

Despite the problems resulting from a breakup, divorce can represent a positive means of reacting to a neglectful, conflict-ridden, or abusive relationship, and women do not feel more upset after a divorce than they did in their high-conflict marriages. Although initially they experience depression and distress, women tend to be happier two years postdivorce than they were during the last year of their marriage (Hetherington, 1993). Further, divorced women are likely to be less depressed than women in unhappy marriages (Hetherington & Stanley-Hagan, 1995).

Additional to relief from leaving a conflict-laden marriage, many women report a variety of positive psychological outcomes—greater feelings of independence and freedom; the ability to meet the challenges of living without a spouse and to function as a single parent, which can produce a new sense of competence (Hetherington, 1993; Riessman, 1990); and, despite the distress they might feel, a greater life satisfaction, compared to women who were never married (Frazier, Arikian, Benson, Losoff, & Maurer, 1996).

Coping with Divorce.   Are there any factors that help women cope more effectively with the strains of divorce? One possibility is employment. According to Gina Basagni and John Eckenrode (1995), employment can facilitate adjustment because it provides an identity outside of women's marital role. In their study, paid work was found to serve as a meaningful outlet—an avenue for productivity and a source of positive distraction and social support for divorced women. Consequently, it was associated with an increase in divorced women's self-esteem and a decrease in their feelings of distress. A teacher, commenting on how helpful it was to have the distraction of her job, stated, "Work filled my time and diverted my mind . . . I was very busy with my job. It kept my mind off things for a while" (Bisagni & Eckenrode, 1995, p. 581). And a clerical worker described the social support she received from her job: "My coworkers really do care. Like when I was going through the divorce, they really wanted to know if I was okay, without trying to pry . . . If I wasn't working here, if I couldn't talk to my coworkers, I probably would've gone to professional help a lot longer" (Bisagni & Eckenrode, p. 580).

Whether or not they work for pay, many divorced women report that social support is vitally important in helping them cope. Women who have a social network of friends and relatives to help them deal with the ramifications of divorce tend to be less depressed in years following the marital breakup (Thabes, 1997). In one study of divorced women, 96 percent of the Latina respondents and 78 percent of the White respondents stressed the importance of family members during the divorce (Parra et al., 1995). Romantic partners are another source of support; women who are in a romantic relationship tend to feel less depressed than those who are not (Thabes, 1997).

Singlehood

Although some women become single at least for a period of time as a result of the breakup of a marriage, others are permanently unmarried. Approximately 4.5 percent of women and 3.7 percent of men in the United States never marry (U.S. Bureau of the Census, 1998e), and women with disabilities are more likely than nondisabled women or men with disabilities to remain single (Hanna & Rogovsky, 1991).

While marriage is still viewed as the expected lifestyle, today there is more freedom in, acceptance of, and support for single lifestyles than in the past. How do never-married heterosexual women feel about being single today? Evidence shows that many are ambivalent about their marital status. On the one hand, they miss the benefits of steady companionship and feel sad about growing old alone, but at the same time, they enjoy their freedom and independence: "I do what I want when I want" (Lewis & Moon, 1997, p. 123). Also, the absence of a marital partner does not mean that single women have no social relationships. Some date or are in committed romantic relationships, and many spend considerable time with nonromantic significant others, such as relatives, friends, and neighbors (Seccombe & Ishii-Kuntz, 1994). In the words of one woman: "It would be nice to be in a relationship, but I don't really need that. My life is fine the way it is. And my life is full of love" (Boston Women's Health Book Collective, 1998, p. 187).

Motherhood

One of the most intimate relationships a woman can experience is her relationship with her child. Consistent with the assumption that motherhood serves as a major source of fulfillment for women (e.g., Hoffnung, 1995), many women view bearing and/or rearing their children as the most meaningful experience of their lives (Josselson, 1996). "For the first time I cared about somebody else more than myself, and I would do anything to nurture and protect her" (Boston Women's Health Book Collective, 1992, p. 488).

This does not mean, however, that parenting leads exclusively to positive emotions. Instead, as Yael Oberman and Ruthellen Josselson (1996) point out, mothers experience a plethora of opposing emotions. Motherhood can bring a great sense of power accompanied by a tremendous burden of responsibility. As one woman said, "The first month was awful. I loved my baby but felt apprehensive about my ability to satisfy this totally dependent tiny creature. Every time she cried I could feel myself tense up and panic" (Boston Women's Health Book Collective, 1998, p. 511). Mothers can experience an overwhelming joy along with waves of guilt or resentment. Motherhood can produce an expansion of personal identity as well as the loss of self. Mothers can feel exhilarated by their new role and mourn the loss of other aspects of themselves and their lives that might now be less salient, such as involvement in work or community activities, or even commitments to friendships, which necessarily change.

Stereotypes of Mothers

Despite the multidimensionality of women's actual experiences of motherhood, people tend to impose a "good mother" stereotype on them. The good mother stereotype is socially constructed as a warm, forgiving, generous, nurturing, person who repeatedly puts her children's needs before her own (Ganong & Coleman, 1995, Hoffnung, 1995), and is able to guide her children through any type of adversity (Weingarten, Surrey, Coll, & Watkins, 1998). Unfortunately, as Kathy

Weingarten and her colleagues (Weingarten et al., 1998) point out, no mother is able to consistently meet either her own standards or the standards of others, and all suffer at least occasionally because of this idealized image. One mother complained, "I didn't know how to change a diaper any more than my husband did. In fact, I may have been more nervous about it, since I was 'supposed' to know how" (Boston Women's Health Book Collective, 1998, p. 511). This good mother image can lead people to blame mothers for their children's problems (Oberman & Josselson, 1996) because it is the social construction of the mother role, more than the father role, that assumes an all-knowing, self-sacrificing, always-caring parent.

The good mother stereotype illustrates the **motherhood mandate**; *the societal belief that women should have children and that they should be physically available at all times to tend to their young children's needs* (Russo, 1979). This view of motherhood was very evident in North America prior to the women's movement in the 1960s and 1970s, but recent decades have shown a dramatic increase in the employment of women, including those with children (see Chapter 10). Does this mean that the motherhood mandate has waned? Many researchers believe it has come back in a different form. According to Betty Holcomb (1998), an editor of *Working Mother*, the 1990s witnessed "the birth of a new mystique about motherhood" (p. 48), evidenced by the media's glorification of middle-class mothers who leave the workplace to become full-time homemakers combined with the contradictory denigration of women on welfare who stay home with their children.

In addition to communal qualities, Weingarten and her colleagues (Weingarten et al., 1998) contend that there are numerous demographic characteristics included in the societal image of the good mother. According to these researchers, the good mother is expected to be White, heterosexual, and married and to have a job that does not prevent her from spending "adequate" time with her children. The more a mother deviates from this image, the more devalued she is and the less likely her own mothering practices and experiences are seen as valid. In the words of a homeless mother: "People definitely think we're not good mothers—just for the fact that we're homeless, we're not good mothers" (Koch, Lewis, Quinones, 1998, p. 62).

Like many other research findings, the motherhood stereotype reflects the primarily White middle-class viewpoint about White middle-class mothers. A look at some images of Black mothers as viewed by both the White dominant culture and the Black community, gives us a different picture of motherhood. According to clinical psychologist Elizabeth Sparks (1998), three stereotypes of Black mothers have been prominent in the last several decades. The **matriarch stereotype,** an image of Black women constructed by Whites, applies to *the Black mother who not only works outside the home and thus fails to adequately fulfill the mother role, but who antagonizes her male partner to the point that he chooses to leave the family.* This stereotype leads Whites to attribute blame for many societal problems, including unemployment, teenage pregnancies, and a high crime rate to Black mothers. A second image held by Whites is that of the **welfare mother stereotype**, a view of *the Black mother who is lazy, sexually promiscuous, uninvolved emotionally in her children, and* *unable to socialize her children toward hard work.* According to Sparks, a third stereo-type of the Black mother is one that has been embraced by Blacks. This is the **superwoman stereotype** and refers to an *idealized image of a Black woman who sac-rifices her own needs for those of her children and family while contributing to her family's economic security and working to advance the Black community.*

These three images ignore societal conditions and assume that the individual has total responsibility for her own outcomes (Sparks, 1998). They disregard the harsh realities of poverty and prejudice that characterize the lives of many Black families and greatly limit women's opportunities and choices regarding goals and lifestyle. This disregard can result in blaming mothers who do not fulfill the super-woman image. Furthermore, because many Black women have internalized the ideal image of the superwoman, some blame themselves for what they perceive as a personal failure and feel guilty and worthless.

Single Mothers

In the last several decades there has been a significant increase in the percentage of single-parent, mother-headed families. Whereas in 1970 approximately 12 per-cent of families were maintained by a mother only, this figure increased to 27 per-cent in 1997, including 58 percent of Black, 31 percent of Latina, and 21 percent of White families (U.S. Bureau of the Census, 1998a). Who are these single moth-ers? Approximately two-thirds are White, they have a median age of 33, and most have one or two children (Center on Hunger, Poverty and Nutrition Policy, in Schnitzer, 1998). Furthermore, they tend to be very poor. As Table 11.1 shows, approximately 40 percent of female-headed families with dependent children live below the poverty level, and this number is significantly greater among Black and Latina families than White (U.S. Bureau of the Census, 1998d). In addition, the percentage of female single-parent families is considerably higher than that for male single-parent families.

Although there are several types of single mothers, including teen parents and divorced mothers, the most rapidly increasing category is the never-married

TABLE 11.1 Poverty Status of Single-Parent Families with Children under 18 in 1997

Ethnicity	Single-Mother Families % Below the Poverty Level	Single-Father Families % Below the Poverty Level
All Ethnic Groups	41	19
Black	47	26
Latina/o	54	31
White	38	18

Source: U.S. Bureau of the Census (1998d).

adult. Whereas in 1960 only 4 percent of single mothers had never been married, in 1998 that figure increased to 40 percent (Popenoe & Whitehead, 1999). These never-married women include unmarried women living with an other-gender or same-gender partner, women who are not in relationships and who choose to become parents, and unmarried women who are raising their child alone but did not choose this lifestyle (Weinraub & Gringlas, 1995).

What are some of the problems experienced by single mothers? Given the high proportion of single mothers living in poverty and the lower earnings of women compared to men (U.S. Bureau of Labor Statistics, 1999d) (see Chapter 10), it is not surprising that financial problems are a major source of stress (e.g., Richards & Schmiege, 1993). Also, because they are frequently juggling house-keeping, childrearing, and employment responsibilities, single mothers have to deal with problems involving time (Hertz & Ferguson, 1998) and the coordination of activities (Richards & Schmiege, 1993).

How do women cope with the responsibilities of single motherhood? One important factor is social support. Studies of both White middle-class (Hertz & Fer-guson, 1998) and Black and White low-income mothers (Olson & Ceballo, 1996) found that support from family and friends is crucial. This support can come in the form of backup help when there is an emergency, regular assistance with trans-portation to and from day care, and the watchful eye of a neighbor while the mother is at work.

Suzanne Randolph (1995) discusses several strengths of Black families and communities that help Black single mothers cope more effectively. Because Blacks have a long history of maternal employment, single mothers have numerous role models for managing the stressors of coordinating these roles. **Extended families**, in which *at least one other adult family member resides in the same household as the mother and her children* and **augmented families**, in which *adult nonrelatives live with the mother and her children* are family structures in the Black community that can be helpful to single mothers. These families offer additional role models for the children and provide substitute caregivers when the mother is at work or is tend-ing to other responsibilities outside of the home. Because extended families are frequently involved in childrearing in Latina/o and Native American as well as Black families (Coll, Meyer, & Brillon, 1995), they can be helpful to single moth-ers in these communities as well.

Lesbian Mothers

Although North American society tends to think of families from a heterosexual perspective, a lesbian sexual orientation is not inconsistent with motherhood. In fact, an estimated 6–14 million children in the United States are raised by lesbian mothers (Patterson, 1992). The majority of these children were born into prior heterosexual marriages; however, a growing number of lesbians choose to involve children in their lives after they have identified as lesbians. These women make use of artificial insemination, maternal surrogacy, adoption, or foster care (Kirk-patrick, 1996; Parks, 1998).

Because custody battles involving lesbian mothers frequently focus on the psychological adjustment and parenting styles of lesbian mothers, numerous studies have examined lesbians in their motherhood role (Bohan, 1996). These studies show that lesbian mothers are similar to heterosexual mothers in self-esteem and psychological adjustment (Bohan, 1996; Patterson, 1996). This similarity between lesbian and heterosexual mothers is particularly noteworthy when we consider that lesbian mothers face stressors not experienced by heterosexual parents. The intensified social disapproval frequently encountered by lesbian mothers (Mitchell, 1996) makes them feel more isolated (Bohan, 1996). Some lesbians face rejection by their families of origin when they decide to parent (Muzio, 1996). Furthermore, unlike the heterosexual community, the lesbian community is not structured around children, and this, too, can add to lesbians' sense of isolation (Bohan, 1996).

While lesbian women do not differ from heterosexual women in nurturance or commitment to their children (Bohan, 1996), they do raise their daughters and sons in a less gender-stereotypic manner (Bohan, 1996). As models of gender-related behavior, they are less traditional than heterosexual mothers. For example, partners are more likely to equally share financial and family responsibilities and to be involved in feminist activities. Lesbian mothers also are less likely to purchase gender-stereotyped toys for their children and have less traditional gender-related expectations for their daughters.

Just as the research on lesbian mothers showed few differences from heterosexual mothers, studies of children show few differences between those raised by lesbian mothers and those raised by heterosexual mothers. Narrative reviews of this research by Janis Bohan (1996) and Cheryl Parks (1998) conclude that children from lesbian and heterosexual families are similar in psychological adjustment, self-esteem, moral adjustment, and relationships with their peers. In addition to psychological adjustment, researchers have focused on the gender-related development of children raised in lesbian families. Somewhat surprisingly, given that lesbian mothers raise their children in a less gender-stereotypic manner than do heterosexual parents, the children of lesbian and heterosexual mothers do not differ in their toy and activity preferences, their occupational aspirations, or other measures of gender-related attributes (Bohan, 1996; Parks, 1998; Patterson, 1997). Also, children of lesbian mothers, like those of heterosexual mothers, have a gender identity consistent with their biological sex and are no more likely to have a lesbian, gay, or bisexual orientation (Bohan, 1996; Parks, 1998; Patterson, 1997). Fiona Tasker and Susan Golombok followed this exploration into adulthood. See Learn about the Research 11.2 to examine the psychological and social outcomes of adults who were raised by lesbian mothers.

The Postparental Period

Motherhood, as we have seen, is an important aspect of identity for most women (e.g., Simon, 1992). How do mothers experience the **postparental period**, that is, *the period of a parent's life when children no longer live in the parent's home*? Considerable evidence indicates most women react quite positively to this "empty nest" period. Women in midlife frequently feel that the postparental period provides

LEARN ABOUT THE RESEARCH 11.2

Adult Children of Lesbian Mothers

Most of the research on the effects of lesbian mothers on children has focused on school-age children. Fiona Tasker and Susan Golombok expanded on this research by examining the experiences of young adults who had been raised by lesbian mothers and comparing these to the experiences of their counterparts reared by heterosexual mothers. The researchers restricted the heterosexual sample to adults whose mothers had been single for some period while raising them in order to compare two groups of children whose mothers differed in sexual orientation but not in the presence of a man in the household. Twenty-five children of lesbian mothers and 21 children of heterosexual mothers were interviewed.

The findings showed no difference in the psychological well-being of the two groups of adult children. Moreover, adults raised by lesbian mothers were no more likely than those in heterosexual families to have experienced same-gender sexual attraction. However, there was a difference in sexual experimentation. Of those who reported some same-gender interest, children raised by lesbian mothers were more likely than children in heterosexual families to have been involved in a same-gender sexual relationship. These relationships ranged from a single incident of kissing to cohabitation. Also, all of the respondents in both groups had experienced at least one other-gender sexual relationship. "Having a lesbian mother, therefore, appeared to widen the adolescent's view of what constituted acceptable sexual behavior to include same-gender relationships" (p. 212). However, the finding that 23 of the 25 young adults raised by lesbian mothers identified themselves as heterosexuals suggests that consideration of same-gender sexual relationships does not lead to a lesbian or gay sexual identity.

In regard to childhood peer relationships, slightly more of the adults raised in lesbian rather than heterosexual families recalled having been teased about their sexuality. However, the percentage who reported this teasing was low; it included 11 percent of the children of lesbian mothers compared to 4 percent of the children raised by heterosexual mothers.

Source: Tasker & Golombok, (1995).

What Does It Mean?

1. The respondents from heterosexual families had been raised by mothers who had been single for some period of time during the respondent's childhood. Do you think differences between the two groups would have been more pronounced if the adult children of heterosexual mothers had come from homes with both a mother and father? Explain your answer.
2. Prepare an argument in support of or in opposition to lesbian motherhood. Refer to the findings of this study, other material from this chapter, theories of gender typing (see Chapter 3), and any other information that you believe is relevant.
3. Do you think that adults raised by lesbian mothers, versus those reared by heterosexual mothers, differ in the way they raise their own children? Explain your answer.

new opportunities for self-development (Thomas, 1997). Some women pursue new careers, others further their education, and others provide service to their communities. And, because children can be a source of tension in any marriage, women often report higher marital satisfaction once their children have left home (e.g., White & Edwards, 1990).

Of course the postparental period is not experienced the same way by all women. Some women, who are reluctant to let go of their parenting role, may perceive this period as stressful. Mothers who are employed during the childrearing years establish an identity in addition to their motherhood role, and this can ease the difficulty of relinquishing parenting responsibilities (e.g., Lippert, 1997). Also, some midlife women face the return home of their adult children for financial or personal reasons, which can be stressful for some parents (Witkin, 1991). To find out more about experiences of the postparental period, try Get Involved 11.1.

GET INVOLVED **11.1**

Women's Experiences during the Postparental Period

Interview two midlife women whose children have left home. Choose any women available to you, such as relatives, neighbors, classmates, etc. However, if possible, select one woman whose last child left home within the year and another whose children have been gone for several years. Ask each to identify (1) any positive and/or negative experiences.

Also, ask each to indicate (2) any changes in her employment role (e.g., started a new job, increased her work hours), community service, and/or leisure activities as a result of her children's departure, and to indicate (3) whether she perceives these changes as primarily positive or primarily negative.

What Does It Mean?

1. How would you characterize the experiences of your two interviewees? Did they mention more positive or negative experiences? How do their experiences compare to the postparental outcomes reported in the text?
2. What changes, if any, did they make in their life roles? How did they feel about these changes?
3. Were there any differences in the experiences of the woman whose children recently left home and the woman whose children left years earlier? If yes, how do you explain these differences?
4. Do you think the postparental experiences of these midlife women will differ from the future experiences of today's young adults? Why or why not?

Intimate Violence

Another, more negative type of close relationship is intimate violence, or rape and domestic violence. Although it might be surprising that these topics are included in a chapter on close relationships, "violence against women is distinguished by the fact that it is usually perpetrated by intimate male partners or family members" (Stewart, 1996, p. 54).

Rape

The definition of **rape** varies across states. However, a common legal definition is *sexual penetration of any bodily orifice against the victim's will, obtained by physical force, the threat of force, or while the victim is incapable of giving consent because of mental illness, mental retardation, or intoxication* (Koss et al., 1994). Does the incident described by the first-year college student in the opening vignette fit this definition? Yes, it does. First, this student repeatedly communicated her nonconsent and, second, the large size differential between the female student and the perpetrator provided him with the physical force necessary to proceed against her will.

Frequency of Rape.   The FBI estimates that every 6 minutes a woman is raped and that one in four women will be raped during her lifetime (Lonsway & Fitzgerald, 1994). Similarly, several surveys indicate that approximately one-quarter to one-third of both college women (e.g., Abbey, Ross, McDuffie, & McAuslan, 1996; Hickman & Muehlenhard, 1997; Koss, Dinero, Seibel, & Cox, 1988) and noncollege young adult women (Wyatt, 1992) experience rape or attempted rape.

Few studies have included large numbers of people of color. Furthermore, methodological problems, such as ethnic differences in willingness to report rape, make ethnic comparisons difficult. Given these limitations, the available evidence suggests that the rape rate is very high among Native Americans (Koss, Gidycz, & Wisniewski, 1987) and is more prevalent among Whites than among Latinas/os or Asian Americans (Arellano, Kuhn, & Chavez, 1997; Sorenson & Siegel, 1992; Urquiza & Goodlin-Jones, 1994). For example, one multi-ethnic investigation of over 1,800 17- to 34-year-old female Navy trainees found that White women reported the highest rape rate and Asian American women the lowest (Merrill, Newell, Milner, Hervig, & Gold, 1997). Comparisons of Blacks and Whites, however, show inconsistent findings. Some indicate a higher prevalence of rape among Black than White women (Abbey et al., 1996; Urquiza & Goodlin-Jones, 1994), whereas others suggest either the reverse pattern (Koss et al., 1987) or no ethnic difference (Wyatt, 1992). Regardless of ethnic variations in the prevalence of rape, however, perpetrators tend to be of the same ethnicity and social class as their victims (e.g., Koss & Harvey, 1991).

Numerous studies in the 1980s and 1990s have shown that the most frequent form of rape differs from the type of incident typically conceptualized as rape. Many people view "'real rape'... as some greasy guy jumping out from behind a bush," who is a stranger to the victim (Schwartz, 1997, p. xii). In fact, before the 1980s, there was no term for rape committed by a nonstranger. But in 1982, an article published in *Ms.* magazine reported evidence of a common but undiscussed *form of rape*, called "date rape," *that involves perpetrators and victims who know each other* (Warshaw, 1988). Since that time date rape—or the more inclusive term, **acquaintance rape**, has been used to refer to rape by a nonstranger. Subsequent research indicates that 80 percent or more of perpetrators are acquaintances of the victim, many of whom are casual or steady dating partners (Hickman & Muehlenhard, 1997; Koss et al., 1988; Ullman, 1996). Furthermore, it is estimated that 10–14 percent of women have been raped by a spouse or cohabiting partner (Mahoney, 1997), and the majority of these women are raped more than once by their spouse (Peacock, 1998; Russell, 1982). "Often he would rape me while I was still sleeping in my bedroom. I would wake with him inside me. He wouldn't stop even after I asked him to" (Peacock, 1998, p. 229).

Although a large proportion of women have had incidents consistent with the legal definition, few actually label their experience as rape, especially if they are raped by an acquaintance (e.g., Koss, Figueredo, Bell, Tharan, & Tromp, 1996; Koss et al., 1988). How can this be explained? According to Mary Koss and Hobart Cleveland (1997), "women appear to believe that sexual aggression is common and therefore harmless, whereas rape is rare" (p. 16). This enables them to limit the negative implications of their experience by focusing on "what they perceive as relatively normal sexual aggression" (p. 16). In fact, it is not unusual for college women who have been raped by an acquaintance to define their experience as a miscommunication rather than a rape (Koss et al., 1988). Many women (as well as men) are not aware of the broad range of behaviors that constitute rape. Thus, not surprisingly, victims of acquaintance rape who do not acknowledge they have been raped have a narrower definition of rape than those who do acknowledge their victimization. Women who do not label their assault as rape are more likely to think of rape as an incident perpetrated by an unknown assailant and involving physical attack (Kahn, Mathie, & Torgler, 1994).

Very few victims, especially victims of acquaintance rape, report their assault to the police (Koss et al., 1988; Ullman, 1996). One reason is that they frequently engage in self-blame for putting themselves into a risky situation or for failing to more clearly communicate their intentions. They also might not want to go through the highly embarrassing procedures involved in a police investigation and might be aware of widespread lack of support for rape victims (Koss & Cleveland, 1997).

Factors Associated with Acquaintance Rape.   What accounts for the high incidence of acquaintance rape?

Sexual Script.   Koss and her colleagues (e.g., Koss & Cleveland, 1997; Koss et al., 1994) contend that the social construction of the roles of men and women in male-female sexual situations provide a social context in which acquaintance rape can occur. This traditional **sexual script** is *a socialized set of expected behaviors characterized by an aggressive male who initiates and pushes for sexual activity and a gatekeeping female* *who sets the limits*. That is, instead of encouraging similar behaviors and goals, gender socialization teaches males to use any strategy in their pursuit of sexual intercourse and teaches females they are supposed to control men's sexual impulses.

Interpreting roles in this sexual script can lead to rape for a number of reasons. First, some men take the initiator role to the extreme and engage in sexual aggression. Second, as discussed previously in this chapter, men frequently infer sexual interest when it is not intended (e.g., Kowalski, 1993; Tomich & Schuster, 1996). As sexual initiator, a man's misperception of his partner's nonsexual behaviors as sexual interest can fuel his sexual aggressiveness (Bondurant & Donat, 1999). Third, the differing roles within the sexual script can set the framework for misunderstanding because the male assumes the female will attempt to limit sexual activity as part of her role, and he might misinterpret her "no" as token resistance that he translates into "yes," leading him to disregard her objections to sex.

To examine the actual frequency of token resistance to sex, Charlene Muehlenhard and Carie Rodgers (1998) asked college women and men to describe real situations, if any, in which they told a sexually willing partner that they didn't want to have sex although, in actuality, they intended to have sexual intercourse with that partner. Only 14 percent of the women respondents described situations that reflected token resistance to a man who had been a previous sexual partner and less than 2 percent reported token resistance to a man with whom they had never had intercourse. Furthermore, although a common stereotype about sex is that women, but not men, engage in token resistance, Muehlenhard and Rodgers found no significant differences in the percentages of women and men who described experiences with token resistance. Consequently, these researchers concluded that: "Although both women and men sometimes engage in token resistance to sex, most do not. All refusal should be taken seriously. Engaging in sex with someone who does not consent is rape" (p. 462).

Characteristics of Sexually Aggressive Men.   Sexually aggressive men, including both rapists and those who use verbal coercion to gain sexual activity, are more likely than nonaggressive men to have witnessed or experienced family violence (e.g., Malamuth, Sockloskie, Koss, & Tanaka, 1991). Men who are sexually aggressive are likely to hold stereotypical attitudes about gender roles (e.g., Lackie & de Man, 1997), feel hostility toward women (e.g., Koss & Gaines, 1993), and be physically aggressive in other situations (e.g., Lackie & de Man, 1997).

Sexually aggressive men, more than nonaggressive men, tend to have attitudes that facilitate the occurrence of rape (e.g., Hamilton & Yee, 1990; Malamuth et al., 1991). These **rape myths** are *"beliefs that are generally false but are widely and persistently held and that serve to deny and justify male sexual aggression against women"* (Lonsway & Fitzgerald, 1994, p. 134). One such belief is the assumption that women contribute to their own victimization. In one study of college students, 27 percent of the males reported agreement with the belief that women provoke rape (Johnson, Kuck, & Schander, 1997). Other rape myths focus on minimizing the perpetrator's responsibility, as indicated by the 42 percent of males in that study, who believed that men have uncontrollable sexual urges.

As might be expected, men tend to endorse these myths more than women do (e.g., Johnson et al., 1997; Theriault & Holmberg, 1998). Also, Black (Johnson et al., 1997) and Asian American (Mori, Bernat, Glenn, Selle, & Zarate, 1995) men more strongly believe rape myths than do White men. Black men's greater acceptance of rape-supportive beliefs might be related to a long history of racist law enforcement, which has made it even more difficult for Black women than for White women to report rape or to obtain legal justice (Collins, 1990). The endorsement of these beliefs by Asian American men, on the other hand, is probably due to the strong Asian American commitment to patriarchy (Mori et al., 1995). To get firsthand knowledge about rape myth acceptance, try Get Involved 11.2.

GET INVOLVED 11.2
Gender and Rape Myths

Ask two female and two male acquaintances to indicate their degree of agreement with each of the following 4 statements about rape, from *strongly disagree* (1) to *strongly agree* (7). If possible, select participants from different ethnic groups.

_____ 1. Women often provoke rape.
_____ 2. Women enjoy rape.
_____ 3. Women frequently falsely claim they have been raped.
_____ 4. Only men who are psychologically disturbed engage in rape.

What Does It Mean?

Sum the 4 ratings for each respondent. The scores can range from 4 to 28, with higher scores reflecting greater acceptance of rape myths. After scoring each person's answers, average the scores of the two females and those of the two males.

1. Compare the scores of the females and males. Did your male respondents express greater acceptance of rape myths than your female respondents did? If yes, explain. If no, indicate possible reasons why your respondents did not reflect the typically found gender difference.

2. If you tested men of different ethnicities, did you note any difference in their scores? If yes, is this difference consistent with that presented in the text? Was there a difference between women respondents of different ethnicities?

3. Which of these 4 statements received the greatest degree of agreement from your respondents and which received the least agreement? Give possible reasons for these findings.

4. What do you think influences the development of these rape myths?

5. How do you think rape myth acceptance can be reduced?

Characteristics of Victims.   Few characteristics differentiate women who are more likely to be raped from those who are less likely. Any woman can be raped. However, the majority of acquaintance victims are between the ages of 15 and 25 (Parrot, 1991). Moreover, as we saw in Chapter 4, women who are raped in adulthood are more likely than nonvictimized women to have been sexually abused in childhood and/or adolescence (Azar, Ferraro, & Breton, 1998; Greene & Navarro, 1998; Neumann et al., 1996), possibly because early victimization can contribute to feelings of powerlessness (Gidycz, Coble, Latham, & Layman; 1993).

Alcohol Consumption. There is considerable evidence that alcohol consumption by the perpetrator and the victim increases the risk of both sexual coercion and rape or attempted rape (e.g., Abbey et al., 1996; Greene & Navarro, 1998). In part, this is because men assume that drinking victims will be held responsible for their victimization (Ullman, Karabatsos, & Koss, 1999). Another explanation is that alcohol can increase men's misunderstanding (Abbey et al., 1996). Men may misperceive women's drinking as a sign of sexual interest, and when men drink, they may be more likely to misinterpret their partner's intentions.

Effects of Rape.   Rape victims may be psychologically plagued by fear, anxiety, and depression (e.g., Frazier & Seales, 1997) and can experience long-term mistrust of men (Wyatt, 1992), whether they are victims of acquaintance rape or stranger rape. Some symptoms, such as self-blame and powerlessness, are more common among acquaintance victims (Frazier & Seales, 1997), as one college freshman described in her emotional reaction to rape by her resident adviser: "I wouldn't even admit it to myself until about four months later when the guilt and fear that had been eating at me became too much to hide and I came very close to a complete nervous breakdown. I tried to kill myself, but fortunately I chickened out at the last minute" (Warshaw, 1988, pp. 67–68).

Physical problems are also prevalent for some rape victims. Victimized women may suffer chronic pain disorders, such as headaches and back pain. They may develop eating disorders, sleep disturbances, and sexually transmitted diseases (Koss et al., 1994; Wyatt, 1992). Also, some women experience reproductive problems, such as painful menstruation and irregular periods, (Golding, 1996) as well as sexual problems, including diminished interest and enjoyment (Golding, 1996; Wyatt, 1992).

Rape Prevention.   Different types of rape education programs have produced varying effects. What are some features of the most effective types? First, rape education must be focused primarily on men. While education can help individual women learn how to better communicate with male partners or how to avoid high-risk situations, it is only when men's motivation to rape decreases that significant rape reduction might take place (Lonsway, 1996). Second, programs targeted at men should use male trainers (Earle, 1996). These trainers can serve as role models with whom the targeted men can identify. Third, because rape-supportive attitudes and the sexual script are learned at a young age, rape education programs should begin early (Abbey et al., 1996).

In addition to rape education, institutions must develop effective procedures for dealing with complaints. Women who report a rape must be assured that their claim will be fairly investigated and that if guilt is determined, the perpetrator will receive appropriate sanctions (Koss & Cleveland, 1997).

Theories of Rape.   How can rape be explained? Our examination focuses on three theories that posit different mechanisms to account for rape.

Evolutionary Theory.   **Evolutionary theory** (also known as sociobiology) *applies the principles of natural selection and its goal of reproductive survival to an understanding of social behavior, including rape. According to this theory, rape has evolved because in ancestral environments it was one strategy males could use to ensure their genes would be passed on to future generations* (Malamuth & Heilmann, 1998). From an evolutionary perspective, it is to males' reproductive advantage to mate often and with numerous partners because they have abundant sperm, do not have to spend any time gestating offspring, and cannot be sure of paternity of offspring. Thus, although evolutionary theorists believe that rape is inappropriate, they argue it is a natural biological behavior (Thornhill & Palmer, 2000) that has evolved as one method for achieving reproductive success.

What type of support is offered for this perspective? Theorists point to the evidence that forced copulations have been observed in a variety of animal species, such as scorpionflies (Thornhill & Palmer, 2000), mallard ducks (Barash, 1977), and orangutans (Thornhill & Palmer, 2000; Wrangham & Peterson, 1996). Also they note that females of childbearing age are the most likely rape victims (Thornhill & Palmer, 2000) and that rape has occurred throughout human evolutionary history (Malamuth, 1998).

Some critics, on the other hand, contend that it is not appropriate to draw conclusions about rape by observing nonhuman species Human behavior is more complexly determined. Furthermore, Anne Fausto-Sterling (1992) argues that when the term "rape" is applied to insects and ducks, its meaning is altered; it no longer reflects a violation of the victim's will because will is an essentially human construct. She maintains, also, that so-called rape in animals does not have the same implications for females of these species as it does for human females for whom rape arouses fear and influences behavioral choices.

Others question the basic tenet of the theory that frequent copulation with multiple partners is reproductively effective for men. Natalie Angier (1999a) argues that a continuous relationship with one woman might be as reproductively successful as promiscuous mating. Mary Koss (Goode, 2000a) notes that although the majority of rape victims are young women of childbearing age, there are numerous rapes of young children. Furthermore, the observations that some men rape wives and dating partners with whom they have also had consensual sex and that most men do not rape are not consistent with this assumption that the purpose of rape is reproduction (de Waal, 2000).

Feminist Theory.   A different perspective is offered by **feminist theory**, *which contends that rape is rooted in the longstanding and pervasive power imbalance between women* *and men* (Malamuth, 1996). Men have greater legal, economic, and political power, which provides them with more power in interpersonal situations. Men use rape as one mechanism to control women and maintain their dominance.

Support for feminist theory at the societal level is provided by evidence that states (Baron & Straus, 1989) and urban areas (Peterson & Bailey, 1992; Whaley, 1999) with greater gender equality in economic, legal, and political power have lower rape rates than do states and urban areas with less gender equality. Moreover, a man's endorsement of male dominance and restricted rights for women is strongly connected to his acceptance of rape beliefs that are detrimental to women, such as, women want to be raped and enjoy rape (e.g., Anderson, Cooper, & Okamura, 1997; Lackie & de Man, 1997). That is, people who more strongly endorse male power tend to hold more rape-supportive beliefs.

Social Learning theory. **Social learning theory** provides a third perspective to the phenomenon of rape. As discussed in Chapter 3, this theory *contends that social behaviors are learned through observation and reinforcement. This includes learning both rape-supportive attitudes and sexually aggressive behaviors* (Ellis, 1989; Spitzberg, 1998). The theory assumes, for example, that men can develop rape-supportive attitudes or sexually aggressive behaviors via media depictions of sexuality and violence. The theory further holds that their sexual aggressiveness can be reinforced by the widespread acceptance of rape myths which blame the victim and excuse the perpetrator, and by the traditional sexual script which encourages males to be aggressive in sexual situations.

Both of these assumptions have received some research. Consistent with the hypothesized influence of observational learning, Barongan and Hall (1995) found that, for some men, exposure to misogynous rap music increases their aggressive feelings toward women. Also, several studies have shown that experience with violent pornography is related to greater sexual aggressiveness (e.g., Boeringer, 1994; Demare, Lips, & Briere, 1993). However, this relationship could reflect either an effect of pornography on sexual aggressiveness or the possibility that sexually aggressive men choose to view violent pornography. In support of the importance of reinforcement, men who more strongly accept rape myths tend to be more sexually aggressive (e.g., Malamuth et al., 1991).

Domestic Violence

Domestic violence refers to *physical and psychological abuse committed by an intimate partner; that is, a spouse, nonmarital romantic partner, or a former spouse/partner.* Also known as battering, domestic violence can involve moderate forms of physical abuse, such as slapping or throwing objects at the victim, or severe forms, including beating and using a weapon. As described by one woman: "I have had glasses thrown at me. I have been kicked in the abdomen, kicked off the bed, and hit while lying on the floor—while I was pregnant. I have been whipped, kicked, and thrown, picked up and thrown down again" (Boston Women's Health Book Collective, 1998, p. 162). Psychological abuse can include overt attempts to dominate and control, as well as more subtle actions that undermine the victim's sense of self (Marshall, 1997). Although in some cases of domestic violence the woman abuses her partner, the majority of cases involve the male partner as the batterer (Browne & Williams, 1993; Straus & Gelles, 1990). Furthermore, men's attacks on women are likely to be more severe than women's attacks on men (e.g., Brush, 1990), and in 1998 the FBI estimated that about 32 percent of female homicide victims were murdered by an intimate male partner (Goode, 2000b).

Like rape, domestic violence is an underreported crime, but, estimates range from 2 to 4 million women abused each year by their male partners (Jacobson & Gottman, in Brody, 1998a; Plichta, 1996). Women with physical disabilities experience abuse at about the same rate as nondisabled women, but their abusive relationships continue for a longer period of time (Nosek, Howland, & Young, 1997).

Although less is known about violence in lesbian relationships, it does occur, perhaps because some lesbian women internalize the sexism and heterosexism pervasive in our society and turn against their partners (Saakvitne & Pearlman, 1993). One estimate, based on the National Lesbian Health Care Survey, states that 11 percent of lesbians have been abused by their partners (Perry & O'Hanlan, 1998). Similar to violence in heterosexual relationships, this can involve both physical and psychological abuse (Bohan, 1996).

Ethnic Comparisons.   Black women are more likely than White women to be victims of domestic violence (Neff, Holamon, & Schluter, 1995; Sorenson, Upchurch, & Shen, 1996). Moreover, their assaults tend to be more severe (Hampton & Gelles, 1994; Stark, 1990). Given that significantly fewer middle-class than lower-class Black women report physical assault by partners (Lockhart & White, 1989), one possible reason for the ethnic difference is that Black women become the scapegoat for lower-class men's frustration about their lack of opportunities

Approximately 2–4 million women are abused each year by their male partners.

(Harvey, 1986). Additionally, Black women remain longer with their abusive partner and are less likely to seek assistance from social service agencies (Joseph, 1997); hence, the severity of their abuse might escalate over time.

Studies of the prevalence of domestic violence among Latinas/os, compared to other ethnic groups, have yielded inconsistent findings (e.g., Sorenson & Telles, 1991; Sorenson et al., 1996; Straus & Smith, 1990), due, perhaps, in part to variations in recency of immigration. Evidence is consistent, however, that battered Latinas experience their abuse for longer periods of time than either Black or White women (Gondolf, Fisher, & McFerron, 1988; Torres, 1991). This may be due to Latina's perception of violent acts, such as being slapped or pushed, as nonabusive (Torres, 1991). Consequently, they remain in their abusive relationship. Also, the strong cultural value placed on the maintenance of the family might play a role, making it difficult for Latina women to leave their abusive partners, even at the expense of their personal welfare (Torres, 1987).

Research on domestic violence within the Asian American community has been minimal, but intimate violence is known to occur (Ho, 1990). Factors that serve to maintain domestic violence among Asian Americans include the cultural emphasis on the family over the individual, the strong value placed on the male as the authority in the family, and the belief that family affairs must be kept private. These reasons keep Asian American women from seeking assistance for their abuse, and those who do report it are likely to meet with considerable disapproval in their communities (Ho, 1990).

Similarly, little research is available on abuse of Native American women. However, there are indications that domestic violence is at extremely high levels and is related to both alcohol abuse and patriarchal beliefs introduced by the Westernization of Native peoples (Allen, 1990).

Risk Factors.   Although abuse by an intimate partner is not limited to any age or socioeconomic group, there are several demographic factors associated with a higher likelihood of abusing and of being abused. First, men's likelihood of engaging in domestic violence and women's risk for being abused are related to both age and social class. Younger men are more likely to be violent (Keller, 1996) and younger women are more likely to be abused ("One of Three," 1998). Also, men who are poor and less educated are more likely to engage in domestic violence (Keller, 1996) and women who are poor (Business and Professional Women's Foundation, 1997; "One of Three," 1998) and less educated (Plichta, 1996) are more likely to be abused.

While no particular personality characteristics of women are associated with the likelihood of their being abused, the need for power and control are important factors related to men's violence against their female partners (Koss et al., 1994), and substance abuse by batterers in both heterosexual and lesbian relationships is common (Stahly & Lie, 1995). Not surprisingly, a background of violence in one's family of origin is a major risk factor for both male batterers and females who are abused by their partners. Witnessing violence between one's parents and experiencing physical or sexual abuse in childhood are more common to male batterers and abused women than to men and women who are not involved in violent relationships (Hotaling & Sugarman, 1986; Keller, 1996; Koss et al., 1994; Plichta,

1996). In one sample, 65 percent of White and 41 percent of Latina abused women had experienced childhood abuse (Krishnan, Hilbert, VanLeeuwen, & Kolia, 1997). This does not mean that all adults with a history of violence will be involved in an abusive relationship, nor does it imply that all those involved in domestic violence have a history of family battering. However, these findings do suggest that the observation of violence committed by a parental role model gives boys the message that violence is a means for handling anger and conflict and influences the development of negative attitudes toward women (Stahly, 1996). For women, the early experience of family violence can provide a similar message that aggression is a "normal" aspect of close relationships. Also, it can make it more difficult for the abused girl to learn how to accurately screen people and situations for danger (Koss et al., 1994).

Effects of Domestic Violence.   The effects of abuse include a large variety of both physical and psychological problems. Many health problems, including bruises and broken bones, loss of vision or hearing (Commonwealth Fund Commission on Women's Health, 1998a) and reproductive difficulties (Plichta & Abraham, 1996) directly result from an abusive relationship. Additionally, abused women can suffer psychological problems such as lower self-esteem, depression, and anxiety (Ammerman & Hersen, 1993). Furthermore, psychological abuse may have a greater effect on women's mental health than physical violence (Marshall, 1997; Simpson, Stone, Newbauer, Freeman, 1997), perhaps because it involves continual humiliation and the destruction of one's identity (Jacobson, in Brody, 1998a).

Leaving the Abusive Relationship.   Many people wonder why abused women don't leave their batterer. Some even assume that women stay in abusive relationships because they are masochistic; that is, they have an unconscious desire to be hurt (Stahly, 1996). However, experts in domestic violence point out that one of the greatest barriers to leaving is financial concern (Brody, 1998a); many women feel they do not have the economic resources to provide for their family. Another major obstacle is fear of retaliation (Brody, 1998a). Batterers can interpret women's attempt to leave as a loss of control and their violence can accelerate (Stahly, 1996). As one battered woman reported, "The very first time that I attempted to leave he tried to choke me with the sheets to the point where I turned blue" (Sorenson, 1996, p. 129).

Theories of Domestic Violence.   Two theories presented as explanations of rape also are useful in understanding domestic violence. As discussed previously, **feminist theory** emphasizes gender power imbalance as a destructive factor in men's interactions with women. When applied to battering, it contends that men use violence against women as a means to maintain their power and status (Stahly, 1996). **Social learning theory,** with its focus on observation and reinforcement, posits that domestic violence is a learned behavior that can develop from observing violence within the family and from receiving reinforcement for aggressive acts (Stahly & Lie, 1995).

SUMMARY

1. Gender differences in verbal communication include males' greater talkativeness and intrusive interruptions and females' greater affiliative interruptions. Also, females are more likely to use speech characterized as tentative. Explanations for these gender differences focus on females' interpersonal orientation and the gender imbalance in power.

2. Both college women and men like to talk to their friends about the other gender. However, women's conversations more than men's focus on interpersonal issues.

3. Females smile and gaze at their conversational partner more than males do. Also, they are better able to interpret nonverbal messages. These differences might reflect the communal socialization of females. Another possibility is that women's ability to understand others is an adaptive mechanism that stems from their lower societal status.

4. Emotional closeness is important to the friendships of both heterosexual and lesbian women but is more central to women's than men's friendships. Gender socialization and heterosexual males' perceived connection between emotional closeness and homosexuality are two explanations for the gender difference.

5. Heterosexual women are more likely than heterosexual men to value a romantic partner's financial stability and less likely to place importance on physical attractiveness. Similarly, lesbian women put less emphasis on physical attractiveness than gay men do.

6. Dating relationships are commonly characterized by traditional gender-related behaviors and roles. When there is a power imbalance, the male is generally viewed as the more powerful partner. Men are more likely than women to perceive nonsexual behaviors, such as a female asking out a male, as indicative of sexual interest.

7. Most women and men marry, but the age of marriage has gone up in recent years. Emotional expressiveness contributes to marital well-being, and wives are more involved in maintaining this emotional communication than their husbands are. Also, both women and men who are married are happier and healthier than their unmarried counterparts.

8. Cohabitors who do not intend to marry tend to be less satisfied with their relationships than married individuals, in part because of the absence of legal commitment. Also, married couples who previously cohabited are more likely to get divorced. This might be accounted for by a selection effect.

9. Most lesbians are in committed, egalitarian, sexually exclusive relationships. Although many experience stressors not encountered by heterosexuals, they are similar to their heterosexual counterparts in their relationship satisfaction.

10. Approximately 50 percent of marriages end in divorce, and divorce is associated with stressors for both women and their children. However, despite initial emotional problems, both women and children tend to effectively adjust. Moreover, divorced women are generally less depressed than those in unhappy marriages. Employment and social support help women cope during the postdivorce period.

11. Single women tend to experience mixed feelings about being unattached. Some regret the absence of a steady partner, some are satisfied living alone, and some become involved in romantic relationships. Also, many are very involved in social networks of relatives, friends, and neighbors.

12. Stereotypes of mothers, including the good mother stereotype and the matriarch, welfare mother, and superwoman images of Black mothers, can lead to blaming mothers and mothers' self-blame if something goes wrong or if the mothers deviate from the ideal stereotype.

13. Two major challenges faced by single mothers are financial problems and numerous responsibilities. Social support, as well as extended and augmented families, can help single mothers cope.

14. Lesbian and heterosexual mothers are similar in mothering style and adjustment. Also, the children reared in lesbian and heterosexual families are similar in terms of their psychological and social adjustment and their sexual orientation.

15. Most women report positive feelings about the postparental period. Women who were employed during the childrearing years find it easier to relinquish the parental role.

16. An estimated one-quarter to one-third of women experience rape or attempted rape, much of it perpetrated by acquaintances. Physical aggressiveness, hostility toward women, gender-stereotypical attitudes, and a history of family violence differentiate sexually aggressive men from other men. Rape victims can experience a variety of emotional and health problems. Evolutionary, feminist, and social learning theories attempt to account for rape. Although some support for all three has been reported, there are many criticisms of evolutionary theory.

17. An estimated 2–4 million females are victims of domestic violence each year. Battering occurs in both lesbian and heterosexual relationships and across ethnic groups, although it is more frequent among Blacks than Whites. A major risk factor for both perpetrators and victims of domestic violence is a history of family violence. Numerous physical and psychological problems can result from victimization. These include physical injuries, reproductive difficulties, lower self-esteem, anxiety, and depression. Financial problems and fear of the perpetrator are the primary reasons for remaining in an abusive relationship. Feminist and social learning theories help explain domestic violence.

WHAT DO YOU THINK?

1. The text discusses several negative consequences of the strong emphasis placed by men on a romantic partner's appearance. Can you think of other negative ramifications of this strong value? What kind of societal changes might contribute to a deemphasis on physical attractiveness in romantic attraction?

2. Letitia Peplau (1998) contends that research on lesbian and gay couples can help dispel biased stereotypes. What are some common stereotypes about lesbian couples? How can scientific research be made public and accessible so that these stereotypes can be altered? Do you think there should be an attempt to eradicate these stereotypes as well as other unfavorable attitudes? Explain your answer.

3. Do you agree with Holcomb's contention that there has been a resurgence of praise for women who give up their careers for full-time motherhood? If so, how can society reconcile the contradictory assumptions that full-time motherhood is desirable for middle-class mothers but that poor mothers should combine employment with parenthood? How do you think people react to middle-class mothers who choose to continue their employment? How do they react to

fathers who opt for full-time parenting? Explain each of your answers.

4. Using either the feminist or social learning theory as a framework, discuss societal changes that might lead to a reduction both in rape and in domestic violence.

IF YOU WANT TO KNOW MORE

Bergen, R. K. (1998). *Issues in intimate violence*. Thousand Oaks, CA: Sage.

Coll, C. G., Surrey, J. L., & Weingarten, K. (1998). *Mothering against the odds: Diverse voices of contemporary mothers*. New York: Guilford.

Davis, L. J. (1997). *The disability studies reader*. New York: Routledge.

Schwartz, M. D., & DeKeseredy, W. S. (1997). *Sexual assault on the college campus: The role of male peer support*. Thousand Oaks, CA: Sage.

Tasker, F. L., & Golombok, S. (1998). *Growing up in a lesbian family: Effects on child development*. New York: Guilford.

Warshaw, R. (1988). *I never called it rape: The* Ms. *report on recognizing, fighting and surviving date and acquaintance rape*. New York: Harper & Row.

Weinstock, J. S., & Rothblum, E. D. (1996). *Lesbian friendships: For ourselves and each other*. New York: New York University Press.

12 Young and Middle Adulthood

Interpersonal Issues II: Balancing Family and Work

KEY TERMS

traditional couples
dual-career couples
dual-earner couples

role strain
role overload
interrole conflict

scarcity hypothesis
enhancement hypothesis
flextime

The beginning of my (Judith's) academic career in the early 1970s coincided with early parenthood. My daughter was less than 1 year old when I started working as an assistant professor of psychology and my son was born 2 years later. Although I adored my children, loved being their mother, and got enormous satisfaction from my career, juggling the two roles was often stressful. To this day, I can vividly recall the anxiety and confusion that erupted when my daughter or son woke up too sick to go to their caregiver's home or when both were of school age and school was canceled because of snow (a frequent occurrence in our New England community). Also, I remember being plagued by worry that my commitment to my children was preventing me from devoting sufficient time and energy to my career and that my employment was somehow hurting my children. Interestingly, however, I don't recall ever feeling that my husband's job was damaging our children or that being a father was hindering his job advancement.

Historically, women and men had different roles within the family. Men were the economic providers and women the caregivers and homemakers. However, the traditional family comprising children, a provider-father, and a stay-at-home mother is relatively rare today. Whereas 57 percent of children in 1960 were raised in this type of household, only about 14 percent of children are now at home full time with their mothers for their first 3 years of life ("HHS Says Statistics," 1999), and only about 3 percent of American families are characterized by the traditional father and mother roles (Barnett & Rivers, 1996). As we saw in Chapter 10, the majority of women, including married women with children, are now employed. Consequently, there has been a major transformation in women's roles.

This chapter explores issues related to the coordination of women's multiple responsibilities in the domestic and employment domains. We begin with a look at attitudes toward their family and employment roles. Then we examine the impact of women's employment on the division of labor in the home as well as the challenges, costs, and benefits of balancing family and work. Last, we explore employer resources that facilitate this coordination and consider strategies women use to manage family and work responsibilities.

Attitudes toward Women's Family and Employment Roles

We have seen that few U.S. families conform to the male provider–female home-maker model. Although this traditional view of women's and men's family roles was once seen as the expected and desirable family type, most adults today do not perceive it as ideal. In 1977 66 percent of American adults believed that husbands should be providers and wives full-time homemakers. However, in the late 1990s that figure dropped to 40 percent (Cherlin, 1998; Smith, 1999).

There is evidence that this more modern belief is held by individuals of diverse ethnic backgrounds. In one large-scale survey (Taylor, Tucker, & Mitchell-Kernan, 1999) Black, Mexican American, and White respondents all endorsed the belief that women and men should contribute to their family's finances. However, a sizeable minority of the Black and Mexican American respondents, especially those who were recent immigrants, indicated that despite the expectation of joint financial contribution, men should maintain the primary financial responsibility for their family. Possibly, this belief is an attempt to maintain male dignity in a society that makes it difficult for ethnic minority men to fulfill their provider role responsibility. (Taylor et al., 1999)

Although North Americans tend to accept women's employment role, their approval of this role varies greatly depending on the presence and age of a woman's children. For example, a national survey (Smith, 1999) found that the overwhelming majority of adults from Canada and the U.S. approve of women working full time if they have no children or if their children are gone from the home. However, less than half (45 percent) of Americans and only slightly more than half (55 percent) of Canadians believe that mothers should work either full or part time if they have preschool children.

These attitudes are reflected in the personal aspirations of college women. Most college women desire both a career and motherhood (Davey, 1998; Schroeder, Blood, & Maluso, 1992), but want to discontinue their employment for a period of time during their children's early years (e.g., Davey, 1998; Schroeder et al., 1992). Judith and Claire (Bridges & Etaugh, 1996) found that, on average, Black college women want to interrupt their employment until their child is approximately 2½ years old, while White women want to wait until their child is approximately 4 years old.

These personal preferences are consistent with college women's general attitudes about combining motherhood and employment. The majority of college women (and men) believe that mothers *should* stay home with their baby for at least the first few months (Novack & Novack, 1996), so it is not surprising that both college women and men evaluate mothers who resume full-time employment after a brief maternity leave more negatively than mothers who interrupt their employment until their children are in school (Bridges & Etaugh, 1995). Furthermore, college students perceive these full-time employed mothers as less communal than mothers who reduce their work hours after their baby's birth (Etaugh & Folger, 1998).

Although college women tend to have negative attitudes toward early maternal employment, there is some variation in these beliefs. There seems to be a relationship between maternal employment attitudes and the employment history of young women's own mothers. White women's attitudes toward employed mothers are more positive the younger they were when their own mothers got involved in paid work (Novack & Novack, 1996), and the longer their mothers worked during their own childhood, the earlier they want to return to employment after childbearing (Bridges & Etaugh, 1996). Adolescent and young adult children whose mothers were employed during their childhood do not feel they were neglected and actually appreciate the effort their mothers undertook to help provide for the family (Gerson, 1999). Consistent with the assumption that gender is constructed in part from interpersonal experiences, it seems likely that positive experiences with an employed mother early in their childhood lead women to consider the combination of motherhood and employment as acceptable female role choices that are not harmful to children. Try the Get Involved 12.1 activity to examine attitudes toward employed mothers at your college or university.

GET INVOLVED **12.1**

How Do College Students Evaluate Employed Mothers?

For this activity, ask four traditional-aged female students to read a brief description of a mother and indicate their impression of her on several rating scales. Give two participants Description A, followed by the rating scales, and two participants Description B, followed by the same scales.

Description A: Carol is a 34-year-old married woman with a 7-year-old child in second grade. Carol is employed full time as a newspaper reporter. She worked as a reporter before her child was born and then resumed

working full time at the end of her 6-week maternity leave.

Description B: Carol is a 34-year-old married woman with a 7-year-old child in second grade. Carol is employed full time as a newspaper reporter. She worked as a reporter before her child was born and then resumed working full time when her child was in first grade and thus in school all day.

Now indicate how much you like and respect Carol by completing the following two rating scales:

| like her very little | 1 2 3 4 5 6 7 | like her very much |
| respect her very little | 1 2 3 4 5 6 7 | respect her very much |

Based on Bridges & Orza, (1993).

(continued on p. 324)

Calculate the average rating for each respondent. A high score reflects a positive evaluation of the mother and a low score shows a negative evaluation. Next, average the responses given by the two respondents who read the description of the continuously employed mother (Description A) and average the scores of the two who read the paragraph about the mother who interrupted her employment (Description B).

1. As discussed in the text, this study found that mothers who take a brief maternity leave are more negatively evaluated than those who interrupt their employment. Did you find the same results? If yes, give reasons for this finding.

2. Describe any socialization experiences that might be associated with young women's personal beliefs about a brief maternity leave versus interrupted employment.

3. This study on attitudes toward maternal employment and others presented in the text examined traditional-aged college students. Do you think that older women would have different impressions? Explain your answer.

Division of Household Labor

Do the husbands of employed women contribute more to unpaid child care or housekeeping labor than the husbands of nonemployed women? Has this changed over time? Are women and men satisfied with this division of labor? We now explore these questions and others related to the division of family responsibilities.

Women's and Men's Family Responsibilities

Studies published in the 1970s revealed that husbands did not participate more in housework or child care when their wives were employed (Pleck, 1985). Further, research in the 1980s pointed to only a minimal contribution of household labor by husbands. For example, one investigation showed that husbands whose wives were employed spent approximately 13 hours per week on child care and household tasks, compared to their wives' 33 hours (Douhitt, 1989). Another study reported that White fathers spent 10 minutes more per day on child care if their wives were employed than if they were full-time homemakers and Black fathers spent an average of 16 additional minutes per day (Beckett & Smith, 1981). It is unlikely that this extra time had a major impact on wives' ability to accomplish all of their responsibilities.

Has this imbalance been reduced over time? Although husbands have increased their housework participation somewhat since the 1970s, their contribution to household labor does not equal that of their wives. According to a 1997 national survey, among employed couples with no children, wives spend about five more hours per week performing housework than their husbands do, and among couples with children, the combined housework and child-care gap increases to approximately 17 hours (Goldstein, 2000). Also, although some research shows greater husband involvement in household and child care duties in Black, compared to White, families (e.g., John & Shelton, 1997; Kamo & Cohen, 1998; Ross, 1987), employed women still perform a disproportionate share of these responsibilities in Black (e.g., Hossain & Roopnarine, 1993; Kamo & Cohen, 1998; McLoyd, 1993), Asian American (Espiritu, 1997), Latina/o (Valdez & Coltrane, 1993), and White (e.g., Biernat & Wortman, 1991; Stohs, 1995) families. In lesbian families, on the other hand, couples are likely to share both household responsibilities (Kurdek, 1998) and childrearing tasks (Chan, Brooks, Raboy, & Patterson, 1998).

What kinds of tasks are performed more by women than by men? First, let's look at women's caregiving responsibilities. Regardless of their employment role, women continue to have primary responsibility for most child care activities. These include routine tasks such as feeding and bathing young children (e.g., Hossain & Roopnarine, 1993; Valdez & Coltrane, 1993), as well as periodic activities such as attending school conferences and sports events (e.g., Robinson, in Rubenstein, 1998) and taking children to the doctor (e.g., Tuohy, 1998; Valdez & Coltrane, 1993). Employed mothers also have the responsibility of arranging for both routine substitute care as well as atypical care when there is a school vacation or a child is sick (e.g., Biernat & Wortman, 1991; Hughes & Galinsky, 1994). In fact, a study by Monica Biernat and Camille Wortman (1991) showed that the only child-related task performed equally by professional women and their husbands was playing with their children.

Many women are currently fulfilling another caregiving role in addition to raising their children; they are providing informal care to aging parents and other relatives. People over 85 are the fastest-growing age group in the United States (Wellesley Center for Research on Women, 1998). These people need assistance with daily living tasks, such as meal preparation and bathing, with financial management, with transportation to doctors, and with shopping. Family members usually give most of this in-home care (Hooyman, 1994), and as with child caregiving, women are the primary family members who provide this care (e.g., Jutras & Veilleux, 1991; Wellesley Center for Research on Women, 1998). In fact, it has been estimated that women can expect to spend 18 years providing care to an elderly parent (Older Women's League, 1989), a period of time roughly comparable to that devoted to childrearing.

In household duties, women clearly have the main responsibility for traditional female chores, such as meal preparation, vacuuming, and housecleaning, whereas men have more responsibility for traditional male chores such as yard work, repairs, and car maintenance (e.g., Dancer & Gilbert, 1993; Tuohy, 1998; Valdez & Coltrane, 1993). Note that the tasks done by women are generally performed one or more times per day or week, while those by men are done only periodically.

This traditional division of household responsibilities suggests a greater time burden for women than for men. In fact, comparisons of women's and men's total time spent in household role responsibilities confirm that women spend more hours performing role duties than men do (e.g., Duxbury & Higgins, 1994). One study of over 1,300 mothers and fathers who were employed full-time and had a full-time employed spouse showed that mothers contributed 72 hours to family and work duties per week compared to fathers' 65 hours (Barnes-Farrell, Bridges, Davis, & McInerney, 1999).

Although most women perform the bulk of their families' caregiving and household responsibilities, variations occur in the relative balance of household labor, and some husbands and wives equally share these tasks. As might be expected, women in **traditional couples**, in which *the husband is employed and the wife is a full-time homemaker*, provide a higher proportion of household labor than women in couples in which both partners are employed (Dancer & Gilbert, 1993; Perry-Jenkins, Seery, & Crouter, 1992).

Among two-income couples, there is evidence of variation's in the division of household labor according to the spouses' investment in their work role. **Dual-career couples,** those in which *both partners have received considerable training for their work, are strongly invested in their job, and consider their job as highly relevant to their personal identity*, tend to share housework responsibilities more equally than do **dual-earner couples**, couples in which *both partners are employed but have less personal investment in their jobs than do career-oriented individuals*. This difference has been observed among Asian Americans (Espiritu, 1997), Latinas/os (Pesquera, 1993), and Whites (Dancer & Gilbert, 1993).

Why is domestic role sharing greater among dual-career than dual-earner couples? One possibility is that the allocation of household duties is based at least in part on spouses' own gender attitudes (Baxter, 1992; Ferree, 1991; Perry-Jenkins & Crouter, 1990). People with careers are generally more highly educated than other workers, and more-educated individuals tend to hold more nontraditional gender attitudes (John & Shelton, 1997; Hoffman & Kloska, 1995). Another possibility is that career women who are highly committed to their jobs may expect greater household participation from their partners (Dancer & Gilbert, 1993).

Women's Perceptions of the Division of Family Labor

Few heterosexual couples view the division of labor in their home as equal. Women and men agree that women perform the bulk of child care (e.g., Biernat & Wortman, 1991) and housekeeping duties (Kurdek, 1998; Valdez & Coltrane, 1993). In one study of 145 married couples, Lawrence Kurdek (1998) found that only about 20 percent of the wives and husbands reported sharing the bathroom cleaning and slightly less than one-third indicated equal participation in cooking. Another study found that even among dual-career couples, only one-quarter of the wives reported equal sharing of all areas of responsibility (Carlisle, 1994).

Given the consensus that wives do the overwhelming majority of childrearing and housekeeping tasks, how do women feel about the allocation of duties?

Interestingly, women, including those who are employed, tend to be generally satisfied with their family's division of labor (e.g., Biernat & Wortman, 1991; Sanchez & Kane, 1996; Stohs, 1995). What might account for this apparent paradox between women's heavier workload and their sense of satisfaction about the allocation of domestic responsibilities? Possibly, women are satisfied because their expectations are not violated (Kurdek, 1998; Major, 1993). Their own gender socialization might have led them to believe that both childrearing and household work are women's domain. Based on this construction of the female role, there might not be any discrepancy between what they expected and what they experience, so they experience no disappointment. Also, if women do not assume most of what they consider to be women's work, they might feel guilty. Additionally, some women might compare their own household responsibility to that of other women, rather than to their husband's responsibility (Major, 1993) and, therefore, not see themselves as unfairly burdened.

Although many women feel generally satisfied with the division of domestic labor, some think the division is unfair and feel dissatisfied. This perceived inequity does not stem directly from the amount of time they spend on household tasks, but from their *share* of the total time spent by the couple (Sanchez & Kane, 1996). The more time those wives spend relative to their husbands, the more likely they are to view the allocation of family responsibilities as unfair and to feel unhappy about it (Stohs, 1995).

Explanations of the Division of Family Labor

What factors can account for women's disproportionate share of child care and housekeeping duties? This section considers three possible answers to this question.

Time Constraints. One explanation for the unequal division of household labor is that domestic responsibilities are allocated on the basis of each spouse's time availability (e.g., Pittman & Kerpelman, 1993), a perspective that assumes the division of household labor is gender-neutral, with consideration of time constraints only. Consistent with this view, full-time homemakers, who have more time available, spend more time in household tasks than do employed women (e.g., DeMeis & Perkins, 1996; Perry-Jenkins et al., 1992). Furthermore, the more hours wives spend in paid work, the less time they expend in housework (Ferree, 1991; John & Shelton, 1997).

Although spouses' time availability is to some extent related to the amount of time they invest in household labor, some patterns of domestic involvement are inconsistent with this explanation. First, even when comparing spouses with comparable work hours, mothers spend more time than fathers caring for their children (Aldous, Mulligan, & Bjarnason, 1998). Second, while one study found that the more time fathers spend on their jobs, the less time they devote to parenting (Aldous et al., 1998), another study indicates that fathers' time on the job is unrelated to the time they spend in child care (Pleck, 1997). Thus, it appears that time availability plays some role but cannot alone adequately explain the allocation of domestic responsibilities.

Relative Power.   Another possible answer to our question is that women's disproportionate share of household labor results from their lower degree of marital power (Steil, 1997; Thompson & Walker, 1989). According to this view, power in marriage depends, in part, on work-related resources, such as occupational prestige and income. The more resources one partner has in relation to the other, the greater that partner's influence (i.e., power) over the other. Because people tend to dislike household chores and to assign them little prestige, the person with the greater resources will use his or her power to limit engagement in these tasks.

Does research support this view? Evidence indicates that the discrepancy in husbands' and wives' resources explains women's participation in household labor more than it explains men's participation. The lower a woman's occupational status (Pittman & Blanchard, 1996) and earnings (Ferree, 1991; Steil & Weltman, 1991) relative to her husband's, the more housework and child care she performs. However, a power discrepancy does not necessarily affect a husband's involvement in household labor. Although men who have less resource power than their wives have a somewhat greater child care responsibility than men who have less power (Steil & Weltman, 1991), the relative degree of husbands' and wives' resources is unrelated to husbands' participation in housework (Ferree, 1991; Pittman & Blanchard, 1996).

This finding may be due to the definition of marital power as the relative degree of work-related resources, which might not fully capture the meaning of marital power. Society's assumption of male power is so firmly rooted in the social construction of gender (Moen, 1992) that it is not easily dismantled by resource equality. Even when wives and husbands bring similar work resources to the marriage, the impact of our expectations about males' higher status, value, and power remain. Janice Steil and Karen Weltman (1991) found that among professional couples in which wives earned significantly more than their husbands, neither husbands nor wives evaluated the wife's career as more important than the husband's. Furthermore, despite their lower income, husbands maintained greater financial decision-making power. Marital power apparently is influenced by more than occupational resources; men's participation in housework doesn't increase when they have fewer occupational resources than their wives because they maintain other forms of power.

Gender Attitudes.   A third explanation for the division of household labor is that the unequal distribution reflects spouses' personal beliefs about appropriate gender roles (Ferree, 1991; Pleck, 1985). People construct images of the roles expected for each gender, and this construction guides their own behavior. According to this view, many couples, including dual-income couples, have internalized the traditional gender beliefs that managing children and the home is *primarily* the wife's responsibility and that husbands should be the *main* financial providers. These views reflect strong societal norms, and many individuals who are socialized into these beliefs as a result of observation in the home, assigned chores, and media depictions of gender roles may be hard pressed to deviate from them.

Consistent with this explanation, men who have nontraditional attitudes about family roles spend more time doing housework than those with traditional views (John & Shelton, 1997; Perry-Jenkins & Crouter, 1990), whereas women with nontraditional beliefs spend less time in household labor than do women who have traditional attitudes (John & Shelton, 1997; Rowley, 1999).

Family-Work Coordination

Women's Experiences with Maternity Leave

Although we have seen that young college women would like to discontinue their employment for some period of time after the birth of their baby, most women do not follow that pattern. In 1998 57.5 percent of married women with infants 1 year or under were employed (U.S. Bureau of Labor Statistics, 1999c).

The high employment rate of mothers with infants points to the importance of adequate maternity leave policies, and three-quarters of Americans favor paid maternity leave (Smith, 1999). Incredibly, the United States is one of the few industrialized countries in the world without a national policy requiring paid maternity leave. A 1998 report by the International Labour Organization, a United Nations agency, found that 80 percent of industrialized countries provide paid maternity leave, with about one-third allowing paid leaves of more than 14 weeks ("U.S. Maternity Benefits," 1998). In North America there is a stark contrast between Canada, which provides 17 weeks of paid leave, and the United States, which has no federal legislation governing leave with pay. In fact, the only federal law mandating maternity leave in the United States is the Family and Medical Leave Act. This law, which has been in effect since 1993, is applicable only to workplaces with more than 50 employees. It allows workers (women and men) in those companies to take up to 12 weeks of *unpaid* leave for medical conditions or family responsibilities, including the birth or adoption of a child. Although some American women are eligible for at least partial-pay maternity benefits through policies of their employer or state ("U.S. Maternity Benefits," 1998), many women take shorter leaves than they would like to take because their families cannot afford their loss of income.

What other factors are related of the length of a woman's maternity leave? One study found that pregnant women who perceived their employers as supportive of employees' family needs were more committed to their organizations and expected an earlier return to employment after childbirth (Lyness, Thompson, Francesco, & Judiesch, 1999) Possibly, the belief that the employer is sensitive to work-family issues contributes to a greater comfort at work and an expectation that family responsibilities will be accommodated. In addition, this study found that women with more nontraditional attitudes about combining employment and parenting expected to resume working sooner.

Is the length of a mother's maternity leave related to her interactions with her child? One indication that it is comes from a study by Roseanne Clark and her colleagues (Clark, Hyde, Essex, & Klein, 1997). These researchers interviewed employed mothers of 4-month-old infants and videotaped their interactions with their babies. On average, these mothers took $8\frac{1}{2}$ weeks of leave. Those who took shorter maternity leaves (approximately 6 weeks) had more difficult interactions with their infants. Mothers who took longer leaves (approximately 12 weeks) had more positive interactions with their babies. The mothers who had shorter leaves were more likely to be frustrated, to respond inconsistently to their babies, and to show displeasure. Although these findings suggest that short leaves have a negative impact on mothers' interactions with their babies, we cannot be certain about the causal nature of the relationship. Possibly, mothers who are more frustrated in their motherhood role—less nurturant, or less pleased with their babies—*choose* to take shorter leaves than other mothers; that is, mothers' own temperament, feelings about motherhood, or relationships with their infants might influence their decisions about length of leave, rather than length of leave influencing their reactions.

These researchers (Hyde, Klein, Essex, & Clark, 1995) also examined the relationship between the length of maternity leave and mothers' mental health. They found that leave time was not related to psychological state unless the mother experienced other stressors, such as marital problems or an unrewarding job. If these difficulties were present, mothers with shorter leaves were more depressed 4 months after childbirth than those with longer leaves. Perhaps it is too difficult for new mothers to cope with nonparental stressors at the same time as dealing with the demands of balancing family and work. However, by 12 months after the birth, this effect disappears (Klein, Hyde, Essex, & Clark, 1998).

How does maternity leave affect women's experiences on the job? A 1991 survey of over 4,000 employed mothers found that more than two-thirds said their boss supported their taking time off after the birth of their baby and felt their leave did not negatively affect their career (Marshall, n.d.), while one-third felt they were treated less favorably after their leave and approximately half believed that people at their job view women who take maternity leave as less committed to their work.

Women's Experiences Balancing Family and Work

Do you think balancing family and work involves both costs and rewards? What kind of costs and rewards might stem from juggling these roles? Consider these questions, then try Get Involved 12.2 to explore your personal expectations of this issue.

When Judith and Claire (Bridges & Etaugh, 1996) asked White and Black college women to respond to the items presented in Get Involved 12.2, we found that these students estimated the benefits to be more likely than the costs (70 percent versus 55 percent). Although the White and Black students had similarly viewed the probability of benefits, the White students estimated a higher likelihood of negative outcomes from working during motherhood than did the Black students (58 percent versus 49 percent). The long history of Black women's

GET INVOLVED **12.2**

What Psychological Experiences Do You Think You Will Have if You Combine Employment and Motherhood?

Pretend that you have two children and a spouse/partner employed full time outside of the home. Given these circumstances think about the experience you might have if you, also, were employed full time outside the home throughout your childrearing years. For each of the following possible consequences of employment during parenthood, estimate the probability, from 0 percent to 100 percent, that you would experience that outcome.

____ 1. higher self-esteem
____ 2. more guilt feelings
____ 3. greater feeling of missing out on your children's developmental progress (e.g., first steps)

____ 4. greater self-fulfillment
____ 5. greater number of conflicting demands
____ 6. greater intellectual stimulation
____ 7. more resentment from spouse/partner
____ 8. more anxiety about your child
____ 9. more mental exhaustion
____ 10. greater degree of pride
____ 11. more social stimulation
____ 12. more irritability
____ 13. more conflict with your spouse/partner
____ 14. more approval from other people

Based on Bridges & Etaugh, (1996).

What Does It Mean?

Items 2, 3, 5, 7, 8, 9, 12, and 13 are possible costs and items 1, 4, 6, 10, 11, and 14 are possible benefits of employment for mothers. For each of these two sets of outcomes, calculate the average probability that you reported. First, add up the 8 probabilities you specified for the costs and divide that total by 8. Then, sum the probabilities you estimated for the 6 benefits and divide that total by 6. After calculating your averages, read the text's presentation of the findings of this study.

1. Compare your expectations to those reported in the text. Are they similar? If not can you think of reasons for any observed differences?
2. Do you think your expectations will influence your decision about the timing of your employment and childbearing?
3. Do you think your answers would have differed if you were the other gender? Refer to material on gender attitudes and gender socialization to explain your answer.

employment (Broman, 1991) and Black women's perception of the provider role as part of their family role (Malson, 1983) may both contribute to their more positive attitude toward maternal employment. These different views held by Black and White women show that these attitudes are socially constructed from individuals' experiences and do not inevitably arise from one's gender.

In actuality, the effects of performing family and work roles are complex and encompass both negative and positive aspects. Because of this, it is important to examine women's actual experiences associated with these roles as well as explanations of these outcomes.

Concerns.   Previously we saw that employed women perform the bulk of child care and housework duties. Understandably, one major concern expressed by these family-work jugglers is simply finding the time to adequately fulfill all their responsibilities (e.g., Crosby, 1991; Families and Work Institute, 1995), and another primary issue is arranging for good child care. "If I did not find good care, I simply would not work" (Snyder, 1994, p. 166). "I currently would like a different job but can't get too serious about looking because I don't care to take my children out of the center we currently use" (Snyder, 1994, p. 165). Comments like these illustrate the central importance that child care has for employed women. Not surprisingly, worries about child care can lead to high levels of stress for employed mothers (Googins, 1991).

Costs.   As we saw earlier in this chapter, women carry most of the responsibility related to child care and housework. As might be expected, many women, especially mothers, experience **role strain**; that is, *stress stemming from one's roles*. Role strain can stem from **role overload**, *role demands that exceed one's available time and/or energy*, and/or **interrole conflict,** *incompatible demands stemming from two or more roles*. Role overload can occur, for example, when, after 9 hours of work and commuting, a mother does her family's laundry, cooks dinner, washes the dishes, and supervises her children's homework. Interrole conflict, on the other hand, would occur if a mother wants to attend her child's band concert at school but is expected to chair an important business meeting scheduled for the same time. Florence Denmark and her colleagues (Denmark, Novick, & Pinto, 1996, p. 108) describe family-work role strain like this: "Between work and family, women face competing demands on their attention. Some days they may feel they cannot accept one more demand on their time. Too much stress and they are like a balloon ready to pop." In fact, the more role strain women experience, the greater their depression and stress (Berger, Cook, DelCampo, Herrera, & Weigel, 1994; Bird & Rogers, 1998; Simon, 1992) and the lower their job and life satisfaction (Kossek & Ozeki, 1998).

What produces role strain? According to the **scarcity hypothesis**, first developed by William Goode (1960), *excessive role responsibilities deplete the individual's limited supply of time and energy and, consequently, can lead to stress*. When individuals have more responsibilities than they have time or energy for handling them, or when they are overwhelmed by conflicts between their role responsibilities, they can experience frustration, fatigue, or other indications of stress.

Estimates of the percentage of employed women who experience role strain vary from 40 percent (Galinsky & Bond, 1996) to over 80 percent (Carlisle, 1994). This large range is to be expected because experiences related to family-work balancing can be influenced by numerous factors, not the least of which is the presence of children. The wife and worker roles alone are not related to role overload or conflict. It is the addition of the mother role to the worker role that creates women's role strain (Barnett & Baruch, 1985; Ray & Miller, 1994). Also, the less their husbands are involved in child care the more likely it is that employed mothers experience stress or depression (Hughes & Galinsky, 1994; Ross & Mirowsky, 1988).

As we stated above, mothers' perceptions of the quality of their child care arrangements are crucial to their level of role strain (Hughes & Galinsky, 1994). One study showed that professional women were more likely than blue-collar or clerical women to report better child care arrangements and to be able to forget about family issues while at work (Burris, 1991). Possibly, their greater comfort about their children's care enabled them to focus on work without the intrusion of family concerns.

Another factor that influences the degree of role strain experienced by women is whether or not they provide care for elderly or dependent adults. Elder caregivers can experience conflicts with their husbands or children (Hooyman, 1994), as well as interference with their employment role (Gignac, Kelloway, & Gottlieb, 1996; Mui, 1995). Elder caregiving thus can considerably increase women's emotional strain (Mui, 1995), especially if they are experiencing stress in their other roles (Stephens & Townsend, 1997).

Although men are not immune to either role overload or interrole conflict, considerable evidence demonstrates that employed married women are more likely than employed married men to experience both of these and that this gender difference holds across several ethnic groups, including Whites (e.g., Berger et al., 1994; Duxbury & Higgins, 1994), Blacks (McLoyd, 1993), and Latinas/os (Berger et al., 1994). The social construction of women as the major caregivers and homemakers and the construction of men as the primary providers means that women's family and work roles are parallel to one another whereas men's are simultaneous. Women's employment is seen as *additional to* their family role, whereas men's employment is viewed as *part of* their family role (Simon, 1995; Wiley, 1991). Women *add* responsibilities to their domestic role by working outside of the home whereas men *fulfill* their domestic responsibilities through paid employment. All of this leads to greater role strain for women than for men.

In addition to role strain, lesbian role jugglers must face other problems as well. For example, their coworkers and/or supervisors might disapprove of their choice of intimate partner, making the work environment uncomfortable. Furthermore, the lack of insurance benefits available for lesbian families can produce economic pressures (Fassinger, 1995).

Benefits.   Juggling family and work can lead to role overload and interrole conflict, but it can also bring numerous rewards, including higher self-esteem, greater respect from others, and greater economic security (Carlisle, 1994; Gilbert, 1993). As one professional woman put it: "I feel that I would be a much better mother if I combined motherhood with employment. I think I would be more fulfilled and feel a sense of accomplishment about my life" (Granrose & Kaplan, 1996, p. 47).

The benefits of multiple role coordination are explained by the **enhancement hypothesis** (Marks, 1977; Sieber, 1974). According to this perspective, *each additional role provides a new source of self-esteem, social approval, social status, and other benefits.* Successfully applying the different skills required by different roles can lead to achievements in many areas. Consequently, family-work balancers can develop competence in numerous domains and experience greater personal pride and fulfillment.

Aside from any rewards associated with managing several roles, women can benefit by using one role to buffer strains associated with another (Crosby, 1991). That is, positive or neutral events in one role can reduce the psychological impact of negative events in another role. A 35-year-old professional woman describes it like this: "Sometimes I have a really rough day at work and then I come home and these two little kids run to the door. My older daughter says 'I'm really glad *you* got picked to be my mother.' Then, I forget the day at work" (Crosby, 1991, p. 103).

Faye Crosby (1991) discusses three reasons why buffering helps psychological well-being. First, involvement in more than one role offers the opportunity for a time-out, giving the family-work juggler an opportunity to distance herself from the problems in one role while she engages in another role. For instance, a mother who is upset about her child's lack of achievement in school can put that worry aside while she focuses on her employment responsibilities.

Second, challenges in one role help put into perspective worries associated with another role. For example, a woman who is very bothered about interpersonal conflicts with her coworkers might view this problem as less important when faced with her husband's serious illness. When his health improves, she might continue to view this interpersonal tension as minor.

Third, buffering helps protect women's self-esteem. Positive or even neutral events in one role can help restore self-esteem that has been damaged by negative events in another role. Thus, the disappointment of not receiving a promotion at work can be mitigated by a mother's feelings of competence as she helps her child successfully cope with a bully at school.

In addition to benefits earned while juggling family and work roles, there is evidence of long-term positive outcomes. Longitudinal research shows that among women who graduated from college in the 1960s, those who combined family and employment roles in early adulthood have more positive role experiences in middle age and experience greater midlife well-being (Vandewater, Ostrove, & Stewart, 1997).

Gender Attitudes and Family-Work Balancing Experiences.

The effects of women's employment on their well-being are related, in part, to their gender attitudes. Employed women with nontraditional attitudes tend to experience more benefits (Marshall & Barnett, 1993) and less stress (Parry, 1987) than women with traditional beliefs, and nonemployed mothers with nontraditional views tend to be more stressed than those with traditional beliefs (Parry, 1987). For example, mothers of infants who want to work outside the home but are full-time homemakers tend to be more depressed than full-time homemakers who do not want to be employed (Hock & DeMeis, 1990). When women's roles are consistent with their attitudes about appropriate roles, they experience better psychological outcomes.

Ethnic Comparison of Family-Work Balancing Experiences. Few studies have examined the outcomes of family and work roles for women in different ethnic groups, but available limited research points to similar reactions in ethnically diverse women. Latina and White women managing multiple roles report comparable degrees of role overload and distress (Berger et al., 1994). A similar study of Black and White middle-class women found no ethnic differences in the personal costs or benefits related to respondents' family and work roles (Bridges & Orza, 1996).

Effects of Mothers' Employment on Children

In 1995, more preschool children were cared for by paid caregivers than by full-time stay-at-home parents, including 45 percent of infants under age 1 ("HHS Says Statistics," 1999). Some pediatricians and psychologists caution mothers about the dangers of nonmaternal care (Holcomb, 1998). Does research support this advice?

According to psychologist Michael Lamb, it is not scientific evidence, but the gender role belief that women belong at home, that fuels the argument against nonmaternal child care (Holcomb, 1998). In actuality, most researchers conclude that maternal employment and nonmaternal care are not harmful. Although a

Most research shows that day care does not hinder children's social, academic, or motivational development.

few studies indicate some negative social and achievement-related effects of non-family care during the baby's first year (e.g., Belsky, 1988), most show no added risks for children's social, academic, or motivational development nor for their relationships with their mothers, even during infancy (e.g., Clarke-Stewart, All-husen, & Clements, 1995; Harvey, 1999; Lamb, 1998; NICHD Early Child Care Research Network, 1997; Scarr, 1997; Symons, 1998).

Children may even benefit from maternal employment. First, girls and boys whose mothers are employed develop less stereotypical attitudes about gender roles, compared to children with nonemployed mothers (e.g., Wright & Young, 1998). Because the employment role is seen as an agentic role and maternal employment frequently necessitates nonstereotypical structuring of household responsibilities among both parents and children, employed mothers often serve as less traditional role models than do full-time homemakers. Second, adolescent girls whose mothers are employed tend to have higher educational and career aspirations than their counterparts with nonemployed mothers (Etaugh, 1993a), possibly because they observe their mother in an agentic role.

Are there other benefits that accrue directly from out-of-home child care programs? The answer to this question is complex and depends, in part, on the consistency between a particular program and childrearing behaviors and values in the home; on characteristics of the child, such as social class; and on attributes of the program, such as size and the staff-to-child ratio. What is clear is that high-quality care can provide significant benefits to children from disadvantaged homes (e.g., Lamb, 1998; Scarr, 1997, 1998). Sandra Scarr (1997, p. 147) states that for low-income children, "high-quality child care programs supply missing elements of emotional support and intellectual opportunities." Both better academic per-formance and a reduction in adolescent social problems, such as teen pregnancy and delinquency, are associated with high-quality care for children from disad-vantaged backgrounds (e.g., Lamb, 1998; Scarr, 1997).

While there is considerable agreement among researchers that high-quality care can be beneficial, particularly to low-income children, the positive effects of lower-quality programs are debatable. Sandra Scarr (1997, 1998) contends that quality of care has little effect on development. She states that, "within a broad range of safe environments, quality variations in child care have only small and temporary effects on most children's development" (1997, p. 147). Meanwhile, other researchers contend that the quality of care does have an important effect on how the child develops (Lamb, 1998; Van Horn & Newell, 1999). Despite the uncertainty about the degree of importance associated with quality of care, researchers do agree that parents have a much greater impact on children's devel-opment than does any non-family child care program (Lamb, 1998; Scarr, 1998). As stated by Michael Lamb (1998, p. 116), "there is clear evidence that the qual-ity of children's interactions and relationships with their parents and family mem-bers and the quality of care children receive at home continue to be the most important sources of influence on the development of young children, even when they receive substantial amounts of care outside the home." Furthermore, Ellen Galinsky's (1999) interviews with more than 1,000 children in grades 3–12 found that children's perceptions of their mother's parenting ability were not related to whether their mother worked outside the home.

Our exploration of the effects of maternal employment on children's development and our discussion of benefits that might accrue from this employment does not imply that full-time homemakers are detrimental to their children's development. What is important is the consistency between a mother's role (employed or not employed) and her belief about the value of maternal employment for her children. Mothers whose roles match their own attitudes are likely to be more effective parents. Furthermore, adolescent children of mothers whose roles are consistent with their attitudes tend to achieve more in school (Paulson, 1996). A mother who is dissatisfied with her role is less likely to display the type of positive parenting characteristics that can lead to good outcomes for her children (MacEwen & Barling, 1991).

Interestingly, most research on the effects of parental employment on children has focused on maternal employment. Many scholars (e.g., Silverstein, 1996) claim there is no evidence for an instinct that makes women better suited to parenting than men; nonetheless, the social construction of gender leads us to conceptualize parenting within the female gender role. This is so ingrained in our thinking that there has been much less investigation of fathering than mothering (Silverstein & Phares, 1996) Furthermore, because employment is identified more closely with the father role than the mother role, there has been little research on children's outcomes associated with paternal employment. Feminist author Betty Friedan has identified our mother-centered focus on parenting as a problem and encourages psychologists to do more research on fathering (Murray, 1999). However, even graduate students, the voice of future psychology, continue to frame their investigations of parenting within a mother-focused perspective (Silverstein & Phares, 1996).

Effects of Wives' Employment on the Marital Relationship

If women's employment is a modification of traditional gender roles, what are the implications for a husband's well-being when his wife is employed? Does it matter whether the wife views her employment as an essential aspect of her identity (as a career) versus as a means of earning a living (as a job)? Terri Orbuch and Lindsay Custer (1995) examined these questions in study samples of Black and White men married to homemakers, career-oriented wives, or job-oriented wives. Their results showed that husbands of homemakers had the lowest well-being and husbands of women who viewed their employment as a job had the highest. How can these findings be explained? According to Orbuch and Custer, one possibility is that husbands of job-oriented wives benefited from the financial support of a working wife but didn't experience the potentially greater challenge to their traditional role associated with a career-oriented spouse.

Turning to wives' feelings about their marriage, satisfaction is related, in part, to the consistency between wives' roles and their gender-related attitudes. In interviews with married women, Maureen Perry-Jenkins and her colleagues (Perry-Jenkins, Seery, & Crouter, 1992) found that employed women who were uncomfortable about their work role experienced less marital satisfaction than those who wanted to work outside the home, and were less satisfied than full-time homemakers. It appears that positive outcomes can accrue from either full-time homemaking or from combining family and work. What is more important than the actual roles is the attitude toward those roles.

Studies of the relationship between women's employment and wives' and husbands' sexual satisfaction show parallel findings. Janet Shibley Hyde and her colleagues (Hyde, DeLamater, & Hewitt, 1998) studied the association between employment and the sexual experiences of more than 500 heterosexual women and their husbands or intimate partners and found that neither women's employment status nor the number of hours they spent at work was related to their sexual frequency or enjoyment. What was important was the quality of their jobs. Both women and men reported greater sexual satisfaction when they had more rewarding work experiences. This could be because positive experiences in the workplace help couples more fully enjoy their sexual relationship or because a satisfactory sex life contributes to enjoyment on the job. Or, it may be that neither domain influences the other but that well-adjusted adults lead lives that are satisfying in many domains, including work and sexual relationships.

Solutions to Family-Work Balancing Difficulties

As we have seen, the numerous rewards that can accrue from combining family and work roles do not eliminate the challenges jugglers face in managing their roles. What approaches can help reduce these difficulties?

Resources Offered by Employers. Given the kinds of information we have examined in this chapter, it is not surprising that a 1999 national survey of workers in the United States found that 97 percent said balancing family and work is their most important concern, taking precedence over issues such as job security and salary ("W/F Balance," 1999). Organizational resources could help parents coordinate their family and work roles in many ways. One is by offering paid parental leave. As discussed previously, adequate leaves are not available to many parents. Mothers and fathers would benefit from leave policies that provide sufficient time to adjust to parenthood, to develop an understanding of the specific needs of one's baby, and, for biological mothers, to recuperate from the physical stresses of pregnancy and childbearing.

A second benefit sought by women is flexible work hours (Galinsky & Bond, 1996; Lee & Duxbury, 1998; "W/F Balance," 1999). **Flextime**, *flexible work scheduling that allows the employee to choose the arrival and departure time within a set of possible options offered by the employer,* can enable parents to better accommodate their work hours to their children's regular child care or school schedules and to deal with unforeseen and unscheduled family demands.

A third option that would help some workers is telecommuting. The rise in technology can make this option to work from home attractive to certain types of workers ("W/F Balance," 1999), although it would not, at the present time, be relevant to the majority.

Fourth, employer help with childcare would ease a major burden faced by employed parents (Lee & Duxbury, 1998). Child care assistance programs can include referral services and day care subsidies as well as on-site day care. Fifty percent of workers sampled in a national survey desired this last option, which would enable them to spend some time with their children during the course of the work day as well as to more easily transport them to and from day care. ("W/F Balance," 1999). Unfortunately, these services are offered primarily by large companies, yet the majority of workers are employed by small companies. Furthermore, companies that employ better-educated, highly skilled workers are more likely to offer these benefits than are companies with a primarily unskilled labor force (Kleiman, 1993). Thus, access to employer-provided child care assistance is not equally available to all women who work in large companies.

Other Child Care Resources.   Only a limited number of child care services are available through employers. Given that child care is one of employed parents' greatest worries, the strong need for additional child care options for infants and preschool children must be addressed. According to the National Women's Law Center, the cost of child care ranges from approximately $4,000–$10,000 per year ("HHS Says Statistics," 1999); therefore, these options must include more affordable care. Also, it is clear that more must be done to ensure that child care facilities are safe environments for children. A study of both for-profit and nonprofit centers conducted by the U.S. Consumer Product Safety Commission found that two-thirds of the centers studied had at least one physical hazard, ranging from unsafe cribs to poorly maintained playground surfaces ("Government Study," 1999).

Parents additionally need assistance with care of older children. School programs that provide before- and after-school care not only would provide safe and stimulating activities for children but would reduce parental worry and eliminate the need for parents to coordinate multiple daily child care arrangements. Similarly, school- or community-based programs for snow days, teachers conferences, and school vacations would be helpful.

Support from Other People.   Enlisting the aid of others to reduce their domestic burden can be effective for some family-work jugglers. Women who have the financial resources can purchase services they would otherwise perform, such as housecleaning and meal preparation. Other women rely on the assistance of family members. Are the children of employed mothers more involved in household chores than the children of full-time homemakers? While research shows mixed findings (Bartko & McHale, 1991; Bianchi & Robinson, 1997), one major factor clearly influences the ease with which women coordinate their family and work roles: the degree of help they receive from their spouses or partners. Women's well-being is positively related to their husbands' greater participation in child care and housework (Galinsky & Bond, 1996; Ozer, 1995) as well as to husbands' emotional support (Lee & Duxbury, 1998; Matire, Stephens, & Townsend, 1998). Keep in mind, however, that support from husbands or male partners is frequently construed as "help," not as a shared responsibility, underscoring the social construction of different and unequal roles for women and men.

Some employed couples work alternating shift schedules to deal with childcare difficulties, thereby sharing the childcare duties and reducing or eliminating the need for nonparental care. For a close look at the gender attitudes of some working-class couples who use this strategy, turn to Learn about the Research 12.1.

LEARN ABOUT THE RESEARCH 12.1

How do Working Class Couples with Alternating Shifts Reconcile Their Own Roles with Their Traditional Gender Attitudes?

Francine Deutsch and Susan Saxon explored the ways working-class couples with alternating work shifts reconciled inconsistencies between their attitudes toward women's and men's gender roles and their actual gender roles. The researchers interviewed 23 primarily White working-class parents. Although these couples had traditional views about parental, marital, and employment roles, they alternated their work shifts, so that one parent would be able to take care of the children while the other parent worked outside the home. Husbands worked an average of 46 hours per week in blue-collar occupations, such as custodian and electrician, and wives worked an average of 33 hours per week in a variety of jobs, including clerical worker and food service worker.

Some of the couples handled the inconsistency between their gender attitudes and their own roles by modifying their traditional views. For example, one woman commented, "When we first married, Larry felt like I was his wife. I was there to be his wife, to do the dishes, to clean the house, to take care of the kids. Things have changed since then. We're more equals. It's more like I'm his wife, not his slave" (p. 344).

Other ways that these couples handled inconsistencies between their attitudes and roles was to maintain the belief that their family roles still reflected three core elements of traditional gender roles. First, they continued to hold the view that the husband was the primary provider. As one husband said, "I have to work and I have to be the breadwinner" (p. 349). Second, these couples, especially the husbands, did not view the worker role as a primary aspect of the mother's identity. Instead they saw it as a financial necessity. One husband said, "I think it would be great if she could be home all the time . . . Right now she's really got no choice because we need the money, but if it were her decision . . . and she wanted to stay home, hey great" (p. 350). Interestingly, however, many of the wives viewed their jobs as providing rewards beyond the financial one. As one woman said, "I look forward to 5:30 every night, I really do . . . taking off in the car by myself. . . . I really enjoy it . . . I love it, I love my job. . . . I love doing the paperwork and working with numbers . . . anyone asks me a question, 9 out of 10 times I have an answer for them and it's wonderful. I feel very successful" (p. 351). Third, these mothers and fathers saw the mother as the primary caregiver. One mother stated it like this, "As much as we try to do everything 50/50, if Jimmy gets hurt and he cries, I think I'm the one that should take care of him" (p. 356).

The authors conclude that these couples were able to reconcile potentially discrepant attitudes and role behaviors by viewing their roles as constrained by financial considerations and maintaining their beliefs that the husband was still the primary breadwinner and the wife, the primary caregiver.

From Deutsch & Saxon, (1998).

(continued on p. 341)

What Does It Mean?

1. The couples examined in this study were primarily White and working class. Do you think middle-class couples or couples with different ethnicities might reconcile their attitudes and roles in a different way? Give reasons for your answer.

2. What are the advantages and disadvantages to the children of parents who work alternating shifts?
3. What are the advantages and disadvantages to the marriage of alternating shifts?

Personal Coping Strategies.   Unfortunately, some women receive no support from others, or the help they do receive is insufficient. Under these circumstances, women use several personal strategies to manage their numerous role responsibilities. One is to modify their role definitions by negotiating with their employer about reduced hours (McLoyd, 1993). Women who reduce their work hours as a means of coping with family and work responsibilities experience both benefits and costs. Kathleen Barker (1993) reported that women who work part time experience greater satisfaction at home than do women employed full time. However, at work, they can feel excluded from interpersonal contact and job development opportunities.

Another strategy for women is to change their perceptions of their responsibilities (McLoyd, 1993). They might, for example, lower their standards for housecleaning or accept the possibility that a promotion might take longer to achieve. Many employed women utilize this strategy at least to some extent. As we saw earlier in this chapter, employed mothers spend fewer hours caring for their homes than do stay-at-home mothers (e.g., DeMeis & Perkins, 1996).

A third approach women use to coordinate family and work roles is to carefully plan time and put in extra time in order to handle all role responsibilities (McLoyd, 1993). This approach can be very difficult and exhausting, and women who use it are sometimes referred to as supermoms. The exercise in Get Involved 12.3 will help you gain firsthand information about women's experiences balancing family and work roles.

GET INVOLVED **12.3**

Women's Experiences Coordinating Family and Work Roles.

Interview two employed mothers. If possible, select mothers who have children under 6. However, if not possible, interview mothers with children of any age. Ask each to talk about the following experiences: (1) time problems, if any, performing all of their responsibilities, (2) conflicts, if any, between demands from different roles, (3) problems, if any, arranging for child care, (4) psychological benefits they receive from their mother role, (5) psychological benefits they receive from their work role, (6) personal coping strategies and/or employer benefits that have helped them deal with any time problems, conflicts, or child care difficulties, and (7) additional employer benefits they would find beneficial.

(continued on p. 342)

What Does It Mean?

1. What new information did you learn from these mothers' experiences that you did not learn from the text?

2. Did the responses of these women enhance your understanding of the costs and benefits of balancing motherhood and employment? Explain your answer.

3. Which solution do you think is the most effective for dealing with family-work balancing? Explain your answer.

4. Which family-work balancing hypothesis best accounts for these mothers' experiences? Explain your answer.

SUMMARY

1. The majority of North Americans approve of women's employment. However, only half believe mothers of preschool children should work.

2. Most college women want to combine a career with motherhood. However, students would like to interrupt their employment for childrearing and believe mothers should stay home for a period of time. Also, they more negatively evaluate mothers who continue their employment after the birth of their baby than mothers who interrupt their employment for childrearing.

3. Women perform most of the child care and housekeeping duties in the family. This pattern exists across ethnic groups. Equal distribution of these responsibilities is more likely in dual-career than in dual-earner or traditional couples.

4. Women tend to be satisfied with the division of labor, although they perform the greater share. This might be because women have been socialized to view household duties as their domain. Also, they might view their obligations as fair in comparison to those of other women.

5. Explanations for the unequal division of labor focus on time constraints, relative power, and gender attitudes. There is more support for the latter two than for the first.

6. The United States is one of the few industrialized countries that does not have federal legislation mandating paid maternity leave.

7. One study found that pregnant women who perceived their employers as supportive of workers' with family needs and those with nontraditional attitudes about combining work and parenting expected an earlier return to employment after childbirth

8. There is some evidence that mothers who take short maternity leaves are more likely than those who take longer leaves to have negative interactions with their babies, but the findings do not indicate whether the negative reactions are caused by the length of the leave. Also, mothers who experience marital or work stressors in the first few months after birth tend to be more depressed if they take shorter maternity leaves. However,

by 12 months after birth, a mother's depression is not related to the length of her maternity leave.

9. Women across ethnic groups experience role strain as well as numerous benefits from multiple role juggling. Role strain can be explained by the scarcity hypothesis; and benefits, such as self-esteem and approval from others, can be explained by the enhancement hypothesis. Another benefit of engaging in both family and work roles is that one role can buffer strains associated with the other.

10. Most research shows no negative effects of maternal employment on children. Day care, even during infancy, generally does not hinder the child's social, academic, or motivational development. Furthermore, it can provide benefits to some children. Day care can help improve school performance and reduce the social problems of children from low-income homes. Also, children with employed mothers have less stereotypical attitudes about gender roles than children of full-time homemakers.

11. Positive psychological feelings, good parenting, and marital satisfaction are more likely when a woman feels comfortable about her role, whether as a full-time homemaker or employed wife and mother.

12. Employer resources, such as flextime and child care assistance, and husbands' participation in family responsibilities and provision of emotional support can help women more effectively manage their multiple demands. Also, personal adjustments, such as altering one's role definitions, changing one's perceptions of responsibilities, and attempting to perform all role duties, are types of strategies women use to balance their family and work roles.

WHAT DO YOU THINK?

1. Use any theory of gender typing (see Chapter 3) to explain the current division of household labor as presented in the text. Would this theory predict a greater equality of child care and household responsibility in the future? Explain your answer.

2. Recall that women seem to be satisfied with an unequal division of household labor. Do you agree with the explanations given in the text? Are there other factors that can account for this phenomenon? Explain your answers.

3. Explain why young Black women, compared to White women, desire an earlier return to employment after they have children. Refer to material in previous chapters and any other information that addresses the question.

4. Women now experience more role strain than men. Do you think this will change in the future? Explain your answer.

5. Does any of the material in this chapter have public policy implications related to maternity leave? That is, does it point to the importance of new maternity leave legislation? Explain your answer.

6. Discuss the origins and implications of the widespread conceptualization of parenting as a female role. What benefits to mothers, fathers, and children would stem from a more inclusive view of parenting?

IF YOU WANT TO KNOW MORE

Barnett, R. C., & Rivers, C. (1996). *She works, he works: How two-income families are happy, healthy, and thriving*. Cambridge, MA: Harvard University Press.

Chira, S. (1998). *A mother's place: Taking the debate about working mothers beyond guilt and blame*. New York: HarperCollins.

Dunne, G. A. (Ed.). (1998). *Living "difference": Lesbian perspectives on work and family life*. Binghamton, NY: Haworth Press.

Granrose, C. S., & Kaplan, E. E. (1996). *Work-family role choices for women in their 20s and 30s: From college plans to life experiences*. Westport, CT: Praeger.

Holcomb, B. (1998). *Not guilty: The good news about working mothers*. New York: Scribner.

Peters, J. K. (1997). *When mothers work: Loving our children without sacrificing our selves*. Reading, MA: Addison-Wesley.

13 Later Adulthood

Physical Development and Health

Physical Development

Sexuality

Benefits of Sexual Activity in Later Life

Sexual Behavior of the Elderly

Factors Affecting Sexual Behavior

Enhancing Sexuality in Later Life

AIDS

Childbearing in the Later Years

Physical Health

Gender Differences in Mortality

Social Class and Ethnic Differences

Gender Differences in Illness

Disability

Mental Health

Depression

Suicide

Health Services

The Physician-Patient Relationship

Type and Quality of Care

Women of Color and Health Care

Health Insurance

Promoting Good Health

Physical Activity and Exercise

Factors Linked to Women's Activity Levels

Nutrition

KEY TERMS

mortality

morbidity

gender paradox

activities of daily living (ADLs)

instrumental activities of
daily living (IADLs)

Medicare

Medicaid

spending down

fee-for-service insurance

managed care

We didn't have the choice of time when the kids were young. Now we have time during the day. We seldom make love at nighttime. Now we can choose. It might be 10 A.M. or 2 P.M. — whenever we're feeling turned on (a 65-year-old woman, in Doress-Worters & Siegal, 1994, p. 85).

Were you surprised when you read the age of the woman who made this statement? Older women often are perceived as being sexually unappealing and as having little or no interest in sex. As we shall see in the next three chapters, this is but one of several myths that portray older women in an unflattering light.

In this chapter, we focus on physical and health issues of older women, including physical development, sexuality, and physical and mental health. We follow this with an exploration of older women and the health care system and conclude with a discussion of factors that promote health.

Physical Development

Normal physical aging results from both genetic and environmental factors. In both sexes certain organs—the kidneys, lungs, and skin—age much faster than others, such as the heart and liver. On the other hand, the cardiovascular, muscular, skeletal, and reproductive systems age at different times for females and males (Leventhal, 1994). These changes are relevant to gender differences in health and illness in later life.

Two major age-related changes in the heart are the accumulation of fat deposits and the stiffening of the heart muscle, as connective tissue replaces muscle tissue. The walls of the arteries stiffen ("harden") as elastic fibers are replaced with less elastic ones, often leading to a rise in blood pressure (Belsky, 1999). Women are largely protected from these changes during their reproductive years. Once estrogen levels drop after menopause, women's hearts begin to show the same changes as men's.

Although both sexes lose muscle mass as they age, men maintain greater muscle strength than women. Loss of bone tissue also occurs in both women and men, as we saw in Chapter 9, but after menopause women lose bone mass faster than men (Kail & Cavanaugh, 2000). Accelerated bone loss and loss of muscle mass are responsible not only for a diminished exercise capacity in women but also for their greater vulnerability to fractures and immobilization (Whitbourne, 1998).

Gender differences are most pronounced in the aging of the reproductive system. Menopause, as noted in Chapter 9, is accompanied by sharp decreases in the levels of estrogen and progesterone, changes in the reproductive organs, and loss of the ability to have children. Men, on the other hand, do not have a physiological event to mark reproductive changes. While men's sperm production decreases gradually throughout life, a man in his eighties still is half as fertile as he was at 25, and remains capable of fathering a child (Kail & Cavanaugh, 2000).

Sexuality

Before reading this section, try Get Involved 13.1. See how your attitudes and those of friends compare to the information in the chapter.

Sexual activity can be as gratifying in the later years as in the younger years (Butler, Lewis, Hoffman, & Whitehead, 1994). Unfortunately, as Get Involved 13.1 demonstrates, there are a number of myths and stereotypes about sexuality in later life. Most of today's older Americans grew up at a time when attitudes toward sexuality were more restrictive than they are today, particularly for women (Hodson & Skeen, 1994). Unlike men, many women were taught that they should not enjoy sex and should not initiate it. This "double standard" of sexuality for women and men (see Chapter 7) exists for adults of all ages. Older women also are subjected to the "double standard" of aging discussed in Chapter 9. Women in their later years are perceived as sexually inactive and sexually unattractive. Men tend to choose

GET INVOLVED **13.1**

Attitudes toward Sexuality in Later Life

On a scale from 1 (strongly disagree) to 7 (strongly agree) indicate the extent to which you disagree or agree with each of the following statements. Also, ask three female and three male acquaintances who vary in age to respond to these statements.

1. Older people lose their interest in sex and no longer engage in sexual activity.
2. Changes in hormone levels that occur during and after menopause cause women to find sex unsatisfying and unpleasant.

3. Women who are beyond the childbearing years lose their sexual desire and their sexual desirability.
4. In order to have a full and satisfying sex life, a woman must have a male partner.
5. Older women who still enjoy sex were probably nymphomaniacs when they were younger.
6. Older people with chronic illness or physical disabilities should cease sexual activity completely.

Source: Doress-Worters & Siegal, (1994, pp. 82–83); Gibson, (1996).

What Does It Mean?

Add up the ratings you gave to these six statements. Do the same for each of your respondents. Note that each statement reflects a myth based on folklore and misconceptions. Therefore, the higher the score, the more the respondent holds unfounded beliefs about sexuality in later life.

1. Are there differences between the views of your female and male respondents? Explain your answer.

2. Are there differences between the views of respondents who vary in age? Explain your answer.
3. Could society's attitudes toward aging and the elderly be related to the persistence of these myths about sexuality in later life? Explain your answer.

younger women or women who look young as their sexual partners and mates (Daniluk, 1998; Doress-Worters & Siegal, 1994).

We first examine older women's sexuality—the benefits of sexual activity in later life, sexual behaviors and the factors affecting them, and enhancement of sexual experience in the later years. We then turn to the topics of AIDS and childbearing in later life.

Benefits of Sexual Activity in Later Life

Sexual activity can have physical, psychological, and emotional benefits for the elderly (Hodson & Skeen, 1994). The physical benefits include improving circulation, maintaining a greater range and motion of joints and limbs in arthritic persons, and controlling weight gain (Butler et al., 1994; Leitner & Leitner, 1996). In one study of adults ranging from 60 to 91 years of age, other reported physical benefits of sex included reducing tension and helping one sleep (Dortess-Worters & Siegal, 1994). Sexual activity among the elderly has psychological and emotional benefits as well. It can improve one's sense of well-being, increase life satisfaction, enhance a women's feeling of femininity and desirability, offer an outlet for emotions, and provide a shared pleasurable experience (Leitner & Leitner, 1996). In the later years, sexual activities other than intercourse—oral sex, manual stimulation, caressing—bring pleasure with or without orgasm (Rathus et al., 2000; Starr, 1995).

Some women find sex more satisfying and their attitudes toward sex more positive and open in later life. In a recent nationwide survey of Americans over age 60, 70 percent of sexually active women said they were as satisfied, or even more satisfied, with their sex lives than they were in their forties (Leary, 1998). Once grown children have left the nest, couples may experience a "second honeymoon" as marital satisfaction increases. (Recall the vignette at the beginning of the chapter.)

Sexual Behavior of the Elderly

Interest in sexual activity remains fairly high throughout adult life, declining only gradually in the later years. In one study of older women and men, 90 percent of those over age 70 expressed a desire for sexual intimacy at least once a week (Wiley & Bortz, 1996). In a Duke University longitudinal study of adults ages 60 to 94, 50 percent of individuals 80 years and older reported still having sexual desires (Leitner & Leitner, 1996).

Some elderly individuals desire to be more sexually active than they currently are. In the nationwide survey mentioned earlier (Leary, 1998), nearly 40 percent of older women and men wished they had sex more frequently. One reason for this discrepancy between interest and activity, particularly among women, is the lack of a partner (Rowe & Kahn, 1998). In the AARP (1999b) study discussed in Chapter 9, for example, 58 percent of men but only 21 percent of women 75 and older reported having sexual partners. How does lack of a partner affect sexual activity? One study of Black and White women and men ages 60 to 93 years found that 54 percent of married individuals were sexually active, compared with only 7 percent of unmarried persons (Leitner & Leitner, 1996). Similarly, in the Duke University study mentioned earlier, 24 percent of the females but only 14 percent of the males had ceased sexual activity. The most common reason given by the females for stopping was lack of a male partner; the most common reason given by men was health. It is probably no coincidence that while the

Sexual activity can be as gratifying in later life as in the younger years.

incidence of masturbation peaks in the teenage years for males and then declines, the opposite trend applies to women. The lack of available partners for elderly women is a likely explanation for these findings (Leitner & Leitner, 1996).

Factors Affecting Sexual Behavior

A number of both physical and psychological factors influence sexual behavior in older women.

Physical Factors.   The physical changes in the reproductive system that begin in midlife (see Chapter 9) become more pronounced in the later years, as estrogen levels continue to decline gradually. Although physical changes, illness, chronic disabilities and medication can affect sexuality in later life, even the most serious conditions should not stop women and men from engaging in satisfying sexual activity (National Institute on Aging [NIA], 1994). Heart disease, especially if one has had a heart attack, leads many older adults to give up sex, fearing it will cause another attack. But the risk of this is low. Most people can resume sexual activity in 12 to 16 weeks. Stroke rarely damages sexual function and it is unlikely that sexual exertion will cause another stroke. Arthritis, the most common chronic disability, causes joint pain that can limit sexual activity. Surgery and drugs can relieve the pain, but in some cases the medications decrease sexual desire. Exercise, rest, warm baths, and changing the positions or timing of sexual activity can be helpful. Medications such as certain antidepressants and tranquilizers also can reduce a woman's sexual desire. However, a physician can often prescribe a different medication without this side effect.

Psychosocial Factors. A person's attitudes toward sex-related physical changes can interfere with sexual activity more than the actual changes themselves. A major psychosocial constraint is the societal view that sexual desire in the elderly is abnormal (Wright, 1997). As a result, older adults who want to fulfill their sexual desires may feel apprehensive and guilty. Another constraint for residents of nursing homes is that the attitudes of nursing home staff often are not supportive of sexual behavior. Many nursing home administrators feel that sexual activity on the part of residents "causes problems," even if the individuals are married. Even masturbation may be strongly discouraged (Leitner & Leitner, 1996).

Enhancing Sexuality in Later Life

Sexual activity can be more rewarding for older adults if people come to realize that sexual expression is a normal part of life regardless of age. Sex counseling can help remove inhibitions restricting an older person's sexual behavior. Emphasizing the quality of the sexual relationship rather than performance can make sexual experiences more enjoyable for the elderly (Hillman & Stricker, 1994; Leitner & Leitner, 1996). Elderly people who are in supervised living arrangements need to be given opportunities to have private time together for intimate contact (Butler et al., 1994; Levy, 1994). Health care professionals should provide information and counseling to the elderly regarding the impact of both normal physical changes and medical conditions on sexual functioning (Richardson & Lazur, 1995).

The many older women who are not in an ongoing physical relationship need to feel it is permissible to express their sexuality in whatever way is comfortable for them, whether it be enjoying their fantasies, self-massaging, or using a vibrator, or whether it is acceptance of an asexual lifestyle (Rice, 1989). While some older women are celibate because they lack the opportunity to meet partners, other choose to be celibate but still enjoy sensuous experiences:

> In Colette's novel, Break of Day, I discovered celibacy as a strategy for older women who too often see themselves as stripped of identity without a partner. Colette sees age fifty-five as the end of having lovers, but the beginning of an aloneness that is joyous and drenched in sensuality—particularly for the artist in all of us. It is a great gift to be one's self at last (Marilyn Zuckerman, a poet in her sixties, in Doress-Worters & Siegal, 1994, p. 88).

AIDS

Whatever a woman's age or sexual orientation, if she is sexually active, she is at risk for contracting sexually transmitted diseases, including HIV, the virus that causes AIDS. Since older women generally are viewed as sexually disinterested and inactive, they are less likely to be given information about safer sex (Doress-Worters & Siegal, 1994).

Today, however, HIV infection is increasing at a faster rate among women than among men (Donatelle & Davis, 1998). Women age 40 and over make up one-third of AIDS cases among females. Over 3,100 cases of AIDS among women age 60 and older have been diagnosed and the number of new cases per year has grown steadily, from 38 in 1985 to 350 in 1999 (National Center for Health Statistics, 1999). In the mid-1980s, most AIDS cases among women in that age group were caused by blood transfusions. Now, heterosexual contact leads to almost 70 percent of them, and that figure is expected to rise (Stock, 1997). One factor putting older women at increased risk during heterosexual contact is the increased thinning of the vaginal tissues and the decrease in lubrication after menopause. These conditions can lead to small skin tears or abrasions during sexual activity that increase the chance of HIV entering the bloodstream (Doress-Worters & Siegal, 1994).

Older women who have HIV infection may have a harder time than infected younger women in obtaining a correct diagnosis and treatment. Physicians do not expect to see AIDS in older women (McCray, 1998), and therefore they are more likely to make a late diagnosis or a misdiagnosis. Symptoms of AIDS resemble those of various age-related diseases including Alzheimer's, which is one of the most common misdiagnoses (Stock, 1997; Strong et al., 1999). Women of this age group also are less likely to think of themselves as being at risk for AIDS, and so they may not think to ask for an HIV test (Stock, 1997). Failure to diagnose HIV early can have serious consequences at any age since it is harder to arrest the disease when it becomes more advanced. But older adults with HIV are even more likely to deteriorate rapidly because of their already weakened immune system.

HIV infection takes an enormous emotional toll on older women, many of whom live alone and already are trying to cope with physical, economic and personal losses. While today's younger women are used to talking more freely about sexual problems, this is difficult for many older women. They feel ashamed and may suffer alone, avoiding telling friends and family. Some avoid intimate contact with grandchildren, such as kissing on the lips, for fear of endangering the youngsters. Those women who join therapy groups often find them to be a great source of emotional support (Stock, 1997).

Childbearing in the Later Years

Claire remembers seeing an amusing comic strip several years ago that featured an elderly couple sitting in rocking chairs. The woman, knitting a tiny sweater, was obviously pregnant. Looking at her husband with an irritated expression on her face, she exclaimed "You and your 'once more for old times' sake!'" The humor of the situation was based on the impossibility of an elderly woman's becoming pregnant. But this is no longer a laughing matter.

Late in 1996, Arceli Keh gave birth in California to a healthy baby girl. News of the event spread like wildfire around the globe. What made this birth so special? Arceli Keh was 63 years old. Her husband's sperm fertilized a young woman's donor egg in a test tube, and the resulting embryo was implanted in Arceli Keh's hormonally readied uterus. Most fertility clinics set an age limit of 50 to 55 for a woman seeking in vitro fertilization. Arceli Keh listed her age as 10 years younger than it actually was in order to be eligible for the procedure (Angell, 1997; Belkin, 1997). Recent breakthroughs in transplanting ovarian tissue further raise the possibility that women may be able to bear children well into their golden years (Grady, 1999b)

Controversy swirls around the issue of whether postmenopausal women should be denied help in becoming pregnant. Those who support this view cite several reasons: (1) Such pregnancies risk the mother's health; (2) An older mother is less likely than a younger one to live long enough to raise her child to adulthood; (3) It is unnatural and a perverse use of technology that has been widely accepted for younger women for over 20 years.

These arguments have been rebutted by others who claim that (1) The complications that could affect the older mother's health also occur in younger women, although less frequently, and are treatable; (2) Any responsible mother, regardless of age, should make provisions for the care of her child in the event that she dies before the child is grown. Some younger women with severe medical conditions have babies. Should they also be barred from reproducing? (3) If the reproductive technology exists, why shouldn't an older woman take advantage of it? Should older women be denied other medical advances such as coronary bypass surgery? (Claire's mother-in-law had this procedure when she was in her early eighties. As of this writing, she is still going strong at age 98. She does not, however, contemplate having another child.)

Marcia Angell, a physician and executive editor of the New England Journal of Medicine, believes that both age discrimination and gender discrimination are at the root of society's discomfort about older women's having babies (Angell, 1997). Think of people's reactions to the news of men becoming fathers in their seventies and eighties: comedian Charlie Chaplin, actor Tony Randall, and former U.S. Senator Strom Thurmond, to mention but a few. Rather than disapproval, there is acceptance and even admiration of the sexual prowess of these older men.

Physical Health

In this section, we examine factors contributing to women's health and illness in old age. We also explore gender differences in **mortality** (*death rates*) and in **morbidity** (*illness*), look at disability in old age and, finally, at the conditions which promote good health.

Gender Differences in Mortality

Women are sicker; Men die quicker. This old saying sums up what is often referred to as the **gender paradox**: *women live longer than men, but in poorer health* (Goldman & Hatch, 2000).

The female-male mortality gap begins before birth. While more males are conceived than females, the rate of stillbirths is higher for males. Although about 106 live males are born for every 100 live females, more male babies die in infancy and at every age thereafter throughout life. Between ages 65 and 69, only 81 males survive for every 100 females. Between ages 80 and 84, the ratio is down to 53 to 100, and by age 100, it has dropped to 22 to 100 (Cavanaugh, 1997; Krach & Velkoff, 1999).

At the turn of the century, life expectancy in the United States was about 51 years for women and 48 years for men. Over the century the gender gap has widened. Life expectancy at birth now is about 79 for women and 6 years less for men. The gender gap exists for both Blacks and Whites. White women tend to outlive White men by 5.6 years (79.9 versus 74.3) and Black women, on average, outlive Black men by 7.5 years (74.7 versus 67.2) (National Center for Health Statistics, 1999). Why do women outlive men? Some explanations focus on biological factors, others on lifestyle behavioral differences.

Biology.   One biological explanation is that women's second X chromosome protects them against certain lethal diseases—such as hemophilia and some forms of muscular dystrophy—that are more apt to occur in individuals (men) who have only one X chromosome. Another biological reason for women's greater longevity is their higher estrogen levels, which seem to provide protection against fatal conditions such as heart disease. In addition, women have a lower rate of metabolism, which is linked to greater longevity. Another suggestion is that women's immune systems are more robust than men's, making men more susceptible to contracting certain fatal diseases (Hayflick, 1994).

Lifestyle Behaviors.   One lifestyle factor accounting for the gender gap in mortality is that males are more likely than females to engage in potentially risky behaviors such as smoking, drinking, violence, and reckless driving (Angier, 1999b; Byrnes, Miller, & Schafer, 1999; Krieger & Fee, 1998). They also may be exposed to more hazardous workplace conditions. Table 13.1 shows that accidents and unintentional injuries are the fourth leading cause of death of males, but the seventh leading cause for females. Cirrhosis, caused largely by excessive drinking, and homicide are the ninth and tenth most common causes of death for males, but do not appear on the "Top Ten" list for females.

As women's lifestyles have become more similar to men's so have some of their health behaviors. For example, while the frequency of men's smoking has declined, that of women's has increased. The result is that deaths from lung cancer among women nearly tripled between 1970 and 1997, whereas the increase for men was only 2 percent (National Center for Health Statistics, 1999). This is

TABLE 13.1   Ten Leading Causes of Death for Females and Males in 1997

Rank	Women	Men
1	Heart disease	Heart Disease
2	Cancer	Cancer
3	Cerebrovascular diseases (stroke)	Cerebrovascular diseases (stroke)
4	Chronic obstructive lung disease (asthma, bronchitis)	Accidents and unintentional injuries
5	Pneumonia and influenza	Chronic obstructive lung disease (asthma, bronchitis)
6	Diabetes	Pneumonia and influenza
7	Accidents and unintentional injuries	Diabetes
8	Alzheimer's disease	Suicide
9	Kidney disease	Chronic liver disease and cirrhosis
10	Septicemia (infection of the blood)	Homicide

Source: National Center for Health Statistics, 1999

one of the reasons that lung cancer has surpassed breast cancer as the leading cause of cancer deaths among women (Collins, Bussell, & Wenzel, 1997; Wingo et al., 1998).

Another behavioral difference is that women make greater use of preventive health services and are more likely to seek medical treatment when they are ill (Cowley, 1999; Lipsyte, 1999). This may help explain why women live longer than men after the diagnosis of a potentially fatal disease. Women's greater tendency to visit the doctor's office suggests that they are more health-conscious than men. Women generally know more than men about health, do more to prevent illness, are more aware of symptoms, and are more likely to talk about their health concerns (Elder, 1997; Papalia, Olds, & Feldman,1998; "Women Heed Warnings," 1998).

Women also outlive men because of their more extensive social support networks involving family, friends, and formal organizational memberships. Involvement in social relationships is related to living longer, perhaps because social ties reduce the impact of life stresses (Belsky, 1999; Unger & Seeman, 2000).

Social Class and Ethnic Differences

Women live longer than men regardless of social class and ethnic membership. Nevertheless, there are differences in longevity among women of different social classes and ethnic groups.

Social Class.   Women and men with higher incomes and more education have longer life expectancies and better health. Some of this difference can be accounted for by a higher incidence of unhealthy behavior, particularly smoking, among the poor and working class. People with lower incomes are less able to afford decent medical care or even adequate food and experience higher levels of chronic stress as a result of such experiences as financial difficulties and job loss. The combination of all these factors shortens life expectancy and increase rates of illness and disease (Bee, 2000; Lantz et al., 1998).

Ethnicity.   Health risks and mortality rates for women vary by ethnic group (See Table 13.2). Mortality rates from all of the major causes of death (except car accidents, chronic obstructive lung disease, and suicide) are higher for Black women than for White women (U.S. Bureau of the Census, 1998d). Black, Latina, and Native American women are more likely than White women to die of diabetes (National Center for Health Statistics, 1999). Native American women have the shortest life expectancy of any group and Asian Americans the longest (Stanford & DuBois, 1992). Asian American women, compared to White women, have lower mortality rates from heart disease; stroke; lung, breast, cervical and colorectal cancer; diabetes; cirrhosis; and chronic obstructive lung disease (Centers for Disease Control, 2000; Commonwealth Fund, 1996a). Differences in mortality rates for women of different ethnic groups are related to their economic status throughout their lives. Blacks and Native Americans, for example, have high mortality rates and low lifetime family incomes while Asian Americans have some of the highest family incomes and lower mortality rates (Torrez, 1997).

Gender Differences in Illness

Although they live longer than men, women have more chronic conditions that cause suffering but do not kill. This is true in every country in which these statistics have been gathered, including developing nations (Rahman, Strauss, Gertler,

TABLE 13.2   Leading Causes of Death for Females by Ethnicity, 1997

Rank	White	Black	Native American	Asian/Pacific Islander	Latina
1	Heart disease	Heart disease	Heart disease	Cancer	Heart disease
2	Cancer	Cancer	Cancer	Heart disease	Cancer
3	Cerebrovascular disease	Cerebrovascular disease	Accidents/ unintentional injuries	Cerebrovascular disease	Cerebrovascular disease
4	Chronic obstructive lung disease	Diabetes	Diabetes	Accidents/ unintentional injuries	Diabetes
5	Pneumonia and influenza	Accidents/ unintentional injuries	Cerebrovascular disease	Pneumonia and influenza	Accidents/ unintentional injuries

Note: Native American includes American Indian and Alaskan Native females.

Source: National Center for Health Statistics, 1999

Ashley, & Fox, 1994; Smith & Baltes, 1999). Women have higher rates of arthritis, sciatica, dermatitis, cataracts, spinal degeneration, gallstones and other digestive system disorders, thyroid conditions, migraine headaches, anemia, bladder infections, urinary incontinence, varicose veins, and chronic sinusitis (Jette, 1996; U.S. Bureau of the Census, 1998c).

These statistics do not mean, however, that women are more likely than men to develop health problems. Women spend 64 of their years in good health and free of disability, compared with only 59 years for men. But because women live longer than men, it is women who more often live many years with chronic, often disabling illnesses (Altman, 1997; Crose et al., 1997). Keep in mind that a person may have one or more chronic diseases without being disabled. The key issue is whether the chronic condition restricts daily life or reduces the ability to take care of oneself (Bee, 2000).

Disability

The degree of disability resulting from chronic conditions is assessed by measuring how well individuals can carry out two groups of activities: (1) **Activities of daily living (ADLs)**, which include *basic self-caring activities such as feeding, bathing, toileting, walking, and getting in and out of a bed or chair*; and (2) **instrumental activities of daily living (IADLs)**, which *go beyond personal care to include preparing meals, doing housework, shopping, doing laundry, attending social activities, using the telephone, taking medications, and managing money* (Unger & Seeman, 2000). Older women living in the community are more likely than older men to have some difficulty with both ADLs and IADLs (Clancy, 2000; U.S. Bureau of the Census, 1998b).

Among women ages 65 to 74, six percent need help with ADLs such as bathing and dressing, while 18 percent need assistance with IADLs such as shopping and household chores (Campbell et al., 1999). Poor women are more likely to report chronic and/or disabling conditions than women who are not. As you might imagine, life satisfaction is considerably lower for women who have serious health problems. Over 40 percent of women with disabilities report lower life satisfaction, compared with 18 percent of women with fair or poor health and 6 percent of all women (Commonwealth Fund, 1993a).

Mental Health

Depression

The most common form of mental illness among older adults is depression, including minor depressed mood as well as full-blown clinical depression. Women consistently have higher rates of depression than men at all ages (Crose et al., 1997; Gatz, Harris, & Turk-Charles, 1995; Smith & Baltes, 1999). Women of color, women in ill health, and poor, less educated, and unemployed women are more likely than other women to experience depression (Earle, Smith, Harris, & Longino, 1998). Women's depression overall seems to peak at midlife and then decline somewhat in old age (Commonwealth Fund, 1993a).

Somewhere between 15 and 25 percent of the elderly in nursing homes are depressed. Among adults 65 and older who live in the community, almost 15 percent show symptoms of depression, with 3 percent estimated to have major clinical depression. Among widows and widowers, one-third are clinically depressed in the first month following the spouse's death, and half of these widowed individuals continue to be depressed a year later (Adler, 1992; Rimer, 1999).

These statistics may be underestimates, however, because 75 to 90 percent of the depressed elderly are undiagnosed and untreated (Adler, 1992; Goleman, 1995; Rimer, 1999). Studies of older adults who committed suicide as a result of depression have found that while 75 percent had visited a doctor within a month of their deaths, only 25 percent of those individuals were diagnosed as being depressed (Goleman, 1995). Older adults do not always experience the classic symptoms of depression: sleeplessness, fatigue, low energy, loss of appetite, guilt feelings, and depressed mood. Rather, depressed elderly individuals may show malaise, confusion, and physical complaints (Crose et al., 1997; DeAngelis, 1997b; Friedrich, 1999). Some symptoms, such as sudden irritability and fault-finding, or pessimism and little hope for the future, may be dismissed as typical personality changes that accompany aging. Even the classic symptoms of low energy, loss of appetite, or loss of interest in former sources of enjoyment may be seen by doctors simply as characteristics of a frail older person. Some health professionals may feel that depression in the elderly is "normal" because of medical, financial, or family difficulties or the losses that come with age (Brozan, 1998). But most older people confront their problems without becoming clinically depressed. Depression in the elderly is often a side effect of medications given for conditions such as heart disease. A change in medication frequently gets rid of the depression. When older adults are correctly diagnosed and treated for depression, they improve about 80 percent of the time (Adler, 1992; DeAngelis, 1997b; Goleman, 1995). Unfortunately, older women are less likely than younger women to receive psychotherapy, and women 75 and over are more likely to receive no treatment at all (Glied, 1998).

Suicide

Most older adults are satisfied with their lives and are able to cope with the challenges of aging. For others, however, later life is a time of physical pain, psychological distress, and dissatisfaction with life, which produce feelings of hopelessness and depression. Some of these individuals may attempt to commit suicide (AARP, 1993).

After declining for 40 years, the suicide rate among adults increased 9 percent from 17.6 suicides per 100,000 in 1980 to 21.8 in 1993 ("Suicide Rate," 1996). These overall figures conceal major differences in gender and ethnicity. As Figure 13.1 shows, the striking increase in suicide rates in the elderly occurs only among White males, whose suicide rate is higher at every age. Black men show a

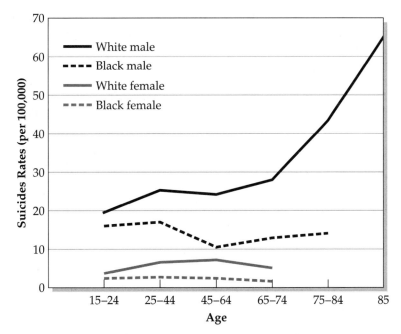

FIGURE 13.1   Suicide Rates in the United States in 1995 (per 100,000)
Source: National Center for Health Statistics, 1999, data from Table 47, pp. 192–194.

decrease after their mid-forties, with a slight increase at age 65. Black and White women's rates increase slightly with age, peak in middle adulthood, and decline in later life. Women in other ethnic groups also show low rates of suicide throughout adulthood (National Center for Health Statistics, 1999).

Suicide attempts in the elderly are more serious than those in the young. Among young people, the ratio of attempted to completed suicides is estimated to be about 7:1, but in individuals over 65, completed suicides outnumber attempts by nearly 8:1. Attempts by younger persons may be more likely to be cries for attention or help. Older adults show a much stronger intention to die. They use more lethal means and less often communicate their intentions to others (Cavanaugh, 1997; DeLeo & Ormskerk, 1991).

Besides gender, other risk factors associated with suicide in later life are the death of a loved one; physical illness; uncontrollable pain; the specter of dying a prolonged death that harms family members emotionally and financially; fear of institutionalization, social isolation and loneliness; and major changes in social roles, such as retirement. Also at high risk are those who abuse alcohol and other drugs, are depressed, or suffer from other mental disorders. Mental disorders are present during the year before suicide for two-thirds of elderly women and one-quarter of men who commit suicide (AARP, 1993; DeLeo & Ormskerk, 1991; Kennedy, 1998; U.S. Public Health Service, 1999).

On a positive note, remember that most older people with health and other problems do not become depressed and suicidal. According to Maggie Kuhn, an older-woman activist:

> *Old age is not a disaster. It is a triumph over disappointment, failure, loss, illness. When we reach this point in life, we have great experience with failure. I always know that if one of the things that I've initiated falters and fails, it won't be the end. I'll find a way to learn from it and begin again.* (Kuhn, 1991, p. 214).

Health Services

We noted in Chapter 7 that until recently, women often were excluded from health research. Even when women's health was studied, older women were noticeably absent or underrepresented (Hutchins et al., 1999; Kolata, 2000b). This situation has begun to change. In a major breakthrough for older women, the NIH in 1991 launched the Women's Health Initiative (WHI), a 15-year study of over 160,000 women age 50 to 79. The study focuses on the major causes of death and disability in postmenopausal women: heart disease, stroke, breast and colorectal cancer, osteoporosis, depression, and Alzheimer's disease (Healy, 1999; McDonald, 1999).

We also pointed out in Chapter 7 that women are treated with less respect within the health care system and receive poorer medical care than men. Older women are in double jeopardy because of society's negative attitudes toward aging women. This important issue warrants a closer look at older women's experiences with the health care system.

The Physician-Patient Relationship

We have seen that physicians may trivialize women's health complaints by attributing them to psychosomatic factors. In addition, many male physicians dismiss the importance of older women's complaints about ailments, such as arthritis and incontinence, as normal to aging and thus not requiring medical attention (Sharpe, 1995).

Ageist as well as sexist views of women are found in medical journal advertisements that portray elderly women as disheveled, disoriented, and needing medication for sleep or depression (Hawkins & Aber, 1993). Women also are underrepresented in ads for cardiovascular medication, even though heart disease is the number one killer of both women and men in middle age and later life (Leppard, Ogletree, & Wallen, 1993).

Type and Quality of Care

Discrimination based on gender and age affects not only interpersonal aspects of health care, but also the type and quality of care that older women receive. Older women are less likely than younger women to receive Pap smears or mammograms. In 1997, for example, 42 percent of women age 70 and over had not had a Pap smear within the past two years and one-third had not had a mammogram during that time period. The corresponding figures for women in their 50s were 17 percent and 22 percent, respectively (Blackman, Bennett, & Miller, 1999). Also, older women are less likely than younger women to receive radiation therapy after lumpectomy (Hewitt & Simone, 1999). Women physicians are more likely to give Pap tests and breast examinations to women patients of all ages than are male physicians (Clancy, 2000).

When we look at medical conditions that affect both women and men, women often receive less adequate care even when the severity of the condition is the same for both. As we saw in Chapter 9, women are less likely to receive coronary artery bypass surgery and angioplasty (Underwood, 1999a). Women also are not as likely as men to receive kidney dialysis or a kidney transplant (Clancy, 2000; Haas, 1998). In addition, physicians often attribute a woman's chronic ailments to natural aging and consequently they are less apt to treat these conditions. For example, despite the fact that urinary incontinence, which affects more women than men, can be treated effectively using medical or behavioral means, many health professionals believe that it is an inevitable part of the aging process (McCandless & Conner, 1997).

Women of Color and Health Care

Women of color are more apt than White women to be uninsured and, thus, are less likely to seek preventive health care services such as Pap smears and pelvic exams (see Chapter 7). Women of color over age 50 also are less likely to have mammograms. The good news is that the number of minority women receiving mammograms has risen substantially during the past decade, from 37 percent in 1993 to 66 percent in 1998 for Black women, and from 54 to 64 percent for Latinas (Commonwealth Fund, 1998b).

Older White women use both prescription and over-the-counter medications at a somewhat higher level than older women of color, but older ethnic minority women may be more likely to encounter special difficulties procuring and using medications. Language differences and cultural differences in perceptions of illness make communicating with the doctor especially problematic. As a result, older ethnic minority women may have greater difficulty following a prescribed regimen. Older women of color often have more problems even in obtaining medication because of their poorer economic status (Kail, 1989).

Health Insurance

The types of insurance programs available to U.S. adults can be grouped into public plans (Medicare, Medicaid) and private plans (fee-for-service and managed care). Let us look at these plans and see how they affect women.

Medicare.   **Medicare**, established in 1965, is the *federal program designed to provide medical care for those who are over 65 or permanently disabled, regardless of income.* Medicare covers less than half of medical costs and it does not cover most long-term care, home and supportive care, or prescription drugs. These limitations affect women disproportionately because they have more, and more complex, medical conditions than men (Ongley, 1999). In addition, some physicians do not accept Medicare patients because the reimbursement is low (Iglehart, 1999b).

Medicaid.   **Medicaid**, established the same year as Medicare, is a *combined state and federal program designed to provide medical care for the needy of any age.* Medicaid dollars are largely directed toward aged and institutionalized persons. While individuals age 65 and older make up about 12 percent of the total U.S. population, they account for at least 50 percent of Medicaid expenditures. Over three-fourths of this amount goes to nursing-home care, even though only 5 percent of older adults live in nursing homes at any given time. Eligibility for Medicaid is based on family assets and income, with the amount varying from state to state. Only one-third of the poor elderly actually are eligible for Medicaid. As with Medicare, many health care providers refuse to see Medicaid recipients because of low reimbursement rates. These patients have no choice but to rely on clinics and emergency rooms (Iglehart, 1999a; Meyer & Bellas, 1995; Reisinger, 1995).

Individuals with high medical bills who do not qualify for Medicaid *ultimately become eligible once they have depleted most of their financial resources and assets.* This process, called **spending down**, is most common in residents of nursing homes. Elderly women undergo the process more frequently than elderly men because they are more likely to enter nursing homes (Meyer & Bellas, 1995).

Women rely more heavily than men on both Medicaid and Medicare because they are more likely to be poor and because they live longer (USDHHS, 1998). Whereas women comprise 54 percent of Medicare beneficiaries between the ages of 65 and 74, they account for 71 percent of the 85-and-over Medicare population (Toner, 1999). Women are less likely than men to have insurance through their own employer since they are more likely to work in temporary or part-time jobs or in occupations that do not provide health insurance benefits. A woman who is covered under a spouse's plan risks losing coverage in the event of divorce, death, or the spouse's retirement (Reisinger, 1995).

Private Insurance Plans.   The majority of Americans are covered by private health insurance provided by their own employer or the employer of a family member. One of the two types of private plans is **fee-for-service** insurance (also known as indemnity insurance). *The insurer pays part of the cost (usually 80 percent) for specified services, including hospitalization (up to a certain limit) and diagnostic services, but not preventive care* (Collins, Rowland, Salganicoff, & Chait, 1994).

The second type of private insurance is **managed care**, which has become the leading means of financing health care (Katzenstein, 1999). Managed care *provides services to members for a flat fee, and emphasizes preventive care and early detection of disease more than fee-for-service plans do.* Health maintenance organizations (HMOs) and preferred provider organizations (PPOs) are the most common types of managed care. Providing inexpensive screening procedures such as mammograms and Pap tests makes the services affordable for many women (Older Women's League, 1997a). It is therefore not surprising that women in managed care are more likely than those in fee-for-service plans to receive Pap smears and colon-cancer screening (Katzenstein, 1999). Moreover, women over 65 in HMOs are more likely than fee-for-service patients to have had their cancers diagnosed at an earlier stage (Riley et al., 1999). However, managed care often limits access to specialists and reduces treatment options for many women, particularly older women who frequently have many chronic ailments requiring treatment by different specialists. Limited finances often prevent elderly women from seeing the physicians or purchasing the medications not covered by their managed care insurance (Older Women's League, 1997a, 1999). Moreover, women enrolled in HMOs are more likely to report not getting needed care and having difficulties reaching their physician when needed. Women in HMOs also are less satisfied with their physicians than those not in HMOs (Collins & Simon, 1996).

Older women may view health and health care differently than younger women. To compare how these two groups view health issues, try Get Involved 13.2.

GET INVOLVED 13.2

What Women Say about Their Health

Answer the following questions, which were included in a recent nationwide poll (Elder, 1997; Mansnerus, 1997). Then ask two young adult women and two women age 65 or older to answer the same questions.

1. Whom would you trust more to be your doctor, a woman or a man, or would you trust them equally?
2. Which presents the more serious risk, heart disease or breast cancer?
3. How would you describe your health: excellent, good, fair, or poor?
4. In general, who has more health problems, men or women?
5. Who handles being sick better, women or men?
6. Whose complaints do doctors take more seriously: men's, women's, or about the same for both?
7. How often do doctors talk down to you? Most of the time, some of the time, hardly ever, or never?
8. Where do you get most of your medical information: doctors, television, newspapers and magazines, or the Internet?

What Does It Mean?

1. How do the responses of the older women compare with the information presented in the chapter?
2. How do the responses of the older women compare with the responses of your college-age friends? How can age account for these differences?
3. Can you think of any factors other than age that might account for any differences between the responses of the two groups of women?

Promoting Good Health

In this section we examine practices that promote good health in elderly women. For a closer look at some of these factors, see Learn about the Research 13.1.

Physical Activity and Exercise

Physical Benefits.   The numerous health benefits of physical activity have been well documented. Indeed, some researchers have suggested that about 50 percent of aging decline is preventable by participation in regular physical exercise. As the

---

LEARN ABOUT THE RESEARCH 13.1

Good Health Habits and Longevity

The relationship between good health habits and longevity was demonstrated dramatically in the Alameda County Study, a large-scale longitudinal investigation conducted in Alameda County, California (Breslow & Breslow, 1993; Kaplan, 1992). At the beginning of the study, the researchers asked each of the nearly 7000 randomly chosen adults about their health practices. In a follow-up study done 18 years later, five good health behaviors were found to predict lower rates of death among the participants: keeping physically active, not smoking, drinking moderately, maintaining normal weight and sleeping 7 to 8 hours a night. The most unexpected finding was that being involved in close relationships was as powerful a predictor of life expectancy as good

health practices. Women and men who followed the greatest number of good health practices and who were most involved in social networks were least likely to die over the 18 years of the study. Moreover, these individuals were only half as likely to develop disabilities.

Another recent study suggests that both social activities and other nonstrenuous "productive" activities such as cooking, shopping, gardening, and volunteering may be just as important as physical activity in helping elderly people live longer (Glass, de Leon, Marottoli, & Berkman, 1999). The findings, based on nearly 3,000 women and men age 65 and over living in New Haven, Connecticut, showed that physical, social, and productive activities produced similar benefits in increasing longevity.

What Does it Mean?

1. In this chapter, we have seen that women are more health conscious than men. Why do you think that is? What are the implications for women's greater longevity?
2. How can more women and men be encouraged to develop good health habits?

3. Teenagers and young adults are less likely to engage in good health practices than are middle aged and older adults. What might account for this difference?
4. How would you explain the findings that social and productive activities increase longevity?

old saying goes, "Use it or lose it" (O'Brien & Vertinsky, 1991). Regular physical exercise is linked with a reduction in the incidence of heart disease, breast and colon cancers, hypertension, diabetes, obesity, and osteoporosis. It can increase self-esteem and energy, improve mood, and decrease stress (McDonald, 1998; "Why You Should Exercise," 1999). As we saw in Chapter 9, exercise does not have to be vigorous to be beneficial. A moderate amount of daily physical activity can also achieve health benefits. For individuals who are inactive, even a small increase in activity can improve health, increase life expectancy, and reduce disability (Brown et. al., 1995; Vita, Terry, Hubert, & Fries, 1998)).

Besides a reduction in disease, exercise has other physical benefits. It enhances the range of motion of joints which can help arthritics maintain normal functioning (King & Kiernan, 1997). It also can improve posture by toning and strengthening the postural muscles. In the later years physical activity helps maintain the strength and flexibility essential in performing activities of daily living (ADLs). Regular strength-building exercise can counteract the loss of muscle mass and strength that normally occurs as people age. Muscle weakness, especially in the lower half of the body, contributes to injuries and lack of mobility in old age (Brody, 1990b; Stevens & Olsen, 2000). About 30 percent of people over age 65 fall each year. Falling may cause hip fractures or other serious injuries which can lead to death or immobility in the elderly ("Falling and the Elderly," 1999). Even if there is little or no injury, individuals may fear further falls, and so limit their physical activity, contributing to even greater muscle weakness (Brody, 1990b). Exercise programs designed to improve balance and increase flexibility and strength in elderly women and men reduce the likelihood of falls (Brody, 1999d; Neporent, 1999). A simple walking program or in-home strength-training exercises for older people with osteoarthritis of the knees can improve walking speed and decrease reports of pain and disability (Ettinger et al., 1997). Even the very old can benefit from exercise. Maria Fiatarone and her colleagues (Fiatarone et al., 1994) conducted a study with 100 women and men whose average age was 87 (about one-third were in their nineties). Half worked out vigorously for 45 minutes three times a week on leg-strengthening machines. The program improved walking speed, stair-climbing ability, and overall level of physical activity. Four individuals were able to discard their walkers for canes.

Older women and men tend to approach physical activity in different ways. Men do more structured activities such as formal exercise, whereas older women keep physically active by going out on a regular basis and doing things they enjoy (walking, gardening, shopping, playing with grandchildren). Both styles are linked to health benefits (Strawbridge, Camacho, Cohen, & Kaplan, 1993). A similar gender difference in exercise is related to mortality: The number of days per week older women walk a mile or more is more closely linked to increased life expectancy than is the practice of a regular exercise routine. For older men, regular exercise is a stronger predictor than walking (Rakowski & Mor, 1992).

Psychological Benefits. Regular exercise promotes a sense of well-being, feelings of accomplishment, and increased self-esteem among the elderly. It also decreases tension, anxiety, depression, and anger (Leitner & Leitner, 1996; Misra, Alexy, &

Panigrahi, 1996). Regular exercise improves physical appearance by developing and toning muscles and reducing body fat. Feeling good about personal appearance enhances self-esteem. Regular physical activity can develop increased abilities in one's favorite recreational activities, which also can improve self-esteem (Donatelle & Davis, 1998). Furthermore, physically active older adults outperform the sedentary elderly on tests of memory, reaction time, reasoning, planning ability, mental speed, and mental flexibility. These findings suggest that regular participation in exercise improves cognitive functioning in later life (Leitner & Leitner, 1996; "Walking: A Good Workout," 1999). An alternative explanation, of course, is that smart people may exercise more because they are aware of its benefits!

Factors Linked to Women's Activity Levels

Inactivity increases with age for both women and men. The proportion of North American adults who say they never exercise almost doubles, from 19 percent for individuals under 55 to 36 percent for those 55 and older. One nationwide study found that only 5 to 7.5 percent of adults over 65 showed appropriate activity levels. Forty-two percent reported they were sedentary. Women were less likely than men to report engaging in any exercise at all (O'Brien & Vertinsky, 1991).

In fact, women of all ages are less apt to exercise than are men (National Center for Health Statistics, 1998). More than one-third of women age 18 to 64, and almost one-half (48 percent) over 65 do not exercise. About one-half of Latinas and Black women do not exercise compared with 36 percent of White women and 42 percent of Asian American women (Commonwealth Fund, 1995a). Much of this ethnic difference may be accounted for by differences in educational and income levels (Clark, 1995). Ethnic minority women are more likely to live in poverty and have lower income and educational levels than White women. The proportion of women who engage in exercise rises as educational and income levels increase. Half of women who live in poverty and more than half of those without a high school education do not exercise. By comparison, only 30 percent of women with incomes at least 300 percent above the poverty level and about 30 percent of women with some college education do not exercise (Commonwealth Fund, 1995a).

Another explanation for the low levels of physical activity among older women is the stereotype that exercise is increasingly inappropriate as a person ages. This stereotype applies even more strongly to women than to men because of the societal expectation that at all ages, women are less physically active than men (Leitner & Leitner, 1996). In addition, the social construction of gender dictates that women are the primary caregivers and managers of home and family. Taking time away from domestic responsibilities to indulge in personal leisure may cause some women to feel selfish or guilty .

Older women not only must overcome sexist and ageist views about appropriate physical behavior in later life but also must combat chronic health problems that inhibit many older people from exercising. Arthritic pain and urinary incontinence, chronic conditions that are much more prevalent in older women than in older men, may serve as deterrents to physical activity. Other barriers include the absence of a companion and the lack of convenient transportation to an exercise facility. In addition, some women feel that they are too old to improve their physical condition, fear that exercise may lead to injury or death, or believe that the declines of aging cannot be reversed. Unfortunately, the issue of attractive exercise programming for older women has been largely overlooked by exercise specialists, yet another example of the relative invisibility and lack of power of older women (O'Brien & Vertinsky, 1991).

Nutrition

Good nutrition is a key factor in promoting the health of the elderly. Elderly women and men need fewer calories than younger people, but their need for key nutrients remains the same. According to some nutritionists, one half of all elderly Americans are endangering their health because of inadequate diets. One study of nearly 500 women and men age 65 to 98 found that most did not get enough nourishment and lacked energy. About 20 percent skipped lunch (Ryan, Craig, & Finn, 1992). Malnutrition can cause serious illness in the elderly, or worsen their condition if they already are sick (Bennet, 1992a).

As people age, the obstacles to eating properly increase. Chronic physical conditions may limit their mobility. As a result, walking to the store, carrying groceries home, and cooking may become difficult. Diminished sensitivity of the taste buds and odor receptors can lead to a loss of appetite. People without their natural teeth or with advanced gum disease may be able to eat only soft foods that are low in fiber and other nutrients. Moreover, people with certain chronic conditions may be restricted to bland, unappetizing diets. Some medications suppress hunger or interfere with absorption of food from the digestive tract. Depression and mental deterioration are other obstacles to eating properly. Some elderly people simply are too poor to afford a wholesome diet, or they live alone and may not feel motivated to fix a nourishing meal for one person (Bennet, 1992a; Brody, 1990a).

We saw in Chapter 9 that bone loss increases rapidly in women after menopause, raising the risk for fracture and disability. Adequate calcium intake thus is important to older women. But vitamin D is necessary for calcium absorption, and as people age, they do not absorb vitamin D as readily as they did when younger. High amounts of sodium in the diet also leads to calcium loss. As aging people's taste buds become less sensitive, they may add more salt to their food. The combination of the increased need for calcium, less availability of vitamin D for calcium absorption, and increased sodium hastens the onset and severity of osteoporosis (Donatelle & Davis, 1998; Utiger, 1998). Studies show that calcium plus vitamin D, or extra vitamin D alone, reduces the risk of hip fracture in nursing-home populations (Butler, Collins, Meier, Muller, & Pinn, 1995). Yet few women consume the 1,000 milligrams of calcium recommended during their younger years or the 1,200–1,500 milligrams recommended during the menopausal and post-menopausal years (Donatelle & Davis, 1998). Nearly 60 percent of women age 65 and over do not take calcium supplements (Commonwealth Fund, 1996a).

SUMMARY

1. Organ systems change with age. The muscular and skeletal systems and the gonads age at different times for women and men.

2. Sexual activity can have physical, psychological, and emotional benefits for the elderly. Interest in sexual activity remains fairly high throughout adulthood, declining gradually in the later years. Sexual interest in the elderly is greater than sexual activity. One reason, especially for women, is lack of a partner.

3. Physical changes, illness, disability, and psychosocial factors influence sexual behavior in older women. Sexuality may be enhanced through counseling, changes in societal attitudes, and greater opportunities for intimate contact.

4. HIV infection in older women is less often diagnosed and treated correctly than in younger women.

5. Controversy exists regarding whether postmenopausal women should be denied help in becoming pregnant.

6. At every age, women report more illness and use of health care services than men, yet women consistently outlive men. Both biological factors and lifestyle differences are responsible. Health risks and mortality rates for women differ by social class and ethnic group.

7. Older women are more likely than older men to have some difficulty with various activities of daily living.

8. Older women have higher rates of depression than older men. Depression peaks in midlife and declines in old age. It is more common among women who are poor, unemployed, members of ethnic minority groups, and residents of nursing homes.

9. Suicide rates are low for women in later life. Older White males show a sharp increase in suicide rates. While younger adults are more likely to attempt than to complete suicide, the reverse is true for older adults.

10. Women in their later years continue to be treated with less respect within the health care system and to receive poorer medical care than men.

11. Women rely on public health insurance plans (Medicare and Medicaid) more than men do. Women in managed care plans more often report not getting needed care than women in fee-for-service plans.

12. Practices that promote good health in elderly women include physical activity, and good nutrition.

WHAT DO YOU THINK?

1. Should women in their fifties and sixties have babies? Why or why not?

2. How can knowledge of risk factors for diseases in older White women and older women of color help us in prevention and early detection of these diseases? How can high risk factors be reduced for both groups?

3. How does the current focus of the health care industry on illness and disease influence the quality of life for older women? Which costs more, prevention and early detection or treating disease and functional limitation?

IF YOU WANT TO LEARN MORE ...

Daniluk, J. C. (1998). *Women's sexuality across the life span: Challenging myths, creating meanings*. New York: Guilford.

Doress-Worters, P. B., & Siegal, D. N. (1994). *The new ourselves growing older*. New York: Simon & Schuster.

Gannon, L. R. (1999). *Women and aging: Transcending the myths*. New York: Routledge.

Haseltine, F. B., & Jacobson, B. G. (Eds.). (1997). *Women's health research: A medical and policy primer*. Washington, DC: American Psychiatric Press.

Cassel, C. K. (Ed.). (1999). *The practical guide to aging: What everyone needs to know*. New York: New York University.

14 Later Adulthood

Employment and Economic Issues

KEY TERMS

impingement
feminization of poverty
dual entitlement
vesting

pension integration
non-portability
durable power of attorney

After Helen Martinez's children were grown, she found employment as a secretary with a large corporation. Eventually, she was promoted to executive secretary, a position she held for several years. Helen decided to retire when her husband did. He was 65; she was 61. They did some traveling and joined a local senior citizens group. After 8 years, her husband died. Helen found that her Social Security benefits and the income from her pension were barely enough to support her. At the age of 70, she decided to go back to work for her old firm. She works two-and-a-half days a week, running a job bank. Now 79, she does not plan to retire again unless forced to by poor health.

Helen Martinez is typical of many women workers and retirees in their later years. In this chapter, we first examine the experience of older women workers, including those who enter or reenter the labor force in later life. We next turn to the retirement experience for women. We look at factors that influence women's decision to retire and their adjustment to retirement. We then focus on leisure activities of older women. Finally, we turn to the economic status of women in later life. Conduct the interviews in Get Involved 14.1 to learn about the experiences of individual women in each of these areas.

The Older Woman Worker

Labor force participation of middle-aged and older women has increased sharply over the past four decades. Two-thirds of married women and nearly 70 percent of unmarried women age 45 to 64 now are in the labor force. Over the age of 65, close to 10 percent of single women, 9 percent of married women, and over 8 percent of widowed and divorced women are employed (U.S. Bureau of the Census, 1999c). During the same 40-year period, by contrast, men have been retiring earlier. By 1998, only 84 percent of 45- to 64-year old married men were in the workforce, compared to 94 percent in 1960. Similarly, the participation rate of married men 65 and over dropped from 37 to 18 percent (U.S. Bureau of the Census, 1999c). As a consequence of these changes, which hold across all ethnic groups, the proportion of paid workers 45 and over who are women is higher than ever before.

GET INVOLVED **14.1**

Interview with Older Women

Interview two women, age 65 or older. It is helpful, but not essential, to know your interviewees fairly well. You may interview your mother, grandmothers, great-aunts, great-grandmothers, etc. Keep a record of your interviewees' responses to the questions below. Compare and contrast the responses of the two women.

1. (If employed) How are things going in your job?
2. Have you reached most of the goals you set for yourself in your life?
3. When do you plan on retiring? (or when did you retire?)
4. What are some of the day-to-day activities that you look forward to after retirement? (or that you've enjoyed since retirement?)
5. How will (did) retirement change you and your lifestyle?
6. How will you adjust (or how have you adjusted) to these changes?
7. In general, how would you describe your current financial situation?
8. What do you think of the Social Security system?

What Does It Mean?

1. How do the work and/or retirement experiences of these women compare with the experiences of older women reported in this book?
2. Are the financial situations of your respondents similar or different to those of older women described in the text? In what ways?

Why Do Older Women Work?

Older women work for most of the same reasons as younger women. Economic necessity is a key factor at all ages. In addition, feeling challenged and productive, and meeting new coworkers and friends give women a sense of personal satisfaction and recognition outside the family (Doress-Worters & Siegal, 1994). Active involvement in work and outside interests in women's later years appear to promote physical and psychological well-being. Work-centered women broaden their interests as they grow older and become more satisfied with their lives. Employed older women have higher morale than women retirees, whereas women who have never been employed outside the home have the lowest (Perkins, 1992).

Age Discrimination in the Workplace

In Chapter 10, we discussed the issue of gender discrimination in employment. As women get older, they also confront age discrimination in the workplace. Because many women enter or reenter the workforce when they are older, they face age discrimination at the point of hiring more often than men do (Rayman, Allshouse, & Allen, 1993). The reasons for age discrimination and the age range during which it occurs differ for women and men. Women's complaints filed with the Equal Employment Opportunity Commission primarily concern hiring, promotion, wages, and fringe benefits. Men more often file on the basis of job termination and involuntary retirement (Rayman et al., 1993).

Women also experience age discrimination at a younger age than men (Rife, 1997). This is another example of the "double standard of aging" discussed in Chapter 13. Women are seen as becoming older at an earlier age than men (Sontag, 1979). Our society's emphasis on youthful sexual attractiveness for women, and the stereotype of older women as powerless, weak, sick, helpless, and unproductive, create obstacles for older women who are seeking employment or who wish to remain employed (Perkins, 1992).

Entering the Workforce in Later Life

Many older women have been employed throughout adulthood. For some—working-class women, women of color, and single women—economic necessity has been the driving force. A few women overcame great obstacles to become pioneers in fields almost completely dominated by men. But for many women who are now in later life, a more typical pattern has been movement in and out of the labor force in response to changing family roles and responsibilities (Doress-Worters & Siegal, 1994). For a closer look at the lifelong work patterns of one group of older women, read Learn about the Research 14.1.

Some women decide to reenter the labor force after their children are grown, or following divorce or the death of their spouse. The prospects of entering or reentering the labor force after 25 or 30 years may be daunting to some women who wonder if they have the skills to be hired. Older women should not overlook the wealth of relevant experience they have accumulated through their homemaking, childrearing, and volunteer activities.

Job-assistance programs can be helpful to older women who seek employment. One of these, the National Displaced Homemakers Network, has more than 1,200 programs nationwide. Services often include sessions on goal setting, confidence building, job skills assessment, résumé writing, interview techniques, job search assistance, and job referral (Doress-Worters & Siegal, 1994). If no program exists in a particular geographic area, women can set up their own support group (Jacobs, 1997). Positive social support provided by friends and family members for the older woman's job search efforts, strengthen the intensity of her search activities (Rife, 1995).

LEARN ABOUT THE RESEARCH 14.1

Working Lives of Gifted Women

In 1922, Lewis Terman selected 1528 school children (672 girls and 856 boys) with very high intelligence test scores for a longitudinal study on intellectual giftedness. These individuals now have been followed for over 70 years. The study has yielded an enormous amount of information about all aspects of the lives of these gifted children as they grew up and grew older.

Boys were much more likely than girls to grow up oriented toward educational and occupational life. They went on to distinguish themselves in business, science, literature, the arts or public affairs. Although the proportion of Terman women who had careers was higher than those of other women of their time, over two-thirds became housewives and/or office workers. Their emphasis was on homemaking, childrearing, and supporting their husbands' careers (Holahan & Sears, 1995).

Carol Tomlinson-Keasey (1990; Tomlinson-Keasey & Keasey, 1993) has focused on the working lives of Terman's gifted women. She found that one-third of the women who had not pursued careers would now do so if given a second chance. Tomlinson-Keasey identified four recurring themes in the lives of the gifted women:

Lack of Confidence. Despite the fact that these women were extremely bright, many lacked confidence in their abilities

- *I am afraid I am one of your failures.*
- *I know I shall always be a marginal person.*
- *Frankly, the thought of myself as a gifted child seems very funny to me for I can seriously claim no particular distinction at present.* (Tomlinson-Keasey, 1990, p. 229)

Serendipity in Career Choices. Women often did not plan to pursue a specific career. Rather, they tended to be "pulled" into the workforce as a result of circumstances such as divorce, economic emergencies, and World War II.

Importance of Social Context. Women's career aspirations often were put aside to meet the needs and demands of their family.

Attenuation of Intellectual Growth. The majority of women thought they had used their intellectual gifts "reasonably well," but 40 percent reported that they had not lived up to their intellectual potential.

What Does It Mean?

1. How were the work lives of Terman's gifted women affected by the social construction of women's roles during the first half of the century?

2. In what ways do the four themes identified for Terman's gifted women apply to today's young college-aged women? In what ways do they not apply?

Retirement

Much of what we know about the effects of retirement is based on studies of men, despite the steady increase in women in the workplace over the past 50 years. This bias reflects the assumption that retirement is a less critical event for women than for men because of women's greater involvement in family roles. More recent research indicates that female retirees were just as committed to their work as were male retirees and that retirement from the labor force has important consequences for women (Etaugh, 1993b).

The Retirement Decision

The decision to retire depends upon many factors including health, income, occupational characteristics, and marital and family situations (Weiss, 1995). When men retire, they are leaving a role that has typically dominated their adult years. They are more likely than women to retire for involuntary reasons, such as mandatory retirement, poor health, or age. Women, on the other hand, are more apt to retire for voluntary reasons, such as the retirement of one's husband or the ill health of a relative (Carp, 1997b; Szinovacz & Eckerdt, 1995).

Compared to men, women arrive at the threshold of retirement with a different work and family history, less planning for retirement, and fewer financial resources (Carp, 1997b; Richardson, 1990). As noted earlier, women typically experience greater job discontinuity. They may have had fewer opportunities to obtain personal career goals and therefore may be more reluctant to retire. Given their more discontinuous employment history and their employment in lower-paid jobs, women are not as likely as men to be covered by pension plans and their Social Security benefits are lower (Moen, 1996; Rubin, 1997). Many older women workers with low salaries choose to continue to work as long as they can. These women may not be able to afford the luxury of retirement because of economic pressures, such as inadequate retirement income or sudden loss of a spouse (Perkins, 1992). Previously married (widowed, divorced) women are more apt than married women to report plans for postponed retirement or plans not to retire at all (Szinovacz & Ekerdt, 1995).

In addition, women who have strong work identities have more negative attitudes toward retiring than those with weaker work identities (Erdner & Guy, 1990). Professional women and those who are self-employed, who presumably have strong work identities, are less likely than other women to retire early (Etaugh, 1993b). Older professional women often do not make systematic plans for their retirement, nor do they wish to do so (Onyx & Benton, 1996).

We have seen why some women may delay their retirement. Why do others retire early? Poor health is one of the major determinants of early retirement. Since aging Black women and men tend to be in poorer health than aging Whites, they are likely to retire earlier (Bound, Schoenbaum, & Waidmann, 1996). Health is a more important factor in the retirement decision for men than for women—especially unmarried women—among both Blacks and Whites (Hatch & Thompson, 1992; Honig, 1996). This gender difference may result from the fact that, unlike married men, married women in poor health may withdraw early from the labor force or do not enter it in the first place. Early withdrawal or nonparticipation in the workforce is enabled by having a provider husband and by societal expectations that employment is optional for women.

Women's role as primary caregiver is another factor contributing to their early retirement. Of the 2.2 million people who provide unpaid home care to frail elderly individuals, nearly three-quarters are women. Their average age is 57. Elder care responsibilities often result in increased tardiness and absenteeism at work, as well as health problems for the caregiver (Mor-Barak & Tynan, 1995). Still, most businesses do not offer work flexibility or support to workers who care for elderly relatives. As a result, more than 20 percent of women caregivers reduce their hours or take time off without pay. Of those who continue to work, more than 8 percent are forced to retire earlier than planned (Perkins, 1992). Also, women whose husbands are in poor health are more likely to retire than women whose husbands enjoy good health (Talaga & Beehr, 1995).

Some women, of course, simply want to retire, whether to spend more time with a partner, family, or friends, to start one's own business, to pursue life-long interests, or to develop new ones.

> *I haven't regretted retiring. I didn't quit my job through any dissatisfaction with the job or the people but I just felt that my life needed a change. I noticed that after working an eight-hour day I didn't have much steam left for a social life and fun. It's been pleasant spending these years doing what I want to do because I spent so many years accommodating myself to other people's needs and plans* (a woman in her seventies, in Doress-Worters & Siegal, 1994, p. 183).

Adjustment to Retirement

In 1960, "adjustment to retirement" had a very different meaning for married women than it does today. A typical scenario involved the retiring husband joining his wife at home to travel and engage in leisure pursuits. Today, as we saw at the beginning of the chapter, labor force participation has increased among women age 45 and older, while men of the same age are retiring earlier. What is the result of this shift? Nowadays, retirement is a *couple* event, according to Maximiliane Szinovacz (1991; Szinovacz & Ekerdt, 1995). In the dual-earner family, if one spouse retires before the other, the couple has to adjust to the retirement of the first spouse and then the later retirement of the other. If both retire at the same time, each one must adjust simultaneously to her or his own retirement *and* that of the spouse.

As retirement age approaches, wives and husbands may differ in their readiness to retire. A man who has put in several decades in the workforce may be eager to retire once he meets Social Security and/or pension eligibility requirements. His wife, on the other hand may have entered the labor force later, after children entered school or were launched. In addition to still being enthusiastic about her job, she may want to continue working in order to build up her pension and Social Security benefits. A growing number of women continue to work after their husbands retire. One recent nationwide study of people in their fifties and sixties found that 45 percent of women whose husbands had retired still worked, most of them full time (Uchitelle, 1997). Women who did not work when their children were young, compared to those who did, are more likely to continue working after their husbands retire (Henretta, O'Rand, & Chan, 1993).

How do women respond to their husband's retirement? Research indicates a variety of reactions. One study surveyed couples during the first year of the husband's retirement (Vinick & Eckerdt, 1991). One-third of the wives in the study were employed, half of them full time and half part time. Over half of the women mentioned **impingement**, *the overlap of husbands into the wives' sphere of activity*, as a nuisance or annoyance. One form of impingement mentioned was the disruption of daily routines, such as reshuffling household-chore schedules or not getting as much done around the house. Impingement may also be psychological. Some wives complained about a lack of privacy. Husbands could monitor wives' daily routines, or overhear their telephone conversations. But most women reported that they had adjusted to their husband's retirement within a few months. Sixty percent of wives and husbands reported that their quality of life was "somewhat better" or "much better" since the husbands' retirement. Less than 10 percent described it as worse. Wives often mentioned that the increased leisure time with their husbands was the most satisfying aspect of their husbands' retirement.

Both genders typically adjust well to retirement, although women may take longer to get adjusted (Etaugh, 1993b). In one recent study, newly retired women reported lower morale and greater depression than newly retired men did (Kim, 1999). Men seemed to enjoy the freedom from work pressure when they retired whereas women appeared to experience the retirement transition as a loss of roles. Because women are not under the same socially prescribed pressures to be employed as are men, those who *do* work, whether out of financial need or commitment to their job, may find it more difficult to stop working (Szinovacz, 1991).

For both men and women, a high level of life satisfaction in retirement generally is associated with having good health, adequate income, and a high activity level (Etaugh, 1993b; Johnston, 1999). Marital status is a contributing factor as well. Married people have more positive retirement attitudes and higher retirement satisfaction than unmarried retirees. Married women who have more frequent and a greater variety of social contacts are more satisfied with the timing of their retirement than those who have less contact (Reeves & Darville, 1994). Retention of preretirement friends and social contacts is even more important for the life satisfaction of retired widows than for retired married women. Similarly, visiting with relatives has a greater impact on the retirement adaptation of widowed, as compared with married, women (Szinovacz & Ekerdt, 1995). For women who have never married, retirement can represent an especially significant transition. Although work assumes a greater importance in their lives than in the lives of never-married men and other women, most never-married women appear to be satisfied with retirement. Still, many develop second careers after retirement, or continue to work part time (Rubinstein, 1994).

We saw in Chapter 12 that multiple roles often have positive consequences for women who are employed. What is the effect of multiple role identities on older retired women? Pamela Adelmann (1993) compared Black and White women age 60 and over who considered themselves retired only, homemakers only, or both. Women who called themselves both retired and homemakers had higher self-esteem and lower depression than women identified with only one role, especially the homemaker role. Apparently, multiple-role identities continue to benefit women even after retirement. A woman's adjustment to retirement also is affected by her personality characteristics. Those women who have higher levels of self-esteem and open-mindness adjust more successfully (Neuhs, 1990).

Retirement can have both positive and negative outcomes for women and men. On the positive side, retirement enhances self-esteem and lowers depression in many people (Reitzes, Mutran, & Fernandez, 1996). Retired women and men spend more time in personal hobbies and increase their interactions with friends. Retired women, particularly unmarried ones, are more involved with friends and neighbors than are retired men or lifelong housewives (Carp, 1997b; Etaugh, 1993b). Retired women, compared to retired men, also report more contact with close relatives and greater participation in organizations and volunteer work (Dorfman, 1995). Both women and men are more satisfied in retirement if they continue to participate in socially productive activities, whether volunteer work, community service, or a return to paid work (Dorfman & Rubenstein, 1993).

Retirement also can be associated with negative outcomes. Retirees with health problems and low incomes show poorer adjustment than those who have good health and higher incomes. Retired women are more likely than retired men to report that their incomes are inadequate (Dorfman, 1995; Goetting, Raiser, Martin, Poon, & Johnson, 1995). Financial factors may also account for the fact that Black retirees have lower levels of life satisfaction than White retirees. Black women tend to be slightly less satisfied than Black men (Krause, 1993). For a closer look at the influence of major life changes such as illness, marital transition, and death of loved ones on adaptation to retirement read Learn about the Research 14.2.

Leisure Activities

Leisure or free time in later life is a fairly recent social phenomenon. In 1900, the average work week was over 70 hours. Most adults died by their mid-forties, and worked until their death. Until the Social Security Act of 1935, retirement was not a reality for most Americans. The economic safety net provided by Social Security, along with increased life expectancy, have given older Americans the opportunity for retirement and, consequently, an increased amount of free time (Stanley & Freysinger, 1995).

LEARN ABOUT THE RESEARCH **14.2**
Do Major Life Events Influence Adaption to Retirement?

Many elderly adults are exposed to at least one of the following major life events requiring adjustment: divorce; major injury or illness experienced by oneself, the spouse or other family members; the death of one's spouse, child, other family members, or friends; moving to another dwelling or another town; and moving in with a child, other family member, or friend. How do these events affect one's adaptation to retirement? Do women and men react differently to these events? To find out, Maximiliane Szinovacz and Christine Washo (1992) surveyed people who had retired from state jobs in Florida within a 5-year period. Women reported experiencing more major life events than men, particularly during the period preceding retirement. Recent retirees who had been exposed to two or more major life events were found to be adapting less well to retirement. Women were much more adversely affected than men.

What Does It Mean?

1. Why do retired women experience more major life events than men?
2. Why do you think the women retirees were more affected by major life events than were men? Think about some of the factors that influence women to retire in the first place.

Women and men, regardless of age, vary in the nature of leisure activities they prefer. Elderly women are more likely than elderly men to participate regularly in social activities, baking and canning, sewing and quilting, collecting, and reading. Elderly males are more frequent participants in vigorous or moderate physical activity, yard work, spectator sports, hunting, and fishing. Elderly women and men show little difference in activities such as walking, crafts and painting, cards, and bingo (Mobily, 1992). In retirement, women are more likely than men to integrate their spheres of leisure activity, bringing together their worlds of friends, home, and hobbies (Hanson & Wapner, 1994).

Feminist perspectives on women's leisure suggest that the concept of leisure is different for women and men, with women experiencing less time for leisure in their lives than do men. A common focus of women's leisure, according to this perspective, is the combining of family obligations with leisure opportunities. A woman may perceive the family's leisure as her leisure and vice versa. The home is the most common place in which women's leisure occurs. In this way, leisure can sometimes be combined with household chores. Women may often "double up" their activities and may be engaging in a leisure activity such as watching TV, while at the same time doing housework, such as cooking or mending. Thus,

Women's leisure activities often bring together their worlds of friend, home, and hobbies.

much of women's leisure time may be fragmented rather than occurring in large blocks of time (Henderson, 1990; Wearing, 1998).

Much of the research on leisure activities for the elderly has focused on middle-class Whites and has been studied largely from a male perspective. Very little is known about the context and meanings of leisure for aging, usually poor, minority women. Katherine Allen and Victoria Chin-Sang interviewed 30 retired Black women whose average age was 75. Work had largely dominated the lives of the women. Most of them had worked domestic and service jobs. When asked how their experience of leisure had changed since retirement, most women replied that they had none in the past. The women considered leisure time in older age to be time to relax or to work with and for others as they chose. The church and the senior center provided important contexts for their leisure activities (Allen & Chin-Sang, 1990).

One factor influencing participation in leisure activity is age. A longitudinal study of women and men at age 54 and again at 70 found that the frequency of women's leisure activity involvement was less likely than that of men to be affected by increasing age. Men's participation in all categories of leisure activity declined between the ages of 54 and 70. On the other hand, women's informal social, home, spectatorship, travel, and hobbies/crafts activities showed no change over the 16-year period. Only their participation in sports and volunteering/formal organizations declined (Stanley & Freysinger, 1995). For another look at the relationship between age and leisure activity, try the exercise in Get Involved 14.2.

Other variables affecting leisure involvement are the amount of free time, transportation, and information on and availability of leisure programs. Some

GET INVOLVED **14.2**

Leisure Activities of Elderly and Young Women

1. Make three columns with the following headings:

   | Young Women's Current Activities | Older Women's Current Activities | Older Women's Past Activities |

2. Briefly interview three young adult females about their current leisure activities. List the most common activities in the first column.

3. Briefly interview three women ages 65 or older about their current leisure activities and about their leisure activities when they were in their early twenties. List their most common current activities in the second column, and their most common leisure activities when they were young adults in the third column.

What Does It Mean?

1. How do the leisure activities of the older women compare with the leisure activities of older women reported in this book?
2. How similar are the current leisure activities of the older women to those when they were young women?
3. Are the leisure activities of the older women when they were young adults more similar to their current activities, or to the activities of the young adult females you interviewed? In what way?
4. Based on this exercise, would you predict that young women's leisure activities in later life would be more similar to their present activities or to those of today's older women? Explain your answer.

From Leitner & Leitner, 1996. Reprinted with permission from The Haworth Press.

elderly people (usually the poor, because they have to, and the more educated and affluent, because they want to) continue to work long after the age of 65. Additionally, caring for ill family members, a responsibility usually assumed by women, can severely curtail the amount of available free time. Women, more than men, may be affected by the availability of transportation services, information about recreational facilities and programs, and the availability of such programs. In one study, women were more likely to list the following as obstacles to recreation participation: lack of partners, family commitments, lack of information, lack of transportation, and physical difficulties (Riddick, 1993). The last of these obstacles is likely to become an even greater problem in the future. Because those over 85 (a majority of them women) are the fastest-growing segment of the population, increasing emphasis will need to be given to providing and adapting leisure services for the moderately impaired or low-functioning elderly (Leitner & Leitner, 1996).

Economic Issues

As mentioned earlier in the chapter, older women are generally less well off financially than older men because of their past employment and earnings history and because of biases in retirement income systems. In this section, we examine in greater detail the economic status of women in their later years.

Poverty

The poverty rate of the elderly has decreased markedly since 1970, when it was 25 percent, twice the rate of the general population. Now, only about 11 percent of older adults are poor, slightly under the 14 percent rate for the general population. But poverty is not distributed equally among the various subgroups of the elderly. Women are hit harder than men, and ethnic minorities harder than Whites (U.S. Bureau of the Census, 1998b, 1999c). Women make up 63 percent of the population over 65 in the United States, but they constitute close to 75 percent of the elderly poor and more than 80 percent of the elderly poor who live alone (Perkins, 1995; Ray, 1996).

Older women are nearly twice as likely as older men to be living near or below the federal poverty level. In 1998, 13 percent of women age 65 and older were poor, compared with 7 percent of men the same age (American Association of Retired Persons, 1999). As you can see in Figure 14.1, this discrepancy holds true for Blacks, Latinas, and Whites. Also evident from the figure is that women of color experience poverty at more than twice the rate of White women. Elderly women and men become increasingly poor as they grow older, with women age 100 or more having the highest poverty rate of all (Krach & Velkoff, 1999).

Another factor associated with poverty is marital status. Divorced and separated older women are poorer than widows and all of them are considerably poorer than wives. In 1993, over one-third of older divorced and separated women lived in poverty, compared to 27 percent of widowed women. Among married women, only 5 percent were below the poverty line (Older Women's League, 1997b). But a married woman is just a heartbeat away from widowhood. The income from a husband's pension usually is greatly reduced or eliminated when he dies, quadrupling his widow's risk of plunging into poverty. Since women usually marry older men and outlive them, there is a high likelihood that they will live alone on a meager income as they grow older. The costs of a husband's illness and burial may seriously deplete the couple's savings, leaving the widow in a precarious economic state (Morgan, Megbolugbe, & Rasmussen, 1996). The longer an older woman lives, the further her assets must stretch. This

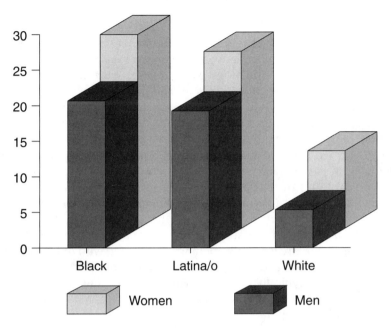

FIGURE 14.1   Percentage of Older Black, Latina/o, and White Women and Men below the Poverty Level in 1997.
Source: Dalaker, J. & Naifeh, M., U.S. Bureau of the Census. Poverty in the United States: 1997. Current population reports; Series P60–201. Washington: U.S. Government Printing Office, 1998.

situation helps explain why the very oldest women have the highest poverty rates. Here is a vivid picture of what it is like for an elderly woman to be poor:

> *After I've paid the rent, I pay the phone bill. My burial plot is all paid for, and I have just a little insurance for my grown children. Then there's my health. My doctor refused Medicaid—after 15 years—and now I have to pay him $27 out of every check. Then it takes $2.50 to do the laundry—you've got to keep your linens clean. I try to buy the cheapest things. I always make my own milk from powder. I only buy bread and chicken, and those no-name paper articles, but it still adds up. If I need clothes, I go across the street to the thrift shop. I watch for yard sales—if you see something for half a buck, there's a Christmas present. If I have 80 cents, I can go to the Council on Aging for a hot lunch. But the last two weeks of the month are always hard. You just can't make it. I'm down to my last $10, and I've got more than two weeks to go* (a woman in her seventies, cited in Doress-Worters & Siegal, 1994, pp. 191–192).

An increasing percentage of all women, not just older women, are living below the poverty line. This phenomenon is referred to as the **feminization of poverty**. Among younger women, this trend is fueled by the increasing proportion of single-parent households headed by women. But what factors account for the relatively high poverty rates of older women? Let's take a look at some of these.

Women's Earning and Labor Force Patterns

In Chapter 10, we discussed the wage differential between female and male workers. You will recall that full-time women workers typically earn only 76 cents for every dollar men make. The wage gap increases with age, however. In 1994, women age 55 to 64 earned 66 percent of the salary of men the same age. Women age 25 to 34, on the other hand, were paid 83 percent of the wages of men of comparable age (Older Women's League, 1997b). Why are older women's earnings depressed? For one thing, older women have spent less time in the labor force than younger women and many started working when employers were free to discriminate in pay between women and men doing the same work. Even now, nearly 40 years after the passage of the 1963 Federal Equal Pay Act, the legacy of once-legal salary discrimination remains (Older Women's League, 1991).

As we have seen, women's family responsibilities often lead to discontinuity in a woman's labor force participation. Women take an average of 11.5 years out of their working life to care for family members, compared with only 1.3 years for men (Barringer, 1992). Also, about 60 percent of today's younger women are employed in occupations that typically are low-paying and offer few, if any, benefits (Older Women's League, 1997b). Furthermore, more employers today are cutting costs by hiring part-time or temporary workers, who are paid less and have minimal or no benefits. Women are more likely than men to hold these jobs, whose flexibility may fit well with a woman's family obligations (Older Women's League, 1997b).

All of these factors adversely affect eligibility and benefits from Social Security and employer's pensions, which are tied to the length of employment (Stock, 1999). Women also are less likely to have accumulated income from savings and investments. The net result is that the income gap between women and men increases in retirement (Porter, Larin, & Primus, 1999). In 1998, women age 65 and older had an average income of $10,054, only 55 percent of the $18,166 income of men of the same age (American Association of Retired Persons, 1999a). Let's take a closer look at each leg of the "three-legged retirement stool"—Social Security, employer pensions, and income from savings and investments.

Social Security

More than 90 percent of older Americans receive Social Security income. Although Social Security originally was designed as an income supplement, its benefits are the major source of income for many elderly adults, especially those who are poor. Social Security provides 40 percent of total income for the elderly population as a whole, but 70 percent of the total income for those who live in poverty (American Association of Retired Persons, 1999a; Meyer & Bellas, 1995). Moreover, Social Security benefits keep about a third of the nation's elderly from sinking into poverty and also narrow the income disparities between older women and men (Porter et al., 1999). Without Social Security, about 53 percent of elderly women and 41 percent of men would be poor. With it, however, these figures are reduced to 15 percent and 8 percent, respectively, cutting the gender gap from 12 to 7 percentage points.

Nearly one-third of older women receive 90 percent of their income from Social Security and almost 20 percent of all older women rely on Social Security as their *only* source of income (Porter et al., 1999). Sole reliance on Social Security can be a financial nightmare. For example, the average Social Security benefit for retired female workers in 1994 was $6,456 a year. This sum was $650 *below* the federal poverty threshold for older adults (Hounsell, 1996). Nearly 60 percent of older women whose only income is from Social Security are poor (Older Women's League, 1997b).

Worker Benefits.   The Social Security system, inaugurated in 1935, was designed to serve the traditional family of that time, which included a breadwinner father, a homemaker mother, and children. Most of today's families do not fit that mold, primarily because the majority of women are in the labor force. Women's different work patterns mean that they are disadvantaged by a Social Security system designed to reward male work histories that often include many uninterrupted years in a relatively high-paying job (Estes, Linkins, & Binney, 1996; Older Woman's League, 1996). The system further penalizes women for adhering to their socially expected role, that of the unpaid homemaker and caregiver (Feldstein, 1998; Meyer & Bellas, 1995).

Ethnic minority women, who tend to be concentrated in lower-paying jobs and to have higher unemployment rates, receive even lower benefits than White women. Because they are more likely than White women to be employed "off the books" where benefits do not accrue, theirs are the lowest of all, while those of White men are the highest. Moreover, many women (75 percent of Whites and 61 percent of Blacks) apply for their benefits early, at age 62, because they are in need of the income. But doing so reduces benefits to 80 percent of their normal amount (Feldstein, 1998; Meyer & Bellas, 1995).

Spousal Benefits.   A lifelong homemaker has no Social Security protection in her own name. She is eligible to receive a spousal benefit equal to half of her husband's benefit if they have been married for at least 10 years. A divorced woman also is eligible to receive half of her ex-husband's benefit if they were married for at least 10 years. If the marriage did not last 10 years, however, she receives no compensation. If a divorced woman remarries, she automatically forfeits her right to her former husband's spousal benefit. In addition, divorced women must wait to receive spousal benefits until their ex-husband retires. In some instances, this can create great economic hardship (Meyer & Bellas, 1995; Older Women's League, 1997b; Social Security Administration, 1999). A widow receives 100 percent of her husband's benefit, although she is ineligible for any benefits until she is 60. If she applies for benefits at age 60 rather than waiting until age 65, however, her benefits are reduced to 72 percent of her normal widow's benefit (Social Security Administration, 1999).

Dual Entitlement. Married women who are wage earners have **dual entitle-ment** but are, in effect, penalized as well. *They qualify for Social Security benefits based on both their own and their husband's work history.* But these women receive the higher of the two benefits to which they are entitled; they do not receive both. Dually entitled women often are eligible for higher benefits based on their hus-band's work record than on their own. Over 60 percent of retired, wage-earning wives draw benefits based on their husband's work records. They would have been entitled to these benefits even if they had never worked a day in their lives. Thus, the Social Security contributions married women make as workers seem unnecessary and unfair (Feldstein, 1998; Meyer & Bellas, 1995; Social Security Administration, 1999).

Pensions

Social Security was never meant to serve as the only source of income for the elderly. The second leg of the retirement stool—private pensions—can be an important source of income for women, lifting them from poverty or near-poverty to a level of economic security. But relatively few women have income from pen-sions. In 1994, only 22 percent of women aged 65 and older received pension income compared with 48 percent of men. Only 15 percent of Black women and 7 percent of Latina women received any pension income. The average pension benefit for newly retired women in 1997 was $4,800 annually, whereas newly retired men received $9,600 (Zaldivar, 1997). Why do so few women receive pen-sion benefits? Let us briefly examine some reasons for this.

Work Patterns. As with Social Security, private pension plans are designed for employees who follow the traditional male work pattern of long continuous years of employment in higher-paying jobs. Women not only work less continuously and in lower-paying jobs, but they also are more likely to work at jobs that have low pension coverage (service jobs, non-union jobs, small businesses). Moreover, women are much more likely than men to work in part-time or temporary jobs, which have little or no pension coverage (Older Women's League, 1996, 1998; Richardson, 1999; Rix, 1994).

Vesting. Women's shorter job tenure also makes it more difficult for them to receive pensions because of a practice known as **vesting**. *The vesting period is the number of years of participation in a company plan that is required to be eligible for a pen-sion.* The majority of plans require 5 years on the job in order to be vested. How-ever, the average job tenure for a woman is only 3.8 years compared with 5.1 years for men (Hounsell, 1996; Older Women's League, 1997b).

Integration. Another troublesome feature of pension plans for women is **pen-sion integration**, in which a *pension is reduced by subtracting part of one's Social Security benefits.* The practice occurs most often in jobs where women are overrepresented. In 1993, for example, 60 percent of sales, clerical, and professional employees in medium to large companies, most of them women, had their pension integrated with Social Security (Older Women's League, 1997b). As a result of integration, workers, especially those with low incomes, receive less in pension benefits than they otherwise would have (Rix, 1990).

Non-Portability.   Women also are disadvantaged because of **non-portability** of pension plans. This means that *most traditional pension plans cannot be taken from one job to another*. This practice affects women more than men, since women are more likely to change jobs frequently. Even if a woman has worked enough years to be vested in a pension plan, she may lose a large portion of her pension benefits if she changes jobs. The reason is that the pension is based on her wages as of the date she leaves the plan. Inflation will severely reduce the value of her benefit by the time she reaches retirement age (Hounsell, 1996; Older Women's League, 1998).

Spousal Benefits.   As with Social Security benefits, a woman is more likely to receive spousal pension benefits as a wife, widow, or divorcée than she is from her own experience as a worker. Widows typically receive a benefit of half the amount the couple received when the husband was alive. Divorced women, too, can receive similar survivor's pension benefits when their former husband dies. On the other hand, she does not automatically receive any of his pension benefits following divorce. Many women do not realize that if they divorce, the divorce settlement can be written to include a share of their husband's pension (Older Women's League, 1997b).

Income from Savings and Investments

The third leg of the retirement stool is income from savings and investments. Nearly 70 percent of retirees have some income from assets, such as interest on savings accounts. Older minority women are much less likely to have such income (25 percent of Black women and 33 percent of Latina women). Asset income averages only a few hundred dollars a year for both women and men and thus is not a major income source (Rix, 1990).

Individual Retirement Accounts (IRAs) are one form of savings. Usually, a worker not already covered by a pension may make a tax-deductible IRA contribution of up to $2000 a year. The income from IRA investments are untaxed until withdrawal at retirement. By the time an individual retires, the savings from an IRA can be sizeable. But low-income earners, including many women and ethnic minorities, are unable to put anything in savings, let alone set aside $2,000 for an IRA (Older Women's League, 1997b; Rix, 1990).

Furthermore, married women wage earners are penalized by IRA laws. Married couples whose income exceeds a certain level are not eligible to make IRA contributions if either spouse has pension coverage. Men, as we have seen, are more likely than women to be vested in a pension plan. The couple is denied IRA participation because of the husband's pension, leaving the wife without either an IRA or a pension benefit in her own name.

Investments can be a source of income for retirement. Women, however, are much more cautious investors than men. In 1997, only 28 percent of women workers invested in stock plans compared with 45 percent of men. Women are more likely to invest in conservative options such as bonds, certificates of deposit, and money-market accounts that pay lower returns than stocks. Because of their discomfort with stock market risk, women don't earn as much from their investments (Rix, 1990; Zaldivar, 1997).

But looking at the "average" older woman often makes us forget the diverse characteristics and qualities of the individuals who make up this group. The stereotype of the older woman's ultraconservative approach to investing is defied by a remarkable group of women who call themselves the Beardstown Ladies Investment Club. In 1984, 16 women in the small farming community of Beardstown, Illinois, formed an investment club to learn how to better manage their personal assets. Thirteen of the women are now in their sixties, seventies and eighties. Most are retired, several are widows, and most knew very little about investing at first. Rather than follow the advice of investment "experts," they did their own homework, handpicked a portfolio of fewer than 20 stocks, and rigorously applied investment principles such as investing regularly, regardless of swings in the market. Their success has been impressive. The annual return on their portfolio one year was reportedly 23.4 percent, more than that of most professional money managers (Beardstown Ladies Investment Club, 1994). The group's claims came under scrutiny in 1998 when audited annual returns were found to be a more modest nine percent. Still, the Beardstown Ladies' self-investment books continue to be best sellers and have led to national television appearances and book-signing tours (Sofradzija, 2000).

Economic Planning for Retirement

The information in this chapter makes it clear that women must take steps early in their adult life to make plans to improve their financial security in retirement. Retirement planning must address the realities of women's current work experience and how those realities translate into life after retirement (Perkins, 1995). Until fairly recently, retirement planning and money management were thought to be best left to husbands (AARP, 1995b). As a result, many women of all ages have relatively little understanding of what retirement planning entails. It is never too early to start thinking about the issues involved. Preretirement planning starting in young adulthood can reduce the number of women who may otherwise find themselves living in poverty during their retirement years (Perkins, 1995). See Table 14.1 for guidelines on how to start planning for retirement *now*.

TABLE 14.1   Retirement planning for women

1. Have your own checking and savings accounts.
2. Once a year, make a list of all your financial assets and liabilities.
3. If your present job does not provide you with health insurance and a pension plan, consider finding a job that does, even if the salary is lower.
4. Learn about Social Security benefits.
5. Get a complete explanation of your payroll benefits.
6. Consider establishing an IRA.
7. Carry enough insurance to cover financial cost of a major loss—life, health, earning power, property.
8. Establish an emergency reserve fund worth at least three months' salary.
9. Learn about investments. Join or form investment clubs with friends.
10. Find a reliable financial advisor.
11. Take a course in personal financial planning.
12. If you have dependents—children, aging parents, disabled partners, or others—make a will *now*.
13. Establish a **durable power of attorney**, *a document in which authorizes someone to handle your financial affairs should you become incompetent.*

Sources: Adapted from Doress-Worters & Siegal, 1994; Perkins, 1995; Patterson, 1996.

SUMMARY

1. Increased numbers of middle-aged and older women are in the labor force. Economic necessity is a key reason. Employment among older women promotes physical and psychological well-being.

2. Women face age discrimination in the workplace at a younger age than men.

3. Job assistance programs can help older women enter or reenter the workforce.

4. Women's retirement decisions depends on many factors. Women earning low wages, including widows and divorcees, tend to delay retirement, as do professional and self-employed women. Older women with caregiving responsibilities tend to retire early.

5. Married women often retire when their husbands do or before. Most adjust to their husband's retirement within a few months. Satisfaction in retirement is associated with having good health, adequate income, high activity level and, for unmarried women, contact with friends and relatives.

6. Older women and men differ in the nature of their preferred leisure activities. Women experience less time for leisure in their lives than do men, and their leisure time may be more fragmented.

7. Older women, especially minorities, are more likely than older men to be poor or near-poor. The poverty rate is greater for very old women and for unmarried women.

8. Because women, compared with men, spend less continuous time in the work-

force, and are in more in low-paying jobs, their eligibility for and benefits from Social Security and pensions suffer. Women also have less income from savings and investments than do men.

9. Preretirement planning in young adulthood can reduce the incidence of poverty among women during later life.

WHAT DO YOU THINK?

1. Given the substantial influx of women into the labor force in the past several decades, the proportion of retired working women to lifelong homemakers will continue to increase among elderly women. What are the implications of this?

2. Why are women more likely than men to integrate friends, home, and leisure activities?

3. What can be done to help ease the "feminization of poverty"?

4. What are some implications of the older woman's greater economic insecurity?

5. What is meant by the statement that elderly minority women are in "triple jeopardy." Provide and discuss examples.

IF YOU WANT TO LEARN MORE

Allen, J., & Pifer, A. (Eds.). (1993). *Women on the front lines: Meeting the challenges of an aging America*. Washington, DC: Urban Institute.

Barusch, A. S. (1994). *Older women in poverty: Private lives and public policy*. New York: Springer.

Bass, S. A. (Ed.). (1995). *Older and active: How Americans over 55 are contributing to society*. New Haven, CT: Yale University Press.

Sinclair, C. (1994). *The women's retirement book*. New York: Random House.

Wearing, B. (1998). *Leisure and feminist theory*. Thousand Oaks, CA: Sage.

15 Later Adulthood

Interpersonal Issues

KEY TERMS

ageism   elder abuse
skip-generation parent   advocate
continuing care retirement
   community

Dorothy Johnson, age 78, is a widow who lives by herself in a small apartment. A broken hip last year has greatly reduced her mobility. She rarely leaves her apartment, and relies on help from her daughter and a home aide to assist with cooking, cleaning, and shopping. Many of her friends have died and she does not have many visitors.

Dorothy Johnson, age 78, is a widow who lives by herself in a small apartment. She is in good health and does her own cooking, cleaning, and shopping. She enjoys taking adult education courses at the nearby community college, and has taken several trips with an Elderhostel group. Two mornings a week, she works as a volunteer tutoring children at the local elementary school. She looks forward to weekly visits with her children and grand-children.

Will the *real* Dorothy Johnson please stand up? Actually, both are real. These descriptions illustrate the wide range of social contacts and relationships experienced by women in their later years. In this chapter, we will examine the social contexts of older women's lives—attitudes toward elderly women, relationships in later life, loss of a spouse or partner, living arrangements, elder abuse, and the vital older woman.

Attitudes toward Elderly Women and Men

One of the challenges facing older people in the United States is the presence of stereotypes (mostly negative) that many people hold about the elderly. Before reading this section, try Get Involved 15.1 to examine your own and your friends' attitudes toward the elderly. Even young children express stereotyped views about older adults, some positive (kind, wonderful, rich) and others negative (mean, lonely, eccentric, feeble) (Davidson et al., 1998; Mellott, 1998). Such stereotypes are part of a concept known as **ageism**. This term refers to *bias against people on the basis of their age* (Byteway, 1995). Ageism can be targeted toward any age group ("Children don't respect their elders; "teenagers are rebellious"). But ageism usually is directed at people in later life. Ageism resembles sexism and racism in that

GET INVOLVED **15.1**

What Are Your Attitudes toward the Elderly?

Answer each of the following items. Circle A if you agree or D if you disagree. Then ask two female and two male friends to do the same.

1. Most older people are socially isolated and lonely . . . . A D
2. Older people can, and are, learning new things all the time . . . . A D
3. The older you get, the more set in your ways you become . . . . A D
4. When people grow old, they generally become cranky. . . . . A D
5. As you grow older, you must expect to depend on others. . . . . . A D
6. Older adults usually can cope with the problems of aging . . . . . . A D
7. Most older people are frail and in poor health. . . . . A D

8. Most older adults are confined to long-term care institutions. . . . . A D
9. Older people cannot be expected to lead satisfying lives . . . . A D
10. Most older people prefer to do some kind of useful work . . . . A D
11. Most older people are forgetful. A D
12. Most older people need caregiving help . . . . A D

Add together the number of A answers you gave for items 2, 6, and 10. Then add together the number of D answers you gave for items 1, 3, 4, 5, 7, 8, 9, 11, and 12. Scores close to 12 indicate positive attitudes toward the elderly.

Based on Turner & Helms, 1989.

What Does It Mean?

1. Do your respondents' answers reflect mostly positive or mostly negative attitudes toward the elderly?
2. Can you think of reasons why many people have negative attitudes toward the elderly?

3. In what ways are your female and male respondents' answers alike? In what ways are they different? Explain the differences and similarities.

all are forms of prejudice that limit people who are the object of that prejudice. Unlike sexism and racism, however, everyone will confront ageism if they live long enough (Laws, 1995).

Ageism seems to be more strongly directed toward women than men. For centuries, unflattering terms have been used to describe middle-aged and older women: crone, hag, wicked old witch, old maid, dreaded mother-in-law (Have you ever heard any jokes about fathers-in-law?) (Markson, 1997; Sherman,

1997). Another example of negative attitudes toward older women is the double standard of aging that we examined in Chapter 9.

Still another example is the relative invisibility of elderly women in the media. When Betty Friedan (1993) examined close to 400 illustrations in the magazines *Ladies Home Journal, Vanity Fair*, and *Vogue*, she located fewer than 10 women who appeared to be 60 or older. Turn on prime-time television and see how many older women are shown. One study found that only 3 percent of prime-time characters are elderly individuals. The few older women who appear are portrayed less favorably than the older men. Moreover, as female characters age, they become less significant to the plot and typically lack clearly defined roles (Vernon, Williams, Phillips, & Wilson, 1991). Whereas prime-time male characters age 65 and older are depicted as active, middle-aged mature adults, women of that age are more likely to be designated as elderly (Signorielli & Bacue, 1999).

Psychologists seem to share society's negative views of older women. In one study, for example, 1,200 psychotherapists were asked to rate characteristics of individuals who were described as either old or young and either White or Black (Turner & Turner, 1991). Older women of both races were viewed as less assertive, less willing to take risks, and less competitive than younger women.

Negative attitudes toward the elderly are far from universal, however. For a look at some of the factors that influence views of older individuals, turn to Learn about the Research 15.1.

LEARN ABOUT THE RESEARCH 15.1

Who Is Ageist?

Many factors are related to attitudes toward the elderly. Two of these are age and ethnicity. Older adults have more positive attitudes toward aging and the elderly than do younger adults (Chasteen, 1998; Harris, Page, & Begay, 1988; Rollins, 1996). In a 1993 *New Woman* magazine survey of over 6,000 of its readers, younger women were more fearful of growing old than older women. Among women in their twenties, 54 percent expressed such a fear compared with only 23 percent of those over 60. Women over age 50 expressed positive views of older women. Half reported that the best part of aging is feeling a firm sense of self. Older women were more satisfied with their lives than younger women. In response to the question "How do you feel about life as a whole?" 26 percent of women over 50 were

"delighted, pleased" and 37 percent were "mostly satisfied," as compared with only 17 percent and 28 percent, respectively, of women under 30 (Perlmutter, Hanlon, & Sangiorgio, 1994). Among younger adults, those with positive, supportive relationships with their grandparents have less negative stereotypes and more positive feelings about older adults (Mitchell & Stricker, 1998).

Views toward older adults also vary among ethnic groups. Whites generally show less favorable attitudes than do ethnic minority groups. In research by Mary Harris and her colleagues (Harris et al., 1988), for example, Whites were less likely to enjoy spending time with the elderly than were Latinos and Native Americans.

(continued on p. 395)

What Does it Mean?

1. Why do you think young women are more afraid of growing old than are older women?

2. Why do you think members of ethnic minority groups hold more positive views of the elderly than Whites do?

3. What are some factors, other than age and ethnicity, that might be related to attitudes toward the elderly?

Although aging women traditionally have been viewed less positively than aging men, there is some indication that attitudes toward older women may be improving. Mary Kite and her colleagues asked college students and adults in the community to list characteristics of 65-year-old and 35-year-old women and men (Kite, Deaux, & Miele, 1991). Similar evaluations were given for the older men and women, although older people generally were evaluated less positively than younger adults.

Another positive sign is what psychologist Margaret Matlin (1998) calls the "Wise and Wonderful Movement." Since the early 1990s, there has been an explosion of books on women who discover themselves in middle or old age. The books present a positive picture of the challenges and opportunities for women in their later years. Two of these books, by Betty Friedan (1993) and Ruth Jacobs (1997), are listed as recommended readings at the end of this chapter.

Relationships in Later Life

Relationships with others shape every aspect of our lives. As women get older, most experience loss or change in many of their closest relationships. Spouses, other family members, and friends may be lost through divorce or death. But many women in the later years maintain supportive social networks by forging new friendships and strengthening existing bonds with family members and friends.

Marriage

Marriage is a central component in the lives of most adults. As life expectancy has increased, so has the incidence of long-term marriages. About 1 marriage in 5 now lasts at least 50 years (Brubaker, 1993). Since women typically marry older men and outlive them and since men are more likely to remarry following widowhood or divorce, many more men than women are married in later life (Smith & Baltes, 1999). Among those age 75 and older, only 30 percent of women are married, compared to 69 percent of men (U.S. Bureau of the Census, 1999c).

Marriage appears to provide numerous benefits in later life, particularly for men. Married people, especially men, live longer. They also have better mental and physical health and more economic resources than unmarried people (Askham, 1995). The majority of older people rate their marriages as happy or very happy, with men more satisfied than women. In part, marital satisfaction in later life probably reflects the selective survival of marriages that did not end in divorce (Huyck, 1995). In one longitudinal study of couples married between 50 and 69 years (Field & Weishaus, 1992), many respondents reported increased satisfaction and feelings of closeness in old age. Marital satisfaction is higher among older couples in which both spouses are either working or retired than among couples with employed wives and retired husbands (Cavanaugh, 1997).

What factors contribute to a successful long-term marriage? In one study of couples who had been married for 45 to 64 years, respondents reported that the most important reason for the success of their marriage was involvement in an intimate relationship with someone they liked and enjoyed being with. Other important factors were commitment to the partner and to the institution of marriage, humor, and agreement on a wide variety of issues (Lauer, Lauer, & Kerr, 1995).

Lesbian Partnerships

As we noted in Chapters 7 and 9, gay and lesbian relationships have long been viewed with disfavor in our society, although the stigma has decreased somewhat in recent years. Aging lesbians must confront the triple obstacles of sexism, ageism, and homophobia (Schoonmaker, 1993). Older lesbians who faced prejudice and discrimination during more hostile times often hid their relationships with other women and limited their contact with other lesbians and gays (Fullmer, Shenk, & Eastland, 1999; Shenk & Fullmer, 1996). Even now, because of social constraints, they may not openly acknowledge the nature of their relationship or use the word lesbian.

On a more positive note, lesbian couples report feeling less lonely than heterosexual married women. Some writers suggest that lesbian couples are advantaged compared with heterosexual wives because they are more likely to have a partner with whom they expect to grow old, to share similar life expectancy, to be less threatened by changes in physical appearance, and to have accumulated their own financial resources through employment (Huyck, 1995).

Elderly lesbians in long-term committed relationships typically provide each other with a mutual support system and the economic benefits of sharing resources and a home (Fullmer, 1995). Having had to cope with the social stigma of homosexuality, many lesbians and gays may be better prepared than heterosexuals to cope with the stigma of aging (Reid, 1995).

Single Women

Among women age 65 and over, 4.7 percent have never married (U.S. Bureau of the Census, 1999c). While many of their experiences are the same as those of other women, there are differences as well. For example, when family caregiving is needed, single women are expected, more so than their married sisters, to provide that caregiving, even at the expense of their own careers. On the flip side of the caregiving coin, the single woman is less apt to have a caregiver for herself when this is needed and as a result she is more likely to be institutionalized (Gottlieb, 1989).

Never-married women typically have developed skills in independent living and in building support systems that stand them in good stead as they get older (Gottlieb, 1989; Newtson & Keith, 1997). Compared with married women, the never-married older woman is better educated, in better health, places a great deal of importance on her job, is less likely to be depressed and commit suicide, values her freedom and autonomy, and has close connections with both siblings and other interpersonal supports (Gottlieb, 1989). The workplace is a significant source of friends for single women, and in retirement these women go on to form new friendships with neighbors or members of organizations to which they belong (Doress-Worters & Siegal, 1994). Single older women have also learned to cope in their earlier years with the "stigma" of not being married and so are better able to deal with the effects of ageism in their later years. Most older, single women are satisfied with their lives and seem at least as happy as married women (Newtson & Keith, 1997; Paradise, 1993).

Adult Children

Women are typically described as the family "kinkeepers," maintaining the bonds between and within generations. Adult daughters maintain closer ties to their parents than do sons. The positive link between grown daughters and their mothers can be enormously satisfying (Moen, 1996), as a recent survey of mothers (average age 73) and their adult daughters (average age 45) revealed. Close mother-daughter ties include satisfying interactions, a history of little conflict, few control issues, and many opportunities for informal contact (Blieszner, Vista, & Mancine, 1996). In the words of three mothers:

> *She has been awfully good to me in every way, when I'm sick and when I'm well, when I'm in a good humor and when I'm in a bad humor.*

> *I can reason with [my daughter] and she understands me. We just sit down and talk it over. We never have an argument. Not that we're perfect, but it's just not necessary.*

> *We go for lunch. We go shopping. . . . I may go three or four days or a week and not see her, but we talk. I feel like that starts my day.* (Blieszner et al., 1996, pp 13–18)

Grandchildren

The stereotyped portrayal of a grandmother is often that of an elderly, white-haired woman providing treats for her young grandchildren. However, grandmothers do not fit into any one pattern. While more than 75 percent of Americans over age 65 are grandparents, some people become grandparents as early as their late twenties (Bee, 2000; Smith, 1995). Over half of women experience this event before the age of 54 and some may spend nearly one-half of their lives as grandmothers (Mark,

1996; Kivett, 1996). Nowadays, many middle-aged grandmothers are in the labor force and may also have responsibilities for caring for their elderly parents (Velkoff & Lawson, 1998). Thus, they may have less time to devote to grandparenting activities.

The grandmother-grandchild relationship provides many benefits to both parties. Grandchildren enjoy the activities shared with the grandmother and the appreciation, individual attention, support, and inspiration she provides (Kalliopuska, 1994). The grandmother feels a sense of biological renewal, emotional self-fulfillment, and vicarious accomplishment (Thomas, 1990). She may look forward to indulging her grandchild in ways she was unable to do with her own children. Grandmothers' involvement with their grandchildren depends on a number of factors, including geographical distance, the grandmother's relationship with her grandchild's parents, and the grandmother's physical and mental health (Roberto, Allen, & Blieszner, 1999).

Earlier in the chapter, we noted that the ties between family generations are maintained largely by women. One example of this is that grandmothers tend to have warmer relationships with their grandchildren than do grandfathers. The maternal grandmother often has the most contact and the closest relationship with grandchildren (Smith, 1995; Walther-Lee & Stricker, 1998). Grandmothers appear to be especially close to the daughters of their daughters (Kivett, 1996).

Just as not all grandparents are old, not all grandchildren are young. More than half of people age 65 and older have at least one adult grandchild (Pruchno & Johnson, 1996). Most adult grandchildren report having a positive relationship with their grandparents (Smith, 1995). Adults who shared a close relationship with a grandparent in childhood continue to maintain regular contact with the grandparent (Hodgson, 1995).

As life expectancy increases, more adults are becoming great-grandparents and even great-great-grandparents. Among those older adults who have ever had a child, nearly half are great-grandparents (Roberto & Stroes, 1992). In one study (Doka & Mertz, 1988), the overwhelming majority of great-grandparents reported that great-grandparenthood renewed their zest for life and reaffirmed the continuance of their families.

An old song proclaims, "Over the river and through the woods to grandmother's house we go." Nowadays this isn't always the case. As more parents separate and divorce, they may refuse to let grandparents see their grandchildren. An estranged parent may deny children access to their grandparents as a means of punishing the spouse. Some grandparents have confronted this situation by suing for visitation and legal rights to grandchildren (Sanger, 2000). As a result, all states now have laws allowing grandparents to petition courts to continue seeing their grandchildren after their child's marriage ends through divorce or death. In some states, grandparents can petition even when a married child just wants to keep the grandparents and children apart (Hafemeister & Jackson, 2000; Lewin, 1999a).

Providing Care and Support for Grandchildren. During their grandchild's infancy, grandmothers often provide the children's parents with considerable emotional support, information, help with infant care and household chores, and to a lesser degree, financial support (Poehlmann, 1999). For nearly one-half of all grandmothers in the United States this help is provided on a regular basis (Baydar & Brooks-Gunn, 1998). The grandmother's role in lending economic, social, and emotional support for her children and grandchildren is more active in many ethnic groups than among Whites. In one study of women over 60 in Southwestern United States, for example, 50 percent of Native American women and 29 percent of Latina women provided child care to their grandchildren, as opposed to only 18 percent of White women (Harris, Begay, & Page, 1989). Latina women are reported to be the most influential and important source of social support for their young adult daughters with children (Ginorio, Gutiérrez, Cauce, & Acosta, 1995), and Black grandmothers are significant figures in the stability and continuity of the family (Shenk, Zablotsky, & Croom, 1998). The involvement of Black grandmothers in single-mother families facilitates the mother's participation in self-improvement activities, increases the quality of child care, and reduces the negative effects of single parenting (Cebello & Olson, 1993; Coley & Chase-Lansdale, 1998; Oyserman, Radin, & Benn, 1993). The presence and support of caring grandparents, especially in homes where a parent was absent or incapacitated, also was found to contribute to the well-being of a low-income, multiracial group of children born and raised on the island of Kauai, Hawaii (Werner & Smith, 1992). In interviews at ages 18 and 30, many of the young people who had overcome their childhood adversities credited their grandparents with the nurturance, structure, and guidance they received in childhood and adolescence.

For some children, grandparents are part of the family household. The number of children living in homes with a grandparent has risen from 2.2 million in 1970 to 3.9 million in 1998 (Biskupic, 2000), including 12.3 percent of Black children, 6.5 percent of Latina/o children, and 3.7 percent of White children (Jendrek, 1994; Pruchno & Johnson, 1996). Some of the increase results from an uncertain economy and the growing number of single mothers, which has sent young adults and their children back to the parental nest (Pebley & Rudkin, 1999). In other cases, elderly adults are moving in with their adult children's families when they can no longer live on their own. New immigrants with a tradition of multigenerational households also have swelled the number of such living arrangements (Ames, 1992). The arrangement benefits all parties. Grandparents and their grandchildren are able to interact on a daily basis, and grandparents may assume some parenting responsibilities.

Raising Grandchildren. Increasing numbers of grandparents now find themselves raising their grandchildren on their own. Even some great-grandparents are serving as primary caregivers for their great-grandchildren (Kail & Cavanaugh, 2000), a role few of them expected to assume. (Claire twice has lived next door to such formidable individuals.)

Of the nearly four million children living in a household with a grandparent, about one-third *are being raised by their grandparents without a parent present* (DeParle, 1999a). These **skip-generation parents** are overwhelmingly (93 percent) grandmothers. According to one study, the most common reason grandparents become full-time caregivers for their grandchildren is child abuse or neglect (39 percent), followed by parental substance abuse (29 percent), and parental psychological or financial problems (21 percent) (Illinois Department of Aging, 1996b). Another cause is the growth of AIDS cases among heterosexuals, whose parents care for their dying children and raise the grandchildren who are left behind (Lombardi, 1997). These children often have emotional scars, which add to the challenges of childrearing. Still, research shows that children reared by their grandparents fare well relative to children in families with one biological parent. They also are no different from children raised in traditional families, with the exception that they have poorer academic performance (Solomon & Marx, 1995).

The belief that caregiving grandmothers are primarily poor ethnic women of color is a myth. Parenting grandmothers can be found across racial and socioeconomic lines (Gilbert, 1998b; Muzi, 2000). More than two-thirds of grandparents raising grandchildren are White, nearly 30 percent are Black, and 10 percent are Latina/o (Sands & Goldberg-Glen, 1998). Black women who are raising their grandchildren, compared to White women, report feeling less burdened and more satisfied in their caregiving role, even though they are generally in poorer health, dealing with more difficult situations, and dealing with them more often alone (Pruchno, 1998).

Rearing a grandchild is full of both rewards and challenges. While parenting a grandchild is an emotionally fulfilling experience, there are psychological, health, and economic costs (Crowther, 1998; Minkler & Roe, 1996; Strawbridge, Wallhagen, Shema & Kaplan, 1997; Solomon & Marx, 1999). A grandmother raising the young child of her drug-addicted adult daughter may concurrently feel delight with her grandchild, shame for her daughter, anxiety about her own future, health, and finances, anger at the loss of retirement leisure, and guilt for feeling angry (Malcolm, 1991).

Grandparents raising grandchildren are often stymied by existing laws that give them no legal status unless they gain custody of the grandchild or become the child's foster parents. Each of these procedures involves considerable time, effort, and expense. Yet without custody or foster parent rights, grandparents may encounter difficulties such as obtaining the child's medical records or enrolling the child in school. In most instances, grandchildren are ineligible for coverage under grandparents' medical insurance, even if they have custody (Chalfie, 1994; Simon-Rusinowitz, Krach, Marks, Piktialis, & Wilson, 1996). Advocates for grandparents' rights are actively seeking legal solutions to these problems (Crowley, 1993).

Siblings

Sisters and brothers play a unique role in the lives of older people, drawing on the shared experiences of childhood and most of the life span (Cavanaugh, 1998). Most older Americans have at least one living sibling. Because women live longer, a surviving sibling is often a sister (Treas & Spence, 1994). Feelings of closeness and compatibility among siblings increase throughout the course of adulthood and generally are strong in later life (Bengston, Rosenthal, & Burton, 1996). Relationships with sisters are emotionally closer than those with brothers. The closer women and men over 65 are to their sisters, the fewer symptoms of depression they have. This is especially true for recently widowed women. For rural aged women, life satisfaction is higher if they simply have a sister living nearby, regardless of the amount of contact they have (Bedford, 1995). Sisters and sisters-in-law are second only to mothers and daughters as sources of companionship and emotional support (Wellman & Wortley, 1989).

> *I have two sisters who live upstairs. People are always surprised that we get along so well, living in the same house. My sisters never go out without coming by to ask me if they can get me anything. We weren't always like that. We were too busy with our own lives. Now we try hard to help each other* (a 70-year-old widow, in Doress-Worters & Siegal, 1994, p. 134).

Parents

While more elderly women are becoming caregivers of their grandchildren, caregiving increasingly is occurring at the other end of the age spectrum as well. As more Americans join the ranks of the "oldest old" (85 and older), growing numbers of elderly "children" find themselves taking care of their parents. One nationwide study found that more than 25 percent of people over 65 care for a family member, friend, or neighbor who is frail, sick, or disabled (Bennet, 1992b). In many cases, the family member is a spouse. But increasingly it is a parent.

Nearly half of all caregivers of the "oldest old" are daughters. Daughters-in-law play a substantial role as well (Bould, Sanborn, & Reif, 1989; Guberman, 1999; Usdansky, 2000). The middle-aged woman as caregiver to aging parents was discussed in Chapter 12. Most of the same issues apply to the elderly woman who is caring for her even older parent, except that the elderly caregiver may herself have some health problems (Rimer, 1998) and is facing her own aging. The sight of her parent becoming more frail and dependent may conjure up a frightening and saddening vision of what is in store for her. Elderly daughters sometimes feel angry and guilty at the sacrifices involved in looking after a parent.

> *My grandmother lived to be almost one-hundred-and-two years old, and my mother cared for her until she was ninety-seven and had to go into a nursing home. Now my mother obviously feels it is her turn, which it is. I am the real problem here, for I have led a very active life and cannot seem to adjust to this demanding and devastating situation. I do not know what to hope for and am almost overcome with the inevitable guilt at my resentment and anger. I have no one to talk to.* (a 72-year old woman, in Doress-Worters & Siegal, 1994, p. 208)

Some caregiving daughters have a different philosophy, enjoying the time spent with their parent(s). One 72-year-old woman takes public transportation every day to visit her 99-year-old father. They chat about their family and she does his grocery shopping. Although she has developed asthma and is not in the best of health, she looks forward to continuing her daily visits (Bennet, 1992b).

The Black community has had a long tradition of grown children, especially daughters, caring for their parents and grandparents. Older Blacks are twice as likely as Whites to be cared for by family members when they are in failing health (Rimer, 1998).

We have been discussing older women's relationships with family and friends. To explore this topic on a more personal level, try Get Involved 15.2.

GET INVOLVED 15.2

Interview with Older Women

Interview two women age 65 or older. It is helpful, but not essential, if you know your respondents fairly well. You may interview your mother, grandmothers, great-aunts, great-grandmothers, etc. Keep a record of your respondents' answers to the questions below. Compare and contrast the responses of the two women.

1. What is one of the nicest things to happen to you recently?
2. How would you describe your relationship with your children?
3. Do you have any sisters and brothers? How would you describe your relationship with them?

4. What do you like about being a grandparent? (if applicable)
5. What types of activities do (did) you enjoy with your grandchildren?
6. Tell me about your best friends and the kinds of things you enjoy doing together.
7. What do you like about your current living situation?
8. What do you dislike about it?
9. In general, what are your feelings on nursing homes?
10. How do you feel about the life you've led?
11. As an experienced woman, what tidbit of wisdom could you pass on to me?

What Does It Mean?

1. How would you characterize the relationships of your interviewees with their adult children? Do they appear to be closer to their daughters than to their sons? If so, why?
2. What kinds of relationships do your interviewees have with their grandchildren? Have either or both participated in child care activities with their grandchildren? How do their experi-

ences compare to those reported in the text?
3. Were there any differences in the relationships of these women with their sisters as compared to their brothers? If yes, how do you explain these differences?
4. How does the discussion in this chapter help you understand your respondents' attitudes toward their current living situation and toward nursing homes?

Friends

Throughout adulthood, friends provide the emotional support and companionship that sustain women as they meet the challenges, changes, and losses of later life. Because so many married women eventually lose their spouses through death or divorce, most women grow old in the company of other women (Doress-Worters & Siegal, 1994). In later life, women are more engaged with friendships and social networks than are men and are more likely both to give and to receive emotional support (Field, 1998; Smith & Baltes, 1999). Friendships among older women enhance physical and mental health and contribute to continued psychological growth (Lewittes, 1989). Older women's close friends tend to be about the same age and socioeconomic status, have the same social and ethnic background, and live close to each other (Adams, 1997; Dykstra, 1990).

Social class influences the way in which friendships are made and maintained. Elderly middle-class women often make friends through membership in an association. The main basis of such friendships is shared interest of the group and its activities. Working-class friendships are more likely to be based on informal mutual aid (Greenberg & Motenko, 1994). Middle-class women and men, compared with working-class individuals, have more contact with friends, are more satisfied with the support they receive from others, and provide more assistance to others (Krause & Borawski-Clark, 1995).

Women's social involvement with their friends includes both home- and community-based activities. The most common social activity of older women and their close friends is getting together for conversation. Frequent topics of discussion are happy and sad events within their families and health problems.

Also, women and their friends help one another with transportation, shopping, and running errands (Adams, 1997). Those who perceive an equal give-and-take in their relationships with friends are more content and happy with the friendships (Roberto, 1996). Long-term friends contribute to a sense of continuity and connection with the past. Over time, friends can come to be considered as family, further increasing one's sense of connectedness (Lewittes, 1989).

Widowhood or Loss of a Partner

Despite the increasing divorce rate, most marriages are terminated not by divorce, but by the death of a spouse. Women are much more likely to become widowed than are men, since women not only have a longer life expectancy but also tend to marry men older than themselves. As of 1998, there were 11 million widows but only 2.6 million widowers in this country, a ratio of more than four to one (U.S. Bureau of the Census, 1999c). About 45 percent of women over the age of 65, but fewer than 15 percent of men the same age are widowed (U.S. Bureau of the Census, 1999c). Among women age 85 or older, four out of five are widowed (Older Women's League, 1999), with Black women widowed earlier than White women (Bradsher, 1997).

Remarriage rates are much higher for widowers than for widows. Widowed men over 65, for example, are seven times more likely to remarry than are widows of the same age (Brandon, 1997). One obvious reason is that unmarried older women greatly outnumber unmarried older men. In 1998, for instance, there were 32 unmarried men aged 65 and over for every 100 unmarried women in that age category (U.S. Bureau of the Census, 1999c). Furthermore, since men tend to marry women younger than themselves, the pool of potential mates expands for an older man but shrinks for an older woman. Thus, elderly women are much more likely to live alone (41 percent) than are elderly men (17 percent) (U.S. Bureau of the Census, 1998c).

Reaction and Adjustment to Widowhood

After losing a spouse people may suffer from restlessness, sleep problems, and feelings of depression, emptiness, anger, and guilt. Most elderly widowed individuals adjust to their spouse's death within 2 to 4 years, although feelings of loneliness, yearning, and missing their partner remain for extended periods of time (Cutter, 1999; O'Bryant, & Hansson, 1995).

As many as 10 to 20 percent of widows, however, experience long-term problems, including clinical depression, abuse of alcohol and prescription drugs, and increased susceptibility to physical illness. Among these are women with a prior history of depression, those whose marriages were less satisfactory, those whose husbands' deaths followed the deaths of other close relatives and friends, and those who depended on their husbands for most social contacts (Cutter, 1999).

Other factors—age, the degree of forewarning of the spouse's death, and financial, social, and personal resources—also affect a woman's reaction to widowhood (Bradsher, 1997). Compared to the young widow, the older widow is more likely to be financially secure, to have no child care responsibilities, to have friends in similar circumstances, and to be more psychologically prepared for her own death and her spouse's (Treas, 1983). Studies comparing the mental and physical health of older widows and older married women generally have not found any differences between these groups (O'Bryant & Hansson, 1995). Younger widows, on the other hand, initially experience greater difficulties in coping with their situation (Bolger & Wortman, 1992; McKiernan, 1996). One reason for the greater distress experienced by young widows may be the greater likelihood that the husband's death was unexpected. In a longitudinal study of widows and widowers younger than 45 years of age, those persons whose spouses died with little or no forewarning had greater difficulty accepting the reality of death, and felt more anger and guilt, than those who had knowledge of the impending death (Parkes & Weiss, 1983). Although younger individuals experience greater distress following their partner's death, the length of recovery is greater for older people (McKiernan, 1996).

Widowhood often results in a substantial reduction in financial resources for women, not only because the husband's income ceases, but also because considerable expenses may be incurred during the husband's final illness (Cutter, 1999;

Doress-Worters & Siegal, 1994). As we saw in Chapter 14, elderly women, especially those living alone, are more likely than elderly men to live in poverty (U.S. Bureau of the Census, 1999c).

Loneliness is another problem faced by widows. About 70 percent of elderly widows live alone (U.S. Bureau of Census, 1998a). Widows who have few social supports report the most loneliness (Rook, 1987). Those who have a support network to stave off loneliness are more satisfied with their lives (Hong & Duff, 1994). Support from families and children, especially daughters, does much to enhance the psychological well-being of widows (McGloshen & O'Bryant, 1988), but social contact with friends and neighbors may have an even more positive impact (Peplau, Bikson, Rook & Goodchilds, 1982). Women friends who are themselves widowed can be particularly supportive (Belsky, 1999). Interestingly, research has found more loneliness among women who have lived with a spouse for many years than among women who live alone (Cohler & Nakamura, 1996).

The importance of economic, social, and personal resources in a woman's adaptation to widowhood was demonstrated in a series of studies by Helene Lopata (1979, 1980), who classified widows in terms of their degree of reengagement in social activities. At one extreme was the active, engaged woman, who initiated changes and retained control of her life after her spouse's death. She was likely to have a greater income, higher educational level, and more friends than other groups of widows. Another type of widow lived in an essentially gender-segregated world, often in an ethnic community. She continued to remain involved with her neighbors, relatives, and church group. At the other extreme was the widow who became a social isolate. She often had a low educational level and had married a man of similar status upon whom she had become quite dependent. Lacking both adequate financial resources and the skills needed to successfully reengage in social activities after her husband's death, she became withdrawn and isolated. To help newly widowed women adjust, Ruth Jacobs offers a number of suggestions (see Table 15.1).

TABLE 15.1   Advice for the Newly Widowed Woman

1. Express your grief. Talk to friends, relatives, counselors, clergy.
2. Educate yourself about the functions your spouse performed, such as handling finances.
3. Seek out support groups.
4. Keep busy after the initial period of intense mourning.
5. Get a paid job or do volunteer work.
6. Seek out new roles; find people and causes where you can make a difference.
7. Don't expect too much too soon. Recovery may take several years.
8. Don't make any major decisions during the first year.
9. Turn to siblings for support.
10. Consider getting a pet.
11. Think of widowhood as sad, but also the beginning of the rest of your life.

Adapted from Jacobs (1997, pp. 255-258).

The death of a spouse takes a heavier toll on men, who suffer more psychological depression, psychiatric disorders, physical illness, death rates, and suicide rates than do widowed women (Angier, 1998; Stroebe & Stroebe, 1993). Moreover, the death rates of widowed men who remarry are lower than those of men who do not, whereas death rates are the same for women who remarry and those who do not (Helsing, Szklo, & Comstock, 1981). Why are widows better able to cope with the death of a spouse? The answer may be in their social support, which serves as a critical buffer against the stresses of widowhood. Women are more apt both to admit a need for support and to have developed broad social networks with friends and relatives (Stroebe & Stroebe, 1993).

Keep in mind that our knowledge of widows has been obtained primarily from older women, most of whom had traditional marriages. When the young women of today become widows, they will be more likely than the current population of widows to have had a different set of life experiences, including a college education and a job or career that will better prepare them for a healthy adjustment to widowhood (Belsky, 1999; Perlmutter & Hall, 1985).

Loss of a Lesbian Partner

Loss of a lesbian's partner is especially stressful if the relationship was not publicly acknowledged, but even when the relationship is open, friends may not comprehend the severity and nature of the loss (Fullmer, Shenk, & Eastland, 1999).

> *Recently, I vacationed with friends who had been friends also with my deceased partner-in-life. A guest arrived with slides of earlier vacations, including pictures of my lover. I objected that if I had been a man who had been recently widowed, they surely would have asked if I would object to showing the pictures. One friend responded she wanted very much to see them. She blanched when I suggested that she might feel differently after the death of her husband. Clearly, she thought that my relationship to Karen differed from her marriage; she evidently also thought my love differed from her friendship with Karen only by degree. Heterosexuals really do not understand what lesbians feel for their partners, even when they know us well. All of these friends had known Karen and me as lovers and had sent me bereavement condolences when Karen died.* (in Doress-Worters & Siegal, 1994, p. 145)

Living Arrangements

A number of housing options are available for elderly women and men. Choices are usually based on physical, emotional, or financial considerations. Let us examine these different types of living arrangements.

Own Home

More than 80 percent of 60- to 75-year-olds own their own homes, compared with 66 percent of the population at large (Brandon, 1997). The overwhelming majority of elderly individuals prefer to stay in their own homes as long as possible. But with incomes fixed and the costs of both renting and owning a home steadily rising, maintaining an affordable home is a major problem, especially for the older woman who lives alone (Carp, 1997a). Housing problems are even more severe for elderly Black and Latina women, who are almost twice as likely as all other older adults to live in rental housing (Doress-Worters & Siegal, 1994).

After widowhood or divorce, elderly persons strongly prefer living alone even when in declining health (Worobey & Angel, 1990). As we noted earlier in the chapter, women are much more likely than men to live alone, a phenomenon that occurs among both Whites and people of color. In 1997, 32 percent of women 65–74 lived alone compared to fewer than 15 percent of men. Similarly, 52 percent of women 75 and older lived alone versus only 21 percent of men (U.S. Bureau of the Census, 1998a). Elderly women who live alone report high levels of psychological well-being and appear to be doing as well as older women who live with others (Burnette & Mui, 1996). Informal and formal caregiving systems in the community contribute to this well-being by enabling older persons to remain at home longer. The elderly usually first seek care from the informal system of family, friends, and neighbors. When informal sources cannot or will not meet their needs, older individuals turn to the formal system. This consists of community groups, organizations, and professionals who offer assistance and services, such as meals on wheels, van service for the disabled, home aides, housekeepers, and visiting nurses (Pynoos & Golant, 1996).

Long-term elderly divorcees are more likely than long-term elderly widows to lack informal support systems. Divorced women generally have fewer children than do widows. As a consequence, they are more likely than widows to rely on paid helpers (Choi, 1995). Divorce, although increasingly common, is a less respectable marital status than widowhood (Etaugh, 1993b). While widowed women often receive sympathy and increased social support, divorced women tend to experience discrimination and to feel more alienated from others (Choi, 1995).

Living with Relatives

One traditional housing choice for older persons has been to move into the home of a relative, usually an adult daughter. This choice often is prompted by infirmity or the death of a spouse. Nearly one in 10 elderly men and 2 in 10 elderly women reside with children, siblings, or other relatives (American Association of Retired Persons, 1999a). Living with an adult child, however, is the least popular residential choice for older people (Bould & Longino, 1997). Most elderly Americans would rather have "intimacy at a distance" than live with relatives. Half of elderly parents do, however, live within 10 miles of a child (Usdansky, 2000). In fact, those who live alone report fewer symptoms of mental disorder and have higher morale than their counterparts who live with children (Magaziner & Cadigan, 1989).

Living with an adult child is more prevalent among ethnic minority elderly than among Whites. Older Asian Americans are most likely to live with their children. Blacks and Latinas/os are less likely to live with their children than Asian Americans, and Whites are least likely to do so (Lubben & Becerra, 1987). As we saw earlier, older ethnic minority women play key roles in their family networks by providing economic, social, and emotional support to their adult children and grandchildren. Poor Black households are predominantly organized around women, with older women at the center. Males are more directly involved in Latina/o and Native American households and families. Still, women in these groups enjoy greater prestige, respect, and domestic authority as they grow older (Padgett, 1989; Sánchez-Ayéndez, 1989).

Retirement Communities

Another housing alternative is the adult retirement community, usually populated by fairly affluent, healthy, active, independent individuals age 55 or older. Approximately 5 percent of Americans age 65 and older live in retirement communities (Leitner & Leitner, 1996). The best-known examples of these are the 45,000-member Sun City in Arizona and Leisure World in Southern California. Residents of these communities enjoy an array of activities, including hobby and academic classes, sports, recreations, and clubs.

Elderly individuals who are unable to manage housekeeping on their own have other options. They can choose to go into **continuing care retirement communities** (CCRCs). This is the newest housing option for the elderly and is the fastest growing. *The purpose of the CCRCs is to provide independent to semi-independent living for the elderly in a supportive environment* (Taylor & Heumann, 1994). Studies of social ties in communities such as these show that friendships flourish for many residents, especially women (Perkinson & Rockemann, 1996). Most residents of CCRCs are widowed women with an average age of 79. They tend to be better educated and more economically advantaged. Typically, the resident pays a large entrance fee as well as a monthly fee. This type of living community unfortunately is not affordable for the large number of elderly women and men with limited incomes.

Nursing Homes

Contrary to popular belief, only 5 percent of individuals age 65 or over live in nursing homes at any given time (Belsky, 1999). However, 20 percent of those 85 and above reside there (American Association of Retired Persons, 1999a; Pynoos & Golant, 1996). For several reasons, older women are almost twice as likely as older men to live in nursing homes (National Center for Health Statistics, 1999). Perhaps the most obvious reason is that women are likely to outlive men. Another reason is that those who live alone are much more likely than married persons to become institutionalized, and older women, as we have seen, are more likely than older men to be widowed, divorced, or single. A third reason is that those with disabilities and chronic illness are more likely to enter nursing homes, and older women are more susceptible than older men to chronic illness (Belsky, 1999; Guralnik et al., 1995). Whites use nursing homes more than Blacks, even when ethnic differences in longevity are taken into account (Kemper & Murtaugh, 1991). One reason for this is that ethnic minority elders are more likely than Whites to live with their families.

Homelessness

Sadly, one housing alternative for some elderly individuals is no housing at all. The homeless elderly population constitutes a relatively small proportion of the overall homeless population (Pynoos & Golant, 1996); however, the number of homeless older people is likely to increase dramatically as post–World War II baby boomers reach their fifties and beyond. More women, particularly those in ethnic minority groups, have joined the ranks of the homeless. The "feminization of poverty" discussed in Chapter 14, has played a major role in this trend (Stoner, 1995). Among the poor, men are still far more likely than women to become homeless. Nevertheless, the percentage of women in the older homeless population is estimated to have grown to 20 percent nationally. There are approximately 1,000 to 1,500 homeless women over age 50 in New York City (Cohen, Ramirez, Teresi, Gallagher, & Sokolovsky, 1997). Moreover, homelessness is not confined to large cities, but reaches the smallest communities as well (Stoner, 1995). Compared to homeless men and younger homeless women, the older homeless woman has lower levels of alcoholism, drug abuse, and criminality but higher levels of serious mental illness (Cohen et al., 1997). One study of 201 older homeless women found that 2 years later, 47 percent were no longer homeless. These women, compared with those remaining homeless, reported having a larger community social support network, were not mentally ill, and had greater financial resources from sources such as Social Security (Cohen et al., 1997). Unfortunately, suitable housing options for older homeless women are scarce.

Living in the City and in the Suburbs

Nearly two-thirds of U.S. women and men age 65 and older live in metropolitan areas. Elderly Latinas are most likely to reside in cities (87 percent), followed by Black women (65 percent) and White women (62 percent) (Markson & Hess, 1997). Older individuals are concentrated in cities because they have "aged in place" while their children have moved to the suburbs. These women are a diverse lot, ranging from the homeless woman to the wealthy widow, but most are on the lower end of the income scale.

One major concern of the older city-dwelling woman is crime. But contrary to popular myth, younger adults are more likely to be victims of crime than the elderly. Why? The old may be fairly easy targets, but they have few resources. More women than men are crime victims. The typical elderly victim is a low-income widow who lives alone. She often is physically disabled and a member of an ethnic minority group (Markson & Hess, 1997). Elderly women, particularly those who live alone, are more fearful than elderly men of being a crime victim.

Socialized to be less assertive and more yielding than men, women are more likely to view themselves as potentially being overpowered by others, particularly men (Markson & Hess, 1997). This is yet another example of the differences in personal power—both real and perceived—between women and men.

Older women who live in the city enjoy some advantages compared to their rural- and suburban-dwelling sisters. Cities have more transportation facilities, and they are more accessible than those in the suburbs. City dwellers also have an easier time obtaining social and medical services that often are located in areas with a high concentration of older adults (Markson & Hess, 1997; Yardley, 1999).

Suburbia is a setting originally created for young families. Many couples moved to the suburbs after World War II, raised their children, and grew old there. Although most older people live in cities, more elderly persons are now living in the suburbs than ever before, and the trend is expected to continue (Carp, 1997a; Hubel, 1999). If this happens we are likely to see more examples of adaptive measures like the elementary school in a suburb of New York City that was closed because of dwindling enrollments and converted to a geriatric center containing an adult day care center and a nursing home (Fein, 1994).

Many of the aging suburban population are widowed women. Those who can no longer drive feel defenseless and isolated. In addition, physical adjustments such as arthritis, make it increasingly difficult to maintain and to get around in large, multilevel homes.

> *Everything is so far away. I used to like that. I used to like not being crowded by neighbors and everything. But now I'm having a hard time managing. I don't want to leave because everything is familiar and I like it here. But its really very hard to cope.* (a 77-year-old widow in Fein, 1994, p. A1)

Elder Abuse

Abuse of older adults is an alarming social phenomenon noted increasingly in recent decades. At least 4 percent of older adults—over two million people in the United States—have been subjected to abuse (American Psychological Association, 1999a; Wolf, 1998). Patterns of abuse vary little among African Americans, Latinas/os and Whites. Asian Americans are less likely than other groups to perceive situations as abusive and are less likely to seek help (Moon & Williams, 1993).

Types of Abuse

Elder abuse *can take several different forms, including physical, psychological, financial, and neglect dimensions*, as shown in Table 15.2. Neglect, the most commonly reported type of abuse, includes inattention, isolation, and withholding items necessary for daily living such as food, medicine, and bathing. Financial and psycho-

TABLE 15.2 Types of Elder Abuse

Type of Abuse	Description
Physical Abuse	Pushing, punching, choking, hair pulling, kicking, burning, cutting, sexually molesting, confining one against her or his will
Psychological Abuse	Frightening, threatening, humiliating, intimidating the person, forcing the person to do degrading things, calling the person names, treating the person like a child, using children or grandchildren as leverage
Financial Abuse	Destroying property or prized possessions, stealing one's money, denying access to one's money, restricting access to household finances
Active Neglect	Depriving person of items needed for daily living (food, warmth, shelter, glasses, dentures, money)
Passive Neglect	Inattention, isolation

Sources: Goldstein (1995); Illinois Department of Aging (1996a).

logical abuse are next in frequency, with physical abuse being the least prevalent (Administration on Aging [AOA], 1998).

Financial exploitation of the elderly has been growing at an disturbing rate. Like much elder abuse, most of these crimes are committed by family members and paid household workers or caregivers. Examples include the housekeeper for a bedridden couple who took thousands of dollars of their cash and possessions before being caught. In another instance, a drug-addicted man took his widowed grandmother's Social Security checks as soon as they arrived. Another man withdrew large sums of money from his ailing mother's bank account to pay for his own expenses, while not letting physicians replace his mother's pacemaker (Nordheimer, 1991).

All states now have laws against elder mistreatment with most mandating that abuse be reported. Yet various studies estimate that only 1 in every 5 or more cases is reported (American Psychological Association, 1999a; AOA, 1998; Rosenblatt et al., 1996). One obstacle is, simply, denial of the problem. For example, it was not until the mid-1970s that the United Kingdom published the first reports of elder abuse (or "granny bashing," as it was called) (Vinton, 1999). In addition, elderly persons themselves may lack the opportunity and the physical and mental ability to report abuse. They often fear not being believed, reprisal, abandonment, and institutionalization. Also, the victimized elderly may wish to protect the abuser, who is most often an adult child or a spouse (Goldstein, 1996).

Who Is Abused and Who Abuses?

The typical victim of elder abuse is a woman over age 75. She often lives at home with adult caregivers but is isolated and fearful. Frequently, she is physically and/or mentally frail (AOA, 1998; Wolf, 1998). Over two-thirds of the abuse is inflicted by children, spouses, or other relatives. The typical abuser is a middle-aged son of the victim. Other perpetrators include spouses, siblings, grandchildren, neighbors, and home–health care providers (Lacks, Williams, O'Brien, Hurst, & Horwitz, 1997). Adult children with mental, alcohol, or drug problems are among the most likely to be abusers. Often, the abuser is the caregiver of the victim and also may be financially dependent upon the victim (American Psychological Association, 1999a; Barnett et al., 1997).

The stress of providing care for an ill relative may contribute to the problem of elder abuse. Some individuals who are caregivers for an older person who is physically ill, frail, or suffers from dementia, may express their frustration by becoming abusive (American Psychological Association, 1999a). The caregiver may be someone who neither chose to do so nor is able to cope with the financial, interpersonal, and time demands placed on him or her (Barnett, Miller-Perrin, & Perrin, 1997).

While acknowledging that caring for an elderly relative can be stressful, one must be careful not to simply "blame the victim" for being abused. (Notice the parallel with inappropriately blaming a woman who has been raped.) The feminist perspective puts elder abuse in a larger social context. From this point of view, elder abuse is part of a spectrum of male violence against women (Whittaker, 1996) that reflects a social context in which men wield more power and dominance over women.

What Can Be Done?

Some of the options that are available to the younger abused woman—deciding to leave a relationship or going to a shelter—are impractical or virtually impossible for most abused elderly. Awareness of the problem is the first step. Education and training are essential to alert the general public and professional service providers to the prevalence of elder abuse and neglect. Professionals must learn to recognize the symptoms of abuse, understand the victim's denial, and strengthen the victim's resolve to end the abuse. The public should be encouraged to report any known or suspected case of abuse. Both the public and the victim must know where to turn for help. New laws have been passed in recent years governing the treatment of victims, especially women, that focus on the need for safety, assistance in accessing the courts, and information about the progress of the proceedings. This emphasis on victims' rights should be ensured by legislation at the state and federal levels. Support groups for victims help validate the victims' experiences, and provide a sense of empowerment that may enable them to change the power structure of the abusive relationship (American Psychological Association, 1999a; Barnett et al., 1997; Decalmer & Glendenning, 1997).

The Vital Older Woman

Don't call me a young woman;
it's not a compliment or courtesy
but rather a grating discourtesy.
Being old is a hard won achievement
not something to be brushed aside
treated as infirmity or ugliness
or apologized away by "young woman."
I am an old woman, a long liver.
I'm proud of it. I revel in it.
I wear my gray hair and wrinkles
as badges of triumphant survival
and I intend to grow even older.
Don't call me a young woman.
I was a young woman for years
But that was then and this is now.
I was a mid-life woman for a time
and I celebrated that good span.
Now I am somebody magnificent, new,
a seer, wise woman, old proud crone,
an example and mentor to the young
who need to learn old women's wisdom.
I look back on jobs well done
and learn to do different tasks now.
I think great thoughts and share them.
Don't call me a young woman.
You reveal your own fears of aging.
Maybe you'd better come learn from
all of us wonderful old women
how to take the sum of your life
with all its experience and knowledge
and show how a fully developed life
can know the joy of a past well done
*and the joy of life left to live.**

Ruth Harriet Jacobs, 1997, pp. 8–9

In the last three chapters, we have explored the life experiences of women in their later years. We have examined a number of challenges faced by many older women: declining health, financial problems, the loss of loved ones, elder abuse. But this does not mean that the later years of a woman's life are filled with frustration and despair. Many older women cope successfully with the challenges that old age brings. They don't just *endure* old age; they *enjoy* it.

Who Are the Vital Older Women?

One of the characteristics of older women who adjust well to later life is the ability to integrate agency and communion (Hubbs-Tait, 1989). You will recall from Chapter 2 that agency refers to such attributes as independence, activity, competitiveness, self-confidence, ambition, and assertiveness. Communion (emotional expressivity) includes such characteristics as affection, compassion, kindness, gentleness, being helpful to others, and awareness of the feelings of others. As we noted in Chapter 3, those individuals who combine both sets of characteristics are referred to as androgynous.

Aging androgynous women show better adjustment, greater feelings of mastery, and higher self-esteem than women who show only the stereotypically feminine traits of communion (Frank, Towell, & Huyck, 1985; Livson, 1983). It may surprise you to learn that most older women cope with life stresses more effectively than do younger women.

Older women in general accept their lives as having been well spent (Hubbs-Tait, 1989). Elderly Black women express significantly more contentment with their lives than do elderly White women, even though Blacks are more disadvantaged socioeconomically and perceive their health as worse than do Whites (Johnson, 1994). How can we explain this? Many aging minority women are able to draw on psychological, social, and cultural strengths, which ease their transition to old age. They have spent their lives marshaling scarce resources to cope with everyday demands and these coping strategies pay off later on as self-reliance. Strengths also arise from family, church, and community networks and shared ethnic identity (Padgett, 1989; Shenk, Zablotsky, & Croom, 1998). In addition, White women may have expectations of life in the later years that are unrealistically high.

Fulfilling Activities in Later Life

How can elderly women make the last half of life as rich as the first? There are many paths to fulfillment. As we saw in Chapter 14, some older women continue to have careers well into later life. Others may devote themselves to pursuits which they had little time for in their younger years. Think of Grandma Moses, for example, who took up painting late in life and became an internationally acclaimed artist.

Many older women become volunteer workers in a wide variety of community settings: schools, hospitals, museums, churches, and service organizations. Devotion to volunteering remains strong until very old age. Twenty-three percent of people 75 and older are still volunteering, compared with only 4 percent who continue to be employed. Nine out of 10 older volunteers feel that their work contributes a great deal to their organization. Of those who volunteer, 71 percent are very satisfied with their lives compared to 58 percent of those who do not volunteer (Commonwealth Fund, 1993b). Similarly, participation in church social activities is positively related to life satisfaction among older widowed women (Neill & Kahn, 1999).

Maggie Kuhn, who founded the Gray Panthers after her forced retirement at age 65, illustrates the active role older women can play as advocates for social change.

Whatever a woman's situation as she ages, there is usually some way in which she can serve as an **advocate**, *a person who plays an active role in making changes in her life, the lives of others, and in society* (Dowling, 1997). For example, women can join and actively participate in any of a number of organizations that advocate for the rights of older persons or specifically for older women. The American Association of Retired Persons (AARP), with over 24 million members, is a powerful advocacy group. The Gray Panthers, a smaller, more activist group, was founded by Maggie Kuhn following her forced retirement at age 65. The Older Women's League (OWL) focuses on social policies affecting midlife and older women (Doress-Worters & Siegal, 1994).

Becoming an activist can transform the life of an older woman. Take the case of Rosemary Bizzell, a widow and grandmother of eight. Prior to joining OWL in 1981, she had never been involved in community affairs. Within 3 years, she had risen to prominence in the city council and in state government. In her words,

> *My self-image as an older woman has improved tremendously in spite of much rejection in job hunting. Apparently I was supposed to count my blessings and not expect to advance. Well, becoming involved in OWL has certainly challenged me. I cannot thank the OWLs enough for opening up a whole new world for older women. I am proud of the opportunity to be part of it.* (in Doress-Worters & Siegel, 1994, p. 436)

SUMMARY

1. Many people hold stereotypes (mostly negative) toward the elderly. Such ageism is more strongly directed toward women. Older adults and ethnic minority groups have more positive attitudes than do the young and Whites.

2. More men than women are married in later life. Couples often report increased marital satisfaction with age.

3. Older lesbians in committed relationships provide each other with a mutual support system and shared economic benefits.

4. Single women have skills in independent living and in building support systems.

5. Older women generally have positive relationships with their daughters and sisters.

6. The grandparent-grandchild relationship has many benefits. Visitation rights for grandparents is a growing social issue. More grandparents than ever live in multigeneration households, particularly members of ethnic minority groups. Increasing numbers of grandmothers are rearing their grandchildren.

7. Growing numbers of elderly adults, especially women, are caregivers of their parents.

8. Friendships among older women enhance physical and mental health.

9. Women are more likely than men to be widowed, but are much less likely to remarry. Reaction to widowhood depends on several factors including age, degree of forewarning of the spouse's death, and financial, social, and personal resources. Loss of a lesbian partner may be very stressful.

10. Most elderly persons own their own homes. Widowed and divorced persons prefer living alone. Living with an adult child is the least popular choice, especially for Whites. Other alternatives include the adult retirement community and the continuing care retirement community. Only 5 percent of those 65 and over live in nursing homes. Women are twice as likely as men to reside there. Most older women live in cities, where crime is a concern but accessible transportation and social services are advantages. Older women in the suburbs may feel isolated. Some older women are homeless.

11. Elder abuse can have physical, psychological, financial, and neglect dimensions. At least 4 percent of older adults are affected, but few cases are reported. The typical victim is a woman age 75 or older who lives with a caregiver. The typical abuser is a middle-aged son who has mental, alcohol, or drug problems. The following are essential in order to combat elder abuse: Educating professionals and the public; reporting abuse cases; passing victims' rights laws; and forming support groups.

12. Older women who cope successfully with aging tend to integrate agency and communion. Some older women continue their careers; others become volunteers, or advocates for social causes.

WHAT DO YOU THINK?

1. What is meant by the saying "To be old is to be a woman?"

2. Do you think that attitudes toward older women are becoming more positive? More negative? Explain your answer.

3. Why have older women been viewed more negatively than older men? Use information from Chapters 1, 2, and 3 to explain your answers.

4. Why do you think older women are closer to their daughters than to their sons?

5. What are the advantages and disadvantages of grandparents rearing their grandchildren?

6. Are elderly widows better off living alone? With family members? In a retirement community? Why?

7. How can public awareness of elder abuse be increased?

IF YOU WANT TO LEARN MORE

Benatovich, B. (Ed.). (1995). *What we know so far: Wisdom among women*. New York: St. Martin's Griffin.

Fridstein, M. (1997). *Grandparenting: A survival guide*. Glenwood Springs, CO: Tageh Press.

Friedan, B. (1993). *The fountain of age*. New York: Simon & Schuster.

Gates, P. (1990). *Suddenly alone: A woman's guide to widowhood*. New York: Harper & Row.

Jacobs, R. H. (1997). *Be an outrageous older woman*. New York: HarperCollins.

Pearsall, M. (Ed.). (1997). *The other within us: Feminist explorations of women and aging*. Boulder, CO: Westview.

CHAPTER

16

A Feminist Future

Goals, Actions, and Attitudes

KEY TERM

ableism

Several years ago, before my (Judith's) daughter left for college, I offered advice about her first-semester courses. Although Rachel accepted a few of my recommendations, she rejected my suggestion of a women's studies course, stating that gender was not an important issue. At age 17, she certainly had no idea the route her academic career would eventually take. Despite her initial protestations, Rachel ultimately registered for a women's studies course in order to fulfill a multicultural curriculum requirement, and this course proved to be a transforming experience. It exposed Rachel to research, theory, and ideology that dramatically affected her attitudes and interests. In fact, this course was the basis for her academic journey that began with a double major in sociology and women studies and culminated in a feminist doctoral dissertation in sociology.

We saw in Chapter 1 that science is not value-free, and as Rachel's experience illustrates, neither is teaching. "The process of education is political" (Wyche & Crosby, 1996, p. 5); that is, both subject matter and teaching methods are influenced by the value system of the instructor and the academic community. Applying this to the field of psychology, Kimberly Kinsler and Sue Rosenberg Zalk (1996) contend that "the greatest value of psychology lies in the field's ability to reveal the psychological processes perpetuating social injustices and to correct the social systems that have an unjust impact on the quality of people's lives" (p. 35). Given this political dimension of teaching, we end this textbook with a look at feminist goals for the future.

Recall that in Chapter 1 we presented three feminist themes that have recurred throughout this book: gender inequality of power, diversity of women, and the social construction of gender. In this chapter we now return to these themes, and translate them into goals for the future, consider actions for achieving these aims, and, because these goals have their root in feminist thought, explore the prevalence of feminist beliefs among North American women.

Feminist Goals

Greater Equality of Power and Focus on the Diversity of Women

Despite legislation that prohibits gender discrimination in employment (Title VII of the Civil Rights Act of 1964) and educational programs (Title IX, 1972), gender differences in organizational and interpersonal power continue to limit women's advancement in the workplace. Antidiscrimination legislation alone cannot change attitudes, and discriminatory policies are hard to monitor. Therefore, as has been noted throughout this text, men, especially White men, continue to have greater access to economic and political resources than women do. They continue to greatly outnumber women at high levels of management and in political office and to own most of the wealth (Chapters 10 and 14).

To combat this inequity, we choose as our first goal for the future greater equality of organizational power. As more and more women attain levels of power currently held by men, gender equality will begin to affect other areas. Women's accessibility to important mentors and social networks will increase, providing even more promotion opportunities for women. And because job level is one factor determining salaries, women's wages will rise and become more similar to those of men. Also the close association between sexual harassment and the power imbalance suggests that a greater power equality will mean less harassment of women.

In addition to greater organizational power, men continue to hold more interpersonal power relative to women. For instance, they tend to have more control over a couple's activities on dates and more influence in marriage (Chapters 11 and 12). A second goal, therefore, is greater equality in relationship power. Women would benefit by having a greater voice in dating decision making and a more balanced division of household labor. The latter, in turn, could reduce women's role overload and interrole conflict. Furthermore, because both rape and domestic violence are due, at least in part, to male dominance, shared interpersonal power would go a long way to reducing intimate violence against women.

Women are disadvantaged due not only to the gender inequality of power, but also to differences within genders that add extra burdens to the lives of many women. White women are advantaged compared to women of color, middle-class women have more power than working-class or poor women, heterosexual women are privileged in comparison to lesbian women, nondisabled women are more advantaged than women with disabilities, and younger women have more power than their older counterparts. We have seen that ethnic minority women and women with disabilities experience even greater wage inequities than White and nondisabled women (Chapter 10). Furthermore, women of color and lesbian women experience more job discrimination and sexual harassment than White and heterosexual women (Chapter 10). Thus, a third power goal is to ensure that increases in female power benefit all women, regardless of ethnicity, class, disability/ability, sexual orientation, or age.

Greater Flexibility in the Social Construction of Gender

We have noted throughout the text that gender is socially constructed; that most gender behaviors and roles—such as career choice (Chapter 8), friendship behaviors (Chapter 11), and contribution to household labor (Chapter 12)—are shaped by interpersonal, societal, and cultural expectations, and are not constrained by biological sex. In examining some of the mechanisms that influence this construction of gender, we explored stereotypes that reflect societal gender expectations (Chapter 2), theoretical perspectives about the mechanisms whereby children learn the behaviors and roles expected for their gender (Chapter 3), and parental shaping of the behaviors and interests of girls and boys (Chapter 4). We saw that it is not the biological nature of females and males that serves as the major foundation for people's view of gender or their gender-related activities and preferences but their conception of what it means to be a female or a male in our society today.

Additionally, power, or rather the imbalance of power, also guides the social construction of gender (e.g., Brown, 1994; Howard & Hollander, 1997). People with more power, who are in dominant positions, are likely to acquire and use different traits and behaviors than people in subordinate positions. Individuals in high-status positions are more likely to display independence, a male gender-related trait that is difficult to embrace if one lacks access to necessary resources in the home, workplace, or social environment. People lacking powerful resources, on the other hand, are more likely to rely instead on emotional connections between people and, consequently, to develop female gender-related traits, such as compassion. Thus, females' and males' development of gender-related traits, behaviors, and roles is constructed via stereotype-based expectations, socialization by parents, peers, and others, and hierarchical status within society.

Unfortunately, a rigid construction of gender is damaging to human potential (e.g., Bem, 1993; Howard & Hollander, 1997; Katz, 1996). It hinders development of our unique talents and interests by guiding us in directions dictated by the social constructs of our biological sex. Judith recalls her days as a new bride when she refused to allow her husband to share the housecleaning, although both she and her husband were employed full time. Her insistence was based on her traditional conception of the "wife" role; a perception that was constructed from television and magazine images and from the roles of many married couples at that time (the 1960s). Her "wife role" behaviors were not based on her own interests, her time availability, or her husband's desires but solely on her construction of this role from the societal images and social behaviors she observed around her.

A fourth goal for women, then, is greater flexibility in the construction of gender. Flexibility can lead to an expansion in career options, more flexible decisions about work and family dilemmas, greater sexual equality, and numerous other reductions in gender-constrained behaviors that limit choices made by both women and men. Flexibility of gender-related behaviors and roles also has the potential to reduce the prevalence of sexual harassment (see Chapters 6, 8, and 10) and acquaintance rape (Chapter 11), both of which are fostered, at least in part, by traditional constructions of the behaviors of men and women. Further, it can enhance communication within heterosexual couples by freeing each partner from constraints expected for her/his gender.

Actions to Achieve These Goals

Research and Teaching

Research and teaching about the psychology of women can play a significant role in achieving feminist goals for several reasons. First, greater knowledge of gender differences in interpersonal and societal power can help clarify the role that power imbalance plays in women's lives. Understanding the extent to which male power influences rape and battering (Chapter 11), serves as the basis for the division of household labor (Chapter 12), and contributes to wage inequities (Chapter 10), means that both female and male students will be aware of the prevalence of male power. A reduction in male dominance cannot occur until more people recognize that it exists (Johnson, 1997). Exposure to this issue within the classroom can increase awareness that can spark the motivation and action necessary for change. The more we (psychologists and students) understand the dynamics and the effects of power differentials, the better armed we are to reduce privilege and its negative consequences for the less powerful.

Second, research and teaching on the psychology of women enlightens us about the way we construct gender in our lives. Scientific investigation gives us a better understanding of the influences on this construction and of the effects our personal images of gender have on our experiences as females or males. Similarly, exploration of these issues in the classroom has the potential to transform. As both women and men learn about the social basis for gender behaviors and roles, they might feel freer to experiment and to make choices that are less traditional but more personally appropriate.

Third, research and teaching about the experiences of diverse women can dispel myths and stereotypes that distort our understanding and reduce tolerance. Also, these activities foster greater understanding, appreciation, and celebration of our similarities and differences and can empower all females, not only those in the most privileged group. Although recent years have brought a greater inclusion of underrepresented groups in both research and educational curricula, to achieve these diversity goals, the field must continue to expand the diversity of its research participants. A more representative body of knowledge can ensure that researchers, instructors, and students do not generalize from one narrow group of females, carrying the implicit message that people in this group are "normal" and any discrepant behaviors, attitudes, or roles on the part of other individuals are "abnormal" (Madden & Hyde, 1998).

Consideration of diverse women's experiences must include a broader scope of topics as well. Research and teaching must address previously underexamined issues, such as employment obstacles for poor women, dating concerns of women with disabilities, experiences of lesbian mothers, outcomes of living in an extended family, and achievement goals of working-class and poor young women. A broader conceptualization of research and teaching topics not only facilitates understanding but can inform policy interventions. For example, although company-supplied day care might ease the work-family burden of women in white-collar and professional jobs, free temporary child care might be a better resource for women on welfare who are seeking job training. Similarly, principles guiding custody decisions for divorced heterosexual women might not apply to divorced lesbian women. It is only through an examination of questions relevant to all types of women that societal interventions can best address the diversity of women's needs.

Although there is much less information available about ethnic minority women, working-class and poor women, women with disabilities, lesbian and bisexual women, and older women, it is essential that we incorporate the knowledge base that does exist into our teaching. As cogently stated by Ann Marie Orza and Jane Torrey (1995), "Teachers and researchers in the psychology of women share the goal of including and understanding not only both sexes but also the great variety of people who also differ from the middle-class European male in race, class, or ethnicity" (p. 212). "Perhaps the most important task confronting women's studies (and all other studies) at this moment in history is to convey the fact that an individual's psychological makeup cannot be understood except in the context of the particular roles he or she plays in the particular culture and community to which he or she belongs" (pp. 211–212). Without this diversity focus in our teaching, students' "educational experience does not reflect social reality and is therefore derelict in preparing them, regardless of race, culture, ethnicity, sexual orientation, and gender, to function in a culturally pluralistic and global society" (Sue, Bingham, Porché-Burke, & Vasquez, 1999, p 1066).

Socialization of Children

Another approach to developing greater flexibility in gender construction is the feminist socialization of children. Parents can bring up their children so that preferences and skills, rather than gender, are the defining characteristics that guide development. How can this be achieved? Read Learn about the Research 16.1 to examine Phyllis Katz's perspective on this topic (1996).

LEARN ABOUT THE RESEARCH 16.1
Why and How Should We Raise Feminist Children?

Phyllis Katz asks what it means to raise a feminist child. One answer is the elimination of all gender-related traits, behaviors, and roles; that is, raising children so that gender is irrelevant. Katz contends, however, that this would not be possible. Children are exposed to influences beyond the home. Consequently, even if parents were to treat their daughters and sons identically, these children would continue to be exposed to other people for whom gender would be important.

Instead Katz advocates raising children to be gender flexible; that is, to select activities and behaviors on the basis of "individual likes and skills rather than being bogged down by gender stereotypes" (pp. 333–334). She notes that because much gender learning takes place during the preschool years, several actions by the parents can play an important role. One is role modeling. For example, maternal employment and nontraditional division of household labor by parents can help develop less stereotypic expectations and behaviors in children. Furthermore, the kinds of activities and goals encouraged by the parents can be instrumental. As examples, discouragement of gender stereotypic activities, toys, and future aspirations can be effective. Also, Katz notes that limiting the amount of television their children can watch might be beneficial because there is some evidence that children who watch less television have less stereotypic conceptions of gender.

Source: Katz, (1996).

(continued on p. 424)

What Does It Mean?

1. Do you think that the development of gender flexibility is a positive goal? Explain your answer.
2. Katz suggests it might not be possible to eliminate all gender-stereotypic influences on children. Do you agree or disagree? Explain your answer.
3. Regardless of your own opinion about gender flexibility, use the knowledge you have gained from this course to suggest other factors besides parental behaviors that might facilitate its development in children and adolescents.

What would be the outcomes of gender-flexible upbringing? First, it would expand the range of activities, behaviors, and roles from which the child and, later, the adult could choose. Instead of assuming, for example, that males make dating decisions, pay for dates, and initiate sex (Chapter 11), whichever dating partner was more comfortable with these behaviors could select them. Furthermore, these might vary depending on the circumstances. This, in turn, could lead to more egalitarian relationships because decision making and instrumental behaviors would not be relegated specifically to males. Similarly, women and men would make occupational choices on the basis of skills, interests, and personal needs without consideration of the gender appropriateness of the field (Chapter 8),

When children observe their parents perform nonstereotypic behaviors they are likely to develop a less rigid construction of gender.

a process that might lead to greater occupational prestige and salaries for women and to greater job satisfaction for both genders.

Second, given the higher status of the male role in North American society, gender flexibility would lead boys to develop a greater understanding and respect for behaviors and roles traditionally associated with females. If boys observe their fathers and other influential adult men performing traditional female behaviors, such as washing the dishes and caring for young children, and if boys are required to perform these chores, they will be more apt to view the traditional female role as worthy and dignified (Goldin, in "A Man's Place," 1999). The far-reaching implications are, of course, that little boys grow up to be men. The values instilled in them in childhood will influence their own involvement in traditional female activities and increase their respect for others who perform such activities. This greater respect could, in turn, carry over to the workplace, where more familiarity with family-related activities might encourage the initiation and support of additional family-friendly policies.

Third, gender flexibility would minimize the extent to which people view and evaluate others on the basis of a rigid construction of gender. For example, girls who play sports would receive the same degree of encouragement as sports-oriented boys (Chapter 4) and women in blue-collar trades would be accepted rather than harassed by their coworkers (Chapter 10). We would evaluate mothers who voluntarily stay home to care for their children or those who elect to work full time in the same way as we would evaluate fathers in these roles. We would have the same reaction to women and men who are fiercely independent and to those who are highly dependent. That is, if our children were brought up with a feminist perspective of equality, their impressions of others would be influenced by their behaviors and roles rather than by the perceived suitability of those behaviors for individuals of one gender or the other, and the choice of roles, for everyone, would be limitless.

Institutional Procedures

Another route for attaining our goals is for institutions to initiate practices that reduce gender inequality and that create hospitable environments for both women and men. In Chapters 10 and 12 we examined organizational procedures that improve working conditions for women (e.g., pay equity, affirmative action) or that facilitate balancing of family and work (e.g., flextime, child care assistance programs). Institutional initiatives can enhance the quality of life for women in other ways as well. For example, Mary Koss and her colleagues (Koss et al., 1994) propose several institutional interventions that can lower the risk of rape and domestic violence by reducing gender inequality and enhancing flexibility of gender-related behaviors and roles.

First, Koss and her associates emphasize the importance of education. They recommend that violence prevention begin in elementary school, when values about females' and males' roles are beginning to form, and continue through college. Although different topics would be appropriate at various educational levels, the curriculum should include an examination and reconceptualization of gender roles, prevention of substance abuse, and exploration of rape myths. This type of curriculum would expose children, adolescents, and young adults to problems inherent in traditional gender-related behaviors and roles, would make them more sensitive to the experiences and pressures of the other gender, and would make them aware of the nature of and influences on violence against women.

Second, these researchers suggest that the church can be involved in reduction of intimate violence. Because some people acquire their view of marital relationships through religious doctrine, programs aimed at reducing domestic violence can be particularly effective for these individuals, if associated with the church.

Third, Koss and her colleagues point to the need for change in media images. Researchers should advance our understanding about how the media contribute to violence against women and about ways they can be used to reduce this violence.

In addition to the prevention of violence against women, Koss and her colleagues address ways that health care institutions can more effectively treat women who have been victimized. They stress the importance for health care providers to have adequate training in treating the physical and mental health problems that arise from rape and battering. Providers must be sensitive to victims' needs and be able to offer effective medical treatment as well as appropriate referrals for psychological counseling or assistance with lifestyle changes, such as leaving their violent relationship.

Individual Actions

Many women seek to achieve success and better their own lives through individual efforts. In fact, consistent with a traditional North American value system that applauds individualism, many American women place greater emphasis on their own hard work in improving their lives than on women's collective efforts (Boxer, 1997; Konek, Kitch, & Shore, 1994). These women think that women's personal effort and success today, more than changes in organizational or governmental policies and practices, will lead to better opportunities for future generations of women (Konek et al., 1994), and they are willing to work hard, assert their rights, seek out opportunities for advancement, and make sacrifices if necessary.

Collective Action

Contrary to the individual approach, many feminist psychologists contend that collective action is necessary in order to achieve significant improvement in women's lives (Worell, 1996a). This does not imply that women should not work hard to attain personal goals. However, it does mean that individual women should strive to empower all women, not just themselves; they should advocate for social change, not just personal betterment. Furthermore, these collective efforts should address the concerns of diverse groups of women.

Unfortunately, the feminist movement, a collective movement aimed at enhancing women's lives, has been focused primarily on the needs of White middle-class women and has been criticized for failing to address racism and classism (e.g., Meara & Day, 2000). It, too, seriously lags behind in dealing with unique problems faced by women of color and poor and working-class women (e.g., Christensen, 1997; Das-Dasgupta, 1998). As a Black college instructor and administrator stated, "Until very recently I did not call myself a feminist. . . . even academic feminism did not include me until the 1980s. Feminism in the United States was pretty monolithic, pretty homogeneous. . . . and these groups were very, very exclusive in terms of what they considered to be priorities. . . . and so until recently, America did not embrace my experiences" (Kmiec, Crosby, & Worell, 1996, p. 58).

As bell hooks (1990) contends, women who differ in ethnicity and class have certain experiences in common by virtue of their gender. However, racism, classism, heterosexism, and **ableism,** *bias against people because of their disability,* contribute to double and triple jeopardies experienced by women who are not in the privileged group. Fortunately, the efforts of women of color, poor women, and lesbian women, have gradually expanded the feminist movement's perspective, and participation by previously excluded groups has increased (Scott, 1998). But this expansion of goals and inclusive participation must continue to grow; attempts to achieve gender equality should, concurrently strive to eradicate inequalities based on ethnicity, class, sexual orientation, physical disability/ability, and age. Only the collective efforts of diverse groups of women working together for the elimination of all types of power inequality can provide a brighter future for all girls and women.

Given that some women ascribe to beliefs in equality but are not oriented toward working for change for others, are there ways to enhance these women's motivation for social activism? Judith Worell (1996a) suggests that communication with other women, learning about the experiences and problems of other women, and exposure to varied situations that involve gender discrimination can broaden one's understanding of women's issues and encourage individuals' greater involvement in advocating for women's rights. Women's studies courses are another valuable resource that can increase students' interest in collective action.

Do our feminist goals for the future coincide with the perspectives of you and your acquaintances? Try Get Involved 16.1 to explore students' fantasies about their ideal futures.

GET INVOLVED **16.1**

A Perfect Future Day

Imagine what you would like your life to be like 10 years in the future. Write a paragraph describing what your ideal typical day would be like. Also, ask one same-gender and two other-gender students to perform the same exercise.

Based on B. Kerr, (1999).

(continued on p. 428)

What Does It Mean?

Read through the four descriptions and record similarities and differences about the following: (1) marital status, (2) presence of children, (3) if married, family responsibilities of each spouse, (4) employment status, (5) if employed, gender-dominance of the occupation, and (6) leisure activities.

1. Do the descriptions written by the women differ from those written by the men in relation to these or any other

topics? If yes, use information learned in this course to explain these differences.

2. Are there any current gender-based expectations about interpersonal or societal roles and behaviors that might hinder your own ideal life from becoming a reality? If yes, what kinds of changes do you think would reduce this impediment? Would you be interested in working for this change?

Feminist Beliefs

We began the text with a discussion of the meaning of feminism, and now we come full circle, back to this topic. Because the goals we have presented and many of the actions taken to achieve these goals are rooted in a feminist perspective, it is important to explore the prevalence and accuracy of feminist beliefs.

Although some North Americans believe that feminism has had a positive impact on women's attainment of greater economic, political, and legal opportunities (Boxer, 1997; Fassinger, 1994), others have argued that feminists are the root of numerous personal and social problems, and especially, are responsible for the decline in the "traditional" American family (Faludi, 1991; Johnson, 1997). Many feminists are, indeed, disturbed about the subordination of women within *patriarchal* families where husbands hold the power and dictate the activities of wives and children (Johnson, 1997), but they are supportive of egalitarian families in which husbands and wives share power and respect. It is untrue to say that most feminists oppose the notion of the family—they oppose the notion of an unequal family.

Another accusation made by some antifeminists is that feminists hate men. While it is true that many feminists object to male power which has oppressed women in the workplace, government, education, and the home (Johnson, 1997), an objection to male *privilege* should not be confused with an objection to men per se.

Sadly, these antifeminist beliefs not only dangerously distort the truth but also discredit feminist ideology. Given that most North Americans are strongly profamily and that males have high status and respect within society, the depiction of feminists as antifamily male-bashers sets them up for ridicule and makes it easier to dismiss their beliefs as extremist. What are your thoughts on feminism? Perform Get Involved 16.2 to reassess your views.

GET INVOLVED **16.2**

How Do You View Feminism?

Answer the following questions without looking back at the answers you gave in Chapter 1.

First, indicate which of the following categories best characterizes your identity as a feminist.

(a) consider myself a feminist and am currently involved in the Women's Movement

(b) consider myself a feminist but am not involved in the Women's Movement

(c) do not consider myself a feminist but agree with at least some of the objectives of feminism

(d) do not consider myself a feminist and disagree with the objectives of feminism

Second, on a scale from 1 (strongly disagree) to 6 (strongly agree), indicate the extent to which you disagree or agree with each of the following statements.

1. Women should be considered as seriously as men as candidates for the Presidency of the United States.

2. Although women can be good leaders, men make better leaders.

3. A woman should have the same job opportunities as a man.

4. Men should respect women more than they currently do.

5. Many women in the work force are taking jobs away from men who need the jobs more.

6. Doctors need to take women's health concerns more seriously.

7. Women have been treated unfairly on the basis of their gender throughout most of human history.

8. Women are already given equal opportunities with men in all important sectors of their lives.

9. Women in the U.S. are treated as second-class citizens.

10. Women can best overcome discrimination by doing the best they can at their jobs, not by wasting time with political activity.

Based on Morgan, (1996).

What Does It Mean?

Before computing your score for the 10 items, reverse the points for statements 2, 5, 8, and 10. That is, for a rating of "1" (strongly disagree), give 6 points, for a rating of "2", give 5 points, and so on. Then sum the points for the 10 items. Note that higher scores reflect greater agreement with feminist beliefs.

1. Compare your feminist identification (Part I) here with your feminist identifi-

cation at the beginning of the course (see Get Involved 1.1). If there has been a change, explain why.

2. Compare your feminist beliefs at the two points in time. If there has been a change, explain why. What specific course material, if any, contributed to this change?

Feminist Identification

According to a recent CBS News poll (Boxer, 1997) and studies of college students (Nelson, Shanahan, & Olivetti, 1997; Williams & Wittig, 1997), only about 25 percent of American women label themselves as feminists, and the percentage of men is even lower (Nelson et al., 1997). Further, the little research available comparing the attitudes of women of different ethnicities, indicates that college women of color are less likely than White college women to label themselves as feminists (Myaskovsky & Wittig, 1997). As stated earlier, the feminist movement has been dominated by White women, and many women of color feel that feminists do not have an interest in their unique experiences and concerns (Myaskovsky & Wittig, 1997). Some women of color, therefore, have embraced woman of color feminism, a form of feminism that addresses racism and other issues of importance to ethnic minority females (see Chapter 1). Rachel Williams and Michele Wittig (1997) see another problem for some women of color—the perception of conflict between the values embraced by their ethnic group and values associated with feminist ideology. These scholars suggest that Asian American and Latina women may feel torn between the more patriarchal belief system of their cultures and the feminist value of egalitarianism.

Interestingly, many women who reject the feminist label, support the goals of feminism (Williams & Wittig, 1997) and believe the women's movement has been a positive force in society (Boxer, 1997). How can these discrepancies between a feminist identification and views about feminist goals or the feminist movement be explained? First, women may be concerned about negative images that some people attach to feminism and feminists. At a personal level, they might want to avoid a negative self-image which they believe would result from identifying themselves with a term that has negative connotations. At a public level they might fear the social disapproval that could follow from their identification as a feminist (Williams & Wittig, 1997). Some of these negative images are illustrated by the following definitions of feminists offered by college students. One student stated, "Feminism is the way females act to lash out at society. They become uptight about men holding doors open for them and yell about equal rights too much!!" (Jackson, Fleury, & Lewandowski, 1996, p. 690). A different negative image, that of feminists as man-haters (Williams & Wittig, 1997) is illustrated by another student's definition of feminism as "opposing the male sex and it's usually rude and crude sarcastic remarks, papers, or books" (Jackson et al., 1996, p. 690).

A second reason that some women refuse to identify as feminists despite their agreement with many feminist goals is that they do not believe women are oppressed or that economic and political systems need to be changed (Nelson, Shanahan, & Olivetti, 1997). Although they value equality of power and opportunity, they believe women have already attained this equality. One study of college women (Foster, 1999) found an association between students' belief that women are disadvantaged relative to men and their participation in activities that enhance the status of women (e.g., talking about women's issues with others, attending talks on women's issues, joining protests). Women who perceived fewer gender differences in social conditions were less likely to be involved in activism.

A third reason some women do not label themselves as feminists is because they believe that a feminist identification implies collective action, but favor individual efforts, rather than group-based actions, for achieving greater power (Williams & Wittig, 1997).

Women's Studies Courses and Feminist Beliefs

According to the Constitution of the National Women's Studies Association (in Bargad & Hyde, 1991), women's studies courses help foster feminist goals by providing students with the knowledge to transform society. How effective have these courses been? Similar to Rachel's experience described in the opening vignette, results from several studies have shown that undergraduate women's studies courses are instrumental in decreasing gender-stereotypic attitudes (e.g., Canetto & Gale, 1997; Harris, Melaas, & Rodacker, 1999; Wilson, 1997), and both undergraduate women's studies courses and graduate gender-sensitive psychology training programs are helpful in increasing commitment to feminism (Thomsen, Basu, & Reinitz, 1995; Worell, Stilwell, Oakley, & Robinson, 1999). Furthermore, Jayne Stake and her colleagues (Stake, Roades, Rose, Ellis, & West, 1994) found, women's studies courses can encourage activism. Their investigations showed that students who took a women's studies course, compared to those who did not, became more active in feminist activities and made more changes in their own roles and/or ways of interacting with others. Moreover, these changes lasted over time (Stake & Rose, 1994). To assess your own involvement in feminist activism, try Get Involved 16.3.

Postscript

We end this exploration of women's lives with two cautionary notes. First, when thinking about the material in this text, keep in mind that the knowledge we have about the psychology of women is situated in a particular time in history; it is strongly connected to existing societal attitudes and to current political, economic, and legal events. Due to economic and attitudinal changes in the last decades of the twentieth century, for example, a major concern for many married mothers at the turn of the century is the balancing of work and family, but this issue would have been irrelevant to stay-at-home mothers in the 1960s. We can expect that some of the information presented here will become obsolete over time. In fact, if women are successful in their efforts, if legislative initiatives and workplace policies address gender inequities in power and opportunities, and if gender roles become more flexible, some current problems, such as wage differentials and sexual harassment, will, hopefully, be eliminated.

GET INVOLVED **16.3**

How Involved in Feminist Activism Are You?

Check each of the following 8 activities you engaged in during the six months prior to the beginning of this semester. Then check each activity you engaged in during this semester.

Before   *During*

____ kept informed on women's rights issues   ____

____ talked with others to influence their attitudes about women's rights issues   ____

____ signed a petition related to women's rights   ____

____ attended a march, rally, or protest related to women's rights   ____

____ wrote letters to politicians or newspapers about women's rights issues   ____

____ contributed money to a women's rights cause or to politicians who supported such causes   ____

____ circulated a petition about a women's right cause   ____

____ worked for a phone bank, letter writing campaign, or political campaign in the cause of women's rights   ____

____ participated in other activity related to women's rights   ____

Based on Stake, Roades, Rose, Ellis, & West, (1994).

What Does It Mean?

1. Has there been an increase in your feminist activities due to this course? If yes, indicate some of the information you learned that contributed to this change.
2. Which of the following types of activities do you believe is the preferable route toward increased rights and opportunities for women: individual effort alone or individual effort combined with collective action? Explain your answer.

Second, as discussed in Chapter 1, teaching does not take place in an ideological vacuum. Even if not explicitly stated, a particular set of values underlies all scholarly research, textbooks, and course content, and this book is no exception. Our feminist values served as the basis for our examination of the lives of girls and women. Regardless of your own commitment to these beliefs, we hope your exploration of the psychology of women has been an enriching experience and that you have achieved an increased understanding of the negative effects of male privilege, a greater appreciation of women's diversity, and a greater awareness of the role interpersonal and societal forces play in shaping gender-based attitudes, behaviors, and goals. And, we sincerely hope you apply what you have learned from this text and course to other academic interests, career pursuits, your own experiences, and perhaps to societal change.

SUMMARY

1. Greater gender equality of organizational and interpersonal power would benefit women in several ways, by increasing opportunities in the workplace, by giving women a greater voice in dating relationships, by creating a more equitable division of household labor, and by reducing intimate violence. It is essential that increases in women's power benefit all women, regardless of ethnicity, class, disability/ability, sexual orientation, or age.

2. The benefits of a flexible construction of gender include behavior and role choices that reflect individual preferences instead of social expectations as well as a reduction in sexual harassment and acquaintance rape.

3. Several actions can facilitate the achievement of these goals including a diversity-oriented psychology of women that can inform about the role of male privilege and the constraints of rigid gender roles and that can enhance our understanding of diversity and increase tolerance.

4. Raising-gender flexible children would free people to make personally appropriate choices, rather than those based on gender-role expectations. Additionally, it would help foster greater appreciation of women's traditional roles and lessen the tendency to evaluate others on the basis of their conformity to gender expectations.

5. Interventions by educational, religious, and health care institutions, as well as the media, can address violence against women.

6. Some women believe that they can enhance their own lives more through their individual efforts than as a result of collective action.

7. Many feminists believe that improvement of the lives of women requires collective action. However, the feminist movement has been focused more on the lives of privileged women than on those who experience double and triple jeopardies stemming from racism, classism, homophobia, and/or ableism.

8. North Americans have mixed views about the value of feminism. Some believe it has helped women. Others believe that feminists are responsible for many personal and social problems.

9. Only 25 percent of American women label themselves as feminists. Some of the women who do not identity themselves as feminists support the goals of feminism. Reasons for this discrepancy include negative images of feminists, the assumption that women have already attained power equality, and the belief that feminism implies collective action.

10. Women's studies courses tend to decrease students' gender-stereotypic attitudes and increase their commitment to feminism and activism.

WHAT DO YOU THINK?

1. The text presented greater equality of power and greater flexibility in the construction of gender as beneficial to girls and women. Do you think there are any disadvantages for females associated with these goals? In what ways would these goals benefit males? In what ways might they be detrimental to males?

2. Which one or more of the various strategies for improving women's lives do you think would be most effective? Explain your answer.

IF YOU WANT TO KNOW MORE

Johnson, A. G. (1997). *The gender knot: Unraveling our patriarchal legacy*. Philadelphia: Temple University Press.

Maglin, N. B., & Perry, D. (Eds.). (1996). *"Bad girls"/"Good girls": Women, sex and power in the nineties*. New Brunswick, NJ: Rutgers University Press.

REFERENCES

Abbassi, V. (1998). Growth and normal puberty. *Pediatrics, 101 (Suppl. 2)*, 507–511.

Abbey, A., Ross, L. T., McDuffie, D., & McAuslan, P. (1996). Alcohol and dating risk factors for sexual assault among college women. *Psychology of Women Quarterly, 20*, 147–169.

Abma, J. C., Chandra, A., Mosher, W. D., Peterson, L., & Piccinino, L. (1997). Fertility, family planning and women's health: New data from the 1995 National Survey of Family Growth. *National Center for Health Statistics. Vital Statistics, 23* (19).

Academe: Bulletin of the American Association of University Professors, 84. (1998, March–April). Washington, DC: AAUP.

Achievements in public health, 1900–1999: Family planning (1999, December 3). *Morbidity and Mortality Weekly Report, 48*, 1073–1080.

Acitelli, L. K. (1992). Gender differences in relationship awareness and marital satisfaction among young married couples. *Personality and Social Psychology Bulletin, 18*, 102–110.

Adams, D. L. (Ed.). (1995). *Health issues for women of color: A cultural diversity perspective*. Thousand Oaks, CA: Sage.

Adams, R. G. (1997). Friendship patterns among older women. In J. M. Coyle (Ed.), *Handbook on women and aging* (pp. 400–417). Westport, CT: Greenwood.

Adams, S., Kuebli, J., Boyle, P. A., & Fivush, R. (1995). Gender differences in parent-child conversations about past emotions: A longitudinal investigation. *Sex Roles, 33*, 309–323.

Adelman, C. (1999). *Answers in the tool box: Academic intensity, attendance patterns, and bachelor's degree attainment*. Jessup, MD: U.S. Department of Education.

Adelmann, P. K. (1993). Psychological well-being and homemaker vs. retiree identity among older women. *Sex Roles, 29*, 195–212.

Ader, D. N., & Johnson, S. B. (1994). Sample description, reporting, and analysis of sex in psychological research: A look at APA and APA division journals in 1990. *American Psychologist, 49*, 216–218.

Adler, N. E., & Smith, L. B. (1998). Abortion. In E. A. Blechman & K. D. Brownell (Eds.), *Behavioral medicine and women: A comprehensive handbook* (pp. 510–514). New York: Guilford.

Adler, T. (1991, December). Abuse within families emerging from closet. *APA Monitor*, p. 16.

Adler, T. (1992, February). For depressed elderly, drugs advised. *APA Monitor*, pp. 16–17.

Administration on Aging. (1998). *The National Elder Abuse Incidence Study*. Washington, DC: Author.

AFL-CIO & the Institute for Women's Policy Research. (1999). *Equal pay for working families: National and state data on the pay gap and its costs*. Washington, DC: Author.

Agency for Health Care Policy and Research. (1998). *AHCPR women's health highlights* (No. 98-P004). Rockville, MD: Author.

Ahrens, J. A., & O'Brien, K. M. (1996). Predicting gender-role attitudes in adolescent females: Ability, agency, and parental factors. *Psychology of Women Quarterly, 20*, 409–417.

Alan Guttmacher Institute. (2000). *Induced abortion*. New York: Author.

Alan Guttmacher Institute. (1998). *Into a new world: Young women's sexual and reproductive lives*. New York: Author.

Alan Guttmacher Institute. (1999a). *Teen sex and pregnancy*. New York: Author.

Alan Guttmacher Institute. (1999b). *Teenage pregnancy: Overall trends and state-by-state information*. New York: Author.

Aldous, J., Mulligan, G. M., & Bjarnason, T. (1998). Fathering over time: What makes the difference? *Journal of Marriage and the Family, 60*, 809–820.

Alfieri, T., Ruble, D. N., & Higgins, E. T. (1996). Gender stereotypes during adolescence: Developmental changes and the transition to junior high school. *Developmental Psychology, 32*, 1129–1137.

Allan, K., & Coltrane, S. (1996). Gender displaying television commercials: A comparative study of television commercials in the 1950s and 1980s. *Sex Roles, 35*, 185–203.

Allen, B. A. (1996). Staying within the academy. In K. F. Wyche & F. J. Crosby (Eds.), *Women's ethnicities: Journeys through psychology* (pp. 9–26). Boulder, CO: Westview.

Allen, J. P., Philliber, S., Herrling, S., & Kuperminc, G. P. (1997). Preventing teen pregnancy and academic failure: Experimental evaluation of a developmentally based approach. *Child Development, 64,* 729–742.

Allen, K. R., & Chin-Sang, V. (1990). A lifetime of work: The context and meanings of leisure for aging black women. *Gerontologist, 30,* 734–740.

Allen, P. G. (1990). Violence and the American Indian woman. *The speaking profits us: Violence in the lives of women of color.* Seattle, WA: SAFECO Insurance Company.

Alsaker, F. D. (1995). Timing of puberty and reactions to pubertal change. In M. Rutter (Ed.), *Psychosocial disturbances in young people: Challenges for prevention* (pp. 37–82). Cambridge, England: Cambridge University Press.

Altman, L. K. (1995, December 3). *Lumpectomy backed in 3 cancer reports.* New York Times, p. Y18.

Altman, L. K. (1997, June 22). Is the longer life the healthier one? *New York Times,* p. WH158.

Altman, L. K. (1998a, May 18). Drug shown to shrink tumors in type of breast cancer by targeting gene defect. *New York Times,* p. A12.

Altman, L. K. (1998b, April 7). Researchers find the first drug known to prevent breast cancer. New York Times, pp. A1, A19.

Altman, L. K. (1998c, April 21). Studies show another drug can prevent breast cancer. *New York Times,* p. A16.

Altman, L. K. (1999a, August 31). Focusing on prevention in fight against AIDS. *New York Times,* p. F5.

Altman, L. K. (1999b, July 15). New means found for reducing AIDS passed to fetus. *New York Times,* pp. A1, A14.

Amato, P. A., & Keith, B. (1991a). Parental divorce and adult well-being: A meta-analysis. *Journal of Marriage and the Family, 53,* 43–58.

Amato, P. A., & Keith, B. (1991b). Parental divorce and child well-being: A meta-analysis. *Psychological Bulletin, 110,* 26–46.

American Academy of Pediatrics. (1999). Contraception and adolescents. *Pediatrics, 104,* 1161–1166.

American Association of Retired Persons (AARP). (1992). *Hormone replacement therapy: Facts to help you decide.* Washington, DC: Author.

American Association of Retired Persons. (1993). *The suicide rate of older men and women: How you can help prevent a tragedy.* Washington, DC: Author.

American Association of Retired Persons. (1995a). *A profile of older Americans.* Washington, DC: Author.

American Association of Retired Persons. (1995b). *Women's issues.* Washington, DC: Author.

American Association of Retired Persons. (1999a). *A profile of older Americans: 1999.* Washington, DC: Author.

American Association of Retired Persons. (1999b). *Sex—What's age got to do with it?* Washington, DC: Author.

American Association of University Women. (1992). *How schools shortchange women: The AAUW Report.* Washington, DC: AAUW Educational Foundation.

American Association of University Women. (1998). *Gender gaps: Where schools still fail our children.* Washington, DC: AAUW Educational Foundation.

American Association of University Women (2000). *Tech-savvy: Educating girls in the new computer age.* Washington, DC: AAUW Educational Foundation.

American Cancer Society. (1998). *Cancer risk report.* Atlanta, GA: Authors.

American Cancer Society. (1999a). *Breast cancer: Treatment guidelines for patients.* Atlanta, GA: Author.

American Cancer Society. (1999b). *For women facing breast cancer.* Atlanta, GA: Author.

American College of Obstetricians and Gynecologists. (1997a). *Hormone replacement therapy.* Washington, DC: Author.

American College of Obstetricians and Gynecologists. (1997b). *The menopause years.* Washington, DC: Author.

American College of Obstetricians and Gynecologists. (1997c). *Preventing osteoporosis.* Washington, DC: Author.

American Heart Association. (1997). *Silent epidemic: The truth about women, heart disease, and stroke.* Dallas, TX: Author.

American Psychiatric Association. (1994). *Diagnostic and statistical manual of mental disorders* (4th ed.). Washington, DC: Author.

American Psychological Association. (1975). Report of the Task Force on Sex Bias and Sex-Role Stereotyping in Psychotherapeutic Practice. *American Psychologist, 30,* 1169–1175.

American Psychological Association. (1994). *Publication manual of the American Psychological Association* (4th ed.). Washington, DC: American Psychological Association.

American Psychological Association. (1999a). *Elder abuse and neglect: In search of solutions.* Washington, DC: Author.

American Psychological Association. (1999b). *Women in the American Psychological Association.* Washington, DC: Author.

Ames, K. (1992, September 14). Cheaper by the dozen. *Newsweek,* pp. 52–53.

Ammerman, R. T., & Hersen, M. (Eds.). (1993). *Assessment of family violence: A clinical and legal sourcebook.* New York: Wiley-Interscience.

Andersen, B. L. (1993). Cancer. In C. Niven & D. Carroll (Eds.), *The health psychology of women* (pp. 75–89). Chur, Switzerland: Harwood Academic.

Andersen, B. L., & Emery, C. (1999, August). *Biobehavioral model of cancer stress: Psychological, behavioral, and biological responses.* Paper presented at the meeting of the American Psychological Association, Boston.

Andersen, R. E., et al. (1999). Effects of lifestyle activity vs. structured aerobic exercise in obese women. *Journal of the American Medical Association, 281,* 335–340.

Anderson, K. B., Cooper, H., & Okamura, L. (1997). Individual differences and attitudes toward rape: A meta-analytic review. *Personality and Social Psychology Bulletin, 23,* 295–315.

Anderson, K. J., & Leaper, C. (1998). Meta-analyses of gender effects on conversational interruption: Who, what, when, where, and how. *Sex Roles, 39,* 225–252.

Angell, M. (1997, April 25). Pregnant at 63? Why not? *New York Times,* p. A27.

Angier, N. (1994, May 3). Male hormone molds women, too, in mind and body. *New York Times,* pp. C1, 13.

Angier, N. (1997a, June 22). Drugs for depression multiply and so do the hard questions. *New York Times,* p. WH11.

Angier, N. (1997b, February 17). In a culture of hysterectomies, many question their necessity. *New York Times,* pp. A1, A10.

Angier, N. (1998, June 21). Men. Are women better off with them or without them? *New York Times,* p. WH10.

Angier, N. (1999a, February 21). Men, women, sex and Darwin. *New York Times Magazine,* pp. 48–53.

Angier, N. (1999b, February 17). Why men don't last: Self-destruction as a way of life. *New York Times,* p. D8.

Annie E. Casey Foundation. (1999). *When teens have sex: Issues and trends.* Baltimore, MD: Author.

Apter, T. (1996). Paths of development in midlife women. *Feminism & Psychology, 6,* 557–562.

Arbona, C., & Novy, D. M. (1991). Career aspirations and expectations of Black, Mexican American, and White students. *The Career Development Quarterly, 39,* 231–239.

Archer, S. L. (1992). A feminist's approach to identity research. In G. R. Adams, T. P. Gullotta, & R. Montemayor (Eds.), *Adolescent identity formation* (pp. 25–49). Newberry Park, CA: Sage.

Archer, S. L. (1993). Identity in relational contexts: A methodological proposal. In J. Krogers (Ed.), *Discussion on ego identity* (pp. 75–99). Hillsdale, NJ: Erlbaum.

Arellano, C. M., Kuhn, J. A., & Chavez, E. L. (1997). Psychosocial correlates of sexual assault among Mexican American and White non-Hispanic adolescent females. *Hispanic Journal of Behavioral Sciences, 19,* 446–460.

Are you getting enough fiber? (1999). *Journal of the American Medical Association, 281,* 602.

Armistead, L., Forehand, R., Steele, R., & Kotchick, B. (1998). Pediatric AIDS. In T. H. Ollendick & M. Hersen (Eds.), *Handbook of child psychopathology* (3rd ed., pp. 463–481). New York: Plenum.

Arnold, K. D. (1993). Academically talented women in the 1970s: The Illinois Valedictorian Project. In K. D. Hulbert, & D. Tickton (Eds.), *Women's lives through time* (pp. 393–414). San Francisco: Jossey-Bass.

Asch, A., & Fine, M. (1992). Beyond pedestals: Revisiting the lives of women with disabilities. In M. Fine (Ed.), *Disruptive voices: The possibilities of feminist research* (pp. 139–171). Ann Arbor, MI: University of Michigan Press.

Askham, J. (1995). The married lives of older people. In S. Arber & J. Ginn (Eds.), *Connecting gender and ageing* (pp. 87–97). Philadelphia: Open University Press.

Assisted reproduction: Who is the mother? (1999). *New England Journal of Medicine, 340,* 650–657.

Astin, A. W. (1993). *What matters in college?* San Francisco: Jossey-Bass.

Awards for Distinguished Scientific Contribution (1998). *American Psychologist, 53,* 365–372.

Azar, B. (1997, October). More study needed on hormone replacement. *APA Monitor,* p. 33.

Azar, S. T., Ferraro, M. H., & Breton, S. J. (1998). Intrafamilial child maltreatment. In T. H. Ollendick

& M. Hersen (Eds.), *Handbook of child psychopathology* (3rd ed., pp. 483–504). New York: Plenum.

Badger, K., Craft, R. C., & Jensen, L. (1998). Age and gender differences in value orientation among American adolescents. *Adolescence, 33,* 591–596.

Baenninger, M. (1997, April). *Sex-related differences in the development of spatial ability.* Paper presented at the meeting of the Society for Research in Child Development, Washington, DC.

Baenninger, M., & Newcombe, N. (1989). The role of experience in spatial test performance: A meta-analysis. *Sex Roles, 20,* 327–344.

Bailey, J. M., Pillard, R. C., Neale, M. C., & Agyei, Y. (1993). Heritable factors influence sexual orientation in women. *Archives of General Psychiatry, 48,* 1089–1096.

Bandura, A. (1965). Influence of model's reinforcement contingencies on the acquisition of imitative responses. *Journal of Personality and Social Psychology, 1,* 589–595.

Bandura, A. (1969). Social-learning theory of identificatory processes. In D. A. Goslin (Ed.), *Handbook of socialization theory and research* (pp. 213–262). Chicago: Rand McNally.

Bank, B. J. (1995). Gendered accounts: Undergraduates explain why they seek their bachelor's degree. *Sex Roles, 32,* 527–544.

Banks, A., & Gartrell, N. K. (1995). Hormones and sexual orientation: A questionable link. *Journal of Homosexuality, 28,* 247–268.

Baram, D. A. (1997). Physiology and symptoms of menopause. In D. E. Stewart & G. E. Robinson (Eds.), *A clinician's guide to menopause* (pp. 9–28). Washington, DC: Health Press International.

Bargad, A., & Hyde, J. S. (1991). Women's studies: A study of feminist identity development in women. *Psychology of Women Quarterly, 15,* 181–201.

Barker, K. (1993). Changing assumptions and contingent solutions: The costs and benefits of women working full- and part-time. *Sex Roles, 28,* 47–71.

Barnard, N. D., Scialli, A. R., Hurlock, D., & Bertron, P. (2000). Diet and sex-hormone binding globulin, dysmenorrhea, and premenstrual symptoms. *Obstetrics & Gynecology, 95,* 240–244.

Barnes-Farrell J. J., Bridges, J. S., Davis, M. A., & McInerney, Z. M. E. (1999). *Effects of the parent and adult caregiving roles on employed women's and men's role strain.* Unpublished manuscript, University of Connecticut at Hartford.

Barnett, O. W., Miller-Perrin, C. L., & Perrin, R. D. (1997). *Family violence across the lifespan: An introduction.* Thousand Oaks, CA: Sage.

Barnett, R. C., & Baruch, G. K. (1985). Women's involvement in multiple roles and psychological distress. *Journal of Personality and Social Psychology, 49,* 135–145.

Barnett, R. C., & Rivers, C. (1996). *She works, he works: How two-income families are happy, healthy, and thriving.* Cambridge, MA: Harvard University Press.

Baron, L., & Straus, M. (1989). *Four theories of rape in American society: A state-level analysis.* New Haven, CT: Yale University Press.

Baron, R. S., Burgess, M. L., & Kao, C. F. (1991). Detecting and labeling prejudice: Do female perpetrators go undetected? *Personality and Social Psychology Bulletin, 17,* 115–123.

Baron, S., & Welty, A. (1996). Elder abuse. *Journal of Gerontological Social Work, 25,* 33–57.

Barongan, C., & Hall, G. C. N. (1995). The influence of misogynous rap music on sexual aggression against women. *Psychology of Women Quarterly, 19,* 195–207.

Barringer, F. (1992, May 7). Insurance gap is seen among older women. *New York Times,* p. A8.

Bartko, W. T., & McHale, S. M. (1991). The household labor of children from dual- versus single-earner families. In J. V. Lerner & N. L. Galambos (Eds.), *Employed mothers and their children* (pp. 159–179). New York: Garland.

Basow, S. A. (1992). *Gender stereotypes and roles* (3rd ed.). Pacific Grove, CA: Brooks-Cole.

Basow, S. A., & Rubin, L. R. (1999). Gender influences on adolescent development. In N. G. Johnson, M. C. Roberts, & J. Worell (Eds.), *Beyond appearance: A new look at adolescent girls* (pp. 25–52). Washington, DC: American Psychological Association.

Bass, E., & Davis, L. (1994). *The courage to heal* (3rd ed.). New York: HarperCollins.

Bassuk, E. L. (1993). Social and economic hardships of homeless and other poor women. *American Journal of Orthopsychiatry, 63,* 340–347.

Bauer, P. J., Liebl, M., & Stennes, L. (1998). Pretty is to dress as brave is to suitcoat: Gender-based property-to-property inferences by 4-year-old children. *Merrill-Palmer Quarterly, 44,* 355–377.

Baxter, J. (1992). Power attitudes and time: The domestic division of labor. *Journal of Comparative Family Studies, 23,* 165–182.

Baydar, N., & Brooks-Gunn, J. (1998). Profiles of grandmothers who help care for their grandchildren in the United States. *Family Relations, 47,* 385–393.

Bazzini, D. G., McIntosh, W. D., Smith, S. M., Cook, S., & Harris, C. (1997). The aging woman in popular film: Underrepresented, unattractive, unfriendly, and unintelligent. *Sex Roles, 36,* 531–543.

Beardstown Ladies Investment Club. (1994). *The Beardstown Ladies common sense investment guide: How we beat the stock market and how you can too.* New York: Hyperion.

Beaton, A. M., Tougas, F., & Joly, S. (1996). Neosexism among male managers: Is it a matter of numbers? *Journal of Applied Social Psychology, 26,* 2189–2203.

Beckett, J., & Smith, A. (1981). Work and family roles: Egalitarian marriage in black and white families. *Social Service Review, 55,* 314–326.

Beckman, L., & Harvey, M. (Eds.). (1998). *The new civil war: The psychology, culture, and politics of abortion.* Washington, DC: American Psychological Association.

Beckman, L. J. (1999, August). *Women's health and the psychology, culture, and politics of abortion.* Paper presented at the meeting of the American Psychological Association, Boston.

Bedford, V. H. (1995). Sibling relationships in middle and old age. In R. Blieszner & V. H. Bedford (Eds.), *Handbook of aging and the family* (pp. 201–222). Westport, CT: Greenwood.

Bee, H. L. (2000). *The journey of adulthood* (4th ed.). Upper Saddle River, NJ: Prentice-Hall.

Begley, S. (1999, Spring/Summer). Understanding perimenopause. *Newsweek,* pp. 31–33.

Belansky, E. S., Early, D. M., & Eccles, J. S. (1993, March). *The impact of mothers and peers on adolescents' gender role traditionality and plans for the future.* Paper presented at the meeting of the Society for Research in Child Development, New Orleans.

Belkin, L. (1997, October 26). Pregnant with complications. *New York Times Magazine,* pp. 34–39, 48–49, 67–68.

Bellamy, C. (1999). *The state of the world's children 1999.* New York: UNICEF.

Belluck, P. (1998, October 12). In small town, USA, AIDS presents new set of hardships. *New York Times,* pp. A1, A13.

Belsky, J. (1988). The "effects" of infant day care reconsidered. *Early Childhood Research Quarterly, 3,* 235–272.

Belsky, J. K. (1999). *The psychology of aging: Theory, research and interventions.* Pacific Grove, CA: Brooks-Cole.

Belsky, J., Steinberg, L., & Draper, P. (1991). Childhood experience, interpersonal development, and reproductive strategy: An evolutionary theory of socialization. *Child Development, 62,* 647–670.

Bem, S. L. (1974). The measurement of psychological androgyny. *Journal of Consulting and Clinical Psychology, 42,* 155–162.

Bem, S. L. (1975). Sex role adaptability: One consequence of psychological androgyny. *Journal of Personality and Social Psychology, 31,* 634–643.

Bem, S. L. (1981). Gender schema theory: A cognitive account of sex typing. *Psychological Review, 88,* 354–364.

Bem, S. L. (1983). Gender schema theory and its implications for child development: Raising gender-aschematic children in a gender-schematic society. *Signs, 8,* 598–616.

Bem, S. L. (1993). *The lenses of gender: Transforming the debate on sexual inequality.* New Haven, CT: Yale University Press.

Benbow, C. P., & Arjmond, O. (1990). Predictors of high academic achievement in mathematics and science by mathematically talented students: A longitudinal study. *Journal of Eductional Psychology, 82,* 430–441.

Benbow, C. P., & Stanley, J. C. (1980). Sex differences in mathematical ability: Fact or artifact? *Science, 210,* 1262–1264.

Benenson, J. F., Morash D., & Petrakos, H. (1998). Gender differences in emotional closeness between preschool children and their mothers. *Sex Roles, 38,* 975–985.

Bengston, V., Rosenthal, C., & Burton, L. (1996). Paradoxes of family and aging. In R. H. Binstock & L. K. George (Eds.), *Handbook of aging and the social sciences* (4th ed., pp. 253–282). New York: Springer.

Bennet, J. (1992a, October 10). Hidden malnutrition worsens health of elderly. *New York Times,* pp. A1, A10.

Bennet, J. (1992b, October 2). More and more, elderly find themselves taking care of their parents. *New York Times,* p. A21.

Bennett, L., & Fineran, S. (1998). Sexual and severe physical violence among high school students: Power beliefs, gender and relationship. *American Journal of Orthopsychiatry, 68,* 645–652.

Beral, V., et al. (1999). Mortality associated with oral contraceptive use: 25 year follow up of cohort of 46,000 women from Royal College of General Practitioners' oral contraception study. *British Medical Journal, 318,* 96–100.

Beren, S. E., Hayden, H. A., Wilfley, D. E., & Striegel-Moore, R. H. (1997). Body dissatisfaction among lesbian college students. *Psychology of Women Quarterly, 21,* 431–445.

Berenbaum, S. A. (1999). Effects of early androgens on sex-typed activities and interests in adolescents with congenital adrenal hyperplasia. *Hormones and Behavior, 35,* 102–110.

Berenbaum, S. A., Duck, S. C., & Bryk, K. (2000). Behavioral effects of prenatal *versus* postnatal androgen excess in children with 21-hydroxylase-deficient congenital adrenal hyperplasia. *Journal of Clinical Endocrinology & Metabolism, 85,* 727–733.

Berenbaum, S. A., & Hines, M. (1992). Early androgens are related to childhood sex-typed toy preferences. *Psychological Science, 3,* 203–206.

Berenbaum, S. A., Korman, K., & Leveroni, C. (1995). Early hormones and sex differences in cognitive abilities [Special issue]. *Learning and Individual Differences, 7,* 303–321.

Berenbaum, S. A., & Resnick, S. M. (1997). Early androgen effects on aggression in children and adults with congenital adrenal hyperplasia. *Psychoneuroendocrinology, 22,* 505–515.

Bergen, D. J., & Williams, J. E. (1991). Sex stereotypes in the United States revisited: 1972–1988. *Sex Roles, 24,* 413–423.

Berger, A. (1999, May 25). What stress can mean to teen-age girls. *New York Times,* p. D8.

Berger, P. S., Cook, A. S., DelCampo, R. L., Herrera, R. S., & Weigel, R. R. (1994). Family/work roles' relation to perceived stress: Do gender and ethnicity matter? *Journal of Family and Economic Issues, 15,* 223–241.

Bergeron, S. M., & Senn, C. Y. (1998). Body image and sociocultural norms: A comparison of heterosexual and lesbian women. *Sex Roles, 22,* 385–401.

Bergum, V. (1997). *A child on her mind: The experience of becoming a mother.* Westport, CT: Bergin & Garvey.

Berk, L. E., Wholeben, B. M., & Bouchey, H. A. (1998). *Instructors resource manual for Berk, L. E. (1998). Development through the lifespan.* Boston: Allyn & Bacon.

Bernstein, N. (1999, January 16). Lawsuit says gay youths in foster care are abused. *New York Times,* p. A16.

Bertakis, K. D. (1998). Physician gender and physician-patient interaction. In E. A. Blechman & K. D. Brownell (Eds.), *Behavioral medicine and women: A comprehensive handbook* (pp. 849–853). New York: Guilford.

Berthiaume, M., David, H., Saucier, J. F., & Borgeat, F. (1996). Correlates of gender role orientation during pregnancy and the postpartum. *Sex Roles, 35,* 781–800.

Best, D. L., & Williams, J. E. (1993). A cross-cultural viewpoint. In A. E. Beall & R. J. Sternberg (Eds.), *The psychology of gender* (pp. 215–248). New York: Guilford.

Betz, N. E. (1994). Basic issues and concepts in career counseling for women. In W. B. Walsh & S. H. Osipow (Eds.), *Career counseling for women* (pp. 1–41). Hillsdale, NJ: Erlbaum.

Betz, N. E., & Hackett, G. (1997). Applications of self-efficacy theory to the career assessment of women. *Journal of Cancer Assessment, 5,* 383–402.

Beyer, S. (1990). Gender differences in the accuracy of self-evaluations of performance. *Journal of Personality and Social Psychology, 59,* 960–970.

Beyer, S. (1997, June). *Gender differences in causal attributions of imagined performance on English, history, and math exams.* Paper presented at the meeting of the American Psychological Society, Washington, DC.

Beyer, S. (1999). Gender differences in the accuracy of grade expectancies and evaluations. *Sex Roles, 41,* 279–296.

Beyer, S., & Bowden, E. M. (1997). Gender differences in self-perceptions: Convergent evidence from three measures of accuracy and bias. *Personality and Social Psychology Bulletin, 23,* 157–172.

Bianchi, S. M., & Robinson, J. (1997). What did you do today? Children's use of time, family composition, and the acquisition of social capital. *Journal of Marriage and the Family, 59,* 332–344.

Biernat, M. (1991). A multicomponent, developmental analysis of sex typing. *Sex Roles, 24,* 567–586.

Biernat, M., & Wortman, C. B. (1991). Sharing of home responsibilities between professionally employed women and their husbands. *Journal of Personality and Social Psychology, 60,* 844–860.

Billy, J. O. G., Brewster, K. L., & Grady, W. R. (1994). Contextual effects on the sexual behavior of adolescent women. *Journal of Marriage and the Family, 56,* 387–404.

Bingham, C. R., Miller, B. C., & Adams, G. R. (1990). Correlates of age at first sexual intercourse in a national sample of young women. *Journal of Adolescent Research, 5,* 18–33.

Bingham, R. P., & Ward, C. M. (1994). Career counseling with ethnic minority women. In W. B. Walsh & S. H. Osipow (Eds.), *Career counseling for women* (pp. 165–195). Hillsdale, NJ: Erlbaum.

Bingham, S. G., & Scherer, L. L. (1993). Factors associated with responses to sexual harassment and satisfaction with outcome. *Sex Roles, 29,* 239–269.

Binion, V. J. (1990). Psychological androgyny: A black female perspective. *Sex Roles, 22,* 487–507.

Bird, C. E., & Rogers, M. L. (1998, November). *Does the presence of children in a household lead to increased depression?: An examination of the effects of children on men's and women's depression levels.* Paper presented at Conference on Work and Family: Today's Realities and Tomorrow's Visions, Boston.

Birenbaum, M., & Kraemer, R. (1995). Gender and ethnic-group differences in causal attributions for success and failure in mathematics and language examinations. *Journal of Cross-Cultural Psychology, 26,* 342–359.

Bisagni, G. M., & Eckenrode, J. (1995). The role of work identity in women's adjustment to divorce. *American Journal of Orthopsychiatry, 65,* 574–583.

Biskupic, J. (1999, January 17). A family affair goes to court. *Washington Post,* pp. 29–30.

Bjorklund, D. F. (2000). *Children's thinking: Developmental function and individual differences* (3rd ed.) Belmont, CA: Wadsworth.

Bjorklund, D. F., & Brown, R. D. (1998). Physical play and cognitive development:Integrating activity, cognition, and education. *Child Development, 69,* 604–606.

Björkvist, K. (1994). Sex differences in physical, verbal, and indirect aggression: A review of recent research. *Sex Roles, 30,* 177–188.

Blackman, D. K., Bennett, E. M., & Miller, D. S. (1999, October 8). Trends in self-reported use of mammograms (1989–1997) and Papanicolaou tests (1991–1997)—Behavioral risk factor surveillance system. *Morbidity and Mortality Weekly Report, 48* (No. SS-6), 1–22.

Blakemore, J. E. O. (1998). The influence of gender and parental attitudes on preschool children's interest in babies: Observations in natural settings. *Sex Roles, 38,* 73–94.

Blieszner, R., Vista, P. M., & Mancine, J. A. (1996). Diversity and dynamics in late-life mother-daughter relationships. *Journal of Women and Aging, 8* (3/4), 5–24.

Blumstein, P. W., & Schwartz, P. (1993). Bisexuality: Some social psychological experiences. In L. D. Garnets & D. C. Kimmel (Eds.), *Psychological perspectives on lesbian and gay male experiences* (pp. 68–184). New York: Columbia University Press.

Boeringer, S. B. (1994). Pornography and sexual aggression: Associations of violent and nonviolent depictions with rape and rape proclivity. *Deviant Behavior, 15,* 289–304.

Bohan, J. S. (1996). *Psychology and sexual orientation.* New York: Routledge.

Bohan, J. S. (1997, August). *The psychology of women, the women of psychology: Recurring questions, persistent themes.* Paper presented at the meeting of the American Psychological Association, Chicago.

Bolger, N., & Wortman, C. (August, 1992). *Age differences in adjustment to widowhood.* Paper presented at the meeting of the American Psychological Association, Washington, DC.

Bondurant, B., & Donat, P. L. N. (1999). Perceptions of women's sexual interest and acquaintance rape. *Psychology of Women Quarterly, 23,* 691–705.

Bornstein, M. H., & Haynes, O. M. (1998). Vocabulary competence in early childhood: Measurement, latent construct, and predictive validity. *Child Development, 69,* 654–671.

Bornstein, M. H., Haynes, O. M., Pascual, L., Painter, K. M., & Galperin, C. (1999). Play in two societies: Pervasiveness of structure. *Child Development, 70,* 317–331.

Bostic, J. Q., Muriel, A. C., Hack, S., Weinstein, S., & Herzog, O. (1997). Anorexia nervosa in a 7-year-old girl. *Journal of Developmental and Behavioral Pediatrics, 18,* 331–333.

Boston Women's Health Book Collective. (1992). *The new our bodies, ourselves: A book by and for women.* New York: Touchstone.

Boston Women's Health Book Collective. (1996). *The new our bodies, ourselves.* New York: Simon & Schuster.

Boston Women's Health Book Collective. (1998). *Our bodies, ourselves for the new century: A book by and for women.* New York: Touchstone.

Bould, S., & Longino, C. F. (1997). Women survivors: The oldest old. In J. M. Coyl (Ed.), *Handbook on women and aging* (pp. 210–222). Westport, CT: Greenwood.

Bould, S., Sanborn, B., & Reif, L. (1989). *Eighty-five plus: The oldest old.* Belmont, CA: Wordsworth.

Bound, J., Schoenbaum, M., & Waidmann, T. (1996). Race differences in labor force attachment and disability status. *Gerontologist, 36,* 311–321.

Bousser, M-G. (1999). Stroke in women. *Circulation, 99*, 463–467.

Boxer, S. (1997, December 14). One casualty of the women's movement: Feminism. *New York Times*, p. WK3.

Boyatzis, C. J., Mallis, M., & Leon, I. (1999). Effects of game type on children's gender-based peer preferences: A naturalistic observational study. *Sex Roles, 40*, 93–105.

Boyer, C. B., Tschann, J. M., & Shafer, M. (1999). Predictors of risk for sexually transmitted diseases in ninth grade urban high school students. *Journal of Adolescent Research, 14*, 448–465.

Brabant, S., & Mooney, L. A. (1997). Sex role stereotyping in the Sunday comics: A twenty year update. *Sex Roles, 37*, 269–281.

Bradford, J., Ryan, C., & Rothblum, E. D. (1994). National lesbian health care survey: Implications for mental health care. *Journal of Consulting and Clinical Psychology, 62*, 228–242.

Bradford, J., & White, J. C. (2000). Lesbian health research. In M. B. Goldman & M. C. Hatch (Eds.), *Women & health* (pp. 64–78). New York: Academic Press.

Bradley, S. J., & Zucker, K. J. (1997). Gender identity disorder: A review of the past 10 years. *Journal of the American Academy of Child and Adolescent Psychiatry, 36*, 872–880.

Bradsher, J. E. (1997). Older women and widowhood. In J. M. Coyle (Ed.), *Handbook on women and aging* (pp. 112–128). Westport, CT: Greenwood.

Brandon, A. (1997, March 9). Longer, healthier, better. *New York Times Magazine*, pp. 44–45.

Brenner, O. C., & Tomkiewicz, J. (1986). Race difference in attitudes of American business school graduates toward the role of women. *Journal of Social Psychology, 126*, 251–253.

Breslow, L., & Breslow, N. (1993). Health practices and disability: Some evidence from Alameda County. *Preventative Medicine, 22*, 86–95.

Brewer, M. B., & Lui, L. L. (1989). The primacy of age and sex in the structure of person categories. *Social Cognition, 7*, 262–274.

Brick, P., & Roffman, D. M. (1998). "Abstinence, no buts" is simplistic. In D. S. DelCampo & R. L. DelCampo (Eds.), *Taking sides: Clashing views on controversial issues in childhood and society* (2nd ed., pp. 324–328). Guilford, CT: Dushkin/McGraw-Hill.

Bridges, J. S. (1987). College females' perceptions of adult roles and occupational fields for women. *Sex Roles, 16*, 591–604.

Bridges, J. S. (1989). Sex differences in occupational values. *Sex Roles, 20*, 205–211.

Bridges, J. S. (1991). Perceptions of date and stranger rape: A difference in sex role expectations and rape-supportive beliefs. *Sex Roles, 24*, 291–307.

Bridges, J. S. (1993). Pink or blue: gender-stereotypic perceptions of infants as conveyed by birth congratulations cards. *Psychology of Women Quarterly, 17*, 193–205.

Bridges, J. S., & Etaugh, C. (1995). College students' perceptions of mothers: Effects of maternal employment-childrearing pattern and motive for employment. *Sex Roles, 32*, 735–751.

Bridges, J. S., & Etaugh, C. (1996). Black and white college women's maternal employment outcome expectations and their desired timing of maternal employment. *Sex Roles, 35*, 543–562.

Bridges, J. S., & Orza, A. M. (1993). Effects of maternal employment-childrearing pattern on college students' perceptions of a mother and her child. *Psychology of Women Quarterly, 17*, 103–117.

Bridges, J. S., & Orza, A. M. (1996). Black and White employed mothers' role experiences. *Sex Roles, 35*, 377–385.

Brindis, C. (1999). Building for the future: Adolescent pregnancy prevention. *Journal of the American Medical Women's Association, 54*, 129–132.

Brinton, L. A., & Schairer, C. (1997). Post menopausal hormone-replacement therapy—Time for a reappraisal? *New England Journal of Medicine, 336*, 1821–1822.

Briton, N. J., & Hall, J. A. (1995a). Beliefs about female and male nonverbal communication. *Sex Roles, 32*, 79–90.

Briton, N. J., & Hall, J. A. (1995b). Gender-based expectancies and observer judgments of smiling. *Journal of Nonverbal Behavior, 19*, 49–65.

Brody, J. E. (1990a, February 8). Changing nutritional needs put the elderly at risk because of inadequate diets. *New York Times*, p. B13.

Brody, J. E. (1990b, August 30). Strength training for the elderly: Discovering an exhilarating road back from muscle atrophy. *New York Times*, p. B17.

Brody, J. E. (1996, August 28). With new treatments, PMS need not be the worry it was just decades ago. *New York Times*, p. C9.

Brody, J. E. (1997a, October 7). Breast cancer awareness may carry its own risks. *New York Times*, pp. B9, B17.

Brody, J. E. (1997b, August 13). Older women often get caught in a bottleneck with managed care. *New York Times*, p. B10.

Brody, J. E. (1997c, September 30). When bones are weakening, several treatments can help save them. *New York Times*, p. B15.

Brody, J. E. (1998a, March 17). Battered women face pit bulls and cobras. *New York Times*, B8–B11.

Brody, J. E. (1998b, June 23). Staying healthy with fins, fur and feathers. New York Times, p. F7.

Brody, J. E. (1998c, January 22). Study challenges idea of PMS as emotional disorder. *New York Times*, pp. A1, A18.

Brody, J. E. (1998d). Teenagers and sex: Younger and more at risk. *New York Times*, p. B15.

Brody, J. E. (1998e, March 10). Test at onset of menopause can avert bone loss. *New York Times*, p. B13.

Brody, J. E. (1999a, February 9). Americans gamble on herbs as medicine. *New York Times*, pp. D1, D7.

Brody, J. E. (1999b, February 2). Another round in drink-a-day debate. *New York Times*, p. D7.

Brody, J. E. (1999c, October 12). Coping with fear: Keeping breast cancer in perspective. *New York Times*, p. D7.

Brody, J. E. (1999d, June 8). Falls by elderly, a perilous yet preventable epidemic. *New York Times*, p. D7.

Brody, J. E. (1999e, April 20). There's plenty of choice in a diet for a healthier heart. *New York Times*, p. D7.

Brody, J. E. (1999f, November 23). Ways to tame menopausal hot flashes, without estrogen. *New York Times*, p. D7.

Brody, J. E. (1999g), November 30). Yesterday's precocious puberty is norm today. *New York Times*, p. D8.

Brody, J. E. (2000a, February 8). The fatty nut finds its place at the table. *New York Times*, p. D8.

Brody, J. E. (2000b, February 1). Hormone replacement: Weighing risks and benefits. *New York Times*, pp. D1, D3.

Brody, S. (1997). *Sex at risk*. New Brunswick, NJ: Transaction.

Broman, C. L. (1991). Gender, work-family roles, and psychological well-being of Blacks. *Journal of Marriage and the Family, 53*, 509–520.

Bronner, E. (1998a, February 1). No sexology, please. We're Americans. *New York Times*, p. WK6.

Bronner, E. (1998b, February 25). U.S. 12th graders rank poorly in math and science, study says. *New York Times*, pp. A1, C20.

Brooke, J. (1998, October 14). Homophobia often found in schools, data show. *New York Times*, p. A17.

Brooks, L., & Forrest, L. (1994). Feminism and career counseling. In W. B. Walsh & S. H. Osipow (Eds.), *Career counseling for women* (pp. 87–134). Hillsdale, NJ: Erlbaum.

Brooks, L., & Perot, A. R. (1991). Reporting sexual harassment: Exploring a predictive model. *Psychology of Women Quarterly, 15*, 31–47.

Brooks, M. G., & Buckner, J. C. (1996). Work and welfare: Job histories, barriers to employment, and predictors of work among low-income single mothers. *American Journal of Orthopsychiatry, 66*, 526–537.

Brooks-Gunn, J., & Chase-Lansdale, P. L. (1995). Adolescent parenthood. In M. Bornstein (Ed.), *Handbook of parenting* (pp. 113–150). Hillsdale, NJ: Erlbaum.

Broverman, I. K., Broverman, D. M., Clarkson, F. E., Rosenkrantz, P. S., & Vogel, S. R. (1970). Sex-role stereotypes and clinical judgements of mental health. *Journal of Consulting Psychology, 34*, 1–7.

Brown, E. R., et al. (1995, October). *Women's health-related behaviors and use of clinical preventive services: A report to the Commonwealth Fund*. Los Angeles: UCLA Center for Health Policy Research.

Brown, L. (1994). *Subversive dialogues: Theory in feminist therapy*. New York: Basic Books.

Brown, L. M., Way, N., & Duff, J. L. (1999). The others in my I: Adolescent girls' friendships and peer relations. In N. G. Johnson, M. C. Roberts, & J. Worell (Eds.), *Beyond appearance: A new look at adolescent girls* (pp. 205–225). Washington, DC: American Psychological Association.

Brown, L. S., & Brodsky, A. M. (1998). The future of feminist therapy. In D. L. Anselmi and A. L. Law (Eds.), *Questions of gender: Perspectives and paradoxes* (pp. 775–782). Boston: McGraw-Hill.

Brown, S. L., & Booth, A. (1996). Cohabitation versus marriage: A comparison of relationship quality. *Journal of Marriage and the Family, 58*, 668–678.

Brown, T. J., & Allgeier, E. R. (1995, June). *The relationship of gender and gender schema to requests for salary information*. Paper presented at the annual meeting of the American Psychological Society, New York.

Browne, A., & Williams, K. R. (1993). Gender, intimacy, and lethal violence: Trends from 1976–1987. *Gender and Society, 7*, 78–98.

Browne, B. A. (1998). Gender stereotypes in advertising on children's television in the 1990s: A cross-national analysis. *Journal of Advertising, 27,* 83–96.

Browning, C. (1998, August). *We are families: Lesbian, gay, bisexual men and women expanding the definition of families.* Division 44 Presidential Address presented at the American Psychological Association, San Francisco.

Brozan, N. (1998, March 16). Decades after midlife mark, a frontier for mental health. *New York Times,* pp. A1, A25.

Brubaker, T. H. (Ed.). (1993). *Family relationships: Current and future directions.* Newbury Park, CA: Sage.

Bruck, M., & Ceci, S. J. (1999). The suggestibility of children's memory. *Annual Review of Psychology, 50,* 419–439.

Bruck, M., Ceci, S. J., & Hembrooke, H. (1998). Reliability and credibility of young children's reports: From research to policy and practice. *American Psychologist, 53,* 136–151.

Brumberg, J. J. (1997). *The body project: An intimate history of American girls.* New York: Random House.

Brush, L. (1990). Violent acts and injurious outcomes in married couples: Methodological issues in the National Survey of Families and Households. *Gender and Society, 4,* 56–67.

Bryant, S., & Demian (Eds.). (1990, May/June). *Partners: Newsletter for gay and lesbian couples.* (Available from Partners, Box 9685, Seattle, WA 98109).

Buhrmester, D. (1996). Need fulfillment, interpersonal competence, and the developmental contexts of early adolescent friendship. In W. M. Bukowski, A. F. Newcomb, & W. W. Hartup (Eds.), *The company they keep: Friendships in childhood and adolescence* (pp. 158–185). New York: Cambridge University Press.

Bukatko, D., & Shedd, J. (1999, April). *Children's evaluations of gender-stereotyped traits, activities and occupations.* Poster presented at the meeting of the Society for Research in Child Development, Albuquerque, NM.

Bumpass, L. L., Martin, T. C., & Sweet, J. A. (1991). The impact of family background and early marital factors on marital disruption. *Journal of Family Issues, 12,* 22–42.

Bumpass, L. L., Sweet, J. A., & Cherlin, A. (1991). The role of cohabitation in the declining rates of marriage. *Journal of Marriage and the Family, 53,* 913–927.

Burckle, M. A., Ryckman, R. M., Gold J. A., Thornton, B., & Audesse, R. J. (1999). Forms of competitive attitude and achievement orientation in relation to disordered eating. *Sex Roles, 40,* 853–870.

Burnette, D., & Mui, A. C. (1996). Psychological well-being among three successive cohorts of older American women who live alone. *Journal of Women and Aging, 8,* 63–80.

Burris, B. H. (1991). Employed mothers: the impact of class and marital status on the prioritizing of family and work. *Social Science Quarterly, 72,* 50–66.

Burros, M. (2000, January 26). Doubts cloud rosy news on soy. *New York Times,* A17.

Bursik, K. (1992). Perceptions of sexual harassment in an academic context. *Sex Roles, 27,* 401–412.

Bush, T. L., & Whiteman, M. K. (1999). Hormone replacement therapy and risk of breast cancer. *Journal of the American Medical Association, 281,* 2140–2141.

Business and Professional Women's Foundation. (1997). *101 facts on the status of working women.* Washington, DC: Author.

Bussey, K., & Bandura, A. (1984). Influence of gender constancy and social power on sex-linked modeling. *Journal of Personality and Social Psychology, 47,* 1292–1302.

Bussey, K., & Bandura, A. (1999). Social cognitive theory of gender development and differentiation. *Psychological Review, 106,* 676–713.

Bussey, K., & Perry, D. G. (1982). Same-sex imitation: The avoidance of cross-sex models or the acceptance of same-sex models? *Sex Roles, 7,* 773–784.

Butler, R. N., Collins, K. S., Meier, D. E., Muller, C. F., & Pinn, V. W. (1995). Older women's health: Clinical care in the postmenopausal years. *Geriatrics, 50* (June), 33–41.

Butler, R. N., Lewis, M. I., Hoffman, E., Whitehead, E. D. (1994). Love and sex after 60: How physical changes affect intimate expression. *Geriatrics, 49* (Sept.), 20–27.

Bux, D. A., Jr. (1996). The epidemiology of problem drinking in gay men and lesbians: A critical review. *Clinical Psychology Review, 16,* 277–298.

Buzi, R. S., Weinman, M. L., & Smith, P. B. (1998). Ethnic differences in STD rates among female adolescents. *Adolescence, 33,* 313–318.

Bylsma, W. H., & Major, B. (1994). Social comparisons and contentment: Exploring the psychological costs of the gender wage gap. *Psychology of Women Quarterly, 18,* 241–249.

Byrnes, J. P., Miller, D. C., & Schafer, W. D. (1999). Gender differences in risk taking: A meta-analysis. *Psychological Bulletin, 125,* 367–383.

Bytheway, B. (1995). *Ageism*. Bristol, PA: Open University Press.

Caetano, R. (1994). Drinking and alcohol-related problems among minority women. *Alcohol Health and Research World, 18,* 333–341.

Call me Madam? No, Sir, call me Ms. and smile when you say it. (1987, July). *Canadian Business, 60,* 12.

Calle, E. E., Thun, M. J., Petrelli, J. M., Rodriguez, C., & Heath, C. W. (1999). Body-mass index and mortality in a prospective cohort of U.S. adults. *New England Journal of Medicine, 341,* 1097–1105.

Calvert, S. L., Stolkin, A., & Lee, J. (1997, April). *Gender and ethnic portrayals in Saturday morning television programs.* Poster presented at the meeting of the Society for Research on Child Development, Washington, DC.

Campbell, P. W. (1999, March 5). Lawmakers push NIH to focus research on minority populations and cancer. *Chronicle of Higher Education,* p. A32.

Campbell, V. A., et al. (1999). Surveillance for sensory impairment, activity, limitation, and health-related quality of life among older adults—United States, 1993–1997. *Morbidity and Mortality Weekly Report, 48,* (SS08), 131–156.

Campion, A. M., & Garske, J. (1998, May). *Antecedents to the development of eating disorders.* Paper presented at the meeting of the Midwestern Psychological Association, Chicago.

Canabal, M. E. (1995). Native Americans in higher education. *College Student Journal, 29,* 455–457.

Canavan, M. M., Meyer, W. J., & Higgs, D. C. (1992). The female experience of sibling incest. *Journal of Marital and Family Therapy, 18,* 129–142.

Canedy, D. (1999, May 14). Wal-Mart decides against selling a contraceptive. *New York Times,* pp. C1, C6.

Canetto, S. S., & Gale, S. R. (1997, August). *Impact of gender studies courses on gender-related attitudes.* Paper presented at the meeting of the American Psychological Association, Chicago.

Cann, A., & Vann, E. D. (1995). Implications of sex and gender differences for self: Perceived advantages and disadvantages of being the other gender. *Sex Roles, 33,* 531–541.

Cano, A., Avery-Leaf, S., Cascardi, M., & O'Leary, K. D. (1998). Dating violence in two high school samples: Discriminating variables. *Journal of Primary Prevention, 18,* 431–446.

Caplan, P. J., & Caplan, J. B. (1999). *Thinking critically about research on sex and gender* (2nd ed.). New York: HarperCollins.

Cappuccio, F. P., Meilahn, E., Zmuda, J. M., & Cauley, J. A. (1999). High blood pressure and bone-mineral loss in elderly White women: A prospective study. *Lancet, 354,* 971–975.

Cardiac regimen aids women most. (1995, August 16). *New York Times,* p. B8.

Carli, L. L. (1990). Gender, language, and influence. *Journal of Personality and Social Psychology, 59,* 941–951.

Carlisle, W. (1994). Sharing home responsibilities: Women in dual-career marriages. In C. W. Konek & S. L. Kitch (Eds.), *Women and careers: Issues and challenges* (pp. 140–152). Thousand Oaks, CA: Sage.

Caron, S. L., & Ulin, M. (1997). Closeting and the quality of lesbian relationships. *Families in Society: The Journal of Contemporary Human Services, 78,* 413–419.

Carp, F. M. (1997a). Living arrangements for midlife and older women. In J. M. Coyle (Ed.), *Handbook on women and aging* (pp. 253–270). Westport, CT: Greenwood.

Carp, F. M. (1997b). Retirement and women. In J. M. Coyle (Ed.), *Handbook on women and aging* (pp. 112–128). Westport, CT: Greenwood.

Carr, D. (1997). The fulfillment of career dreams at midlife: Does it matter for women's mental health? *Journal of Health and Social Behavior, 38,* 331–344.

Carr, J. G., Gilroy, F. D., & Sherman, M. F. (1996). Silencing the self and depression among women. *Psychology of Women Quarterly, 20,* 375–392.

Cash, T. F., Ancis, J. R., & Strachan, M. D. (1997). Gender attitudes, feminist identity, and body images among college women. *Sex Roles, 36,* 443–447.

Cash, T. F., & Deagle, E. A. (1997). The nature and extent of body-image disturbances in anorexia nervosa and bulimia nervosa: A meta-analysis. *International Journal of Eating Disorders, 22,* 107–125.

Cash, T. F., & Henry, P. E. (1995). Women's body images: The results of a national survey in the U.S.A. *Sex Roles, 33,* 19–28.

Cash, T. F., & Roy, R. E. (1999). Pounds of flesh: Weight, gender and body images. In J. Sobal & D. Maurer (Eds.), *Interpreting weight: The social management of fatness and thinness* (pp. 209–228). Hawthorne, NY: Aldine de Gruyter.

Cashdan, E. (1998). Smiles, speech, and body posture: How women and men display sociometric status and power. *Journal of Nonverbal Behavior, 22,* 209–228.

Caspi, A., & Moffitt, T. E. (1991). Individual differences are accentuated during periods of social change: The sample case of girls at puberty. *Journal of Personality and Social Psychology, 61,* 157–168.

Cassell, J., & Jenkins, H. (Eds.) (1998). *From Barbie to Martial Kombat: Gender and computer games.* Cambridge, MA: MIT Press.

Castaneda, D. (1996). Gender issues among Latinas. In J. C. Chrisler, C. Golden, & P. D. Rozee (Eds.), *Lectures on the Psychology of Women* (pp. 167–181). New York: McGraw-Hill.

Castro, I. L. (1997, Spring). Worth more than we earn: Fair pay as a step toward gender equity. *National Forum, 77,* 17–21.

Catsambis, S. (1999). The path to math: Gender and racial-ethnic differences in mathematics participation from middle school to high school. In L. A. Peplau, S. C. DeBro, R. C. Veniegas, & P. L. Taylor (Eds.), *Gender, culture, and ethnicity: Current research about women and men* (pp. 102–120). Mountain View, CA: Mayfield.

Cavanaugh, J. C. (1997). *Adult development and aging* (3rd ed.). Pacific Grove, CA: Brooks-Cole.

Cavanaugh, J. C. (1998). Friendships and social networks among older people. In I. H. Nordhus, G. R. VandenBos, S. Bert, & P. Fromholt (Eds.), *Clinical geropsychology* (pp. 137–140). Washington, DC: American Psychological Association.

Cebello, R., & Olson, S. L. (1993, March). *The role of alternative caregivers in the lives of children from poor single-parent families.* Paper presented at the meeting of the Society for Research in Child Development, New Orleans.

Celis, W., III. (1994, June 8). More college women drinking to get drunk. *New York Times,* p. B8.

Centers for Disease Control and Prevention. (1998a). Abortion surveillance: Preliminary analysis—United States, 1996. *Morbidity and Mortality Weekly Report, 47,* 1025–1028, 1035.

Centers for Disease Control and Prevention. (1998b). 1998 Guidelines for treatment of sexually transmitted diseases. *Morbidity and Mortality Weekly Report, 47,* (No. RR-1).

Centers for Disease Control and Prevention. (1998c). *1996 Assisted reproductive technology success rates: National summary and fertility clinic reports.* Atlanta, GA: Author.

Centers for Disease Control and Prevention. (1998d). Self-reported use of mammography and insurance status among women aged 40 years—United States, 1991–1992 and 1996–1997. *Morbidity and Mortality Weekly Report, 47,* 825–830.

Centers for Disease Control and Prevention. (1999a). *Breast and cervical cancer. Office of Women's Health— Fact sheet.* Atlanta, GA: Author.

Centers for Disease Control and Prevention. (1999b). *Sexually transmitted diseases. Office of Women's Health— Fact sheet.* Atlanta, GA: Author.

Centers for Disease Control and Prevention. (2000). *Women and heart disease: An atlas of racial and ethnic disparities in mortality.* Atlanta, GA: Author.

Chalfie, D. (1994). *Going it alone: A closer look at grandparents parenting grandchildren.* Washington, DC: AARP Women's Initiative.

Chan, R. W., Brooks, R. C., Raboy, B., & Patterson, C. J. (1998), Division of labor among lesbian and heterosexual parents: Associations with children's adjustment. *Journal of Family Psychology, 12,* 402–419.

Chandra, A. (1998). *Surgical sterilization in the United States: Prevalence and characteristics, 1965–95.* Series 23, No. 20 (PHS Publication No. 98-1996). Washington, DC: U.S. Government Printing Office.

Chasteen, A. L. (1998, August). *The role of age and age-related attitudes in perceptions of elderly individuals.* Paper presented a the meeting of the American Psychological Association, San Francisco.

Cherlin, A. J. (1998, April 5). By the numbers. *New York Times Magazine,* pp. 39–41.

Cherlin, A. J., et al. (1991). Longitudinal studies of effects of divorce on children in Great Britain and the United States. *Science, 252,* 1386–1389.

Cherney, I. D., & Ryalls, B. O. (1999). Gender-linked differences in the incidental memory of children and adults. *Journal of Experimental Child Psychology, 72,* 305–328.

Cherry, F., & Deaux, K. (1978). Fear of success versus fear of gender-inappropriate behavior. *Sex Roles, 4,* 97–101.

Chipman, S. F. (1996). Female participation in the study of mathematics: The U.S. situation. In G. Hanna (Ed.), *Towards gender equity in mathematics education: An ICMI study* (pp. 285–296). Norwell, MA: Kluwer.

Chipman, S. F., Krantz, D. H., & Silver, R. (1992). Mathematics anxiety and science careers among able college women. *Psychological Science, 3,* 292–295.

Chira, S. (1994, September 20). Teen-age mothers helped by Ohio plan, study finds. *New York Times,* p. A12.

Chiu, C. (1998). Do professional women have lower job satisfaction than professional men? Lawyers as a case study. *Sex Roles, 38,* 521–537.

Chodorow, N. J. (1990). *Feminism and the psychoanalytic theory.* New Haven, CT: Yale University Press.

Choi, N. G. (1995). Long-term elderly widows and divorcees: Similarities and differences. *Journal of Women and Aging, 7(3),* 69–92.

Chrisler, J. C., & Ghiz, L. (1993). Body image issues of older women. In N. D. Davis, E. Cole, and E. D. Rothblum (Eds.), *Faces of women and aging* (pp. 67–75). New York: Harrington Park Press.

Chrisler, J. C., Johnston, I. K., Champagne, N. M., & Preston K. E. (1994). Menstrual Joy: The construct and its consequences. *Psychology of Women Quarterly, 18,* 347–387.

Christ, M. J., Raszka, W. V., & Dillon, C. A. (1998). Prioritizing education about condom use among sexually active adolescent females. *Adolescence, 33,* 735–744.

Christensen, K. (1997). "With whom do you believe your lot is cast?" White feminists and racism. *Signs, 22,* 617–648.

Chubb, N. H., Fertman, C. I., & Ross, J. L. (1997). Adolescent self-esteem and locus of control: A longitudinal study of gender and age differences. *Adolescence, 32,* 113–129.

Cianni, M., & Romberger, B. (1995). Interactions with senior managers: Perceived differences by race/ethnicity and by gender. *Sex Roles, 32,* 353–373.

Cicchetti, D., & Toth, S. L. (1998a). The development of depression in children and adolescents. *American Psychologist, 53* 221–241.

Cicchetti, D., & Toth, S. L. (1998b). Perspectives on research and practice in developmental psychopathology. In W. Damon (Gen. Ed.), I. E. Sigel, & K. A. Renninger (Vol. Eds.), *Handbook of child psychology: Vol. 4. Child psychology in practice* (pp. 479–583). New York: Wiley.

Cirillo, J. M. (1996). Differential treatment: Considerations for the female alcoholic. *Women and mental health: Annals of the New York Academy of Sciences, 789,* 83–99.

Clancy, C. M. (2000). Gender issues in women's health care. In M. B. Goldman & M. C. Hatch (Eds.), *Women & health* (pp. 50 –64). New York: Academic Press.

Clark, D. O. (1995). Racial and educational differences in physical activity among older adults. *Gerontologist, 35,* 472–480.

Clark, M. L., & Bittle, M. L. (1992). Friendship expectations and the evaluation of present friendships in middle childhood and early adolescence. *Child Study Journal, 22,* 115–135.

Clark, R., Hyde, J. S., Essex, M. J., & Klein, M. H. (1997). Length of maternity leave and quality of mother-infant interactions. *Child Development, 68,* 364–383.

Clark, R. A. (1998). A comparison of topics and objectives in a cross section of young men's and women's everyday conversations. In D. J. Canary & K. Dindia (Eds.), *Sex differences and similarities in communication: Critical essays and empirical investigations of sex and gender in interaction* (pp.303–319). Mahwah, NJ: Erlbaum.

Clarke-Stewart, K. A., Allhusen, V. D., & Clements, D. C. (1995). Nonparental caregiving. In H. H. Bornstein (Ed.), *Handbook of parenting: Vol. 3. Status and social conditions of parenting* (pp. 151–176). Hillsdale, NJ: Erlbaum.

Clewell, B. C. (1991). Increase in minority and female participation in math and science: The important of the middle school years. In R. M. Lerner, A. C. Petersen, & J. Brooks-Gunn (Eds.), *Encyclopedia of adolescence* (pp. 647–657). New York: Garland.

Cochran, C. C., Frazier, P. A., & Olson, A. M. (1997). Predictors of responses to unwanted sexual attention. *Psychology of Women Quarterly, 21,* 207–226.

Cohen, C. I., Ramirez, M., Teresi, J., Gallagher, M., & Sokolovsky, J. (1997). Predictors of becoming redomiciled among older homeless women. *Gerontologist, 37,* 67–74.

Cohen, J. A., & Mannarino, A. P. (1998). Factors that mediate treatment outcome of sexually abused preschool children: Six- and 12-month follow-up. *Journal of the American Academy of Child & Adolescent Psychiatry, 37,* 44–51.

Cohler, B. J., & Nakamura, J. E. (1996). Self and experience across the second half of life. In J. Sadavoy, L. W. Lawrence, L. F. Jarvik, & G. T. Grossberg (Eds.), *Comprehensive review of geriatric psychiatry-II* (2nd., ed., pp. 153–194). Washington, DC: American Psychiatry Press.

Coie, J. D., & Dodge, K. A. (1998). Aggression and antisocial behavior. In W. Damon (Series Ed.) & N. Eisenberg (Vol. Ed.), *Handbook of child psychology: Vol. 3, Social, emotional and personality development* (5th ed., pp. 779–862). New York: Wiley.

Col, N. F., et al. (1997). Patient-specific decisions about hormone replacement therapy in postmenopausal women. *Journal of the American Medical Association, 277,* 1140–1147.

Cole, D. A., Martin, J. M., Peeke, L. A., Seroczynski, A. D., & Fier, J. (1999). Children's over- and under-estimation of academic competence: A longitudinal study of gender differences, depression, and anxiety. *Child Development, 70,* 459–473.

Coley, R. L., & Chase-Lansdale, P. L. (1998). Adolescent pregnancy and parenthood: Recent evidence and future directions. *American Psychologist, 53,* 152–166.

Coll, C. T. G., Meyer, E. C., Brillon, L. (1995). Ethnic and minority parenting. In M. H. Bornstein (Ed.), *Handbook of parenting: Vol. 2. Biology and ecology of parenting* (pp. 189–209). Mahwah, NJ: Erlbaum.

Collins, A. (1997). A psychological approach to the management of menopause. In B. G. Wren (Ed.), *Progress in the management of the menopause,* (pp. 94–98). Pearl River, NY: Parthenon.

Collins, D. W., & Kimura, D. (1997). A large sex difference on a two-dimensional mental rotation task. *Behavioral Neuroscience, 11,* 845–849.

Collins, K. S., Bussell, M. E., & Wenzel, W. (1997). *The health of women in the United States: Gender differences and gender-specific conditions.* New York: Commonwealth Fund.

Collins, K. S., Rowland, D., Salganicoff, A., & Chait, E. (1994). Assessing and improving women's health. In C. Costello & A. J. Stone (Eds.), *The American woman 1994–95: Women and health* (pp. 109–153). New York: Norton.

Collins, K. S., & Simon, L. J. (1996). Women's health and managed care: Promises and challenges. *Women's Health Issues, 6* (1), 39–44.

Collins, P. H. (1990). *Black feminist thought.* Boston: Unwin Hyman.

Collison, B. B. (1994). Mentor: Career women and supervision. In C. W. Konek & S. L. Kitch (Eds.), *Women and careers: Issues and challenges* (pp. 83–96). Thousand Oaks, CA: Sage.

Coltrane, S. (1997, Spring). Families and gender equity. *National Forum, 77,* 31–34.

Coltrane, S., & Adams, M. (1997). Work-family imagery and gender stereotypes: Television and the reproduction of difference. *Journal of Vocational Behavior, 50,* 323–347.

Comas-Díaz, L., & Greene, B. (Eds.). (1994). *Women of color: Integrating ethnic and gender identities in psychotherapy.* New York: Guilford.

Commonwealth Fund. (1993a). *The Commonwealth Fund survey of women's health.* New York: Author.

Commonwealth Fund. (1993b). *The untapped resource: The final report of the Americans over 55 at work program.* New York: Author.

Commonwealth Fund. (1995a). *Fact sheet: Women's health-related behaviors and use of clinical preventive services.* New York: Author.

Commonwealth Fund. (1995b). *Women and mental health: Issues for health reform.* New York: Author.

Commonwealth Fund. (1996a). *Prevention and women's health: A shared responsibility.* New York: Author.

Commonwealth Fund. (1996b). *Violence against women in the United States: A comprehensive background paper.* New York: Author.

Commonwealth Fund. (1997a). *The Commonwealth Fund survey of the health of adolescent girls.* New York: Author.

Commonwealth Fund. (1997b). *In their own words: Adolescent girls discuss health and health care issues.* New York: Author.

Commonwealth Fund. (1998a). *Addressing domestic violence and its consequences.* New York: Author.

Commonwealth Fund. (1998b). *The Commonwealth Fund 1998 survey of women's health.* New York: Author.

Comstock, G. (1991). *Television and the American child.* Orlando, FL: Academic Press.

Connolly, J., & Stevens, V. (1999, April). *Best friends, cliques, and young adolescents' romantic involvement.* Paper presented at the meeting of the Society for Research in Child Development, Albuquerque, NM.

Conti, N. E., & Kimmel, E. B. (1993). *Gender and cultural diversity bias in developmental textbooks.* Paper presented at the annual meeting of the Southeastern Psychological Association, Atlanta, GA (ERIC/CASS, Document Reproduction Service No. ED 359 478)

Cook, L. S., & Weiss, N. S. (2000). Endometrial cancer. In M. B. Goldman & M. C. Hatch (Eds.), *Women & health* (pp. 916–931). New York: Academic Press.

Cooper-Patrick, L. et al. (1999). Race, gender, and partnership in the patient-physician relationship. *Journal of the American Medical Association, 232,* 583–589.

Cortina, L. M., Swan, S., & Fitzgerald, L. F. (1995, May). *Still chilly? The climate for women in academia.* Paper presented at the annual meeting of the Midwestern Psychological Association, Chicago.

Cortina, L. M., Swan, S., Fitzgerald, L. F., & Waldo, C. (1998). Sexual harassment and assault: Chilling the climate for women in academia. *Psychology of Women Quarterly, 22*, 419–441.

Cowley, G. (1999, August 1). So, how's your health? *Newsweek*, pp. 48–53.

Cowley, G., & Underwood, A. (1999, Spring/Summer). Defeating breast cancer. *Newsweek*, pp. 40–44.

Crabb, P. B., & Bielawski, D. (1994). The social representation of material culture and gender in children's books. *Sex Roles, 30*, 69–79.

Craig, R. S. (1992). The effect of television day part on gender portrayals in television commercials: A content analysis. *Sex Roles, 26*, 197–211.

Cramer, D. W., et al. (1998, January 10). Over-the-counter analgesics and risk of ovarian cancer. *Lancet, 351*, (9096), 104.

Cranberg, G. (1992, August 17). Even sensible Iowa bows to the religious right. *The Los Angeles Times*, p. B5.

Crandall, C. S., Tsang, J-A., Goldman, S., & Pennington, J. T. (1999). Newsworthy moral dilemmas: Justice, caring, and gender. *Sex Roles, 40*, 187–209.

Crawford, M., & Chaffin, R. (1997). The meanings of differences: Cognition in social and cultural context. In P. J. Caplan, M. Crawford, J. S. Hyde, & J. T. E. Richardson (Eds.), *Gender differences in human cognition* (pp. 30–51). New York: Oxford University Press.

Crawford, M., & Kimmel, E. (1999). Promoting methodological diversity in feminist research. *Psychology of Women Quarterly, 23*, 1–6.

Crawford, M., & MacLeod, M. (1990). Gender in the college classroom: An assessment of the "chilly climate" for women. *Sex Roles, 23*, 101–122.

Crick, N. R., & Bigbee, M. A. (1998). Relational and overt forms of peer victimization:A multiinformant approach. *Journal of Consulting and Clinical Psychology, 66*, 337–347.

Crick, N. R., Casas, J. F., & Ku, H-C. (1999). Relational and physical forms of victimization in preschool. *Developmental Psychology, 35*, 376–385.

Crockett, L. J. (1991). Sex roles and sex-typing in adolescence. In R. M. Lerner, A. C. Petersen, & J. Brooks-Gunn (Eds.), *Encyclopedia of adolescence, Vol. 2* (pp. 1007–1017). New York: Garland.

Crosby, F. J. (1982). *Relative deprivation and working women*. New York: Oxford University Press.

Crosby, F. J. (1991). *Juggling: The unexpected advantages of balancing career and home for women and their families*. New York: Free Press.

Crose, R., Leventhal, E. A., Haug, M. R., & Burns, E. A. (1997). The challenges of aging. In S. J. Gallant, G. Puryear Keita, & R. Royak-Schaler (Eds.), *Health care for women: Psychological, social, and behavioral influences* (pp. 221–234). Washington, DC: American Psychological Association.

Cross, S. E. (n.d.). *Climate, confidence, and the gender gap in science and engineering*. Unpublished manuscript.

Croteau, J. M., & Von Destinon, M. (1994). A national survey of job search experiences of lesbian, gay, and bisexual affairs professionals. Journal of College Student Development, 35, 40–45.

Crouter, A. C., Manke, B. A., & McHale, S. M. (1995). The family context of gender intensification in early adolescence. *Child Development, 66*, 317–329.

Crowley, S. L. (1993, October). Grandparents to the rescue. *AARP Bulletin*, pp. 1, 16–17.

Crowther, M. R. (1998, May). *African American grandparents as parents*. Paper presented at the meeting of the American Psychological Society, Washington, DC.

Culbertson, A. L., & Rosenfeld, P. (1994). Assessment of sexual harassment in the active-duty Navy. *Military Psychology, 6*, 69–93.

Culbertson, F. M. (1997). Depression and gender: An international review. *American Psychologist, 52*, 25–31.

Culp, L. N., & Beach, S. R. H. (1998). Marriage and depressive symptoms: The role and bases of self-esteem differ by gender. *Psychology of Women Quarterly, 22*, 647–663.

Cummings, S. R., (1999). The effect of raloxifene on risk of breast cancer in postmenopausal women. *Journal of the American Medical Association, 281*, 2189–2197.

Cummings, S. R., Black, D. M., Thompson, D. E., et al. (1998). Effect of alendronate on risk of fracture in women with low bone density but without vertebral fractures. *Journal of the American Medical Association, 280*, 2077–2082.

Cummings, S. R., et al. (2000). Monitoring osteoporosis with bone densitometry. *Journal of the American Medical Association, 283*, 1318–1321.

Curtin, S.C. & Park, M. M. (1999). Trends in the attendant, place, and timing of births, and in the use of obstetric interventions: United States, 1989–97. *National Vital Statistics Reports, 47,* No. 27. Hyattsville, MD: National Center for Health Statistics.

Cusumano, D. L., & Thompson, J. K. (1997). Body image and body shape ideals in magazines: Exposure, awareness, and internalization. *Sex Roles, 37,* 701–721.

Cutter, J. A. (1999, June 13). Coming to terms with grief after a longtime partner dies. *New York Times,* p. WH10.

Daley, S. (1991, January 19). Girls' self-esteem is lost on way to adolescence, new study finds. *New York Times,* pp. B1, B6.

D'Amico, M., Baron, L. J., & Sissons, M. E. (1995). Gender differences in attributions about microcomputer learning in elementary school. *Sex Roles, 33,* 353–385.

Dancer, L. S., & Gilbert, L. A. (1993). Spouses' family work participation and its relation to wives' occupational level. *Sex Roles, 28,* 127–145.

Daniluk, J. C. (1998). *Women's sexuality across the life span: Challenging myths, creating meanings.* New York: Guilford.

Danner, F., Noland, F., McFadden, M., Dewalt, K., & Kotchen, J. M. (1991). Description of the physical activity of young children using movement sensor and observation methods. *Pediatric Exercise Science, 3,* 11–20.

D'Arcy, J. (1998, August 24). Marriage and family vs. career. *Hartford Courant,* pp. F1, F3.

D'Augelli, A. R. (1996). Lesbian, gay and bisexual development during adolescence and young adulthood. In R. P. Cabaj and T. S. Stein (Eds.), *Textbook of homosexuality and mental health* (pp. 267–288). Washington, DC: American Psychiatric Press.

D'Augelli, A. R. (1998). Developmental implications of victimization of lesbian, gay, and bisexual youths. In G. M. Herek (Ed.), *Stigma and sexual orientation: Understanding prejudice against lesbians, gay men, and bisexuals* (pp. 187–210). Thousand Oaks, CA: Sage.

Darling, C. A., Davidson, J. K., Sr., & Jennings, D. A. (1991). The female sexual response revisited: Understanding the multiorgasmic experience in women. *Archives of Sexual Behavior, 20,* 527–540.

Das-Dasgupta, S. (1998). Women's realities: Defining violence against women by immigration, race,

and class. In R. K. Bergen (Ed.), *Issues in intimate violence* (pp. 209–219). Thousand Oaks, CA: Sage.

Daubman, K. A., Heatherington, L., & Ahn, A. (1992). Gender and the self-presentation of academic achievement. *Sex Roles, 27,* 187–204.

Daubman, K. A., & Sigall, H. (1997). Gender differences in perceptions of how others are affected by self-disclosure of achievement. *Sex Roles, 37,* 73–89.

Davey, E. H. (1998). Young women's expected and preferred patterns of employment and child care. *Sex Roles, 38,* 95–102.

David, H. P. (1992). Born unwanted: Long term developmental effects of denied abortion. *Journal of Social Issues, 48* (3), 163–181.

Davidson, D., Luo, Z., Saggar, S., Lewis, J., Lash, D., Mehta, M., & Burden, M. (1998, May). *First- and fifth-grade children's perception and memory for elderly individuals: The effects of stereotypes and descriptive information on children's responses.* Paper presented at the meeting of the Midwestern Psychological Association, Chicago.

Davis, D. M. (1990). Portrayals of women in prime-time network television: Some demographic characteristics. *Sex Roles, 23,* 325–332.

Davis, H., & Gergen, P. (1994). Self-described weight status of Mexican-American adolescents. *Journal of Adolescent Health, 15,* 407–409.

Davis, P. J. (1999). Gender differences in autobiographical memory for childhood emotional experiences. *Journal of Personality and Social Psychology, 76,* 498–510.

Deal, J. J., & Stevenson, M. A. (1998). Perceptions of female and male managers in the 1990s: Plus ca change . . . *Sex Roles, 38,* 287–300.

DeAngelis, T. (1997a, March). Body-image problems affect all groups. *APA Monitor,* pp. 44–45.

DeAngelis, T. (1997b, October). Elderly may be less depressed than the young. *APA Monitor,* p. 25.

DeAngelis, T. (1997c, September). There's new hope for women with postpartum blues. *APA Monitor,* pp. 22–23.

DeAngelis, T. (1997d, August). Women unwittingly uphold wage gap between the sexes. *APA Monitor, 28,* p. 42.

Deaux, K. (1999). An overview of research on gender: Four themes from 3 decades. In W. B. Swann, J. H. Langlois, & L. A. Gilbert (Eds.), *Sexism and stereo-*

types in modern society (pp. 11–35). Washington, DC: American Psychological Association.

Decalmer, P., & Glendenning, F. (Eds.). (1997). *The mistreatment of elderly people* (2nd ed.). Thousand Oaks, CA: Sage.

DeCock, K. M. et al. (2000). Prevention of mother-to-child HIV transmission in resource-poor countries. *Journal of the American Medical Association, 283,* 1175–1182.

Delaney, J., Lupton, M. J., & Toth, E. (1988). *The curse: A cultural history of menstruation* (rev. ed.). Urbana, IL: University of Illinois.

de las Fuentes, C., & Vasquez, M. J. T. (1999). Immigrant adolescent girls of color: Facing American challenges. In N. G. Johnson, M. C. Roberts, & J. Worell (Eds.), *Beyond appearance: A new look at adolescent girls* (pp. 131–150). Washington, DC: American Psychological Association.

DeLeo, D., & Ormskerk, S. C. R. (1991). Suicide in the elderly: General characteristics. *Crisis, 12* (2), 3–17.

De Leon, B. (1995). Sex role identity among college students: A cross-cultural analysis. In A. M. Padilla (Ed.), *Hispanic psychology: Critical issues in theory and research.* Thousand Oaks, CA: Sage.

Delgado, A., López-Fernández, L. A., & deDios Luna, J. (1993). Influence of the doctor's gender in the satisfaction of the users. *Medical Care, 31,* 795–800.

De Lisi, R., & Soundranayagam, L. (1990). The conceptual structure of sex role stereotypes in college students. *Sex Roles, 23,* 593–611.

Delmas, P. D., et al. (1997). Effects of raloxifene on bone mineral density, serum cholesterol concentrations, and uterine endometrium in postmenopausal women. *New England Journal of Medicine, 337,* 1641–1647.

Delmas, P. D., Mitlak, B. H., & Christiansen, C. (1998). To the editor: Effects of raloxifene in postmenopausal women. *New England Journal of Medicine, 338,* 1313–1314.

DeLoach, C. P. (1989). Gender, career choice and occupational outcomes among college alumni with disabilities. *Journal of Applied Rehabilitation Counseling, 20,* 8–12.

Demare, D., Lips, H. M., & Briere, J. (1993). Sexually violent pornography, anti-woman attitudes, and sexual aggression: *A structural equation model. Journal of Research in Personality, 27,* 285–300.

DeMaris, A., & Rao, V. (1992). Premarital cohabitation and subsequent marital stability in the United States: *A reassessment. Journal of Marriage and the Family, 54,* 178–190.

DeMeis, D. K., & Perkins, H. W. (1996). "Super-Moms" of the nineties: Homemaker and employed mothers' performance and perceptions of the motherhood role. *Journal of Family Issues, 17,* 777–792.

Denmark, F. L. (1994). Engendering psychology. *American Psychologist, 49,* 329–334.

Denmark, F. L. (1999). Enhancing the development of adolescent girls. In N. G. Johnson, M. C. Roberts, & J. Worell (Eds.), *Beyond appearance: A new look at adolescent girls* (pp. 337–404). Washington, DC: American Psychological Association.

Denmark, F. L., Novick, K., & Pinto, A. (1996). Women, work, and family: Mental health issues. In J. E. Sechzer, S. M. Pfafflin, F. L. Denmark, A. Griffin, & S. J. Blumental (Eds.), *Women and mental health* (pp. 101–117). New York: NY Academy of Sciences.

Dennerstein, L., & Shelley, J. (Eds.) (1998). *A woman's guide to menopause and hormone replacement therapy.* Washington, DC: American Psychiatric Association.

DeParle, J. (1999a, February 21). As welfare rolls shrink, load on relatives grows. *New York Times,* pp. A1, A20.

DeParle, J. (1999b, November 28). Early sex abuse common among welfare's women. *New York Times,* pp. Y1, Y20.

Derry, P. S., Gallant, S. J., & Woods, N. F (1997). Premenstrual syndrome and menopause. In S. J. Gallant, G. Puryear Keita, & R. Royal-Schaler (Eds.), *Health care for women: Psychological, social and behavioral influences* (pp. 203–220). Washington, DC: American Psychological Association.

Deter, H. C., & Herzog, W. (1994). Anorexia nervosa in a long-term perspective: Results of the Heidelberg-Mannheim study. *Psychosomatic Medicine, 56,* 20–27.

Deutsch, F. M., & Saxon, S. E. (1998). Traditional ideologies, nontraditional lives. *Sex Roles, 38,* 331–362.

Device offers an alternative to hysterectomy (1997, December 14). *New York Times,* p. Y22.

de Waal, F. B. M. (2000, April 2). Survival of the rapist. *New York Times,* Section 7, pp. 24–25.

DeZolt, D. M., & Henning-Stout, M. (1999). Adolescent girls' experiences in school and community settings. In N. G. Johnson., M. C. Roberts, & J. Worell

(Eds.), *Beyond appearance: A new look at adolescent girls* (pp. 253–275). Washington, DC: American Psychological Association.

Diamond, L. M. (2000). Sexual identity, attractions, and behavior among young sexual-minority women over a 2-year period. *Development Psychology, 36,* 241–250.

Diamond, M. (1996). Prenatal predisposition and the clinical management of some pediatric conditions. *Journal of Sex & Marital Therapy, 22,* 139–147.

Diamond, M. (1997). Sexual identity and sexual orientation in children with traumatized or ambiguous genitalia. *Journal of Sex Research, 34,* 199–211.

Diamond, M., Binstock, T., Kohl, J. V. (1996). From fertilization to adult sexual behavior. *Hormones and Behaviors, 30,* 333–353.

Dick, D. M., Rose, R. J., & Viken, R. J. (2000). Pubertal timing and substance use: Associations between and within families across late adolescence. *Developmental Psychology, 36,* 180–189.

Dickersin, K., & Lemaire, G. S. (2000). Hysterectomy. In M. B. Goldman & M. C. Hatch (Eds.), *Women & health* (pp. 253–267). New York: Academic Press.

Diekman, A. B., & Eagly, A. H. (1997, May). *Past, present, and future: Perceptions of change in women and men.* Paper presented at the meeting of the Midwestern Psychological Association, Chicago.

Dietz, T. L. (1998). An examination of violence and gender role portrayals in video games: Implications for gender socialization and aggressive behavior. *Sex Roles, 38,* 425–442.

DiMatteo, M. R., & Kahn, K. L. (1997). Psychosocial aspects of childbirth. In S. J. Gallant, G. Puryear Keita, & R. Royak-Schaler (Eds.), *Health care for women: Psychological, social, and behavioral influences* (pp. 175–186). Washington, DC: American Psychological Association.

Dindia, K., & Allen, M. (1992). Sex differences in self-disclosure: A meta-analysis. *Psychological Bulletin, 112,* 106–124.

Dion, K. L. (1987). What's in a title: The Ms. stereotype and images of women's titles of address. *Psychology of Women Quarterly, 11,* 21–36.

Dion, K. L., & Cota, A. A. (1991). The Ms. stereotype: Its domain and the role of explicitness in title preference. *Psychology of Women Quarterly, 15,* 403–410.

Dion, K. L., & Schuller, R. A. (1990). Ms. and the manager: A tale of two stereotypes. *Sex Roles, 22,* 569–577.

Dobrzynski, J. H. (1996, October 8). Study finds few women in 5 highest company jobs. *New York Times,* p. C3.

Dogar, R. (1999, Spring/Summer). STDs: Better safe than sorry. *Newsweek,* pp. 54–55.

Doka, K. J., & Mertz, M. E. (1988). The meaning and significance of great-grandparenthood. *Gerontologist, 28,* 192–197.

Dolgin, K. G., & Minowa, N. (1997). Gender differences in self-presentation: A comparison of the roles of flatteringness and intimacy in self-disclosure to friends. *Sex Roles, 36,* 371–380.

Donatelle, R. J., & Davis, L. G. (1998). *Access to health* (5th ed.). Boston: Allyn & Bacon.

Donovan, P. (1998). U.S. teenage pregnancy rate now lowest in two decades. *The Guttmacher Report on Public Policy, 1* (5), 6–9.

Doress-Worters, P. B., & Siegal, D. L. (1994). *The new ourselves growing older.* New York: Simon & Schuster.

Dorfman, L. T. (1995). Health, financial status, and social participation of retired rural men and women: Implications for educational intervention. *Educational Gerontology, 21,* 653–669.

Dorfman, L. T., & Rubenstein, L. M. (1993). Paid and unpaid activities and retirement satisfaction among rural seniors. *Physical & Occupational Therapy in Geriatrics, 12,* 45–63.

Douhitt, R. (1989). The division of labor within the home: Have gender roles changed? *Sex Roles, 20,* 693–704.

Dowling, W. (1997). Volunteerism among older women. In J. M. Coyle (Ed.), *Handbook on women and aging* (pp. 242–252). Westport, CT: Greenwood.

Driscoll, J. M., Kelley, F. A., & Fassinger, R. E. (1996). Lesbian identity and disclosure in the workplace: Relation to occupational stress and satisfaction. *Journal of Vocational Behavior, 48,* 229–242.

DuBois, D. L., Bull, C. A., Sherman, M. D., & Roberts, M. (1998). Self-esteem and adjustment in early adolescence: A social-contextual perspective. *Journal of Youth and Adolescence, 27,* 557–583.

Duck, S., & Wright, P. H. (1993). Reexamining gender differences in same-gender friendships: A close look at two kinds of data. *Sex Roles, 28,* 709–727.

Duff, J. L. (1996). *The best of friends: Exploring the moral domain of adolescent friendship.* Unpublished doctoral dissertation, Stanford University.

Duffy, J., Gunther, G., & Walters, L. (1997). Gender and mathematical problem solving. *Sex Roles, 37,* 477–494.

Dugger, K. (1988). Social location and gender-role attitudes: A comparison of black and white women. *Gender & Society, 2,* 425–448.

Dunn, A. L., et al. (1999). Comparison of lifestyle and structured interventions to increase physical activity and cardiorespiratory fitness. *Journal of the American Medical Association, 281,* 327–334.

Duxbury, L., & Higgins, C. (1994). Interference between work and family: A status report on dual-career and dual-earner mothers and fathers. *Employee Assistance Quarterly, 9,* 55–80.

Dweck, C. S., Goetz, T. E., & Strauss, N. C. (1980). Sex differences in learned helplessness: IV. An experimental and naturalistic study of failure generalization and its mediators. *Journal of Personality and Social Psychology, 38,* 441–452.

Dykstra, P. (1990). *Next of (non)kin; The importance of primary relationships for older adults' well-being.* Amsterdam: Swets and Zertlinger.

Eagly, A. H. (1987). *Differences in social behavior: A social role analysis.* Hillsdale, NJ: Erlbaum.

Eagly, A. H. (1995). The science and politics of comparing women and men. *American Psychologist, 50,* 145–158.

Eagly, A. H. (1998). Gender and altruism. In D. L. Anselmi and A. L. Law (Eds.), *Questions of gender: Perspectives and paradoxes* (pp. 405–417). Boston: McGraw-Hill.

Eagly, A. H. (1999, April). *The power elite: Why so few women?* Presidential address at the meeting of the Midwest Psychological Association, Chicago.

Eagly, A. H., & Carli, L. L. (1981). Sex of researchers and sex-typed communications as determinants of sex differences in influenceability: A meta-analysis of social influence studies. *Psychological Bulletin, 90,* 1–20.

Eagly, A. H., Makhijani, M. G., & Klonsky, B. G. (1992). Gender and the evaluation of leaders: A meta-analysis. *Psychological Bulletin, 111,* 3–22.

Eagly, A. H., & Steffen, V. J. (1984). Gender stereotypes stem from the distribution of women and men into social roles. *Journal of Personality and Social Psychology, 46,* 735–754.

Eagly, A. H., & Steffen, V. J. (1986). Gender stereotypes, occupational roles, and beliefs about part-time employees. *Psychology of Women Quarterly, 10,* 252–262.

Eagly, A. H., & Wood, W. (1985). Gender and influenceability: Stereotype versus behavior. In V. E. O'Leary, R. K. Unger, & B. S. Wallston (Eds.), *Women, gender, and social psychology* (pp. 225–256). Hillsdale, NJ: Erlbaum.

Eagly, A. H., & Wood, W. (1999). The origins of sex differences in human behavior: Evolved dispositions versus social roles. *American Psychologist, 54,* 408–423.

Earle, J. P. (1996). Acquaintance rape workshops: Their effectiveness in changing the attitudes of first year college men. *NASPA Journal, 34,* 2–18.

Earle, J. R., Smith, M. H., Harris, C. T., & Longino, C. F. (1998). Women, marital status, and symptoms and depression in a midlife national sample. *Journal of Women & Aging, 10,* 41–57.

Early Breast Cancer Trialists' Collaborative Group. (1998). Tamoxifen for early breast cancer: An overview of the randomised trials. *Lancet, 35,* 1451–1467.

Earned degrees conferred by U.S. institutions, 1995–1996. (1998, November 13). *Chronicle of Higher Education,* p. A41.

East, P. L., Felice, M. E., & Morgan, M. C. (1993). Sisters' and girlfriends' sexual and childbearing behavior: Effects on early adolescent girls' sexual outcomes. *Journal of Marriage and the Family, 55,* 953–963.

Eating Disorders—Part I. (1997, October). *The Harvard Mental Health Letter,* pp. 1–5.

Eating Disorders—Part II. (1997, November). *The Harvard Mental Health Letter,* pp. 1–5.

Eberhardt, J. L., & Fiske, S. T. (1998). Affirmative action in theory and practice: Issues of power, ambiguity, and gender versus race. In D. L. Anselmi & A. L. Law (Eds.), *Questions of gender: Perspectives and paradoxes* (pp. 629–641). Boston: McGraw-Hill.

Eccles, J. S. (1994). Understanding women's educational and occupational choices: Applying the Eccles et al. model of achievement-related choices. *Psychology of Women Quarterly, 18,* 585–609.

Eccles, J. S., Barber, B., & Jozefowicz, D. (1999). Linking gender to educational, occupational, and recreational choices: Applying the Eccles et al. model of achievement-related choices. In W. B. Swann, Jr., J. H. Langlois, & L. A. Gilbert (Eds.), *Sexism and stereotypes in modern society: The gender science of Janet Taylor Spence* (pp. 153–192). Washington, DC: American Psychological Association.

Eccles, J. S., Barber, B., Jozefowicz, D., Malenchuk, O., & Vida, M. (1999). Self-evaluations of competence, task values, and self-esteem. In N. G. Johnson, M. C. Roberts, & J. Worell (Eds.), *Beyond appearance: A new look at adolescent girls* (pp. 55–83). Washington, DC: American Psychological Association.

Eccles, J. S., & Roeser, R. W. (1999). School and community influences on human development. In M. H. Bornstein & M. E. Lamb (Eds.), *Developmental psychology: An advanced textbook* (4th ed., pp. 503–554). Mahwah, NJ: Erlbaum.

Eccles, J. S., Wigfield, A., & Schiefele, U. (1998). Motivation to succeed. In W. Damon (Series Ed.) & N. Eisenberg (Vol. Ed.), *Handbook of child psychology: Vol. 3. Social, emotional and personality development* (5th ed., pp. 1017–1095). New York: Wiley.

EDK Associates. (1994, February). *Women and sexually transmitted diseases: The dangers of denial.* New York: Author.

Edmondson, C. B., & Conger, J. C. (1995). The impact of mode of presentation on gender differences in social perception. *Sex Roles, 32,* 169–183.

Edwards, F. H., Carey, J. S., Grover, F. L., Bero, J. W., & Hartz, R. S. (1998). Impact of gender on coronary bypass operative mortality. *The Annals of Thoracic Surgery, 66,* p. 125.

Eisenberg, N., & Fabes, R. A. (1998). Prosocial development. In W. Damon (Series Ed.) & N. Eisenberg (Vol. Ed.), *Handbook of child psychology: Vol. 3. Social, emotional and personality development* (5th ed., pp. 701–778). New York: Wiley.

Eisenberg, N., Martin, C. L., & Fabes, R. A. (1996). Gender development and gender effects. In D. C. Berliner & R. C. Calfee (Eds.), *The handbook of educational psychology* (pp. 358–396). New York: Simon & Schuster.

Elder, J. (1997, June 22). Poll finds women are the health-savvier sex, and the warier. *New York Times,* p. WH8.

Eley, T. C., Lichtenstein, P., & Stevenson, J. (1999). Sex differences in the etiology of aggressive and nonaggressive antisocial behavior: Results from two twin studies. *Child Development, 70,* 155–168.

Eliason, S. R. (1995). An extension of the Sorensen-Kalleberg theory of the labor market matching and attainment processes. *American Sociological Review, 60,* 247–271.

Ellis, B. J., & Garber, J. (2000). Psychosocial antecedents of variation in girls' pubertal timing: Maternal depression, stepfather presence, and marital and family status. *Child Development, 71,* 485–501.

Ellis, B. J., McFadyen-Ketchum, S., Dodge, K. A., Pettit, G., & Bates, J. (1999). Quality of early family relationships and individual differences in the timing of pubertal maturation in girls: A longitudinal test of an evolutionary model. *Journal of Personality and Social Psychology, 77,* pp. 387–401.

Ellis, L. (1989). *Theories of rape: Inquiries into the causes of sexual aggression.* New York: Hemisphere.

Ellis L. (1996). The role of perinatal factors in determining sexual orientation. In R. C. Savin-Williams & K. Cohen (Eds.), *The lives of lesbians, gays and bisexuals: Children to adults* (pp. 35–70). Fort Worth, TX: Harcourt Brace.

Elrich, D. (1997, July 3). New video games: Despite promises, violence rules. *New York Times,* p. B1.

Emery, R. E., & Laumann-Billings, L. (1998). An overview of the nature, causes, and consequences of abusive family relationships. Toward differentiating maltreatment and violence. *American Psychologist, 53,* 121–135.

Employment and Immigration Canada. (1992). *Annual report: Employment Equity Act.* Ottawa, Canada: Department of Supply and Services Canada.

Erdner, R. A., & Guy, R. F. (1990). Career identification and women's attitudes toward retirement. *International Journal of Aging and Human Development, 30,* 129–139.

Erikson, E. H. (1968). *Identity: Youth and crisis.* New York: Norton.

Erikson, E. H. (1980). *Identity and the life cycle.* New York. Norton.

Erkut, S., Marx, F., Fields, J. P., & Sing, R. (1999). Raising confident and competent girls: One size does not fit all. In L. A. Peplau, S. C. DeBro, R. C. Veniegas, & P. L. Taylor (Eds.), *Gender, culture, and ethnicity: Current research about women and men,* (pp 83–101). Mountain View, CA: Mayfield.

Erkut, S., & Tracy, A. (1999, August). *Protective effects of sports participation on girls' sexual behavior.* Paper presented at the meeting of the American Psychological Association, Boston.

Espiritu, Y. L. (1997). *Asian American women and men: Labor, laws, and love.* Thousand Oaks, CA: Sage.

Estes, C. L., Linkins, K. W., & Binney, E. A. (1996). The political economy of aging. In R. H. Binstock & L. K. George (Eds.), *Handbook of aging and the social sciences* (4th ed., pp. 346–361). San Diego, CA: Academic Press.

Estrogens au naturel (1997, June 22). *New York Times,* p. WH3.

Etaugh, C. (1993a). Maternal employment: Effects on children. In J. Frankel (Ed.), *The employed mother and the family context* (pp. 68–88). New York: Springer.

Etaugh, C. (1993b). Women in the middle and later years. In F. Denmark & M. Paludi (Eds.), *Handbook on the psychology of women* (pp. 213–246). Westport, CT: Greenwood.

Etaugh, C., Bridges, J. S., Cummings-Hill, M., & Cohen, J. (1999). "Names can never hurt me?" The effects of surname use on perceptions of married women. *Psychology of Women Quarterly, 23,* pp. 819–823.

Etaugh, C., & Duits, T. (1990). Development of gender discrimination: Role of stereotypic and counter-stereotypic gender cues. *Sex Roles, 23,* 215–222.

Etaugh, C., & Folger, D. (1998). Perceptions of parents whose work and parenting behaviors deviate from role expectations. *Sex Roles, 39,* 215–223.

Etaugh, C., & Fulton, A. (1995, June). *Perceptions of unmarried adults: Gender and sexual orientation (not social attractiveness) matter.* Paper presented at the meeting of the American Psychological Association, New York.

Etaugh, C., Grinnell, K., & Etaugh, A. (1989). Development of gender labeling: Effect of age of pictured children. *Sex Roles, 21,* 769–773.

Etaugh, C., Jones, N. A., & Patterson, K. (1995, August). *Gender comparisons and stereotypes: Changing views in introductory psychology textbooks.* Paper presented at the meeting of the American Psychological Association, New York City.

Etaugh, C., Levine, D., & Mennella, A. (1984). Development of sex biases in children: Forty years later. *Sex Roles, 10,* 913–924.

Etaugh, C., & Liss, M. B. (1992). Home, school, and playroom: Training grounds for adult gender roles. *Sex Roles, 26,* 129–146.

Etaugh, C., & Nekolny, K. (1990). Effects of employment status and marital status on perceptions of mothers. *Sex Roles, 23,* 273–280.

Etaugh, C., & Rathus, S. (1995). *The world of children.* Fort Worth, TX: Harcourt Brace.

Etaugh, C., & Stern, J. (1984). Person perception: Effects of sex, marital status, and sex-typed occupation. *Sex Roles, 11,* 413–424.

Ettinger, B., et al. (1999). Reduction of verbal fracture risk in postmenopausal women with osteoporosis treated with raloxifene. *Journal of the American Medical Association, 282,* 637–649.

Ettinger, W. H., et al. (1997). The Fitness Arthritis and Seniors Trial (FAST): A randomized trial comparing aerobic exercise and resistance exercise to a health education program on physical disability in older people with knee osteoarthritis. *Journal of the American Medical Association, 277,* 25–31.

Evans, N. J., & D'Augelli, A. R. (1996). Lesbians, gay men, and bisexual people in college. In R. C. Savin-Williams & K. Cohen (Eds), *The lives of lesbians, gays, and bisexuals: Children to adults* (pp. 201–226). Fort Worth, TX: Harcourt Brace.

Fabes, R. A., Eisenberg, N., Jones, S., Smith, M., Guthrie, I., Poulin, R., Shepard, S., & Friedman, J. (1999). Regulation, emotionality, and preschoolers' socially competent peer interactions. *Child Development, 70,* 432–442.

Fabrikant, G. (1996, April 8). The young and restless audience: Computers and videos cut into children's time for watching TV and ads. *New York Times,* p. C1.

Fagot, B. I. (1995). Parenting boys and girls. In M. H. Bornstein (Ed.), *Handbook of parenting: Vol. 1. Children and parenting* (pp. 163–183). Mahwah, NJ: Erlbaum.

Fagot, B. I., & Leinbach, M. D. (1993). Gender-role development in young children: From discrimination to labeling. *Developmental Review, 13,* 205–224.

Fagot, B. I., Leinbach, M. D., & O'Boyle, C. (1992). Gender labeling, gender stereotyping, and parenting behaviors. *Developmental Psychology, 28,* 225–230.

Falling and the elderly. (1999). *Journal of the American Medical Association, 281,* 1871.

Fallon, A. E. (1994). Body image and the regulation of weight. In V. J. Adesso, D-M. Reddy, & R. Fleming (Eds.), *Psychological perspectives on women's health* (pp. 127–180). Washington, DC: Taylor & Francis.

Faludi, S. (1991). *Backlash: The undeclared war against women.* New York: Crown.

Families and Work Institute. (1995, May). *Women: The new providers* (Whirlpool Foundation Study, part one). New York: Author.

Faria, G., & Belohlavek. (1995). Treating female adult survivors of childhood incest. In F. J. Turner (Ed.), *Differential diagnosis and treatment in social work* (4th ed., pp. 744–753). New York: Free Press.

Farmer, H. S. (1997). Women's motivation related to mastery, career salience, and career aspiration: A multivariate model focusing on the effects of sex role socialization. *Journal of Career Assessment, 5,* 355–381.

Farmer, H. S. (Ed.). (1997). *Diversity and women's career development: From adolescence to adulthood.* Thousand Oaks, CA: Sage.

Fassinger, R. E. (1994). Development and testing of the attitudes toward feminism and the women's movement (FWM) Scale. *Psychology of Women Quarterly, 18,* 389–402.

Fassinger, R. E. (1995). From invisibility to integration: lesbian identity in the workplace. *The Career Development Quarterly, 44,* 148–167.

Fausto-Sterling, A. (1992). *Myths of gender: Biological theories about women and men* (2nd ed.). New York: Basic Books.

Federal Glass Ceiling Commission. (1995a, March). *Good for business: Making full use of the nation's human capital.* Washington, DC: Author.

Federal Glass Ceiling Commission. (1995b, November). *A solid investment: Making full use of the nation's human capital.* Washington, DC: Author.

Fein, E. B. (1994, July 19). Elderly find hardship in haven for young. *New York Times,* pp. A1, A12.

Fein, E. B. (1998, February 22). Calling infertility a disease, couples battle with insurers. *New York Times,* pp. Y1, Y40.

Feingold, A. (1988). Cognitive gender differences are disappearing. *American Psychologist, 43,* 95–103.

Feingold, A. (1990). Gender differences in effects of physical attractiveness on romantic attraction: A comparison across five research paradigms. *Journal of Personality and Social Psychology, 59,* 981–993.

Feingold, A. (1993). Cognitive gender differences: A developmental perspective. *Sex Roles, 29,* 91–112.

Feingold, A., & Mazzella, R. (1998). Gender differences in body image are increasing. *Psychological Science, 9,* 32–37.

Feinman, S. (1984). A status theory of the evaluation of sex-role and age-role behavior. *Sex Roles, 10,* 445–456.

Feldman, R. S. (1998). Social psychology (2nd. ed.). Upper Saddle River, NJ: Prentice-Hall.

Feldman, R. S. (2000). *Development across the life span* (2nd ed.). Upper Saddle River, NJ: Prentice-Hall.

Feldman, S. S., & Gowen, L. K. (1998). Conflict negotiation tactics in romantic relationships in high school students. *Journal of Youth and Adolescence, 27,* 691–717.

Feldstein, K. (1998, April 13). Social Security's gender gap. *New York Times,* p. A27.

Felmlee, D. H. (1994). Who's on top? Power in romantic relationships. *Sex Roles, 31,* 275–295.

Fennema, E. (1990). Teachers' beliefs and gender differences in mathematics. In E. Fennema & G. C. Leder (Eds.), *Mathematics and gender* (pp. 169–187). New York: Teachers College Press.

Ferree, M. M. (1991). The gender division of labor in two-earner marriages: Dimensions of variability and change. *Journal of Family Issues, 12,* 158–180.

Fewer high school students having sex, poll shows (1998, September 18). *New York Times,* p. A18.

Fiatarone, M. A., et al. (1994). Exercise training and nutritional supplementation for physical frailty in very elderly people. *New England Journal of Medicine, 33,* 1769–1775.

Field, D. (1998, July). *Women and men in advanced old age: Continuity or change in social relations?* Paper presented at the meeting of the International Society for the Study of Behavioral Development. Basel, Switzerland.

Field, D., & Weishaus, S. (1992). Marriage over half a century: A longitudinal study. In M. Bloom (Ed.), *Changing lives* (pp. 269–273). Columbia, SC: University of South Carolina Press.

Field, T., Schanberg, S., Kuhn, C., Field, T., Fierro, K., Henteleff, T. Mueller, C., Yando, R., Shaw, S., & Burman, I. (1998). Bulimic adolescents benefit from massage therapy. *Adolescence, 33,* 555–563.

Fielding, E. N. (1999, August). *Passing the power: Gender differences in computer use in the elementary classroom.* Paper presented at the meeting of the American Psychological Association, Boston.

Finer, L. B., Darroch, J. E., & Singh, S. (1999). Sexual partnership patterns as a behavioral risk factor for sexually transmitted diseases. *Family Planning Perspectives, 31,* 228–236.

Finkelhor, D. (1990). Early and long-term effects of child sexual abuse: An update. *Professional Psychology: Research and Practice, 21,* 325–330.

Finn, R. (1999, March 7). Harassment a concern as women's sports grow. *New York Times,* pp. A1, A16.

Firestein, B. A. (Ed.), (1996). *Bisexuality: The psychology and politics of an invisible minority.* Thousand Oaks, CA: Sage.

Firestone, J. M., & Harris, R. J. (1997). Organizational climate, leadership and individual responses to sexual harassment in the active duty military. *Free Inquiry in Creative Sociology, 25,* 1–7.

Fiscella, K., Kitzman, H. J., Cole, R. E., Sidora, K. J., & Olds, D. (1998). Does child abuse predict adolescent pregnancy? *Pediatrics, 101,* 620–624.

Fisher, M., et al. (1995). Eating disorders in adolescents: A background paper. *Journal of Adolescent Health, 16,* 420–437.

Fisher-Thompson, D. (1991, August). *Toys children request and receive: Sex and gender schema effects.* Paper presented at the meeting of the American Psychological Association, San Francisco.

Fisher-Thompson, D., Sausa, A. D., & Wright, T. F. (1995). Toy selection for children: Personality and toy request influences. *Sex Roles, 33,* 239–255.

Fiske, S. T., Bersoff, D. N., Borgida, E., Deaux, K., & Heilman, M. E. (1991). Social science research on trial: Use of sex stereotyping research in *Price Waterhouse v. Hopkins. American Psychologist, 46,* 1049–1060.

Fiske, S. T., & Glick, P. (1995). Ambivalence and stereotypes cause sexual harassment: A theory with implications for organizational change. *Journal of Social Issues, 51,* 97–115.

Fiske, S. T., & Stevens, L. A. (1993). What's so special about sex? Gender stereotyping and discrimination. In S. Oskamp & M. Costanzo (Eds.), *Gender issues in contemporary society* (pp. 173–196). Newbury Park, CA: Sage.

Fitch, R. H., Cowell, P. E., & Denenberg, V. H. (1998). The female phenotype: Nature's default? *Developmental Neuropsychology, 14,* (pp. 213–231).

Fitzgerald, L. F. (1993). Sexual harassment: Violence against women in the workplace. *American Psychologist, 48,* 1070–1076.

Fitzgerald, L. F. (1996). Sexual harassment: The definition and measurement of a construct. In M. A. Paludi (Ed.), *Sexual harassment on college campuses: Abusing the ivory power* (pp. 25–47). Albany, NY: SUNY.

Fitzgerald, L. F., & Ormerod, A. J. (1997, August). *Assessing the invisible variable: Examining the effects of sexual harassment on women's work adjustment.* Paper presented at the meeting of the American Psychological Association, Chicago.

Fitzgerald, L. F., Swan, S., & Fischer, K. (1995). Why didn't she just report him? The psychological and legal implications of women's responses to sexual harassment. *Journal of Social Issues, 51,* 117–138.

Fitzgerald, M. H. (1990). The interplay of culture and symptoms: Menstrual symptoms among Samoans. *Medical Anthropology, 12,* 145–167.

Flanagan, C. (1993). Gender and social class: Intersecting issues in women's achievement. *Educational Psychologist, 28,* 357–378.

Flannagan, D., Baker-Ward, L., & Graham, L. (1995). Talk about preschool: Patterns of topic discussion and elaboration related to gender and ethnicity. *Sex Roles, 32,* 1–15.

Flannagan, D., & Perese, S. (1998). Emotional references in mother-daughter and mother-son dyads' conversations about school. *Sex Roles, 39,* 353–367.

Follette, V. M., Alexander, P. C., & Higgs, D. C. (1991). Individual predictors of outcome in group treatment for incest survivors. *Journal of Consulting and Clinical Psychology, 59,* 150–155.

Foote, D., & Seibert, S. (1999, Spring/Summer). The age of anxiety. *Newsweek,* pp. 68–72.

For gay teens, a desperate cry for help. (1999, May 18). *New York Times,* p D8.

For Pap smears, the matter of timing. (1999, February 16). *New York Times,* p. D7.

Forehand, R., Wierson, M., Thomas, A. M., Fauber, R., Armistead, L., Kemptom, T., & Long, N. (1991). A short-term longitudinal examination of young adolescent functioning following divorce: The role of family factors. *Journal of Abnormal Child Psychology, 19,* 97–111.

Foschi, M., Sigerson, K., & Lebesis, M. (1995). Assessing job applicants: the relative effects of gender, academic record, and decision type. *Small Group Research, 26,* 328–352.

Foshee, V. A., Bauman, K. E., & Fletcher, G. (1999). Family violence and the perpetration of adolescent dating violence: Examining social learning and social control processes. *Journal of Marriage and the Family, 61,* 331–342.

Foster, M. D. (1999). Acting out against gender discrimination: The effects of different social identities. *Sex Roles, 40,* 167–186.

Fouts, G., & Burggraf, K. (1999). Television situation comedies: Female body images and verbal reinforcements. *Sex Roles, 40,* 473–481.

Fowers, B. J. (1991). His and her marriage: A multivariate study of gender and marital satisfaction. *Sex Roles, 24,* 209–221.

Fowers, B. J., Applegate, B., Tredinnick, M., & Slusher, J. (1996). His and her individualisms? Sex bias and individualism in psychologists' responses to case vignettes. *Journal of Psychology, 130,* 159–174.

Frank, A. (1995). *The diary of a young girl: The definitive edition.* New York: Bantam Books.

Frank, E. (2000). *Gender and its effects on psychopathology.* Washington, DC: American Psychiatric Publishing Group.

Frank, S. J., Towell, P. A., & Huyk, M. (1985). The effects of sex-role traits on three aspects of psychological well-being in a sample of middle-aged women. *Sex Roles, 12,* 1073–1087.

Frankie, R., & Leary, M. R. (1991). Disclosure of sexual orientation by lesbians and gay men: A comparison of private and public processes. *Journal of Social and Clinical Psychology, 10,* 262–269.

Franklin, K. (1998, August). *Psychosocial motivations of hate crime perpetrators: Implications for educational interventions.* Paper presented at the meeting of the American Psychological Association, San Francisco.

Fraser, D. M., Brockert, J. E., & Ward, R. H. (1995). Association of young maternal age with adverse reproductive outcomes. *New England Journal of Medicine, 332,* 1113–1117.

Frazier, P., Arikian, N., Benson, S., Losoff, A., & Maurer, S. (1996). Desire for marriage and life satisfaction among unmarried heterosexual adults. *Journal of Social and Personal Relationships, 13,* 225–239.

Frazier, P. A., & Seales, L. M. (1997). Acquaintance rape is real rape. In M. D. Schwartz (Ed.), *Researching sexual violence against women: Methodological and personal perspectives* (pp. 54–64). Thousand Oaks, CA: Sage.

Fredrickson, B. L., & Roberts, T. A. (1997). Objectification theory: Toward understanding women's lived experiences and mental health risks. *Psychology of Women Quarterly, 21,* 173–206.

Freud, S. (1925/1989). Some psychological consequences of the anatomical distinction between the sexes. In P. Gay (Ed.), *The Freud Reader* (pp. 670–678). New York: Norton.

Freud, S. (1933/1965). Femininity. In J. Strachey (Ed.), *New introductory lectures on psychoanalysis* (pp. 112–135). New York: Norton.

Freud, S. (1938). The transformation of puberty. In A. A. Brill (Ed. and Trans.), *The basic writings of Sigmund Freud* (pp. 604–629). New York: Random House.

Freudenheim, M. (1998, January 10). Aetna is reducing fertility benefits. *New York Times,* pp. A1, A8.

Frey, K. S., & Ruble, D. N. (1992). Gender constancy and the "cost" of sex-typed behavior. A test of the conflict hypothesis. *Developmental Psychology, 28,* 714–721.

Freyd, J. J., & Quina, K. (2000). Feminist ethics in the practice of science: The contested memory controversy as an example. In M. M. Brabeck (Ed.), *Practicing feminist ethics in psychology* (pp. 101–123). Washington, DC: American Psychological Association.

Friedan, B. (1963). *The feminine mystique.* New York: Norton.

Friedan, B. (1993). *The fountain of age.* New York: Simon & Schuster.

Friedman, R. C., & Downey, J. I. (1994). Homosexuality. *New England Journal of Medicine, 331,* 923–930.

Friedrich, M. J. (1999, October 6). Recognizing and treating depression in the elderly. *Journal of the American Medical Association, 282,* 1215.

Fritzsche, B. A., & Mayfield, H. E., Jr. (1997, August). *Sex bias in judgments of actual resumes.* Poster presented at the meeting of the American Psychological Association, Chicago.

Frost, J. J., & Forrest, J. D. (1995). Understanding the impact of effective teenage pregnancy prevention programs. *Family Planning Perspectives, 27,* 188–195.

Frye, J. C. (1996). Affirmative action: Understanding the past and present. In C. Costello & B. K. Krimgold (Eds.), *The American woman 1996–97* (pp. 33–43). New York: Norton.

Fullmer, E. M. (1995). Challenging biases against families of older gays and lesbians. In G. C. Smith, S. S. Tobin, E. A. Robertson, T. Chabo, & P. W. Power (Eds.), *Strengthening aging families: Diversity in practice and policy* (pp. 99–119). Thousand Oaks, CA: Sage.

Fullmer, E. M., Shenk, D., & Eastland, L. J. (1999). Negating identity: A feminist analysis of the social invisibility of older lesbians. *Journal of Women & Aging, 11,* (2/3), 131–148.

Fulton, S. A., & Sabornie, E. J. (1994). Evidence of employment inequality among females with disabilities. *Journal of Special Education, 28,* 149–165.

Furman, W., Brown, B. B., & Feiring, C. (Eds.). (1999). *The development of romantic relationships in adolescence.* Cambridge, England: Cambridge University Press.

Furnham, A., Abramsky, S., & Gunter, B. (1997). A cross-cultural content analysis of children's television advertisements. *Sex Roles, 37,* 91–99.

Furstenberg, F. F., Jr. (1991). Pregnancy and childbearing: Effects on teen mothers. In R. M. Lerner, A. C. Petersen, & J. Brooks-Gunn (Eds.), *Encyclopedia of adolescence* (pp. 803–807). New York: Garland.

Fyock, J., & Stangor, C. (1994). The role of memory biases in stereotype maintenance. *British Journal of Social Psychology, 33,* 331–343.

Gagliano, C. K. (1995). Group treatment for sexually abused girls. In F. J. Turner (Ed.), *Differential diagnosis and treatment in social work* (4th ed., pp. 721–730). New York: Free Press.

Galambos, N. L., Almeida, D. M., & Petersen, A. C. (1990). Masculinity, femininity, and sex role attitudes in early adolescence: Exploring gender intensification. *Child Development, 61,* 1905–1914.

Galinsky, E. (1999, August 30). Do working parents make the grade? *Newsweek,* pp. 52–56.

Galinsky, E., & Bond, J. T. (1996). Work and family: The experiences of mothers and fathers in the U.S. labor force. In C. Costello & B. K. Krimgold (Eds.), *The American woman 1996–1997* (pp. 79–103). New York: Norton.

Gallagher, C., & Busch-Rossnagal, N. A. (1991, March). *Self-disclosure and social support in the relationships of black and white female adolescents.* Poster presented at the Society for Research in Child Development, Seattle, WA.

Gallant, S. J., & Derry, P. S. (1995). Menarche, menstruation, and menopause: Psychological research and future directions. In A. L. Stanton & S. J. Gallant (Eds.), *The psychology of women's health: Progress and challenges in research and application* (pp. 199–259). Washington, DC: American Psychological Association.

Galliher, R. V., Rostosky, S. S., Welsh, D. P., & Kawaguchi, M. C. (1999). Power and psychological well-being in late adolescent romantic relationships. *Sex Roles, 40,* 689–710.

Gammon, M. D., John, E. M., & Britton, J. A. (1998). Review: Recreational and occupational physical activities and risk of breast cancer. *Journal of the National Cancer Institute, 90,* 100–117.

Gander, A. (1992). Reasons for divorce: Age and gender differences. *Women and Aging, 4,* 47–60.

Gannon, L., & Ekstrom, B. (1993). Attitudes toward menopause: The influence of sociocultural paradigms. *Psychology of Women Quarterly, 17,* 275–288.

Gannon, L., Luchetta, T., Rhodes, K., Pardie, L., & Segrist, D. (1992). Sex bias in psychological research: Progress or complacency? *American Psychologist, 47,* 389–396.

Gannon, L., & Stevens, J. (1998). Portraits of menopause in the mass media. *Women and Health, 27,* 1–15.

Gannon, L. R. (1999). *Women and aging: Transcending the myths.* New York: Routledge.

Ganong, L. H., & Coleman, M. (1995). The content of mother stereotypes. *Sex Roles, 32,* 495–512.

Ganong, L. H., Coleman, M., Thompson, A., & Goodwin-Watkins, C. (1996). African American and European American college students' expectations for self and future partners. *Journal of Family Issues, 17,* 758–775.

Garnefski, N., & Diekstra, R. F. W. (1997). Child sexual abuse and emotional and behavioral problems in adolescence: Gender differences. *Journal of the American Academy of Child and Adolescent Psychiatry, 36,* 323–329.

Gastil, J. (1990). Generic pronouns and sexist language: The oxymoronic character of masculine generics. *Sex Roles, 23,* 629–643.

Gater, R., Tansella, M., Korten, A.,. Tiemens, B. G., Mavreas, V. G., & Olatawura, M. O. (1998). Sex differences in the prevalence and detection of depressive and anxiety disorders in general health care settings. *Archives of General Psychiatry, 55,* 405–413.

Gatz, M., Harris, J. R., & Turk-Charles, S. (1995). The meaning of health for older women. In A. L. Stanton & S. J. Gallant (Eds), *The psychology of women's health: Progress and challenges in research and application* (pp. 491–529). Washington, DC: American Psychological Association.

Gavey, N., & McPhillips, K. (1999). Subject to romance: Heterosexual passivity as an obstacle to women initiating condom use. *Psychology of Women Quarterly, 23,* 349–367.

Ge, X., Conger, R. D., & Elder, G. H., Jr. (1996). Coming of age too early: Pubertal influences on girls' vulnerability to psychological distress. *Child Development, 67,* 3386–3400.

Geary, D. (1999). Evolution and developmental sex differences. *Current Directions in Psychological Science, 8,* 115–120.

Geary, D. C. (1996). Sexual selection and sex differences in mathematical abilities. *Behavioral and Brain Sciences, 19,* 229–284.

Geleijnse, J. M., et al. (1999). Tea flavonoids may protect against atherosclerosis: The Rotterdam Study. *Archives of Internal Medicine, 159,* 2170–2174.

Genant, H. K., et al. (1997). Low-dose esterfied estrogen therapy: Effects on bone, plasma, estradiol concentrations, endometrium, and lipid levels. *Archives of Internal Medicine, 157,* 2609–2615.

Gender bias on the campus. (1999, March 28). New York Times, p. WK16.

Gender gap in drug abuse said to close. (1996, June 6). *New York Times*, p. A14.

Gentry, M. (1998). The sexual double standard: The influence of number of relationships and level of sexual activity on judgements of women and men. *Sex Roles, 22,* 505–511.

George, D., Carroll, P., Kersnick, R., & Calderon, K. (1998). Gender-related patterns of helping among friends. *Psychology of Women Quarterly, 22,* 685–704.

George, G. H. M., & Spector, T. D. (1997). Arthritis, menopause and estrogens. In B. G. Wren (Ed.), *Progress in the management of the menopause,* (pp. 323–327). Pearl River, NY: Parthenon.

Gerson, K. (1999). Children of the gender revolution: Some theoretical questions and preliminary notes from the filed–selected excerpts. *Work-family researchers electronic network: Selected excerpts from the on-line newsletter.* Boston: Boston College Center for Work & Family.

Gettelman, T. E., & Thompson, J. K. (1993). Actual differences and stereotypical perception in body image and eating disturbance: A comparison of male and female heterosexual and homosexual samples. *Sex Roles, 29,* 545–562.

Gibbons, J. L., Lynn, M., & Stiles, D. A. (1997). Cross-national gender differences in adolescents' preferences for free-time activities. *Cross-Cultural Research, 31,* 55–69.

Gibson, H. B. (1996). Sexual functioning in later life. In R. T. Woods (Ed.), *Handbook of the clinical psychology of aging* (pp. 183–193). New York: Wiley.

Gidycz, C. A., Coble, C. H., Latham, L., & Layman, M. J. (1993). Sexual assault experience in adulthood and prior victimization experiences: A prospective analysis. *Psychology of Women Quarterly, 17,* 151–168.

Giesbrecht, N. (1998). Gender patterns of psychosocial development. *Sex Roles, 39,* 463–478.

Gignac, M. A. M., Kelloway, E. K., & Gottlieb, B. H. (1996). The impact of caregiving on employment: A mediational model of work-family conflict. *Canadian Journal on Aging, 15,* 525–542.

Gil, R. M. (1996). Hispanic women and mental health. *Women and Mental Health. Annals of the New York Academy of Sciences, 789,* 147–159.

Gilbert, L. A. (1993). *Two careers/one family.* Newberry Park, CA: Sage.

Gilbert, L. A. (1994). Reclaiming and returning gender to context: Examples from studies of heterosex-ual dual-earner families. *Psychology of Women Quarterly, 18,* 539–558.

Gilbert, L. A., & Scher, M. (1999). *Gender and sex in counseling and psychotherapy.* Boston: Allyn and Bacon.

Gilbert, S. (1996, October 2). Estrogen may help prevent osteoarthritis. *New York Times*, p. B8.

Gilbert, S. (1998a, May 19). Benefits of assistant for childbirth go far beyond the birthing room. *New York Times*, p. B17.

Gilbert, S. (1998b, July 28). Raising grandchildren, rising stress. *New York Times*, p. B8.

Gilbert S. (1999a, August 3). For some children, it's an after-school pressure cooker. *New York Times*, p. D7.

Gilbert, S. (1999b, April 6). A less invasive alternative for fibroids. *New York Times*, p. D7.

Gilligan, C. (1982). *In a different voice.* Cambridge, MA: Harvard University Press.

Gilligan, C. (1993). Joining the resistance: Psychology, politics, girls and women. In L. Weis & M. Fine (Eds.), *Beyond silenced voices* (pp. 143–168). Albany, NY: SUNY Press.

Ginorio, A. B., Gutiérrez, L., Cauce, A. M., & Acosta, M. (1995). Psychological issues for Latinas. In H. Landrine (Ed.), *Bringing cultural diversity to feminist psychology: Theory, research and practice* (pp. 241–263). Washington, DC: American Psychological Association.

Gise, L. H. (1997). Psychosocial aspects. In D. E. Stewart & G. E. Robinson (Eds.), *A clinician's guide to menopause* (pp. 29–44). Washington, DC: Health Press International.

Glasier, A., & Baird, D. (1998). The effects of self-administering emergency contraception. *New England Journal of Medicine, 339,* 1–4.

Glass, T. A., de Leon, C. M., Marottoli, R. A., & Berkman, L. F. (1999). Population based study of social and productive activities as predictors of survival among elderly Americans. *British Medical Journal, 319,* 478–483.

Glick, P. (1991). Trait-based and sex-based discrimination in occupational prestige, occupational salary, and hiring. *Sex Roles, 25,* 351–378.

Glick, P., & Fiske, S. T. (1997). Hostile and benevolent sexism: Measuring ambivalent sexist attitudes toward women. *Psychology of Women Quarterly, 21,* 119–135.

Glied, S. (1998). The diagnosis and treatment of mental health problems among older women. *Jour-*

nal of the American Medical Women's Association, 53, 187–191.

Glomb, T. M., Munson, L. J., Hulin, C. L., Bergman, M. E., & Drasgow, F. (1999). Structural equation models of sexual harassment: Longitudinal explorations and cross-sectional generalizations. *Journal of Applied Psychology, 84,* 14–28.

Godard, B. (1998). Risk factors for familial and sporadic ovarian cancer among French Canadians: A case-control study. *American Journal of Obstetrics and Gynecology, 179,* 403–410.

Godbey, J. K., & Hutchinson, S. A. (1996). Healing from incest: Resurrecting the buried self. *Archives of Psychiatric Nursing, 10,* 304–310.

Goetting, M. A., Raiser, M. V., Martin, P., Poon, L., & Johnson, M. A. (1995). Older women's financial resources and perception of financial adequacy. *Journal of Women and Aging, 7* (4), 67–81.

Goldberg, C. (1998, September 8). Getting to the truth in child abuse cases: New methods. *New York Times,* p. B10.

Goldberg, C. (1999a, October 27). Just another girl, unlike any other. *New York Times,* p. A14.

Goldberg, C. (1999b, May 16). Wellesley grads find delicate balance. *Hartford Courant,* p. G3.

Goldberg, C. (2000, March 17). Vermont house passes bill on rights for gay couples. *New York Times,* pp. A1, A18.

Goldberg, C., & Elder, J. (1998, January 16). Public still backs abortion, but wants limits, poll says. *New York Times,* pp. A1, A16.

Golding, J. M. (1996). Sexual assault history and women's reproductive and sexual health. *Psychology of Women Quarterly, 20,* 101–121.

Golding, J. M. (1999). Sexual-assault history and long-term physical health problems: Evidence from clinical and population epidemiology. *Current Directions in Psychological Science, 8,* 191–194.

Goldman, M. B., & Hatch, M.C. (2000). An overview of women's health. In M. B. Goldman & M. C. Hatch (Eds.), *Women & health* (pp. 5–14). New York: Academic Press.

Goldman, M. B., Missmer, S. A., & Barbieri, R. L. (2000). Infertility. In M. B. Goldman & M. C. Hatch (Eds.), *Women & health* (pp. 196–214). New York: Academic Press.

Goldstein, A. (2000, February 29). Breadwinning wives are on the rise. *Hartford Courant,* pp. A1, A7.

Goldstein, M. Z. (1995). Maltreatment of elderly persons. *Psychiatric Services, 46,* 1219–1225.

Goldstein, M. Z. (1996). Elderly maltreatment and post-traumatic stress disorder. In P. E. Ruskin & J. A. Talbott (Eds.), *Aging and posttraumatic stress disorder* (pp. 127–135). Washington, DC: American Psychiatric Press.

Goleman, D. (1993, October 6). Abuse-prevention efforts and children. *New York Times,* p. C13.

Goleman, D. (1995, September 6). Elderly depression tied to stroke. *New York Times,* p. B6.

Golub, S. (1992). *Periods: From menarche to menopause.* Newbury Park, CA: Sage.

Golub, S., & Catalano, J. (1983). Recollections of menarche and women's subsequent experiences with menstruation. *Women & Health, 8* (1), 49–61.

Gomberg, E. S. L. (1994). Risk factors for drinking over a woman's life span. *Alcohol Health and Research World, 18,* 220–227.

Gondolf, E. W., Fisher, E., & McFerron, J. R. (1988). Racial differences among shelter residents: A comparison of Anglo, Black, and Hispanic battered women. *Journal of Family Violence, 3,* 39–51.

Gonsiorek, J. C. (1996). Mental health and sexual orientation. In R. C. Savin-Williams & K. Cohen (Eds.), *The lives of lesbians, gays and bisexuals: Children to adults* (pp. 462–478). Fort Worth, TX: Hartcourt Brace.

Gonzalez, F. J., & Espin, O. M. (1996). Latino men, Latina women, and homosexuality. In R. P. Cabaj, & T. S. Stein (Eds.), *Textbook of homosexuality and mental health.* (pp. 583–593). Washington, DC: American Psychiatric Press.

Gonzalez, M. H., & Meyers, S. A. (1993). "Your mother would like me.": Self-presentation in the personal ads of heterosexual and homosexual men and women. *Personality and Social Psychology Bulletin, 19,* 131–142.

Goode, E. (1999a, February 16). New study finds middle age is prime of life. *New York Times,* p. D6.

Goode, E. (1999b, May 20). Study finds TV trims Fiji girls' body image and eating habits. *New York Times,* p. A13.

Goode, E. (2000a, January 15). What provokes a rapist to rape? *New York Times,* pp. A21, A23.

Goode, E. (2000b, February 15). When women find love is fatal. *New York Times,* D1, D6.

Goode, W. J. (1960). A theory of role strain. *American Sociological Review, 25,* 483–496.

Goodman, G. S., Emery, R. E., & Haugaard, J. J. (1998). Developmental psychology and law: Divorce, child maltreatment, foster care, and adoption. In

W. Damon (Series Ed.), I. E. Sigel, & K. A. Renninger (Vol. Eds.), *Handbook of child psychology: Vol. 4. Child psychology in practice* (5th ed., pp. 775–874). New York: Wiley.

Googins, B. K. (1991). *Work/family conflicts*. New York: Auburn House.

Gordon, M. (1993, Fall). Sexual slang and gender. *Women and Language, 16,* 16–21.

Gose, B. (1995, February 10). Second thoughts at women's colleges. *Chronicle of Higher Education,* pp. A22–24.

Gotlib, I. H. (1998). Postpartum depression. In E. A. Blechman & K. D. Brownell (Eds.), *Behavioral medicine and women: A comprehensive handbook* (pp. 489–494). New York: Guilford.

Gottlieb, N. (1989). Families, work and the lives of older women. In J. D. Garner & S. O. Mercer (Eds.), *Women as they age: Challenge, opportunity, and triumph* (pp. 217–244). Binghamton, NY: Haworth.

Gould, L. (1990). X: A fabulous child's story. In A. G. Halberstadt & S. L. Ellyson (Eds.), *Social psychology readings: A century of research* (pp. 251–257). Boston: McGraw-Hill.

Government study finds 2 of 3 child care facilities have a safety hazard. (1999, April 20). *The National Report on Work & Family, 12,* 67.

Graber, J. A., & Brooks-Gunn, J. (1998). Puberty. In E. A. Blechman & K.D. Brownell (Eds.), *Behavioral medicine and women: A comprehensive handbook* (pp. 51–58). New York: Guilford.

Graber, J. A., Brooks-Gunn, J., & Warren M. P. (1995). The antecedents of menarcheal age: Heredity, family, environment, and stressful life events. *Child Development, 66,* 346–359.

Grady, D. (1998, October 20). Surrogate mothers report few regrets. *New York Times,* p. D12.

Grady, D. (1999a, May 4). As heart attacks wane, heart failure is on the rise. *New York Times,* pp. D1, D4.

Grady, D. (1999b, September 25). Ballerina's ovarian tissue transplant gives hope to other young women facing infertility. *New York Times,* p. A8.

Grady, D. (1999c, February 23). Experts urge chemotherapy for invasive cancer concern. *New York Times,* pp. A1, A15.

Grady, D. (1999d, January 26). In breast cancer data, hope, fear and confusion. *New York Times,* pp. D1, D4.

Grady, D. (1999e, February 17). New ways to help sperm get up and go. *New York Times,* p. D12.

Grady, D. (1999f, January 26). Software to compute women's cancer risk. *New York Times,* p. D4.

Grady, D. (2000a, January 5). New test for cancer surpasses the Pap one, studies show. *New York Times,* p. A18.

Grady, D. (2000b, January 27). Study backs hormone link to cancer for women. *New York Times,* p. A17.

Graham, S. (1997). "Most of the subjects were White and middle class": Trends in published research on African Americans in selected APA journals, 1970–1989. In L. A. Peplau & S. E. Taylor (Eds.), *Sociocultural perspectives in social psychology: Current readings* (pp. 52–71). Upper Saddle River, NJ: Prentice-Hall.

Granrose, C. S., & Kaplan, E. E. (1996). *Work-family role choices for women in their 20s and 30s: From college plans to life experiences*. Westport, CT: Praeger.

Grant, B. F., & Dawson, D. A. (1997). Age at onset of alcohol use and its association with DSM-IV alcohol use and dependence: Results from the National Longitudinal Alcohol Epidemiologic Survey. *Journal of Substance Abuse, 9,* 103–110.

Gray, J. (1992). *Men are from Mars, women are from Venus*. New York: HarperCollins.

Gray, P., & Feldman, J. (1997). Patterns of age mixing and gender mixing among children and adolescents at an ungraded democratic school. *Merrill-Palmer Quarterly, 43,* 67–86.

Gray-Little, B., & Hafdahl, A. R. (2000). Factors influencing racial comparisons of self-esteem: A quantitative review. *Psychological Bulletin, 126,* 26–54.

Green, B. L., & Russo, N. F. (1993). Work and family roles: Selected issues. In F. L. Denmark & M. A. Paludi (Eds.), *Psychology of women: A handbook of issues and theories* (pp. 685–719). Westport, CT: Greenwood.

Greenberg, B. S., & Brand, J. D. (1993). Cultural diversity on Saturday morning television. In G. L. Berry & J. K. Asamen (Eds.), *Children & television: Images in a changing sociocultural world* (pp. 1132–142). Newbury Park, CA: Sage.

Greenberg, S., & Motenko, A.K. (1994). Women growing older: Partnerships for change. In M.P. Mirkin (Ed.), *Women in context: Toward a feminist reconstruction of psychotherapy* (pp. 96–117). New York: Guilford.

Greenberg, S. H., & Westreich, J. (1999, Spring/Summer). Beyond the blues. *Newsweek,* p. 75.

Greene, B. (1996). African-American women: Considering diverse identities and societal barriers in psychotherapy. *Women and Mental Health. Annals of the New York Academy of Sciences, 789,* 191–209.

Greene, B., & Sanchez-Hucles, J. (1997). Diversity: Advancing an inclusive feminist psychology. In J. Worell & N. G. Johnson (Eds.), *Shaping the future of feminist psychology: Education, research and practice* (pp. 173–202). Washington, DC: American Psychological Association.

Greene, B. A., DeBacker, T., Ravindran, B., & Krows, A. J. (1999). Goals, values, and beliefs as predictors of achievement and effort in high school mathematics classes. *Sex Roles, 40,* 421–458.

Greene, C. K., & Stitt-Gohdes, W. L. (1997). Factors that influence women's choices to work in the trades. *Journal of Career Development, 23,* 265–278.

Greene, D. M., & Navarro, R. L. (1998). Situation-specific assertiveness in the epidemiology of sexual victimization among university women: A prospective path analysis. *Psychology of Women Quarterly, 22,* 589–604.

Greenspan S. (1999). A 73-year-old woman with osteoporosis. *Journal of the American Medical Association, 281,* 1531–1540.

Grimmell, D., & Stern, G. S. (1992). The relationship between gender role ideals and psychological well-being. *Sex Roles, 27,* 487–497.

Grodstein, F., et al. (1997). Postmenopausal hormone therapy and mortality. *New England Journal of Medicine, 336,* 1769–1775.

Gross, J. (1998, November 29). In quest for the perfect look, more girls choose the scalpel. *New York Times,* pp. Y1, Y38.

Grossman, A. L., & Tucker, J. S. (1997). Gender differences and sexism in the knowledge and use of slang. *Sex Roles, 37,* 101–110.

Growing older in good health. (2000). *Journal of the American Medical Association, 283,* 560.

Gruber, J. E., Smith, M., & Kauppinen-Toropainen, K. (1996). Sexual harassment types and severity: Linking research and policy. In M. S. Stockdale (Ed.), *Sexual harassment in the workplace: Perspectives, frontiers, and response strategies* (pp. 151–173). Thousand Oaks, CA: Sage.

Gu, K., Cowie, C. C., & Harris, M. I. (1999). Diabetes and decline in heart disease mortality in U.S. adults. *Journal of the American Medical Association, 281,* 1291–1297.

Guberman, N. (1999). Daughters-in-law as caregivers: How and why do they come to care? *Journal of Women & Aging, 11,* 85–102.

Guerrero, L. K. (1997). Nonverbal involvement across interactions with same-sex friends, opposite-sex friends and romantic partners: Consistency or change. *Journal of Social and Personal Relationships, 14,* 31–58.

Guerrero, L. K., & Reiter, R. L. (1998). Expressing emotion: Sex differences in social skills and communicative responses to anger, sadness, and jealousy. In D. J. Canary & K. Dindia (Eds.), *Sex differences and similarities in communication: Critical essays and empirical investigations of sex and gender in interaction* (pp. 321–350). Mahwah, NJ: Erlbaum.

Guille, C., & Chrisler, J. C. (1999). Does feminism serve a protective function against eating disorders? *Journal of Lesbian Studies, 3,* (4) 141–148.

Gump, J. P. (1980). Reality and myth: Employment and sex-role identity in black women. In J. Sherman & F. L. Denmark (Eds.), *The psychology of women: Directions in research* (pp. 349–380). New York: Psychological Dimensions.

Guralnik, J. M., et al. (Eds.) (1995). *The Women's Health and Aging Study: Health and social characteristics of older women with disability.* (NIH Pub. No. 95-4009) Bethesda, MD: National Institute on Aging.

Guse, K. E. (1998, May). *Components of love: Links to attachment style, gender, and relationship type.* Poster session presented at the Annual Convention of the American Psychological Society, Washington, DC.

Gutek, B. A. (1985). *Sex and the workplace.* San Francisco: Jossey-Bass.

Gutek, B. A. (1993). Responses to sexual harassment. In S. Oskamp & M. Costanzo (Eds.), *Gender issues in contemporary society* (pp. 197–216). Newbury Park, CA: Sage.

Hackett, G., Betz, N. E., Casas, J. M., & Rocha-Singh, I. A. (1992). Gender, ethnicity, and social cognitive factors predicting the academic achievement of students in engineering. *Journal of Counseling Psychology, 39,* 527–538.

Haden, C. A., Haine, R. A., & Fivush, R. (1997). Developing narrative structure in parent-child reminiscing across the preschool years. *Developmental Psychology, 33,* 295–307.

Hafemeister, T. L., & Jackson, S. (2000, February). Grandparent visitation: Who should decide? *APA Monitor,* p. 81.

Hafner, K., (1998, September 10). Girl games: Plenty and pink. *New York Times,* p. D8.

Half of America's women are not getting the mammograms they should (1997). *Women and Aging Letter, 2* (2), 1–9.

Hall, C. C. I., & Crum, M. J. (1994). Women and "body-isms" in television beer commercials. *Sex Roles, 31,* 329–337.

Hall, J. A. (1996). Touch, status, and gender at professional meetings. *Journal of Nonverbal Behavior, 20,* 23–44.

Hall, J. A. (1998). How big are nonverbal sex differences? The case of smiling and sensitivity to nonverbal cues. In D. J. Canary & K. Dindia (Eds.), *Sex differences and similarities in communication: Critical essays and empirical investigations of sex and gender in interaction* (pp. 155–177). Mahwah, NJ: Erlbaum.

Hall, J. A., & Veccia, E. M. (1992). Touch asymmetry between the sexes. In C. L. Ridgeway (Ed.), *Gender, interaction, and inequality* (pp. 81–96). New York: Springer.

Hall, R. M., & Sandler, B. R. (1982). *The classroom climate: A chilly one for women?* Project on the Status and Education of Women. Washington, DC: Association of American Colleges.

Halmi, K. A. (1996). Eating disorder research in the past decade. *Women and Mental Health. Annals of the New York Academy of Sciences, 789,* 67–77.

Halmi, K. A. (2000). Eating disorders. In M. B. Goldman & M. C. Hatch (Ed.),. *Women & health.* (pp. 114–125). New York: Academic Press.

Halpern, D. F. (1992). *Sex differences in cognitive abilities* (2nd ed.). Hillsdale, NJ: Erlbaum.

Halpern, D. F. (1997). Sex differences in intelligence. *American Psychologist, 52,* 1091–1102.

Hamida, S. B., Mineka, S., & Bailey, J. M. (1998). Sex differences in perceived controllability of mate value: An evolutionary perspective. *Journal of Personality and Social Psychology, 75,* 953–966.

Hamilton, M. C. (1991). Masculine bias in the attribution of personhood: People = male, male = people. *Psychology of Women Quarterly, 15,* 393–402.

Hamilton, M., & Yee, J. (1990). Rape knowledge and propensity to rape. *Journal of Sex Research, 24,* 111–122.

Hampton, R. L., & Gelles, R. J. (1994). Violence toward Black women in a nationally representative sample of Black families. *Journal of Comparative Family Studies, 25,* 105–120.

Hamrick, F. (1994). Perceptions of equity: Career women and discrimination. In C. W. Konek & S. L. Kitch (Eds.), *Women and careers: Issues and challenges* (pp. 99–137). Thousand Oaks, CA: Sage.

Hankinson, S. E., et al. (1998). Circulating concentrations of insulin-like growth factor I and risk of breast cancer. *Lancet, 351,* 1393–1396.

Hanna, W. J., & Rogovsky, B. (1991). Women with disabilities: two handicaps plus. *Disability, Handicap & Society, 6,* 49–63.

Hanna, W. J., & Rogovsky, E. (1992). On the situation of African-American women with physical disabilities. *Journal of Applied Rehabilitation Counseling, 23,* 39–45.

Hanson, K., & Wapner, S. (1994). Transition to retirement: Gender differences. *International Journal of Aging and Human Development, 39,* 189–208.

Harden, T. (1999, June 13). Diagnosing fibroids is simple; deciding what to do is hard. *New York Times,* p. WH14.

Hardie, E. A. (1997). Prevalence and predictors of cyclic and noncyclic affective change. *Psychology of Women Quarterly, 21,* 299–314.

Hare-Mustin, R., & Marecek, J. (1988). The meaning of difference: Gender theory, postmodernism, and psychology. *American Psychologist, 43,* 455–464.

Hare-Mustin, R. T., & Marecek, J. (1990a). Gender and the meaning of difference. In R. T. Hare-Mustin and J. Marecek (Eds.), *Making a difference: Psychology and the construction of gender* (pp. 22–64). New Haven, CT: Yale University Press.

Hare-Mustin, R. T., & Marecek, J. (1990b). On making a difference. In R. T. Hare-Mustin and J. Marecek (Eds.), *Making a difference: Psychology and the construction of gender* (pp. 1–21). New Haven, CT: Yale University Press.

Harper, L. V., & Huie, K. S. (1998). Free play use of space by preschoolers from diverse backgrounds: Factors influencing activity choices. *Merrill-Palmer Quarterly, 44,* 423–446.

Harris, A. C. (1994). Ethnicity as a determinant of sex role identity: A replication study of item selection for the Bem Sex Role Inventory. *Sex Roles, 31,* 241–273.

Harris, K. L., Melaas, K., & Rodacker, E. (1999). The impact of women's studies courses on college students of the 1990s. *Sex Roles, 40,* 969–977.

Harris, M. B. (1994). Growing old gracefully: Age concealment and gender. *Journal of Gerontology: Psychological Sciences, 49,* 149–158.

Harris, M. B., Begay, C., & Page, P. (1989). Activities, family relationships and feelings about aging in a multicultural elderly sample. *International Journal of Aging and Human Development, 29,* 104–110.

Harris, M. B., & Knight-Bohnhoff, K. (1996). Gender and aggression II: Personal aggressiveness. *Sex Roles, 35,* 27–42.

Harris, M. B., Page, P., & Begay, C. (1988). Attitudes toward aging in a southwestern sample: Effects of ethnicity, age, and sex. *Psychological Reports, 62,* 735–746.

Harris, R. J., & Firestone, J. M. (1998). Changes in predictors of gender role ideologies among women: A multivariate analysis. *Sex Roles, 38,* 239–252.

Harris, S. M. (1993). The influence of personal and family factors on achievement needs and concerns of African-American and Euro-American college women. *Sex Roles, 29,* 671–689.

Harris, S. M. (1995). Family, self, and sociocultural contributions to body-image attitudes of African-American women. *Psychology of Women Quarterly, 19,* 129–145.

Hart, B. I., & Thompson, J. M. (1996). Gender role characteristics and depressive symptomatology among adolescents. *Journal of Early Adolescence, 16,* 407–426.

Harter, S. (1990). Adolescent self and identity development. In S. S. Feldman & G. R. Elliot (Eds.), *At the threshold: The developing adolescent* (pp. 352–387). Cambridge, MA: Harvard University Press.

Harter, S. (1998). The development of self-representations. In W. Damon (Series Ed.) & N. Eisenberg (Vol. Ed.), *Handbook of child psychology: Vol. 3. Social, emotional and personality development* (5th ed., pp. 553–617). New York: Wiley.

Harter, S. (1999). *The construction of the self: A developmental perspective.* New York: Guilford.

Hartup, W. W. (1993). Adolescents and their friends. In B. Laursen (Ed.), *New directions in child development: No. 60. Close friendships in adolescence* (pp. 3–22). San Francisco: Jossey-Bass.

Hartup, W. W., & Stevens, N. (1999). Friendships and adaptation across the life span. *Current Directions in Psychological Science, 8,* 76–79.

Harvey, E. (1999). Short-term and long-term effects of early parental employment on children of the National Longitudinal Survey of Youth. *Developmental Psychology, 35,* 445–459.

Harvey, W. B. (1986). Homicide among young lack adults: Life in the subculture of exasperation. In D. F.

Hawkins (Ed.), *Homicide among Black Americans* (pp. 153–171). Lanham, MD: University Press of America.

Haskell, M. (1998, February 8). Where the old boy always get the girl. *New York Times,* p. AR11.

Haskell, M., & Harmetz, A. (1998, March-April). Star power. *Modern Maturity, 41,* 32–40.

Hatala, M. N., & Prehodka, J. (1996). Content analysis of gay male and lesbian personal advertisements. *Psychological Reports, 78,* 371–374.

Hatch, L. R., & Thompson, A. (1992). Family responsibilities and women's retirement. In M. Szinovacz, D. J. Ekerdt, & B. H. Vinick (Eds.), *Families and retirement* (pp. 99–113). Newbury Park, CA: Sage.

Hawkes, K., O'Connell, J. F., & Blurton-Jones, N. G. (1997). Hadza women's time allocation, offspring provisioning, and the evolution of long postmenopausal life spans. *Current Anthropology, 38,* 551–565.

Hawkins, J. W., & Aber, C. S. (1993). Women in advertisements in medical journals. *Sex Roles, 28,* 233–244.

Hayflick, L. (1994). *How and why we age.* New York: Ballantine Books.

Healy, B. (1999, Spring/Summer). A medical revolution. *Newsweek,* pp. 64–65.

Heart disease: Women at risk. (1993, May). *Consumer Reports,* pp. 300–304.

Heatherington, L., Daubman, K. A., Bates, C., Ahn, A., Brown, H., & Preston, C. (1993). Two investigations of "female modesty" in achievement situations. *Sex Roles, 29,* 739–754.

Hebl, M. (1995). Gender bias in leader selection. *Teaching of Psychology, 22,* 186–188.

Hedley, M. (1994). The presentation of gendered conflict in popular movies: Affective stereotypes, cultural sentiments, and men's motivation. *Sex Roles, 31,* 721–740.

Hefferman, K. (1999). Lesbians and the internalization of societal standards of weight and appearance. *Journal of Lesbian Studies, 3* (4), 121–127.

Helgeson, V. S. (1994). Relation of agency and communion to well-being: Evidence and potential explanations. *Psychological Bulletin, 116,* 412–428.

Helsing, K. J., Szklo, M., & Comstock, G. W. (1981). Factors associated with mortality after widowhood. *American Journal of Public Health, 71,* 802–809.

Helson, R. (1992). Women's difficult times and the rewriting of the life story. *Psychology of Women Quarterly, 16,* 331–347.

Helwig, A. A. (1998). Gender-role stereotyping: Testing theory with a longitudinal sample. *Sex Roles, 38,* 403–423.

Henderson, K. A. (1990). The meaning of leisure for women: An integrative review of the research. *Journal of Leisure Research, 22,* 228–243.

Henley, N. M. (1973). Status and sex: Some touching observations. *Bulletin of the Psychonomic Society, 2,* 91–93.

Henley, N. M., Meng, K., O'Brien, D., McCarthy, W. J., & Sockloskie, R. J. (1998). Developing a scale to measure the diversity of feminist attitudes. *Psychology of Women Quarterly, 22,* 317–348.

Henretta, J. C., O'Rand, A. M., & Chan, C. G. (1993). Gender differences in employment after spouse's retirement. *Research on Aging, 15,* 148–149.

Henrion, C. (1997). *Women in mathematics: The addition of difference.* Bloomington, IN: University of Indiana Press.

Henriques, G. , Calhoun, L., & Cann, A. (1996). Ethnic differences in women's body satisfaction: An experimental investigation. *Journal of Social Psychology, 136,* 689–697.

Herdt, G. H., & Davidson, J. (1988). The Sambia "turnim-man": Sociocultural and clinical aspects of gender formation in male pseudohermaphrodites with 5-alpha-reductase deficiency in Papua, New Guinea. *Archives of Sexual Behavior, 17,* 33–56.

Herek, G. M. (1996). Heterosexism and homophobia. In R. P. Cabaj and T. S. Stein (Eds.), *Textbook of homosexuality and mental health* (pp. 101–113). Washington, DC: American Psychiatric Press.

Herman-Giddens, M. E., et al. (1997). Secondary sexual characteristics and menses in young girls seen in office practice: A study from the Pediatric Research in Office Settings network. *Pediatrics, 99,* 505–512.

Hertz, R., & Ferguson, F. I. (1998). Only one pair of hands: Ways that single mothers stretch work and family resources. *Community, Work, & Family, 1,* 13–37.

Hetherington, E. M. (1993). An overview of the Virginia longitudinal study of divorce and remarriage with a focus on early adolescence. *Journal of Family Psychology, 7,* 1–18.

Hetherington, E. M. (1999). Social capital and the development of youth from non-divorced, divorced, and remarried families. In W. A. Collins & B. Laursen (Eds.), *Relationships as developmental contexts. The Minnesota Symposia on Child Psychology, Vol. 30* (pp. 177–209). Mahwah, NJ: Erlbaum.

Hetherington, E. M., Clingempeel, W. G., Anderson, E. R., Deal, J. E., Stanley-Hagan, M., Hollier, E. A., & Lindner, M. S. (1992). Coping with marital transitions: A family systems perspective. *Monographs of the Society for Research in Child Development 57,* (2–3, Serial No. 227).

Hetherington, E. M., & Stanley-Hagan, M. M. (1995). Parenting in divorced and remarried families. In M. H. Bornstein (Ed.), *Handbook of parenting: Vol. 3. Status and social conditions of parenting* (pp. 233–254). Mahwah, NJ: Erlbaum.

Hewitt, M., & Simone, J. (Eds.). (1999). *Ensuring quality cancer care.* Washington, DC: National Academic Press.

Hewstone, M., Hantzi, A., & Johnston, L. (1991). Social categorisation and person memory: The pervasiveness of race as an organizing principle. *European Journal of Social Psychology, 21,* 517–528.

Heywood, L. (1999, January 8). Despite the positive rhetoric about women's sports, female athletes face a culture of sexual harassment. *Chronicle of Higher Education,* pp. B4–B5.

HHS says statistics back up need for more federal child care funding. (1999, April 6). *The National Report on Work & Family, 12,* 57.

Hickman, S. E., & Muehlenhard, C. L. (1997). College women's fears and precautionary behaviors related to acquaintance rape and stranger rape. *Psychology of Women Quarterly, 21,* 527–547.

Hiedemann, B., Suhomlinova, O., & O'Rand, A. M. (1998). Economic independence, economic status, and empty nest in midlife marital disruption. *Journal of Marriage and the Family, 60,* 219–231.

Higginbotham, E., & Weber, L. (1996). Moving up with kin and community: Upward social mobility for Black and White women. In E. N. Chow, D. Wilkinson, & M. B. Zinn (Eds.), *Race, class, & gender: Common bonds, different voices* (pp. 125–148). Thousand Oaks, CA: Sage .

High percentage of inmates say they were abused as children. (1999, April 12). *New York Times,* p. A19.

Hillman, J. L., & Stricker, G. (1994). A linkage of knowledge and attitudes toward elderly sexuality: Not necessarily a uniform relationship. *Gerontologist, 34,* 256–260.

Hines, M., & Kaufman, F. R. (1994). Androgen and the development of human sex-typical behavior: Rough-and-tumble play and sex of preferred playmates in children with congenital adrenal hyperplasia (CAH). *Child Development, 65,* 1042–1053.

Hitt, J. (1999, October 24). The battle of the binge. *New York Times Magazine,* pp. 31–32.

HIV infection rate steady, but rate of AIDS has slowed. (1998, April 25). *New York Times,* p. A7.

Ho, C. K. (1990). An analysis of domestic violence in Asian-American communities: A multicultural approach to counseling. In L. S. Brown & M. P. P. Root (Eds.), *Diversity and complexity in feminist therapy* (pp. 129–150). New York: Haworth Press.

Hock, E., & DeMeis, D. K. (1990). Depression in mothers of infants: The role of maternal employment. *Developmental Psychology, 26,* 285–291.

Hodgson, L. G. (1995). Adult grandchildren and their grandparents: The enduring bond. In J. Hendrick (Ed.), *The ties of later life* (pp. 155–170). Amityville, NY: Baywood.

Hodson, D. S., & Skeen, P. (1994). Sexuality and aging: The hammerlock of myths. *Journal of Applied Gerontology, 13* (3), 219–235.

Hoffmann, F. L. (1986). Sexual harassment in academia: Feminist theory and institutional practice. *Harvard Educational Review, 56,* 105–121.

Hoffman, L. W., & Kloska, D. D. (1995). Parents' gender-based attitudes toward marital roles and child rearing: Development and validation of new measures. *Sex Roles, 32,* 273–295.

Hoffnung, M. (1995). Motherhood: Contemporary conflict for women. In J. Freeman (Ed.), *Women: A feminist perspective* (pp. 162–181). Mountain View, CA: Mayfield.

Hogan, J. D., & Sexton, V. S. (1991). Women and the American Psychological Association. *Psychology of Women Quarterly, 15,* 623–634.

Holahan, C. K., & Sears, R. R. (1995). *The gifted group in later maturity.* Stanford, CA: Stanford University Press.

Holcomb, B. (1998). *Not guilty: The good news about working mothers.* New York: Scribner.

Holcomb, L. P., & Giesen, C. B. (1995). Coping with challenges: College experiences of older women and women with disabilities. In J. C. Chrisler & A. H. Hemstreet (Eds.), *Variations on a theme: Diversity and the psychology of women.* Albany, NY: SUNY.

Holland, A., & Andre, T. (1992). College students' attitudes toward women: A three-dimensional approach. *College Student Journal, 26,* 253–259.

Holland, D. C., & Eisenhart, M. A. (1990). *Educated in romance: Women, achievement, and college culture.* Chicago: University of Chicago Press.

Hollenshead, C. S., Wenzel, S. A., Lazarus, B. B., & Nair, I. (1996). The graduate experience in the sciences and engineering: Rethinking a gendered institution. In D. S. Davis, A. B. Ginorio, C. S. Hollenshead, B. B. Lazarus, & P. M. Raymond (Eds.), *The equity equation* (pp. 122–162). San Francisco: Jossey-Bass.

Hollingsworth, M. A., Tomlinson, M. J., & Fassinger, R. E. (1997, August). *Working it out : Career development among prominent lesbian women.* Paper presented at the meeting of the American Psychological Association, Chicago.

Holmes, M. D., Hunter, D. J., Colditz, G. A., et al. (1999). Association of dietary intake of fat and fatty acids with risk of breast cancer. *Journal of the American Medical Association, 281,* 914–920.

Holubkar, R., & Reis, S. E. (2000). Diagnosis and treatment of heart disease in women. In M. B. Goldman & M. C. Hatch (Eds.), *Women & health* (pp. 771–781). New York: Academic Press.

Hong, L. K., & Duff, R. W. (1994). Widows in retirement communities: The social context of subjective well-being. *The Gerontologist, 34,* 347–352.

Honig, M. (1996). Retirement expectations: Differences by race, ethnicity, and gender. *Gerontologist, 36,* 373–382.

Hood, K. E., Draper, P., Crockett, L. J., Petersen, A. C. (1987). The ontogeny and phylogeny of sex differences in development: A biopsychosocial synthesis. In D. B. Carter (Ed.), *Current conceptions of sex roles and sex typing: Theory and research* (pp. 49–77). New York: Praeger.

hooks, b. (1990). Feminism: A transformational politic. In D. L. Rhode (Ed.), *Theoretical perspectives in sexual difference* (pp. 185–193). New Haven, CT: Yale University Press.

Hooyman, N. R. (1994). Caregiving to older relatives. In A. Monk (Ed.), *The Columbia retirement handbook* (pp. 463–485), New York: Columbia University Press.

Hopkins, A. B. (1996). *So ordered: Making partner the hard way.* Amherst, MA: University of Massachusetts Press.

Hopkins, B., Raja, S., Ruderman, A., & Tassava, S. (1997, August). *A review of risk factors for bulimia.* Paper presented at the meeting of the American Psychological Association, Chicago.

Hopkins, N. (1999, June 11). MIT and gender bias: Following up on victory. *Chronicle of Higher Education* pp. B4–B5.

Hopkins-Best, M., Wiianamaki, M., & Yurcisin, A. (1985). Career education for college women with disabilities. *Journal of College Student Personnel, 26,* 220–223.

Hornbacher, M. (1998). *Wasted: A memoir of anorexia and bulimia.* New York: Harper Perennial.

Horner, M. S. (1972). Toward an understanding of achievement-related conflicts in women. *Journal of Social Issues, 28,* 157–176.

Horney, K. (1926/1974). The flight from womanhood: The masculinity-complex in women as viewed by men and women. In J. Strouse (Ed.), *Women and analysis: Dialogues on psychoanalytic views of femininity* (pp. 171–186). New York: Viking.

Hortobagyi, G. N. (1998). Treatment of breast cancer. *New England Journal of Medicare, 339,* 974–984.

Horwitz, A. V., & White, H. R. (1998). The relationship of cohabitation and mental health: A study of a young adult cohort. *Journal of Marriage and the Family, 60,* 505–514.

Hossain, Z., & Roopnarine, J. L. (1993). Division of household labor and child care in dual-earner African-American families with infants. *Sex Roles, 29,* 571–583.

Hotaling, G. T., & Sugarman, D. B. (1986). An analysis of risk markers in husband to wife violence: the current state of knowledge. *Violence and Victims, 1,* 101–124.

Hounsell, C. (1996). Women and pensions: A policy agenda. In C. Costello, & B. K. Krimgold (Eds.), *The American woman 1996–97: Women and work.* New York: Norton.

Howard, J. A., & Hollander, J. (1997). *Gendered situations, gendered selves: A gender lens on social psychology.* Thousand Oaks, CA: Sage.

Huang, Z., et al. (1997). Dual effects of weight and weight gain on breast cancer risk. *Journal of the American Medical Association, 278,* 1407–1411.

Hubbs-Tait, L. (1989). Coping patterns of aging women: A developmental perspective. In J. D. Garner & S. O. Mercer (Eds.), *Women as they age: Challenge, opportunity, and triumph,* (pp. 95–117). Binghamton, NY: Haworth.

Hubel, J. A. (1999, March 21). I like it here. The house is paid for. I think I'll stay. *New York Times,* p. WH7.

Huffman, T., Chang, K., Rausch, P., & Schaffer, N. (1994). Gender differences and factors related to the disposition toward cohabitation. *Family Therapy, 21,* 171–184.

Hughes, D. L., & Galinsky, E. (1994). Gender, job and family conditions, and psychological symptoms. *Psychology of Women Quarterly, 18,* 251–270.

Hunt, K. (1997). A "cure for all ills"? Constructions of the menopause and the chequered fortune of hormone replacement therapy. In S. Wilkinson & C. Kitzinger (Eds.), *Women and health: Feminist perspectives* (pp. 141–165). Bristol, PA: Taylor & Francis.

Hunter College Women's Studies Collective. (1995). *Women's realities, women's choices.* New York: Oxford University Press.

Hupka, R. B., & Bank, A. L. (1996). Sex differences in jealousy: Evolution or social construction? *Cross-Cultural Research, 30,* 24–59.

Huston, A. C., & Alvarez, M. M. (1990). The socialization context of gender role development in early adolescence. In R. Montemayor, G. R. Adams, & T. P. Gullotta (Eds.), *From childhood to adolescence: A transitional period? Vol. 2* (pp. 156–179). New York: Sage.

Huston, A. C., & Wright, J. C. (1998). Mass media and children's development. In W. Damon (Series Ed.), I. E. Sigel, & K. A. Renninger (Vol. Eds.), *Handbook of child psychology: Vol. 4. Child psychology in practice* (5th ed., pp. 999–1058). New York: Wiley.

Huston, A. C., Wright, J. C., Marquis, J., & Green, S. B. (1999). How young children spend their time: Television and other activities. *Developmental Psychology, 35,* 912–925.

Hutchins, L. F., et al. (1999). Underrepresentation of patients 65 years of age or older in cancer-treatment trials. *New England Journal of Medicine, 341,* 2061–2067.

Huyck, M. H. (1995). Marriage and close relationships of the marital kind. In R. Blieszner & V. H. Bedford (Eds.), *Handbook of aging and the family* (pp. 181–200). Westport, CT: Greenwood.

Hyde, J. S. (1994). Should psychologists study gender differences? Yes, with some guidelines. *Feminism & Psychology, 4,* 507–512.

Hyde, J. S., DeLamater, J. D., & Hewitt, E. C. (1998). Sexuality and the dual-earner couple: Multiple roles and sexual functioning. *Journal of Family Psychology, 12,* 354–368.

Hyde, J. S., Fennema, E., & Lamon, S. J. (1990). Gender differences in mathematics performance: A meta-analysis. *Psychological Bulletin, 107,* 139–155.

Hyde, J. S., Klein, M. H., Essex, M. J., & Clark, R. (1995). Maternity leave and women's mental health. *Psychology of Women Quarterly, 19,* 257–285.

Hyde, J. S., & Linn, M. C. (1988). Gender differences in verbal ability: A meta-analysis. *Psychological Bulletin, 104,* 53–69.

Hyde, J. S., & McKinley, N. M. (1997). Gender differences in cognition: Results from meta-analyses. In P. J. Caplan, M. Crawford, J. S. Hyde, & J. T. E. Richardson (Eds.), *Gender differences in human cognition* (pp. 30–51). New York: Oxford University Press.

Hyde, J. S., & Plant, E. A. (1995). Magnitude of psychological gender differences. *American Psychologist, 50,* 159–161.

Hyman, I., & Pentland, J. (1996). The role of mental imagery in the creation of false childhood memories. *Journal of Memory & Languages, 35,* 101–117.

Hynie, M., & Lydon, J. E. (1995). Women's perceptions of female contraceptive behavior: Experimental evidence of the sexual double standard. *Psychology of Women Quarterly, 19,* 563–581.

Hynie, M., Lydon, J. E., & Taradash, A. (1997). Commitment, intimacy, and women's perceptions of premarital sex and contraceptive readiness. *Psychology of Women Quarterly, 21,* 447–464.

Iglehart, J. K. (1999a). The American health care system—Medicaid. *New England Journal of Medicine, 340,* 403–408.

Iglehart, J. K. (1999b). The American health care system—Medicare. *New England Journal of Medicine, 340,* 327–332.

Illinois Department of Aging. (1996a). *Elder abuse and neglect.* Springfield, IL: Author.

Illinois Department of Aging. (1996b). *Grandparents raising grandchildren.* Springfield, IL: Author.

Imperato-McGinley, J., Peterson, R. E., Gautier, T., & Sturla, E. (1979). Androgens and the evolution of male-gender identity among male pseudohermaphrodites with 5 alpha-reductase deficiency. *New England Journal of Medicine, 300,* 1233–1237.

The importance of a Pap test. (1999). *Journal of the American Medical Association, 281,* 1565.

Institute for Women's Policy Research. (1997, February). *Research in brief: The wage gap: Women's and men's earnings.* Washington, DC: Author.

International Perinatal HIV Group. (1999). The mode of delivery and the risk of vertical transmission of human immunodeficiency virus type 1—A meta-analysis of 15 prospective cohort studies. *New England Journal of Medicine, 340,* 977.

Jack, D. C. (1991). *Silencing the self: Women and depression.* Cambridge, MA: Harvard University Press.

Jack, D. C. (1999). Silencing the self: Inner dialogues and outer realities. In T. Joiner and J. C. Coyne (Eds.), *The interactional nature of depression: Advances in interpersonal approaches* (pp. 221–246). Washington, DC: American Psychological Association.

Jackson, L. A. (1989). Relative deprivation and the gender wage gap. *Journal of Social Issues, 45,* 117–133.

Jackson, L. A. (1992). *Physical appearance and gender.* Albany, NY: State University of New York Press.

Jackson, L. A., & Ervin, K. S. (1991). The frequency and portrayal of Black females in fashion advertisements. *The Journal of Black Psychology, 18,* 67–70.

Jackson, L. A., Fleury, R. E., & Lewandowski, D. A. (1996). Feminism: Definitions, support, and correlates of support among female and male college students. *Sex Roles, 34,* 687–693.

Jackson, L. A., Gardner, P. D., Sullivan, L. A. (1992). Explaining gender differences in self-pay expectations: Social comparison standards and perceptions of fair pay. *Journal of Applied Psychology, 77,* 651–661.

Jackson, L. A., & Grabski, S. V. (1988). Perceptions of fair pay and the gender wage gap. *Journal of Applied Social Psychology, 18,* 606–625.

Jackson, L. A., & McGill, O. D. (1996). Body type preferences and body characteristics associated with attractive and unattractive bodies by African Americans and Anglo Americans. *Sex Roles, 35,* 295–307.

Jacobs, R. H. (1997). *Be an outrageous older woman.* New York: HarperCollins.

Jaffe, M. L. (1998). *Adolescence.* New York: Wiley.

James, T. W., & Kimura, D. (1997). Sex differences in remembering the locations of objects in an array: Location shifts versus location exchanges. *Evolution and Human Behavior, 18,* 155–163.

Janelli, L. M. (1993). Are there body image differences between older men and women? *Western Journal of Nursing Research, 15,* 327–339.

Jarrell, A. (2000, April 3). The face of teenage sex grows younger. *New York Times,* pp. B1, B8.

Jemmott, J. B., Jemmott, L.S., & Fong, G.T. (1998). Abstinence and safer sex HIV risk-reduction interventions for African American adolescents. *Journal of the American Medical Association, 279,* 1529–1536.

Jendrek, M. P. (1994). Grandparents who parent their grandchildren: Circumstances and decisions. *Gerontologist, 34,* 206–216.

Jessell, J. C., & Beymer, L. (1992). The effects of job title vs. job description on occupational sex typing. *Sex Roles, 27,* 73–83.

Jette, A. M. (1996). Disability trends and transitions. In R. H. Binstock & L. K. George (Eds.), *Handbook of aging and the social science* (4th ed.), pp. 94–116. San Diego, CA: Academic Press.

Jetter, A. (2000, February 22). Breast cancer in blacks spurs hunt for answers. *New York Times*, pp. D5, D8.

Jezl, D. R., Molidor, C. S., & Wright, T. L. (1996). Physical, sexual and psychological abuse in high school dating relationships: Prevalence rates and self-esteem issues. *Child and Adolescent Social Work Journal, 13*, 69–87.

John, D., & Shelton, B. A. (1997). The production of gender among Black and White women and men: The case of household labor. *Sex Roles, 36*, 171–193.

Johnson, A. G. (1997). *The gender knot: Unraveling our patriarchal legacy*. Philadelphia: Temple University Press.

Johnson, B. E., Kuck, D. L., & Schander, P. R. (1997). Rape myth acceptance and sociodemographic characteristics: A multidimensional analysis. *Sex Roles, 36*, 693–707.

Johnson, C. L. (1994). Differential expectations and realities: Race, socioeconomic status, and health of the oldest old. *International Journal of Aging and Human Development, 38*, 13–27.

Johnson, D. R., & Scheuble, L. K. (1995). Women's marital naming in two generations: A national study. *Journal of Marriage and the Family, 57*, 724–732.

Johnston, D. C. (1999, March 21). A growing gap between the savers and the save-nots. *New York Times*, p. WH12.

Johnston, J., & Ettema, J. S. (1982). *Positive images: Breaking stereotypes with children's television*. Beverly Hills, CA: Sage

Johnston, L. D., O'Malley, P. M., & Bachman, J. G. (1999a). *National survey results on drug use from the Monitoring the Future Study, 1975–1998: Vol. 1. Secondary school students*. Rockville, MD: National Institute on Drug Abuse.

Johnston, L. D., O'Malley, P. M., & Bachman, J. G. (1999b). *National survey results on drug use from the Monitoring the Future Study, 1975–1998: Vol. 2. College students and young adults*. Rockville, MD: National Institute on Drug Abuse.

Joiner, G. W., & Kashubeck, S. (1996). Acculturation, body image, self-esteem and eating-disorder symptomatology in adolescent Mexican American women. *Psychology of Women Quarterly, 20*, 419–435.

Jones, B. E., & Hill, M. J. (1996). African-American lesbians, gay men and bisexuals. In R. P. Cabaj and T. S. Stein (Eds.), *Textbook of homosexuality and mental health* (pp. 549–561). Washington, DC: American Psychiatric Press.

Jones, B. H., & McNamara, K. (1991). Attitudes toward women and their work roles: Effects of intrinsic and extrinsic religious orientations. *Sex Roles, 24*, 21–29.

Jones, S. E. (1986). Sex differences in touch communication. *Western Journal of Speech Communication, 50*, 227–241.

Jordan, J. V. (Ed.). (1997). *Women's growth in diversity: More writings from the Stone Center*. New York: Guilford.

Jordan, J. V., Kaplan, A. G., Miller, J. B., Stiver, J. L., & Surrey, L. P. (Eds.). (1991). *Women's growth in connection*. New York: Guilford.

Joseph, J. (1997). Woman battering: A comparative analysis of Black and White women. In G. K. Kantor & J. L. Jasinski (Eds.), *Out of the darkness: Contemporary perspectives on family violence* (pp. 161–169). Thousand Oaks, CA: Sage.

Josselson, R. (1994). Identity and relatedness in the life cycle. In H. A. Bosma, T. L. G. Graafsma, H. D. Groterant, & D. J. de Levita (Eds.), *Identity and development: An interdisciplinary approach* (pp. 81–102). Thousand Oaks, CA: Sage.

Josselson, R. (1996). *Revising herself: The story of women's identity from college to midlife*. New York: Oxford University Press.

Jovanovic, J., & Dreves, C. (1997, April). *Sex differences in students competency perceptions in science: Do classroom interactions play a role?* Paper presented at the meeting of the Society for Research in Child Development, Washington, DC.

Jutras, S., & Veilleux, F. (1991). Gender roles and care giving to the elderly: An empirical study. *Sex Roles, 25*, 1–18.

Kaemingk, K., & Paquette, A. (1999). Effects of prenatal alcohol exposure on neuropsychological functioning. *Developmental Neuropsychology, 15*, 111–140.

Kahn, A. S., Mathie, V. A., & Torgler, C. (1994). Rape scripts and rape acknowledgement. *Psychology of Women Quarterly, 18*, 53–66.

Kail, B. L. (1989). Drugs, gender, and ethnicity: Is the older minority woman at risk? *Journal of Drug Issues, 19*, 171–189.

Kail, R. V., & Cavanaugh, J. C. (2000). *Human development: A lifespan view.* Belmont, CA: Wadsworth.

Kalb, C. (1999, August 9). Our quest to be perfect. *Newsweek,* pp. 52–59.

Kalichman, S. C. (1998). *Preventing AIDS: A sourcebook for behavioral interventions.* Mahwah, NJ: Erlbaum.

Kalliopuska, M. (1994). Relations of retired people and their grandchildren. *Psychological Reports, 75,* 1083–1088.

Kamo, Y., & Cohen, E. (1998). Division of household work between partners: A comparison of Black and White couples. *Journal of Comparative Family Studies, 29,* 131–145.

Kaplan, G. A. (1992). Health and aging in the Alameda County Study. In K. W. Schaie, D. Balzer, & J. S. House (Eds.), *Aging health behaviors and health outcomes* (pp. 69–88). Hillsdale, NJ: Erlbaum.

Kaplowitz, P. B., Oberfield, S. E., & the Drug and Therapeutics and Executive Committees of the Lawson Wilkens Pediatric Endocrine Society. (1999). Reexamination of the age limit for defining when puberty is precocious in girls in the United States: Implications for evaluation and treatment. *Pediatrics, 104,* 936–941.

Karlsson, M. K., et al. (2000). Exercise during growth and bone mineral density and fractures in old age. *Lancet, 355,* 469.

Karniol, R., Gabay, R., Ochion, Y., & Harari, Y. (1998). Is gender or gender-role orientation a better predictor of empathy in adolescence? *Sex Roles, 39,* 45–59.

Karraker, K. H., Vogel, D. A., & Lake, M. A. (1995). Parents' gender-stereotyped perceptions of newborns: The eye of the beholder revisited. *Sex Roles, 33,* 687–701.

Kassirer, J. P., & Angell, M. (1998). Losing weight—An ill-fated New Year's resolution. *The New England Journal of Medicine, 338,* 52–54.

Kates, E. (1996). Educational pathways out of poverty: Responding to the realities of women's lives. *American Journal of Orthopsychiatry, 66,* 548–556.

Katz, P. A. (1987). Variations in family constellation: Effects on gender schema. In L. S. Liben & M. L. Signorella (Eds.), *Children's gender schema: New directions for child development* (Vol. 38, pp. 39–56). San Francisco: Jossey-Bass.

Katz, P. A. (1996). Raising feminists. *Psychology of Women Quarterly, 20,* 323–340.

Katz, P. A., & Walsh, V., (1991). Modification of children's gender-stereotyped behavior. *Child Development, 62,* 338–351.

Katz, R. C., Hannon, R., & Whitten, L. (1996). Effects of gender and situation on the perception of sexual harassment. *Sex Roles, 34,* 35–42.

Katzenstein, L. (1999, June 13). Beyond the horror stories, good news about managed care. *New York Times,* p. WH6.

Kauffman, J. A., & Joseph-Fox, Y. K. (1996). American Indian and Alaska Native women. In M. Bayne-Smith (Ed.), *Race, gender and health* (pp. 68–93). Thousand Oaks, CA: Sage.

Kaufmann, J. A. (1996). Teenage parents and their offspring. *Women and Mental Health. Annals of the New York Academy of Sciences, 789,* 17–30.

Keel, P. K., & Mitchell, J. E. (1997). Outcome in bulimia nervosa. *Journal of Psychiatry, 154,* 313–321.

Keel, P. K., Mitchell, J. E., Miller, K. B., Davis, T. L., Crow S. J. (1999). Long-term outcome of bulimia nervosa. *Archives of General Psychiatry, 56,* 63–69.

Keller, E. L. (1996). Invisible victims: Battered women in psychiatric and medical emergency rooms. *Bulletin of the Menninger Clinic, 60,* 1–21.

Kelley, T. (2000, February 13). On campuses, warnings about violence in relationships. *New York Times,* p. L40.

Kelso, W. M., Nicholls, M. E. R., & Warne, G. L. (1999). Effects of prenatal androgen exposure on cerebral lateralization in patients with congenital adrenal hyperplasia (CAH). *Brain and Cognition, 40,* 153–156.

Kemper, P., & Murtaugh, C. M. (1991). Lifetime use of nursing home care. *New England Journal of Medicine, 324,* 595–600.

Kendall-Tackett, K. A., Kantor, G. K. (1993). *Postpartum depression: A comprehensive approach for nurses.* Newbury Park, CA: Sage.

Kendall-Tackett, K. A., Williams, L. M., & Finkelhor, D. (1993). Impact of sexual abuse on children: A review and synthesis of recent empirical studies. *Psychological Bulletin, 113,* 164–180.

Kennedy, J. R. (1998, May). *Hopelessness and suicide among adults: A review and meta-analysis.* Paper presented at the meeting of the American Psychological Society, Washington, DC.

Kennell, J. H., Klaus, M. H., McGrath, S., Robertson, S., & Hinkley, C. (1991). Continuous emotional support during labor in a U.S. hospital: A randomized clinical trial. *Journal of the American Medical Association, 265,* 2197–2201.

Kennell, J. H., & McGrath, S. (1993, March). *Perinatal effects of labor support.* Paper presented at the meeting of the Society for Research in Child Development, New Orleans.

Kerr, B. (1999, March 5). When dreams differ: Male-female relations on campus. *Chronicle of Higher Education,* pp. 87, 88.

Kilborn, P. T. (1999a, May 31). Disabled spouses increasingly face a life alone and a loss of income. *New York Times,* p. A8.

Kilborn, P. T. (1999b, April 9). Third of Hispanic Americans do without health coverage. *New York Times,* pp. A1, A18.

Kim, J. E. (1999, August). *Couples' work status and psychological well-being in older adults.* Paper presented at the meeting of the American Psychological Association, Boston.

Kimball, M. M. (1989). A new perspective on women's math achievement. *Psychological Bulletin, 105,* 198–214.

Kimball, M. M. (1995). *Feminist visions of gender similarities and differences.* New York: Harrington Park.

Kimball, M. M. (1998). Gender and math: What makes a difference? In D. L. Anselmi and A. L. Law (Eds.), *Questions of gender: Perspectives and paradoxes* (pp. 446–460). Boston: McGraw-Hill.

Kimmel, D. C., & Sang, B. E. Lesbians and gay men in midlife. (1995). In A. R. D'Augelli & C. J. Patterson (Eds.), *Lesbian, gay, and bisexual identities over the lifespan: Psychological perspectives* (pp. 190–214). New York: Oxford University Press.

Kimura, D. (1992). Sex differences in the brain. *Scientific American, 267,* 118–125.

King, A. C., & Kiernan, M. (1997). Physical activity and womens health: Issues and future directions. In S. J. Gallant, G. Puryear Keita, & R. Royak-Schaler (Eds.), *Health care for women: Psychological, social and behavioral influences* (pp. 133–146). Washington, DC: American Psychological Association.

King, L. A., & King, D. W. (1990). Abbreviated measures of sex role egalitarian attitudes. *Sex Roles, 23,* 659–673.

King, Y. (1997). The other body: Reflections on difference, disability, and identity politics. In M. Crawford & R. Unger (Eds.), *In your own words: Readings on the psychology of women and gender* (pp. 107–111). New York: McGraw-Hill.

Kinsey, A. C., Pomeroy, W. B., Martin, C. E., & Gebhard, P. H. (1953). *Sexual behavior in the human female.* Philadelphia: Saunders.

Kinsler, K., & Zalk, S. R. (1996). Teaching is a political act: Contextualizing gender and ethnic voices. In K. F. Wyche & F. J. Crosby (Eds.), *Women's ethnicities: Journeys through psychology* (pp. 27–48). Boulder, CO: Westview.

Kirkpatrick, M. (1996). Lesbians as parents. In R. P. Cabaj & T. S. Stein (Eds.), *Textbook of homosexuality and mental health.* (pp. 353–370). Washington, DC: American Psychiatric Press.

Kitano, M. K. (1998). Gifted Latina women. *Journal for the Education of the Gifted, 21,* 131–159.

Kitch, S. L. (1994). "We're all in this alone": Career women's attitudes toward feminism. In C. W. Konek & S. L. Kitch (Eds.), *Women and careers: Issues and challenges* (pp. 21–62). Thousand Oaks, CA: Sage.

Kite, M. E., Deaux, K., & Miele, M. (1991). Stereotypes of young and old: Does age outweigh gender? *Psychology and Aging, 6,* 19–27.

Kite, M. E., & Whitley, B. E. (1996). Sex differences in attitudes toward homosexual persons, behaviors, and civil rights: A meta-analysis. *Personality and Social Psychology Bulletin, 22,* 336–353.

Kitto, J. (1989). Gender reference terms: Separating the women from the girls. *British Journal of Social Psychology, 28,* 185–187.

Kivett, V. R. (1996). The saliency of the grandmother-granddaughter relationship: Predictors of association. *Journal of Women and Aging, 8* (3/4), 25–39.

Kleiman, C. (1993, February 8). Study shows job status skews family benefits. *Chicago Tribune,* p. C3.

Klein, M. H., Hyde, J. S., Essex, M. J., & Clark, R. (1998). Maternity leave, role quality, work involvement, and mental health one year after delivery. *Psychology of Women Quarterly, 22,* 239–266.

Kling, K. C., Hyde, J. S., Showers, C. J., & Buswell, B. N. (1999). Gender differences in self-esteem: A meta-analysis. *Psychological Bulletin, 125,* 470–500.

Klinger, R. L. (1996). Lesbian couples. In R. P. Cabaj & T. S. Stein, *Textbook of homosexuality and mental health* (pp. 339–352). Washington, DC: American Psychiatric Association.

Klinkenberg, D., & Rose, S. (1994). Dating scripts of gay men and lesbians. *Journal of Homosexuality, 260,* 23–35.

Klonoff, E. A., & Landrine, H. (1995). The schedule of sexist events: A measure of lifetime and recent sexist discrimination in women's lives. *Psychology of Women Quarterly, 19,* 439–472.

Kmiec, J., Crosby, J. F., & Worell, J. (1996). Walking the talk: On stage and behind the scenes. In K. F. Wyche & F. J. Crosby (Eds.), *Women's ethnicities: Journeys through psychology* (pp. 49–61). Boulder, CO: Westview.

Know your options for breast cancer. (1999). *Journal of the American Medical Association, 281,* 772.

Knox, M., Funk, J., Elliott, R., & Bush, E. G. (1998). Adolescent_ possible selves and their relationship to global self-esteem. *Sex Roles, 39,* 61–80.

Knox, S. S., & Czajkowski, S. (1997). The influence of behavioral and psychosocial factors on cardiovascular health in women. In S. J. Gallant, G. Puryear Keita, & R. Royak-Schaler (Eds.), *Health care for women: Psychological, social and behavioral influences* (pp. 257–272). Washington, DC: American Psychological Association.

Kobrynowicz, D., & Branscombe, N. R. (1997). Who considers themselves victims of discrimination? Individual difference predictors of perceived gender discrimination in women and men. *Psychology of Women Quarterly, 21,* 347–363.

Koch, R., Lewis, M. T., Quinones, W. (1998). Homeless: Mothering at rock bottom. In C. G. Coll, J. L. Surrey, & K. Weingarten (Eds.), *Mothering against the odds: Diverse voices of contemporary mothers* (pp. 61–84). New York: Guilford.

Koff, E., & Rierdan, J. (1995). Preparing girls for menstruation: Recommendations from adolescent girls. *Adolescence, 30,* 795–811.

Koff, E., & Rierdan, J. (1996). Premenarcheal expectations and post-Menarcheal experiences of positive and negative menstrual related changes. *Journal of Adolescent Health, 18,* 286–291.

Kohlberg, L. (1966). A cognitive-developmental analysis of children's sex-role concepts and attitudes. In E. Maccoby (Ed.), *The development of sex differences* (pp. 82–173). Stanford, CA: Stanford University Press.

Kohlberg, L. (1985). *The psychology of moral development.* San Francisco: Harper & Row.

Kolata, G. (1994, August 3). Deadliness of breast cancer in blacks defies easy answer. *New York Times,* p. C10.

Kolata, G. (1998a, January 11). The fat's in the fire, again. *New York Times,* p. WK4.

Kolata, G. (1998b, February 25). Soaring price of donor eggs sets off debate. *New York Times,* pp. A1, A14.

Kolata, G. (2000a, April 6). Estrogen question gets tougher. *New York Times,* pp. A20.

Kolata, G. (2000b, February 15). New emphasis in cancer drug tests: The elderly. *New York Times,* pp. D1, D6.

Konek, C. W., Kitch, S. L., & Shore, E. R. (1994). The future of women and careers: Issues and challenges. In C. W. Konek & S. L. Kitch (Eds.), *Women and careers: Issues and challenges* (pp. 234–248). Thousand Oaks, CA: Sage.

Kortenhaus, C. M., & Demarest, J. (1993). Gender role stereotyping in children's literature: An update. *Sex Roles, 28,* 219–232.

Koss, M. P., & Cleveland, H. H. (1997). Stepping on toes: Social roots of date rape lead to intractability and politicization. In M. D. Schwartz (Ed.), *Researching sexual violence against women: methodological and personal perspectives* (pp. 4–21). Thousand Oaks, CA: Sage.

Koss, M. P., Dinero, T. E., Seibel, C. A., & Cox, S. L. (1988). Stranger and acquaintance rape: Are there differences in the victim's experience? *Psychology of Women Quarterly, 12,* 1–24.

Koss, M. P., Figueredo, A. J., Bell, I., Tharan, M., & Tromp, S. (1996). Traumatic memory characteristics: A cross-validated mediational model to response to rape among employed women. *Journal of Abnormal Psychology, 105,* 421–432.

Koss, M. P., & Gaines, J. A. (1993). The prediction of sexual aggression by alcohol use, athletic participation, and fraternity affiliation. *Journal of Interpersonal Violence, 8,* 94–108.

Koss, M. P., Gidycz, C. A., & Wisniewski, N. (1987). The scope of rape: Incidence and prevalence of sexual aggression and victimization in a national sample of higher education students. *Journal of Consulting and Clinical Psychology, 55,* 162–170.

Koss, M. P., Goodman, L. A., Browne, A., Fitzgerald, L. F., Keita, G. P., & Russo, N. F. (1994). *No safe haven: Male violence against women at home, at work, and in the community.* Washington, DC: American Psychological Association.

Koss, M. P., & Harvey, M. R. (1991). *The rape victim: Clinical and community interventions.* Newbury Park, CA: Sage.

Kossek, E. E., & Ozeki, C. (1998). Work-family conflict, policies, and the job-life satisfaction relationship: A review and directions for organizational behavior-human resources research. *Journal of Applied Psychology, 83,* 139–149.

Kowalski, R. M. (1993). Inferring sexual interest from behavioral cues: Effects of gender and sexually relevant attitudes. *Sex Roles, 29,* 13–36.

Krach, C. A., & Velkoff, V. A. (1999). *Centenarians in the United States.* (U.S. Bureau of the Census, Current Population Reports, Series P23–199). Washington, DC: U.S. Government Printing Office.

Krahé, B., Scheinberger-Olwig, R., Waizenhöfer, E., & Kolpin, S. (1999). Childhood sexual abuse and revictimization in adolescence. *Child Abuse & Neglect, 23,* 383–394.

Krause, N. (1993). Race differences in life satisfaction among aged men and women. *Journal of Gerontology: Social Sciences, 48,* S235–S244.

Krause, N., & Borawski-Clark, E. (1995). Social class differences in social support among older adults. *Gerontologist, 35,* 498–508.

Kresevich, D. M. (1993, March). *Traditional and nontraditional career choices of elementary aged children.* Paper presented at the meeting of the Society for Research in Child Development, New Orleans.

Krieger, N. (1990). Racial and gender discrimination: Risk factors for high blood pressure? *Social Science and Medicine, 30,* 1273–1281.

Krieger, N., & Fee, E. (1998). Man-made medicine and women's health: The biopolitics of sex/gender and race/ethnicity. In D. L. Anselmi & A. L. Law (Eds.), *Questions of gender: Perspectives and paradoxes* (pp. 678–690). Boston: McGraw-Hill.

Krishnan, S. P., Hilbert, J. C., VanLeeuwen, D., & Kolia, R. (1997). Documenting domestic violence among ethnically diverse populations: Results from a preliminary study. *Family Community Health, 20,* 32–48.

Kuhn, M. (1991). *No stone unturned.* New York: Ballatine Books.

Kujala, V. M., Kaprio, J., Sarna, S., Koskenvuo, M. (1998). Relationship of leisure-time, physical activity and mortality. *Journal of the American Medical Association, 279,* 440–441.

Kurdek, L. A. (1994). The nature and correlates of relationship quality in gay, lesbian, and heterosexual cohabiting couples: A test of the individual difference, interdependence, and discrepancy models.

In B. Greene & G. M. Herek (Eds.), *Lesbian and gay psychology* (pp. 133–155). Thousand Oaks, CA: Sage.

Kurdek, L. A. (1998). The allocation of household labor in gay, lesbian, and heterosexual married couples. In D. L. Anselmi & A. L. Law (Eds.), *Questions of gender: Perspectives and paradoxes* (pp. 582–591). Boston: McGraw-Hill.

Kurth, S. B., Spiller, S. S., & Travis, C. B. (2000). Consent, power, and sexual scripts: Deconstructing sexual harassment. In C. B. Travis & J. W. White (Eds.), *Sexuality, society, and feminism* (pp. 323–354). Washington DC: APA.

Kuttner, R. (1999). The American health care system—Health insurance coverage. *New England Journal of Medicine, 340,* 163–168.

Lackie, L., & de Man, A. F. (1997). Correlates of sexual aggression among male university students. *Sex Roles, 37,* 451–457.

Lacks, M. S., Williams, C., O'Brien, S., Hurst, L., & Horwitz, R. (1997). Risk factors for reported elder abuse and neglect: A nine-year observational cohort study. *Gerontologist, 37,* 469–474.

LaFrance, M., & Henley, N. M. (1994). On oppressing hypotheses: Or differences in nonverbal sensitivity revisited. In H. L. Radtke & H. J. Stam (Eds.), *Power/gender: Social relations in theory and practice. Inquiries in social construction* (pp. 287–311). London: Sage.

LaFromboise, T. D., Berman, J. S., & Sohi, B. K. (1994). American Indian women. In L. Comas-Díaz & B. Greene (Eds.), *Women of color: Integrating ethnic and gender identities in psychotherapy* (pp. 30–71). New York: Guilford.

LaFromboise, T. D., Heyle, A. M., & Ozer, E. J. (1990). Changing and diverse roles of women in American Indian cultures. *Sex Roles, 22,* 455–476.

Lakkis, J., Ricciardelli, L. A., & Williams, R. J. (1999). Role of sexual orientation and gender-related traits in disordered eating. *Sex Roles, 41,* 1–16.

Lakoff, R. (1973). Language and woman's place. *Language in Society, 2,* 45–80.

Lakoff, R. (1975). *Language and woman's place.* New York: Harper and Row.

Lamb, M. E. (1998). Nonparental child care: Context, quality, correlates, and consequences. In W. Damon (Ed.), *Handbook of child psychology (5th ed.): Vol. 4. Child psychology in practice* (pp. 73–133). New York: Wiley.

Lamberg, L. (1999). Safety of antidepressant use in pregnant and nursing women. *Journal of the American Medical Association, 282,* 222–223.

Lamont, J. A. (1997). Sexuality. In D. E. Stewart & G. E. Robinson (Eds.), *A clinician's guide to menopause* (pp. 63–76). Washington, DC: Health Press International.

Landau, J. (1995). The relationship of race and gender to managers' ratings of promotion potential. *Journal of Organizational Behavior, 16,* 391–400.

Landrine, H. (1985). Race ¥ class stereotypes of women. *Sex Roles, 13,* 65–75.

Laner, M. R., & Ventrone, N. A. (1998). Egalitarian daters/Traditionalist dates. *Journal of Family Issues, 19,* 468–477.

Lang, A. A. (1999, June 13). Doctors are second-guessing the "miracle" of multiple births. *New York Times,* p. WH4.

Lanis, K., & Covell, K. (1995). Images of women in advertisements: Effects on attitudes related to sexual aggression. *Sex Roles, 32,* 639–649.

Lannin, D. R., et al. (1998). Influence of socioeconomic and cultural factors on racial differences in late-stage presentation of breast cancer. *Journal of the American Medical Association, 279,* 1801–1807.

Lantz, P. M., et al. (1998). Socioeconomic factors, health behaviors and mortality: Results from a nationally representative prospective study of U.S. adults. *Journal of the American Medical Association, 279,* 1703–1708.

LaRocca, M. A., & Kromrey, J. D. (1999). The perception of sexual harassment in higher education: Impact of gender and attractiveness. *Sex Roles, 40,* 921–940.

Larson, R. W., & Verma, S. (1999). How children and adolescents spend time across the world: Work, play, and developmental opportunities. *Psychological Bulletin, 125,* 701–736.

Lauer, R. H., Lauer, J. C., & Kerr, S. T. (1995). The long-term marriage: Perceptions of stability and satisfactions. In. J. Hendricks (Ed.), *The ties of later life* (pp. 35–41). Amityville, NY: Baywood.

Laumann, E. O., Gagnon, J. H., Michael, R. T., & Michaels, S. (1994). *The social organization of sexuality: Sexual practices in the United States.* Chicago: University of Chicago Press.

Laumann, E. O., Paik, A., & Rosen, R. C. (1999). Sexual dysfunction in the United States: Prevalence and predictors. *Journal of the American Medical Association, 281,* 537–544.

Lavender, T., & Walkinshaw, S. A. (1998). Can midwives reduce postpartum psychological morbidity? A randomized trial. *Birth, 25,* 215–219.

Law, D. J., Pellegrino, J. W., & Hunt, E. B. (1993). Comparing the tortoise and the hare: Gender differences and experience in dynamic spatial reasoning tasks. *Psychological Science, 4,* 35–40.

Laws, G. (1995). Understanding ageism: Lessons from feminism and postmodernism. *Gerontologist, 35,* 112–118.

Lawton, C. A., & Morrin, K. A. (1999). Gender differences in pointing accuracy in computer-simulated 3D mazes. *Sex Roles, 40,* 73–92.

Leaper, C. (Ed.). (1994). *Childhood gender segregation: Causes and consequences.* San Francisco: Jossey-Bass.

Leaper, C., Anderson, C. J., & Sanders, P. (1998). Moderators of gender effects on parents' talk to their children: A meta-analysis. *Developmental Psychology, 34,* 3–27.

Leary, W. E. (1998, September 29). Older people enjoy sex, survey says. *New York Times,* p. B16.

LeBoff, M. S., et al. (1999). Occult Vitamin D deficiency in postmenopausal U.S. women with acute hip fracture. *Journal of the American Medical Association, 281,* 1505–1511.

Ledman, R. E., Miller, M., & Brown, D. R. (1995). Successful women and women's colleges: Is there an intervening variable in the reported relationship? *Sex Roles, 33,* 489–497.

Lee, C. M., & Duxbury, L. (1998). Employed parents' support from partners, employers, and friends. *Journal of Social Psychology, 138,* 303–322.

Lee, S., & Kite, M. (1998, May). *Structure of attitudes toward gay men and lesbians.* Paper presented at the meeting of the Midwestern Psychological Association, Chicago.

Legato, M. J. (1998, May 15). Research on the biology of women will improve health care for men, too. *Chronicle of Higher Education, 44,* pp. B4, B5.

Leiblum, S. R. (1990). Sexuality and the midlife woman. *Psychology of Women Quarterly, 14,* 495–508.

Leiblum, S. R. (Ed.). (1997). *Infertility: Psychological issues and counseling strategies.* New York: Wiley.

Leinbach, M. D., & Fagot, B. I. (1993). Categorical habituation to male and female faces: Gender schematic processing in infancy. *Infant Behavior and Development, 16,* 317–322.

Leitner, M. J., & Leitner, S. F. (1996). *Leisure in later life* (2nd ed.). Binghamton, NY: Haworth.

Leland, J. (2000, March 20). Shades of gays. *Newsweek*, pp. 46–49.

Leland, J., & Miller M. (1998, August 17). Can gays convert? *Newsweek*, pp. 47–50.

Lemaitre, R. N., Siscovick, D. S., Raghunathan, T. E., Weinmann, S., Arbogast, P., & Lin, D. (1999). Leisure-time physical activity and the risk of primary cardiac arrest. *Archives of Internal Medicine, 159*, 686–690.

Leonard, D., & Jlang, J. (1999). Gender bias and the college predictions of the SATs: A cry of despair. *Research in Higher Education, 40*, 375.

LePage-Lees, P. (1997). Struggling with a nontraditional past: Academically successful women from disadvantaged backgrounds discuss their relationship with "disadvantage." *Psychology of Women Quarterly, 21*, 365–385.

Leppard, W., Ogletree, S. M., & Wallen, E. (1993). Gender stereotyping in medical advertising: Much ado about something? *Sex Roles, 29*, 829–838.

Leung, S. A., Conoley, C. W., & Scheel, M. J. (1994). The career and educational aspirations of gifted high school students: A retrospective study. *Journal of Counseling Development, 27*, 298–303.

Leung, S. A., Ivey, D., Suzuki, L. (1994). Factors affecting the career aspirations of Asian Americans. *Journal of Counseling & Development, 72*, 404–410.

Levant, R. F. (1997, August). *Deconstructing Disney: Gender socialization through the lens of the cinema.* Paper presented at the meeting of the American Psychological Association, Chicago.

Leventhal, E. A. (1994). Gender and aging: Women and their aging. In V. J. Adesso, D. M. Reddy, and R. Flemming (Eds.), *Psychological perspectives on women's health* (pp. 11–35). Washington, DC: Taylor & Francis.

Levine, M., & Leonard, R. (1984). Discrimination against lesbians in the work force. *Signs: Journal of Women in Culture & Society, 9*, 700–710.

Levine, S. C., Huttenlocher, J., Taylor, A., & Langrock, A. (1999). Early sex differences in spatial skill. *Developmental Psychology, 35*, 940–949.

Levinson, W., & Altkorn, D. (1998). Primary prevention of postmenopausal osteoporosis. *Journal of the American Medical Association, 280*, 1821–1822.

Levy, G. D. (1998). Effects of gender constancy and figure's height and sex on young children's gender-typed attributions. *Journal of General Psychology, 125*, 65–88.

Levy, G. D., Barth, J. M., & Zimmerman, B. J. (1998). Associations among cognitive and behavioral aspects of preschoolers' gender role development. *Journal of Genetic Psychology, 159*, 121–126.

Levy, G., Zimmerman, B., Barber, J., Martin N., & Malone, C. (1998, May). *Preverbal awareness of gender roles in toddlers.* Poster presented at the meeting of the American Psychological Society, Washington, DC.

Levy, J. A. (1994). Sex and sexuality in later life stages. In A. S. Rossi (Ed.), *Sexuality across the life course* (pp. 287–309). Chicago: University of Chicago Press.

Lew, A. S., Allen, R., Papouchis, N., & Ritzler, B. (1998). Achievement orientation and fear of success in Asian American college students. *Journal of Clinical Psychology, 54*, 97–108.

Lewin, T. (1997a, September 30). Little talk on sexual diseases. *New York Times*, p. B15.

Lewin, T. (1997b, December 21). A new procedure makes abortions possible earlier. *New York Times*, pp. Y1, Y8.

Lewin, T. (1998a, January 17). Debate distant for many having abortions. *New York Times*, pp. A1, A7.

Lewin, T. (1998b, April 15). Men assuming bigger share at home, new survey shows. *New York Times*, p. A16.

Lewin, T. (1999a, October 3). Defining who can see the children. *New York Times*, p. WK3.

Lewin, T. (1999b, April 14). Programs about abstinence have an impact nationwide. *New York Times*, p. Y16.

Lewis, K. G., Moon, S. (1997). Always single and single again women: A qualitative study. *Journal of Marital and Family Therapy, 23*, 115–134.

Lewis, T., & Phillipsen, L. C. (1998). Interactions on an elementary school playground: Variations by age, gender, race, group size, and playground area. *Child Study Journal, 28*, 309–320.

Lewittes, H. J. (1989). Just being friendly means a lot—women, friendship, and aging. In L. Grace & I. Susser (Eds.), *Women in the later years: Health, social, and cultural perspectives* (pp. 139–159). New York: Harrington Park Press.

Lex, B. W. (1994). Alcohol and other drug abuse among women. *Alcohol Health & Research World, 18*, 212–219.

Lickona, T. (1998). Where sex education went wrong. In D. S. DelCampo & R. L. DelCampo (Eds.), *Taking sides: Clashing views on controversial issues in childhood and society* (2nd ed., pp. 316–323). Guilford, CT: Dushkin/McGraw-Hill.

Lin, C. A. (1998). Uses of sex appeals in prime-time commercials. *Sex Roles, 38,* 461–475.

Lindsey, E. W., Mize, J., & Pettit, G. S. (1997). Differential play patterns of mothers and fathers of sons and daughters: Implications for children's gender-role development. *Sex Roles, 37,* 643–661.

Linn, M. C., & Petersen, A. C. (1986). A meta-analysis of gender differences in spatial ability: Implications for mathematics and science achievement. In J. S. Hyde & M. C. Linn (Eds.), *The psychology of gender: Advances through meta-analysis* (pp. 67–101). Baltimore, MD: Johns Hopkins University Press.

Lippert, L. (1997). Women at midlife: Implications for theories of women's adult development. *Journal of Counseling & Development, 76,* 16–22.

Lips, H. M. (1997). *Sex and gender: An introduction* (3rd ed.). Mountain View, CA: Mayfield.

Lipsyte, R. (1999, February 17). Don't take your medicine like a man. *New York Times,* pp. D1, D8.

Lisi, D. (1993). Found voices: Women, disability, and cultural transformation. *Women & Therapy, 14,* 195–209.

Litt, I. F. (1997). *Taking our pulse: The health of America's women.* Stanford, CA: Stanford University Press.

Littleton, K., Light, P., Barnes, P., Messer, D., & Joiner, R. (March, 1993). *Gender and software effects in computer based problem solving.* Paper presented at the meeting of the Society for Research in Child Development, New Orleans.

Liu, E., Kahan, M. & Wilson, L. (1999, August). *Physician attitudes and behavior towards male and female problem drinkers.* Paper presented at the meeting of the American Psychological Association, Boston.

Livson, F. B. (1983). Gender identity: A life span view of sex role development. In R. Weg (Ed.), *Aging: An international annual: Vol. 1. Sexuality in the later years: roles and behavior* (pp. 105–14). Menlo Park, CA: Addison-Wesley.

Lloyd-Jones, D. M., Larson, M. G., Beiser, A., & Levy, D. (1999). Lifetime risk of developing coronary heart disease. *Lancet, 353,* 89–92.

Lobel, T. E., & Menashri, J. (1993). Relations of conceptions of gender-role transgressions and gender constancy to gender-typed toy preferences. *Developmental Psychology, 29,* 150–155.

Lock, L. M. (1993). *Encounters with aging: Mythologies of menopause in Japan and North America.* Berkeley, CA: University of California Press.

Lockhart, L., & White, B. (1989). Understanding marital violence in the Black community. *Journal of Interpersonal Violence, 4,* 421–436.

Loeber, R., & Hay, D. (1997). Key issues in the development of aggression and violence from childhood to early adulthood. *Annual Review of Psychology, 48,* 371–410.

Loeber, R., & Stouthamer-Loeber, M. (1998). Development of juvenile aggression and violence: Some common misperceptions and controversies. *American Psychologist, 53,* 242–259.

Loftus, E. F., & Pickrell, J. (1995). The formation of false memories. *Psychiatric Annals, 25,* 720–725.

Lombardi, K. S. (1997, June 22). Many grandparents find themselves parenting again. *New York Times,* pp. WC1, WC10.

Lonsway, K. A. (1996). Preventing acquaintance rape through education: What do we know? *Psychology of Women Quarterly, 20,* 229–265.

Lonsway, K. A., & Fitzgerald, L. F. (1994). Rape myths: In review. *Psychology of Women Quarterly, 18,* 133–164.

Lopata, H. Z. (1979). *Women as widows.* New York: Elsevier.

Lopata, H. Z. (1980). The widowed family member. In N. Datan & W. Lohman (Eds.), *Transitions of aging* (pp. 93–118). New York: Academic Press.

Lorenz, F. O., Simons, R. L., Conger, R. D., Elder, G. H., Jr., Johnson, C., & Chao, W. (1997). Married and recently divorced mothers' stressful events and distress: Tracing change across time. *Journal of Marriage and the Family, 59,* 219–232.

Lottes, I. L., & Kuriloff, P. J. (1992). The effects of gender, race, religion, and political orientation on the sex role attitudes of college freshmen. *Adolescence, 27,* 675–688.

Lubben, J. E., & Becerra, R. M. (1987). Social support among Black, Mexican, and Chinese elderly. In D. E. Gelford & C. M. Barresi (Eds.), *Ethnic dimensions of aging* (pp. 130–144). New York: Springer.

Lubinski, D., & Benbow, C. P. (1992). Gender differences in abilities and preferences among the gifted: Implications for the math-science pipeline. *Current Directions in Psychological Science, 1,* 61–66.

Lucas, V. A. (1992). An investigation of the health care preferences of the lesbian population. *Health Care for Women International, 13,* (2), 221–228.

Luecke, A. D., Anderson, D. R., Collins, P. A., & Schmitt, K. L. (1995). Gender constancy and television viewing. *Developmental Psychology, 31,* 773–780.

Lummis, M., & Stevenson, H. W. (1990). Gender differences in beliefs and achievement: A cross-cultural study. *Developmental Psychology, 26,* 254–563.

Lundy, B., Field, T., McBride, C., Field, T., & Largie, S. (1998). Same-sex and opposite-sex best friend interactions among high school juniors and seniors. *Adolescence, 33,* 279–289.

Luster, T., & Small, S. A. (1997). Sexual abuse history and number of sex partners among female adolescents. *Family Planning Perspectives, 29,* 204–211.

Lutzker, J. R., Bigelow, K. M., Swenson, C. C., Doctor, R. M., Kessler, M. L. (1999). Problems related to child abuse and neglect. In S. D. Netherton, D. Holmes, & C. E. Walker (Eds.), *Child and adolescent psychological disorders: A comprehensive textbook* (pp. 520–548). New York: Oxford University Press.

Lynch, S. A. (1998). Who supports whom: How age and gender affect the perceived quality of support from family and friends. *The Gerontologist, 38,* 231–238.

Lyness, K. S., Thompson, C. A., Francesco, A. M., & Judiesch, M. K. (1999). Work and pregnancy: Individual and organizational factors influencing organizational commitment, timing of maternity leave, and return to work. *Sex Roles, 41,* 485–508.

Lyness, K. S., & Thompson, D. E. (1997). Above the glass ceiling? A comparison of matched samples of female and male executives. *Journal of Applied Psychology, 82,* 359–375.

Lytton, H., & Romney, D. M. (1991). Parents' differential socialization of boys and girls: A meta-analysis. *Psychological Bulletin, 109,* 267–296.

Maccoby, E. E. (1998a). Gender and relationships: a developmental account. In D. L. Anselmi and A. L. Law (Eds.), *Questions of gender: Perspectives and paradoxes* (pp. 294–305). Boston: McGraw-Hill.

Maccoby, E. E. (1998b). *The two sexes: Growing up apart, coming together.* Cambridge, MA: Harvard University Press.

Maccoby, E. E., & Jacklin, C. N. (1974). *The psychology of sex differences.* Stanford, CA: Stanford University Press.

Maccoby, E. E., & Jacklin, C. N. (1987). Gender segregation in childhood. In H. W. Reese (Ed.), *Advances in child development and behavior: Vol. 20* (pp. 239–288). New York: Academic Press.

MacDorman, M. F., & Singh, G. K. (1998). Midwifery care social and medical risk factors, and birth outcomes in the USA. *Journal of Epidemiology and Community Health, 52,* 310–317.

MacEwen, K. E., & Barling, J. (1991). Effects of maternal employment on children's behavior via mood, cognitive difficulties, and parenting behavior. *Journal of Marriage and the Family, 53,* 635–644.

MacKinnon, C. A. (1979). *Sexual harassment of working women: A case of sex discrimination.* New Haven, CT: Yale University Press.

Madden, M. E., & Hyde, J. S. (1998). Integrating gender and ethnicity into psychology courses. *Psychology of Women Quarterly, 22,* 1–12.

Magaziner, J., & Cadigan, D. A. (1989). Community caring of older women living alone. In L. Grace & I. Susser (Eds.), *Women in the later years: Health, social, and cultural perspectives* (pp. 121–138). New York: Harrington Park Press.

Magley, V. J., Hulin, C. L., Fitzgerald, L. F., & DeNardo, M. (1999). Outcomes of self-labeling sexual harassment. *Journal of Applied Psychology, 84,* 390–402.

Mahoney, P. (1997, Fall). Falling through the cracks: women sexually assaulted by their husbands/cohabiting partners. *Research Report, 2* (pp. 1–2). Wellesley, MA: Wellesley Center for Research on Women.

Major, B. (1989). Gender differences in comparisons and entitlement: Implications for comparable worth. *Journal of Social Issues, 45,* 99–115.

Major, B. (1993). Gender, entitlement, and the distribution of family labor. *Journal of Social Issues, 49,* 141–159.

Major, B., Barr, L., Zubek, J., & Babey, S. H. (1999). Gender and self-esteem: A meta-analysis. In W. B. Swann, J. H. Langlois, & L. A. Gilbert (Eds.), *Sexism and stereotypes in modern society* (pp. 223–254). Washington, DC: American Psychological Association.

Major, B., & Cozzarelli, C. (1992). Psychosocial predictors of adjustment to abortion. *Journal of Social Issues, 48,* 121–142.

Major, B., Richards, C., Cooper, M. L., Cozzarelli, C., & Zubek, J. (1998). Personal resilience, cognitive appraisals, and coping: An integrative model of adjustment to abortion. *Journal of Personality and Social Psychology, 74,* 735–752.

Malacrida, R., et al. (1998). A comparison of the early outcome of acute myocardial infarction in women and men. *New England Journal of Medicine, 338,* 8–14.

Malamuth, N. M. (1996). The confluence model of sexual aggression: Feminist and evolutionary perspectives. In D. M. Buss & N. M. Malamuth (Eds.), *Sex, power, conflict: Evolutionary and feminist perspectives* (pp. 269–295). New York: Oxford University Press.

Malamuth, N. M. (1998). An evolutionary-based model integrating research on the characteristics of sexually coercive men. In J. G. Adair, D. Belanger, & K. L. Dion (Eds.), *Advances in psychological science, Vol. 1*, (pp. 151–184). Hove, UK: Psychology Press.

Malamuth, N. M., & Heilmann, M. F. (1998). Evolutionary psychology and sexual aggression. In C. Crawford & D. L. Krebs (Eds.), *Handbook of evolutionary psychology: Ideas, issues and applications* (pp. 515–542). Mahwah, NJ: Erlbaum.

Malamuth, N. M., Sockloskie, R. J., Koss, M. P., & Tanaka, J. S. (1991). Characteristics of aggressors against women: Testing a model using a national sample of college students. *Journal of Consulting and Clinical Psychology, 59*, 670–681.

Malcolm, A. H. (1991, November 19). Lending help when grandparents become parents again. *New York Times*, p. C13.

Malkin, A. R., Wornian, K., & Chrisler, J. C. (1999). Women and weight: Gendered messages on magazine covers. *Sex Roles, 40*, 647–655.

Malovich, N. J., & Stake, J. E. (1990). Sexual harassment on campus: Individual differences in attitudes and beliefs. *Psychology of Women Quarterly, 14*, 63–81.

Malson, M. R. (1983). Black women's sex roles: The social context for a new ideology. *Journal of Social Issues, 39*, 101–113.

Mandelbrot, L., et al. (1998). Perinatal HIV-1 transmission. Interaction between zidorudine prophylaxis and mode of delivery in the French perinatal cohort. *Journal of the American Medical Association, 280*, 55–60.

Manger, T., & Eikeland, O. (1998). The effect of mathematics self-concept on girls' and boys' mathematical achievement. *School Psychology International, 19*, 5–18.

Mansfield, P. K., Koch, P. B., Henderson, J., Vicary, J. R., Cohn, M., & Young, E. W. (1991). The job climate for women in traditionally male blue-collar occupations. *Sex Roles, 25*, 63–79.

Mansfield, P. K., Koch, P. B., & Voda, A. M. (1998). Qualities midlife women desire in their sexual relationships and their changing sexual response. *Psychology of Women Quarterly, 22*, 285–303.

Mansfield, P. K., Voda, A. M., & Koch, P. B.(1995). Predictions of sexual response changes in heterosexual midlife women. *Health Values, 19*, 10–20.

Manson, J. E., et al. (1999). A prospective study of walking as compared with vigorous exercise in the prevention of coronary heart disease in women. *New England Journal of Medicine, 341*, 650–658.

A man's place. (1999, May 16). *New York Times Magazine*, pp. 48, 64, 66, 68, 73–74.

Marano, H. E. (1997, July 1). Puberty may start at 6 as hormones surge. *New York Times*, pp. B9, B12.

Marano, H. E. (1998, August 4). Debunking the marriage myth: It works for women, too. *New York Times*, p. B8.

Marcia, J. E. (1993). The relational roots of identity. In J. Krogers (Ed.), *Discussion on ego identity* (pp. 101–120). Hillsdale, NJ: Erlbaum.

Marecek, J., & Hare-Mustin, R. T. (1998). A short history of the future: Feminism and clinical psychology. In D. L. Anselmi and A. L. Law (Eds.), *Questions of gender: Perspectives and paradoxes* (pp. 748–758). Boston: McGraw-Hill.

Mark, N. F. (1996). Social demographic diversity among American midlife parents. In C. D. Ryff & M. M. Seltzer (Eds.), *The parental experience in midlife* (pp. 29–75). Chicago: University of Chicago Press.

Marklein, M. B. (1997, June 17). Title IX also aided women academically. *USA Today*, p. 1A.

Marks, M. A., & Nelson, E. S. (1993). Sexual harassment on campus: Effects of professor gender on perception of sexually harassing behaviors. *Sex Roles, 28*, 207–217.

Marks, S. R. (1977). Multiple roles and role strain: Some notes on human energy, time and commitment. *American Sociological Review, 41*, 921–936.

Markson, E. W. (1997). Sagacious, sinful or superfluous? The social construction of older women. In J. M. Coyle (Ed.), *Handbook on women and aging* (pp. 53–71). Westport, CT: Greenwood.

Markson, E. W., & Hess, B. B. (1997). Older women in the city. In M. Pearsall (Ed.), *The other within us: Feminist explorations of women and aging* (pp. 57–70). Boulder, CO: Westview.

Markson, E. W., & Taylor, C. A. (1993). Real versus reel world: Older women and the Academy Awards. In N. D. Davis, E. Cole, & E. Rothblum (Eds.), *Faces of women and aging*, (pp. 157–175). New York: Harrington Park Press.

Marlowe, C. M., Schneider, S. L., & Nelson, C. E. (1996). Gender and attractiveness biases in hiring decisions: Are more experienced managers less biased? *Journal of Applied Psychology, 81*, 11–21.

Marquez, S. A. (1994). Distorting the image of Hispanic women in sociology: Problematic strategies of presentation in the introductory text. *Teaching Sociology, 22,* 231–236.

Marrugat, J., Sala, J., Masia, R., et al. (1998). Mortality differences between men and women following first myocardial infarction. *Journal of the American Medical Association, 280,* 1405–1409.

Marshall, L. L. (1997, July). *Effects of subtle and overt psychological abuse on the well-being of 834 low-income women.* Paper presented at the International Family Violence Research Conference, Durham, NH.

Marshall, N. L. (n.d.). Women's experiences with maternity leave. *Center for Research on Women: Working Papers Series* (Project Paper 04). Wellesley, MA: Center for Research on Women.

Marshall, N. L., & Barnett, R. C. (1993). Work-family strains and gains among two-earner couples. *Journal of Community Psychology, 21,* 64–78.

Martin, C. L. (1990). Attitudes and expectations about children with nontraditional and traditional gender roles. *Sex Roles, 22,* 151–165.

Martin, C. L. (1994). Cognitive influences on the development and maintenance of gender segregation. In C. Leaper (Ed.), *Childhood gender segregation: Causes and consequences. New directions for child development* (Vol. 65, pp. 35–51). San Francisco: Jossey-Bass.

Martin, C. L. (1995). Stereotypes about children with traditional and nontraditional gender roles. *Sex Roles, 33,* 727–751.

Martin, C. L. (1999). A developmental perspective on gender effects and gender concepts. In W. B. Swann, J. H. Langlois, & L. A. Gilbert (Eds.), *Sexism and stereotypes in modern society* (pp. 45–74). Washington, DC: American Psychological Association.

Martin, C. L., & Little, J. K. (1990). The relation of gender understanding to children's sex-typed preferences and gender stereotypes. *Child Development, 61,* 1327–1439.

Mason, E. S. (1995). Gender differences in job satisfaction. *Journal of Social Psychology, 135,* 143–151.

Masters, W. H., & Johnson, V. E. (1966). *Human sexual response.* Boston: Little, Brown.

Matire, L. M., Stephens, M. A. P., & Townsend, A. L. (1998). Emotional support and well-being of midlife women: Role-specific mastery as a mediational mechanism. *Psychology and Aging, 13,* 396–404.

Matlin, M. W. (1998, August). *Wise and wonderful . . . or wrinkled and wretched: How psychology, the general public, and the media view older women.* Invited address, American Psychological Association, San Francisco.

Mattson, S. N., Riley, E. P., Gramling, L., Delis, D. C., & Jones, K. L. (1998). Neuropsychological comparison of alcohol-exposed children with or without physical features of fetal alcohol syndrome. *Neuropsychology, 12,* 146–153.

McCandless, N. J., & Conner, F. P. (1999). Older women and the health care system: A time for change. *Journal of Women & Aging, 11,* (2/3), 13–27.

McClelland, D. (1961). *The achieving society.* New York: Van Nostrand.

McConnell, A. R., & Fazio, R. H. (1996). Women as men and people: Effects of gender-marked language. *Personality & Social Psychology Bulletin, 22,* 1004–1013.

McCowan, C. J., & Alston, R. J. (1998). Racial identity, African self-consciousness, and career decision making in African American college women. *Journal of Multicultural Counseling and Development, 26,* 28–38.

McCray, C. C. (1998). Ageism in the preclinical years. *Journal of the American Medical Association, 279,* 1035.

McCreary, D. R. (1994). The male role and avoiding femininity. *Sex Roles, 31,* 517–531.

McDonald, K. A. (1998, September 25). Sports scientists gain new respect as they shift focus to the elderly. *Chronicle of Higher Education,* pp. A15, A16.

McDonald, K. A. (1999, June 25). Studies of women's health produce a wealth of knowledge on the biology of gender differences. *Chronicle of Higher Education,* pp. A19, A22.

McFadden, D., & Pasanen, E. G. (1996). Comparison of the auditory systems of heterosexuals and homosexuals: Click-evoked otoacoustic emissions. *Proceedings of the National Academy of Sciences, 95,* 2709–2713.

McFarlane, J. M., & William, T. M. (1994). Placing premenstrual syndrome in perspective. *Psychology of Women Quarterly, 18,* 339–373.

McGloshen, T. H., & O'Bryant, S. L. (1988). The psychological well-being of older, recent widows. *Psychology of Women Quarterly, 12,* 99–116.

McGue, M. (1999). The behavioral genetics of alcoholism. *Current Directions in Psychological Science, 8,* 109–115.

McHale, S. M., Crouter, A. C., & Tucker, C. J. (1999). Family context and gender role socialization in middle childhood comparing girls to boys and sisters to brothers. *Child Development, 70,* 990–1004.

McKiernan, F. (1996). Bereavement and attitudes towards death. In R. T. Woods (Ed.), *Handbook of the clinical psychology of aging* (pp. 159–182). New York: Wiley.

McLanahan, S. S., & Booth, K. (1989). Mother-only families: Problems, prospects, and politics. *Journal of Marriage and the Family, 51,* 557–580.

McLanahan, S. S., & Sandefur, G. (1994). *Growing up with a single parent.* Cambridge, MA: Harvard University Press.

McLoyd, V. C. (1993). Employment among African-American mothers in dual-earner families: Antecedents and consequences for family life and child development. In J. Frankel (Ed.), *The employed mother and the family context.* New York: Springer.

McNeilly-Choque, M. K., Hart, C. H., Robinson, C. C., Nelson, L. J., & Olsen, S. F. (1996). Overt and relational aggression on the playground: Correspondence among different informants. *Journal of Research in Childhood Education, 11,* 47–67.

McQuaide, S. (1998). Women at midlife. *Social Work, 43,* 21–31.

McRae, M. B. (1994). Influence of sex role stereotypes on personnel decisions of black managers. *Journal of Applied Psychology, 79,* 306–309.

McSweeney, J. C. (1998). Women's narratives: Evolving symptoms of myocardial infarction. *Journal of Women & Aging, 10,* 67–83.

Meara, N. M., & Day, J. D. (2000). Epilogue: Feminist visions and virtues of ethnical psychological practice. In M. M. Brabeck (Ed.), *Practicing feminist ethics in psychology* (249–268). Washington, DC: APA.

Medicine, B. (1988). Native American (Indian) women: A call for research. *Anthropology & Education Quarterly, 19,* 86–92.

Mednick, M. T., & Thomas, V. G. (1993). Women and the psychology of achievement: A view from the eighties. In F. L. Denmark & M. A. Paludi (Eds.), *Psychology of women: A handbook of issues and theories* (pp. 585–626). Westport, CT: Greenwood.

Mellott, D. S. (1998, May). *Do older adults show automatic ageism?* Paper presented at the meeting of the Midwestern Psychological Assocation, Chicago.

Mendelsohn, M. E., & Karas, R. H. (1999). Mechanisms of disease: The protective effects of estrogen on the cardiovascular system. *New England Journal of Medicine, 340,* 1801–1811.

Menopause: A guide to smart choices (1999, January). *Consumer Reports,* pp. 50–54.

Meredith, K., & Bathon, R. (1997). A comprehensive center for women with HIV. In M. G. Winiarski (Ed.), *HIV mental health for the 21st century* (pp. 257–271). New York: New York University Press.

Merikangas, K. R., & Pollock, R. A. (2000). Anxiety disorders in women. In M. B. Goldman & M. C. Hatch (Eds.), *Women & health* (pp. 1010–1023). New York: Academic Press.

Merrill, L. L., Newel, C. E., Milner, J. S., Hervig, L. K., & Gold, S. R. (1997). Prevalence of premilitary adult sexual victimization and aggression in a Navy basic trainee sample. *U.S. Naval Health Research Center Report* (No. 97-4, pp. 1–14).

Merskin, D. (1999). Adolescence, advertising, and the ideology of menstruation. *Sex Roles, 40,* 941–957.

Messner, M. A., Duncan, M. C., & Jensen, K. (1993). Separating the men from the girls: The gendered language of televised sports. *Gender & Society, 7,* 121–137.

Meyer, M. H., & Bellas, M. L. (1995). U.S. old-age policy and the family. In R. Bleiszner & V. H. Bedford (Eds.), *Handbook of aging and the family* (pp. 263–283). Westport, CT: Greenwood.

Michael, R. T., Gagnon, J. H., Laumann, E. O., & Kolata, G. (1994). *Sex in America: A definitive survey.* Boston: Little, Brown.

Milar, K. S. (in press). The first generation of women psychologists and the psychology of women. *American Psychologist.*

Milette, J., & Howard, A. (1998, June). *Sex differences and perception of desirable traits in potential mates.* Poster presented at the meeting of the American Psychological Society, Washington, DC.

Miller, A., & Raymond, J. (1999, Spring/Summer). The infertility challenge. *Newsweek,* pp. 26–28.

Miller, B. C., & Moore, K. A. (1990). Adolescent sexual behavior, pregnancy, and parenting: Research through the 1980s. *Journal of Marriage and the Family, 52,* 1025–1044.

Miller, C., & Swift, K. (1991). *Words and women: Updated.* New York: HarperCollins.

Miller, J. B., & Stiver, I. P. (1997). *The healing connection.* Boston: Beacon Press.

Miller, K. S., Levin, M. L., Whittaker, D. J., & Xu, X. (1998). Patterns of condom use among adolescents: The impact of mother-adolescent communication. *American Journal of Public Health, 88,* 1542–1544.

Miller, L. J. (Ed.). (1999). *Postpartum mood disorders.* Washington, DC: American Psychiatric Press.

Minkler, M., & Roe, K. M. (1996). Grandparents as surrogate parents. *Generations, 20* (1), 34–38.

Mintz, L. B., & Kashubeck, S. (1999). Body image and disordered eating among Asian American and Caucasian college students: An examination of race and gender differences. *Psychology of Women Quarterly, 23,* 781–796.

Mirkin, M. P., & Okun, B. (1994). The sociopolitical context of abortion. In M. P. Mirkin (Ed.), *Women in context: Toward a feminist reconstruction of psychotherapy.* New York: Guilford.

Mischel, W. (1966). A social-learning view of sex differences in behavior. In E. Maccoby (Ed.), *The development of sex differences* (pp. 56–81). Stanford, CA: Stanford University Press.

Misra, R., Alexy, B., & Panigrahi, B. (1996). The relationships among self-esteem, exercise, and self-related health in older women. *Journal of Women and Aging, 8,* 81–94.

Mitchell, B. S., & Stricker, G. (1998, August). *The quality of the grandparent-young adult relationship: How does it relate to attitudes toward older persons and personal anxiety towards aging?* Paper presented at the meeting of the American Psychological Association, San Francisco.

Mitchell, V. (1996). Two moms: Contribution of the planned lesbian family to the deconstruction of gendered parenting. In J. Laird & R-J Green (Eds.), *Lesbians and gays in couples and families* (pp. 343–357). San Francisco: Jossey-Bass.

Mobily, K. E. (1992). Leisure, lifestyle, and lifespan. In M. L. Teague & R. D. MacNeil (Eds.), Aging and leisure: Vitality in later life (2nd ed., pp. 179–206). Dubuque, IA: Brown & Benchmark.

Moen, P. (1992). *Women's two roles: A contemporary dilemma.* New York: Auburn House.

Moen, P. (1996). Gender, age, and the life course. In R. H. Binstock, & L. K. George (Eds.), *Handbook of aging and the social sciences* (4th ed., pp. 171–187). San Diego, CA: Academic Press.

Moffat, S. C., & Hampson, E. (1996). A curvilinear relationship between testosterone and spatial cognition in humans: Possible influence of hand preference. *Psychoneuroendocrinology, 21,* 323–337.

Moller, L. C., & Serbin, L. A. (1996). Antecedents of toddler gender segregation: cognitive consonance, gender-typed toy preferences and behavioral compatibility. *Sex Roles, 35,* 445–460.

Molloy, B. L., & Herzberger, S. D. (1998). Body image and self-esteem: A comparison of African-American and Caucasian women. *Sex Roles, 38,* 631–643.

Monaghan, P. (1999, July 30). Making babies with new technologies. *Chronicle of Higher Education,* pp. A10–11.

Money, J. (1993). Prenatal hormones that masculinize the female brain. In *The Adam principle: Genes, genitals, hormones, & gender: Selected readings in sexology* (pp. 94–106). Buffalo, NY: Prometheus.

Money, J., & Ehrhardt, A. A. (1972). *Man & woman, boy & girl: The differentiation and dimorphism of gender identity from conception to maturity.* Baltimore, MD: Johns Hopkins.

Mongeau, P. A., Carey, C. M., & Williams, M. L. M. (1998). First date initiation and enactment: An expectancy violation approach. In D. J. Canary & K. Dindia (Eds.), *Sex differences and similarities in communication: Critical essays and empirical investigations of sex and gender in interaction* (pp. 413–426). Mahwah, NJ: Erlbaum.

Mookherjee, H. N. (1997). Marital status, gender, and perception of well-being. *Journal of Social Psychology, 137,* 95–105.

Moon, A., & Williams, O. (1993). Perceptions of elder abuse and help-seeking patterns among African American, Caucasian American and Korean American elderly women. *Gerontologist, 33,* 386–395.

Moore, K. (1999). *Anti-lesbian, gay, bisexual and transgender violence in 1998.* New York: National Coalition of Anti-Violence Programs.

Moore, S. (1995). Girls' understanding and social construction of menarche. *Journal of Adolescence, 18,* 87–104.

Moore, S., & Boldero, J. (1991). Psychosocial development and friendship functions in adolescence. *Sex Roles, 25,* 521–536.

Moos, R. (1985). *Perimenstrual symptoms: A manual and overview of research with the menstrual distress questionnaire.* Stanford, CA: Stanford University.

Morahan-Martin J., & Schumacher, P. (1998, August). *Are Internet and computer experiences and attitudes related?: Gender differences.* Paper presented at the meeting of the American Psychological Association, San Francisco.

Mor-Barak, M. E., & Tynan, M. (1995). Older workers and the workplace. In F. J. Turner (Ed.), *Differential diagnosis and treatment in social work* (4th ed.). New York: Free Press.

Morgan, B. A., Megbolugbe, I. F., & Rasmussen, D. W. (1996). Reverse mortgages and the economic status of elderly women. *Gerontologist, 36,* 400–405.

Morgan, B. L. (1996). Putting the feminism into feminism scales: Introduction of a Liberal Feminist Attitude and Ideology Scale (LFAIS). *Sex Roles, 34,* 359–390.

Morgan, K. S. (1992). Caucasian lesbians_ use of psychotherapy: A matter of attitude? *Psychology of Women Quarterly, 16,* 127–130.

Mori, L., Bernat, J. A., Glenn, P. A., Selle, L. L., & Zarate, M. G. (1995). Attitudes toward rape: Gender and ethnic differences across Asian and Caucasian college students. *Sex Roles, 32,* 457–467.

Morinaga, Y., Frieze, I. H., & Ferligoj, A. (1993). Career plans and gender-role attitudes of college students in the United States, Japan, and Slovenia. *Sex Roles, 29,* 317–334.

Morisset, C., Barnard, K., & Booth C. (1995). Toddlers' language development: Sex differences within social risk. *Developmental Psychology, 31,* 851–865.

Morokoff, P. J., Mays, V. M., & Coons, H. L. (1997). HIV infection and AIDS. In S. J. Gallant, G. Puryear Keita, & R. Royak-Schaler (Eds.), *Health care for women: Psychological, social and behavioral influences* (pp. 273–293). Washington, DC: American Psychological Association.

Morris, J. F. (1998, August). *Use of therapy by lesbian and bisexual women of color.* Paper presented at the meeting of the American Psychological Association, San Francisco.

Morrow, D. J. (1999, September 9). A movable epidemic: Makers of AIDS drugs struggle to keep up with market. *New York Times,* pp. C1, C21.

Morrow, S. L., Gore, P. A., Jr., & Campbell, B. W. (1996). The application of a sociocognitive framework to the career development of lesbian women and gay men. *Journal of Vocational Behavior, 48,* 136–148.

Morse, C. A. (1997). Menopause transition. In B. G. Wren (Ed.), *Progress in the management of the menopause,* (pp. 50–57). Pearl River, NY: Parthenon.

Mortola, J. F. (2000). Premenstrual syndrome. In M. B. Goldman & M. C. Hatch (Eds.), *Women & health* (pp. 114–125). New York: Academic Press.

Muehlenhard, C. L., & Rodgers, C. S. (1998). Token resistance to sex: New perspectives on an old stereotype. *Psychology of Women Quarterly, 22,* 443–463.

Mueller, K. A., & Yoder, J. D. (1997). Gendered norms for family size, employment, and occupation:

Are there personal costs for violating them? *Sex Roles, 36,* 207–220.

Mui, A. C. (1995). Caring for frail elderly parents: A comparison of adult sons and daughters. *Gerontologist, 35,* 86–93.

Mulac, A. (1998). The gender-linked language effect: Do language differences really make a difference? In D. J. Canary & K. Dindia (Eds.), *Sex differences and similarities in communication: Critical essays and empirical investigations of sex and gender in interaction* (pp. 127–153). Mahwah, NJ: Erlbaum.

Mullen, B., & Riordan, C. A. (1988). Self-serving attributions for performance in naturalistic settings: A meta-analytic review. *Journal of Applied Social Psychology, 18,* 3–22.

Mullis, I. V. S., Dossey, J. A., Campbell, J. R., Gentile, C. A., O'Sullivan, C., Latham, A. S. (1994). *NAEP, 1992, Trends in academic progress.* Washington, DC: U.S. Government Printing Office.

Murphy, J. M., Kinnaird, P., Sellers, P., Crutchfield, A., & Jordan, H. (1999, August). *Acceptance of homosexuals: The influence of religious and demographic characteristics.* Paper presented at the meeting of the American Psychological Association, Boston.

Murray, B. (1998, October). Survey reveals concerns of today's girls. *APA Monitor,* p. 12.

Murray, B. (1999, May). Friedan calls for more research on fathers and parenting. *APA Monitor, 30,* p. 10.

Murrell, A. J. (1996). Sexual harassment and women of color: Issues, challenges, and future directions. In M. S. Stockdale (Ed.), *Sexual harassment in the workplace: Perspectives, frontiers, and response strategies* (pp. 51–66). Thousand Oaks, CA: Sage.

Murrell, A. J., Frieze, I. H., & Frost, J. L. (1991). Aspiring to careers in male- and female-dominated professions: A study of black and white college women. *Psychology of Women Quarterly, 15,* 103–126.

Murrell, A. J., & Jones, R. (1996). Assessing affirmative action: Past, present, and future. *Journal of Social Issues, 52,* 77–92.

Murry, V. M. (1994). Black adolescent females: A comparison of early versus late coital initiators. *Family Relations, 43,* 342–348.

Muth, J. L., & Cash, T. F. (1997). Body-image attitudes: What differences does gender make? *Journal of Applied Social Psychology, 27,* 1438–1452.

Muzi, M. J. (2000). *The experience of parenting.* Upper Saddle River, NJ: Prentice-Hall.

Muzio, C. (1996). Lesbians choosing children: Creating families, creating narratives. In J. Laird & R-J Green (Eds.), *Lesbians and gays in couples and families* (pp. 358–369). San Francisco: Jossey-Bass.

Myaskovsky, L., & Wittig, M. A. (1997). Predictors of feminist social identity among college women. *Sex Roles, 37,* 861–883.

Myers, D. J., & Dugan, K. B. (1996). Sexism in graduate school classrooms: Consequences for students and faculty. *Gender & Society, 10,* 330–350.

Nagourney, E. (2000, February 15). Study finds families bypassing marriage. *New York Times,* D8.

Nardi, P. M. (1992). "Seamless soul": An introduction to men's friendships. In P. M. Nardi (Ed.), *Men's friendships* (pp. 1–14). Newbury Park, CA: Sage.

Nash, H. C., & Chrisler, J. C. (1997). Is a little (psychiatric) knowledge a dangerous thing? The impact of premenstrual dysphoric disorder on perceptions of premenstrual women. *Psychology of Women Quarterly, 21,* 315–322.

National Center on Addiction and Substance Abuse (1999). *Dangerous liaisons: Substance abuse and sex.* New York, NY: Author.

National Center for Health Statistics. (1999). *Health, United States, 1999 with health and aging chart book,* Hyattsville, MD: Author.

National Committee on Pay Equity. (1998). *Questions and answers on pay equity.* Washington, DC: Author.

National Council on Aging. (1997). *Myths and perceptions about aging and women's health.* Washington, DC: Author.

National Institute on Aging (NIA). (1991). *Age page: Smoking: It's never too late to stop.* Washington, DC: U.S. Government Printing Office.

National Institute on Aging (NIA). (1994). *Age page: Sexuality in later life.* Washington, DC: U.S. Government Printing Office.

National Institute on Alcohol Abuse and Alcoholism (NIAAA)(1997). *Alcohol alert.* Washington, DC: Author.

National Institutes of Health. (1999). *Agenda for research on women's health for the 21st century, a report of the Task Force on the NIH Women's Health Research Agenda for the 21st Century* (NIH Pub. No. 99-4386). Bethesda, MD: Author.

National Osteoporosis Foundation. (2000). *The physician's guide to prevention and treatment of osteoporosis.* Washington, DC: Author.

National Partnership for Women & Families. (1998). *Balancing acts: Work/family issues on prime-time TV.* Washington, DC: Author.

Neff, J. A., Holamon, B., & Schluter, T. D. (1995). Spousal violence among Anglos, Blacks, and Mexican Americans: The role of demographic variables, psychosocial predictors, and alcohol consumption. *Journal of Family Violence, 10,* 1–21.

Neill, C. M., & Kahn, A. S. (1999). The role of personal spirituality and religious social activity on the life satisfaction of older widowed women. *Sex Roles, 40,* 319–329.

Nelson, L. J., Shanahan, S. B., & Olivetti, J. (1997). Power, empowerment, and equality: Evidence for the motives of feminists, nonfeminists, and antifeminists. *Sex Roles, 37,* 227–249.

Neporent, L. (1999, January 12). Balance drills for the sake of safety. *New York Times,* p. D8.

Neppl, T. K., & Murray, A. D. (1997). Social dominance and play patterns among preschoolers: Gender comparisons. *Sex Roles, 36,* 381–393.

Neufeldt, V., & Guralnik, D. B. (1994). *Webster's new world dictionary of American English* (3rd college ed.). New York: Macmillan.

Neugarten, B. L., & Datan, N. (1974). The middle years. In S. Arieti (Ed.), *American handbook of psychiatry: Vol. I.* (2nd ed., pp. 592–608). New York: Basic Books.

Neumann, D. A., Houskamp, B. M., Pollock, V. E., & Briere, J. (1996). The long-term sequelae of childhood sexual abuse in women: A meta-analytic review. *Child Maltreatment, 1,* 6–16.

Newman, L. S., Cooper, J. N., & Ruble, D. N. (1995). Gender and computers, II. The interactive effects of knowledge and constancy on gender-stereotyped attitudes. *Sex Roles, 33,* 325–351.

Newton, K. M., Lacroix, A. Z., & Buist, D. S. M. (2000). Overview of risk factors for cardiovascular disease. In M. B. Goldman & M. C. Hatch (Eds.), *Women & health* (pp. 757–770). New York: Academic Press.

Newtson, R. L., & Keith, P. M. (1997). Single women in later life. In J. M. Coyle (Ed.), *Handbook on women and aging* (pp. 385–399). Westport, CT: Greenwood.

NICHD Early Child Care Research Network. (1997). The effects of infant child care on infant-mother attachment security: Results of the NICHD study of early child care. *Child Development, 68,* 860–879.

Nichols, M. (1994). Therapy with bisexual women: Working on the edge of emerging cultural and personal identities. In M. P. Mirkin (Ed.), *Women in context: Toward a feminist reconstruction of psychotherapy* (pp. 149–169). New York: Guilford.

Nicol-Smith, L. (1996). Causality, menopause and depression: A critical review of the literature. *British Medical Journal, 313,* 1229–1232.

Niemann, Y. F., Jennings, L., Rozelle, R. M., Baxter, J. C., & Sullivan, E. (1994). Use of free responses and cluster analysis to determine stereotypes of eight groups. *Personality and Social Psychology Bulletin, 20,* 379–390.

Noble, H. B. (1999, June 1). Steroid use by teen-age girls is rising. *New York Times,* p. D8.

Nock, S. L. (1995). A comparison of marriages and cohabiting relationships. *Journal of Family Issues, 16,* 53–76.

Nolen-Hoeksema, S. (1995). Epidemiology and theories of gender differences in unipolar depression. In M. V. Seeman (Ed.), *Gender and psychopathology* (pp. 63–87). Washington, DC: American Psychiatric Press.

Nolen-Hoeksema, S. (1999, August). *Women think, men drink: Rumination, depression and alcohol use.* Paper presented at the meeting of the American Psychological Association, Boston.

Nolen-Hoeksema, S. K., & Girgus, J. S. (1994). The emergence of gender differences in depression during adolescence. *Psychological Bulletin, 115,* 424–443.

Nolen-Hoeksema, S. K., & Girgus, J. S. (1998, August). *Worried girls: Rumination and the transition into adolescence.* Paper presented at the meeting of the American Psychological Association, San Francisco.

Nolen-Hoeksema, S., Larson, J., & Grayson, C. (1999). Explaining the gender difference in depressive symptoms. *Journal of Personality and Social Psychology, 77,* 1061–1072.

Nordheimer, J. (1991, December 16). A new abuse of elderly: Theft by kin and friends. *New York Times,* pp. A1, A12.

Nordvik, H., & Amponsah, B. (1998). Gender differences in spatial abilities and spatial activity among university students in an egalitarian educational system. *Sex Roles, 38,* 1009–1023.

Nosek, B., Banaji, M. R., & Greenwald, A. G. (1998, May). *Me = female, math = male, therefore math ± me.* Paper presented at the meeting of the American Psychological Society, Washington, DC.

Nosek, M. A., Howland, C. A., & Young, M. E. (1997). Abuse of women with disabilities: Policy implications. *Journal of Disability Policy Studies, 8,* 157–175.

Nosek, M. A., Howland, C. A., Young, M. E., Georgiou, D., Rintala, D. H., Foley, C. C., Bennett, J. L, & Smith, Q. (1994). Wellness models and sexuality among women with physcial disabilities. *Journal of Applied Rehabilation Counseling, 25,* 50–57.

Novack, L. L., & Novack, D. R. (1996). Being female in the eighties and nineties: Conflicts between new opportunities and traditional expectations among white, middle class, heterosexual college women. *Sex Roles, 35,* 57–77.

Nowell, A., & Hedges, L. V. (1998). Trends in gender differences in academic achievement from 1960 to 1994: An analysis of differences in mean, variance, and extreme scores. *Sex Roles, 39,* 21–43.

Nye, S. S., & Johnson, C. L. (1999). Eating disorders. In S. D. Netherton, D. Holmes, & C. E. Walker (Eds.), *Child and adolescent psychological disorders: A comprehensive textbook* (pp.397–414). New York: Oxford University Press.

Oakley, G. P. (1998). Eat right and take a multivitamin. *New England Journal of Medicine, 338,* 1060–1061.

Obeidallah, D. A., McHale, S. M., & Silbereisen, R. K. (1996). Gender role socialization and adolescents reports of depression: Why some girls and not others? *Journal of Youth and Adolescence, 25,* 776–786.

Oberman, Y., & Josselson, R. (1996). Matrix of tensions: A model of mothering. *Psychology of Women Quarterly, 20,* 341–359.

O'Brien, S. J., & Vertinsky, P. A. (1991). Unfit survivors: Exercise as a resource for aging women. *Gerontologist, 31,* 347–357.

O'Bryant, S. L., & Hansson, R. O. (1995). Widowhood. In R. Blieszner & V. H. Bedford (Eds.), *Handbook of aging and the family* (pp. 440–458). Westport, CT: Greenwood.

O'Connell, A. N., & Russo, N. F. (Eds.). (1990). *Women in psychology: A bio-bibliographic sourcebook.* New York: Greenwood.

O'Connell, A. N., & Russo, N. F. (1991). Women's heritage in psychology. *Psychology of Women Quarterly, 15,* 495–504.

O'Dea, J. A., & Abraham, S. (1999). Association between self-concept and body weight, gender, and pubertal development among male and female adolescents. *Adolescence, 34,* 69–79.

Oggins, J., Veroff, J., & Leber, D. (1993). Perceptions of marital interaction among Black and White newlyweds. *Journal of Personality and Social Psychology, 65,* 494–511.

Ogletree, S. M., Williams, S. W., Raffeld, P., Mason, B., & Fricke, K. (1990). Female attractiveness and eating disorders: Do children's television commercials play a role? *Sex Roles, 22,* 791–797.

O'Keefe, M. (1997). Predictors of dating violence among high school students. *Journal of Interpersonal Violence, 12,* 546–568.

Older Women's League. (1989, May). *Failing America's caregivers: A status report on women who care.* Washington, DC: Author.

Older Women's League. (1991, May). *Paying for prejudice: A report on midlife and older women in America's labor force.* Washington, DC: Author.

Older Women's League. (1994). *Women and pensions.* Washington, DC: Author.

Older Women's League. (1995). *Osteoporosis: A challenge for midlife and older women.* Washington, DC: Author.

Older Women's League. (1996). *Secure women, secure lives: Women and Social Security.* Washington, DC: Author.

Older Women's League. (1997a). *Managed care: Opportunities and risks for mid-life and older women.* Washington, DC: Author.

Older Women's League. (1997b). *The path to poverty: An analysis of women's retirement income.* Washington, DC: Author.

Older Women's League. (1998). *Women, work, and pensions: Improving the odds for a secure retirement.* Washington, DC: Author.

Older Women's League. (1999). *The face of Medicare is a woman you know.* Washington, DC: Author.

Olian, J. D., Schwab, D. P., & Haberfeld, Y. (1988). The impact of applicant gender compared to qualifications on hiring decisions: A meta-analysis of experimental studies. *Organizational Behavior and Human Decision Processes, 41,* 180–195.

Oliver, M. B., & Hyde, J. S. (1993). Gender differences in sexuality: A meta-analysis. *Psychological Bulletin, 114,* 29–51.

Oliver, M. B., & Sedikides, C. (1992). Effects of sexual permissiveness on desirability of partner as a function of love and high commitment to relationship. *Social Psychology Quarterly, 55,* 321–333.

Olson, S. L., & Ceballo, R. E. (1996). Emotional well-being and parenting behavior among low-income single mothers: Social support and ethnicity as contexts of adjustment. In K. F. Wyche & F. J. Crosby (Eds.), *Women's ethnicities: Journeys through psychology* (pp. 105–123). Boulder, CO: Westview.

O'Neil, J. (1999, February 2). Happy endings after difficult journeys. *New York Times,* p. D7.

O'Neill, J. (2000, April 18). Strong bones from hardy gardens grow. *New York Times,* p. D8.

Once behind the scenes, now in the fore (1999, December). *APA Monitor,* p. 23. 1 of 3 women experience emotional or physical abuse: Greater awareness of domestic abuse needed in hospital emergency departments. (1998). *Journal of the American Medical Association, 280,* pp. 433–438.

Ongley, B. L. (1999). Medicare and Social Security: A challenge for OWL. *OWL Observer, 20* (1), 4.

Onyx, J., & Benton, P. (1996). Retirement: A problematic concept for older women. *Journal of Women and Aging, 8,* 19–34.

Orbuch, T. L., & Custer, L. (1995). The social context of married women's work and its impact on Black husbands and White husbands. *Journal of Marriage and the Family, 57,* 333–345.

Orenstein, P. (1994). *School girls: Young women, self-esteem, and the confidence gap.* New York: Doubleday.

Orza, A. M., & Torrey, J. W. (1995). Teaching the psychology of women. In J. C. Chrisler & A. H. Hemstreet (Eds.), *Variations on a theme: Diversity and the psychology of women* (pp. 201–224). Albany, NY: SUNY Press.

Ott, P. J., & Levy, S. M. (1994). Cancer in women. In V. J. Adesso, D. M. Reddy, & R. Fleming (Eds.), *Psychological perspective on women's health* (pp. 83–98). Washington, DC: Taylor & Francis.

Oyserman, D., Radin, N., & Benn, R. (1993). Dynamics in a three-generational family: Teens, grandparents, and babies. *Developmental Psychology, 29,* 564–572.

Ozer, E. M. (1995). The impact of childcare responsibility and self-efficacy on the psychological health of professional working mothers. *Psychology of Women Quarterly, 19,* 315–335.

Padgett, C. (1989). Aging minority women: Issues in research and health policy. In L. Grace & I. Susser (Eds.), *Women in the later years: Health, social and cultural perspectives* (pp. 213–237). New York: Harrington Park Press.

Palmer, H. T., & Lee, J. A. (1990). Female workers' acceptance in traditionally male-dominated blue-collar jobs. *Sex Roles, 22,* 607–626.

Paludi, M. A. (1996). Sexual harassment in college and university settings. In J. C. Chrisler, C. Golden, & P. D. Rozee (Eds.), *Lectures on the Psychology of Women* (pp. 325–337). New York: McGraw-Hill.

Paludi, M. A. (1998). *The psychology of women.* Upper Saddle River, NJ: Prentice Hall.

Panchaud, C., Singh, S., Feivelson, D., & Darroch, J. E. (2000). Sexually transmitted diseases among adolescents in developed countries. *Family Planning Perspectives, 32* (1), 24–32, 45.

Papalia, D. E., Olds, S. W., & Feldman, R. D. (1998). *Human development* (7th ed.). Boston: McGraw-Hill.

Paradise, S. A. (1993). Older never married women: A cross cultural investigation. In N. D. Davis, E. Cole & E. Rothblum (Eds.), *Faces of women and aging,* (pp. 129–139). New York: Harrington Park Press.

Parke, R. D., & Buriel, R. (1998). Socialization in the family: Ethnic and ecological perspectives. In W. Damon (Series Ed.) & N. Eisenberg (Vol. Ed.), *Handbook of child psychology: Vol. 3. Social, emotional and personality development* (5th ed.) (pp. 463–552). New York: Wiley.

Parks, C. A. (1998). Lesbian parenthood: A review of the literature. *American Journal of Orthopsychiatry, 68,* 376–389.

Parkes, C. M., & Weiss, R. S. (1983). *Recovery from bereavement.* New York: Basic Books.

Parnell, K., Sargent, R., Thompson, S. H., Duhe, S. F., Valois, R. F., & Kemper, R. C. (1996). Black and White adolescent females_ perceptions of ideal body size. *Journal of School Health, 66,* 112–118.

Parra, E. B., Arkowitz, H., Hannah, M. T., & Vasquez, A. M. (1995). Coping strategies and emotional reactions to separation and divorce in Anglo, Chicana, and Mexicana women. *Journal of Divorce & Remarriage, 23,* 117–129.

Parrot, A. (1991). Medical community response to acquaintance rape—recommendations. In A. Parrot & L. Bechhofer (Eds.), *Acquaintance rape: The hidden crime* (pp. 304–316). New York: Wiley.

Parry, G. (1987). Sex-role beliefs, work attitudes and mental health in employed and non-employed mothers. *British Journal of Social Psychology, 26,* 47–58.

Pastore, D., Fisher, M., & Friedman, S. (1996). Abnormalities in weight status, eating attitudes, and eating behaviors among urban high school students: Correlations with self-esteem and anxiety. *Journal of Adolescent Health, 18,* 312–319.

Patterson, C. J. (1992). Children of lesbian and gay parents. *Child Development, 63,* 1025–1042.

Patterson, C. J. (1995). Lesbian and gay parenthood. In M. H. Bornstein (Ed.), *Handbook of parenting: Vol. 3. Status and social conditions of parenting* (pp. 255–274). Mahwah, NJ: Erlbaum.

Patterson, C. J. (1996). Lesbian mothers and their children: Findings from the Bay Area families study. In J. Laird & R-J. Green (Eds.), *Lesbians and gays in couples and families* (pp. 420–437). San Francisco: Jossey-Bass.

Patterson, C. J. (1997). Children of lesbian and gay parents. In T. H. Ollendick & R. J. Prinz (Eds.), *Advances in clinical child psychology, Vol. 19* (pp. 235–282). New York: Plenum.

Patterson, M. P. (1996). Women's employment patterns, pension coverage, and retirement planning. In C. Costello & B. K. Krimgold (Eds.), *The American woman 1996–1997: Women and work* (pp. 148–165). New York: Norton.

Paulson, S. E. (1996). Maternal employment and adolescent achievement revisited: An ecological perspective. *Family Relations, 45,* 201–208.

Peacock, P. (1998). Marital rape. In R. K. Bergen (Ed.), *Issues in intimate violence* (pp. 225–235). Thousand Oaks, CA: Sage.

Pearlman, S. F. (1993). Late mid-life astonishment: Disruptions to identity and self-esteem. In N. D. Davis, E. Cole, and E. D. Rothblum (Eds.), *Faces of women and aging* (pp. 67–75). New York: Harrington Park Press.

Pearson, J. C., & Cooks, L. (1995). Gender and power. In P. J. Kalbfleisch & L. Cooks (Eds.), *Gender, power, and communication in human relationships* (pp. 331–349). Hillsdale, NJ: Erlbaum.

Pebley, A. R., & Rudkin, L. L. (1999). Grandparents caring for grandchildren: What do we know? *Journal of Family Issues, 20,* 218–242.

Peirce, K. (1990). A feminist theoretical perspective on the socialization of teenage girls through Seventeen magazine. *Sex Roles, 23,* 491–500.

Peirce, K. (1993). Socialization of teenage girls through teen-magazine fiction: The making of a new woman or an old lady? *Sex Roles, 29,* 59–68.

Peirce, K. (1997). Women's magazine fiction: A content analysis of the roles, attributes, and occupations of main characters. *Sex Roles, 37,* 581–593.

Pellegrini, A. D., & Smith, P. K. (1998). Physical activity play: The nature and function of a neglected aspect of play. *Child Development, 69,* 577–598.

Peplau, L. A. (1998). Lesbian and gay relationships. In D. L. Anselmi & A. L. Law (Eds.), *Questions of gender: Perspectives & paradoxes* (pp. 505–519). Boston: McGraw-Hill.

Peplau, L. A., Bikson, T. K., Rook, K. S., & Goodchilds, J. S. (1982). Being old and living alone. In L.

A. Peplau & D. Perlman (Eds.), *Loneliness* (pp. 327–347). New York: Wiley.

Perkins, D. F., Luster, T., Villarruel, F. A., & Small, S. (1998). An ecological risk-factor examination of adolescents' sexual activity in three ethnic groups. *Journal of Marriage and the Family, 60,* 660–673.

Perkins, K. P. (1992). Psychosocial implications of women and retirement. *Social Work, 37,* 526–532.

Perkins, K. P. (1995). Social (in)security: Retirement planning for women. *Journal of Women & Aging, 7,* 37–53.

Perkins, K. R. (1996). The influence of television images on Black females' self-perceptions of physical attractiveness. *Journal of Black Psychology, 22,* 453–469.

Perkinson, M. A., & Rockemann, D. D. (1996). Older women living in a continuing care retirement community: Marital status and friendship formation. *Journal of Women & Aging, 8* (3/4), 159–177.

Perlmutter, C., Hanlon, T., & Sangiorgio, M. (1994, August). Triumph over menopause. *Prevention, 78–87,* 142.

Perlmutter, M., & Hall, E. (1985). *Adult development and aging.* New York: Wiley.

Perry, M. J., & O'Hanlan, K. A. (1998). Lesbian health. In E. A. Blechman & K. D. Brownell (Eds.), *Behavioral medicine and women: A comprehensive handbook* (pp. 843–848). New York: Guilford.

Perry-Jenkins, M., & Crouter, A. C. (1990). Men's provider-role attitudes: Implications for household work and marital satisfaction. *Journal of Family Issues, 11,* 136–156.

Perry-Jenkins, M., Seery, B., & Crouter, A. C. (1992). Linkages between women's provider-role attitudes, psychological well-being, and family relationships. *Psychology of Women Quarterly, 16,* 311–329.

Pesquera, B. M. (1993). In the beginning he wouldn't even lift a spoon: The division of household labor. In A. de la Torre & M. B. Pesquera (Eds.), *Building with our hands: New directions in Chicana studies* (pp. 181–195). Berkeley, CA: University of California Press.

Petersen, A. C. (1993). Creating adolescents: The role of context and process in developmental transitions. *Journal of Research on Adolescents, 3* (1), 1–18.

Peterson, R. D., & Bailey, W. C. (1992). Rape and dimensions of gender socioeconomic inequality in U.S. metropolitan areas. *Journal of Research in Crime and Delinquency, 29,* 162–177.

Peto, R., et al. (1998). Tamoxifen for early breast cancer: An overview of the randomized trials. *Lancet, 351,* 1451–1467.

Peyser, M. (1998, August 17). Battling backlash. *Newsweek,* pp. 50–52.

Peyser, M. (1999, Spring/Summer). The estrogen dilemma. *Newsweek,* pp. 35–37.

Phillips, D. F. (1998). Reproductive Medicare experts till an increasingly fertile field. *Journal of the American Medical Association, 280,* 1893–1895.

Phillips, K-A., Glendon, G., & Knight, J. A. (1999). Putting the risk of breast cancer in perspective. *New England Journal of Medicine, 340,* 141–144.

Phillips, S. D., & Imhoff, A. R. (1997). Women and career development: A decade of research. *Annual Review of Psychology, 48,* 31–59.

Phipps, B. J. (1995). Career dreams of preadolescent students. *Journal of Career Development, 22,* 19–32.

Pike, K. M., & Striegel-Moore, R. H. (1997). Disordered eating and eating disorders. In S. J. Gallant, G. P. Keita, & R. Royak-Schaler (Eds.), *Health care for women: Psychological, social and behavioral influences* (pp. 97–114). Washington, DC: American Psychological Association.

Piller, C. (1998, September). Women avoiding computer field as gender gap goes high tech. *Hartford Courant,* pp. A12–13.

Pincus, H. A., et al. (1998). Prescribing trends in psychotropic medications: Primary care, psychiatry and other medical specialties. *Journal of the American Medical Association, 279,* 526–531.

Pines, A. M. (1998). A prospective study of personality and gender differences in romantic attraction. *Personality and Individual Differences, 25,* 147–157.

Pittman, J. F., & Blanchard, D. (1996). The effects of work history and timing of marriage on the division of household labor: A life-course perspective. *Journal of Marriage and the Family, 58,* 78–90.

Pittman, J. F., & Kerpelman, J. L. (1993). Family work of husbands and fathers in dual-earner marriages. In J. Frankel (Ed.), *The employed mother and the family context* (pp. 89–112). New York: Springer.

Pleck, J. H. (1985). *Working wives/working husbands.* Beverly Hills, CA: Sage.

Pleck, J. H. (1992). Work-family policies in the United States. In H. Kahne & J. Giele (Eds.), *Women's lives and women's work: Parallels and contrasts in modernizing and industrial countries.* Boulder, Co: Westview.

Pleck, J. H. (1997). Paternal involvement: Levels, sources, and consequences. In M. E. Lamb (Ed.), *The role of the fathers in child development* (pp. 66–103). New York: Wiley.

Plichta, S. B. (1996). Violence and abuse: Implications for women's health. In M. M. Falik & K. S. Collins (Eds.), *Women's health: The Commonwealth Fund survey* (pp. 237–270). Baltimore, MD: Johns Hopkins University Press.

Plichta, S. B., & Abraham, C. (1996). Violence and gynecologic health in women <50 years old. *American Journal of Obstetrics and Gynecology, 174,* 903–907.

Plous, S., & Neptune, D. (1997). Racial and gender biases in magazine advertising: A content-analytic study. *Psychology of Women Quarterly, 21,* 627–644.

Poehlmann, J. (1999, April). *Functions of grandmother contact and support for mothers and their 12 –month-old infants.* Poster presented at the meeting of the Society for Research in Child Development, Albuquerque, NM.

Polce-Lynch, M., Myers, B. J., Kilmartin, C. T., Forssmann-Falck, R., & Kliewer, W. (1998). Gender and age patterns in emotional expression, body image, and self-esteem: A qualitative analysis. *Sex Roles, 38,* 1025–1048.

Pollack, A. (1998, May 22). Drug used against advanced breast cancer is also effective in early treatment, study finds. *New York Times,* p. A14.

Pomerantz, E. M., & Ruble, D. N. (1998). The role of maternal control in the development of sex differences in child self-evaluative factors. *Child Development, 69,* 458–478.

Pomerleau, A., Bolduc, D., Malcuit, G., & Cossette, L. (1990). Pink or blue: Environmental gender stereotypes in the first two years of life. *Sex Roles, 22,* 359–367.

Ponterotto, J. G. (1990). Racial/ethnic minority and women students in higher education: A status report. *New Directions for Student Services, 52,* 45–59.

Poole, D. A., & Lamb, M. E. (1998). *Investigative interviews of children: A guide for helping professionals.* Washington, DC: American Psychological Association.

Pope, K. S. (1997). Science as careful questioning: Are claims of a false memory syndrome epidemic based on empirical evidence? *American Psychologist, 52,* 997–1006.

Pope, K. S., & Brown, L. S. (1996). Recovered memories of abuse: *Assessment, therapy, forensics.* Washington, DC: American Psychological Association.

Popenoe, D., & Whitehead, B. D. (1999). *The state of our unions: The social health of marriage in America.* New Brunswick, NJ: National Marriage Project at Rutgers University.

Population Action International. (1998). *Educating girls: Gender gaps and gains.* Washington, DC: Author.

Porter, K. H., Larin, K., & Primus, W. (1999). *Social security and poverty: A national and state perspective.* Washington, DC: Center on Budget and Policy Priorities.

Poulin-Dubois, D., Serbin, L. A., & Derbyshire, A. (1998). Toddlers' intermodal and verbal knowledge about gender. *Merrill-Palmer Quarterly, 44,* 338–354.

Poulin-Dubois, D., Serbin, L., & Eischedt, J. (1997, April). *The construction of gender concepts between 12 and 24 months.* Paper presented at the meeting of the Society for Research in Child Development, Washington, DC.

Powell, S. R., & Yanico, B. J. (1991). A multimethod attitude study about women's roles and issues. *Psychology of Women Quarterly, 15,* 97–101.

Powlishta, K. K. (1995). Gender bias in children's perception of personality traits. *Sex Roles, 32,* 17–28.

Powlishta, K. K. (1997, May). *Social categorization and gender-role development.* Paper presented at the meeting of the Midwestern Psychological Association, Chicago.

Prevent hip fractures. (1999). *Journal of the American Medical Association, 282,* 1396.

Protect against cervical cancer (2000). *Journal of the American Medical Association, 282,* 1094.

Provenzo, E. F. (1991). *Video kids: Making sense of Nintendo.* Cambridge, MA: Harvard University Press.

Pruchno, R. A. (1998). Personal communication.

Pruchno, R. A., & Johnson, K. W. (1996). Research on grandparenting: Review of current studies and future needs. *Generations, 20* (1), 65–69.

Pryor, J. B. (1987). Sexual harassment proclivities in men. *Sex Roles, 17,* 269–290.

Pryor, J. B., & Day, J. D. (1988). Interpretations of sexual harassment: An attributional analysis. *Sex Roles, 18,* 405–417.

Pryor, J. B., LaVite, C. M., & Stoller, L. M. (1993). A social psychological analysis of sexual harassment: The person/situation interaction. *Journal of Vocational Behavior, 42,* 68–83.

Pryor, T., & Wiederman, M. W. (1998). Personality features and expressed concerns of adolescents with eating disorders. *Adolescence, 33,* 291–300.

Purcell, P., & Stewart, L. (1990). Dick and Jane in 1989. *Sex Roles, 22,* 177–185.

Purdy, L. M. (1992). Another look at contract pregnancy. In H. B. Holmes (Ed.), *Issues in reproductive technology* (pp. 303–320). New York: Garland.

Pynoos, J., & Golant, S. C. (1996). Housing and living arrangements for the elderly. In R. H. Binstock & L. K. George (Eds.), *Handbook of aging and the social sciences* (4th ed., pp. 303–324). San Diego, CA: Academic Press.

Queenan, R. A., & Beauregard, L. (1997). Diseases that affect only women. In F. P. Haseltine & B. G. Jackson (Eds.), *Women's health research: A medical and policy primer* (pp. 87–130). Washington, DC: American Psychiatric Press.

Raag, T., & Rackliff, C. L. (1998). Preschoolers' awareness of social expectations of gender: Relationships to toy choices. *Sex Roles, 38,* 685–700.

Rabasca, L. (1998, August). Psychological barriers keep women from seeking care. *APA Monitor,* p. 39.

Radner, G. (1990). *It's always something.* New York: Avon.

Ragins, B. R. (1998, August). *The effect of legislation on workplace discrimination against gay employees.* Paper presented at the meeting of the American Psychological Association, San Francisco.

Ragins, B. R., & Cotton, J. L. (1999). Mentor functions and outcomes: A comparison of men and women in formal and informal mentoring relationships. *Journal of Applied Psychology, 84,* 529–550.

Ragins, B. R., & Scandura, T. A. (1995). Antecedents and work-related correlates of reported sexual harassment: An empirical investigation of competing hypotheses. *Sex Roles, 32,* 429–455.

Ragsdale, J. D. (1996). Gender, satisfaction level and the use of relational maintenance strategies in marriage. *Communication Monographs, 63,* 354–369.

Rahman, O., Strauss, J., Gertler, P., Ashley, D., & Fox, K. (1994). Gender differences in adult health: An international comparison. *Gerontologist, 34,* 463–469.

Raisz, L. G. (1998). Estrogen and the risk of fracture—New data, new questions. *New England Journal of Medicine, 339,* 767–768.

Rakowski, W., & Mor, V. (1992). The association of physical activity with mortality among older adults in the Longitudinal Study of Aging (1984–1988). *Journal of Gerontology: Medical Sciences, 47,* M122–M129.

Ramey, F. H. (1995). Obstacles faced by African American women administrators in higher education: How they cope. *Western Journal of Black Studies, 19,* 113–119.

Randolph, S. M. (1995). African American children in single-mother families. In B. J. Dickerson (Ed.), *African American single mothers: Understanding their lives and families* (pp. 117–145). Thousand Oaks, CA: Sage.

Ratey, J., & Johnson, C. (1997). *Shadow syndromes.* New York: Random House.

Rathus, S., Nevid, J., & Fichner-Rathus, L. (2000). *Human sexuality in a world of diversity* (4th ed). Boston: Allyn & Bacon.

Ratner, E. (1999). *The feisty woman's breast cancer book.* New York: Hunter House.

Ray, E. B., & Miller, K. I. (1994). Social support, home/work stress, and burnout: Who can help? *Journal of Applied Behavioral Science, 30,* 357–373.

Ray, R. E. (1996). A postmodern perspective on feminist gerontology. *Gerontologist, 36,* 674–680.

Rayman, P., Allshouse, K., & Allen, J. (1993). Resiliency amidst inequity: Older women workers in an aging United States. In J. Allen & A. Pifer (Eds.), *Women on the frontlines: Meeting the challenge of an aging America* (pp. 133–166). Washington, DC: Urban Institute Press.

Raymond, C. L., & Benbow, C. P. (1986). Gender differences in mathematics: A function of parental support and student sex typing? *Developmental Psychology, 22,* 808–819.

Raymond, J. G. (1993). *Women as wombs: Reproductive technologies and the battle over women's freedom.* New York: HarperCollins.

Recker, R. R., Davies, K. M., Dowd, R. M., & Heany, R. P. (1999). The effect of low-dose continuous estrogen and progesterone therapy with calcium and vitamin D on bone in elderly women: A randomized controlled trial. *Annals of Internal Medicine, 130,* 898–904.

Redman, S., Saltman, D., Straton, J., & Young, B. (1994). Determinants of career choices among women and men medical students and interns. *Medical Education, 28,* 361–371.

Reeves, J. B., & Darville, R. L. (1994). Social contact patterns and satisfaction with retirement of women in dual-career/earner families. *International Journal of Aging and Human Development, 39,* 163–175.

Reibstein, L. (1998, January 26). Arguing at fever pitch. *Newsweek,* pp. 66–67.

Reid, J. D. (1995). Development in later life: Older lesbian and gay life. In A. R. D'Augelli & C. J. Patterson (Eds.), *Lesbian, gay and bisexual identities over the lifespan: Psychological perspectives* (pp. 215–240). New York: Oxford University Press.

Reid, P. T. (1993). Poor women in psychological research: Shut up and shut out. *Psychology of Women Quarterly, 17,* 133–150.

Reid, P. T., & Kelly, E. (1994). Research on women of color: From ignorance to awareness. *Psychology of Women Quarterly, 18,* 477–486.

Reis, H. T. (1998). Gender differences in intimacy and related behaviors: Context and process. In D. J. Canary & K. Dindia (Eds.), *Sex differences and similarities in communication: Critical essays and empirical investigations of sex and gender in interaction* (pp. 203–231). Mahwah, NJ: Erlbaum.

Reisberg, L., (2000, January 28). Student stress is rising, especially among women. *Chronicle of Higher Education,* pp. A49 –A52.

Reisinger, A. L. (1995). *Health insurance and access to care: Issues for women.* New York: Commonwealth Fund.

Reitzes, D. C., Mutran, E. J., & Fernandez, M. E. (1996). Does retirement hurt well-being? Factors influencing self-esteem and depression among retirees and workers. *Gerontologist, 36,* 649–656.

Remafedi, G. (1999). Sexual orientation and youth suicide. *Journal of the American Medical Association, 282,* 1291–1292.

Reskin, B. F., & Padavic, I. (1994). *Women and men at work.* Thousand Oaks, CA: Pine Forge Press.

Resnick, M. D., et al. (1997). Protecting adolescents from harm: Findings from the National Longitudinal Study in Adolescent Health. *Journal of the American Medical Association, 278,* 823–832.

Rhodes, J. C., et al. (1999). Hysterectomy and sexual functioning. *Journal of the American Medical Association, 282,* 1934–1941.

Rice, S. (1989). Sexuality and intimacy for aging women: A changing perspective. In J. D. Garner & S. O. Mercer (Eds.), *Women as they age: Challenge, opportunity, and triumph* (pp. 245–264). Binghamton, NY: Haworth.

Richards, L. N., & Schmiege, C. J. (1993). Problems and strengths of single-parent families: Implications for practice and policy. *Family Relations, 42,* 277–285.

Richards, M. H., Crowe, P. A., Larson, R., & Swarr, A. (1998). Developmental patterns and gender differences in the experience of peer companionship during adolescence. *Child Development, 69,* 154–163.

Richardson, P., & Lazur (1995). Sexuality in the nursing home patient. *American Family Physician, 51,* 121–124.

Richardson, V. (1990). Gender differences in retirement planning among educators: Implications for practice with older women. *Journal of Women and Aging, 2(3),* 27–40.

Richardson, V. E. (1999). Women and retirement. *Journal of Women & Aging, 11 (2/3),* 49–66.

Richie, B. S., Fassinger, R. E., Prosser, J., Linn, S. G., Johnson, J., & Robinson, S. (1997). Persistence, connection, and passion: A qualitative study of the career development of highly achieving African American-Black and White women. *Journal of Counseling Psychology, 44,* 133–148.

Rickert, V. I., Wiemann, C. M., & Berenson, A. B. (2000). Ethnic differences in depressive symptomatology in young women vary according to ethnicity and include physical or sexual assault, recent substance abuse, unemployment, age, and limited education. *Obstetrics & Gynecology, 95,* 55–60.

Riddick, C. C. (1993). Older women's leisure activity and quality of life. In J. R. Kelly (Ed.), *Activity and aging: Staying involved in later life* (pp. 86–98). Newbury Park, CA: Sage.

Rierdan, J., Koff, E., & Stubbs, M. L. (1989). Timing of menarche, preparation, and initial menstrual experience: Replication and further analyses in a prospective study. *Journal of Youth and Adolescence, 18,* 413–425.

Riessmann, C. K. (1990). *Divorce talk: Women and men make sense of personal relationships.* New Brunswick, NJ: Rutgers University Press.

Rife, J. C. (1995). Older unemployed women and job search activity: The role of social support. *Journal of Women & Aging, 7,* 55–68.

Rife, J. C. (1997). Middle-aged and older women in the work force. In J. M. Coyle (Ed.), *Handbook on women and aging* (pp. 93–111). Westport, CT: Greenwood.

Riger, S. (1992). Epistemological debates, feminist voices: Science, social values, and the study of women. *American Psychologist, 47,* 730–740.

Riggs, J. M. (1997). Mandates for mothers and fathers: Perceptions of breadwinners and care givers. *Sex Roles, 37,* 565–580.

Riley, G. F., et al. (1999). Stage at diagnosis and treatment patterns among older women and breast cancer: An HMO and fee-for-service comparison. *Journal of the American Medical Association, 281,* 720–726.

Rimer, S. (1998, March 15). Tradition of care thrives in black families. *New York Times,* pp. Y1, Y16.

Rimer, S. (1999, September 5). Gaps seen in treatment of depression in elderly. *New York Times,* pp. Y1, Y16.

Rimm, E. B., et al. (1998). Folate and vitamin B6 from diet and supplements in relation to risk of coronary heart disease among women. *Journal of the American Medical Association, 279,* 359–364.

Rind, B., Tromovitch, P., & Bauserman, R. (1998). A meta-analytic examination of assumed properties of child sexual abuse using college samples. *Psychological Bulletin, 124,* 22–53.

Ringle, J., & LaVoie, J. C. (1997, April). *Same-sex and cross-sex relationship development in 13–22 year olds.* Paper presented at the Society for Research in Child Development, Washington, DC.

Rintala, D. H., Howland, C. A., Nosek, M. A., Bennett, J. L., Young, M. E., Foley, C. C., Rossi, C. D., & Chanpong, G. (1997). Dating issues for women with physical disabilities. *Sexuality and Disability, 15,* 219–242.

Rivers, I. (1999, August). *The impact of homonegativism at school over the lifespan.* Paper presented at the meeting of the American Psychological Association, Boston.

Rix, Sara E. (1990). Who pays for what? Ensuring financial security in retirement. In C. L. Hayes & J. M. Deren (Eds.), *Preretirement planning for women: Program design and research* (pp. 5–26). New York: Springer.

Rix, Sara E. (1994). Retirement and the American woman. In A. Monk (Ed.), *The Columbia retirement handbook* (pp. 433–447). New York: Columbia University Press.

Roberto, K. A. (1996). Friendships between older women: Interactions and reactions. *Journal of Women & Aging, 8* (3/4), 55–73.

Roberto, K. A., Allen, K. R., & Blieszner, R. (1999). Older women, their children and grandchildren: A feminist perspective on family relationships. *Journal of Women & Aging, 11,* (2/3), 67–84.

Roberto, K. A., & Stroes, J. (1992). Grandchildren and grandparents: Roles, influences and relationships. International *Journal of Aging and Human Development, 34,* 227–239.

Roberts, B. W. (1997). Plaster or plasticity: Are adult work experiences associated with personality change in women? *Journal of Personality, 65,* 205–232.

Roberts, D. F., Foehr, U. G., Rideout, V. J., & Brodie, M. (1999). *Kids & media @ the new millenium.* Menlo Park, CA: Henry J. Kaiser Family Foundation.

Robertson, J., & Fitzgerald, L. F. (1990). The (mis)treatment of men: Effects of client gender role and life-style on diagnosis and attribution of pathology. *Journal of Counseling Psychology, 37,* 3–9.

Robinson, C. C., & Morris, J. T. (1986). The gender-stereotyped nature of Christmas toys received by 36-, 48-, and 60-month-old children: A comparison between nonrequested vs. requested toys. *Sex Roles, 15,* 21–32.

Robinson, G. E., & Stewart, D. E. (1993). Postpartum disorders. In D. E. Stewart & N. L. Stotland (Eds.), *Psychological aspects of women's health care: The interface between psychiatry and obstetrics and gynecology* (pp. 115–138). Washington, DC: American Psychiatric Press.

Robinson, T., Killen, J., Litt, I., Hammer, L., Wilson, D., Haydel, K., Hayward, C., & Taylor, B. (1996). Ethnicity and body dissatisfaction: Are Hispanic and Asian girls at increased risk for eating disorders? *Journal of Adolescent Health, 19,* 384–393.

Rochon, P. A., & Gurwitz, J. H. (1999). Prescribing for seniors: Neither too much nor too little. *Journal of the American Medical Association, 282,* 113–115.

Rockhill, B., et al. (1999). A prospective study of recreational physical activity and breast cancer guidelines. *Archives of Internal Medicine, 159,* 2290–2296.

Rodgers, C. S., Fagot, B. I., & Winebarger, A. (1998). Gender-typed toy play in dizygotic twin pairs: A test of hormone transfer theory. *Sex Roles, 39,* 173–184.

Rodin, J. (1986). Aging and health: Effects of the sense of control. *Science, 233,* 1271–1276.

Roger, V. et al. (2000). Sex differences in evaluation and outcome of unstable angina. *Journal of the American Medical Association, 283,* 646–652.

Rogers, S. J., & Amato, P. R. (1997). Is marital quality declining? The evidence from two generations. *Social Forces, 75,* 1089–1100.

Rohsenow, D. J. (1998). Alcholism. In E. A. Blechman & K. D. Brownell (Eds.), *Behavioral medicine and women: A comprehensive handbook* (pp. 402–406). New York: Guilford.

Rollins, J. R. (1996). *Women's minds/women's bodies: The psychology of women in a biosocial context.* Upper Saddle River, NJ: Prentice-Hall.

Romaine, S. (1999). *Communicating gender.* Mahwah, NJ: Erlbaum.

Rook, K. S. (1987). Reciprocity of social exchange and social satisfaction among older women. *Journal of Personality and Social Psychology, 52,* 145–154.

Roosa, M. W., Reinholtz, C., & Angelini, P. J. (1999). The relation of child sexual abuse and depression in young women: Comparisons across four ethnic groups. *Journal of Abnormal Child Psychology, 27,* 65–76.

Roosa, M. W., Tein, J. Y., Reinholtz, C., & Angelini, P. J. (1997). The relationship of childhood sexual abuse to teenage pregnancy. *Journal of Marriage and the Family, 59,* 119, 130.

Rose, S., & Frieze, I. H. (1993). Young singles contemporary dating scripts. *Sex Roles, 28,* 499–509.

Rosenblatt, E. D., Cho, K. H., & Durance, P. W. (1996). Reporting mistreatment of older adults: The role of physicians. *Journal of the American Geriatrics Society, 44,* 65–70.

Rosenblum C. (1991, October 31). Yipes! An eery metamorphosis is turning girls into turtles. *New York Times,* p. B1.

Rosenblum, G. D., & Lewis, M. (1999). The relations among body image, physical attractiveness, and body mass in adolescence. *Child Development, 70,* 50–64.

Rosenbluth, S. (1997). Is sexual orientation a matter of choice? *Psychology of Women Quarterly, 21,* 595–610.

Rosenthal, R. (1995). Writing meta-analytic reviews. *Psychological Bulletin, 118,* 183–192.

Ross, C. E. (1987). The division of labor at home. *Social Forces, 65,* 816–833.

Ross, C. E., & Mirowsky, J. (1988). Child care and emotional adjustment to wives' employment. *Journal of Health and Social Behavior, 29,* 127–138.

Ross, L. E., & Davis, A. C. (1996). Black-White college students attitudes and expectations in paying for dates. *Sex Roles, 35,* 43–56.

Rostosky, S. S., & Travis, C. B. (1996). Menopause research and the dominance of the biomedical model 1984–1994. *Psychology of Women Quarterly, 20,* 285–312.

Roter, D. L., & Hall, J. A. (1997). Gender differences in patient-physician communication. In S. J. Gallant, G. Puryear Keita, & R. Royak-Schaler (Eds.), *Health care for women: Psychological, social, and behavioral influences* (pp. 57–71). Washington, DC: American Psychological Association.

Rothblum, E. D., & Brehony, K. A. (1991). The Boston marriage today: Romantic but asexual relationships among lesbians. In C. Silverstein (Ed.). *Gays, lesbians, and their therapists: Studies in psychotherapy* (pp. 210–226). NY: W. Norton.

Rothblum, E. D., Mintz, B., Cowan, D. B., & Haller, C. (1995). Lesbian baby boomers at midlife. In K. Jay (Ed.), *Dyke life: From growing up to growing old, a celebration of the lesbian experience.* New York: Basic Books.

Rowe, D. C. (1999). Environmental and genetic influences on pubertal development: Evolutionary life history traits? In J. L. Rogers, D. C. Rowe, & W. B. Miller (Eds.), *Genetic influences on human fertility and sexuality: Recent empirical and theoretical findings* (pp. 1–21). Boston: Kluwer.

Rowe, J. W., & Kahn, R. L. (1998). *Successful aging.* New York: Pantheon.

Rowley, L. M. C. (1999, August). *Women in dual-earner marriages: The impact of religious commitment on household task and management performance.* Paper presented at the meeting of the American Psychological Association, Boston.

Royak-Schaler, R., Stanton, A. L., & Danoff-Burg, S. (1997). Breast cancer: Psychosocial factors influencing risk perception, screening, diagnosis, and treatment. In S. J. Gallant, G. Puryear Keita, & R. Royak-Schaler (Eds.), *Health care for women: Psychological, social and behavioral influences* (pp. 295–314). Washington, DC: American Psychological Association.

Rubin, J. Z., Provenzano, R., & Luria, Z. (1974). The eye of the beholder: Parents views on sex of newborns. *American Journal of Orthopsychiatry, 44,* 512–519.

Rubin, K. H., Bukowski, W., & Parker, J. G. (1998). Peer interactions, relationships, and groups. In W. Damon (Series Ed.) & N. Eisenberg (Vol. Ed.), *Handbook of child psychology: Vol. 3. Social, emotional and personality development* (5th ed., pp. 619–700). New York: Wiley.

Rubin, R. M. (1997). The economic status of older women. In J. M. Coyle (Ed.), *Handbook on women and aging* (pp. 75–92). Westport, CT: Greenwood.

Rubin, R. T., Reinisch, J. M., & Haskett, R. F. (1981). Postnatal gonadal steroid effects on human behavior. *Science, 211*, 1318–1324.

Rubinstein, R. L. (1994). Adaptation to retirement among the never married, childless, divorced, gay and lesbian, and widowed. In A. Monk (Ed.), *The Columbia retirement handbook* (pp. 448–461). New York: Columbia University Press.

Ruble, D. N., & Martin, C. L. (1998). Gender development. In W. Damon (Series Ed.) & N. Eisenberg (Vol. Ed.), *Handbook of child psychology: Vol. 3. Social, emotional and personality development* (5th ed., pp. 933–1016). New York: Wiley.

Rudolph, K. D., & Hammen, C. (1999). Age and gender as determinants of stress exposure, generation, and reactions in youngsters: A transactional perspective. *Child Development, 70*, 660–677.

Russell, D. E. H. (1982). *Rape in marriage.* New York: Macmillan.

Russell, M., Testa, M., & Wilsnack, S. (2000). Alcohol use and abuse. In M. B. Goldman & M. C. Hatch (Eds.), *Women & health* (pp. 589–598). New York: Academic Press.

Russo, N. F. (1979). Overview: Roles, fertility and the motherhood mandate. *Psychology of Women Quarterly, 4*, 7–15.

Russo, N. F. (1998). Measuring feminist attitudes: Just what does it mean to be a feminist? *Psychology of Women Quarterly, 22*, 313–315.

Ryan, A. S., Craig, L. D., & Finn, S. C. (1992). Nutrient intakes in dietary patterns of older Americans: A national study. *Journal of Gerontology: Medical Sciences, 47* (5), M145–M150.

Saakvitne, K. W., & Pearlman, L. A. (1993). The impact of internalized misogyny and violence against women on feminine identity. In E. P. Cook (Ed.), *Women, relationships, and power: Implications for counseling* (pp. 247–274). Alexandria, VA: American Counseling Association.

Sacco, R. L., Elkind, M., Boden-Albala, B., et al. (1999). The protective effect of moderate alcohol consumption on ischemic stroke. *Journal of the American Medical Association, 281*, 53–60.

Sachs, B. P., Kobelin, C., Castro, M. A., & Frigoletto, F. (1999). The risks of lowering the cesarean-delivery rate. *New England Journal of Medicine, 340*, 54–57.

Sadker, M., & Sadker, D. (1994). *Failing at fairness: How America's schools cheat girls.* New York: Scribner.

Samter, W., Whaley, B. B., Mortenson, S. T., & Burleson, B. R. (1997). Ethnicity and emotional support in same-sex friendship: A comparison of Asian-Americans, African-Americans, and Euro-Americans. *Personal Relationships, 4*, 413–430.

Sanchez, L., & Kane, E. W. (1996). Women's and men's constructions of perceptions of housework fairness. *Journal of Family Issues, 17*, 358–387.

Sánchez-Ayéndez, M. (1989). Puerto Rican elderly women: The cultural dimension of social support networks. In L. Grace & I. Susser (Eds.), *Women in the later years: Health, social and cultural perspectives* (pp. 239–252). New York: Harrington Park Press.

Sanderson, C. A., & Cantor, N. (1995). Social dating goal in late adolescence: Implications for safer sexual activities. *Journal of Personality and Social Psychology, 68*, 1121–1134.

Sandnabba, N. K., & Ahlberg, C. (1999). Parents' attitudes and expectations about children's cross-gender behavior. *Sex Roles, 40*, 249–263.

Sands, R. G. (1998). Gender and the perception of diversity and intimidation among university students. *Sex Roles, 39*, 801–815.

Sands, R. G., & Goldberg-Glen, R. S. (1998). The impact of employment and serious illness on grandmothers who are raising their grandchildren. *Journal of Women & Aging, 10*, 41–58.

Sanger, C. (2000, January 5). The needs of the children. *New York Times,* p. A25.

Savin-Williams, R. C. (1998). The disclosure to families of same-sex attractions by lesbian, gay, and bisexual youths. *Journal of Research on Adolescence, 8*, 49–68.

Savin-Williams, R. C., & Berndt, T. J. (1990). Friendship and peer relations. In S. Feldman & G. Elliott (Eds.), *At the threshold: The developing adolescent* (pp. 277–307). Cambridge, MA: Harvard University Press.

Savin-Williams, R. C., & Diamond, L. M. (1997). Sexual orientation as a developmental context for lesbians, gays, and bisexuals: Biological perspectives. In N. L. Segal, G. E. Weisfeld, & C. C. Weisfeld (Eds.), *Uniting psychology and biology: Integrating per-*

spectives on human development (pp. 217–238). Washington, DC: American Psychological Association.

Savin-Williams, R. C., & Dubé, E. M. (1998). Parental reactions to their childs disclosure of a gay/lesbian identity. *Family Relations, 47,* pp. 7–13.

Scarr, S. (1997). Why child care has little impact on most children's development. *Current Directions in Psychological Science, 6,* 143–148.

Scarr, S. (1998). American child care today. *American Psychologist, 53,* 95–108.

Scarr, S., Phillips, D., & McCartney, K. (1989). Working mothers and their families. *American Psychologist, 44,* 1402–1409.

Schairer, C. et al. (2000). Menopausal estrogen and estrogen—progestin replacement therapy and breast cancer risk. *Journal of the American Medical Association, 282,* 485–560.

Schellenberg, E. G., Hirt, J., & Sears, A. (1999). Attitudes toward homosexuals among students at a Canadian university. *Sex Roles, 40,* 139–152.

Schlenker, J. A., Caron, S. L., & Halteman, W. A. (1998). A feminist analysis of *Seventeen* magazine: Content analysis from 1945 to 1995. Sex Roles, 38, 135–150.

Schmidt, P. J., Nieman, L. K., Danaceau, M. A., Adams, L. F., & Rubinow, D. R. (1998). Differential behavioral effects of gonadal steroids in women with and in those without premenstrual syndrome. *New England Journal of Medicine, 338,* 209–216.

Schnitzer, P. K. (1998). He needs his father: The clinical discourse and politics of single mothering. In C. G. Coll, J. L. Surrey, & K. Weingarten (Eds.), *Mothering against the odds: Diverse voices of contemporary mothers* (pp. 151–172). New York: Guilford.

Schodolski, V. J. (1998, September 10). Unionization drive targets nation's day-care workers. *Hartford Courant,* p. A20.

Scholl, T. O. (2000). Puberty and adolescent pregnancy. In M. B. Goldman & M. C. Hatch (Eds.), *Women & health* (pp. 85–98). New York: Academic Press.

Schoonmaker, C. V. (1993). Aging lesbians: Bearing the burden of triple shame. In N. D. Davis, E. Cole, & E. D. Rothblum (Eds.), *Faces of women and aging* (pp. 21–31). New York: Harrington Park Press.

Schreiber, G., Robins, M., Striegel-Moore, R., Obarzanek, E., Morrison, J., & Wright, D. (1996). Weight modification efforts reported by black and white preadolescent girls: National Heart, Lung, and Blood Institute Growth and Health Study. *Pediatrics, 98,* 63–70.

Schroeder, K. A., Blood, L. L., & Maluso, D. (1992). An intergenerational analysis of expectations for women's career and family roles. *Sex Roles, 26,* 273–291.

Schulman, K. A., et al. (1999). The effect of race and sex on physicians' recommendations for cardiac catheterization. *New England Journal of Medicine, 340,* 618–626.

Schumm, W. R., Resnick, G., Bollman, S. R., & Jurich, A. P. (1998). Gender effects and marital satisfaction: A brief report from a sample of dual military couples from the 1992 Department of Defense Worldwide Survey of Members and Spouses. *Psychological Reports, 82,* 161–162.

Schumm, W. R., Webb, F. J., & Bollman, S. R. (1998). Gender and martial satisfaction: Data from the National Survey of Families and Households. *Psychological Reports, 83,* 319–327.

Schwartz, J. A. J., Gladstone, T. R. G., & Kaslow, N. J. (1998). Depressive disorders. In T. H. Ollendick & M. Hersen (Eds.), *Handbook of child psychopathology* (3rd ed., pp. 269–289). New York: Plenum.

Schwartz, L. A., & Markham, W. T. (1985). Sex stereotyping in children's toy advertisements. *Sex Roles, 12,* 157–170.

Schwartz, M. (1995). *Guidelines for bias-free writing.* Indianapolis, IN: Indiana University Press.

Schwartz, M., O'Leary, S. G., & Kendziora, K. T. (1997). Dating aggression among high school students. *Violence and Victims, 12,* 295–305.

Schwartz, M. D. (Ed.). (1997). *Researching sexual violence against women: Methodological and personal perspectives.* Thousand Oaks, CA: Sage.

Schwartz, M. S., & Abell, S. C. (1999, August). *Body shape satisfaction and self-esteem: Exploring racial differences.* Paper presented at the meeting of the American Psychological Association, Boston.

Schwartz, P., & Rutter, V. (1998). *The gender of sexuality.* Thousand Oaks, CA: Pine Forge Press.

Schweingruber, H. (1997, April). *The effects of gender and exposure to advanced mathematics on achievement and attitudes in four countires.* Poster presented at the meeting of the Society for Research in Child Development, Washington, DC.

Scott, E. K. (1998). Creating partnerships for change: Alliances and betrayals in the racial politics of two feminist organizations. *Gender & Society, 12,* 400–423.

Scott, K. D., Berkowitz, B., & Klaus, M. H. (1999). A comparison of intermittent and continuous support during labor: A meta-analysis. *American Journal of Obstetrics and Gynecology, 180,* 1054–1059.

Sears, D. O. (1997). College sophomores in the laboratory: Influences of a narrow data base on psychology's view of human nature. In L. A. Peplau & S. E. Taylor (Eds.), *Sociocultural perspectives in social psychology: Current readings* (pp. 20–51). Upper Saddle River, NJ: Prentice-Hall.

Seccombe, K., & Ishii-Kuntz, M. (1994). Gender and social relationships among the never-married. *Sex Roles, 30,* 585–603.

Seegmiller, B. (1993). Pregnancy. In F. L. Denmark & M. A. Paludi (Eds.), *Psychology of women: A handbook of issues and theories* (pp. 437–474). Westport, CT: Greenwood.

Segraves, R. T., & Segraves, K. B. (1993). Female sexual disorders. In D. E. Steward & N. L. Stotland (Eds.), *Psychological aspects of women's health care: The interface between psychiatry and obstetrics and gynecology* (pp. 351–373). Washington, DC: American Psychiatric Press.

Seiffge-Krenke, I. (1993). Close friendships and imaginary companions in adolescence (1993). In B. Laursen (Ed.), *New directions in child development: No. 60. Close friendships in adolescence* (pp. 73–87). San Francisco: Jossey-Bass.

Seitz, V. (1996). Adolescent pregnancy and parenting. In E. F. Ziegler, L. Kagen, & N. W. Hall (Eds.), *Children, families and government* (pp. 268–287). New York: Cambridge University Press.

Selingo, J. (1998, February 20). Science-oriented campuses strive to attract more women. *Chronicle of Higher Education,* A53–A54.

Sells, L. (1982). Leverage for equal opportunity through mastery of mathematics. In S. M. Humphreys (Ed.), *Women and minorities in science* (pp. 7–26). Boulder, CO: Westview.

Serbin, L. A., Moller, L. C., & Gulko, J. (1993). The development of sex-typing in middle childhood. *Monographs of the Society for Research in Child Development, 58* (Serial No. 232).

Serbin, L. A., Moller, L. C., Gulko, J., Powlishta, K. K., & Colburne, K. A. (1994). The emergence of gender segregation in toddler playgroups. In C. Leaper (Ed.), *Childhood gender segregation: Causes and consequences. New directions for child development* (Vol. 65, pp. 7–17). San Francisco: Jossey-Bass.

Serdula, M. K., et al. (1999). Prevalence of attempting weight loss and strategies for controlling weight. *Journal of the American Medical Association, 282,* 1353–1358.

Shain, R. N., et al. (1999). A randomized controlled trial of a behavioral intervention to prevent sexually transmitted disease among minority women. *New England Journal of Medicine, 340,* 93–100.

Shakin, M., Shakin, D., & Sternglanz, S. H. (1985). Infant clothing: Sex labeling for strangers. *Sex Roles, 12,* 955–964.

Sharpe, P. A. (1995). Older women and health services: Moving from ageism toward empowerment. *Women & Health, 22,* 9–23.

Sharps, M. J., Welton, A. L., & Price, J. L. (1993). Gender and task in the determination of spatial cognitive performance. *Psychology of Women Quarterly, 17,* 71–83.

Shaw-Taylor, Y., Benokraitis, N. V. (1995). The presentation of minorities in marriage and family textbooks. *Teaching Sociology, 23,* 122–135.

Sheehy, G. (1991). *The silent passage.* New York: Random House.

Sheeran, P., Abraham, C., & Orbell, S. (1999). Psychosocial correlates of heterosexual condom use: A meta-analysis. *Psychological Bulletin, 125,* 90–132.

Shenk, D., & Fullmer, E. (1996). Significant relationships among older women: Cultural and personal constructions of lesbianism. *Journal of Women & Aging, 8* (3/4), 75–89.

Shenk, D., Zablotsky, D., & Croom, M. B. (1998). Thriving older African American women: Aging after Jim Crow. *Journal of Women & Aging, 10,* 75–95.

Shepela, S. T., & Levesque, L. L. (1998). Poisoned waters: Sexual harassment and the college climate. *Sex Roles, 38,* 589–611.

Sherman, P. J., & Spence, J. T. (1997). A comparison of two cohorts of college students in responses to the male-female relations questionnaire. *Psychology of Women Quarterly, 21,* 265–278.

Sherman, S. R. (1997). Images of middle-aged and older women: Historical, cultural, and personal. In J. M. Coyle (Ed.), *Handbook on women and aging* (pp. 14–28). Westport, CT: Greenwood.

Shorter-Gooden, K., & Washington, N. C. (1996). Young, Black and female: The challenge of weaving an identity. *Journal of Adolescence, 19,* 465–475.

Shum, L. M. (1996). Asian-American women: Cultural and mental health issues. *Women and Mental Health: Annals of the New York Academy of Sciences, 789,* 181–190.

Siann, G. (1997). We can, we don't want to: Factors influencing women's participation in computing. In

R. Lander & A. Adam (Eds.), *Women in computing* (pp. 113–121). Exeter, England: Intellect Books.

Sieber, S. (1974). Toward a theory of role accumulation. *American Sociological Review, 39,* 567–578.

Sieving, R., et al. (1997). Cognitive and behavioral predictors of sexually transmitted disease risk behavior among sexually active adolescents. *Archives of Pediatric and Adolescent Medicine, 151,* 243–251.

Signorella, M. L., Bigler, R. S., & Liben, L. S. (1993). Developmental differences in children's gender schemata about others: A meta-analytic review. *Developmental Review, 13,* 147–183.

Signorella, M. L., Bigler, R. S., & Liben, L. S. (1997). A meta-analysis of children's memories for own-sex and other-sex information. *Journal of Applied Developmental Psychology, 18,* 429–445.

Signorella, M. L., & Frieze, I. H. (1989). Gender schemes in college students. *Psychology: A Journal of Human Behavior, 26,* 16–23.

Signorielli, N. (1993). Television, the portrayal of women, and children's attitudes. In G. L. Berry & J. K. Asamen (Eds.), *Children & television: Images in a changing sociocultural world* (pp. 229–242). Newbury Park, CA: Sage.

Signorielli, N. (1997, April). *A content analysis: Reflections of girls in the media.* Menlo Park, CA: Children Now and the Henry J. Kaiser Family Foundation.

Signorielli, N., & Bacue, A. (1999). Recognition and respect: A content analysis of prime-time television characters across the decades. *Sex Roles, 40,* 527–544.

Signorielli, N., & Lears, M. (1992). Children, television, and conceptions about chores: Attitudes and behaviors. *Sex Roles, 27,* 157–170.

Silence about sexual problems can hurt relationships. (1999). *Journal of the American Medical Association, 281,* 584.

Silverstein, L. B. (1996). Fathering is a feminist issue. *Psychology of Women Quarterly, 20,* 3–37.

Silverstein, L. B., & Phares, V. (1996). Expanding the mother-child paradigm: An examination of dissertation research 1986–1994. *Psychology of Women Quarterly, 20,* 39–53.

Simi, N. L., & Mahalik, J. R. (1997). Comparison of feminist versus psychoanalytic/dynamic and other therapists on self-disclosure. *Psychology of Women Quarterly, 21,* 465–483.

Simmons, R. G., & Blyth, D. A. (1987). *Moving into adolescence: The impact of pubertal change and school context.* Hawthorne, NY: Aldine de Gruyter.

Simon, J. G., & Feather, N. T. (1973). Causal attributions for success and failure at university examinations. *Journal of Educational Psychology, 64,* 45–56.

Simon, R. J. (1998, October 2). What are the most pressing issues today in relations between men and women? Race and class drive most conflict now. *Chronicle of Higher Education,* p. B6.

Simon, R. W. (1992). Parental role strains, salience of parental identity and gender differences in psychological distress. *Journal of Health and Social Behavior, 33,* 25–35.

Simon, R. W. (1995). Gender, multiple roles, role meaning, and mental health. *Journal of Health and Social Behavior, 36,* 182–194.

Simon-Rusinowitz, L., Krach, C. A., Marks, L. N., Piktialis, D., & Wilson, L. B. (1996). Grandparents in the workplace: The effects of economic and labor trends. *Generations, 20* (1), 41–44.

Simons, R. L. (1996). The effect of divorce on adult and child adjustment. In R. L. Simons & Associates, *Understanding differences between divorced and intact families: Stress, interaction, and child outcome* (pp. 3–20). Thousand Oaks, CA: Sage.

Simpson, G. (1996). Factors influencing the choice of law as a career by black women. *Journal of Career Development, 22,* 197–209.

Simpson, J. E., Stone, M., Newbauer, J., & Freeman, A. (1997, August). *Depression among battered women: A shelter sample.* Paper presented at the meeting of the American Psychological Association, Chicago.

Sims, M., Hutchins, T., & Taylor, M. (1998). Gender segregation in young children's conflict behavior in child care settings. *Child Study Journal, 28* (1), 1–16.

Singh, K., Robinson, A., & Williams-Green, J. (1995). Differences in perceptions of African American women and men faculty and administrators. *Journal of Negro Education, 64,* 401–408.

Singh, S., & Darroch, J. E. (2000). Adolescent pregnancy and childbearing: Levels and trends in developed countries. *Family Planning Perspectives, 32* (1), 14–23.

Sippola, L. K., Bukowski, W. M., & Noll, R. B. (1997). Dimensions of liking and disliking underlying the same-sex preference in childhood and early adolescence. *Merrill-Palmer Quarterly, 43,* 591–609.

Slijper, F. M. E., Drop, S. L. S., Molenaar J. C., de Muinck, K. S., & Sabine, M. P. F. (1998). Long-term psychological evaluation of intersex children. *Archives of Sexual Behavior, 27,* 125–144.

Small, F. L., & Schultz, R. W. (1990). Quantifying gender differences in physical performance: A developmental perspective. *Developmental Psychology, 26,* 360–369.

Small, S., & Luster, T. (1994). Adolescent sexual activity: An ecological risk-factor approach. *Journal of Marriage and the Family, 56,* 181–192.

Smith, D. G. (1990). Women's colleges and coed colleges: Is there a difference for women? *Journal of Higher Education, 61,* 181–195.

Smith, J., & Baltes, M. M. (1998). The role of gender in very old age: Profiles of functioning and everyday life patterns. *Psychology and Aging, 13,* 676–695.

Smith, J., & Baltes, P. B. (1999). Life-span perspectives on development. In M. H. Bornstein & M. E. Lamb (Eds.), *Developmental psychology: An advanced textbook* (4th ed., pp. 47–72). Mahwah, NJ: Erlbaum.

Smith, J. E., Waldorf, V. A., & Trembath, D. L. (1990). "Single white male looking for thin, very attractive . . ." *Sex Roles, 23,* 675–685.

Smith, K. A., Fairburn, C. G., & Cowen, P. J. (1999). Symptomatic relapse in bulimia nervosa following acute tryptophan deletion. *Archives of General Psychiatry, 56,* 171–176.

Smith, M. (1980). Sex bias in counseling and psychotherapy. *Psychological Bulletin, 87,* 392–407.

Smith, P. K. (1995). Grandparenthood. In M. H. Bornstein (Ed.), *Handbook of parenting: Vol. 3. Status and social conditions of parenting* (pp. 89–112). Mahwah, NJ: Erlbaum.

Smith, T. W. (1994). Attitudes toward sexual permissiveness: Trends, correlates, and behavioral connections. In A. S. Rossi (Ed.), *Sexuality across the life course* (pp. 63–97). Chicago: University of Chicago Press.

Smith, T. W. (1999). *The emerging 21st century American family.* Chicago: University of Chicago, National Opinion Research Center.

Smith-Warner, S. A., et al. (1998). Alcohol and breast cancer in women. *Journal of the American Medical Association, 279,* 535–540.

Snow, M., Jacklin, C., & Maccoby, E. E. (1983). Sex-of-child differences in father-child interaction at one year of age. *Child Development, 54,* 227–232.

Snyder, N. M. (1994). Career women and motherhood: Child care dilemmas and choices. In C. W. Konek & S. L. Kitch (Eds.), *Women and careers: Issues and challenges* (pp. 155–172). Thousand Oaks, CA: Sage.

Sobal, J., & Maurer, D. (Eds.). (1999). *Weighty issues: Fatness and thinness as social problems.* Hawthorne, NY: Aldine de Gruyter.

Social Security Administration. (1999). *Social Security: What every woman should know* (SSA Publication No. 05-10127). Washington, DC: Author.

Sofradzija, O. (2000, April 17). Beardstown Ladies member dies. *Peoria Journal Star,* p. 82.

Solarz, A. L. (Ed.). (1999). *Lesbian health: Current assessment and directions for the future.* Washington, DC: National Academy Press.

Solinger, R. (Ed.). (1998). *Abortion wars: A half century of struggle, 1950–2000.* Berkeley, CA: University of California Press.

Solomon, D., & Schiffman, M. (2000). Cervical cancer screening. In M. B. Goldman & M. C. Hatch (Eds.), *Women & health* (pp. 942–948). New York: Academic Press.

Solomon, J. C., & Marx, J. (1995). "To grandmother's house we go": Health and school adjustment of children raised solely by grandparents. *Gerontologist, 35,* 386–394.

Solomon, J. C., & Marx, J. (1999). Who cares? Grandparent/grandchild households. *Journal of Women & Aging, 11,* 3–25.

Sommer, B., et al. (1999). Attitudes toward menopause and aging across ethnic/racial groups. *Psychosomatic Medicine, 61,* (6), 868–875.

Sommer, K. S., Keogh, D., & Whitman, T. L. (1995, March). *Prenatal predictors of cognitive and emotional development in children of adolescent mothers.* Paper presented at the meeting of the Society for Research in Child Development, Indianapolis, IN.

Sommers-Flanagan, R., Sommers-Flanagan, J., & Davis, B. (1993). What's happening on music television? A gender role content analysis. *Sex Roles, 28,* 745–753.

Sonnert, G., & Holton, G. (1996). Career patterns of women and men in the sciences. *American Scientist, 84,* 63–71.

Sontag, S. (1979). The double standard of aging. In J. H. Williams (Ed.), *Psychology of women: Selected readings* (pp. 462–478). New York: Norton.

Sorenson, S. B. (1996). Violence against women: Examining ethnic differences and commonalities. *Evaluation Review, 20,* 123–145.

Sorenson, S. B., & Siegel, J. M. (1992). Gender, ethnicity, and sexual assault: Findings from a Los Angeles study. *Journal of Social Issues, 48,* 93–104.

Sorenson, S. B., & Telles, C. A. (1991). Self-reports of spousal violence in a Mexican American and non-Hispanic White population. *Violence and Victims, 6,* 3–16.

Sorenson, S. B., Upchurch, D. M., & Shen, H. (1996). Violence and injury in marital arguments. *American Journal of Public Health, 86,* 35–40.

Spaccarelli, S., & Fuchs, C. (1997). Variability in symptom expression among sexually abused girls: Developing multivariate models. *Journal of Clinical Child Psychology, 26,* 24–35.

Spade, J. Z., & Reese, C. A. (1991). We've come a long way maybe: College student's plans for work and family. *Sex Roles, 24,* 309–321.

Spanier, B. B. (1997). Sexism and scientific research. *National Forum, 77* (2), 26–30.

Sparks, E. E. (1998). Overcoming stereotypes of mothers in the African American context. In D. L. Anselmi & A. L. Law (Eds.), *Questions of gender: Perspectives & Paradoxes* (pp. 220–232). Boston: McGraw-Hill.

Sparks, E. E., & Park, A. H. (2000). The integration of feminism and multiculturalism: Ethical dilemmas at the border. In M. M. Brabeck (Ed.) *Practicing feminist ethics in psychology* (pp. 203–224). Washington, DC: American Psychological Association.

Spence, J. T., & Hahn, E. D. (1997). The Attitudes Toward Women Scale and attitude change in college students. *Psychology of Women Quarterly, 21,* 17–34.

Spence, J. T., & Helmreich, R. L. (1978). *Masculinity & femininity: Their psychological dimensions, correlates, & antecedents.* Austin, TX: University of Texas Press.

Spence, J. T., Helmreich, R. L., & Stapp, J. (1974). The Personal Attributes Questionnaire: A measure of sex-role stereotypes and masculinity-femininity. *JSAS Catalog of Selected Documents in Psychology, 4,* (Ms. No. 617).

Spicher, C. H., & Hudak, M. A. (1997, August). *Gender role portrayal on Saturday morning cartoons: An update.* Paper presented at the convention of the American Psychological Association, Chicago.

Spiegel, D. (1998). Getting there is half the fun: Relating happiness to health. *Psychological Inquiry, 9,* 66–68.

Spiegel, D., Bloom, J. R., Kraemer, H. C., & Gottheil, E. (1989). Effect of psychosocial treatment on survival of patients with metastatic breast cancer. *Lancet, 2,* 888–891.

Spitz, I. M., Bardin, C. W., Benton, L., & Robbins, A. (1998). Early pregnancy termination with mifepristone and misoprostol in the United States. *New England Journal of Medicine, 338,* 1241–1247.

Spitzberg, B. H. (1998). Sexual coercion in courtship relations. In B. H. Spitzberg & W. R. Cupach (Eds.), *The dark side of close relationships* (pp. 179–232). Mahwah, NJ: Erlbaum.

Spitzer, B. L., Henderson, K. A., & Zivian, M. T. (1999). Gender differences in population versus media body sizes: A comparison over four decades. *Sex Roles, 40,* 545–565.

Sprecher, S., & Felmlee, D. (1997). The balance of power in romantic heterosexual couples over time from "his" and "her" perspectives. *Sex Roles, 37,* 361–379.

Sprock, J., & Yoder, C. Y. (1997). Women and depression: An update on the report of the APA Task Force. *Sex Roles, 36,* 269–303.

Sroufe, L. A., Bennett, C., Englund, M., Urban, J., & Shulman, S. (1993). The significance of gender boundaries in preadolescence: Contemporary correlates and antecedents of boundary violation and maintenance. *Child Development, 64,* 455–466.

Stack, S., & Eshleman, J. R. (1998). Marital status and happiness: A 17-nation study. *Journal of Marriage and the Family, 60,* 527–536.

Stahly, G. B. (1996). Battered women: Why don't they just leave? In J. C. Chrisler, C. Golden, & P. D. Rozee (Eds.), *Lectures on the psychology of women* (pp. 289–306). New York: McGraw-Hill.

Stahly, G. B., & Lie, G-Y. (1995). Women and violence: A comparison of lesbian and heterosexual battering relationships. In J. C. Chrisler & A. H. Hemstreet (Eds.), *Variations on a theme: Diversity and the psychology of women* (pp. 51–78). Albany, NY: SUNY Press.

Stake, J. E. (1997). Integrating expressiveness and instrumentality in real-life settings: A new perspective on the benefits of androgyny. *Sex Roles, 37,* 541–564.

Stake, J. E., Roades, L., Rose, S., Ellis, L., & West, C. (1994). The women's studies experience: Impetus for feminist activism. *Sex Roles. 18,* 17–24.

Stake, J. E., & Rose, S. (1994). The long-term impact of women's studies on students' personal lives and political activism. *Psychology of Women Quarterly, 18,* 403-412.

Stamler, J., et al. (1999). Low risk-factor profile and long-term cardiovascular and noncardiovascular mortality and life expectancy. *Journal of the American Medical Association, 282,* 2012–2018.

Stanford, P., & DuBois, B. C. (1992). Gender and ethnicity. In J. E. Birren, R. B. Sloane, & G. D. Cohen (Eds.), *Handbook of mental health and aging* (pp. 99–110). San Diego, CA: Academic Press.

Stanley, D., & Freysinger, V. J.(1995). The impact of age, health, and sex on the frequency of older adult's leisure activity participation: A longitudinal study. *Activities, Adaptation & Aging, 19,* 31–42.

Stanley, J. P. (1977). Paradigmatic woman: The prostitute. In D. L. Shores & C. P. Hines (Eds.), *Papers in language variation* (pp. 303–321). Tuscaloosa, AL: University of Alabama Press.

Stanton, A. L. (1995). Psychology of women's health: Barriers and pathways to knowledge. In A. L. Stanton & S. J. Gallant (Eds.), The psychology of women's health: *Progress and challenges in research and application* (pp. 3–21). Washington, DC: American Psychological Association.

Stark, E. (1990). Rethinking homicide: Violence, race, and the policies of gender. *International Journal of Health Sciences, 20,* 3–26.

Starr, B. D. (1995). Sexuality. In G. L. Maddox (Ed.), *Encyclopedia of aging* (pp. 854–857). New York: Springer.

Stedman, N. (1999, June 13). *Young athletes with old bones.* New York Times, p. WH3.

Steele, C. M. (1997a). Race and the schooling of Black Americans. In L. A. Peplau & S. E. Taylor (Eds.), *Sociocultural perspectives in social psychology: Current readings* (pp. 359–371). Upper Saddle River, NJ: Prentice-Hall.

Steele, C. M. (1997b). A threat in the air: How stereotypes shape intellectual identity and performance. *American Psychologist, 52,* 613–629.

Steil, J. M. (1997). *Marital equality: Its relationship to the well-being of husbands and wives.* Thousand Oaks, CA: Sage.

Steil, J. M., & Weltman, K. (1991). Marital inequality: The importance of resources, personal attributes, and social norms on career valuing and the allocation of domestic responsibilities. *Sex Roles, 24,* 161–179.

Steiner-Adair, C. (1990). The body politic: Normal female adolescent development and the development of eating disorders. In C. Gilligan, N. P. Lyons, & T. J. Hammer (Eds.), *Making connections* (pp. 162–182). Cambridge, MA: Harvard University Press.

Steinhauer, J. (1999, March 1). For women in medicine, a road to compromise, not perks. *New York Times,* pp. A1, A21.

Steinpreis, R. E., Anders, K. A., & Ritzke, D. (1999). The impact of gender on the review of the curricula vitae of job applicants and tenure candidates: A national empirical study. *Sex Roles, 41,* 509–528.

Stephens, M. A. P., & Townsend, A. L. (1997). Stress of parent care: Positive and negative effects of women's other roles. *Psychology and Aging, 12,* 376–386.

Stephenson, J. (1999). Experts debate drugs for healthy women with breast cancer risk. *Journal of the American Medical Association, 282,* 117–118.

Stern, M., & Karraker, K. H. (1989). Sex stereotyping of infants: A review of gender labeling studies. *Sex Roles, 20,* 501–521.

Stevens, J., et al. (1998). The effect of age on the association between body-mass index and mortality. *New England Journal of Medicine, 338,* 1–7.

Stevenson, J. (1999). The treatment of long-term sequelae of child abuse. *Journal of Child Psychology and Psychiatry, 40,* 89–111.

Stevens, J. A., & Olson, S. (2000, March 31). Reducing falls and resulting hip fractures among older women. *Morbidity and Mortality Weekly Report, 49* (RR02), 1–12.

Stewart, A. (1997). *Separating together: How divorce transforms families.* New York: Guilford.

Stewart, A., & Ostrove, J. M. (1998). Women's personality in middle age: Gender history, and midcourse corrections. *American Psychologist, 53,* 1185–1194.

Stewart, A. J., & Chester, N. (1982). Sex differences in human social motives: Achievement, affiliation, and power. In A. J. Stewart (Ed.), *Motivation and society* (pp. 172–218). San Francisco: Jossey-Bass.

Stewart, A. J., & Vandewater, E. A. (1999). "If I had it to do over again . . .": Midlife review, midcourse corrections, and women's well-being in midlife. *Journal of Personality and Social Psychology, 76,* 270–283.

Stewart, D. E. (1996). Violence and women's mental health. *Harvard Review of Psychiatry, 4,* 54–57.

Stock, J. L., Bell, M. A., Boyer, D. K., & Connell, F. A. (1997). Adolescent pregnancy and sexual risk-taking among sexually abused girls. *Family Planning Perspectives, 29,* 200–203, 227.

Stock, R. W. (1997, July 31). When older women contract the AIDS virus. *New York Times,* pp. B1, 4.

Stock, R. W. (1999, March 21). Not an age, but an expanding state of mind. *New York Times,* pp. WH 1, WH 15.

Stohs, J. H. (1995). Predictors of conflict over the household division of labor among women employed full-time. *Sex Roles, 33,* 257–275.

Stokes, J., Riger, S., & Sullivan, M. (1995). Measuring perceptions of the working environment for women in corporate settings. *Psychology of Women, 19,* 533–549.

Stolberg, S. G. (1997a, December 14). For the infertile, a high-tech treadmill. *New York Times,* pp. Y2, Y24.

Stolberg, S. G. (1997b, December 19). U.S. publishes first guide to treatment of infertility. *New York Times,* p. A14.

Stolberg, S. G. (1998a). Concern among Jews is heightened as scientists deepen gene studies. *New York Times,* p. A24.

Stolberg, S. G. (1998b). Quandary on donor eggs: What to tell the children. *New York Times,* pp. Y1, Y14.

Stolberg, S. G. (1998c, March 9). U.S. awakes to epidemic of sexual diseases. *New York Times,* pp. A1, A14.

Stoner, M. R. (1995). Homelessness. In F. J. Turner (Ed.), *Differential diagnosis and treatment in social work* (4th ed., pp. 1285–1298). New York: Free Press.

Storkamp, B., & McCluskey-Fawcett, K. (1998, August). *The relationship between child sexual abuse and adolescent pregnancy.* Paper presented at the meeting of the American Psychological Association, San Francisco.

Stotland, N. L. (1998). *Abortion: Facts and feelings.* Washington, DC: American Psychiatric Press.

Straus, M. A., & Gelles, R. J. (Eds.). (1990). *Physical violence in American families.* New Brunswick, NJ: Transaction.

Straus, M. A., & Smith, C. (1990). Violence in Hispanic families in the United States: Incidence rates and structural interpretations. In M. A. Straus & R. J. Gelles (Eds.), *Physical violence in American families: Risk factors and adaptations to violence in 8,145 families* (pp. 341–367). New Brunswick, NJ: Transaction.

Strauss, R. S. (2000). Childhood obesity and self-esteem. *Pediatrics, 105,* (1), p. e15.

Strawbridge, W. J., Camacho, T. C., Cohen, R. D., & Kaplan, G. A. (1993). Gender differences in factors associated with change in physical functioning in old age: A 6-year longitudinal study. *Gerontologist, 33,* 603–609.

Strawbridge, W. J., Wallhagen, M. I., Shema, S. J., & Kaplan, G. A. (1997). New burdens or more of the same? Comparing grandparent, spouse and adult-child caregivers. *Gerontologist, 37,* 505–510.

Street, S., Kimmel, E. B., & Kromrey, J. D. (1995). Revisiting university student gender role perceptions. *Sex Roles, 33,* 183–201.

Street, S., Kromrey, J. D., & Kimmel, E. (1995). University faculty gender roles perceptions. *Sex Roles, 32,* 407–422.

Streissguth, A. P., Barr, H. M., Bookstein, F. L., Sampson, P. D., & Olson, H. C. (1999). The long-term neurocognitive consequences of prenatal alcohol exposure: A 14-year study. *Psychological Science, 10,* 186–190.

Striegel-Moore, R. H., & Cachelin, F. M. (1999). Body image concerns and disordered eating in adolescent girls: Risk and protective factors. In N. G. Johnson, M. C. Roberts, & J. Worell (Eds.), *Beyond appearance: A new look at adolescent girls* (pp. 85–113). Washington, DC: American Psychological Association.

Stroebe, M. S., & Stroebe, W. (1993). The mortality of bereavement: A review. In M. S. Stroebe, W. Stroebe, & R. D. Hanson (Eds.), *Handbook of bereavement* (pp. 208–226). London: Cambridge University Press.

Strong, B., DeVault, C., & Sayad, B. W. (1999). *Human sexuality: Diversity in contemporary America* (3rd ed.). Mountain View, CA: Mayfield.

Stubbs, M. L., Rierdan, J., & Koff, E. (1989). Developmental differences in menstrual attitudes. *Journal of Early Adolescence, 9,* 480–498.

Students and sexual harassment. (1999, May 25). *New York Times,* p. A30.

Study shows that Zoloft helps women suffering from PMS. (1997, September 30). *New York Times,* p. B14.

Stumpf, H., & Stanley, J. C. (1998). Stability and change in gender-related differences on the College Board Advanced Placement and Achievement Tests. *Current Directions in Psychological Science, 7,* 192–196.

Sue, D. W., Bingham, R. P., PorchJ-Burke, L., & Vasquez, M. (1999). The diversification of psychology: A multicultural revolution. *American Psychologist, 54,* 1061–1069

Suggs, W. (2000). Uneven progress for women's sports. *Chronical of Higher Education,* pp. A52–A57.

Suicide rate among elderly climbs by 9% over 12 years (1996, January 12). *New York Times,* p. A11.

Sumner, K. E., & Brown, T. J. (1996). Men, women, and money: Exploring the role of gender, gender-linkage of college major and career-information sources in salary expectations. *Sex Roles, 34,* 823–839.

Swanston, H. Y., Tebbutt, J. S., O'Toole, B. I., & Oates, R. K. (1997). Sexually abused children 5 years after presentation: A case-control study. *Pediatrics, 100,* 600–608.

Swim, J. K., Aikin, K. J., Hall, W. S., & Hunter, B. A. (1995). Sexism and racism: Old-fashioned and modern prejudices. *Journal of Personality and Social Psychology, 68,* 199–214.

Swim, J. K., Borgida, E., Maruyama, G., & Myers, D. G. (1989). Joan McKay versus John McKay: Do gender stereotypes bias evaluations? *Psychological Bulletin, 105,* 409–429.

Swim, J. K., & Cohen, L. L. (1997). Overt, covert, and subtle sexism: A comparison between the attitudes toward women and modern sexism scales. *Psychology of Women Quarterly, 21,* 103–118.

Switzer, J. Y. (1990). The impact of generic word choices: An empirical investigation of age- and sex-related differences. *Sex Roles, 22,* 69–82.

Symons, D. K. (1998). Post-partum employment patterns, family-based care arrangements, and the mother-infant relationship at age two. *Canadian Journal of Behavioral Science, 30,* 121–131.

Szinovacz, M. (1991). Women and retirement. In B. B. Hess & E. W. Markson (Eds.), *Growing old in America* (4th ed., pp. 293–303). New Brunswick, NJ: Transaction.

Szinovacz, M. (1992). Social activities and retirement adaptation: Gender and family variations. In M. Szinovacz, D. J. Ekerdt, & B. H. Vinick (Eds.), *Families and retirement* (pp. 236–253). Newbury Park, CA: Sage.

Szinovacz, M., & Ekerdt, D. J. (1995). Families and retirement. In R. Blieszner & V. H. Bedford (Eds.), *Handbook of aging and the family* (pp. 375–400). Westport, CT: Greenwood.

Szinovacz, M., & Washo, C. (1992). Gender differences in exposure to life events and adaptation to retirement. *Journal of Gerontology: Social Science, 47,* S191–S196.

Talaga, J. A., & Beehr, T. A. (1995). Are there gender differences in predicting retirement decisions? *Journal of Applied Psychology, 80,* 16–28.

Talbot, M. (1999, July 11). The little white bombshell. *New York Times Magazine,* pp. 39–43, 48, 61–63.

Tang, M-X., et al., (1998). The APOE-4 allele and the risk of Alzheimer disease among African Americans, Whites, and Hispanics. *Journal of the American Medical Association, 279,* 751–766.

Tanner, J. M. (1991). Secular trend in age of menarche. In R. M. Lerner, A. C. Petersen, & J. Brooks-Gunn (Eds.), *Encyclopedia of Adolescence* (pp. 637–641). New York: Garland.

Tasker, F., & Golombok, S. (1995). Adults raised as children in lesbian families. *American Journal of Orthopsychiatry, 65,* 203–215.

Taylor, C. R., Lee, J. Y., & Stern, B. B. (1995). Portrayals of African, Hispanic, and Asian Americans in magazine advertising. *American Behavioral Scientist, 38,* 608–621.

Taylor, J. M., Gilligan, C., & Sullivan, A. M. (1995). *Between voice and silence.* Cambridge, MA: Harvard University Press.

Taylor, P. L., Tucker, M. B., & Mitchell-Kernan, C. (1999). Ethnic variations in perceptions of men's provider role. *Psychology of Women Quarterly, 23,* 741–761.

Taylor, P. S., & Heumann, L. F. (1994). Housing with assistance: Opportunities for the less independent retiree. In A. Monk (Ed.), *The Columbia retirement handbook* (pp. 384–404). New York: Columbia University Press.

Taylor, S. E., & Langer, E. J. (1977). Pregnancy: A social stigma? *Sex Roles, 3,* 27–35.

Teegen, F. (1999). Childhood sexual abuse and long-term sequelae. In A. Maercker, M. Schützwohl, & Z. Solomon (Eds.), *Post-traumatic stress disorder: A lifespan developmental perspective* (pp. 97–112). Seattle, WA: Hografe & Huber.

Tepper, C. A., & Cassidy, K. W. (1999). Gender differences in emotional language in children's picture books. *Sex Roles, 40,* 265–280.

teVelde, E. R., & Cohlen, B. J. (1999). The management of infertility. *New England Journal of Medicine, 340,* 224–226.

Thabes, V. (1997). A survey analysis of women's long-term, postdivorce adjustment. *Journal of Divorce & Remarriage, 27,* 163–175.

Theriault, S. W., & Holmberg, D. (1998). The new old-fashioned girl: Effects of gender and social desirability on reported gender-role ideology. *Sex Roles, 39,* 97–112.

Thoma, S. J. (1986). Estimating gender differences in the comprehension and preference of moral issues. Developmental *Review, 6,* 165–180.

Thomas, A., & White, R. (1996). A study of gender differences among school psychologists. *Psychology in the Schools, 33,* 351–359.

Thomas, J. L. (1990). Grandparenthood and mental health: Implications for the practitioner. *Journal of Applied Gerontology, 9,* 464–479.

Thomas, J. R., & French, K. E. (1985). Gender differences across age in motor performance: A meta-analysis. *Psychological Bulletin, 98,* 260–282.

Thomas, S. P. (1997). Psychosocial correlates of women's self-rated physical health in middle adulthood. In M. E. Lachman & J. B. James (Eds.), *Multiple paths of midlife development* (pp. 257–291). Chicago: University of Chicago Press.

Thompson, G. (1999, March 30). New clinics seek patients among lesbians, who often shun health care. *New York Times,* p. 25.

Thompson, J. K. (Ed.). (1996). *Body image, eating disorders, and obesity: An integrative guide to assessment and treatment.* Washington, DC: American Psychological Association.

Thompson, J. K., Heinberg, L. J., Altabe, M., & Tantleff-Dunn, S. (1999). *Exacting beauty: Theory, assessment and treatment of body image disturbance.* Washington, DC: American Psychological Association.

Thompson, L., & Walker, A. J. (1989). Gender in families: Women and men in marriage, work, and parenthood. *Journal of Marriage and the Family, 51,* 945–871.

Thompson, T. L., & Zerbinos, E. (1995). Gender roles in animated cartoons: Has the picture changed in 20 years? *Sex Roles, 32,* 651–673.

Thomsen, C. J., Basu, A. M., & Reinitz, M. T. (1995). Effects of women's studies courses on gender-related attitudes of women and men. *Psychology of Women Quarterly, 19,* 419–426.

Thorne, B. (1993). *Gender play: Girls and boys in school.* New Brunswick, NJ: Rutgers University Press.

Thornhill, R., & Palmer, C. T. (2000). *A natural history of rape: Biological bases of sexual coercion.* Cambridge, MA: M. I. T. Press.

Thornhill, R., & Thornhill, N. W. (1983). Human rape: An evolutionary analysis. *Ethology and Sociobiology, 4,* 137–173.

Thornton, B., & Maurice, J. K. (1999). Physical attractiveness contrast effect and the moderating influence of self-consciousness. *Sex Roles, 40,* 379–392.

Thorogood, M. (1999). Risk of stroke in users of oral contraceptives. *Journal of the American Medical Association, 281,* 1255–1256.

Thun, M. J., et al. (1997). Alcohol consumption and mortality among middle-aged and elderly U.S. adults. *New England Journal of Medicine, 337,* 1705–1714.

Thune, I., Benn, T., Lund, E., & Gaard, M. (1997). Physical activity and the risk of breast cancer. *New England Journal of Medicine, 336,* 1269–1275.

Thys-Jacob, S., Starkey, P., Bernstein, D., & Tian, J. (1998). Calcium carbonate and the premenstrual syndrome: Effects on premenstrual and menstrual symptoms. *American Journal of Obstetrics and Gynecology, 179,* 444–452.

Tidball, M. E., Smith, D. G., Tidball, C. S., & Wolf-Wendel, L. E. (1999). *Taking women seriously: Lessons and legacies for educating the majority.* Phoenix, AZ: American Council on Education.

Tilberis, L. (1998). *No time to die.* London: Little, Brown.

Tomich, P. L., & Schuster, P. M. (1996). Gender differences in the perception of sexuality: Methodological considerations. *Sex Roles, 34,* 865–874.

Tomlinson-Keasey, C. (1990). The working lives of Terman's gifted women. In H. Y. Grossman & N. L. Chester (Eds.), *The experience and meaning of work in women's lives* (pp. 213–239). Hillsdale, NJ: Erlbaum.

Tomlinson-Keasey, C., & Keasey, C. B. (1993). Graduating from college in the 1930s: The Terman genetic studies of genius. In K. D. Hulbert & D. Tickton (Eds.), *Womens' lives through time* (pp. 63–93). San Francisco: Jossey-Bass.

Toner, R. (1999, September 13). Debate on aid for the elderly focuses on women. *New York Times,* pp. A1, A14.

Torres, S. (1987). Hispanic-American battered women: Why consider cultural differences? *Response to the Victimization of Women and Children, 10,* 20–21.

Torres, S. (1991). A comparison of wife abuse between two cultures: Perception, attitudes, nature, and extent. *Issues in Mental Health Nursing: Psychiatric Nursing for the 90's: New Concepts, New Therapies, 12,* 113–131.

Torrez, D. J. (1997). The health of older women: A diverse experience. In J. M. Coyle (Ed.), *Handbook on women and aging* (pp. 131–148). Westport, CT: Greenwood.

Tosi, H. L., & Einbender, S. W. (1985). The effects of the type and amount of information in sex discrimination research: A meta-analysis. *Academy of Management Journal, 28,* 712–723.

Tougas, F., Brown, R., Beaton, A. M., & Joly, S. (1995). Neosexism: Plus ça change, plus c'est pareil. *Personality and Social Psychology Bulletin, 21,* 842–849.

Treas, J. (1983). Aging and the family. In D. C. Woodruff, & J. E. Birren (Eds.), *Aging: Scientific perspectives and social issues* (2nd ed., pp. 94–109). Monterey, CA: Brooks-Cole.

Treas, J., & Spence, M. (1994). Family life in retirement. In A. Monk (Ed.), *The Columbia retirement handbook* (pp. 419–432). New York: Columbia University Press.

Tremblay, R. E., Schaal, B., Boulerice, B., Arseneault, L., Soussignan, R. G., Paquette, D., & Laurent, D. (1998). Testosterone, physical aggression, dominance, and physical development in early adolescence. *International Journal of Behavioral Development, 22,* 753–777.

Trends in HIV-related sexual risk behaviors among high school students—selected U.S. cities, 1991–1997. (1999). *Mortality and Morbidity Weekly Report, 48,* 440–443.

Trentham, S., & Larwood, L. (1998). Gender discrimination and the workplace: An examination of rational bias theory. *Sex Roles, 38,* 1–28.

Trice, A. D., Hughes, M. A., Odom, C., Woods, K., & McClellan, N. C. (1995). The origins of children's career aspirations: IV. Testing hypotheses from four theories. *Career Development Quarterly, 43,* 307–322.

Trickett, P. K., & Putnam, F. W. (1998). The developmental consequences of child sexual abuse. In P. Trickett & C. Schellenbach (Eds.), *Violence against children in the family and the community* (pp. 39–56). Washington, DC: American Psychological Association.

Tripp, M. M., & Petrie, T. A. (1999, August). *Sexual abuse and disturbed eating patterns in college women.* Paper presented at the meeting of the American Psychological Association, Boston.

Trippet, S. E., & Bain, J. (1992). Reasons American lesbians fail to seek traditional health care. *Health Care for Women International, 13* (2), 145–153.

Troisi, R., & Hartge, P. (2000). Ovarian cancer. In M. B. Goldman & M. C. Hatch (Eds.), *Women & health* (pp. 907–915). New York: Academic Press.

Trussell, J., & Vaughan, B. (1999). Contraceptive failure, method-related discontinuation and resumption of use: Results from the 1995 National Survey of Family Growth. *Family Planning Perspectives, 31* (2), 64–72, 93.

Tsui, L. (1998). The effects of gender, education, and personal skills self-confidence on income in business management. *Sex Roles, 38,* 363–373.

Tucker, M. B., & Mitchell-Kernan, C. (1995). *The decline in marriage among African Americans: Causes, consequences, and policy implications.* New York: Russell Sage.

Tuohy, L. (1998, October 1). Don't touch that mop! *Hartford Courant,* pp. A1 & A17.

Turiel, E. (1998). The development of morality. In W. Damon (Series Ed.) & N. Eisenberg (Vol. Ed.), *Handbook of child psychology: Vol. 3. Social, emotional and personality development* (5th ed., pp. 863–932). New York: Wiley.

Turner, B. F., & Turner, C. B. (1991). Through a glass, darkly: Gender stereotypes for men and women varying in age and race. In B. B. Hess, & E. W. Markson (Eds.), *Growing old in America* (4th ed., pp. 137–150). New Brunswick, NJ: Transaction.

Turner, J. S., & Helms, D. B. (1989). *Contemporary adulthood* (4th ed.). Fort Worth, TX: Holt, Rinehart, & Winston.

Turner, L. W., Taylor, J. E., & Hunt, S. (1998). Predictors for osteoporosis diagnosis among postmenopausal women: Results from a national survey. *Journal of Women & Aging, 10,* 79–96.

Turner, P. J., & Gervai, J. (1995). A multidemensional study of gender typing in preschool children and their parents: Personality, attitudes, preferences, behavior, and cultural differences. *Developmental Psychology, 31,* 759–772.

Turner-Bowker, D. M. (1996). Gender stereotyped descriptors in children's picture books: Does "Curious Jane" exist in the literature? *Sex Roles, 35,* 461–488.

Twenge, J. M. (1997a). Attitudes toward women, 1970–1995: A meta-analysis. *Psychology of Women Quarterly, 21,* 35–51.

Twenge, J. M. (1997b). Changes in masculine and feminine traits over time: A meta-analysis. *Sex Roles, 36,* 305–325.

Two studies show sex harassment in high schools. (1998). *About Women on Campus, 7* (2), 8.

Uchitelle, L. (1997, December 14). She's wound up in her career, but he's ready to wind down. *New York Times*, pp. BU 1, 13.

Udry, J. R., & Campbell, B. C. (1994). Getting started on sexual behavior. In A. S. Rossi (Ed.), *Sexuality across the life course* (pp. 187–207). Chicago: University of Chicago Press.

Uhlenberg, P., Cooney, T., & Boyd, R. (1990). Divorce for women after midlife. *Journal of Gerontology: Social Sciences, 45*, S3–S11.

Ullman, S. E. (1996). Social reactions, coping strategies, and self-blame attributions in adjustment to sexual assault. *Psychology of Women Quarterly, 20*, 505–526.

Ullman, S. E., Karabatsos, G., & Koss, M. P. (1999). Alcohol and sexual aggression in a national sample of college men. *Psychology of Women Quarterly, 23*, 673–689.

Underwood, A. (1999a, Spring/Summer). The heart of women's health. *Newsweek*, pp.58–59.

Underwood, A. (1999b, Spring/Summer). The ovarian cancer conundrum. *Newsweek*, p. 44.

UK Trial of Early Detection of Breast Cancer Group. (1999). 16-year mortality from breast cancer in the UK Trial of Early Detection of Cancer. *Lancet, 353*, 1909–1914.

U.S. approves device to test bone density. (1998, March 15). *New York Times*, p. Y21.

U.S. Bureau of the Census. (1992). *Studies in marriage and the family: Married couple families with children.* (Current Population Reports, P-23, No. 162). Washington, DC: U.S. Government Printing Office.

U.S. Bureau of the Census. (1997). *Annual demographic survey: March supplement.* Washington, DC: U.S. Government Printing Office.

U.S. Bureau of the Census. (1998a). *All parent/child situations, by type, race, and Hispanic origin of household or reference person: 1970 to present.* (Table FM-2) [On-line]. Available: http://www.census.gov/population/socdemo/hh-fam/htabFM-2.txt

U.S. Bureau of the Census. (1998b). *Marital status and living arrangements: March 1997.* Washington, DC: U.S. Government Printing Office.

U.S. Bureau of the Census. (1998c). *Population profile of the United States: 1997.* Washington, DC: U.S. Government Printing Office.

U.S. Bureau of the Census. (1998d). *Poverty status of families, by type of family, presence of related children, race, and Hispanic origin: 1959–1997.* (Table 4) [On-line]. Available: http://www.census.gov/hhes/poverty/histpov/hstpov4.html

U.S. Bureau of the Census. (1999a). *Estimated median age at first marriage, by sex: 1890 to the present.* (Table MS-2) [On-line]. Available: http://www.census.gov/population/socdemo/ms-la/tabms-2.txt

U.S. Bureau of the Census. (1999b). *Poverty in the United States: 1998* (Current Population Survey P 60–207). Washington, DC: U.S. Government Printing Office.

U.S. Bureau of the Census. (1999c). *Statistical abstract of the United States* (119th ed.). Washington, DC: U.S. Government Printing Office.

U.S. Bureau of Labor Statistics. (1999a). *Employed persons by occupation, race, and sex.* (Table A-20) [On-line]. Available: http://www.bls.gov/cpsee.htm

U.S. Bureau of Labor Statistics. (1999b). Employment status of the civilian population by race, sex, age, and Hispanic origin. *The employment situation news release.* (Table A-2) [On-line]. Available: http://www.bls.gov/news.release/empsit.t02.htm

U.S. Bureau of Labor Statistics. (1999c). *Labor force statistics from the current population survey.* (Tables 4, 5, & 6) [On-line]. Available: http://www.bls.gov/news.release/famee.t04.htm; t05.htm, t06.htm.

U.S. Bureau of Labor Statistics. (1999d). *Quarterly Tables from Employment and Earnings.* (Table D-20) [On-line]. Available: http://www.bls.gov/cpseeq.htm

U.S. Department of Education. (1997). *National assessment of educational progress* (Indicator 32: Writing Proficiency). Washington, DC: Author.

U.S. Department of Education. (1999). *1998 Reading report card for the nation.* Washington, DC: Author.

U.S. Department of Education, National Center for Education Statistics. (1996). *Digest of Education Statistics 1996,* (NCES 96-133). Washington, DC: U.S. Government Printing Office.

U.S. Department of Health and Human Services (USDHHS). (1998). *Child maltreatment 1996: Reports from the states to the National Child Abuse and Neglect Data System.* Washington, DC: U.S. Government Printing Office.

U.S. Department of Health and Human Services (USDHHS). (1999). *1998 National Household Survey on Drug Abuse.* Washington, DC: U.S. Government Printing Office.

U.S. Department of Labor, Employment Standards Administration. (1999, April 22). Texaco to pay $3.1

million to women professionals and executives in largest pay discrimination settlement. Washington, DC: Author.

U.S. Department of Labor, Employment Standards Administration, Office of Federal Contract Compliance Programs. (n.d.). *Affirmative action at OFCCP: A sound policy and a good investment*. Washington, DC: Author.

U.S. Department of Labor, Women's Bureau. (1999). *20 leading occupations of employed women 1998 annual averages*. [On-Line]. Available: http://www. dol.gov/dol/wb/public/wb_pubs/20lead98.htm.

U.S. maternity benefits fall short, report says. (1998, February 16). *Hartford Courant*.

U.S. Public Health Service (1999). *The Surgeon General's call to action to prevent suicide*. Washington, DC: Author.

Upchurch, D. M., Levy-Storms, L., Sucoff, C. A., & Aneshensel, C. S. (1998). Gender and ethnic differences in the timing of first sexual intercourse. *Family Planning Perspectives, 30* (3), 121–127.

Urquiza, A. J., & Goodlin-Jones, B. L. (1994). Child sexual abuse and adult revictimization with women of color. *Violence and Victims, 9,* 223–232.

Usdansky, M. L. (2000, March 8). Numbers show families growing closer as they pull part. *New York Times,* p. 10.

Utiger, R. D. (1998). The need for more Vitamin D. *New England Journal of Medicine, 338,* 828–829.

Valdez, E. O., & Coltrane, S. (1993). Work, family and the Chicana: Power, perception, and equity. In J. Frankel (Ed.), *The employed mother and the family context* (pp. 153–179). New York: Springer.

Valmadrid, C. T., Klein, R., Moss, S., Klein, B. E. K., & Cruikshanks, K. J. (1999). Alcohol intake and the risk of coronary heart disease mortality in persons with older-onset diabetes mellitus. *Journal of the American Medical Association, 282,* 239–246.

Vandewater, E. A., Ostrove, J. M., & Stewart, A. J. (1997). Predicting women's well-being in midlife: The importance of personality development and social role involvements. *Journal of Personality and Social Psychology, 72,* 1147–1160.

Vandewater, E. A., & Stewart, A. J. (1997). Women's career commitment patterns and personality development. In M. E. Lachman & J. B. James (Eds.), *Multiple paths of midlife development* (pp. 375–410). Chicago: University of Chicago Press.

Vangelisti, A. L., & Daly, J. A. (1997). Gender differences in standards for romantic relationships: Dif-

ferent cultures or different experiences? *Personal Relationships, 4,* 203–219.

Van Horn, M. L., & Newell, W. (1999). Costs and benefits of quality child care. *American Psychologist, 54,* 142–143.

Vasquez, M. J. T., & de las Fuentes, C. (1999). American-born Asian, African, Latina, and American Indian adolescent girls: Challenges and strengths. In N. G. Johnson, M. C. Roberts, & J. Worell (Eds.), *Beyond appearance: A new look at adolescent girls* (pp. 151–173). Washington, DC: American Psychological Association.

Vasta, R., Knott, J. A., & Gaze, C. E. (1996). Can spatial training erase the gender differences on the water-level task? *Psychology of Women Quarterly, 20,* 549–567.

Vazquez-Nuttall, E., Romero-Garcia, I., & De Leon, B. (1987). Sex roles and perceptions of femininity and masculinity of Hispanic women: A review of the literature. *Psychology of Women Quarterly, 11,* 409–425.

Velkoff, V. A., & Lawson, V. A. (1998). *Gender and aging: Caregiving*. (1B/98-3). Washington, DC: U.S. Bureau of the Census.

Veniegas, R. C., & Peplau, L. A. (1997). Power and the quality of same-sex friendships. *Psychology of Women Quarterly, 21,* 279–297.

Ventura, S. J., Mathews, T. J., & Curtin, S. C. (1999). Declines in teenage birth rates, 1991–98: Update of national and state trends. *National Vital Statistics Reports, 47,* No. 26. Hyattsville, MD: National Center for Health Statistics.

Vermeulen, M. E., & Minor, C. W. (1998). Context of career decisions: Women reared in a rural community. *Career Development Quarterly, 46,* 230–245.

Vernon, J. A., Williams, J. A., Phillips, T., & Wilson, J. (1991). Media stereotyping: A comparison of the way elderly women and men are protrayed on prime-time television. *Journal of Women and Aging, 2,* 55–68.

Villarosa, L. (1999, June 22). Tri-fold ailment stalks female athletes. *New York Times,* p. D7.

Vinick, B. H., & Ekerdt, D. J. (1991). The transition to retirement: Responses of husbands and wives. In B. B. Hess & E. W. Markson (Eds.), *Growing old in America* (4th ed., pp. 305–317). New Brunswick, NJ: Transaction.

Vinton, L. (1999). Working with abused older women from a feminist perspective. *Journal of Women & Aging, 11,* (2/3), 85–100.

Vita, A. J., Terry, R. B., Hubert, H. B., & Fries, J. F. (1998). Aging, health risks, and cumulative disability. *New England Journal of Medicine, 338,* 1035–1041.

Vogeltanz, N. D., & Wilsnack, S. C. (1997). Alcohol problems in women: Risk factors, consequences, and treatment strategies. In S. J. Gallant, G. Puryear Keita, & R. Royak-Schaler (Eds.), *Health care for women: Psychological, social and behavioral influences* (pp. 75–96). Washington, DC: American Psychological Association.

Vogt, A. (1997, August 24). Even in virtrual reality, it is still a man's world. *Chicago Tribune,* Sec. 13, pp. 1, 6.

Voyer, D., Voyer, S., & Bryden, M. P. (1995). Magnitude of sex differences in spatial abilities: A meta-analysis and consideration of critical variables. *Psychological Bulletin, 117,* 250–270.

Wade, N. A., et al. (1998). Abbreviated regimens of zidovudine prophylaxis and periatal transmission of the human immunodeficiency virus. *New England Journal of Medicine, 339,* 1409–1414.

Wagner, M. (1992, April). *Being female—A secondary disability? Gender differences in the transition experiences of young people with disabilities.* Paper presented at the meeting of the American Educational Research Association, San Francisco.

Wagner, R. M. (1993). Psychosocial adjustments during the first year of single parenthood: A comparison of Mexican-American and Anglo women. *Journal of Divorce & Remarriage, 19,* 121–142.

Wainer, H., & Steinberg, L. S. (1992). Sex differences in performance in the mathematics section of the Scholastic Aptitude Test: A bidirectional validity test. *Harvard Educational Review, 62,* 323–336.

Waisberg, J., & Page, S.(1988). Gender role nonconformity and perceptions of mental illness. *Women & Health, 14,* 3–16.

Waldo, C. R., Hesson-McInnis, M. S., & D'Augelli, A. R. (1998). Antecedents and consequences of victimization of lesbian, gay and bisexual young people: A structural model comparing rural university and urban samples. *American Journal of Community Psychology, 26,* 307–334.

Walitzer, K. S., & Sher, K. J. (1996). A prospective study of self-esteem and alcohol use disorders in early adulthood: Evidence for gender differences. *Alcoholism: Clinical and Experimental Research, 20,* 1118–1124.

Walker, A. E. (1998). *The menstrual cycle.* New York: Routledge.

Walker, K. (1998). Men, women, and friendship: What they say, what they do. In D. L. Anselmi & A. L. Law (Eds.), *Questions of gender: Perspectives & paradoxes* (pp. 493–505). Boston: McGraw-Hill.

Walker, L. J. (1984). Sex differences in the development of moral reasoning: A critical review. *Child Development, 55,* 677–691.

Walker, L. J. (1991). Sex differences in moral reasoning. In W. M. Kurtines & J. L. Gewirtz (Eds.), *Handbook of moral behavior and development: Vol 2. Research* (pp. 333–367). Hillsdale, NJ: Erlbaum.

Walking: A good workout for older minds. (1999, August 3). *New York Times,* p. D10.

Walsh, B. W., et al. (1998). Effects of raloxifene on serum lipids and coagulation factors in healthy postmenopausal women. *Journal of the American Medical Association, 479,* 1445–1451.

Walsh, P. V., Katz, P. A., & Downey, E. P. (1991, April). *A longitudinal perspective on race and socialization in infants and toddlers.* Paper presented at the meeting of the Society for Research in Child Development, Kansas City, KS.

Walsh-Bowers, R. (1999). Fundamentalism in psychological science: The Publication Manual as bible. *Psychology of Women Quarterly, 23,* 375–392.

Walther-Lee, D., & Stricker, G. (1998, August). *The basis of closeness between grandchildren and grandparents.* Paper presented at the meeting of the American Psychological Association, San Francisco.

Wangby, M., Bergman, L. R., & Magnusson, D. (1999). Development of adjustment problems in girls: What syndromes emerge? *Child Development, 70,* 678–699.

Warshaw, R. (1988). *I never called it rape: The* Ms. *report on recognizing, fighting, and surviving date and acquaintance rape.* New York: Harper & Row.

Watson, M., Haviland, J. S., Greer, S., Davidson, J., & Bliss, J. M. (1999). Influence of psychological response on survival in breast cancer: A population-based cohort study. *Lancet, 354,* 1331–1336.

Way, N. (1995). "Can't you see the courage, the strength that I have?" Listening to urban adolescent girls speak about their relationships. *Psychology of Women Quarterly, 19,* 107–128.

Way, N. (1998). *Everyday courage: The lives and stories of urban teenagers.* New York: New York University Press.

Wearing, B. (1998). *Leisure and feminist theory.* Thousand Oaks, CA: Sage.

Weatherall, A. (1999). Exploring a teaching/research nexus as a possible site for feminist methodological innovation in psychology. *Psychology of Women Quarterly, 23,* 199–214.

Weber, L. (1998). A conceptual framework for understanding race, class, gender, and sexuality. *Psychology of Women Quarterly, 22,* 13–32.

Weber, L., & Higginbotham, E. (1997). Black and white professional-managerial women's perceptions of racism and sexism in the workplace. In E. Higginbotham & M. Romero (Eds.), *Women and work: Exploring race ethnicity, and class* (pp. 153–175). Thousand Oaks, CA: Sage.

Weeks, W. A., & Nantel, J. (1995). The effects of gender and career stage on job satisfaction and performance behavior: A case study. *Journal of Social Behavior and Personality, 10,* 273–288.

W/F balance becomes the major job concern; telework a potential solution. (1999, March 23). *The National Report on Work & Family, 12,* 45.

Weg, R. B. (1989). Sensuality/sexuality of the middle years. In S. Hunter & M. Sundel (Eds.), *Midlife myths* (pp. 31–50). Newbury Park, CA: Sage.

Weinberg, M. S., Williams, C. J., & Pryor, D. W. (1994). *Dual attraction: Understanding bisexuality.* New York: Oxford University Press.

Weingarten, K., Surrey, J. L., Coll, C. G., & Watkins, M. (1998). Introduction. In C. G. Coll, J. L. Surrey, & K. Weingarten (Eds.), *Mothering against the odds: Diverse voices of contemporary mothers* (pp. 1–14). New York: Guilford.

Weinraub, M., Clemens, L. P., Sockloff, A., Ethridge, R., Gracely, E., & Myers, B. (1984). The development of sex role stereotypes in the third year: Relationships to gender labeling, gender identity, sex-typed toy preferences, and family characteristics. *Child Development, 55,* 1493–1503.

Weinraub, M., & Gringlas, M. B. (1995). Single parenthood. In M. H. Bornstein (Ed.), *Handbook of parenting: Volume 3. Status and social conditions of parenting* (pp. 65–87). Mahwah, NJ: Erlbaum.

Weinstock, J. S. (1997, March). *Lesbian friendships: Simply an alternative or is this a revolution?* Paper presented at the annual meeting of the Association of Women in Psychology, Pittsburgh, PA.

Weisner, T. S., Garnier, H., & Loucky, J. (1994). Domestic tasks, gender egalitarian values and children's gender typing in conventional and nonconventional families. *Sex Roles, 30,* 23–54.

Weiss, R. S. (1995). Processes of retirement. In F. C. Gamst (Ed.), *Meanings of work: Considerations for the twenty-first century* (pp. 233–250). Albany: SUNY Press.

Weissman, M. M., et al. (1996). Cross-national epidemiology of major depression and bipolar disorder. *Journal of the American Medical Association, 276,* 293–299.

Weitz, R., & Gordon, L. (1993). Images of Black women among Anglo college students. *Sex Roles, 28,* 19–34.

Wellesley Center for Research on Women. (1998, Spring). Skills training for caregivers: A policy-relevant supportive service. *Research Report, 2,* 1, 11.

Wellman, B. (1992). Men in networks: Private communities, domestic friendships. In P. M. Nardi (Ed.), *Men's friendships* (pp. 74–114). Newbury Park, CA: Sage.

Wellman, B., & Wortley, S. (1989). Brothers' keepers: Situating kinship relations in broader networks of social support. *Sociological Perspectives, 32,* 273–306.

Werner, E. E., & Smith, R. S. (1992). *Overcoming the odds.* Ithaca, NY: Cornell University Press.

Werner-Wilson, R. J. (1998). Gender differences in adolescent sexual attitudes: The influence of individual and family factors. *Adolescence, 33,* 519–531.

Wexler, L. F. (1999). Studies of acute coronary syndromes in women: Lessons for everyone. *New England Journal of Medicine, 341,* 275–276.

Whaley, R. B. (1999, April). *Reconciling the apparent contradictory effects of gender equality on rape: A city-level analysis: 1970–1990.* Paper presented at the meeting of the Pacific Sociological Association, Portland, OR.

Whitbourne, S. K. (1998). Physical changes in the aging individual: Clinical implications. In I. H. Nordhus, G. R. VandenBos, S. Bert, & P. Fromholt (Eds.), *Clinical geropsychology* (pp. 33–48). Washington, DC: American Psychological Association.

White, J. W., & Kowalski, R. M. (1994). Deconstructing the myth of the nonaggressive woman: A feminist analysis. *Psychology of Women Quarterly, 18,* 487–508.

White, L., & Edwards, J. N. (1990). Emptying the nest and parental well-being: An analysis of national panel data. *American Sociological Review, 55,* 235–242.

Whitley, B. E., Jr. (1983). Sex role orientation and self-esteem: A critical meta-analytic review. *Journal of Personality and Social Psychology, 44,* 765–778.

Whitley, B. E., Jr., McHugh, M. C., & Frieze, I. H. (1986). Assessing the theoretical models for sex differences in causal attributions of success and failure. In J. S. Hyde & M. C. Linn (Eds.), *The psychology of gender: Advances through meta-analysis* (pp. 102–135). Baltimore, MD: Johns Hopkins.

Whitley, B. E., Jr., & Richardson, A. J. (2000, May). *Gender-role variables and attitudes toward homosexuality: A meta-analysis*. Paper presented at the Midwestern Psychological Association, Chicago.

Whittaker, T. (1996). Violence, gender and elder abuse. In B. Fawcett, B. Featherstone, J. Hearn, & C. Toft (Eds.), *Violence and gender relations: Theories and interventions* (pp. 147–160). Thousand Oaks, CA: Sage.

Whorf, B. L. (1956). *Language, thought, and reality.* Cambridge, MA: MIT Press.

Why you should exercise. (1999, January 27). *Journal of the American Medical Association, 281,* 394.

Wichstrom, L. (1999). The emergence of gender differences in depressed mood during adolescence: The role of intensified gender socialization. *Developmental Psychology, 35,* 232–245.

Wiederman, M. W., Sansone, R .A., & Sansone, L. A. (1998). Disordered eating and perceptions of childhood abuse among women in a primary care setting. *Sex Roles, 22,* 505–511.

Wigfield, A., & Eccles, J. S. (1992). The development of achievement task values: A theoretical analysis. *Developmental Review, 12,* 265–310.

Wilcox, S. (1997). Age and gender in relation to body attitudes: Is there a double standard of aging? *Psychology of Women Quarterly, 21,* 549–555.

Wilcox, S., & Stefanik, M. L. (1999). Knowledge and perceived risk of major diseases in middle-aged and older women. *Health Psychology, 18,* 346–353.

Wiley, D., & Bortz, W. M., II. (1996). Sexuality and aging—Usual and successful. *Journal of Gerontology: Medical Science, 51A* (3), M142–M146.

Wiley, M. G. (1991). Gender, work, and stress: The potential impact of role-identity salience and commitment. *Sociological Quarterly, 32,* 495–510.

Willetts-Bloom, M. C., & Nock, S. L. (1994). The influence of maternal employment on gender role attitudes of men and women. *Sex Roles, 30,* 371–389.

Williams, C. L. (1992). The glass escalator: Hidden advantages for men in the "female" professions. *Social Problems, 39,* 253–267.

Williams, J. E., & Best, D. L. (1990). *Measuring sex stereotypes: A multination study.* Newbury Park, CA: Sage.

Williams, L. R. (1983). Beliefs and attitudes of young girls regarding menstruation. In S. Golub (Ed.), *Menarche* (pp. 139–148). Lexington, MA: Lexington Books.

Williams, R., & Wittig, M. A. (1997). "I'm not a feminist, but . . ." Factors contributing to the discrepancy between pro-feminist orientation and feminist social identity. *Sex Roles, 37,* 885–904.

Williams, S. (1999, Spring/Summer). You can prevent osteoporosis. *Newsweek,* pp. 61–62.

Williams, T. J., et al. (2000). Finger-length ratios and sexual orientation. *Nature, 404,* 455–456.

Williams, V. L. (1999, June 18). A new harassment ruling: Implications for colleges. *Chronicle of Higher Education,* p. A56.

Williamson, D. A., Bentz, B. G., & Rabalais, J. Y. (1998). Eating disorders. In T. H. Ollendick & M. Hersen (Eds.), *Handbook of child psychopathology* (3rd ed., pp. 291–305). New York: Plenum.

Willis, F. N., & Carlson, R. A. (1993). Singles ads: Gender, social class, and time. *Sex Roles, 29,* 387–404.

Wilson C. C., III, & Gutierrez, F. (1995). *Race, multiculturalism, and the media.* Thousand Oaks, CA: Sage.

Wilson, J. F. (1997). Changes in female students' attitudes toward women's lifestyles and career choices during a psychology of women course. *Teaching of Psychology, 24,* 50–52.

Wingo, P. A., & McTiernan, A. (2000). The risks and benefits of hormone replacement therapy: Weighing the evidence. In M. B. Goldman & M. C. Hatch (Eds.), *Women & health* (pp. 1169–1182). New York: Academic Press.

Wingo, P. A., Ries, L. A. G., Giovine, G. A. (1999). Annual report to the nation on the status of cancer, 1993–1996, with a special section on lung cancer and tobacco smoking. *Journal of the National Cancer Institute, 91,* 675–690.

Wingo, P. A., Ries, L. A. Rosenberg, H. M. (1998). Cancer incidence and mortality, 1973–1995. *Cancer, 82,* 1197–1207.

Winkleby, M. A., Kraemer, H. C., Ahn, D. K., & Varady, A. N. (1998). Ethnic and socioeconomic differences in cardiovascular disease risk factors: Findings for women from the third National Health and Nutrition Examination Survey, 1988–1994.

Journal of the American Medical Association, 280, 356–362.

Winkler, K. J. (1997, July 11). Scholars explore the blurred lines of race, gender, and ethnicity. *Chronicle of Higher Education,* pp. A11–A12.

Witkin, G. (1991). *The female stress syndrome* (2nd ed.). New York: Newmarket Press.

Wolf, R. S. (1998). Domestic elder abuse and neglect. In I. H. Nordhus, G. R. VandenBos, S. Bert, & P. Fromholt (Eds.), *Clinical geropsychology* (pp. 161–166). Washington, DC: American Psychological Association.

Wolfe, A. (1998, February 8). The homosexual exception. *New York Times Magazine,* pp. 46–47.

Wolfe, D. A., Wekerle, C., Reitzel-Jaffe, D., & Lefebvre, L. (1998). Factors associated with abusive relationships among maltreated and nonmaltreated youth. *Development & Psychopathology, 10,* 61–85.

Wolfe, J., Sharkansky, E. J., Read, J. P., Dawson, R., Martin, J. A., Ouimette, P. C. (1998). Sexual harassment and assault as predictors of PTSD symptomatology among U.S. Female Persian Gulf War military personnel. *Journal of Interpersonal Violence, 13,* 40–57.

Wolk, A., et al. (1998). A prospective study of association of monounsaturated fat and other types of fat with risk of breast cancer. *Archives of Internal Medicine, 158,* 41–45.

Women heed warnings about stroke better than men do. (1998, March). *APA Monitor,* p. 9.

Women more likely than men to earn bachelor's degrees. (1999, January 25). *Higher Education and National Affairs, 48,* 2.

Women's cholesterol undertreated. (1997, April 23). *New York Times,* p. B10.

Women's Sports Foundation. (1998). *Gender equality report card: A survey of athletic opportunity in American higher education.* East Meadow, NY: Author.

Wood, J. T. (1994). *Gendered lives: Communication, gender, and culture.* Belmont, CA: Wadsworth.

Woods, N. F., & Jacobson, B. G. (1997). Diseases that manifest differently in women and men. In F. B. Haseltine & B. G. Jacobson (Eds.), *Women's health research: A medical and policy primer* (pp. 159–187). Washington, DC: American Psychiatric Press.

Woodside, D. B., & Kennedy, S. H. (1995). Gender difference in eating disorders. In M. V. Seeman (Ed.), *Gender and psychopathology* (pp. 253–268). Washington, DC: American Psychiatric Press.

Worell, J. (1996a). Feminist identity in a gendered world. In J. C. Chrisler, C. Golden, & P. D. Rozee (Eds.), *Lectures on the psychology of women* (pp. 359–370). New York: McGraw-Hill.

Worell, J. (1996b). Opening doors to feminist research. *Psychology of Women Quarterly, 20,* 469–485.

Worell, J., & Etaugh, C. (1994). Transforming theory and research with women: Themes and variations. *Psychology of Women Quarterly, 18,* 443–450.

Worell, J., Stilwell, D., Oakley, D., & Robinson, D. (1999). Educating about women and gender: Cognitive, personal, and professional outcomes. *Psychology of Women Quarterly, 23,* 797–811.

Worling, J. R. (1995). Adolescent sibling-incest offenders: Differences in family and individual functioning when compared to adolescent non-sibling sex offenders. *Child Abuse and Neglect, 19,* 633–643.

Worobey, J. L., & Angel, R. J. (1990). Functional capacity and living arrangements of unmarried elderly persons. *Journal of Gerontology, 45,* 95–101.

Wrangham, R., & Peterson, D. (1996). *Demonic males: Apes and the origins of human violence.* New York: Houghton Mifflin.

Wright, D. W., & Young, R. (1998). The effects of family structure and maternal employment on the development of gender-related attitudes among men and women. *Journal of Family Issues, 19,* 300–314.

Wright, H. J. (1997). The female perspective: Women's attitudes toward urogenital aging. In B. G. Wren (Ed.), *Progress in the management of the menopause* (pp. 476–480). Pearl River, NY: Parthenon.

Wright, P. H. (1998). Toward an expanded orientation to the study of sex differences in friendship. In D. J. Canary & K. Dindia (Eds.), *Sex differences and similarities in communication: Critical essays and empirical investigations of sex and gender in interaction* (pp. 41–63). Mahwah, NJ: Erlbaum.

Writing Group for the PEPI Trial. (1996). Effects of hormone therapy on bone mineral density: Results from the Postmenopausal Estrogen/Progestin Interventions (PEPI) Trial. *Journal of the American Medical Association, 276,* 1389–1396.

Wu, X., & DeMaris, A. (1996). Gender and marital status differences in depression: The effects of chronic strains. *Sex Roles, 34,* 299–318.

Wu, Z., & Penning, M. J. (1997). Marital instability after midlife. *Journal of Family Issues, 18,* 459–478.

Wyatt, G. E. (1992). The sociocultrual context of African-American and White American women's rape. *Journal of Social Issues, 48,* 77–91.

Wyatt, G. E., & Riederle, M. (1994). Sexual harassment and prior sexual trauma among African-American and White American women. *Violence and Victims, 9,* 233–247.

Wyche, K. F. (1993). Psychology and African-American women: Findings from applied research. *Applied & Preventive Psychology, 2,* 115–121.

Wyche, K. F., & Crosby, F. J. (Eds.). (1996). *Women's ethnicities: Journeys through psychology.* Boulder, CO: Westview.

Wyche, K. F., & Rice, J. K. (1997). Feminist therapy: From dialogue to tenets. In J. Worell & N. G. Johnson (Eds.), *Shaping the future of feminist psychology: Education, research and practice* (pp. 57–71). Washington, DC: American Psychological Association.

Yaffe, K., Sawaya, G., Lieberburg, I., & Grady, D. (1998). Estrogen therapy in postmenopausal women: Effects on cognitive function and dementia. *Journal of the American Medical Association, 279,* 688–695.

Yoder, J. D., & Aniakudo, P. (1996). When pranks become harassment: The case of African American women firefighters. *Sex Roles, 35,* 253–270.

Yoder, J. D., & Aniakudo, P. (1997). "Outsider" within the firehouse: Subordination and difference in the social interactions of African American women firefighters. *Gender & Society, 11,* 324–341.

Yoder, J. D., & Kahn, A. S. (1992). Toward a feminist understanding of women and power. *Psychology of Women Quarterly, 16,* 381–388.

Yoder, J. D., & Kahn, A. S. (1993). Working toward an inclusive psychology of women. *American Psychologist, 48,* 846–850.

Younger, B. A., & Fearing, D. D. (1999). Parsing items into separate categories: Developmental change in infant categorization. *Child Development, 70,* 291–303.

Zaldivar, R. A. (1997, November 30). In retirement, women face gender gap. *Hartford Courant,* pp. A1, A10.

Zalk, S. R. (1991, Fall). Task force report response of mainstream journals to feminist submissions. *Psychology of Women: Newsletter,* pp. 10–12.

Zea, M. C., Reisen, C. A., & Poppen, P. J. (1999). Psychological well-being among Latino lesbians and gay men. *Cultural Diversity and Ethnic Minority Psychology, 5,* 371–379.

Zhang, S., et al. (1999). A prospective study of folate intake and the risk of breast cancer. *Journal of the American Medical Association, 281,* 1632–1637.

Zirkel, S. (1997). *Should I stay or should I go? Why men and women leave undergraduate engineering programs.* Unpublished manuscript, Saybrook Graduate School at San Francisco.

Zucker, A. N. (1999). The psychological impact of reproductive difficulties on women's lives. *Sex Roles, 40,* 767–786.

Zucker, K. J., Bradley, S. J., Oliver, G., & Blake, J. (1996). Psychosexual development of women with congenital adrenal hyperplasia. *Hormones and Behavior, 30,* 300–318.

Zuger, A. (1998a, January 6). Do breast self-exams save lives? Science still doesn't have answer. *New York Times,* pp. B9, B15.

Zuger, A. (1998b, July 28). A fist of hostility is found in women. *New York Times,* pp. B9, B12.

Zuger, A. (1998c, June 21). What doctors of both sexes think of patients of both sexes. *New York Times,* p. WH20.

NAME INDEX

SUBJECT INDEX

Photo Credits

Page 1: Steve Mason, PhotoDisk, Inc.; Page 8: Courtesy American Psychological Association; Page 25: Reprinted with permission of Robert A. Baron; Page 49: Reprinted with permission of The Knoxville News-Sentinel Company; Page 53; Will Faller; Page 59: Reprinted with permission of Johns Hopkins University Press; Page 100: Robert Harbison; Page 110: Robert Harbison; Page 130: ©Oscar Burriel, Science Source/Photo Researchers; Page 140: Will Faller; Page 157: Will Hart; Page 162: Stone/Roger Tully; Page 185: Jonathan Nourok, PhotoEdit; Page 188: Stone/David Joel; Page 217: Steve Smith, FPG International; Page 234: Jim Cummins, FPG International; Page 267: John Coletti; Page 283: Stone/Zigy Kaluzny; Page 314: Ansell Horn, Impact Visuals; Page 320: Stone/Natalie Fobes; Page 335: Robert Harbison; Page 345: Will Hart; Page 350: Cleo Photography, PhotoEdit; Page 380: Stone/Bruce Ayres; Page 391: Will Faller; Page 415: ©Bettmann/Corbis; Page 418: ©Leif Skoogfors, Corbis; Page 424: Ron Rovtar, FPG International.